Mass Communication in Canada

Mass Communication in Canada

SIXTH EDITION

Rowland Lorimer   •   Mike Gasher   •   David Skinner

OXFORD

UNIVERSITY PRESS

OXFORD
UNIVERSITY PRESS

70 Wynford Drive, Don Mills, Ontario M3C 1J9
www.oup.com/ca

Oxford University Press is a department of the University of Oxford.
It furthers the University's objective of excellence in research, scholarship,
and education by publishing worldwide in

Oxford   New York

Auckland Bangkok Buenos Aires Cape Town Chennai
Dar es Salaam Delhi Hong Kong Istanbul Karachi Kolkata
Kuala Lumpur Madrid Melbourne Mexico City Mumbai Nairobi
São Paulo Shanghai Taipei Tokyo Toronto

Oxford is a trade mark of Oxford University Press
in the UK and in certain other countries

Published in Canada
by Oxford University Press

Statistics Canada information is used with the permission of the Minister of Industry, as Minister
responsible for Statistics Canada. Information on the availability of the wide range of data
from Statistics Canada can be obtained from Statistics Canada's Regional offices,
its World Wide Web site at http://www.statcan.ca, and its toll-free access number 1-800-263-1136

National Library of Canada Cataloguing in Publication

Lorimer, Rowland, 1944- Mass communication in Canada/
Rowland Lorimer, Mike Gasher and David Skinner. —6th ed.

Includes bibliographical references and index.

ISBN 978-0-19-542535-2

1.Mass media.   2. Mass media—Canada.   I. Gasher, Mike, 1954-   II. Title/

P92.C3L672003   302.23   C2003-904604-4

Cover Design: Sherill Chapman
Cover Image: Louie Psihoyos/Getty Images

1 2 3 4 - 11 10 09 08
This book is printed on permanent (acid-free) paper ∞.
Printed in Canada

Table of Contents

Part III: Major Influences on Media Functioning

Part IV: Our Evolving Communications World

Additional Credits

Chapter 2, p.. 29-30. Excerpts from Denis McQuail, *Mass Communication Theory: An Introduction*. Reproduced by permission of SAGE Publications, London, Los Angeles, New Delhi and Singapore, Copyright © Denis McQuail, 1983.

Chapter 10, p. 267, Excerpt from Creative Commons Licence. Creative Commons is a trademark of Creative Commons Inc. (USA). Licence excerpt courtesy of Creative Commons Canada: www.creativecommons.ca. Copyright 2006.

Chapter 11, p. 283. Excerpts from Edward Herman and Robert McChesney, *The Global Media: The New Missionaries of Global Capitalism*. Copyright. Reprinted with the permission of the publisher, The Continuum International Publishing Group.

Chapter 12, Excerpt from *Report of the Events Relating to Maher Arar: Analysis and Recommendations*, pp. 46, 47, 2006. Reproduced courtesy of The Privy Council Office, with the permission of the Minister of Public Works and Government Services, 2007.

Preface

With each revision of this book, we come to realize how much the world of communication has changed over the years since the preceding edition. This revision is no different and to provide a comprehensive textbook we have added David Skinner as a third author. It is a wonderful privilege to consider changes to the media and mass communication every four or five years as we have been able to do with each successive edition of this textbook. For the past three editions we have marvelled at the major changes that have taken place in the media. To some extent, we assumed tacitly that such changes could not go on forever. They won't go on forever, of course. But with each passing edition it seems that there will continue to be major restructurings for years to come—20 years at least, maybe a century. Generally speaking, as the world of media and communication enlarges, the world itself gets smaller and more integrated because of that enlargement. While expansion of the activities of the historic core of mass communication—the media industries—is vast, changes in person-to-person communication, in part facilitated by emerging media industries, are challenging the dominance of centralized media production and distribution of cultural products. Interpersonal communication is capturing leisure time to a degree that is nothing short of astonishing.

The internet has become the agora of the world, the virtual space where the world gathers to interact. Web display technology and a massive communicative infrastructure are transforming the audience from consumers to producing consumers; interactivity is replacing passive reception. As we explain in Chapter 2, mass communication now includes the mass distribution of centrally produced media products *and* mass interchange of words, sounds, and images.

This massive change calls for reassessment, which reverberates throughout this sixth edition. Notable changes include the following.

Chapter 2 simplifies and refines the definitions offered of mass communication, the mass media, and the interaction of communicational dynamics and society. Chapter 3 has been substantially changed and revised. New sections on general media history have been added, as well as discussion of media as social and cultural forms. The discussion of media develop-

ment in the Canadian context has also been considerably revised.

The discussion of media theory in Chapters 4 and 5 has been significantly revised and restructured, with particular attention to making these theories more accessible to first-year students and providing examples of the application of the theories. For instance, in Chapter 4 new sections, illustrations, and text boxes frame media production and consumption as part of a complex process of encoding and decoding as well as illustrate how different theories provide different approaches to these processes. A new section on communication theory as social theory addresses the question 'What is social theory?' and explains the purposes of studying and using social theory in the analysis of communication. We have also added discussion of how theories of the media are often related to theories of society, and a range of theoretical perspectives on media content such as discourse analysis, organizational analysis, and content analysis have been updated and added. In Chapter 5, discussion of the role of culture as a 'meaning-generating system' has been revised and updated. The discussion of theoretical perspectives on audiences has been given fuller explanation and these perspectives have been linked back to their larger historical and theoretical foundations. Discussion and illustration of the shifting definition and character of the audiences in the context of the internet have also been added.

Chapters 6 and 7, which address the Canadian communications policy framework, have been completely updated. Chapter 6 includes the pertinent findings contained in the 2006 final report of the Telecommunications Policy Review Panel. Chapter 7, which covers the cultural industries, pays particular attention to what downloading means for the music recording industry and addresses ongoing trends in the burgeoning arena of new media.

Chapter 8, on ownership, provides an up-to-date picture of media holdings, particularly by the converged conglomerates, and includes a new section on the media reform and alternative media movements. Chapter 9 provides new data on Canadian journalists, particularly with respect to questions of race and gender.

For some time we have been somewhat uneasy about our treatment of technology in Chapter 10. With the help of John Maxwell, this chapter has been almost entirely rewritten and is greatly strengthened in it social analysis of technology. Chapter 11, on globalization, has been completely rewritten, with a more thorough theorization of international communication flows.

In summarizing the book and examining the implications of its content in Chapter 12, we have added two final sections, first, dealing with two important books that advance the discussion of communication, culture, and economics, and, finally, examining the implications of the Maher Arar case both for the Canadian polity and for the relationship between media and the state in a democratic society.

As a whole, this book can be thought of as having four parts. Understanding those parts should help readers to assimilate more readily the ideas of the book as a whole.

Part I: Communication and Society

The first part is meant to orient the reader to the major elements of the field of mass communication: Chapter 1 speaks of communication and its importance to the creation and maintenance of society; Chapter 2 defines mass communication and the mass media (as part of communication as a whole); and Chapter 3 discusses the role of the mass media in society in the context of history, political values, and cultural dynamics.

Chapter 1 introduces communication and discusses how it affects society in three ways. The first is the breadth of its influence. Communication is involved in all social acts and we discuss nine dimensions of social activity and how communication affects them. The second way in which communication affects society is in the dual role as a conduit or transmitter of information and as a transformative agent. And the third way communication affects society is through the transformative dynamics of the dominant communication forms—oral speech, written language, visual imagery, and electronic communication.

Chapter 2 defines mass communication and the mass media. The richness and complexity of the concepts of mass communication and the mass media are discussed here and a foundation for understanding is laid down.

Having thoroughly discussed the mass media both as facilitators of information transmission among members of society and as institutions that disseminate information and entertainment products to audiences, we turn in Chapter 3 to the historical and political contexts of the media. This chapter examines the development of the press out of Enlightenment values and presents the media as a complex cultural form that was given shape by the rise of industrial society. The chapter also introduces ways in which the media have been conceptualized and considers how the distinctive characteristics of the Canadian state have shaped the mass media and their operation within Canadian society. It pays particular attention to the interaction between the media and Canada's political system and culture.

Part II: Content and Audiences

A McLuhanite might suggest that our first three chapters are a beginning discussion of how the medium is the message, in other words, how the structure of the media, quite apart from content, influences society. While at one level of analysis the organization of the media is more important than many realize, it would be folly to suggest that content and the interaction between content and members of various audiences are unimportant. Chapter 4 examines content and the various ways in which content is discussed by communication theorists. It begins with consideration of a concept called 'indeterminacy of representation'. Essentially, this means that an idea may be represented in many different ways. Fifteen different people would probably summarize a television program or a real event in 15 different ways. The greater the complexity of what they were describing, or the greater the difference between the backgrounds of the people doing the describing, probably the more significant would be the variability in the descriptions. Take this multiplicity one step further. The various representations are not more or less correct. Rather, the nature of representation is that one invents a reality on the foundation of, for instance, the material world. A glass is not a glass until it is created into a glass by a person who perceives it as a container from which to drink. Communication studies are concerned with the dynamics of the invention of meaning, what some call symbolic production. Indeterminacy of representation distinguishes communication studies from studies that attempt to find definitive answers, as science does.

Chapter 4, then, reviews various theoretical approaches to the study of content. These include:

- the context in which the content was created;
- the intent of the author;
- the structure of ideas;
- the assumptions behind the structure of ideas;
- the frequency of concepts and expressions;
- the economic interests of those involved;
- genres and other defining elements of a media form.

With these theoretical perspectives in place the chapter takes a closer look at the interaction between media content and society.

Chapter 5 explores the role of the audience. The beginning of the chapter offers an overview on how to conceive audiences—not as consumers of produced content but rather as individuals who engage with newspapers, magazines, books, television, movies, and music to a greater or lesser extent and interpret them according to context, their background, their desire to find something meaningful, elements of the content that may speak loudly to them, and so on. In the same way that the media invent meaning, so, as in our example of the glass, individual members of the audience invent meaning from media content, as do cultures in creating social systems within which the media operate. The chapter continues with a review of the various theoretical perspectives frequently used for scholarly research on audiences.

The remainder of the chapter examines what information the media industries collect on audiences and how they use that information. While we use the Print Measurement Bureau's data on Canadian magazines and their audiences, as we point out, other organizations, such as the Bureau of Broadcast Measurement, provide the same types of data for the broadcasting industries. Certain communication scholars tend to demean these types of data by claiming that what scholars study treats audience members as thinking citizens with certain needs and wants, while industry-based research treats audiences as commodities to be bought and sold and, at best, as consumers of content. The two approaches are quite different. But this does not mean that a scholar or student cannot gain valuable insights from examining industry-generated audience figures. By examining certain statistical data on the magazine industry— who reads what magazines, which are on upward and which are on downward trends, which have large circulations and in what parts of the country, what the age and gender mix of readership is—one can appreciate some of the changing dynamics of society, and not just for the purpose of selling audience attention to advertisers.

Part III: Major Influences on Media Functioning

Law, policy, ownership, content production, and technology are all part of the institutional structure of mass communication; they shape the contexts in which mass communication occurs and they all continue to evolve. And because they are mutually constitutive, it is not easy to decide which should come first. Some students better appreciate the significance of law and policy after they have come to grips with ownership structures and the various tensions between owners, content producers, and technology. On the other hand, others appreciate that law and policy set the rules of the game within which owners, content producers, and technology make their influence felt, and thus it is with law and policy that we begin this section.

At a time of considerable resistance to state intervention in all areas of the economy—usually regarded as state interference—it is important for readers to understand that laws and policies, discussed in Chapter 6, are not simply reactions or afterthoughts that address already existing economic and technological determinants. Rather, laws and policies help constitute media environments and are, when well-conceived, designed to anticipate future directions in ownership, content production, and technology. Media environments are not primarily the products of free-market economics and technology; they are socially constructed environments in which laws, policies, the goals and ideals of content producers, and economic and technological forces all come into play.

The laws and policies established by each national government determine how the media operate within that nation. Further, international laws and policies govern how the media operate at the international level, how, for instance, copyright applies across many countries, how the broadcast spectrum is allocated to various countries and to various user groups, and how places for communication satellites in geostationary orbit are allocated to various countries. This structure and these rules are created by formal statutes, in which case they are laws, and/or in government plans of action, in which case they are policy. And while laws derive from statutes, regulations derive from policy.

After discussing how policy is developed, Chapter 6 examines telecommunications policy and then broadcasting policy. Telecommunications policy, based in Canada on the Telecommunications Act, governs the technological infrastructure upon which are based all of broadcasting and land-line telephones, cell-phones, and other wireless communication devices, emergency communication, military communication, taxis, and other point-to-point communications systems. With the expansion of the internet, telecommunications law will only increase in importance. In addition, who controls the hardware infrastructure can be critically important to a nation's affairs.

Broadcasting policy is determined by the Broadcasting Act. Historically, Canadian broadcasting policy has been implicated in the nation-building project of the federal government. If originally that meant linking the far reaches of the country into a national public radio network, today it means providing content that speaks to the broad diversity of the Canadian people and providing access to the radio and television airwaves for journalists, creators, and performers of all backgrounds.

Chapter 7 examines the cultural industries, cinema, music recording, book publishing, magazine publishing, newspaper publishing (which also receives greater attention in Chapters 8 and 9), and new media. In contrast to broadcasting, there are no overarching statutes to determine policy direction for these media. Yet, government does play a role in each of these cultural industries. To ensure that Canadians have a presence in film, books, magazines, music, and newspapers, policy must be put in place to ensure that the dynamics of the marketplace do not silence Canadian voices. In a marketplace dominated by US producers who have the advantages of an English-speaking market more than 10 times the size of Canada's, a government determined to advance the interests of its producers, and an ideology that denies the integrity of collectivities in favour of the rights of individuals, the distribution systems for Canadian cultural products, as well as the opportunities for creating content in the first place, could easily be overwhelmed. Chapter 7 delves into the basic policies that have encouraged Canadian cultural expression and have given Canada a place on the world stage in music, book authorship, film, and television program-

ming. It also discusses how legislation has ensured that Canadian magazines and newspapers have been strengthened over the years and how that legislation has been challenged and renewed.

With the policy framework for the media laid out in Chapters 6 and 7, Chapter 8 goes on to discuss the structure and role of media ownership. Here, our point about the social construction of the media environment is reinforced. From the outset, the chapter establishes that there is no natural or inevitable way to structure the media economically—every society adapts its own media to its own needs, and ownership forms can be quite distinct from medium to medium within the same country. The chapter describes the two principal types of media ownership—public (or government-owned) and private—but notes that all media participate in the Canadian economy and that no media industry operates exclusively on the basis of free-market principles. The restructuring of the media economy by large, converging conglomerates is also addressed.

Chapter 9 brings content producers into the picture, concentrating on the example that journalists provide. Journalists do not simply gather news, nor do they simply mirror society. Instead, like other kinds of cultural workers—filmmakers, fiction writers, photographers, and musicians—they actively produce their material by seeking out and presenting the stories they believe are the most important, most relevant, and most interesting to their audiences' daily lives. Although journalism is similar to other forms of content production because it is produced and because news is told in story form, journalists are expected to adhere to certain well-known ideals, such as objectivity, fairness, balance, and accuracy, all in the service of their quest for truth. The pursuit of these ideals by journalists is set in the actual political, legal, and economic contexts of Canadian society for the purpose of underlining the structural tensions inherent to its practice.

Chapter 10 introduces technology as the fourth of the four major factors that influence how the media operate, the first three being law and policy, ownership, and professionalism. Almost completely rewritten to encompass developments in theories of technology, this chapter expands the discussion of various viewpoints that tend to dominate discussions of the social nature of technology. In this reconceptualization, following theorists such as Feenberg, we note how technology and the handling of technology are situated within society. Stated differently, what we call technology is an element of society that involves the development of machines and systems to address desired outcomes. At its core is instrumental thought to address the achievement of those outcomes that are expressed in material artifacts, which, like social mores, encourage closure on social behaviour. Such closure leads to a deterministic fallacy that every technological society must overcome to maintain a trajectory of development. The chapter concludes with an overview of recent technological developments and how they are changing the manner in which society operates.

Part IV: Our Evolving Communications World

Both Chapters 11 and 12 look back over the phenomena discussed in the previous chapters. Chapter 11 is conceptual and focused in its overview. Chapter 12 is descriptive.

Chapter 11 has both an empirical and a theoretical foundation. When policy, ownership, professional activity, content production, and technology come together, the most noticeable direction in which they take society is towards global integration. Electronic communications technology allows for instantaneous transmission of content around the world. Economies of scale encourage concentration of ownership and hence the creation of larger and larger enterprises. Facilitated by technology and increasingly larger transnational corporations whose reach is global, content production takes place with an eye on many national markets. Even in law and policy, governments have found it desirable over the past decade or so to create laws and policies in the form of international trade regimes to facilitate the flow of media products. And, of course, the internet is a global communications system.

The dynamics of globalization are both positive and negative. While bringing technically sophisticated and aesthetically pleasing cultural products to broader audiences and a wider variety of locations, individuals may benefit. They gain information; they are amused; they are enlightened. But by the same token, this wide distribution carries with it the material realities, cultural values, and even the language of the producing culture. Simultaneously, globalization produces gratitude and resentment, sometimes in the mind of the same person, sometimes gratitude in some people and resentment in others. In a world of vast differences in standards of living, we ignore this double reality at our peril, as the attacks on New York and Washington on 11 September 2001 illustrated. As Marshall McLuhan would say, and this is the theoretical foundation of the chapter, through electronic communication we have created a global village that has brought us all into each others' backyards, with all the difficulties as well as advantages that this entails.

Chapter 12 is a descriptive overview of the book. It follows through each of the chapters, describes what each contributes to our overall understanding of mass communication, and looks forward to the future. As noted above, it ends with mind-opening examinations of two important books—Peter Grant and Chris Wood's *Blockbusters and Trade Wars* and Chris Anderson's *The Long Tail*—and of the Arar case.

Rowland Lorimer, Vancouver
Mike Gasher, Montreal
David Skinner, Toronto

Acknowledgements

We owe particular thanks to Dianne Arbuckle, Chantal Basch-Tetreault, Anne Carscallen, Richard Smith, Stefan Lorimer, Conor Lorimer, Julia Lorimer, John Maxwell, David Mitchell, Ed Slopek, and our anonymous readers for their comments and contributions to this edition. We also would like to thank the editorial, management, and sales teams at Oxford University Press Canada for their work and support.

PART ONE

Communication
and Society

CHAPTER 1

Communication and Society

Introduction

This first chapter outlines the nature of the interaction between communication and society. After an overview that provides a sense of the quickly expanding communications universe as well as both optimistic and pessimistic views of that universe, the chapter proceeds to its three main points: (1) communication is part of all social behaviour; (2) communication encompasses both transmission and transformation; and (3) at the highest level of generality, the transformational dynamics of communication can be described by orality, literacy, and electronic processes.

An Ever-Changing Communications Universe

The internet has now joined broadcasting and film as a major media industry. However, unlike broadcasting and film, and indeed sound recording, the internet has more to offer in terms of communications processes. In joining computing power with transmission capacity, thousands of hitherto unimaginable services have become available, from banking and investing to medical diagnosis, distance-delivered education, and telecommuting (working at home for a company that may be located halfway around the world). Yet the internet offers even more. It allows anyone, anywhere, at any time to communicate with anyone else in a wide variety of locations around the world.

By joining broadcasting and film—and, to a lesser extent, books, magazines, recorded music, and newspapers—as a key medium of mass communication, the internet has disrupted both the media and society. The relatively controlled environment of the centralized production and wide dissemination of media products has become far more open. This new environment encompasses websites from any organization intending to serve anyone outside its immediate physical proximity; blogs by a myriad of individuals who feel they have something to offer the world; and text and voice messaging among individuals in or out of real time. In short, the internet has introduced a tremendous decentralizing and less controllable media environment.

Yet the internet is not unique. Rather, it is one in a series of major technological innovations introduced in the twentieth century. The others were:

- the displacement of newspapers and live theatre by radio broadcasting and silent film and then talkies in the early decades of the century;
- the advent of television in the 1950s;
- the creation of cable distribution for television in the 1960s and 1970s that brought forward a challenge to national broadcasting **networks** by specialty channels.

Each of these media developments has fragmented the audience and hence fragmented the focus of citizens of nearly all societies around the world. Programs have turned from a focus on general-interest news and entertainment, which contribute to an overall coherence in society, to content targeted towards a demographically narrower but spatially broader audience, thereby weakening national citizenship. 'Think globally, act locally' captures some of that pan-nationalism. Gone are the days when whole nations watched the 6 p.m. or 11 p.m. news. The now-fragmented audience assembles only for the most unusual of circumstances, as when terrorist attacks struck the United States on 9/11, when the US invaded Iraq, when terrorists bombed the subways of Madrid and London, or when major natural, technological, or political disasters occur, such as with the Asian tsunami of December 2004 or in August 2005 when Hurricane Katrina crashed into New Orleans, exposing the underbelly of racism and poverty of America's homegrown less developed world. Gone also are the days when the majority of the population watched television in the evening. Currently, leisure time is disappearing as increasing numbers have second jobs while other are fully engaged on the internet or using ever-cheaper phone rates.

The technology available is stupendous. For instance, as the Arctic ice cap melts, you can take a phone on your voyage through the Northwest Passage, or anywhere else in the world, and for about $2.50 per minute talk to the rescue agency of your choice. With a GPS unit attached to your watch and a satellite phone (or a cellphone if you are near a city) you can call for help and give your exact location. Soon you will be able to see television from any country in the world virtually anywhere, providing you can afford the receiving technology.

The temptation of new technologies diverts public investment from direct public service (i.e., funding national public broadcasters) to stimulating economic growth through investment in technological infrastructure. The goal is to provide Canadians with a comparative advantage by creating opportunities for a wide range of commercial information, entertainment, and communications enterprises serving every conceivable audience and taking advantage of every possible technological permutation. The motivation of government is that once this is accomplished, and even as it is being implemented, the resulting communication system will be transformed from a public service expenditure into tax revenue and employment. The temptation of new technologies also encourages concentration of ownership, not only to raise the needed capital but also to allow firms to take advantage of convergence: the multiple exploitation of research and content, for example, for both a newspaper article and a television news item. This temptation causes governments to set aside social impacts and the interests of their citizens with the rationale that businesses will seek opportunities to do this once a marketplace becomes possible.

There are a considerable number of problems with this approach. One is that a communications system designed on the basis of marketplace principles serves producers and investors, not citizens, because of its overarching need to make a profit. Raymond Williams, a British media scholar, once noted that people are free to say anything as long as they say it profitably. Because new (and old) commercial communications enterprises seek revenue from advertisers, they must serve the needs of these advertisers. Advertisers need to sell goods and services to people. They seek out certain audiences (those with disposable incomes) by delivering particular content (that which encourages product consumption). Their interest in supporting content that makes a positive contribution to society or that is well produced is secondary. Advertisers support such programming because it generates goodwill or a richer society and, ultimately,

increased consumption. Without long- or short-term payoff advertisers will withdraw. The matter for commercial communications corporations is one of fiduciary responsibility—the requirement of a publicly traded corporation to look after the economic interests of its shareholders. Some may argue that such a system also serves consumers. It may, to a degree, although it provides increased competitive advantage to the largest and richest corporations. But such a system serves consumers and consumption, not people, not citizens, not children growing up who need care and nurturing, not the aged. In short, those who have money and spend it are those the advertisers wish to reach.

The net result is that what commercial communications enterprises provide is all subject to a commercial equation. Whether it celebrates plurality, balances the rights of the individual with the rights of the community, or considers social values like medicare, a television program appears because that program makes commercial sense. To be sure, commercial sense has wide parameters, because audience members have a wide range of tastes. But, in all cases, for the com-

The marriage between Hollywood movies and consumer products is a very profitable one. Sean (Diddy) Combs, record producer, entertainer, writer, arranger, actor, and Grammy Award-winning rapper, now has a clothing line, a popular fragrance, and a restaurant chain. (CP/Devan/INFphoto.com)

mercial sector, the bottom line is profit. Hollywood's proud claim of providing 'pure entertainment' was silenced in the 1980s and buried in the 1990s. Movies have become purveyors of placed products. While they deliver content to the audience, they deliver the attention of the audience to firms that have paid for product placement. Some movies are little more than a launching pad for derivative records, toys, books, and T-shirts. Others are merely excuses to sell over-priced popcorn and candy.

And so the market is coming to reign supreme. Sell the funky boots made in Newfoundland. Sell the beer that will surround you with every person and object you ever dreamed of. Sell the politician who will build a new tomorrow, create lots of jobs, and get rid of the debt—all painlessly. Sell the law that will rid the streets of criminals. Sell the drug that will free you of all pain, worry, or inconvenient personality traits. Sell the operation that will create for you the ideal body, complete with self-selected race and gender characteristics. Sell the investigative reporter who will reveal the hidden truth, like CNN's Anderson Cooper trolling the back streets of post-Katrina New Orleans to find people drowned in their attics. Sell the evan-

gelist who will extract money from lonely and well-meaning people with a genuine desire to help others.

Or is this too jaded a view?

The promoters of communication technology present an alternative view of the communications landscape: they claim that communication technology can deliver to mass society true participatory democracy on a global scale. The internet and home computers can bring the entire world into every home and every country. The communications industries claim that they can turn every home and every country into an information or entertainment production centre. Informed citizens, the technology enthusiasts argue, are the foundation of democracy. True, they admit, our past communications accomplishments have been no mean feat. Our media systems have been able to bring us the best actors, locations, and information and analysis the world had to offer. We have experienced television and radio programs created by the world's greatest producers. Books written by the greatest authors, past and present, have been available in every language with interpretations by the world's best literary critics. Movies by the world's greatest directors have been shown in

Queen's University is among a number of Canadian universities that offer distance education programs. The following ad, adapted to local markets, appeared in Montreal, Toronto, Ottawa, Winnipeg, Edmonton, Calgary, and Vancouver newspapers.

local cinemas for decades. In terms of the right 'to receive information from any source', as outlined in Article 19 of the United Nations Universal Declaration of Human Rights, we have been well served.

But we (or they) can do even better! Bringing the best to our local movie houses or our living rooms puts audience members in a passive position. The internet and the computer in its many forms (from cell-phones to desktop computers) allow citizens to participate in making meaning, making programs, compiling songs, or writing books. In other words, while we have been able to receive the best available from any source, the internet opens up our ability to seek and especially to impart information, the two other elements of Article 19 of the Declaration of Human Rights (see Chapter 9). With internet technology, not only are we able to explore the masterpieces of civilization according to our individual tastes, but also we can share our insights about that exploration, or anything else, with anyone in the world who might be interested. With Google Print, any book ever written may soon be desktop accessible. A universe of information and entertainment, instantaneously available everywhere and produced by anyone, is at hand—at least for those who have the time, equipment, and knowledge to use the internet.

Want to know what feminists or environmentalists think about a specific issue? Look it up on the web. Want to set up an exchange of views between Canada and Turkey? Put the word out on the net and wait a few days for an answer. Want to share your insights on viticulture with the vintners of France, Chile, California, Australia, or Bulgaria? Join the International Viticulture Association and its on-line discussion group. It's all possible for next to nothing—once you have a computer, internet access, and no time charges on your data line.

How about extending your education? Over the past decade numerous universities, such as Queen's,

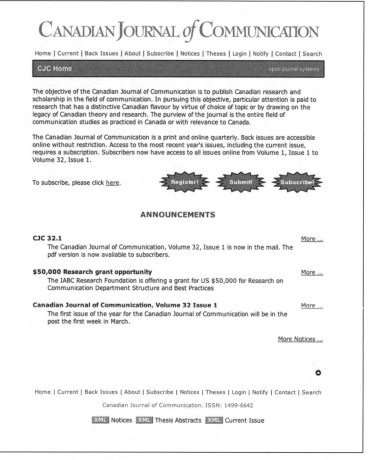

The *Canadian Journal of Communication* website (www.cjc-online.ca) is one of the earliest scholarly journal sites, made possible largely as a result of the efforts of Professor Richard Smith at Simon Fraser University and his students, particularly Paul Wolstenholme. (Permission granted by the publisher.)

University of Toronto, Athabasca, Simon Fraser, and Waterloo, have developed distance education programs, which you can undertake without leaving your home. You may enrol in a variety of courses and will be provided with reading lists, lists of lectures, lecture notes and transcripts, video recordings of lectures and special presentations, and access to on-line tutorials and discussion groups. In some programs the instructors make visits to locations that have class-sized enrolments. They hold formal and informal discussions and provide social and intellectual stimulation.

In the library world it is usually possible for anyone anywhere to obtain access to the best collections through direct document delivery service. In Canada, CISTI, the Canada Institute for Scientific and Technical Information, serves the needs of scientific researchers and in fact provides free access to its 15 different journals to anyone with a dot.ca address (www.nrc.ca/cgi-bin/cisti/journals/rp/rp2_jour_e). The *Canadian Journal of Communication* has been on-line for nearly a decade and makes all but the most recent content available freely (www.cjc-online.ca). And a national project awaiting funding is designed to allow every Canadian social science and humanities journal to publish on-line.

In the world of interaction one can text-message anywhere by phone or by computer. Equally, at least in 2007, using Skype, one can voice-message for no charge beyond internet access.

Thus, one can just as well speak of technological promise as about the downgrading of social services. And arguably that investment in technology can increase the ability of our national communication system to address goals of public interest.

So, are society and its citizens winning or losing? Is technology going to help in creating a better, more equitable world? Or is it going to increase the gap between the rich and the poor—the digital divide? Ultimately, what are the implications of the current monumental changes in communications? Are we collapsing into a totally commercialized society that insufficiently differentiates between the worthwhile and the trivial, or are we evolving into a more equitable, freer, information-rich, just, and exciting society? It is very difficult to say.

In the late spring of 1998 a proposal brought forward by the United States to the Organization for Economic Co-operation and Development (OECD) was defeated by a coalition of public interest groups. The Multilateral Agreement on Investment (MAI) was essentially an international bill of rights for corporations that would have placed the right to do business ahead of the rights of individual governments to set rules for doing business within their jurisdictions. The defeat of the MAI was made possible by a combination of resistance within OECD countries, resistance by certain members of the OECD, and the sharing of information over the internet by anti-MAI groups. The ability of groups to obtain information and share it quickly was an obvious contributing factor to the defeat of this agreement.

On a more positive note, in October 2005 the United Nations Educational, Scientific and Cultural Organization (UNESCO) voted to approve a Convention on the Protection and Promotion of the Diversity of Cultural Expressions. The fruit of a long international effort (largely spearheaded by Canada and former Liberal Heritage Minister Sheila Copps) to develop a New International Instrument on Cultural Diversity (NIICD), the Convention was then sent to UNESCO's member states for ratification. It calls for special treatment in trading agreements for cultural products on the grounds that culture contributes to the integrity and diversity of society and thus must not be treated as a mere product with only economic value. In short, it is intended to put the brakes on absolute domination by the US entertainment industry that, for example, sells broadcast rights of Johnny Depp movies to Trinidad and Tobago for $250. How can even a local news program compete with such prices?

The point, and one can argue on either side of the issue, is that even with the passing of the dot-com bubble, we are nonetheless going through a technological revolution in communication. The technology at the base of this revolution is integrating the information and entertainment systems of the world. Whether the net result is for good or for ill remains to be seen. As we will see in Chapter 10, technology doesn't so much solve problems. It introduces new social realities and hence a new set of dynamics with which society must cope. And whether technology is for good or ill depends, in part, on the resolve of those who have the power to insist that the communications infrastructure we create will be for good.

Communication and Social Behaviour

Communication in general, and mass communication in particular, affects every dimension of society. Communication does not simply carry content; it also transforms the content it carries. More than the message matters. The medium through which a message is expressed transforms the content. As the Canadian communications theoretician Marshall McLuhan stated it, *the medium is the message*. Television creates couch potatoes. Radio causes us to imagine. Books make us think and separate us from social interaction. Magazines involve.

The All-Pervasive Range of Influence of Communication

How communication permeates virtually every aspect of our lives was outlined in a report commissioned by UNESCO. The MacBride Report (after the commission chairman, the noted Irish statesman Séan

MacBride) discussed how communication impinges on our lives along six dimensions: the social, political, economic, educational, cultural, and technological (UNESCO, 1980). To that list of six we add two more dimensions: the familial and individual.

THE SOCIAL DIMENSION

Communication fills a *social need*. It provides an information base around which a society, community, or group can coalesce and interact, ideally contributing to social cohesion, a sense of belonging on the part of all members of society. All Canadians in communities of 500 persons or more have access to CBC radio and television and usually at least one commercial station. Thanks to communications satellites, families with receiving dishes have gained access to additional programming. The existence of this Canadian communication system, augmented by telephones, newspapers, books, magazines, videos, films, and the internet, provides a context within which Canadians can see themselves as a single nation.

Canada's modern communications system is historically rooted in transportation. While it is true that Sir John A. Macdonald had the CPR built primarily to ensure the flow of goods and immigrants, with the flow of both came the flow of information—through the mail and the telegraph. The post office instituted inexpensive second-class mail rates to encourage the circulation of newspapers and magazines to help knit the country together. These, and other commercial communications—for example, Eaton's catalogue— gave Canadians a sense of connection with their compatriots elsewhere in the country. Ordering a pump organ from Berlin or Clinton, Ontario, or a wood stove from Sackville, New Brunswick, or Elmira, Ontario, for instance, gave western Canadians both an economic link and a social connection to eastern Canada. However, even then, as today, Canadian communications carried a great deal of foreign content, especially from the United Kingdom and the United States. This foreign content has always been a part of the social fabric of the Canadian nation and though it has been the subject of controversy, it has given Canadians a certain worldliness.

THE POLITICAL DIMENSION

Communication is a *political instrument*. Probably the most famous English-Canadian example of communication being used as a political instrument is of William Lyon Mackenzie politicizing Upper Canadians through his newspaper, the *Colonial Advocate*, and eventually leading some of them into rebellion in 1837. Similarly, Pierre Bédard spread his political ideas in *Le Canadien*, the newspaper he helped to establish. As the leader of the Parti Canadien (later the Parti Patriote), Bédard used *Le Canadien* as a nationalist party organ to oppose the Château Clique, the ruling elite group of Lower Canada. Even earlier, in 1778, through *La Gazette littéraire* (precursor to *La Gazette de Montréal* [1785]), Fleury Mesplet, a colleague of Benjamin Franklin, spread the ideals of the American Revolution in French Canada.

This overt political influence of communication, especially through newspapers, has remained. For instance, the controlling shareholder of CanWest Media Works, the Asper family of Winnipeg, has made it clear that they see control of editorial perspective as a privilege of ownership (see Chapter 8). As well, in Quebec, *Le Devoir* is a staunch supporter of Quebec sovereignty, whereas the Desmarais family's *La Presse* supports the federal Liberals. Governments also employ the press to advance their own interests. For instance, the federal government frequently announces initiatives that will benefit one or another group and claims the credit for making any positive change. And when governments become dissatisfied with normal media coverage, they create media events to orchestrate the release of significant information, or they advertise in order to speak directly to the public.

The political role of communication, however, is constrained on the one side by a concern with **freedom of information** and on the other by a concern for **privacy**. For instance, governments collect vast amounts of information through surveys, censuses, satellites, clandestine activities, and mandatory reporting mechanisms such as income tax statements. Certain parties, usually businesses trying to sell products, wish to have access to this information, and they often argue in favour of the free circulation of government information. Yet, those same companies and many individuals have concerns over the circulation of information they regard as private. Why should anyone have access to your medical record without your permission, even if your name is removed? How much power should the state have to collect information about individuals? The risk is that information collected can be disseminated, whether intentionally or not. Certainly there has been abuse. For example, the RCMP has had illegal or unexpected access to some individuals' tax records, as well as health records. In Vancouver in 1995 an anti-abortionist was obtaining, apparently from police sources, the names of the owners of vehicles parked near abortion clinics (Bolan, 1995).

In the post-9/11 world the US government, with very little resistance from its freedom-loving citizens, has put in place vast schemes, led by The Patriot Act, for the invasion of privacy of both US citizens and those who have any dealings with the US. The Canadian government has been less hysterical about homeland security but is following the same path.

Privacy concerns have led the government to keep information to itself in order to protect individual rights. In doing so, the government also protects itself against political scandal or accusations of ineptitude. However, it also jeopardizes the ability of its citizens to use this information to their advantage, whether that advantage is accumulation of wealth, political reform, or cultural development.

In short, communication can be a political instrument working in the interests of reform, in the effort to suppress individuals and information, or in myriad other ways. It can benefit the state, the community, the individual, commerce, and culture all at the same time or it can work for one or more of these to the detriment of the others.

THE ECONOMIC DIMENSION

Communication is an *economic force*. It makes itself felt in various ways. As described above, the information a government collects has potential economic benefit for groups and individuals. The collection of information about markets or weather conditions, for instance, can be useful to certain groups, such as agricultural producers. For example, a violent storm hit Britain in the late 1980s causing death and destruction. The storm was described as having arrived without warning—this was not true. It turned out that the weather service had been recently **privatized** and only those who subscribed to a top level of service were aware of the coming storm. The nation as a whole was not aware because certain institutions, including the media, subscribed to a lower level of service. This disaster was a result of Margaret Thatcher's attempts to create private knowledge-based industries on a foundation of public-sector information with no safeguards for public emergencies.

Because of the enhanced availability of information, nations and companies producing goods for export can gain knowledge of market trends as sophisticated as that available to domestic producers. Exporters are no longer confined to producing basic products with characteristics that change very slowly and for which there is a steady, predictable demand. They can now participate in markets where yearly trends determine which products will sell for a premium price and which will be down-market items. In fact, as demonstrated in the electronics industry, foreign producers like Sony can lead the industry, introducing new products and new styles of products—for example, the Walkman, Discman, and so forth. The severe loss of market share by North American car producers in the 1970s and 1980s is another example of how foreign producers can both participate in a market determined by style and even set the style. During these decades, Japanese car producers seized the small-car industry of North America through sound market analysis and quality products. From that base they have come to dominate around the world.

Similarly, a number of 'colonial upstarts', such as Canadians Roy Thomson and Conrad Black, as well as Australian Rupert Murdoch, seized control of a variety of money-losing British newspapers and turned them into cash cows. Knowing the size and stability of the market and the necessary costs of production, they purchased the papers and turned red ink to black—mainly by firing sometimes more than half the labour force. Automation helped, but more important were knowledge of market and production costs and a willingness to confront the unions. From a communications perspective the information a foreign producer can access matches what any local producer has, as long as the producer can pay for the information.

The economic force of communications also depends on one's ability to analyze it. The MacBride Report recommended that each nation achieve a capability to take available information and analyze it from its own national or industrial perspective. For example, planning on the basis of weather forecasts only makes sense if you can predict for your precise area and your precise activity.

THE EDUCATIONAL DIMENSION

Communication has *educational potential*. New communications technologies or facilities are customarily announced in the context of the humanitarian benefits they can contribute. These benefits are of two types: medical and educational. In countries such as Canada new developments in communications are described in terms of enhanced opportunities for people in outlying regions. For example, satellites currently facilitate both medical diagnosis and the delivery of educational courses to outlying areas. In countries with high rates of illiteracy the educational potential of communications is even greater. Telemedicine exemplifies how doctors are able to spread their expertise within the profession. In Montreal, for example, Info-Santé allows people to contact health professionals by telephone 24 hours a day, seven days a week. Other projects are developing on-line diagnostic services. Already, medical diagnostic packages have been developed and sold to interested buyers. And medical services in the developing world have been enhanced via telemedicine.

However, the educational potential of communication has, in some cases, the power to exclude. For instance, the professions—engineering, medicine, law—have access to information and a knowledge of the procedures for using that information that are not readily accessible to others. They also have permission to use that information in certain crucial settings, such as hospitals or the courts. As media expert Joshua Meyrowitz has stated, 'The information possessed by very high status people must appear to be not only unknown, but unknowable, creating in the general population both mystery and mystification' (1985: 64–5). The power of computers to store such information and retrieve it in a selective and flexible manner could open that knowledge to a much larger group of individuals (see Lorimer and Webber, 1987). But as we are seeing on the internet, once an open information system is created, determining veracity becomes essential.

THE CULTURAL DIMENSION

Communication is both *an impulse and a threat to culture*. As the MacBride Report phrased it, communication systems have the ability to distribute information or items of quality (rich visual, audio, and dramatic presentations) widely. At the same time communication has the potential to threaten or eclipse local culture. Lavish entertainment productions and educational programs can provide the basis for invidious comparisons of the quality of life. Hollywood cinema is the norm. Rather than being evaluated on its own merits, local cinema is compared to that norm, as implied by names such as Hollywood North

for Canadian film and Bollywood for Indian film.

Culture is the core issue in debates surrounding globalization and respect for culture is the foundation of resentment that eventually brings about the downfall of empires. Concern for culture drives all of the policies and support programs for broadcasting, film, newspapers, magazines, broadcasting, and music recording in Canada and in every other country except the US and the UK. And while from the 1950s through to the 1990s local products, especially local films, were largely spurned, the tide seems to have turned. As late as the 1980s audiences tended to see movies as an escape from reality into a dream world (Knelman, 1977). Currently, engagement reigns, whether it is in the computer graphics, the stunts, or the social reality. Audiences seem to desire to celebrate media products as extensions of themselves—in a scenery they know, in the artist, author, or actor who comes from their country, province, or city.

In *Blockbusters and Trade Wars* Peter Grant and Chris Wood consider the struggle of nations other than the US to maintain a dynamic culture in the face of the bombardment of American cultural products. In summarizing the language used in the NIICD they clarify what culture is and what the cultural dimension of communication is all about. The aim of the NIICD, they say, is to 'sustain the diversity of thought and expression essential to societies' resilience, adaptation and regeneration and growth' (Grant and Wood, 2004: 315). The measures contained within the NIICD must not stop societies from changing. Nor should they stop foreign products from being heard or seen. Their purpose is to invigorate culture by creating an interaction between the domestic and the international. The rationale behind the NIICD rests on the right to and need for cultural diversity (ibid.).

THE TECHNOLOGICAL DIMENSION

Communication also represents a *technological dilemma*. Many imagine that technological advance is rapid and independent of society, that society has a difficult time keeping up with technological change. As we point out in later chapters, technological advance does not occur as a beneficial side effect in the pursuit of scientific knowledge. Communications technology—from radios to HDTV to satellites—is not a spinoff but an extension of conceptual thought to create devices that are technologically feasible and have a market value. Radio, television, iPods—in fact, books, newspapers, and magazines—are all examples of intentionally created communications devices that gained a place and survived in the marketplace.

The introduction of new technology usually provides a wider range of access to services. However, with it come both industrial and cultural repercussions. For example, **direct-to-home (DTH) satellites** provide digital, and hence high-quality, signals that can be received by a flat round antenna the size of a large pizza pan, thereby threatening cable companies. Digital radio is now delivering the same quality in audio signals, thereby threatening Canadian radio broadcasters. Cable and phone companies vie with each other and satellite services to provide internet services. All this competition increases viewer choice. However, each company and each sector manage to introduce choice not to maximize viewer satisfaction but to maintain their own business in competition with others.

THE FAMILIAL OR PRIMARY SOCIAL GROUP DIMENSION

Just as societies must cope with communications, so must small social groups and families. The difference in the amount and the perspective of the information received by children and their elders can contribute to a lack of understanding between generations.

The penetration of communications into family living rooms in developed countries and into the communities and villages of developing countries *changes the dynamics of the group*. Children are exposed to a much wider range of information and sometimes to a whole different language from that of their parents' generation. Children are also exposed to potential role models who may behave in ways quite contradictory to what their parents or community see as desirable. For instance, in cultures that favour clothing promoting physical modesty, parents may have a very difficult time if their teenage daughters prefer tight clothes and bare midriffs. As well, programs designed explicitly for children can encourage consumption far beyond the financial ability of the family. Christmas can be a time of special anxiety for families when media-driven desires overextend family means. It would be difficult to argue that the constant advertising of junk foods is not contributing both to obesity and to resulting family tensions, given recent studies demonstrating a positive correlation between obesity and television watching.

THE INDIVIDUAL DIMENSION

Communication both aids and constrains the development of *individual identity*. On the one hand, communication provides us with models of behaviour and helps us shape our 'selves'. On the other hand, by reinforcing certain character types and simplifying non-mainstream lifestyles, it actually may narrow the choices people tend to make in the roles they will adopt. In the arena of new communications devices, people's patterns of use can define who they are. For example, searching out and finding favourite websites via computers can transform what information people have and what perspective they take on certain issues. Cellphone users can be 'in touch' with anyone, all day, every day, or at least until the batteries need a recharge. Commuters often catch up on messages on the way to work while families and young people take over the cellphone frequencies in the free-time evenings.

Communication as Transmission and as Transformation

It goes almost without saying that communication involves the **transmission** or **carriage** of information. To communicate is to extend knowledge, to transfer meaning from one sentient entity to another, whether an animal or a machine. As a phrase from the 1960s had it, one cannot not communicate.

The best model for thinking about the transmission characteristics of communication was proposed in 1949, by Claude Shannon and Warren Weaver. Shannon and Weaver's so-called mathematical model of communication makes reference to the basic technical characteristics of communications technology. In this model, seen in Figure 1.1, a person, the encoder, formulates a message, for example, by putting an idea into words. Words are symbols for ideas: the word 'chair' represents the object 'chair'. The person (or device) receiving the message, the decoder, unravels the signals and, on the basis of the symbols sent, formulates meaningful content. In this example, the decoder would formulate an idea of the object 'chair' and code it into speech or writing by making a sound or typing a word on a keyboard.

The 'channel' is the medium through which the message is conducted, for example, a human voice in air or print on paper. The decoder may then give the encoder 'feedback', that is, let the encoder know that she or he has understood the message. By virtue of

Figure 1.1 Shannon and Weaver's Mathematical Model of Communication (1949)

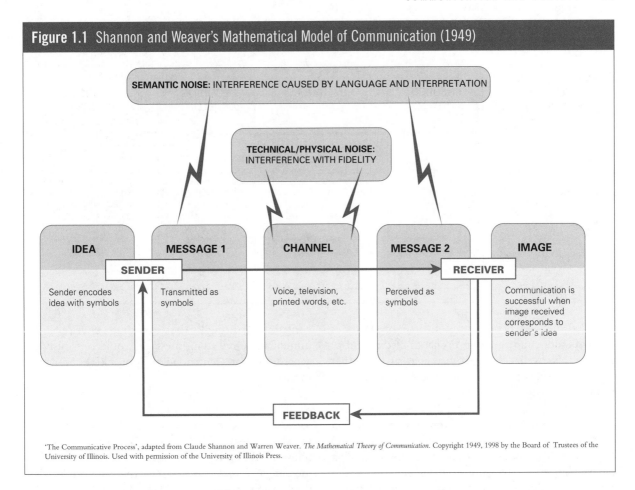

sending a message back, the decoder becomes an encoder. This feedback might be produced by means of a simple non-verbal nod of the head and a smile. Or, the decoder might carry on the discourse, taking it in a new direction, for example, 'Which chair?' All these responses are feedback and they are also new messages soliciting feedback from the original encoder (or others).

Any interference in the transmission of the intended message (signified by the lightning bolts in the diagram) is referred to as noise. Noise may be loud background noise that makes it difficult to hear, a heavy unfamiliar accent, the snow on a television screen, static on the radio, a misplaced paragraph in a newspaper, or the imperfect encoding into words of the idea that the encoder has in his or her mind.

Shannon and Weaver's model works well for engineers and technicians who speak in terms of fidelity and message transmission. But it works less well for sociologists and others concerned with the social nature of communication, as we are in this book. In fact, it banishes consideration of the transformative element of communication.

TRANSFORMATION

To communicate is also to transform. Writing a poem about a person represents that person differently than does a photograph or a biography. Films adapted from books transform the works on which they are based—authors often point out that their books are ruined when made into movies.

The social and transformational nature of communication can be seen in Figure 1.2. This social model emphasizes social and media-related variables that account for the transformative nature of communication. For example, the social context within which message formulation takes place is termed the 'encoding envelope'. At the other end, the 'decoding envelope' represents the context of ideas and understandings that the decoder brings to deciphering the

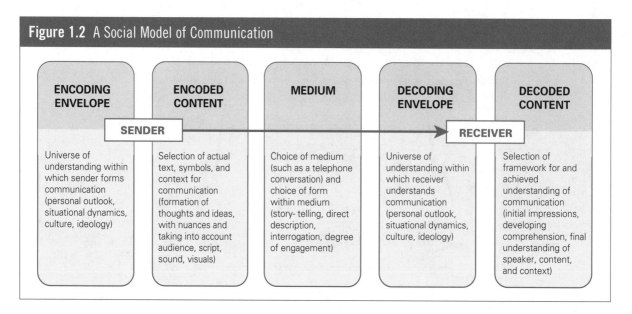

Figure 1.2 A Social Model of Communication

ENCODING ENVELOPE	ENCODED CONTENT	MEDIUM	DECODING ENVELOPE	DECODED CONTENT
SENDER →			RECEIVER	
Universe of understanding within which sender forms communication (personal outlook, situational dynamics, culture, ideology)	Selection of actual text, symbols, and context for communication (formation of thoughts and ideas, with nuances and taking into account audience, script, sound, visuals)	Choice of medium (such as a telephone conversation) and choice of form within medium (story-telling, direct description, interrogation, degree of engagement)	Universe of understanding within which receiver understands communication (personal outlook, situational dynamics, culture, ideology)	Selection of framework for and achieved understanding of communication (initial impressions, developing comprehension, final understanding of speaker, content, and context)

encoded message. (The nature of these envelopes of understanding and meaning exchange is the stuff of semiotics, as well as of discourse analysis and other theories of meaning generation and communicative interaction that we will explore in Chapters 4 and 5.)

In between the encoding and decoding process, the social model turns away from the transmission channel and the distortion that noise introduces and focuses on the transformation of any message that any medium (or channel) introduces. For instance, to put an idea into words is not the same as painting a picture in an attempt to communicate the same idea. Or, a news story on television is not the same as a newspaper write-up of the same story. Similarly, a novel differs from its movie adaptation. In fact, talking to a child, a friend, or a person in a position of authority transforms both the content of the message and the choice of medium as well as the manner in which the chosen medium is used. In encoding, the envelope of activities in which the person doing the encoding engages includes taking into account the physical and social context as well as the person for whom the message is intended. In transmitting, the medium transforms the message by encouraging a certain structure in the encoding process, and further transforms it by making certain elements predominant for decoding. Television emphasizes the picture. Writing emphasizes linearity and logic. Oral speech emphasizes social context and body language, the individual instance rather than the general case. Although feedback is not indicated in this model, it

contributes through the encoding envelope. An immediately preceding message would obviously be a predominant element in the formation of a new message.

This model provides a foundation for a simple social definition of communication. Viewed from a social perspective, communication is the process by which a message (content, meaning) is encoded, transmitted, and decoded and the manner in which a message (content, meaning) is transformed by that three-part process.

Two Canadians, Harold Innis and Marshall McLuhan, were the first scholars to bring serious attention to the transformative elements of communication. They approached the issue in broad terms, arguing that the dominant forms of communication shape a society, its economic life, politics, and culture. Innis (1950) was the first to articulate this perspective. He claimed that oral communication tends to maintain cultural practices while written communication favours the establishment and maintenance of empires—power blocs spread over large geographic areas and across many different cultures. He used the Roman Empire as his example. To conquer and then co-ordinate, administer, and police such a vast empire required a written system for recording and communicating messages on a portable medium. Laws were created, written down accurately, and transported to the far reaches of the Empire. As well, from this communication system emerged an educated elite to maintain the system.

Harold Innis had a broad and profound impact on Canadian scholarship—his ideas have been applied in various disciplines, from communications to political science and economics. (Courtesy National Archives of Canada/C-003407)

Innis wrote about the **media bias** of each communications medium and its transformative properties. For instance, he claimed that oral communication and early hieroglyphic writing on clay emphasized the preservation of outlooks, values, and understanding over long periods of time. Later, written communication, using the phonetic alphabet on papyrus and paper, emphasized basic social control (the rule of Roman law) across space (the entirety of the Empire). Such biases of the dominant media a society uses shape the characteristics of that society.

McLuhan, a scholar of English literature, took up Innis's ideas and extended them to the modern period. McLuhan first studied the impact of printing, capturing its influence on society by coining the term 'typographical man', which referred to humanity after the invention of printing with movable type (in the West) by Johann Gutenberg in 1454. McLuhan and many scholars since have demonstrated how the printed book transformed humanity so that all Western societies came to accept logical, linear thought, as well as individualism, conceptuality, science, and indeed monotheism. The printed book was

a tremendously powerful means of communicating ideas and knowledge in early modern Europe (McLuhan, 1962). (However, David Ze [1995] and others have argued that printing with movable type had no parallel effect in Korea and China, where it had been invented several hundred years earlier.) Printing with movable type created print culture, which dominated the Western world until electronic communication was developed and harnessed by such men as Guglielmo Marconi (radio transmission) and Canadians Reginald Fessenden (radio transmission) and Alexander Graham Bell (telephone).

After examining print culture, McLuhan turned to electronic society (1964), revealing its dynamics to an unbelieving world. He was the first real analyst of the impact of the new media of communication (radio, TV, photography, film) on what we think of as modern societies, although certain British modernists, such as Wyndham Lewis, preceded him and had a parallel concern (Tiessen, 1993). McLuhan expressed his ideas in a distinctive, aphoristic way, referring to them as **probes**. And while many scholars dismissed them, his ideas had a great impact in the 1960s in North America and Europe, spreading to politics, the advertising world, even the media. McLuhan's observations

Marshall McLuhan was one of Canada's most prominent intellectuals of the twentieth century. (©1973, Mohan Juneja. Reprinted by permission.)

Inventor of the telephone (and various other things) Alexander Graham Bell patented his invention for transmitting speech over wires in 1876. (Courtesy National Archives of Canada/C-017335)

made the media and their influence an important issue. In the same way that Sigmund Freud identified the unconscious as an unknown force affecting our behaviour and that Albert Einstein posited interactions at the level of atoms that were awesomely powerful, so McLuhan was telling us that the media were transforming society before our very eyes though we couldn't observe it—until his theory revealed it. As the quintessentially sophisticated US journalist of the period, Tom Wolfe, observed, 'What if he's right?'

McLuhan argued that the electronic media created, for the very first time in history, the possibility of instant communication between any two points on the globe: he referred to this reality as the **global village**. Although now, in the age of the internet and the World Wide Web, we are beginning to understand the significance of instant worldwide communication and electronic communication as an 'outered nervous system', in the 1960s, when hardly a single computer existed and not a single non-military communications satellite flew above us, McLuhan's writing was particularly prescient.

Like print, electronic media have powerful transforming effects on the social character of time and space. It is increasingly difficult not to have some

knowledge of what is happening elsewhere in the world today. Global television, a global telephone and fax network, and the internet are all very real. When hundreds of millions of people scattered all over the world have simultaneous access to an event, such as the recent Iraq War or the Olympic Games (Dayan and Katz, 1992), or when certain television programs are watched in over a hundred different countries around the world (see Silj, 1988; Liebes and Katz, 1986; and Ang, 1985, for their analyses of the TV program *Dallas*), it is clear that electronic media contribute to the formation of a global culture, underpinned by global capitalism. Similarly, when 20 people around the world who share a common interest or expertise can be in daily e-mail contact, or when anyone anywhere can access a website with no thought whatsoever of location, a different globalism can emerge, but one that is somewhat freer from global capitalism.

Both Innis (1950) and McLuhan (1962), as well as the **Toronto School** that followed in their wake (for example, Ong [1982] and Goody [1977]), placed their emphasis on media writ large. However, it is useful to explore the dynamics of oral, literate, and electronic societies in some detail in order to understand the influence of communication overall.

Oral Society

Innis claimed that the means of communication set the basic parameters for the functioning of any society. As such, in oral societies people are governed by the knowledge vested in the community and specifically preserved by certain members of society. For instance, in classical Greece, such individuals maintained and transmitted their knowledge by means of epic poems and what Innis called epic technique (1951). Epic technique involved creating poems in rhythmic six-beat lines—hexameters—that had certain rigidities and elasticities. The rigidities were the parts that were memorized. The elasticities permitted the adaptation of certain elements according to time and place. Forms, words, stock expressions, and phrases acted as aids, while the local language and situation provided the basis for ornamental gloss. The development of such techniques meant that epic poetry was in the hands of persons with excellent memories and poetic and linguistic abilities. The techniques for memorizing and reciting epics were often passed on within families of professional storytellers and minstrels. According to Innis, such families probably built up a system of memory aids that were private and carefully guarded. Catholic priest and linguist Walter Ong has described the oral process in greater detail:

> You have to do your thinking in mnemonic patterns, shaped for ready oral recurrence. Your thought must come into being in heavily rhythmic balanced patterns, in repetitions or antitheses, in alliterations and assonances, in epithetic and other formulary expression, in standard thematic settings, in proverbs, or in other mnemonic form. Mnemonic needs determine even syntax. (Ong, 1982: 34)

The epics permitted constant adaptation, as required by the oral tradition, and also allowed for the emergence of completely new content to describe conditions of social change. What was socially relevant was remembered, what was not was forgotten. As well, the flexibility permitted the incorporation of sacred myths from other civilizations, with these myths being transformed and humanized as they were turned into the content of an epic poem. The Greeks could thereby foster the development of an inclusive ideology as they expanded their empire, and this ideology could serve colonizing efforts extremely well.

While the above description may seem attractive, there are those who have viewed oral societies as especially vulnerable to power politics. Karl Popper (1945, 1962) referred to them as closed societies and saw the transformation to literate society as a movement from a closed to an open society—open to the expression of individual freedoms.

The dynamics of the oral tradition in a modern context are illustrated in the *Delgamuukw* decision, a landmark decision of the Supreme Court of Canada in which Aboriginal oral history has been accepted as a legally valid foundation for pursuing land claims. While such a decision may seem only right and proper, it has taken centuries for our literate culture to accept the veracity and authority of oral culture. In part, that acceptance has come about because of our understanding of oral communication and oral culture (see, for example, *Globe and Mail*, 15 Dec. 1997, A23, for an illustration of how we now understand oral culture).

Oral history has also been shown to be quite accurate. For instance, according to Maori oral history, New Zealand was settled by their Polynesian ancestors about 800 years ago, when eight to ten canoes of settlers set out in December from Eastern Polynesia to establish themselves in New Zealand. Recent genetic research confirms the oral history. Tracing changes in mitochondrial DNA, a genetic researcher has found that, in all likelihood, New Zealand was indeed settled by about 70 women (mitochondrial DNA is passed from mother to daughter) and their men approximately 800 years ago. Since the large canoes of the Polynesians carried about 20 people and there would have been approximately 150 settlers (not counting children) it appears they would have needed about eight to ten canoes (see *Globe and Mail*, 5 Sept. 1998).

Providing a sense of the difference between oral and literate societies, anthropologist A.B. Lord explores in *The Singer of Tales* (1964) the dynamics of a modern oral tradition (rural Yugoslavia, 1937–59). Lord notes that, for the oral bard, the recording of the words of a song is a totally foreign experience. It preserves a particular performance at a particular time in a particular setting, in a dead, utterly useless form. It does not represent the correct or best version because there is no correct or best version. Rather like Grateful Dead and, more recently, Phish concerts, each performance is unique in itself. The Canadian pianist Glenn Gould's 'literate' perspective was the antithesis of this: he believed a perfect performance, especially of the work of a composer such as Bach, could be created in the recording studio by splicing the best bits from many different performances (Payzant, 1984). He believed the concert stage merely interfered with musical perfection. Communications theorist Simon Frith (1988) carries the literate perspective one step further. He notes that whereas the record used to be a reminder of a performance, today the live performance (complete with taped inputs and pre-programmed amp settings) is a simulacrum of the record.

The oral tradition and its ability to preserve the past, to transform that past as necessary, to base law in custom, and to explain all events within a natural cosmology point to the stability of oral societies and their tendency to preserve, extend, and adapt culture. Rather than being concerned with the continued existence of formal structures and institutions, oral societies are most successful at extending the dynamics of interaction. As Innis phrased it, they have a **time bias**, that is, they tend to extend themselves over the

TIME BIAS

Societies have both history and geography—or, as Harold Innis would put it, societies occupy both time and space. One way societies occupy time and space is through their communications media, which, Innis argued, have characteristic biases that make some media more conducive to carrying messages through time—e.g., heavy, durable materials like clay or the brick walls of buildings—and some media more conducive to carrying messages through space—e.g., light, easily transportable materials like parchment or paper.

Time-biased media are time-binding media, in that they connect us to the past through their enduring images and messages. Think of the stained-glass windows in churches that relate Biblical tales, war memorials that ask us to remember fallen ancestors, or buildings that carry the names of their founders etched in stone or concrete. Historical murals, such as those in Chemainus, British Columbia, or Vankleek Hill, Ontario (see photo), offer both residents and visitors a sense of the town's past.

(Photograph by Mike Gasher. Reprinted with permission from artist, Elizabeth Skelly.)

centuries. Change in such societies often induces an adaptation that preserves ways of acting, but in new circumstances. The ancient Greeks, for example, established a stable, continuous, but adapting culture.

Today, every community has its oral processes. Music seems to play an especially strong catalytic role in helping oral societies bond. For instance, in Eastern European countries under Communist rule, jazz music was both popular and suppressed. Communist governments were especially frightened of jazz. Perhaps it was because of the African-American roots

of jazz, or perhaps it was because it seemed so uncontrolled and expressive of basic emotions. Whatever the reason, jazz was often banned. In Western countries today, there are restrictions instead of absolute bans on particular types of music. For example, rock-music stations and television broadcast channels do not play certain songs and videos, many of which are oral expressions of youth culture, although these may be available through record and video stores. For both political and cultural reasons, the hugely popular country singers, the Dixie Chicks, were banned from

'WRITTEN ORALITY'

Found orality in written form (on a birthday card to a 14-year-old Canadian girl from another).

Booface (Granny P, Judie)

Hey Granny, I may not be your sister but I think I'm your third cousin twice removed then re-added by your mom's aunt's cousin's sister's brother. In other words you're my grandma. (Don't pinch my cheeks) HAHA-HAHA!!!!!!

—Lots of love. Lesbo.

The word and relationship play in the above passage is more typical of speaking than writing. In speaking, the passage generates good-natured confusion and bonding. In writing, on a birthday card, the context maintains that bonding. Here, in a textbook, it invites analysis for logical sense.

hundreds of US radio stations and music stores after their lead singer told a concert audience in London, England, in 2003, shortly before the American war on Iraq, that they were ashamed to be from the same state as US President George W. Bush.

The ways in which oral societies preserve knowledge and cultural integrity are fundamentally different from those of literate society. Where literate cultures emphasize the 'letter of the law', oral cultures emphasize its meaning. In an oral society organizing and originating myths serve to justify present-day reality rather than a chronology of historical events. In literate cultures, where the meaning of history can go unstated even though it is recorded in detail, history eventually becomes both synchronic and diachronic—ideas that span time and narratives that are faithful to chronology can exist simultaneously. The result, in literate society, is that each generation remakes its history in the light of the ideas of the day, but also within the chronology of recorded events. As such, history is continually rewritten in literate societies.

Literate Society

Whereas Greece, for Innis, represented an oral society, Rome represented a literate society. It was not that Greece was unaffected by writing. On the contrary, a number of authors, notably Eric Havelock (1976), claim that the basis of the enormous contribution

Greek civilization made to modern civilization is to be found in writing, in their invention of the phonetic alphabet. In fact, Innis cites Greek sources from the period when writing emerged that express the significance of the change from oral to written modes. For example, in Plato's *Phaedrus* Socrates reports a conversation between the Egyptian god Thoth, the inventor of letters, and the god Amon. Amon says:

> This discovery of yours will create forgetfulness in the learners' souls, because they will not use their memories; they will trust to the external written characters and not remember of themselves. The specific you have discovered is an aid not to memory, but to reminiscence, and you give your disciples not truth but only the semblance of truth; they will be bearers of many things and will have learned nothing; they will appear to be omniscient and will generally know nothing; they will be tiresome company, having the show of wisdom without the reality.

After relaying the conversation, Socrates states:

> I cannot help feeling, Phaedrus, that writing is unfortunately like painting; for the creations of the painter have the attitude of life, and yet if you ask them a question, they preserve a solemn silence, and the same may be said of speeches. You would imagine that they had intelligence, but if you want to know anything and put a question to one of them, the speaker always gives one unvarying answer. (Plato, 1973: 84)

This conversation resembles discussions of television, especially those that focus on its numbing effect on the mind. This is not surprising, for the transformation from an oral to a literate society was as major a change as from a literate to an electronic society. The discourse also points out the degree to which knowledge and wisdom were negotiated in oral discourse, rather than derived from a linear conceptual exposition.

Rome and the Roman Empire represent the origin of literate society because the operating concepts and processes of Rome were derived from the written rather than the spoken word. In legal proceedings, for example, the influence of writing can be seen in the fact that trained lawyers were responsible for defining the exact nature of a dispute within written laws (a literate function). Nonetheless, once the dispute was defined, the case was handed to laymen (a jury) to determine a settlement among the claimants (an oral community function). The development of contract law illustrates the Romans' ability to supplant oral practices with written ones. A contract changes an oral pact into a legal obligation and permits a much more complex and contingent agreement. It is a precise written record of an agreed obligation between persons or other legal entities. Such literate inventions allowed for both an orderly and a vast expansion of the Roman Empire. As Innis (1950, 1951) phrased it, the Roman Empire had a **space bias**, that is, a tendency to extend itself over a larger and larger territory. At the greatest extent of the Empire, in the third century AD, the Romans maintained control of the lands and people around the entire perimeter of the Mediterranean, from Southern and Central Europe to the Middle East, North Africa, and the Iberian Peninsula, and on to the north and west through present-day France and Great Britain. Crucial to the exercise of administrative power in the Roman Empire was the formation of abstract laws to apply in all situations, which were then written down on a portable medium, such as parchment, so they could be consulted in any location.

The development of literate society in Western civilization reflected an attempt to replace spoken, poetic, emotive language with clear, ordered, unambiguous, logical, written prose. This, in turn, led to the emergence of new ideas and concepts. For instance, in their writings, Cicero (106–43 BC) and other Stoic philosophers invented ideas that are now fundamental to modern thought, including the notions of a world state, natural law and justice, and universal citizenship. All these became characteristics of literate societies, as did libraries, which were scattered throughout the Roman Empire. Such ideas and institutions were nurtured by writing—a technology that allows the static representation of ideas, so that the eye can juxtapose and compare two ideas, and that allows one to see many individual instances and abstract the general case.

Most other writings about literate societies focus on modern societies. While they discuss the influence of writing they do so within a context of an evolved technology and developed social, political, and legal institutions (see, for example, McLuhan, 1962; Goody, 1977; Olson, 1980). The basic claim of these authors is that writing has favoured the development of logical, linear, sequential, and conceptual thinking. Written dis-

WHO SAYS TV IS BAD FOR YOU ANYWAY?

The following historical anecdotes are meant to underline that, just like newspapers and books, television is an important medium that brings valuable information and perspectives to members of society.

Like Moses Znaimer, *Globe and Mail* TV critic John Doyle is a person who harbours no prejudice against television. In fact, it is hugely important and, Doyle figures, can be good for you. His argument runs in a four-part series that began on 26 May 2001. Behind his argument were a number of milestones that highlighted the contribution of television to modern history. Some of those milestones were:

May 1939 RCA broadcast the first live sports event, a baseball game. The broadcast laid the foundation of sports television and the new sports economy.

Fall 1951 *I Love Lucy* establishes a whole new pop culture comedy genre.

March 1954 Television cameras capture the bullying of Sen. Joseph McCarthy with contemptuous narration by Edward R. Murrow, thereby hastening an end to the Senator's witch-hunting career.

Fall 1960 Television watchers are convinced that John F. Kennedy wins his television debate against Richard Nixon. Radio listeners are of the opposite opinion. The TV politician has arrived.

Fall 1966 *W-Five* is launched by CTV as a detective-style public affairs show exposing corruption in politics and business.

July 1969 Humanity walks on the moon and is linked to earth by live broadcast.

November 1969 *Sesame Street* is created and is enormously popular for its role in helping children to learn.

September, 1972 Paul Henderson scores the TV-captured winning goal in the Canada–Russia hockey series.

June 1985 The rock concert Live Aid links two concerts in London and Philadelphia and raises millions for famine relief in Africa.

Fall 1996 CBC airs *The Newsroom*, created by Winnipegger Ken Finkleman, which satirizes the network. Finkleman becomes a television auteur.

SPACE BIAS

The notion of space bias does not come easily to some, perhaps because the word 'bias' most commonly has negative connotations. Innis used the word to mean tendency or emphasis. Thus, literacy favours or promotes the development of cultures spanning large geographic spaces. The following footprint diagram illustrates the space bias of satellite technology. By beaming down a signal to a particular area of the earth's surface, a satellite creates, at least to some degree, a community—a community of all those receiving the same signal. Of course, people choose whether to watch and which channel to watch, and different satellite footprints can carry the same content. However, the broadcast of a news program from a particular city to widespread geographic areas creates an artificial spatial extension of that city. To take another example, in some ways CNN and the BBC are extensions of Atlanta, Georgia, and London, England, just as the *Globe and Mail* is an extension of Toronto. These are all instances of space bias.

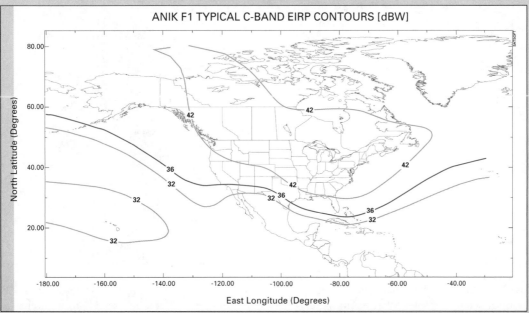

Telesat Canada's Anik F1 satellite creates a primary spatial community encompassing virtually all of Canada and much of the US. As the map shows, weather signals extend that community to the rest of Canada and the US. (Footprint courtesy of Telesat Canada.)

course is logical because it is presented in such a way that anyone can understand the meaning of a written passage without the benefit of knowing the context within which the passage was written and without the possibility of further reference to the author. It can stand by itself as a statement that is consistent both internally and with reference to other common knowledge. Literate thought is conceptual because it encourages the abstraction of salient variables within a framework of analysis and can present both the specific and general. Literate thought is linear and sequential because only one idea can be presented at a time, followed by another, and then another, each building on its predecessor. This contrasts with what can be done in some electronic media such as television, where a picture can provide context while a spoken text presents other aspects of meaning. It also contrasts with what is available to a speaker, who can communicate, with facial or bodily gesture, certain aspects of a message while communicating other aspects in words.

Electronic Society

So central are literate dynamics to modern society that when Marshall McLuhan introduced his notion of electronic society in the early 1960s, it seemed

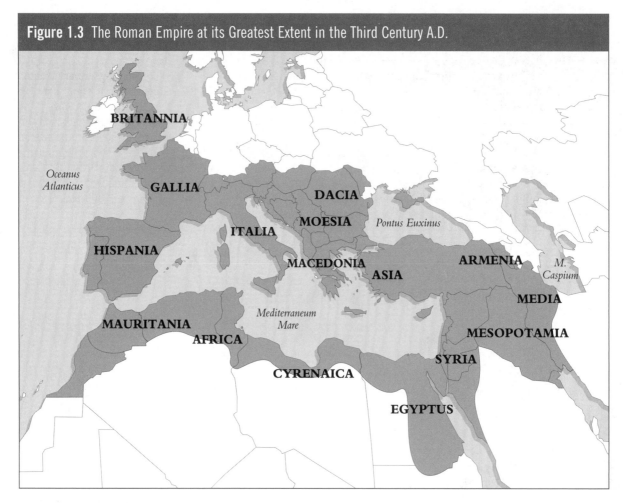

Figure 1.3 The Roman Empire at its Greatest Extent in the Third Century A.D.

both audacious and trivial to claim that somehow television, telephones, radio, and telex (the technologies that predominated in this period) were going to be as influential as writing, print, and literacy had been. It has taken a long time for academic discourse to fully incorporate McLuhan's ideas about the transformations in our society that result from a growing reliance on electronic communications. Perhaps because scholars depend so heavily on what we associate with writing, that is, the ability to write clearly and think logically and conceptually, we have not been able to imagine how electronic information processes can change society so dramatically. In trying to understand electronic society, McLuhan introduced the notion of a global village. By that he meant that electronic society has vast information-gathering and transmission capacities sufficient to make us intimately (perhaps too intimately) aware of the goings-on of people in every kind of situation all around the

world. Though our linkage with the whole world is always incomplete, it becomes steadily more inclusive as technology and communications organizations and professionals extend our realm of knowledge, thereby transforming our local and global environments. That capacity for awareness and information-processing is fundamentally affecting our society.

Joshua Meyrowitz (1985) has argued that electronic media, above all TV, weaken the once strong link between physical place and social space. Whereas previously, place and space were inseparable, communications technologies, such as the telephone and e-mail, allow two people in distant physical places to share the same social, communicative space (for example, love on the internet). Drawing heavily on the perspectives of McLuhan and Canadian sociologist Erving Goffman (1959), Meyrowitz has argued that electronic media tend to undermine traditional settings of social interaction that maintained distinct and separate social identities, for instance, the boundaries between children and adults or men and women. By invading social spaces hitherto undisturbed, broadcasting affects the character of social relationships. For instance, in India the social organization of domestic space in the household tended to keep men, women, and children apart for much of the time, thereby maintaining their distinct and traditional social roles and identities. The arrival of TVs in the households of rural India has considerably disturbed traditional relations between the sexes and between young and old by breaking segregation barriers in the family (Malik, 1989). Electronic media's influence on social space is not confined to societies such as India's. In North America, for example, TV ads for feminine hygiene products take men and children into a world from which they were previously separated.

Television has become a medium that demands both the enactment of a small drama and visual interest. British theatre critic Martin Eslin (1980) has argued that, with the advent of television, dramatization has become the predominant mode of argumentation or presentation of facts. Theatricality has replaced reasoned analysis. Information is not collected and later transformed into a form presentable through television; rather, events are often staged, and TV crews select short 'clips' for television use. Indeed, this was even the case in the Iraq War of 2003, where television reporters 'embedded' with American and British troops often presented a narrow, selected view of a broad and politically complex crisis. The presentation of news on television is a matter of careful selection. Those who can create good television are those who become newsworthy. The idea of newsworthiness itself shifts the focus away from logically or politically interesting items to the visually or dramatically interesting.

Another feature of television that has affected our electronic society can be captured in the following, recast phrase: *the camera never tells the whole truth*. We never know what is going on outside the frame. As media analyst Antonia Zerbisias (2003: A14) wrote of the widely and repeatedly broadcast toppling, by American troops, of a Saddam Hussein statue in Baghdad, 'Never mind how that video was tightly framed, showing a chanting crowd, when wider shots would have revealed a very different picture: a very large, mostly empty square surrounded by US tanks.' We never know what happened the instant before the camera was turned on or the instant after it was turned off. We never know if what was filmed is typical or atypical. And while we never know 'what is not said or printed' in any means of communication, we are much more apt to feel with visual communication that we can 'trust our own eyes'. In short, the camera never presents the temporal or spatial frame.

This trust was further undermined with the development of digital technology that allows film and television producers to make the person on camera look as if he is saying what is being said—it is the same technology that is used to make animals appear as if they are speaking.

In an effort to combat the 'bad press' that television sometimes gets, Moses Znaimer, of CityTV in Toronto, created a documentary, *TVTV: The Television Revolution*, to challenge what he calls 'print dogma'. Some communication scholars took his challenge seriously: they created a McLuhanesque-style book, *TVTV: The Debate*, in which they challenged Znaimer's 'television dogma' and gave him a chance to reply (Anderson et al., 1996). The book and the documentary together provide a foundation for an in-depth discussion of the nature and influence of print and television.

From the publication of McLuhan's book, *Understanding Media* (1964), to the 1990s, discussions of electronic society were focused on television because television was the dominant medium of this period. With the development of and widespread access to personal computers and then the internet, everyone, from communications scholars to government planners and members of the general public, has begun to realize just how profound are the social changes being brought about by electronic communications. The nature of education, e-commerce, electronic publication of scientific journals, and direct communication with friends and those from around the world we have never met all reflect that how we do things and the dynamics of cultures, political systems, and markets are being changed fundamentally by electronic communications.

Today, the basic principles of electronic communication, above and beyond television, are essentially as McLuhan outlined. Communication is instantaneous. Therefore, location and distance decrease in their importance. Electronic communication can encompass images, sound, and text. Therefore, we are far less restricted to one mode of expression. Electronic communication is as powerful as, if not more powerful than, print—because access to it is less restricted.

TV AS RELIGION?

Moses Znaimer's Ten Commandments of television are:

1. Television is the triumph of the image over the printed word.
2. Print created illiteracy. TV is democratic. Everybody gets it.
3. The true nature of television is flow, not show; process, not conclusion.
4. As worldwide television expands, the demand for local programming increases.
5. The best TV tells me what happened to me, today.
6. TV is as much about the people bringing you the story as the story itself.
7. In the past, TV's chief operating skill was political. In the future it will be, it will have to be, mastery of the craft itself.
8. TV creates immediate consensus, subject to immediate change.
9. There was never a mass audience, except by compulsion.
10. Television is not a problem to be managed, but an instrument to be played.

Source: Anderson et al. (1996: 14).

Therefore, determining who controls it is of increased importance. This is why the fate of Microsoft is so very important to everyone, not just Bill Gates and his competitors. It is also why so many are determined to preserve part of the internet as a place for public discourse, not merely as a medium for business.

Modes of Communication

Given the historical development of communication—from oral to literate to electronic society—as well as the theories and analysis of this development, we now turn to the underlying features of each of these communication modes. The following provides an overview of the characteristics of oral and literate forms of communication, as well as the different kinds of electronic communication: oral, audiovisual, and digital.

ORAL AND LITERATE COMMUNICATION

As anthropologist E.T. Hall (1980) has so vividly explained, oral communication incorporates lived cultural patterns—how close we stand to one another, how much inflection we put into our words through facial and bodily gesture, how we use our eyes, and so forth. The radical side of oral communication is conversation: anyone may say anything in any manner and thereby accomplish anything, from entirely preserving the achieved social relations to disrupting them completely. Investigations in a variety of disciplines, including anthropology (Goody,

1977), communications (McLuhan, 1962, 1964; Innis, 1950, 1951; Ong, 1982), and classics (Havelock, 1976), have also shown that when people engage in conversation, they focus on the intent of the person with whom they are speaking or listening to, whether those conversationalists are human beings or gods. Oral communication leads to belief systems in which environmental constants, such as the sun, moon, stars, earth, air, seas, rivers, trees, rocks, animals, and so forth, are made into persons or metaphors of persons. Oral communication also favours the formation of groups of like-minded people. The pluralism inherent in this system of environmental constants, all with their own dynamics, provides for a variety of interpretative structures that vie for allegiance and are not necessarily consistent with one another.

Oral chants are the conservative side of oral communication. By means of exact repetition they affirm the fundamental shared realities of a community. They utilize voice and body, often adding adornments to the voice—rhythm, music, tone of voice—and adornments to the person, such as items of symbolic significance—masks, speaking sticks, incense burners. Such adornments heighten various senses, such as sight, smell, touch, hearing, as well as the overall perception and conception of the chant. Oral chants encourage affirmation of the group through an emergent sense of the whole being greater than the sum of its parts. The orientation is one of consolidation, of affirming the whole community, and of its constituent members playing out

TWO EXPERIMENTS IN ORAL COMMUNICATION

You can test out one of the variables surrounding oral communication. E.T. Hall called it social distance. Pick out a place near to where you are having your conversation and see if you can move the person with whom you are speaking to that spot. You can use one of two methods. One is to stand closer than usual to your fellow conversationalist. The other is to stand slightly further away. Either way, you can usually push or pull them to that spot as long as they are not conscious of your intent.

Ethnomethodologists such as Garfinkel (1984) were intent on demonstrating that conversation, at least in certain social settings, has implicit rules. They would take a behaviour from one social setting and insert it into another, such as getting up in the middle of a dinner and warmly greeting the hostess of the dinner as if one were first arriving at a dinner party. The surprised reactions of the other dinner guests confirmed, for Garfinkel, that there were implicit rules in such social situations. Notwithstanding this, conversation is a form of communication with radical potential. You can try an ethnomethodological experiment such as this, but for it to work you must not insert a behaviour that others might think you wanted to do anyway, such as planting a drive-by passionate kiss. The Quebec-produced no-dialogue TV program, *Just for Laughs,* is a marvellous source of such experiments.

their various established roles.

Literate communication is also divided into two forms, the prosaic and the poetic. The prose text must have internal consistency and comprehensiveness. It must be capable of standing apart from its author as a meaningful statement in and by itself. Its associated analysis framework is linear—moving from one logical point to the next. It is not situationally contextualized, for example, by body language and tone of voice. Contextualization must be inherent in the text through the use of modifying words or the creation of images. Prosaic literate communication leads to the development of general and specific explanatory concepts. These explanatory concepts have a hierarchical relation to one another and, over the course of time, form an explanatory framework. Such a framework can be, for instance, a scientific theory. For example, the behaviour of objects relative to other objects was defined by a number of specific laws until Newton suggested the notion of gravity to explain such behaviour. Later, Einstein proposed his general theory of relativity, and Newton's notions were recast as specific instances within Einstein's more encompassing framework. In such a case, old concepts were eclipsed by new ones.

The hierarchical nature of prosaic literate communication results from a focus on producing and testing conceptual constants to prove the supremacy of single general concepts that seem to explain all related phenomena. Consistent with this tendency, literate societies are less amenable than are oral societies to a plurality of explanatory frameworks that gain or lose apparent validity, and hence the allegiance of followers, as events unfold. They favour a single, logically supportable, perspective.

Written poetry diverges from written prose in the analytical framework it encourages. Rather than encouraging logical and hierarchical thinking, poets strive to evoke images in the mind of the reader and, through those images, to provide insight into the real or the imaginary. The social philosophy consistent with poetic mode focuses on both the created images and the poet. On the one hand it may encourage elitism (few have the talent to work with words to produce images that resonate with an audience of any size), and on the other hand it may encourage plurality as a result of the multiplicity of images that the poets create. In addition, how poets are cast in society—as agents of the court, voices of the people, or as noble instead of corrupt—constrains both their role and the power of their images.

ELECTRONIC ORAL COMMUNICATION

Electronic society is complex and needs to be divided up to be understood. First are electronic oral communication and its two submodes, *broadcast* and *point-to-point* systems. Radio typifies the broadcast mode, while the telephone typifies point-to-point. Ironically, cellphones are really a restricted broadcast form, which is why (in analogue versions at least) they can be monitored. Cellphones are more accurately called cellular radio.

Electronic oral communication is not closely confined by space but it is confined by time. Radio waves reach many listeners, depending on their power and depending on which part of the radio spectrum they use—short-wave signals can bounce more than halfway around the world, especially at night. Telephone similarly reaches around the world. Even more than oral communication, electronic oral communication is focused on speaking, that is, the rhetorical structure of the message, and the human voice itself—there is nothing else, no person, no gestures. Like oral communication, electronic oral communication exists in the passing moment and is not preserved except in the memory of the listener and, at times, in electronic archives. It relies for its effect on immediate impression and the echoes of that impression in the listener's mind. Oral broadcasts often mimic the giving of speeches or lectures in that they may be created first in written form and then delivered orally, as in newscasts. In other instances, oral broadcasts are confined to a particular topic, or only certain individuals speak (for example, a host and a panel of experts), and certain distinctive rules are observed (see Scannell, 1991). Point-to-point electronic oral communication (the telephone in various forms) usually provides access to everyone and replaces face-to-face communication.

Electronic oral communication is affected by: (1) voice modulation (radio professionals are trained to speak in a certain manner); (2) the choice of words and whether the ideas are expressed within a narrative mode; and (3) the sequencing of ideas or, for example, the opposing ideas of different speakers. To some degree electronic oral communication is narrative or dramatic performance. It is impressionistic of both the message and the messenger. As the words go by, some phrases stick in your mind, not just their meaning but also the exact words. And the exact words are framed both more broadly, in the vaguely remembered whole, and more vividly, in the imputed personality of the speaker—the kind of person that would speak that way on that subject. Understanding is nuanced by perceived and projected interpretations consistent with the inferred character of the speaker.

The effectiveness of electronic oral communication can rest on the ability of certain speakers to capture, in ringing tones, the often unarticulated attitudes and understandings of the audience—sometimes called the *Zeitgeist*. The phrase 'does it ring true' is often operative. This perspective can lead to a view of certain speakers, such as talk-show hosts or investigative reporters, as believable whether or not their content stands up to detailed scrutiny. Smooth-talking politicians, especially those who wear the mantle of power well, can use this media 'bias' to their advantage. The phrases 'he sounds sincere' and 'you can tell she knows just from the sound of her voice' are germane to understanding how people evaluate electronic oral performance.

TRANSFORMING THE MESSAGE

A cartoonist for the Los Angeles Times Syndicate, Jeff Danzinger, captured the transformative aspects of communication in a cartoon which shows Monica Lewinsky telling her story to a would-be ghost writer. There are two ways of reading this description of a cartoon. The one probably intended by the cartoonist was the scattered nature of supposed oral discourse of Monica Lewinsky and the ordered logical thought of the ghost writer. A far different reading is possible insofar as much of anyone's talk is neither strictly logical nor linear and it does not follow along a single track.

So then I said to my mother . . . 'Oh! I know what I wanted to tell you. Like yesterday? I was shopping my brains out and I remembered that the creep like, you know, no wait, it was the otherr day, not the otherr day you know. And, so I bought this, this, this thing thing, a kind of whatever thing and then I thought, well sure, like so what, I can win. Nah-uh, so Vernon said Monica, he said fine like whatever. Do you know what I mean? I mean.

The cartoon shows the balding, middle-aged writer typing into his laptop with a title-page on his left reading Butthead's Ashes by Monica Lewinsky. He translates as he types:

My mother was a great comfort to me during those challenging days, and often when I reminisce, while shopping or just letting my thoughts roam about the cards life has dealt me and the way others treated me . . .

ELECTRONIC AUDIOVISUAL COMMUNICATION

Electronic audiovisual communication is most obviously exemplified by television, including both national network broadcasting and **narrowcasting**, that is, television focusing on a sector of the audience (though, in some cases, such as CNN or BBC World, this audience may stretch around the world). It also includes community television or, more accurately, community-access television. This form of television usually consists of a local cable channel made available to the public so they can make their voices heard. And while to include film would be technologically anomalous and impure according to McLuhanites, film does fit here the best. (Some would argue that film is not an electronic medium but rather, in its method of projecting images, an extension of painting.)

Electronic audiovisual communication attempts to 're-create' or 're-present' the social through its moving pictures and spoken words. In broadcasting, it combines access to special people (celebrities) in special settings (famous, meaningful, opulent) under special circumstances (orchestras in the wings). Based on its orientation to visual images, which convey its power and also allow mediated intimate contact, electronic audiovisual communication can be said to be an iconic or image-oriented medium (see Bruner, 1978). It shares with electronic oral communication the characteristic of being a narrative and dramatic medium. It presents stories of people usually within the context of a given problem and its resolution.

The production of audiovisual images is a process that, in the final analysis, is usually directed by a single individual but involves a large and diverse team of specialists. Each member contributes to a complement of images through lighting, framing, dialogue, ambience, or editing style, which combine to create the intended impression. In some sense, electronic audiovisual communication is the re-creation of face-to-face communication in a fully visualized context conceived by the literate mind.

The cost of the creative process marks the major difference between community television and its rich sisters. The low production values of resource-starved community television contrasts with the glossy output of mainstream channels. This contrast provides daily legitimization of the position of power that the commercial channels occupy. High production values imbue media celebrities with an aura of legitimacy. Indeed, the supreme position of authority on television is that of the news anchor.

The investment demanded for the production of sophisticated audiovisual images has meant that television has fallen under the control of two types of owners: governments and large commercial organizations. Even community stations have been given over to the commercial sector, which provides access to groups and individuals as a kind of freebie in exchange for its monopoly position.

Because an infinite number of images and impressions can be created by even slight variations—the way a camera frames a person—the derivative analytic framework for this form of communication emphasizes flexibility and room for difference of opinion. In general, the television-based perspective on the world is pluralistic: it involves an acceptance of variety, particularity, and novelty. However, it is a restricted pluralism. It is peopled by a feudal court of celebrity personalities. It also has the dubious power to command the forces of communication so effectively that visual rhetoric prevails as the foundation of effective communication. The attractiveness of the image plays a very large part in determining the effectiveness of the communication of the message.

ELECTRONIC DIGITAL COMMUNICATION

Now here is a problem. If radio is electronic oral, and television is electronic audiovisual, what is the proper term for information transmission and telecommunications, exclusive of broadcasting? Until this edition, we have called it what the heading says, electronic digital communication. But everything—radio, television, sound, video—is going digital. All web technologies are digital. To consider information transmission and telecommunications, exclusive of broadcasting, as electronic data communication is also a problem because digital data are exactly what are created in all electronic digital forms, whether images, sounds, text, or instances of purchasing. As recently as 1995, data communication was dominated by large organizations—banks, travel agents, hotel chains, central governments, stock analysts, global ad agencies, even large urban public libraries. Now, with the burgeoning of websites and the digitizing of broadcasting, 'digital electronic communication' is an all-encompassing term.

This said, what we used to mean by the term 'electronic digital communication' involved the communication of data that could involve an individual creating input and another or that same individual doing some final interpretations of output. However, programmed computers can suffice for all aspects—inputting, reception, and analysis. The information typical to this mode of communication is monitored (the number of items sold at a particular cash register, the number of hits to a website) or sampled (a market or political poll). The communicators involved—both information creators and receivers—have the capacity to analyze and benefit from vast quantities of detailed information. At its most sophisticated level, descriptive and inferential mathematical analysis and statistics can be used for summarizing data patterns, thereby revealing the secrets of brainwaves or weather patterns. Such possibilities encourage the ascendancy of planners and strategists and expert interpreters knowledgeable of both trends and trend analysis.

But what to call it? Perhaps we will have to live with ambiguity. In the same way that telecommunication encompasses broadcasting, so 'electronic data communication' seems the most suitable term, even if, strictly speaking, it encompasses digital broadcasting and web activity.

Other Derivative and Different Viewpoints

Though Innis and McLuhan were the first to theorize on communication and its transformative effects, the shortcoming of their frameworks is that they tend towards a **technological determinism**. In other words, they tend to make us think that technology is the fundamental shaping variable and society is a mere expression of the dynamics of technology (a phenomenon explored in greater detail in Chapters 10 and 11). It is not that either author was an avowed technological determinist. McLuhan, for instance, once noted: 'we shape our tools; thereafter our tools shape us.' Thus it might be claimed that McLuhan begins his analysis with **human agency**, not technology. But it might also be claimed that McLuhan had very little to say about the 'we' in that statement (the nature of human agency). Certainly McLuhan inspired others, notably Elizabeth Eisenstein (1983), to place technology at the centre of their explanatory frameworks. They, too, deny that they are technological determinists. But rather than emphasizing human agency and social interaction, which shape both technology and the uses made of it, they slide into technologically derived descriptions of the social process.

They fail to portray technology as a tool employed by those with power to advance their own interests.

Other viewpoints address and examine communications media. They are mainly rooted in material realities. They range from pure **Marxism** to current cultural theories and audience theories. (Such perspectives are introduced in later chapters, especially Chapters 4 and 5.) Raymond Williams (1974), for example, notes that communications technologies arise from the organization of society and reflect that organization. In his doctoral dissertation, 'Printing as an Agent of Stability in China', David Ze (1995) challenges Elizabeth Eisenstein's (1983) thesis in her book, *The Printing Press as an Agent of Change*. Ze makes the case that it is not technology that is important but its social organization. He argues that even though the Chinese invented movable type before it was invented in Europe, printing was an agent of social stability rather than change. The basic points of his argument are that: printing was controlled by Chinese emperors; it was used to transmit official versions of a limited number of texts; printers had everything to lose and nothing to gain in printing original material; and wood blocks were the most efficient means of reproducing texts as demand emerged. He concludes that the existence of a technology does not necessarily affect society significantly. However, if society can benefit from a technology, and people can see that benefit, then technology can speed and consolidate the evolution of a new social organization.

Summary

The purpose of this chapter has been to convey the importance of communication in the affairs of society. We did so, first, by introducing some current elements of communications: the rapidly changing technology; the growing trend of supporting communication that is financially lucrative; and the exercise of control over technology (particularly the 'who' and 'how' of control). We then discussed the extensive range of influence of communication, how communication is bound up in all social activity. We summarized eight dimensions of its influence on human activity: the social, political, economic, educational, cultural, technological, familial, and individual.

After a brief nod to the obvious fact that communication transmits content, we discussed how communication transforms the content it carries. We reviewed how oral, literate, and various modes of electronic communication have affected the basic functioning of all societies throughout history and prehistory.

The importance of communication in society cannot be overestimated. We have argued that communication is a force that contributes to social cohesion and is therefore a structuring force in society, both facilitating and constraining. Human affairs cannot be divorced from the communication system used to represent or discuss them. The design of our communication systems impinges on every element of our present and future lives.

RELATED WEBSITES

Canadian Journal of Communication: www.cjc-online.ca
The *Canadian Journal of Communication* is Canada's principal communication journal. Students can make good use of it by accessing the site and searching on essay topics. The *CJC* is a leading proponent of on-line journal publishing and makes its back issues accessible on the internet.

Council of Canadians: www.canadians.org
The Council of Canadians involves itself in a wide range of issues where it feels that Canadians have a distinct set of interests.

Harold Innis Research Foundation: www.utoronto.ca/hirf
The Harold Innis Research Foundation at the University of Toronto fosters research and other activities, including a research bulletin that focuses on the theories of Harold Innis. The University of Toronto also has a college named Innis College.

McLuhan Research Centre: www.mcluhan.utoronto.ca/
The McLuhan Centre has quite a dynamic website. It runs courses and a web log along with many other McLuhanesque and McLuhan-oriented activities.

MZTV museum: www.mztv.com
Broadcaster and TV mogul Moses Znaimer is founder of the MZTV museum.

FURTHER READINGS

Canadian Journal of Communication, Special Issue, 1996. 'TVTV: The Television Revolution, The Debate', eds Robert Anderson, Richard Gruneau, and Paul Heyer. This special issue offers a number of essays critical of Moses Znaimer's ideas, as presented in the documentary *TVTV: The Television Revolution*. Znaimer's ideas could be called McLuhanesque.

Eisenstein, Elizabeth. 198379. *The Printing Revolution in Early Modern Europe*. Cambridge: Cambridge University Press. Eisenstein examines the role of the printing press and movable type.

McLuhan, Marshall. 1962. *The Gutenberg Galaxy: The Making of Typographic Man*. Toronto: University of Toronto Press. This was the first of McLuhan's two major works. It outlines orality and literacy and their historical development. Its key thesis is that typography created the world as we know it.

———. 1964. *Understanding Media: The Extensions of Man*. Toronto: McGraw-Hill. Here McLuhan focuses on the influence of the media on the modern world. The various essays that make up the text explore the implications of (largely) electronic information systems. The book is interesting for both its insight and its foresight.

Ong, Walter. 1982. *Orality and Literacy: The Technologizing of the Word*. London: Methuen. Following McLuhan's basic ideas plus ideas from classicists, Walter Ong examines the nature of orality in greater depth than did McLuhan.

STUDY QUESTIONS

1. Communication affects the full range of human activity, from how we think about ourselves and how we act in the world to the interaction between nations. Describe the range of influence of communication and its significance for the evolution of society.
2. The influence of communication is not confined to its capacity to transfer information. Explain.
3. What are the fundamental differences between the mathematical and the social models of communication?
4. Summarize the path-breaking writings of Marshall McLuhan and the characteristics he attributes to oral societies, literate societies, and electronic societies.
5. In some sense, electronic audiovisual communication is the re-creation of face-to-face communication in a fully visualized context conceived by the literate mind. Explain.
6. How are new media influencing the structure of our society?
7. The current mass media system serves consumers, not people, not citizens, not children, not all groups within society, but consumers. Discuss.

LEARNING OUTCOMES

*   To provide the understanding that communication is part of virtually every aspect of our lives, including our ideas of ourselves.
*   To introduce the notion that communication is transmissive and transformative in function.
*   To outline the characteristics of a mathematical or technical model of communication.
*   To introduce Canadians Marshall McLuhan and Harold Innis as major communication theorists.
*   To provide a basic sense of the varying transformative natures of oral, literate, and electronic media and their influence on society.
*   To introduce Innis's notions of space bias and time bias.
*   To illustrate the dynamics of electronic communication and how it encompasses oral and electronic communication.
*   To explain briefly the technological emphasis inherent in the frameworks discussed.

CHAPTER 2

Mass Communication and Modern Society

Introduction: Definitions

Chapter 1 explored the influence of communication on society. It noted that communication affects the whole of the social world as a result of its transmission function and also through the transformative influences of oral, literate, and electronic communication processes. Each medium has a distinctive influence on the social process. This chapter narrows the focus in two ways: from communication of all types to mass communication, and from society through the ages to modern society.

Mass communication encompasses the traditional mass communication industries such as broadcasting and newspapers, the more recent decentralized production of information for mass communication that now takes place via the internet, e.g., health or transportation information, and third, the vastly expanded world of person-to-person communication on a mass scale that also takes place via the internet, phone systems, and postal systems. Whereas mass communication traditionally has involved in large part the centralized production and dissemination of information and entertainment products, technology has finally brought to a substantial majority of members of developed societies—and an increasing number of citizens of the developing world—the ability to communicate with others worldwide. No longer are people confined to being solely audience members for corporate products that are increasingly injected with commercial messages; they can engage in the production and exchange of text, sound, and image, singly or in combination with others of their choosing (and sometimes not of their choosing). Today, we are confined, more than anything, by language rather than by geography, a confinement gradually being chipped away by automatic translation programs. To be concrete, the internet has joined with the postal system and a much enhanced phone system to make communication between and among members of society on a mass or wide scale as important to, and as influential on, society as the mass distribution of centrally produced information and entertainment products by

broadcasters, newspaper, magazine, and book publishers, filmmakers, and the music recording industry.

This chapter begins by discussing the word 'mass'. It expands the discussion of communication outlined in the first chapter. It then examines mass communication, public communication, and the nature and operation of the mass media.

THE MEANING OF 'MASS'

The *Concise Oxford Dictionary* (ninth edn, p. 838) offers various meanings of the noun 'mass'. Included are: a coherent body of matter of indefinite shape; a dense aggregation of objects; a large number or amount; the majority; the ordinary people (in the plural); affecting a large number of people or things; large scale. The purpose of our including so many definitions is to point out, moving into semiotics for a moment, that the word 'mass' is complex and extensive, truly polysemic. And, extensive as the definitions of 'mass' are, the *Concise Oxford* does not wholly recognize the use of 'mass' by social theorists. The closest it comes is to provide an example of large scale: '(mass audience, mass action, mass murder)'.

Sociologist and media theorist Herbert Blumer provides further context to the use of the word 'mass' in a communication context. In an early article, Blumer (1939) contrasted a number of different kinds of collectivities to arrive at a meaning for 'mass'. Simplifying and adapting Blumer's ideas somewhat, we can say that in a small group all members know each other and are aware of their common membership. The crowd is limited to a single physical space, is temporary in its existence and composition, and if it acts as a unit it rarely does so rationally. The public is customarily large and widely dispersed. It is often represented by largely self-appointed, 'informed' people who speak publicly and in rational discourse to validate their statements and appointment.

Denis McQuail (1983: 36) has summarized the meaning Blumer arrived at for 'mass':

The term 'mass' captures several features of the new audience for cinema and radio which were missing or not linked together by any of these three existing concepts [small group, crowd, public]. It was often very large—larger than most groups, crowds or publics. It was very widely dispersed and its members were usually unknown to each other or to whoever brought the audience into existence. It lacked self-awareness and self-identity and was incapable of acting together in an organized way to secure objectives. It was marked by a shifting composition within changing boundaries. It did not act for itself, but was rather 'acted upon'. It was heterogeneous, in consisting of large numbers from all social strata and demographic groups, but homogeneous in its behaviour of choosing a particular object of interest and in the perception of those who would like to 'manipulate' it.

McQuail, in each edition of his introduction to mass communication (1983, 1987, 1994), and Tim O'Sullivan and his colleagues, writing in 1983 in *Key Concepts in Communication*, note what they term 'mass society theory' of the early twentieth century. This model of industrialist/capitalist societies portrayed them as composed of elites (capitalist owners, politicians, the clergy, landowners, artists, intellectuals) and workers, 'a vast work-force of atomized, isolated individuals without traditional bonds of locality or kinship, who were alienated from their labour by its repetitive, unskilled tendencies and by their subjection to the vagaries of the market. Such individuals were entirely at the mercy of (i) totalitarian ideologies and propaganda; and (ii) influence by the mass media (comprising, in this period, the emergent cinema and radio)' (O'Sullivan et al., 1983: 131). No mention is made of Marx or the Frankfurt School (see Chapter 4) but, presumably, the authors had these theorists in mind when they were writing. O'Sullivan et al. point out that 'mass society theory has been refuted by historical evidence' but they also note that the concept of the alienated majority of society has survived. Indeed, it appears to have survived the more than 20 years since the publication of the work of O'Sullivan and his colleagues to the present day. The moral force of the view of people who work, which portrays ordinary people as alienated from participating in the structuring of their own society and hence their own lives, seems to have invested itself in much social commentary on the evils of globalization.

However, as the *Concise Oxford* attests and O'Sullivan and his colleagues point out, one need not imbue the word 'mass' with a sense of alienation or totalitarian tendencies. It can indeed mean, simply, large scale. This is how we mean it in this book.

MASS COMMUNICATION

In Chapter 1, we defined **communication** as the process by which a message (content, meaning) is encoded, transmitted, and decoded and the manner in which a message (content, meaning) is transformed by that three-part process. If we were to carry forward the above definition of communication, we would see mass communication as communication on a mass scale, in other words, a lot of messages being encoded, transmitted, received, and decoded.

Some of mass communication is exactly that—many people talking on the telephone, sending and receiving e-mail, blogging, and writing and receiving letters. Yet, as noted in the opening of this chapter, the traditional meaning of 'mass communication' did not describe that process at all, or if it included such processes, it did so weakly. What was, until the turn of the century, more often termed 'mass communication' is the communication that happens by means of movies, large daily newspapers, and broadcasting, that is, *the centralized creation, production, and mass distribution of information and entertainment*. O'Sullivan and his colleagues captured that type of mass communication quite well:

> Mass communication is the practice and product of providing leisure entertainment and information to an unknown audience by means of corporately financed, industrially produced, state regulated, high-technology, privately consumed commodities in the modern print, screen, audio and broadcast media. (O'Sullivan et al., 1983: 131)

This definition was written prior to the development of the internet, CD-ROM games, cellphones with cameras and MP3 players, Blackberries, transmitting GPS units, Google, blogs, and wikis and therefore does not encompass them.

O'Sullivan et al. pointed out that this usage of the term 'mass communication' had the potential to mislead. They advised that, following in the after-currents of mass society theory, the word 'mass' encourages many to think of the audience as a vast, undifferentiated agglomeration of unthinking individuals, likely to behave in a non-rational, if not irrational, manner (recall the dictionary definition noted above). This conception of the audience is misleading, they noted. In reality, those who watch television, read newspapers, or go to movies are a heterogeneous group who bring many different contexts (encoding envelopes, see Chapter 1) to any message. Moreover, they added, the word 'communication' masks the industrial nature of the media and promotes a tendency to think of them as analogous to interpersonal communication, that is, person-to-person communication on a mass scale. Back in 1983, with these caveats in place, the O'Sullivan definition was generally accepted and used. Parallel definitions were put forward by others, including DeFleur and Ball-Rokeach (1989). These definitions, although fading, are still in use today.

However, times and technology have changed. Beginning about 1990, when the internet began to be embraced, the possibilities for person-to-person communication on a mass scale expanded dramatically. Suddenly, it became possible to post an e-mail to an address anywhere in the world that had an e-mail system, where the message would await access by the user. The transmission was instantaneous and free—no writing paper, envelope, postage stamp, mailbox, mail pickup, imperfect post office sorting and handling, travel by air, land, or sea, resorting, and delivery; nor, alternatively, any dictation over a phone to a telegrapher at an exorbitant charge per word; nor, alternatively again, any need for a dedicated machine to create a graphic to be sent over phone lines to arrive in fuzzy facsimile (fax) form at the other end.

In quick succession, a number of technologies were added to text-exchange protocols so that by 2000, digital files of any type—text, sound, image—could be exchanged between any computer user and any other computer user for an insignificant cost. (By 2006, movie files and three-dimensional images had been added to the list.) Moreover, with the deployment of World Wide Web technology, alongside platform-independent file writing and reading, the foundations of centralized mass communication (that is, corporately financed, industrially produced, state-regulated, high-technology institutions) as the only form of mass communication began to unravel. By 2000, it had also become possible for any person, with a bit of effort and little more expense than a computer, some software, and internet access, to create a website that was accessible around the world.

By 2005, still more major innovations had taken place. First blogs—diary-type web logs or postings, usually done by individuals, of text, images, and links to other blogs, web pages, and other media—multiplied into the millions. Then wikis—websites that encourage collaboration, allowing users to add, delete, edit, or otherwise change content—came into widespread use: Wikipedia.com is the best-known public example of the use of such technology.

By 2006, the idea of a transformed web, dubbed **Web 2.0**, was being promoted to describe the extension of the web though the addition of new communication and interaction options. In the main, Web 2.0 applications change static informational sites to electronic communication facilities where people can discuss, collaborate, or otherwise interact. Coupled with RSS (Really Simple Syndication), that is, notifications of new content postings, such applications allow people to monitor and participate in forums central to their interests.

In short, while the internet started off as a means for person-to-person communication (on a mass scale), with the success of WWW technology and its increasing use by the business community and other organizations, the internet has become both a mass person-to-person communication system and a mass (decentralized) broadcast or dissemination system. The internet has quickly evolved into a large-scale communication and interaction-capable system open to and welcoming (by its affordability) the public. It allows anyone, in Canada or in many other countries, to create content for next to nothing (after equipment or access costs) and make that content available to the world (i.e., broadcast it and open it for interaction)—facilitated, of course, by now ubiquitous search engines. Four notable sites in early 2007 that allow many different people to post content for the world to see are Post Secret (postsecret.blogspot.com), Fanfiction (www.fanfiction.net), KYOU Radio (www.kyouradio.com), and Soundclick (www.soundclick.com). Given that millions use the internet daily, all these developments increase substantially the effectiveness of the technology as a means of mass communication and interaction. Various institutions have contributed to making information public by uploading substantial content that is available to all internet users. Four examples are: the Public Library of Science (www.plos.org), Science Commons (sciencecommons.org), MIT OpenCourse Ware (ocw.mit.edu), and Project Gutenberg (www.gutenberg.org/wiki/Main_Page).

These many and continuing developments change the nature of mass communication fundamentally. O'Sullivan et al. described what they saw in the context of their time. What they could not imagine was the development of technology that would so powerfully enable interpersonal communication and interaction on a mass scale that it would transform our social contacts and society as a whole. No one else could imagine this either, except Marshall McLuhan, and few understood fully or believed what McLuhan actually claimed. Back in the 1960s, McLuhan claimed that in the age of television we were living in a world of instantaneous communication everywhere. In fact, instantaneous communication everywhere was far off. McLuhan's genius was to see that, using electronic communications technology, the world would eventually reach that state. As of the first decade of the twenty-first century, in the developed world and in pockets within developing economies, we have reached that instantaneous state. Everywhere is yet to come.

Thus, the traditional definition of 'mass communication', from our current perspective, does not describe mass communication at all but rather the mass distribution of information and entertainment products. Looked at today, such a definition is incomplete. In our changed world, and in a nutshell, *mass communication encompasses the transmission and transformation of meaning on a large scale*. Such a definition involves three different organizational forms:

1. *Mass communication is the production and dissemination of mass information and entertainment*—the traditional definition. This form of communication involves the corporately financed industrial production of entertainment and information to large, unknown audiences by means of print, screen, audio, broadcast, audiovisual, and internet technologies or public performance for both private and public consumption. In certain instances (e.g., broadcasting and, less often, print) it is state-regulated. Some examples are: radio, television, newspapers, film, magazines, books, recorded and performed music, and advertising.

2. The second form has the same general organization but allows for greater participation by many members of society as part of either their work or leisure. *Mass communication is the decentralized production and wide accessibility of information and entertainment*. Such communication is sometimes cor- porately financed, sometimes industrially produced, and often intended for small or niche audiences. It is rarely state-regulated and is undertaken by many individuals, organizations, and institutions. It includes websites, podcasts, blogs, print, film, audio, broadcast, and public performance.

3. The third form of mass communication is quite different and, currently, ever-changing as new technologies are developed. *Mass communication is the interactive exchange of information (or messages or intelligence) on a mass scale*. Its defining attribute is **interactivity**. Such interactivity encompasses the exchange of information that takes place among individuals and groups by means of public access to communication channels. This form of mass communication encompasses the interactivity inherent in the Web 2.0 paradigm. This exchange of information on a mass scale includes the mass communication that takes place by wired and wireless phone, the mail, e-mail, pagers, two-way radio, and fax. It is an increasingly robust, decentralized, two-way exchange of information and creative expression. This form of mass communication encompasses such technologies as computer-facilitated phone technology (e.g., Skype, VOIP (Voice Over Internet Protocol), cellphones that themselves encompass GPS (Global Positioning System) functionality and MP3-facilitated music recording and playback), file exchange facilitated through e-mail (instead of faxes), and enhanced security and electronic signature functions. A particularly interesting extension of interactivity is the collaborative creation of software that frees users from having to purchase commercial software at a relatively high cost. Joomla (www.joomla.org) and SourceForge (sourceforge.net) are two examples. Still others allow users access to differentiated sound tracks that they can remix to create new musical expression. Examples are ccMixter (ccmixter.org) and a collaboration among Britain's Open University, Channel 4 (a non-BBC public service television channel), the British Film Institute, and the BBC, the motto of which is 'find it, rip it, mix it' (see copyfight.corante.com/archives/2005/04/13/bbc_rips_mixes_creative_commons.php).

Such a three-part definition of mass communication—within the overall definition offered above: the transmission and transformation of meaning on a large scale—repositions centralized and industrialized production and dissemination of information and entertainment products as simply one form of mass communication rather than its being the central and dominant feature. This is especially so because of the vast expansion of decentralized two-way information exchange with its public access and interactivity. The decreased dominance of the production and distribution of industrialized media product gives greater prominence to citizen participation in the provision and exchange of information and interactivity. Members of society, who were previously confined to limited one-to-one media such as telephones and the postage system, are now understood to have access to the creation and dissemination of media products. By including public access to communication and interaction technologies, this three-part definition reflects a major evolution of mass communication towards addressing the desires and needs of members of society. No longer are people merely provided with information and entertainment and hence positioned as audience members who may (or may not) actively interpret and engage with media products. In different terms, given the contemporary evolution of mass communication, we are entering an era in which two-way flows of information, rather than simply one-way flows, are of considerable significance.

Our job as textbook authors is not to project the future, but it is too tempting not to conjecture about the relative influence of these three forms of communication. It seems that the timeless desire of people to interact socially with one another may assert itself as dominant over the interest people have in watching, hearing, or reading about a small pantheon of celebrities acting out pseudo realities. Why?

- The traditional media forms, such as television networks, movie makers, and magazines, are having difficulty in maintaining their audiences.
- Person-to-person communicative activity on cellphones, blogs, and wikis continues to increase.
- Individuals have a greater capability of creating and exchanging high-quality multimedia content.

That said, as discussed in Chapter 10, the evolution of major brands as mediators of interaction—MySpace, YouTube, even Google and Facebook—may dictate otherwise.

DEFINING 'MASS MEDIA' AND 'NEW MEDIA'

The term **mass media** is really a contraction of 'mass communication media'. O'Sullivan et al. (1983: 130) define mass media by providing a list: 'Usually understood as newspapers, magazines, cinema, television, radio and advertising; sometimes including book publishing (especially popular fiction) and music (the pop industry)'. However, in the context of technological change and the three-part definition of mass communication introduced above, the media of mass communication, a.k.a. mass media, have become something quite different. Taking technological change into account and paying attention to common usage among professionals, we find the following to be an appropriate definition:

> *The mass media are technologies, practices, and institutions that make possible information and entertainment production and dissemination through newspapers, magazines, cinema, television, radio, advertising, book publishing, music publishing, recording, and performance.*

These products and/or access to them are sold or given away to large, unknown audiences for both private and public consumption.

Other mass media forms are worthy of note, and in some ways they reflect the decentralized mass communication discussed above. These include buildings, pictures, statues, coins, banners, stained glass, songs, medallions, social practices, and rituals of all kinds (see Curran, 1982: 202). They are mass media in that they often involve institutions communicating with many members of society. While they are media of mass communication we tend not talk about them as mass media (because their existence as media of communication is secondary to their primary function—housing people, commemorating history, serving as medium of exchange, etc.).

The term **new media** can also be said to be a contraction, of 'new mass communication media'. New media are different from the mass media in that they do not focus on centralized institutional production and mass dissemination. Rather, first and foremost, they provide public access to opportunities to create content—messages that are informative and/or entertaining. Hence they are decentralized. In being decentralized they encourage wider participation and in some cases facilitate ongoing participation in the production and exchange of meaning on a mass scale.

THE VARIOUS WAYS WE COMMUNICATE

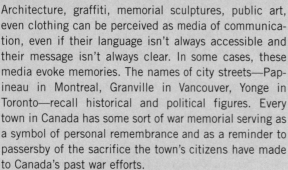

Architecture, graffiti, memorial sculptures, public art, even clothing can be perceived as media of communication, even if their language isn't always accessible and their message isn't always clear. In some cases, these media evoke memories. The names of city streets—Papineau in Montreal, Granville in Vancouver, Yonge in Toronto—recall historical and political figures. Every town in Canada has some sort of war memorial serving as a symbol of personal remembrance and as a reminder to passersby of the sacrifice the town's citizens have made to Canada's past war efforts.

Building styles, too, can recall specific historical periods or they can make a statement about the community, or part of town, they inhabit. The number, size, and structural splendour of Montreal's churches speak to the power the Roman Catholic Church once wielded in Quebec. The new Vancouver Public Library's obvious architectural reference to the Roman Coliseum (see photo) remains controversial because it privileges the city's European roots over its Asian heritage. Besides its phallic symbolism, the CN Tower (see photo) is a clear reminder that Toronto is the country's communications centre—it's a telecommunications tower serving 16 Canadian television and radio stations—as well as a major rail, air, and road transportation hub.

If these media draw much of their authority by being sanctioned, permanent community symbols, graffiti draw their communicative efficacy from their ephemeral and rebellious qualities. Often dismissed simply as vandalism, graffiti nonetheless speak to people. Sometimes the message is a straightforward 'I was here', as in the 'tags' or signatures we see on city buildings, or in the names of people spray-painted on rock faces at various spots along the Trans-Canada Highway. Or the message—often profane—can be one of protest or dissent. Whatever the case, graffiti serve very much as a 'voice of the voiceless' (see photo).

New media can be seen to have two forms and can be defined as follows:

New media are technologies, practices, and institutions designed to encourage public participation in information creation, production, and exchange (i.e., communication) on a mass scale.

New media take two forms. (1) The *decentralized new media* extend participation in meaning-making—otherwise known as symbolic production—in an even more powerful way than small-time book and magazine publishing, documentary filmmaking, public performing, and local theatre do as compared with worldwide book and magazine publishers such as Bertelsmann, Hollywood movie production companies such as Disney, and national and international television networks such as NBC, the CBC, and the BBC. In music production, independent labels and groups that post their material on the web represent decentralized production in comparison with the Sonys and Time Warners with their massive investments in each title and equally massive marketing campaigns and block booking of theatre screens (see Chapter 7). The most notable form of decentralized new media is websites.

(2) *Interactive new media* carry symbolic production one step further. Their purest (new) forms, definitionally speaking, are MSN, e-mail, phone text-messaging, and file transfers from one person to another, and these technologies parallel the telephone and the postal system. But the interactive new media extend to blogs and wikis in that both these forms can be seen as decentralized broadcasters—to whatever person might happen upon them, i.e., an unknown member of society if not exactly an 'audience' member. These same forms can and mostly do include interactivity—the ability to comment on or to change entirely the content of a posting, as in Wikipedia.

To reiterate, the new media provide the wherewithal for increasingly easy and inexpensive public participation in meaning-making and transmission. That's the decentralization element. Second is interactivity, which over the past few years has been building. It began with websites, where a user selects and the site transforms and displays. It has progressed to wikis and similarly structured technology that encourage collaboration and interaction, sometimes in real time. Specific software focuses on particular types of interaction. For example, Google Docs allows a group to write collaboratively from a variety of locations with each contributor able to see the actions of the others.

Formally speaking, just to keep our terms straight, as with mass communication, mass media and new media are, generally speaking, both part of the mass media. The established mass media are typified by industrial production and dissemination of products. New media more and more reflect communication interaction on a mass scale. As such, they are extensions of the social process for all members of society, and because they extend the social process they are becoming increasingly powerful.

A final point should be made. We are accustomed to thinking of the established mass media as a group of technologies, practices, and institutions that are integrated into a single effort, i.e., television broadcasting or newspaper publishing. This single effort encompasses what are called 'content' and 'carriage', that is, the creation of content and the means of delivery are combined. For new media, content and carriage are usually separate. The institutions that provide the technology for the internet, together with those that sell or otherwise provide internet access, are the carriers. Those who provide the content, the owners of websites or the senders of e-mail, are the content providers. Notably, and Chapter 10 will elaborate on this, the carriers tend to be large institutions while the content generators are a wide variety of institutions and individuals.

In the remainder of this chapter, we will elaborate on the functioning of the mass media and new media in an attempt to provide a thorough understanding of their impact on society. This elaboration will give a sense of the nature and operation of all modern mass media and lay the foundation for later chapters.

The Mass Media

In 1983, British media researcher Denis McQuail provided a detailed overview of the mass media appropriate for the time. Here we adapt McQuail's overview to bring our discussion of mass media up to date. The mass and new media:

1. are *a distinct set of activities*;
2. involving *particular technological configurations*;
3. associated, to some degree, with *formally constituted institutions*;
4. acting within *certain laws, rules, and understandings*;
5. carried out by *persons occupying certain roles*;

6. which, together, convey *information, entertainment, images, and symbols* and may facilitate communicative interaction;
7. to or among *members of society*.

A DISTINCT SET OF ACTIVITIES

From a technical perspective that concentrates on transmission or carriage, following Shannon and Weaver's mathematical model of communication (see Figure 1.1), the mass media are indeed a distinct set of activities in their communicative form and function. The mass media, for example, ensure that a device, such as a microphone, is connected to a transmission device, a carrier, conduit, or **conductor**. The signal—analogue or digital—travels along the conduit either as light in a glass fibre or as electricity in a copper wire or coaxial cable. Mass media carriers ensure that, at the receiving end, the signal is decoded and reconstituted into sound, usually amplified and made available to an audience, members of which make meaning out of these transmitted sounds. New media involve a bevy of hardware and software devices and protocols that ensure that texts, sound, and images are transmitted with substantial fidelity.

The social model of communication, with its greater focus on content, stresses that the transmission function (moving meaning from one place or one person to another) is also transforming. The social model stresses the role of both the encoders/decoders and the media themselves as active symbol- or meaning-producing agents that contribute to defining key and subordinate characteristics of reality, that is, what is important and what is not.

Two media theorists, Peter Berger and Thomas Luckmann (1966), describe this transforming function in the operation of the mass media as a construction function. Through representing objects, events, and ideas in certain ways, the mass media 'construct' images and encourage certain perceptions in the same way as builders using bricks and mortar to construct a house. The mass media use the elements at hand—people, events, objects, settings—to create a meaningful whole. Semioticians use the word 'signify' to mean much the same thing as Berger and Luckmann's 'construct'. As Chapter 4 explains in more detail, semioticians, who are also media theorists, work with *signifiers*, that is, symbols or sounds (for example, words); *signifieds*, that is, objects or events to which the words refer; and *signs*, the totality of meanings we associate with the signifiers and signifieds.

A good example is a photograph. For many, a photograph represents what is, or was, there. This undervalues the work of professional photographers because they go to considerable effort to compose their work, taking into account light, background, foreground, the mood of the subject, and so on. Faced with a professional photograph, a person may describe the photographer as lucky to have captured the scene in the way he or she did. Such a statement effectively denies the construction function of the photographer. As Stephen Osborne says, even when we say 'smile for the camera' we are engaging in the construction of the visual object. We are creating a reality for a viewer. This concept is explained more fully in the box, opposite. (See also Osborne's website: www.phototaxis.ca.)

New media practitioners construct meaning in the same way as mass media practitioners; first, by selection, and second, by forming elements into a whole. Part of their construction, mostly lacking the mass media, is the set of opportunities the creator provides for interaction, whether pauses or questions in talking on the phone or provision for comments on a blog.

In summary, both the mass media and new media are distinct sets of activities because they are the primary tools societies use to make or manufacture meaning and to signify or construct reality. The mass media are major contributors to our perceptions because of both the information they carry (transmission) and the interpretation they place on that information (transformation). However, our own constructions of reality now being made more powerful by new media and the constructions of the mass media are both important.

PARTICULAR TECHNOLOGICAL CONFIGURATIONS

The ideas of Marshall McLuhan and Harold Innis outlined in Chapter 1, especially their emphasis on oral, literate, and electronic communication processes, illustrate how the means of communication affect how a message is formed or constructed and then communicated. By examining the particular technological configurations used by the mass and new media we are extending the ideas of Innis and McLuhan.

Raymond Williams (1974) has pointed out that technologies do not arise from the brain of a genius working in isolation from any social context. For example, television did not emerge as an inevitable

CONSTRUCTING THE VISUAL OBJECT

Photographs offer an imprint of the world, a trace of things that were; as rubbings taken from gravestones attest to the authenticity of an original, so photographs attest to the authenticity of the past. This is the forensic dimension of photography, embedded in what John Berger calls the 'enigma of the visual'. Two men in a photograph stare at a TV set at the edge of a river. They are sitting on the end of a log partially hidden by thick grass; they may have had to clear away the grass in order to sit down. The TV set is a wooden cabinet model, built in an age when television sets were trying to look like real furniture. A television expert might name an epoch, a time when people were likely to be throwing away obsolete TVs like this one, even carrying them down to the riverbank. The TV in the photograph seems to have been carefully positioned on its mound of grass. The men in the photograph could be inhabiting any moment in the last 50 years: their clothing and outward aspect suggest little more. Above them a ghostly limb resembling a tree trunk leans impossibly into the space of the photograph: it casts no reflection in the water, and then we see that it is not in the photograph at all: it is a crease in its paper surface, a trace of the object that provided the original of this image. The television screen is blank. The surface of the river is limpid, as flat as the sky, and utterly still; the silhouette of scrubby trees drips into the river like ink. The two men are certainly aware of the camera (a photographer—unknown to us today—accompanies them), and, although they cannot see what we see, they anticipate us looking at them now, in the future.

–Mandelbrot, *Geist* no. 43 (Winter 2001): 3.

offshoot of the search for scientific knowledge. Rather, it emerged from the interests and conceptions of technical investigators and industrial entrepreneurs who were able to imagine an electronic medium of sound and visual communication for use in the home. Inventors such as Marconi, Edison, and Bell were more driven by the idea of inventing something that would be used by many people in a social context than by intellectual curiosity. Their aggressive registration of patents is evidence of this.

Just as the inventions of new technology are shaped by societal forces, how they are used is also shaped by society. The typewriter was originally built as a toy. Radio originated as a two-way medium. The original fax machine was a flop—no one could see any use for it, and as file exchange becomes more common the use of faxes is dwindling again.

The current technological configuration of television allows owners, actors, advertisers, technicians, actors, and many others to make money. Commercial television allows the creation and production of content to be delivered almost free, subsidized as it is by the price we pay for advertised products. TV also allows large, established companies that manufacture brand-name goods to keep their products at the forefront of people's minds. It serves the capitalist system by providing jobs in the entertainment sector. It also serves mass society by allowing for atomized diversion, entertainment, and a bit of education for people during their leisure time. So television, as it is now used, is well entrenched in society. But that does not mean that this particular technological configuration could not be changed so that television could serve an entirely different purpose. (Equally, one might claim that the National Hockey League has colonized the game of hockey for the benefit of players, team owners, arena owners, commentators, television sports, and so on. It is not just communication technology that exists as both a technology and a social practice.)

Television is but one example of a modern mass medium. A more

recent example is the digital camera. For years it languished as an inadequate device with insufficient processing power. By early in the twenty-first century, however, those inadequacies had been overcome so that affordable cameras with sufficient resolution had all but replaced film cameras. A less obvious example is the increasingly ubiquitous new media form, the cellphone. In 1990 a cellphone had the weight necessary to double as a club. Today, however, its light weight, together with the capacity of its microphone to pick up the voice of the user and its ability to act as a music player as well as a location transmitter, has played a large part in it becoming the contact instrument of choice among people from all walks of life.

In summary, the modern mass and new media are a set of technological configurations that bring us information and entertainment in a variety of forms. In the print medium there are broadsheet and tabloid newspapers, magazines, journals, and books—mass paperbacks, quality paperbacks, hardcovers, textbooks, school books, limited editions, coffee-table books, talking books, large-print books, children's literature. In the electronic media we have public, community,

In another Canadian communications first, in 1973, while working at Motorola in New York, Canadian-born Martin Cooper developed the first modern cellphone (weight 1.2 kilograms) based on technology developed at Bell labs in 1945. In 1985, 12 years after its invention, there were only approximately 6,000 registered cellphones in Canada. By 1995 there were 2.8 million, and by March 2006 there were 16.6 million (52 per cent of the Canadian population). In February 2006, the number of users in China surpassed 400 million. One consulting group predicts that by 2010, 65 per cent of Canadians (21.7 million) will use cellphones.

educational, and commercial television, and radio is delivered by broadcast, cable, and satellite. In addition, there are both feature films and non-theatrical films. Sound recordings are available on vinyl, audio cassettes, CDs, MP3s, and DVDs as well as, in their promotional version, on video cassettes. Each year, new media forms provide unexpected functionality. Disposable chips are now available that can track the location of a purchased object. Garbage bags can be scanned for chip content to pry into the consumptions patterns of their owners. The recent technological configurations that allow for interactivity are particularly significant because such technology transforms the communications system from a carrier of cultural and commercial products to audiences to a mode whereby individuals can communicate with one another.

FORMALLY CONSTITUTED INSTITUTIONS

The mass and new media capture distinct meaning-making activities using particular technologies. Most often in the mass media, these activities are associated with formally constituted industrial production structures—media companies—for the production, processing, carriage, and marketing of content. In new media, with its roots in person-to-person communication on a mass scale, the industrial structures are more akin in basic function to telephone companies—they provide the technology to allow people to communicate with one another. Yet, they are not quite the same as telephone companies. Portal institutions such as MySpace, YouTube, Flickr, and PostSecret are establishing and branding themselves as carriers of content and hence content providers. Certainly, at the level of content provision, it is a free-for-all in which individuals, groups, and formal organizations and institutions—in fact, a wide swath of society—participate in providing content. And there is little question that MySpace and YouTube and the many parallel services are trying to turn themselves into significant media players. The day might even come when the mass media and new media converge into indistinguishable institutions. This would happen if the mass media loosened their control over production—which they are already doing with 'idol' and 'reality' shows—and new media portals provided users with quality ratings by providing user commentaries combined with traffic data. The assiduous seeking after advertising dollars by both the mass

and new media make such a convergence highly likely, a development that would parallel the competitive struggles between the cable industry and the phone companies.

Whatever the exact future, both the mass and new media may be under **private ownership** (commercial institutions owned by shareholders) or **public ownership** (in Canadian terms, **Crown corporations**). On the other hand, content production is increasingly available to individuals and is not circumscribed by being within or associated with institutions.

Commercial Institutions

Commercial media institutions may be defined as corporations owning media enterprises for profit. Their primary purpose is to optimize revenues and minimize costs. This principle of action guides the entire scope of their operations. However, that principle must be and is applied in a sophisticated manner that enhances the opportunities for survival and expansion.

Commercial media institutions use content to build audiences. They do so by spending money to provide content that will interest their target audiences. Revenues come from the sale of content to audiences (e.g., newspaper or magazine subscriptions and newsstand sales) and/or from the sale of audiences to advertisers (newspaper, magazine, and TV ads). Revenue is also generated through the sale of content to other organizations that must similarly build audiences (network TV **syndication**).

Notice how the above paragraph also applies to new media (carriage) institutions. They spend money on the hardware and software infrastructure and connectivity and then offer people uploading opportunities. By doing so, they obtain content and that content allows them to build audiences. Generally, they don't usually sell content to audiences—although some magazines and newspapers do—but rather, like television, they sell audiences (i.e., user traffic) to advertisers. They even gain revenue by selling content to other organizations via linking.

An examination of the finances of a broadcasting station, newspaper, book publishing house, or film studio makes the parallels seem even closer between the mass and new media. For mass media institutions, purchasing content accounts for only about 10 to 15 per cent of expenditures. (The parallel costs for new media carriers or portals are zero.) Other housekeeping activities, such as maintaining a physical plant, administration, sales of advertising space/time, subscriptions, and distribution, take up the remaining 85 to 90 per cent of costs. For new media, expenditures on infrastructure functionality, a different form of housekeeping, are closer to 100 per cent of all costs and serve to attract content. The content then attracts the users and the users are then sold to advertisers.

For the mass media, content expenditures can be relatively high in the pursuit of large audiences. For instance, the US networks will spend over $1 million to produce a single episode of a TV drama series that they then can sell in many different markets. But by the same token, new media expenditures on functionality can also be high. The mass media networks sell by territory and the selling price reflects both the number of users and anticipated advertising dollars the purchaser can raise by selling advertising. Thus, million-dollar programs in rerun can be purchased in Canada for about $10,000. (In Trinidad and Tobago one-time broadcast rights to Bruce Willis movies sell for $250.) These production/distribution economics mean that neither Canada nor Trinidad and Tobago can compete financially in the production of content at anything near the same level of quality for anything close to the price of an import.

In the case of the new media, the audience can be calculated much more precisely. All traffic can be recorded and a portal such as MySpace can provide content opportunities for free and collect advertising dollars for bringing users to advertised products. A fair exchange? Different people have different opinions. Independent of the question of fairness, consider what kinds of products most benefit from such a system. The short answer is international brands, certainly not local products without widespread marketing and distribution.

Commercial mass media outlets are socializing institutions. In broadcasting, outlets exist by virtue of receiving a licence from the state in exchange for a promise of performance, a legal document that outlines how their programming will contribute to the community. Such institutions must weigh their costs and profits against their perceived responsibility to the community. They must also take into account audience sensitivity. For instance, failure to provide local and national news and public affairs programs—a preference of most audience members—may alienate an audience. For new media, fewer strictures exist. There is no promise of performance, no obligation to

make a social contribution. After all, and again, more like phone companies, the carriers are merely providing the technology to facilitate the exposure of content created by all comers.

In a few instances, privately owned mass media enterprises emphasize their social contribution over the bottom line. In the case of newspapers, *The Times* (London) is an example, as are *Le Monde* (Paris), the *New York Times*, *Le Devoir* (Montreal), and, at certain points in their histories, the *Globe and Mail* (Toronto) and the *Jerusalem Post*. In their glory days, each of these papers was able to trade on its prestige as the paper of the elite to support its service to the community. More recently, such papers have either become prestige papers or flagship dailies of conglomerates, which maintain them as prestige outlets and for the generation of content that can then be used throughout the conglomerate. (*Le Devoir* is the exception here—it remains independent of a larger chain and is managed by its employees under the oversight of an outside board of directors.) Such papers might also be seen as loss leaders in a conglomerate's attempt to maintain its hold on the consuming public.

The new media equivalent can be seen in Google's investment in scanning out-of-print books and making them available on the internet. It is an investment that can be seen as a social good. But it also attracts traffic as a flagship newspaper attracts readers and generates goodwill.

Public-Sector Institutions

The other major type of formally constituted media institution is the **public-sector institution**, which, in most Western countries, is owned and/or regulated but not controlled by the state. In other words, the directors of the institution are charged with guiding the institution with the public interest in mind. They are not employees of a government ministry, nor are they responsible for carrying out the minister's orders. This structure keeps the influence of partisan politics somewhat at a distance from the day-to-day operations of such media institutions.

In Western nations, public-sector media corporations usually operate at 'arm's length' from control of the government (although the length of the arm varies greatly). In socialist countries, public ownership of the mass media is achieved by means of state institutions not unlike government departments—a structure that is also emerging in developing countries. In various countries of Eastern Europe, for instance, commercial media operations often exist at the pleasure of the state, usually the president, and within a set of constraints defined in the constitution (see the discussion of public media in various countries in *Canadian Journal of Communication* 20, 1 [1995]). It remains to be seen whether these media will evolve into reasonably independent institutions. Two types of institutions appear to be evolving: commercial enterprises featuring entertainment and co-owned by old Communists or media moguls like Rupert Murdoch, and state corporations operating under the watchful eye of either the president or the parliament.

Public-sector media corporations in Canada, like commercial institutions, must balance their revenues and costs. The advantage public-sector institutions have is the revenues they receive from government. These revenues, however, are not unconditional gifts. They are funds to help them fulfill the special public-service responsibilities that they have been assigned in the Broadcasting Act, over and above those of the commercial sector. For example, the CBC must attempt to make its signals available to all Canadians in both languages. Its programs must appeal to all ages, not just those audiences in which advertisers have an interest. As a result of government grants, which can be generous or miserly, the publicly owned media have a greater but still limited freedom to produce programming of value to the community.

The new media, at first glance, don't seem to have an equivalent to a national public broadcaster like the CBC. In fact, however, the plethora of websites created by government and non-governmental organizations in pursuit of the public interest are, as a group, a (decentralized) new media equivalent to a publicly owned broadcaster. An example of a government site is Culturescope.ca, Canada's 'Cultural Observatory' site intended primarily for people engaged in delivering cultural programs or concerned with policy-making. While the site is somewhat confusing in that it seems to be trying to do too much, if you access the 'In Focus' pieces that are within the 'Research Themes' section, you can access some very sophisticated discussions. One example is a discussion created by the Copyright Policy Branch of the Department of Canadian Heritage. Its title is 'The Challenges and Opportunities of Online Music: Technology Measures, Business Models, Stakeholder Impact and Emerging Trends' (www.canadianheritage.gc.ca/progs/ac-ca/progs/pda-cpb/pubs/online_music/

tdm_e.cfm). In the non-governmental sphere, there are countless sites. We found www.yspace.net as a result of a typo. It is a network, based in Australia, formed to foster and support the development across nations of youth-inclusive policy and practice in the design and management of public- and community-accessed spaces. The Council of Canadians has a site at www.canadians.org to promote the interests of Canada and Canadians. And of course, there are many health-related sites, just one of which is that of the Mayo Clinic at www.mayoclinic.com/. Taken as a group, such sites represent a significant contribution by public-sector institutions and organizations to the public interest.

Public versus Commercial Institutions

Whether the media are owned publicly or commercially is obviously a major factor affecting the relationship among the media, the state, and the public. Where private ownership is dominant, considerations of profit-making and advertiser interests focusing on groups with disposable income prevail over considerations of **public service**. (It is, of course, possible for private ownership of a mass media system to be organized on a non-profit basis. It occurs in the Netherlands, but it is relatively rare.) Where public ownership prevails the wide range of interests among members of the public are better served. True, a danger exists that those determining the public interest may do a poor job—many long-time CBC viewers and listeners are unhappy about the many attempts of the CBC to appeal to youth by cancelling old programs. And potential advertisers complain of an inability to get information to consumers, while consumers sometimes complain of the lack of escapist programming. Nonetheless, Canadians continue to show support for the CBC in poll after poll.

CERTAIN LAWS, RULES, AND UNDERSTANDINGS

In a nutshell, the laws McQuail had in mind were the specific statutes of a country governing broadcasting and other laws such as libel and copyright. The rules to which he was referring were the requirements of regulatory bodies such as the Canadian Radio-television and Telecommunications Commission. The understandings were the socialization role played by the media to keep a society informed and entertained and, generally, to promote the status quo while, perhaps, mildly challenging it.

Stated more formally, because the mass media tend to operate within specific national societies, they are subject to formal legal constraints as well as less formal patterns of expectation that exist within that society. For years Canada was a partial exception to this rule, in that US signals from border stations have circulated within the country and yet are not controlled by Canadian law (except insofar as they are carried by Canadian cable companies who must act within Canadian law). For example, US reporters have been known to attend Canadian trials and then, in spite of a publication ban by a Canadian court, report the proceedings in US border media that are accessible to Canadians. For whatever reason, Canadian governments and our courts have not taken much action in face of such lack of respect for Canadian law. At most, a reporter is not welcomed back into the country. With the deployment of communication satellites, the Canadian exception has become the rule around the world. Signals are made available in countries that do not regulate their circulation. This is particularly the case for international services such as the ABC group—Qatar-based Al Jazeera, the BBC World Service, and CNN. Each must conform to the laws of the country within which it operates, but it is not responsible to the many countries where the signals are received. That said, in countries such as China signals are regulated to such an extent that what a visitor can receive in a hotel room is different from what a Chinese resident can receive at his home next door.

In terms of formal laws, in the case of broadcasting, the desire to ensure social benefit from programming obliges national governments to exercise some control, in the form of licensing requirements, so that broadcasters have sufficient revenues to be able to afford to meet such requirements. In the case of newspaper and magazine publishing, most developed countries exercise little overt control. No licences are required and media content is not restricted, except by broad laws directed at libel, sedition, hate, and pornography. However, various indirect controls, such as taxation, subsidies, business policies, and distribution subsidies, can be and are employed. France is a good example of a country that uses such devices.

In Canada, the Broadcasting Act (1991) is the pre-eminent statute controlling broadcasting (see Chapter 6). There are no equivalent statutes for Canadian newspapers, magazines, books, or recorded music, although Section 19 of the Income Act encourages Canadian ownership of newspapers and magazines (see Chapter 7). The reasons why broadcasting has received such particular attention in legislation are partly constitutional (the federal government has clear, undivided power over 'radio communication', which includes broadcasting); partly social (a widely held belief in Canada is that centralized broadcasting is particularly important to nation-building); and partly technological (the sudden development and uptake of broadcasting technology was a significant political force that nations felt needed control). In addition to other formalities, such as defining broadcast undertakings, who can own outlets, and technical matters, the Broadcasting Act outlines what broadcasting should do for society. In other words, it provides a framework for policy. The Act addresses the tacitly accepted values and ideals of Canadian society and the means by which broadcasting can contribute to their achievement.

The Broadcasting Act also provides for the existence of an agency to ensure adherence to the Act. This organization, the Ottawa-based Canadian Radio-television and Telecommunications Commission (CRTC), administers the policies and provisions enunciated in the Broadcasting Act. The CRTC translates the principles of the Act into rules for broadcasters. It mediates between the ideals and values outlined in the Act and the practical realities of running broadcasting undertakings. This mediation has led to the development of many issues of concern, some short-lived and others recurring. As will become apparent throughout this book, and especially in Chapter 6, the recurring issues are valuable indicators of critical points of tension in Canada's broadcasting system.

A second key statute is the Copyright Act, which creates **intellectual property**. It transforms the expression of one's intellectual efforts, for example a poem, a script, or a movie, into a piece of property that can be owned. Moreover, it attaches certain rights and privileges to that ownership. **Copyright** law stimulates creators to create by providing a means for them to require payment for their efforts and by prohibiting the use of their creation without their permission and/or payment. Copyright does not protect ideas; it protects the expression of ideas. The Copyright Act provides a framework for the way in which publishers pay royalties to authors in return for the right to publish and distribute their books. It also affects how persons who make movies based on books buy the movie rights for the book.

Other statutes also influence how the media operate, but the Copyright and Broadcasting Acts are of primary importance. Both of these Acts have resulted in the creation of certain concrete rules that are consistent with the principles of the legislation. Radio provides a good example of the effects of the Copyright Act and the Broadcasting Act and of how Canadian artists are remunerated for their intellectual property according to how often their songs are played. To comply with the Copyright Act, radio stations pay songwriters (and others) for the right to play their songs. To administer the royalty system for the performing rights of musical compositions, the Society of Composers, Authors, and Musicians of Canada (SOCAN) surveys each radio station five to six times a year. These surveys are undertaken on different days for different stations, so that sampling is occurring at all times. The radio station is required to submit a complete playlist of all songs played over a three-day period. SOCAN analyzes the playlist to determine what songs by which artists have been played, and then, based on the relative number of times a song has been played, distributes the money to the song's creators, music composer, lyricist, performer, and publishing company. No more than 50 per cent of performing rights royalties are paid to the music publisher, and SOCAN works with any relative division of royalties it is informed of between the song's various creators. Each radio station must also contribute 3.2 per cent of its gross advertising revenue to SOCAN. In general, SOCAN 'licenses the public performance and telecommunication of the world's repertoire of copyright-protected musical works in Canada and then distributes royalties to its members and affiliated international societies' (www.socan.ca/jsp/en/about/).

With the authority provided to it through the Broadcasting Act, the CRTC determines content rules. For example, the CRTC requires AM and FM radio stations that specialize in popular music to devote at least 35 per cent of their play time to Canadian selections. This **Canadian content** rule has had a positive impact on a number of Canadian recordings and artists, as seen by the number of them making it to radio 'top 10' charts.

The laws and rules that govern the behaviour of the mass media have developed from society's understanding of the potential value of a centralized, content-producing media. At a most general level, the media in Western societies are encouraged to provide

Nelly Furtado is one of many Canadian music artists who are increasingly gaining in popularity, both domestically and internationally. (CP/Roger Wong/INFphoto.com)

'continuity, order, integration, motivation, guidance and adaptation' (McQuail, 1983: 64). More recently, the media have been seen as contributors to social cohesion in heterogeneous societies within a globalizing world. A special issue of the *Canadian Journal of Communication* (27, 2–3), titled 'Making Connections: Culture and Social Cohesion in the New Millennium', provides interesting explorations of social cohesion from around the world. In a complex, liberal democracy, where the values and goals of society are both known in general terms and are a matter of continuing debate, the media have substantial latitude for making their social contributions. Of course, that debate also encompasses whether the media are contributing appropriately. Certain media spokespersons claim that if people are watching television (since they have the freedom not to watch), the television station is obviously making an appropriate contribution to the enjoyment of their leisure time. At the other end of the spectrum, others claim that the media should set for themselves much more ambi-

INTERPRETING THE BROADCASTING ACT

As time passes societies change. Less frequently do statutes change. And so it is important to write statutes in such a way that they can be interpreted within the context of the time. For example, Section 3d(iii) of the Broadcasting Act declares that 'the Canadian broadcasting system should through its programming and the employment opportunities arising out of its operations, serve the needs and interests and reflect the circumstances and aspirations, of Canadian men, women and children, including equal rights, the linguistic duality and multicultural and multiracial nature of Canadian society and the special place of aboriginal people within that society.' And Section 3i(i) notes that 'the programming provided by the Canadian broadcasting system should be varied and comprehensive, providing a balance of information, enlightenment and entertainment for men, women and children of all ages, interests and tastes.'

These two clauses address directly two basic differences in society, race and gender, and less directly a third, class. All three are often associated with inequality. The Act provides the framework and the media strive to address the changing norms and ideals of society with respect to race, class, and gender.

tious goals—to provide, for example, enlightening rather than escapist entertainment. This debate, which will receive further attention in later chapters, is over what constitutes the **public interest**. The point here is that both the spirit and the exact content of laws matter. On the basis of those laws certain rules are developed, and the laws themselves are founded on certain broad understandings of the role of a centralized media in a democratic society.

In addition to the Broadcasting and Copyright Acts, an important communications statute that receives less attention in discussions of the mass media is the Telecommunications Act. This is because, in the social operation of the mass media, telecommunications is an infrastructural transmission element that exists behind the scenes. It is the carriage alone, not the content. Within a social context, telecommunications is generally discussed in terms of the provision of equitable access for all citizens to telephone services. The Telecommunications Act gives the common carriers, for example, phone companies that serve everyone, the responsibility to average out their costs so that people in rural areas, on islands, or in the Far North do not end up paying dearly for phone service while city dwellers bask in low prices. They are charged not necessarily an equal monthly fee but an equitable fee, one that balances cost against the social goal of providing inexpensive access to all citizens.

The social dynamics of telecommunications service provision increases in importance when we consider the new mass media and the interactive media.

Who owns and controls service provision, to whom it is sold, and on what terms all have an impact over the long term. Clearly, the provision of telecommunications services has social impact, just as did the provision of postal and telephone service over our history. Currently, the laws, and especially the rules and understandings that apply to the telecommunication services that are the backbone of both the new mass media and the interactive media, are much less extensive than those that apply to the traditional mass media. As stated previously, the two main reasons for this are that the service providers are carriers who lack control over content and there is greater public access to content creation and distribution—content is not centrally produced by a few for the many.

The kinds of considerations that are applicable to telecommunications are applicable to new media. For example, intellectual property and privacy laws are as applicable to new media as they are to all other communications activity, as are laws related to speech regulation, liability, and jurisdiction. Specific to new media are laws relevant to domain-name governance and internet commerce.

Other actions by government that affect new media tend to be supportive of its development, rather than regulatory or restrictive. In an attempt to secure a Canadian on-line presence, various departments in government have sought to stimulate and support Canadian participation in the development of the internet. For example, the Department of Canadian Heritage has a number of support programs and Industry Canada has invested substantially in stimulating on-line business activity. Generally speaking, and following the recommendations of the Information Highway Advisory Council, the CRTC has declined to weigh in with content regulations. Stated differently, neither informal understandings nor actual restrictive or regulatory rules have been developed. This is why there is an ongoing debate about on-line pornography.

PERSONS OCCUPYING CERTAIN ROLES

The number of people involved in the mass media and the number of roles people play are vast. The most obvious players are the journalists. But there are also owners, editors, printers, producers, studio technicians, actors, administrators, designers, advertisers, members of regulatory bodies like the CRTC, politicians who control the purse strings (of public-sector

VIEWING HOURS AND THE CBC

Commercial broadcasters worry about competition in the marketplace, about the total programs available to viewers, and about other media. As a public enterprise with a cultural and political mandate, the CBC often considers the total programming and other types of programming available out of a concern to provide a wide range of information and entertainment to all Canadians. For example, the CBC asks questions like how many hours of programming are available for every hour of television watched? It turns out to be 120 hours. In 1999 the CBC sought out the available hours of English-language programming over the previous 15 years and compared them with the per-capita hours of viewing per week. As shown in Figure 2.1 the number of TV viewing hours per week has remained fairly steady. On the other hand, the number of available hours of viewing increased steadily until 1995–6, when, with the explosion of specialty channels, it rose quite sharply. However, this increase in available viewing hours has had relatively no impact on viewing.

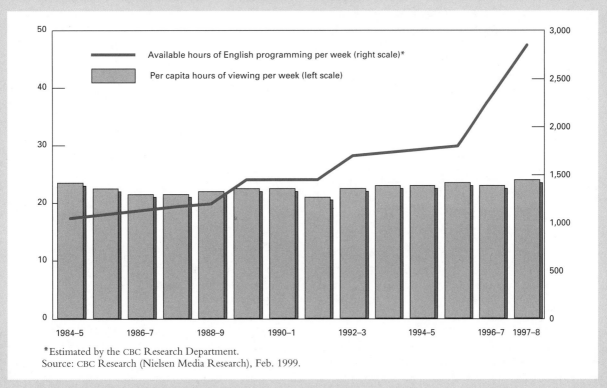

*Estimated by the CBC Research Department.
Source: CBC Research (Nielsen Media Research), Feb. 1999.

Source: *Globe and Mail*, 22 Feb. 1999. Reprinted by permission of CBC Research.

companies), lawyers, public-interest groups, and the audience. These various players can be divided into six major groups, four operating outside the structure of the mass media—business, government, the legal system, and the audience—and two operating inside—owners and media professionals.

Business Influences from outside the Media

The influence of business on the mass media is exercised through ownership and advertising. We will deal with owners, who are insiders, later. With regard to advertisers, decisions by businesses on where to advertise and how much to spend affect the fortunes of individual media enterprises. To attract advertisers, media managers are careful to ensure that content does not clash with advertisers' messages. Such clashes may be specific, such as a consumer-oriented article or program that criticizes the products of a particular advertiser; or they may be more diffuse, such as descriptions of a non-consumer or anti-consumer lifestyle. Neither would fit well with the consumerism promoted in advertising. The video *Pack of Lies* (Foundation for Media Education, 1992) discusses the relationship between content and advertising, taking a *Newsweek* story on cancer as an example. The gist of their argument is that the commercial media cannot be trusted to tell the whole truth about companies who advertise on their pages or during their programming. This argument has been supported in many studies and is now quite broadly accepted.

To avoid offending advertisers, media enterprises normally tailor their content to correspond to advertisers' interests. Generally speaking, mass media content encourages consumption, especially of nice clothes, fancy cars, travel, liquor and other drugs, and entertainment. More specifically, media enterprises may make a special effort to avoid offending certain constituencies. It is not uncommon for the media to notify advertisers, through their advertising agency, that they might not want to advertise in a particular issue (because of an editorial message that conflicts with their product). As a matter of routine, airline commercials are rarely placed anywhere near stories of an airline hijacking or of an airplane crash. Drug abuse stories will not be found next to drug company ads. Ads for designer clothes will not be found next to stories on the exploitation of offshore labour. This live-and-let-live philosophy is an accommodation that allows for a range of opinion without confrontation of interests.

It is a myth that the two types of material—content and ads—are managed quite separately and that journalists or program producers are insulated from advertiser influence. In reality, as the *Report of the Royal Commission on Newspapers* (Canada, 1981) points out, it does not work that way. For instance, in the summer and fall of 1990 an informal but determined boycott of the *Kingston Whig-Standard* by local real estate agents took place in response to one of the newspaper's articles, which outlined the advantages of self-selling by owners. Such events are unusual because the rules of the game are generally known within the industry. (The general operation of the *Kingston Whig-Standard*, an important small paper until it was taken over by Thomson and subsequently Southam, has been documented by Fetherling [1993].)

Even media such as book publishing experience pressures from business. The bookstore chain, Chapters, has been known to reduce its orders dramatically from publishers who negatively comment

---

NEWSPAPER CREDIBILITY

Every year in September, NADbank (National Audience Databank Inc.) releases annual readership figures. Funnily enough, each paper appears to be a winner over its competition, at least this was the case in 2001. The headline in the *Globe and Mail* was, 'Readership success for The Globe'. The headline in the *National Post* was 'Over 2 million read the *Post*'. The story in the *Post* noted that over two million Canadians read the *Post* every week (not every day) and, it boasted, the *Post* had achieved a stunning growth of 18 per cent in Toronto while the comparable figure for the *Globe and Mail* was a 10 per cent loss.

The story in the *Globe* had the following lead sentence: 'With 1,006,000 readers a day and 2.5 million a week, the *Globe and Mail* continues to be Canada's largest and most influential national newspaper. . . . Cumulative weekly readership has risen sharply over the year, up 15 per cent across Canada.'

This magazine, in which the above ad arguing against the privatization of Canada's health-care system, provides a friendly media environment for the social activist agenda of the Canadian Auto Workers and the Centre for Social Justice. (By permission of CAW-Canada)

Outside business influence on the new media is confined mainly to the role advertisers play in controlling content. Because these services are funded by advertisers, their attitudes are important. That said, advertisers tolerate a broader spectrum of content on the internet than they do on broadcast television. As well, vast numbers of websites and e-mail services are not influenced by business because they are not advertiser-funded.

Inside business influences are quite another thing. As is obvious to everyone, a great many websites exist as on-line retail or wholesale businesses. They are pure business communication. On-line businesses engage in commercial discourse, directly promoting products and telling the user how to buy them. As such, they are far different from the phenomenon of media self-censorship in the coverage of news based on a perceived need not to offend advertisers. Others are good Samaritan sites where the site owner expects no gain but has a desire to help others to repair a car or a clothes dryer or know the dangers as well as the benefits of a drug.

Government Influences from outside the Media

The influence of government on the mass media has several dimensions (see Chapter 3 for a more detailed discussion). In a federal state such as Canada, more than one level of government influence is at work. Within any one

on the business practices of Chapters. Similarly, books that deal with subject matter unwanted by the owners, Heather Reisman and financial mogul, Gerry Schwartz, are sometimes not to be found on Chapters' shelves. The need for Chapters to determine what books and magazines should not be seen by Canadians is open to question, especially when the content deals with matters involving the ethnicity of the owners. Certainly, as owners, they have the right to sell what they please. But as controllers of more than 50 per cent of bookstore sales in the country, these owners have a social responsibility to look beyond their own personal preferences.

government, we can also distinguish between bureaucratic (or departmental) structures and political structures. At the bureaucratic level, the government is a major source of information for the mass media; it is often the only source for specific types of information. The flow of information from government to the mass media benefits both parties. To inform the general public of its programs and expenditures, the government needs access to media outlets. The mass media need the information supplied by governments as a readily usable source of content for news, current affairs, and public affairs items.

The relationship between the media and govern-

ACCESS TO GOVERNMENT INFORMATION

In an attempt to increase access to information that governments want citizens to have, all federal government departments have created their own websites. A good example is that of the Department of Canadian Heritage. The English-language address for the cultural part of the site is www.pch.gc.ca/culture/english.htm. An interesting exercise in examining the impact of government information, and especially press releases, is to go to the section labelled 'press releases', find one or two, and then try to find stories that built from those releases on radio and television or in the newspapers. For newspapers, in addition to purchasing a copy, you can go to the websites of the *Globe and Mail* (www.globeandmail.com) or the *National Post* (www.nationalpost.com) and try to find resulting articles. You will see how little some information is followed up, the angle or perspective taken by the newspapers, and the degree to which they rely on the supplied government information.

ment, however, has its drawbacks. For instance, because of time constraints and limited resources, media workers tend to rely heavily on the news releases and handouts prepared by the government, but, by failing to look behind these announcements, the media outlets run the risk of acting as the propaganda arm of the government. The drawback for the government is in the sheer volume of materials pumped out by numerous departments, agencies, and ministries. The mass media cannot publish or broadcast all of it, and from the government's viewpoint the selection of items can be quite arbitrary.

Related to both the bureaucratic and political levels of government is government advertising. Government advertisements come in many forms: they can provide information on government programs; they can be straightforward political campaigning; or they can be in the grey area of general promotion of a given federal or provincial government. Total advertising revenues from government sources form a substantial part of the media's advertising revenues, especially for Canadian newspapers; the federal government outspends any one commercial advertiser. As well, a number of government-funded organizations also spend liberally on advertising.

In addition to being a source of information, the subject of news, and the source of advertising revenues, government also influences the mass media through its power to regulate and control them. Both at the federal and provincial levels, government has the authority to approve legislation, to impose taxes, and, in various other ways, to affect the manner in which mass media organizations conduct their operations. Commercial enterprises have a strong tendency to resist or seek to reduce government control over their operations by raising the banners of 'freedom of the press' and 'freedom of the marketplace'. However, constraints on their freedom, under legislation related to restriction of competition, for example, are more apparent than real. In recent history successful prosecutions of media companies have been extremely rare and court interpretations of Canada's competition legislation have further weakened it. Nevertheless, mass media owners continue to argue that the freedom essential to a democratic press is threatened by excessive use of government power.

The conflicts between commercial mass media institutions and government exist at many levels and are not resolvable by allowing commercial corporations a free hand to operate mass media outlets. As for public corporations, their relationships to government are also complex. Tensions tend not to focus on issues of freedom of the press, but on issues related to public funding and accountability. The CBC in particular has a long history of difficulties in ensuring its ability to maintain the proper balance between political freedom and public accountability.

The point with respect to these government/business/media relationships is not that these issues can be resolved. Rather, they are continuing tensions that must be managed in the context of the time and of democratic values. Their public debate is healthy in a democracy as it reminds us of the existence of different interests and the need for them to be resolved to best advantage. In the long run, the manner in which governments handle such interest differences contributes to their ability to be elected.

Government influence on new media, at least in Canada, tends to be facilitative through investment in

Patents will be pending

Some of Canada's brightest minds are converging in Saskatoon, Saskatchewan. The Canadian Light Source synchrotron project at the University of Saskatchewan is Canada's largest science project in decades. Synchrotron light lets scientists analyse matter at the atomic level. This promises exciting breakthroughs in pharmaceuticals, computer microchips, new metal alloys, and environmental clean-up to name a few. There's a lot of science to discover in Saskatchewan. To learn how resourceful we are, visit our Web site or call 1-866-SASK-HAS.

Saskatchewan
Our Future is Wide Open ™

wideopenfuture.ca

Dr. Bill Thomlinson, Executive Director of the Canadian Light Source, Saskatoon
"The Canadian Light Source will take its place among the great synchrotrons of the world and provide a tool that will help Canada maintain its position as an innovative technological nation."

The Canadian Light Source, opening in January 2004, will use brilliant light, millions of times brighter than sunlight, in diverse fields of research ranging from medical radiation therapy to cleaner-burning fossil fuels.

 Government of Saskatchewan

Advertising allows governments to reach the public and accounts for a substantial portion of media advertising revenues. (Saskatchewan Industry and Resources)

internet access is controlled. In still other countries, infrastructure development has been slow because it has been left totally in the hands of business.

Legal Influences

In addition to the impact of laws and policies affecting the mass media, lawyers, judges, and others in the legal profession play certain roles and thereby influence both the mass media and new media. The courts must interpret existing statutes in instances where specific media practitioners or owners are thought to have operated outside the law. A much more widespread influence on content, however, is exercised with various sections of the Criminal Code that cover offences such as sedition, promulgating obscenity, propagating hate literature, issuing false messages, and interfering with the rights of an accused to a fair trial. Court decisions on cases of these kinds tend to influence all mass media practitioners—particularly journalists—and are used as indicators to guide future actions taken in the selection of media content. On-line seduction of people below the age of consent has created a certain number of headlines.

the infrastructure and assistance with the provision of on-line services, not least of which is government on-line. While the government has yet to commit to the provision of broadband services for all Canadians, it is only a matter of time before that point is reached. The Canadian government has also invested in all sorts of projects to assist businesses and social organizations to have internet access. Canadians can count themselves lucky for the support and freedom provided to the new mass media and the interactive media. In Europe, internet usage is more costly. In other parts of the world, such as India and Africa, it is virtually unaffordable for the vast majority. In China,

Legislatures have a special influence on new media through their enactment of laws to cover new realities. For example, copyright legislation assists those who undertake intellectual work by allowing them to receive payment for that work. There is an ongoing discussion about copyright being outdated in the age of the internet. While some of it is naive, such developments as the Creative Commons (www.creativecommons.org) open source programming and the General Public Licence (www.gnu.org/) are realistic attempts to balance the interests of creators and the public.

Audience and User Influences from outside the Media

The fourth outside influence on the mass media is the audience. Denis McQuail, writing in 1983 before new media, suggested that the audience can influence media content in six different ways (168–70).

1. As critics and fans, audience members (and now, we would add, users) can comment (with both approval and disapproval) on the nature of specific content pieces or content producers. Numerous publications and opportunities exist to reflect critics' opinions and the preferences of fans and users regarding media content.

2. Through institutionalized accountability, audience members can seek to influence mass media organizations. This is often easier to do with public corporations than with commercial enterprises. In Canada, the CRTC is obliged to regulate the broadcasting system 'in the public interest' and, in doing so, seeks the opinions and preferences of viewers and listeners across the country. For the print media, press councils—made up of representatives of owners, journalists, and the public—can act on behalf of readers who complain about specific content in newspapers. Some media outlets also have ombudspersons who mediate between the audience and the outlet.

3. Through the market, audience members and users can choose among media outlets and services and, through such choices (revealed in ratings), exert some influence on the mass and new media to the extent that they are audience/user dependent.

4. Through direct feedback to mass media outlets audiences can make their views known and hope to influence future actions in the same way that users of new media can. 'Letters to the editor' are the standard form of feedback for the press, while broadcasting stations rely on phone calls and e-mail messages.

5. Through the use of audience and user group images formed in the minds of content producers and service providers, the audience can influence media content. However, understanding exactly how these images are generated and changing them is a real challenge.

6. Through audience and traffic research, media professionals can gain a more precise idea of audience interests and responses to specific media content. However, as McQuail points out, the type of audience most likely to be influential is that which can be delineated with statistical findings (audience size and breakdown) and that which matches the practitioners' own views about audience preferences.

Do these six types of mechanisms translate into new media? To some degree yes, but consider this. There is a certain irony in considering the influence of new media users in that, to an ever greater extent, as a result of interactivity, 'users' are far different from 'audience members'. The irony is captured by the phrase 'media participants formerly known as the audience'. So extensive have new media become with their decentralized and interactive elements that it hardly seems appropriate to compare, let's say, a blogger or podcaster to an avid TV watcher, movie goer, or even book reader. One produces. The other consumes. Yet, in a way, large companies such as Google, MySpace, YouTube, Netflix, Rhapsody, and Apple's Itunes are branding themselves as focal portals where users post their creations and explore what others have done and they track their hits to see if anyone is paying attention to them. The challenge of each big brand is to establish and maintain a distinct, energetic, and attractive identity that brings users repeatedly to the site. (We will revisit this dynamic in the final chapter, taking a lead from the editor of *Wired* magazine, Chris Anderson, and his book, *The Long Tail* [2006].)

What does such branding and user attraction sound like? Large organizations like Google and Rhapsody look more and more like traditional newspapers (which bring together the output of reporters, columnists, and wire services) or television networks (which bring together the output of various producers). Like the traditional media, they add a certain aesthetic, sell ads, and make barrels of cash. Whether a person is posting new content or browsing the content of others, his or her screen is awash with ads, and selling the attention of potential customers to advertisers is what the media are all about. So even though the communicative activity is quite different, the large net organizations are transforming that activity into something they can exploit in the same way that the traditional media do.

So indeed, following McQuail's six points, as fans of certain services, users influence how they operate; because the new media have so little social responsibility, user influence via this means is weak. Traffic patterns and click-throughs are the foundation for the attention-market, hence users also have an influence here. Users also can make their influence felt through comments to the services they use, and how they present their needs and wants to services also has an influence. Finally, through the wide variety of measures the services use to evaluate user behaviour, the users also have an impact.

But more than the above, as *producers* and *participants* of new media, users directly control content rather than influence it. Podcasting and blogging are perfect examples. As well, it is useful to recall that in many cases feedback is content. In fact, the prevalence of feedback (plus facilitating technology) has led the traditional mass media to augment substantially the ability of audience members to provide comment on programs. The ability to track user behaviour—where users go, how much time they spend where they are, whether they retrieve available files for download—allows new media practitioners to understand their user groups.

The mass media are in the business of selling attention. They sell the attention of their audiences either to advertisers or, if they are publicly funded, to politicians or funding bodies such as governments. While the commercial new media are still working out business models, to an increasing extent they, too, are selling the attention of users to advertisers. On the other hand, the not-for-profit participants in the new media—individuals and organizations—are simply acting, creating, and producing out of self-interest or in the public interest.

The Inside Influences of Owners, Media Professionals, and Other Content Creators

Thus far, we have been looking at outside influences on the operation of both mass media organizations and new media. The internal structures of these organizations and the people who work in them also exert considerable influence. Technicians keep the presses operating or the broadcaster broadcasting; other technicians (e.g., camera operators, text layout artists) bring professional practice to bear as they do their work; researchers provide raw information; and teams of 'creatives' (authors, actors, set designers, and such) interpret and express the content provided to them, sometimes under the prior or following direction of others (e.g., movie directors, book editors). In most examples of the mass media, media profession-

als (sometimes in combination with amateurs) are directly engaged in the production of media content. They do this within an organizational structure operated by media management (who are also media professionals but of a different sort), which may have several levels to it (see Chapter 9 for more on this). Media professionals have a dual allegiance to their profession and to the company for which they work. How they play out these roles and the social system that emerges within the corporation can greatly influence the resulting output of the station, network, magazine, or newspaper. Of particular interest is the way creative people are attracted to organizations in which they may thrive but that inevitably place some restrictions on their creativity. British media professor Margaret Gallagher (1982) provides an insightful account of how these individuals and their organizations negotiate in such a way that there is not only control and predictability over programs but also room for creativity.

The new media are not that much different except that, at this point in history, there is a greater prevalence of amateurs. However, increasingly, professional groups, including programmers, database managers, website designers, usability experts, and website managers, are emerging in the new media. Programmers determine what is feasible; database managers keep information up to date, expand functionality, and ensure that queries are processed smoothly and quickly; website designers determine the look, feel, and navigation of the site; usability experts assess whether sites are intuitive in their design; and website managers update site-based information. On the other hand, websites can be created by relatively naive web users operating by themselves or by using prepared generalized templates and services provided by those who create websites and those who access the websites of others. It is fair to say that, in general, and specifically within the context of the influence of media professionals (and owners), there is a greater structural difference between amateur and commercial new media than there is between mass media and new media enterprises. That said, it is important to bear in mind that a great many more new media entities are extensions of other activities (business, governments, institutions) than there are mass media extensions of other activities.

The owners of the media corporations (or the owners' representatives) have a substantial influence on the operation of the media. In the case of public corporations and institutions, while the owners are the taxpaying public, through Parliament and other governmental bodies, responsibility is vested in a governing board that sets strategic direction. In the case of commercial corporations, the owners are shareholders or individual entrepreneurs (usually the former). Shares may be widely held among many investors or closely held by the members of a particular family. Owners may be actively involved in managing the media corporation or may rely largely or even entirely on senior managers. Internally, media corporations can be viewed as social systems with their own structures and history.

With respect to new media, the situation differs in two ways. The portal services are more like a telephone company than a television station or newspaper. They provide communications services and those using the service use it because it offers unfettered free expression. In other words, owners are restricted in their influence in the type of service they provide and because the content creators are neither media professionals nor employees of the service provider. Owners, even of content services such as Wikipedia, must make the decision whether the content service will be centrally controlled or web-controlled, i.e., controlled by users. (An article in *The Atlantic* tells a great story of the struggle between the founding editor and founding owner of Wikipedia. The editor wanted to exercise editorial control but the owner wanted to let users do what they thought best [Poe, 2006].)

The influence of the owner of content creation is the exact opposite to that of the service providers or for Wikipedia. New media operations are customarily extensions of business, social, and ideological groups as well as ideologically driven individuals. They create and control content absolutely. Owner influence is owner control and it is absolutely the norm.

The most important, ever-strengthening, long-term trend in owner influence (explored further in Chapter 8) is increasing editorial control by the owner based on his/her ideological interests. Media owners are unapologetically placing ideological and political constraints on what they own. The Asper family, owner of CanWest Global, has followed this path, as did Conrad Black when he was a major media mogul, and as do the previously noted owners of Chapters bookstores. The major exception to this rule has been the Thomson family, owners of the *Globe and*

Mail. Until recently, the owner's financial interests tended to keep owner influence at bay, but with the success of notably ideologically biased media outlets such as those owned by Rupert Murdoch, there is little to hold owner influence in check.

Information, Entertainment, Images, and Symbols

The terms 'information', 'entertainment', 'images', and 'symbols' cover what is known as content. Television provides information programming (news, current affairs, documentaries) and entertainment programming (sitcoms, music, drama, sports). For analytical purposes it is useful to distinguish between the two categories, but we must bear in mind that entertainment is also—or is taken to be—informative, just as information can be entertaining. For example, people do not watch the news merely to become better informed, nor do they listen to music or go to a concert simply to be entertained. In newspapers, information is included in news and sports, opinions in editorials and columns, advertisements, and even cartoons, while entertainment is provided in travel, leisure, gossip columns, the comics, and sports. Similarly, information and entertainment are provided by the fiction and non-fiction in magazines such as *Maclean's*, *Saturday Night*, *Canadian Living*, *The Walrus*, *Geist*, *Canadian Geographic*, and *This* magazine. The content of the mass media brings us direct reports of the world through information programming and indirect reports of the state of living through entertainment programs. Similarly, new media provide information and entertainment and, increasingly, formats are arising dedicated to health information, news, blogging, wikis, music, and personal content that access information from other sites.

To say that the media convey images and symbols is to look at content from a different angle. Whether through words or pictures, in print or electronically, the media present us with images of the world—images that fall into two classes (discussed in greater detail in Chapter 4). The first is denotative, that is, those images that are explicit, objective, there for anyone to see. A descriptive analysis of a photograph that identifies its various elements or a rational argument—each presents us with denotative images. The second class of images is connotative: they are associations that are implied and/or that we infer from the context that surrounds the denotative images. Take, for instance, a travel advertisement: the photo of a boat sailing on a calm lake on a sunny day would be the denotative image, whereas the peacefulness and enjoyment implied and inferred from such an image is connotative. The focus of our discussion, and the emphasis in communications literature, is on connotative images, which may derive from very different sources. Connotative images may arise from rhetorical argument. They may have a visual base and derive from the composition of a still photograph, or from the timing and juxtaposition of a series of video shots, or even from the layout of a printed page.

Symbols can include anything, from letters of the alphabet to something as complex as a religious icon directly related to a Biblical story, which, in turn, has a particular meaning. Here we use the term in a general sense, stressing the interpretive tendencies of the audience. Thus, at every level of our existence, from the biological to the psychological—the social, the cultural, the political—the meaning of a symbol is an interaction between the composition of the image and the interpretive predispositions of the audience. A death mask has a biological base; a flag has a sociocultural as well as an aesthetic base and, perhaps, a political base. Symbolic meaning can also be understood to have connotative value.

The images the mass media present are rich in symbolic meaning or connotative value, whether or not the media intend them to be. To some degree, the success of all media products, from movies and books to television programs and newspapers, depends on the presentation of images that are layered with symbolic meaning. The sum of the meaning of the images and symbols presented to us by the media represents the ideological currents and community norms of society. In this way, the media play a fundamental role in articulating and consolidating ideological control and community behaviour in society. The contrast between mass media and new media images and symbols to some degree reflects the difference between what society expects from institutions and what individuals, groups, business, and other social institutions acting without constraint offer up to society.

Members of Society: The Mass Audience

As noted at the beginning of this chapter, a **mass audience** is not to be thought of as a mob or as an unthinking mass of individuals vulnerable to the intentional or unintentional manipulations of media

practitioners. Rather, it is a convenient shorthand term for the great number of people who consume mass entertainment and information. And, again, as noted, rather than being homogeneous, vulnerable, and passive, the mass audience is better conceived as consisting of individuals who, from their diverse backgrounds, bring varying degrees of engagement and a variety of readings or interpretations to media content—readings that are derived from their psychological, social, economic, political, cultural, and spiritual roots, as well as their age, region, and gender. The mass audience should also be distinguished from both the 'populace' (all members of society) and those members of society who tend to be self-appointed public spokespeople and who have an interest in society's present-day order and/or its evolution towards greater equity and justice.

Mass audiences are still a reality. They form around certain events or international spectacles like the Olympics or the soccer World Cup. They watch, read, or listen to so-called genre leaders, such as the Grey Cup or Super Bowl, election coverage, or news coverage of disaster, but after that point the audience fragments, as it does in watching the various reality TV programs, reading a wide selection of books or magazines, listening to a wide variety of music, and so on. One might then say that the mass audience consumes reality TV rather than a specific program.

The success of the new media, which facilitate 'many-to-many' communication by members of the public, can be interpreted as indicating a strong and, to some extent, repressed desire in a mass media-dominated age to interact with others using language, music, images, and moving images. In short, the new media reflect a desire to act socially (in a virtual environment that may or may not have very real consequences), and that desire appears to be outstripping a desire to be audience members in someone else's play. To use a word now gone out of fashion, such communication is empowering. It provides many people with greater power to act in the world, to make their voices heard. Pressure groups can organize with considerable effectiveness against the World Trade Organization and its good-for-business mentality that privileges standard of living over the concerns of citizens for quality of life. Individuals can take a legitimate grievance to the public and sometimes see it addressed. Groups and individuals can reach further afield and enjoy themselves in extending their contacts and/or helping others. In short, our participation

IDENTIFICATION AND INTERACTION

Notwithstanding the definitions introduced in this chapter, it is a good experiment to try to think of counter examples. At a communications conference held in Salvador, Brazil, a number of papers discussed soap operas. It was apparent that the Brazilian academics saw Brazilian soap operas (*telenovelas*) as very much their product and their export success to the rest of the world.

At the same conference, a number of Canadian academics spoke of interactive media, the web, and video games.

The question arose, if an audience identifies very strongly with the content of a TV format, or an individual show, in what way is this not 'interaction', while pressing buttons or looking up information on the internet is?

through communication media with the world as a whole is no longer confined to assembling together or individually in our atomized spaces for the delivery of packaged entertainment and information products. We can now engage in person-to-person communication with others from around the world, in real time or not, and organize and participate in defining and acting on our own realities.

The power to do so is fundamentally realigning the social and representational world, that is, the creation and production of interpretations of the social. As this chapter makes clear, mass communication is evolving into a more equal balance between the distribution of centrally produced media products to large audiences and the interchange of symbolic representation from person to person on a mass scale. Society will not be the same for it.

Summary

This chapter began with a series of definitions—'mass' and 'communication' in both technical and social senses, 'mass communication', 'mass media', and 'new media'. Most importantly, it introduced a new definition of 'mass communication' encompassing three elements: (1) the centralized production and dissemination of information and entertainment products; (2) the decentralized production and provision of access to information and entertainment; and (3) the exchange of intelligence on a mass scale by members of society.

The chapter then offered new definitions of the mass media and new media.

- The mass media are technologies, practices, and institutions that make possible information and entertainment production and dissemination.

These products and/or access to them are sold or given away to large, unknown audiences for both private and public consumption.
- New media are technologies, practices, and institutions designed to encourage public participation in information creation, production, and exchange on a mass scale, leading towards communicative interaction on a mass scale. They take two forms: decentralized new media and interactive new media.

The chapter then explored the nature of the mass and new media by means of a seven-part outline. Both types of media were discussed as:

1. a distinct set of activities;
2. involving particular technological configurations;
3. associated, to some degree, with formally constituted institutions;
4. acting within certain laws, rules, and understandings;
5. carried out by persons occupying certain roles;
6. which, together, convey information, entertainment, images, and symbols, and facilitate communicative interaction;
7. to or among members of society.

The major elements of both mass and new media were considered, and we saw that the new media and mass media differ in important ways. Overall, mass media of communication are woven into the societies of which they are a part through a legal and regulatory framework, certain types of proprietorship, professions, associated institutions, particular technology, available leisure time, and content—the images and symbols employed and the information and entertainment provided. In contrast, new media are an extension of the natural tendency of people wanting to communicate with each other in an ever more communicative world.

It was also stressed that society is being changed fundamentally by new media, which are open to far greater participation by all. While this participation opens up flows of information and allows members of society to enhance their participation in personal, social, and political affairs, it also transforms the mass media from being socializing institutions to being, more simply, reflections of human activity at work and at play.

RELATED WEBSITES

Backbone Magazine: www.backbonemag.com/
  Backbone is a Canadian magazine with insights into technology and the web.

BBC: Find, Rip, Mix, Reuse: copyfight.corante.com/archives/2005/04/13/bbc_rips_mixes_creative_commons.php
  Open University, Channel 4, the British Film Institute (BFI), and the BBC are making their archived programs, films, and other materials available on the internet for the public, free of charge, so that others may use them for other creative projects.

Berne Convention (copyright): www.law.cornell.edu/treaties/berne/overview.html
  This is the pre-eminent world statute dealing with copyright. Its various clauses and levels are to be found at this site.

Canada's Copyright Act: laws.justice.gc.ca/en/C-42/text.html
  Canadian legislation on copyright conforms to the Berne Convention and provides the foundation for copyright protection in Canada for both Canadian and foreign creators. This is the site of the statute.

Canadian Association of Journalists: www.eagle.ca/caj/
  This site provides journalists with professional information and, from time to time, it takes up issues of interest to all Canadian journalists.

Canadian Broadcast Standards Council: www.cbsc.ca
  The CBSC sets broadcasting standards such as how much advertising broadcasters should put in a half-hour of programming.

Canadian Radio-television and Telecommunications Commission (CRTC): www.crtc.gc.ca
  The CRTC provides everything you might want to know about its activities regulating Canada's media.

CBC: www.cbc.ca
  The CBC site highlights CBC programs and issues dealt with on the CBC. The site changes continuously. An interesting alternative site directed primarily at people in their twenties and thirties is www.cbcradio3.com.

CBC journalistic code of conduct: www.cbc.radio-canada.ca/policies/journalistic.htm
  This code of conduct is not only a guide to journalists but also an indication to the public that CBC journalists work within a set of standards.

CBC media policy: www.cbc.radio-canada.ca/htmen/policies/
  The policy framework within which the CBC operates is found here.

CBC's *The National*: www.tv.cbc.ca/national
  This site provides headlines of the day's news as it is carried on the program, features, further elaboration on certain stories, and even a subscription service.

ccMixter: ccmixter.org/
  A community music site featuring remixes licensed under Creative Commons. Users can listen to, sample, mash-up, or interact with music however they please.

Fanfiction.net: www.fanfiction.net/
  Individuals can post fictions they have written based on books, movies, or TV shows using the same characters and sometimes the same situations. The site is a resource for writing, reviewing, and reading.

Joomla: www.joomla.org/
  An open-source solution free to all, Joomla is a content management system (CMS) that helps build websites and other on-line applications.

KYOU Radio: www.kyouradio.com/
  The world's first radio station to broadcast podcasts full of original content created and chosen by the artists and the listeners. The site provides music and talk radio programming straight from the source.

MIT OpenCourseWare: ocw.mit.edu/index.html
  A site that makes course materials from virtually all of MIT's courses available on the web free of charge.

PostSecret: postsecret.blogspot.com/
  Individuals can anonymously send a postcard revealing a secret to an address given on the website and the postcard will be posted on the site. The postcards are mostly very artsy.

Project Gutenberg: www.gutenberg.org/wiki/Main_Page
  A library site of 17,000 free e-books whose copyright has expired in the US.

Public Library of Science (PLoS): www.plos.org/
  Non-profit organization that through its website is making the world's medical and scientific literature available and free to everyone.

Science Commons: sciencecommons.org/
  Open access to scholarly literature and data that helps the movement of information, tools, and data through the scientific research cycle.

Society of Composers, Authors, and Musicians of Canada (SOCAN): www.socan.ca

The SOCAN site presents information for musicians, users of music, and the general public.

SourceForge: sourceforge.net/

SourceForge is the world's largest open-source software development website and manages projects, issues, communications, and code.

Wikipedia: www.wikipedia.org

Wikipedia is a credible source of information about the media, and a whole lot else.

Wired **magazine:** www.wired.com/

Wired magazine is a wonderful source of insight into the media. It touts Marshall McLuhan as its patron saint.

FURTHER READINGS

Curran, James. 1982. 'Communications, power, and social order', in Michael Gurevitch, Tony Bennett, James Curran, and Jane Woollacott, eds, *Culture, Society and the Media*. Toronto: Methuen. Curran discusses the historical elements of the mass media from an interesting, and wider, perspective.

McQuail, Denis. 1983 (see also fifth edition, 2005). *Mass Communication Theory: An Introduction*. Beverly Hills, Calif.: Sage. McQuail has written over a dozen books on the media. He is now emeritus professor at the University of Amsterdam. Some notes about his work on media accountability can be found at: www.grady.uga.edu/cox-center/activities/activities0102/act042.htm.

O'Sullivan, T., J. Hartley, D. Saunders, and J. Fiske. 1983. *Key Concepts in Communication*. Toronto: Methuen. While somewhat dated, this work provides a useful listing of critical terms—not quite a dictionary but almost.

STUDY QUESTIONS

1. Define 'communication' and 'mass' (as used in this chapter).
2. Define 'mass communication' and its three parts.
3. Define and distinguish between the mass media and new media.
4. In what way is the internet a mass medium? In what way is it a new medium?
5. The media construct reality. Explain.
6. How do publicly owned broadcast institutions differ in their basic purpose and mission from commercial or private broadcast institutions?
7. Define, in a few words for each, the roles played by owners, media professionals, advertisers, politicians, interest groups, the legal system, and audience members in influencing the media.
8. Discuss how definitions structure our understanding.

LEARNING OUTCOMES

• To provide an understanding of the mass distribution of centrally produced symbolic or communication products, i.e., the traditional mass media.
• To explain and define the mass distribution of decentralized production of information and entertainment, i.e., the new mass media.
• To explain and define the interactive mass media as consisting of communication on a mass scale.
• To explain how traditional, interactive, and new mass media are all part of what can be considered mass communication.
• To explain how the internet has fundamentally transformed mass communication and therefore the modern mass media and consequently is in the process of fundamentally changing society.
• To outline the many roles played by individuals associated with the media.
• To illustrate how definitions structure understanding.

CHAPTER 3

Media: History, Culture, and Politics

Introduction

The mass media are far more than activities that generate information and entertainment. They are key elements of industrial society and key elements in the culture and politics of contemporary states. This chapter examines both the historical and current roles of communication and information in Western societies. It considers the developmental context of mass media and several perspectives for understanding the roles they play in political life. The distinctive characteristics of the development of the Canadian media are examined, as well as how they reflect and nurture Canadian culture and political values. The chapter ends with a comment on Canadian cultural concerns in an international context.

The European Roots of Media and Western Society

While both papermaking and movable type were first developed in Asia, it might be said that the modern mass media began to emerge in mid-fifteenth-century Europe with Johann Gutenberg's development of the printing press in Mainz, Germany, in 1454. This advance in technology is often used to designate the end of the Middle Ages and the beginning of the Renaissance—a transition from a social order where people were subservient to the powerful Church and monarch to a social order more sympathetic to the freedom of both individuals and ideas. The Renaissance and the movements and conceptual developments that followed it—humanism, the Reformation, the Counter-Reformation, the Enlightenment, and finally, the Industrial Revolution—paved the way for liberal democratic industrial societies and modern forms of mass media.

A major aspect of the Renaissance was a rediscovery and revival of literature and learning from antiquity, especially of the Greek and Roman Empires, which had been lost and suppressed during the Middle Ages. This recovered knowledge helped to re-establish faith in humanity and nature. Led by Italian

thinkers and artists, the Renaissance was the beginning of a reassertion of reason and the senses that had characterized classical Greece. Underlying the Renaissance was humanism, a broad philosophy that celebrated human achievement and capacity. Although often couched in religious contexts—in art, sculpture, and architecture—humanism celebrated the human form and encouraged an empirical understanding of the world. The great works of art and architecture that characterize the period were grounded in an understanding of mathematics, mechanics, and geometry, an awareness of perspective, and a theory of light and colour. In the practice of this empirical knowledge, humanism emphasized people's abilities to know and understand the world outside of the teachings of the Church.

At this point in European history the dominant ideology held that the world was ordered by a divine hand and that true knowledge of the world might only come from God or through his emissaries on earth, the pope and priests of the Church. Tradition was the principal element structuring society. In the feudal system of production that characterized the times, social position and responsibilities were inherited by birth, and royalty and aristocrats both held their stations and governed by divine right. Through demonstrating the abilities of individuals to understand and shape the world, the humanism that underlay the Italian Renaissance began to sow the seeds of a secularized society within this traditional order.

The dissemination of humanist ideas was facilitated by the technologies of writing and printing, which allowed individuals to develop and record their ideas and communicate them in a manner understandable by many. Printing presses were established throughout Europe over the next centuries and encouraged the spread of literacy. As literacy spread, so, too, did the thirst for ideas. With printing, ideas rejected by the ruling elite in one regime could be exported into others, leading to a destabilization in these states. As American historian Robert Darnton (1982) has demonstrated, a regular business of printing in Switzerland and smuggling books into France was an

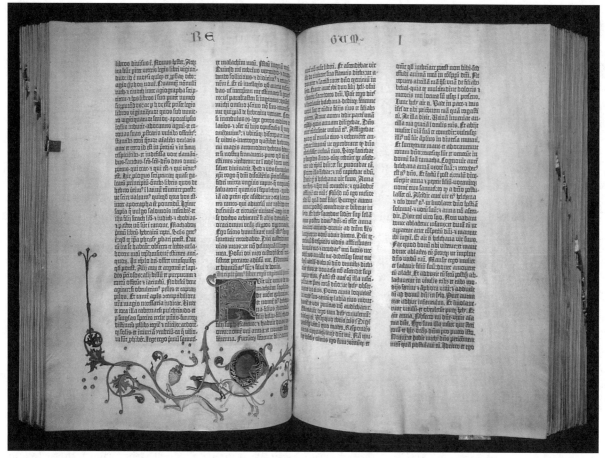

The printing process has changed dramatically since this Gutenberg Bible was published, *circa* 1455. (© Huntington Library/SuperStock)

important precursor to the French Revolution.

The following passage from the writings of Italian printer Aldus Manutius (1450–1515) gives a sense of the times and the significance of early printers in their societies.

ALDUS MANUTIUS BASIANAS ROMANUS
gives his most devoted greetings to all students

Ever since I started this enterprise seven years ago, I have not had a single quiet hour, this I can swear. Everyone without exception says our discovery is most useful & beautiful, & it is widely praised & admired. To me, however, this striving for perfection & the eagerness to be of service to you, to supply you with the best books, has developed into an instrument of torture. I tell my friends, when they come to see me, two Greek proverbs which most aptly describe my situation.

The first is: 'The thrush drops its own misfortune', or, more elegantly, as Plautus expresses it: 'The bird is father to its own death.' For it is said that bird lime (for trapping birds) is produced entirely from bird droppings, especially those of pigeons & thrushes. . . . The second proverb is: 'We draw ills upon ourselves like Caecias the clouds.' Aristotle tells us that Caecias, the wind, blows in such a way that the clouds are not driven away, as they are in other winds, but rather that he draws & summons them toward himself. This is exactly what happened to me: I have begot my own misfortune. I have provided myself with trouble & over burdened myself with great labours. My only consolation is the assurance that my labours are helpful to all, & that the fame & the use of my books increase from day to day, so even the 'book-buriers' are now bringing their books out of their cellars and offering them for sale.

The transposition of Renaissance ideas from Italy to Germany led to a quite different manifestation of the search for knowledge, affirmation of the human spirit, and exploration of ideas. To capture the matter in a few words, the Italian Renaissance overcame what had been an avenging Church (which for centuries had taken vengeance against individuals for actions deemed not in keeping with the Church's preferred rules of living) and established a freedom of intelligence that led to a vibrant culture. The German Reformation followed with a freedom of conscience from institutionalization (the Roman Catholic Church)—arguing that each individual could come to know God directly—and attempted to redefine religion and morality on a more individual basis. The Reformation began in earnest with Martin Luther's nailing of his 95 theses to the castle church door in 1517 in Wittenberg to protest against the selling of indulgences. The theses, written in Latin, were quickly translated into German, printed, and circulated throughout Germany. Luther also translated the Bible into German. As Elizabeth Eisenstein (1983: 273–4) points out in *The Printing Revolution in Early Modern Europe*, 'Intellectual and spiritual life . . . were profoundly transformed by the multiplication of new tools for duplicating books in fifteenth-century Europe. The communications shift altered the way Western Christians viewed their sacred book and the natural world. It made the word of God appear more multiform and his handiwork more uniform. The printing press laid the basis for both literal fundamentalism and modern science.' By making the Bible more accessible, printing undermined the power of the Catholic Church and its priests to act as intermediaries in delivering religion to the people and led to mounting support for a restructuring or 'reformation' of Church doctrine and to the development of Protestantism.

Both the Reformation and the Renaissance were brought to a close in Europe during the sixteenth and seventeenth centuries by the Counter-Reformation, a conservative backlash that re-established monarchical absolutism in both Church and state. Its most extreme manifestation was the Spanish Inquisition. During the Counter-Reformation, European states, recognizing the powerful role of ideas, writing, printing, and communication in general, put in place severe controls on printing to limit the dissemination of ideas. Various printers and writers were branded as heretics and were tortured and executed. Nevertheless, writers and printers persisted. In 1644 in England, writer John Milton penned his anti-censorship essay, *Areopagitica*, advocating the free flow of ideas. His essay was motivated by a 1643 decree that renewed a ban on type founding and maintained the monopoly of Oxford, Cambridge, and London over printing. Only in 1695, with the lapse of the Licensing Act, did printing in England gain its freedom—a freedom later confirmed in the first copyright act, the Statute of Anne, in 1710. Nonetheless, attempts to restrict publishing continued for some time after. For instance, freedom to publish in France was granted with the Revolution in 1793 but was lost under Napoleon and not restored until 1870.

The backlash against humanism that characterized the Counter-Reformation was not to last, however, and in the early eighteenth century a new try at humanism based on a combination of logic and empiricism introduced the Age of Reason or, as otherwise known, the Enlightenment. The Enlightenment was distinguished by an intellectual approach based on a scientific and rational perspective on the world. It introduced a fundamental shift in world view that championed science over religion, justice over the abuse of power, and a social contract that specified individual rights and freedoms over the absolutist rule of kings and popes.

The writings of Enlightenment philosophers such as John Locke (1632–1704), Voltaire (1694–1778), Jean Jacques Rousseau (1712–88), and Adam Smith (1723–90) worked to undermine the inherited right of kings and the Church to control government. They argued the people possessed natural, inalienable social rights, and they championed the market over feudal forms of production and exchange. These shifts in social ideas that characterized the Enlightenment were fuelled by an emerging elite competing for power with the aristocracy. An expanding, materialist, prosperous, and educated 'bourgeoisie'—or new landowning class—had been building with the accelerated development of the market economy and colonial trade from about the sixteenth century. Through the eighteenth and early nineteenth centuries, the Enlightenment's legacy of scientific reason combined with the growing wealth of the bourgeoisie to fuel change in social and political structure. First with the American War of Independence (1775–83) and later with the French Revolution (1789–99), both Europe and North America were gripped in conflict as a new social order took form. The result was a massive upheaval in European society that laid the ground for yet another change in social structure, the shift from an agrarian to an industrial society—a transformation that was, again, fertilized by communication.

From the invention of the printing press onward, the spread of knowledge laid the foundation for the profound political and social change from feudalism to democracy, from farming to industry, from medieval to Renaissance and then to Enlightenment world view. In the realm of politics, the acquisition of knowledge in the context of humanism and reason allowed a new class of citizens to emerge and gain enough education to compete for the right to govern. Similarly, in culture, talented and knowledgeable creative artists brought forward more secular literary, musical, and artistic works that were to be appreciated by the viewer for their manifest beauty. Knowledge, reason, and information institutions became, and have remained, essential to the process of government because they inform the public about the important issues of the day and the various solutions proposed by the competing elites who wish to govern.

In summary, the printing press served a key role in informing citizens on matters both important and trivial. Printers were one of the first groups of early capitalists—skill-based entrepreneurs who took the risk to print news sheets, pamphlets, and books and then to sell them to booksellers and the public. At first printers busied themselves with the dissemination of ancient knowledge, but as that was assimilated and individualism began to take hold, authorship by living people emerged. With the emergence of contemporary authorship, the already established struggle between those in power and those who wished to gain power was intensified. A wealth of documentation prior to and including the beginnings of copyright tells us much about the various attempts by those in power to control the output of information by their rivals, especially when it was directed at the general population. In the main, those who wished to gain power spoke in the name of the bourgeoisie and the manufacturers who required greater freedoms to operate. As they achieved these freedoms others began to speak in the interests of workers. A great cacophony of voices emerged.

The Industrial Revolution, Communication, and Social Form

Just as the Enlightenment gave rise to new ways of thinking about people's relations to both each other and the world, so the Industrial Revolution intro-

duced a major change in social organization. With the application of growing scientific knowledge to production, industry began to take hold in the late eighteenth century. As landlords moved to turn their lands to commercial agriculture, people were forced to migrate, either into the swelling cities and towns where the new 'manufactories' were taking form or across the oceans to developing colonies, which increasingly served as sites for raw materials for industrial production. In this context, new forms of transportation—such as railways and steamships—provided means for moving people, raw materials, and finished goods, while new forms of communication—such as the telegraph and newspapers—provided vehicles for co-ordinating buyers and sellers, workers and employers, and governments and citizens.

The growth of industry gave rise to increasingly complex social relationships as both urbanization and migration stamped the landscape with the spatial and temporal edifices and rhythms of industrial production. Industrial production demanded the co-ordination of social action across ever increasing physical distances as both raw materials for factory processes and foodstuffs for rising populations converged upon burgeoning urban centres. Industrial life also redrew the dimensions of family life. The traditional extended family whereby mother and father, children, grandparents, and aunts and uncles might live in close proximity—even in the same home—gave way to the nuclear family, a more flexible form of social organization that was easily moved from place to place following work opportunities. Industrial production also shifted the temporal dimensions of social life. Working in a rural, agricultural setting is an ongoing, relatively slow-paced way of life in which the rhythm of work and daily living blend together throughout the daily and annual cycles, structured by the necessities of animal husbandry, raising crops, and sustaining and maintaining the family and the household. Industrial production demanded a different temporal division of the day and a distinction arose between work and leisure time.

It was in this context that modern communications media took form. In the face of the changes wrought by the new industrial way of life, the media developed what Raymond Williams has called 'specialized means' to close the geographical and social distances created by industrial production and to serve new social interests and needs. As Williams (1974: 22–3) illustrates, in this context 'the press

CYBER WORLD IS CHANGING THE REAL ONE

Harvard's . . . Professor John Putnam said six years ago that the jury was still out on the question of how the internet will affect modern society. New findings from Statistics Canada this week say that is still true, but also show how quickly and deeply the new medium has permeated society.

Putnam's 2000 book *Bowling Alone* examined the decline in what he calls 'social capital' in America—all the voluntary connections that weld individuals together. Bowling leagues, political meetings, churches, square-dancing clubs—all such institutions and habits tie a community or a country together. McGill ethicist Margaret Somerville says social capital reflects 'embedded trust'—how much confidence people have in one another. Higher social capital correlates with fewer social problems.

Putnam found social capital was dwindling rapidly in the United States as the tightly knit Second World War generation departs and as two-career families, suburban sprawl and the nightly allure of the television set all whittled away at neighbourhood interactions. (He focused on the United States, but Canadians will recognize themselves in what he found.)

At first glance, each family's internet connection, like its TV cable, serves to draw people away from chatting over the back fence and reduces them to staring at dancing electrons. However, Putnam speculated internet connectivity could also spawn unforeseen new connections among groups and individuals. And that, up to a point, is what StatsCan found. In its 2005 General Social Survey, the agency looked into many aspects of the way we live now, by asking people how they spend their time.

Logically enough, StatsCan found those it calls heavy internet users—more than an hour a day online not counting on-the-job time—spend less time doing other things. Specifically, such people reported that they sleep less, relax less, go to fewer movies and do less volunteer work than other people. They also spend less time with other family members, and on housekeeping.

Careful, as usual, to report but not decide, StatsCan said heavy net users are not necessarily anti-social, but rather 'differently social'. Anyone who has watched teenagers deep into instant messaging and touring their friends' MySpace sites will understand that there might well be more communication, not less, going on. Similarly the internet allows special-interest groups to flourish without regard for geography. And don't you have at least one old friend, living far away, with whom you're in closer touch thanks to e-mail than you were 10 or 15 years ago?

Ultimately, a reasonable amount of face-to-face interaction is, one suspects, important to individuals and to society. But 'society' is always changing. No doubt somebody once complained that people spending time with those new-fangled printed books were not spending enough time playing with the kids. And many people wasted lots of time quite successfully before YouTube and gossip sites.

For better and for worse, the internet, astonishingly important already, is just getting started. Hang on: It's going to be quite a ride.

Source: Adapted from *The Gazette* (Montreal),
4 Aug. 2006, A18.

[developed] for political and economic information; the photograph for community, family and personal life; the motion picture for curiosity and entertainment; [and] telegraphy and telephony for business information and some important personal messages.'

In the context of developing industrial society, the telegraph greatly enhanced the co-ordination of people and goods across vast distances. It was a key advance in what Karl Marx described as people's abilities to 'shrink space through time'. It forestalled the necessity of physically sending messages from one place to another and enabled communication literally at the speed of light. Both government and industry could respond much more quickly to developing events, accomplishing so much more in shorter periods of time that it seemed as though space—or the distances between places and things—had actually become smaller. Governments were quicker to learn of revolts in far-flung parts of their territories, respond with troops, and thereby secure more readily the supply of resources and markets. Manufacturers could order raw materials from suppliers a continent away, while orders for goods could be taken from cities and towns scattered across the country. The telephone built upon and enhanced the economic relations created by the telegraph, and although today we think of the telephone as primarily for personal communication, it was first, foremost, and generally remains a business tool.

The photograph, on the face of it a simple technique for capturing images on light-sensitive glass or paper, became a way of constructing family and community at a time when traditional kin and friendship ties were being torn apart. As Susan Sontag (1999: 177) points out:

> Photography becomes a rite of family life just when, in the industrializing countries of Europe and America, the very institution of the family starts undergoing radical change. . . . Those ghostly traces, photographs, supply the token presence of dispersed relatives. A family's photograph album is generally about the extended family—and often it is all that remains of it.

With the rise of the industrial press in the late nineteenth century, the photograph also becomes a way of familiarizing readers with political and business leaders—of 'putting a face to the name'—as well as,

through images, linking them with far-off events. In this way, photography helped sew the seams of the emerging industrial-based social fabric.

While the photograph was woven into the context of new familial and community relationships, motion pictures, an extension of the photographic image, were given cultural form by the new rhythm of the industrial day that divided time between work and leisure. Through the early twentieth century, an increasing number of urban dwellers had both free time and disposable income. Entrepreneurs worked to find ways to capitalize on these circumstances, and new products or 'commodities' (see box) were created to sell to this growing body of consumers, among them the motion picture. The motion picture was also the product of the economies of scale engendered through industrial production. Many copies or prints of the same film could be shown simultaneously in scattered cities and towns, thereby spreading the cost of production among many audience members.

Of all the modern media given both form and function by the development of industrial society, however, the newspaper was both the earliest to develop and the most pervasive.

THE COMMODITY AND COMMUNICATION

One of the most dynamic features of capitalism as an economic system is the way it works to convert things for which we find need and uses in our lives into products for which we must pay market price. Critical commentators call this the commodification of everyday life—that is, what Karl Marx highlighted as the process of turning 'use value' into 'exchange value' (see Mosco, 1996). Others celebrate this as the entrepreneurial spirit of capitalism.

Think of all the different elements of the process of communication that have been commodified over the last few years. Television and radio used to arrive free over the air. Now the monthly cable or satellite bill can eat up a day's pay. Time spent in movie theatres—particularly the time between when people take their seats and the film starts—has been commodified as the theatre owners have used advertising to turn that time into a product they can sell to advertisers. Internet access is now sold in a range of different speeds. Telephone service has evolved into an ever-increasing array of products

such as voice mail, text messaging, and various web-based telecom services. Even the ring tones for cellphones have become products for sale. And, increasingly, information itself—such as news, government reports and statistics, and course readings—is becoming a product for sale.

As we shall see in the following chapters, this ongoing commodification of communication products and processes lies at the heart of what people call the 'communication economy' or the 'communication revolution' and is seen as a key factor in economic growth. At the same time, however, it creates a growing divide between the communication 'haves' and 'have-nots', between the 'information rich' and the 'information poor'. And, given that communication products and processes play key roles in our knowledge and understanding of the world, the commodification of communication and information can't help but undermine people's abilities to exercise their full rights and responsibilities as citizens.

The Beginnings of the Modern Press

In the eighteenth and early nineteenth centuries, some degree of organization was brought to the cacophony of publishing voices created by the printing press as newspapers began to be aligned with (and sometimes even owned by) political parties. This pattern—the emergence of many voices and their reduction to a few, often politically aligned, newspapers—has been repeated in many Western countries at various points in their histories. And just as this pattern has repeated itself, so has the subsequent transition of control of newspapers from political parties to business. In books and magazines a variation on the same pattern can be seen, with control first being established in the hands of wealthy patrons, then among liberal members of the elite, and finally passing, sometimes first through political hands, to the hands of business enterprises.

In Canada, newspapers in the early to mid-1800s were generally under the control of partisan political interests. As Robert Hackett and Yuezhi Zhao note in *Sustaining Democracy: Journalism and the Politics of Objectivity*:

> Often owned by a group of wealthy partisans . . . papers had the explicit purpose of representing a political party. Overall, they tended to serve the ruling political and business elites. . . . Newspapers often counted on financial support from government patronage or direct party subsidies. Shaped by party affiliations, the journalism of the time was replete not only with special pleading for the politicians who financially supported each paper, but also with vicious personal attacks on political foes. (Hackett and Zhao, 1998: 20)

By the early twentieth century, however, the cost of producing newspapers drove them into the hands of business. Perhaps the largest influence on this shift in ownership was the development of industrial society. Around the end of the nineteenth century, the growth in industry and urban populations led to developments in both mass production and mass marketing. As Minko Sotiron (1997: 4) explains in *From Politics to Profit*, the modern newspaper in Canada is rooted in the period '1890–1920, when among other things, a rapidly expanding urban population, increased literacy, the economic boom of the Laurier era, and a growing national market of consumer markets contributed to the profitability of new newspaper ventures.'

Newspaper publishers found that providing marketers with a vehicle to reach the increasing numbers of consumers was more profitable than direct alliances with political parties, and advertising soon became their major source of revenue. As modern newspapers took form in the context of industrial society, they crossed the boundary between the public life of work and community and the private home. In this guise they began to serve multiple roles. Not only were they the source of political and community news, but also they provided a wide range of other information important to a population confronted with an increasingly complex society. Want ads linked job seekers and employers, merchandise and service ads linked growing numbers of workers with a growing number of products, and personal ads helped people locate partners and friends in the increasingly impersonal urban environment. New technologies animated these changes. Cheap newsprint and faster printing presses lowered the cost of newspapers, while the telegraph and later the telephone were plentiful conduits for the information needed to fill pages and attract readers. Thus, just as the photograph, the motion picture, the telegraph, and the telephone took form and function in the emerging structure of industrial society, so, too, did newspapers (Schudson, 1978).

Journalism also changed to meet the new industrial regime. In news, 'objectivity' replaced partisan reporting as papers sought to reach a wider readership and increase both circulation and profits (see Hackett and Zhao, 1998). The use of headlines and photographs to capture the attention of potential readers became popular, as did partitioning newspapers into different sections and offering a range of different features—such as serialized novels—to attract a diverse set of readers.

As the press became more of a business, publishers also promoted their own interests, emphasizing the freedom to pursue profitability in the marketplace unencumbered by state restrictions (see Chapter 8). Similarly, journalists have developed a complementary ethic by stressing the need for independence from the state for reportage and analysis. This dual business and journalistic thrust has allowed the press to establish some distance from the politicians of the day. This is not to say that in claiming their independence newspapers, and the media as a whole, represent the interests of all citizens. On the contrary, as we will see

Early on, Canadian legislators recognized radio's ability to operate on the principle of free speech and its potential to create a national community. (Courtesy Library and Archives Canada/C-080917)

in the following chapters, the media generally represent the interests of the power elites in society—mostly business interests, but also the interests of the political and intellectual elites.

Perspectives on the Press

Since its inception the role of the printing press in developing and circulating ideas has been controversial. In Martin Luther's day, it was used to undermine the traditional power of the Catholic Church. As newspapers developed through the seventeenth and eighteenth centuries governments in Britain and Europe used a range of measures to censor and control the circulation of news in order to maintain social and political control. Through the late eighteenth and early nineteenth centuries, however, early liberal writers such as Jeremy Bentham, James Mill, and John Stuart Mill advocated that a press independent from government regulation (a 'free' press) was central to

good government and democracy. It was in this context that in a speech to the British House of Common Edmund Burke referred to the press as the **fourth estate**, meaning that—alongside the other 'estates' or insititutions of social governance such as the government (the first estate), the judiciary (the second estate), and the church (the third estate)—the press played an important role in acting as a kind of political watchdog, guarding the rights of citizens through publicly reporting on affairs of state. In the wake of the long struggle to wrest political control from the hands of monarchs, as John Thompson (1999: 122) points out, 'There is considerable force in the argument that the struggle for an independent press, capable of reporting and commenting on events with a minimum of state interference and control, played a key role in the development of the modern constitutional state.' Consequently, over the last several centuries **freedom of the press** from government interference became an important political ideal reflected in the Constitution of the United States, the United Nations' Universal Declaration of Human Rights, and the Canadian Charter of Rights and Freedoms.

But while newspapers did contribute to political freedoms, as they came to be operated as commercial enterprises there has been a growing concern that corporate interest—that is, the pursuit of private profit—has dominated over the public interest in free and unfettered expression of and access to information. Press barons of the late nineteenth century were known to sensationalize news, and sometimes even to make it up, in their efforts to attract readers. And today there are many examples of how news production is often tilted towards the interests of shareholders rather than the public (see Chapter 8).

Still, defining the social role of the press, and subsequently that of the media, is a matter of some debate and depends largely upon the theoretical perspective one uses to approach the issue. For instance, in liberal theory the function of the mass media is to preserve liberal democracy—in other words, the political system within which the media now exist. The media are seen as monitoring abuses of power and attempting to ensure that the will of the people is carried out. They assist in ensuring that governments and institutions are flexible and sensitive to the changing needs and desires of society. According to this theory, the media provide the information necessary for public participation in the political process and aid in the dissemination of information about public programs and services. In short, they provide citizens with information about matters that are part of the political and socio-economic system in which they live—information that most citizens do not otherwise receive.

In contrast to liberal political theory, the Marxist approach (see Chapter 4) describes the media's activities not as working on behalf of the community as a whole, but rather as promoting the ideology and the interests of the dominant classes of society. Marxists point out that while the media may propose revisions and small reforms, such as the election of an opposition party in place of a continuation of a current government, they do so to preserve the existing political system rather than opting for a new, more equitable system. In putting forward a limited range of ideas and analysis, the media present different manifestations of the same basic political perspective and thus reinforce existing power relations and ideology. In short, the media reflect the interests of their capitalist owners in maintaining a politically stable society.

Critical scholars such as James Curran (1990) and John Fiske (1987, 1989a, 1989b, 1989c) have carved out a somewhat middle ground in describing the role of the media in Western society. Like the Marxists they claim that the media are intimately involved in relations of social power, but they see them as contributing information and analysis on a wide variety of subjects and from a fairly broad set of perspectives. The media do so in the context of various competing groups and individuals and, sifting through these different perspectives, seek to interpret the 'real' meaning of events. For example, in the case of Aboriginal land claims one can, at various times, see the point of view of First Nations, the provincial and federal governments, business, residents on the land, or ordinary Canadians who are not direct stakeholders. At times the contributions of the media are made with the interests of the public in mind; at other times they are more self-interested or represent the interests of a particular group. If major reforms are called for on a particular issue, the media may eventually present and discuss that possibility. In the end, however, for a variety of reasons we will examine in following chapters, Fiske and Curran claim that the media generally entrench the status quo.

Which of these theoretical perspectives is the true or correct one? Indeed, all three approaches provide insight on media operations. As we saw in Chapters 1 and 2, the social role and structure of the media are complex. To understand what role they play in any specific instance we need to examine the relations of power they are implicated in at that point. In other words, the media may play different social roles at the same time.

Given the various conceptions of the media, considerable attention and debate have been directed at the ownership and control of the media: where does it or should it rest? Analysts have identified four different sites where the power of media ownership and control are located in society:

- within the state;
- as part of social or political movements or parties;
- as private enterprises; and
- as public enterprises at arm's length from the state.

Each of these locations tilts the interests and the orientation of the media in a particular direction. Each introduces a bias focused on the interests of those who control the site in question.

Various scholars have discussed the implications of the media operating from each site, in terms of ownership, content production, and societal functioning. In the hands of the state the media strengthen state control, as has been the case in one-party totalitarian states and in certain developing countries where the state maintains close control over the media. In the hands of social and political movements they tend to fragment and politicize society, as in Italy, unless there is both a delicate balance of interests and a calm political climate, as in the Netherlands. In the hands of business, business interests are advanced at the expense of the interests of the community as a whole. In the hands of public enterprise, education, enlightenment, and, sometimes, talent development tend to become the primary values, with the interests of advertisers becoming secondary.

The Traditional Mass Media and Canadian Realities: History and Structure

Just as larger social, political, and economic events such as the Enlightenment and the Industrial Revolution have given form to communications media in general, so, too, the development and structure of the Canadian state, as well as a distinctive Canadian culture, have nuanced the structure and operation of media in Canada.

In the early nineteenth century European settlement of the geography that is now Canada took the form of a collection of colonies scattered across the vast northern half of North America. Industry, such as it was, was largely devoted to the export of staples or raw materials for manufacturing in Great Britain and the United States. In this context, the lines of communication followed the lines of commerce and ran either overseas to Britain or north–south into the US. But by mid-1800s both Britain and the US had enacted trade restrictions on the colonies, forcing them to look to themselves for development. Confederation in 1867 was the first step to building an economic unit out of these colonies.

In 1879 Prime Minister John A. Macdonald introduced Canada's first National Policy, a set of initiatives designed to turn the idea of an east–west economy into a reality. The National Policy had three particularly important components:

1. the building of transcontinental railway;
2. a tariff designed to limit the entry of manufactured goods from the US and Britain; and
3. efforts to entice immigrants to settle the prairies.

The purpose of the railway was to provide a reliable line of transportation for people and goods across the country, and particularly to move raw materials from the margins of the country to the industrial heartland in central Canada where they would be manufactured into goods and shipped back out to market. It was to bind the country into a cohesive political economic unit with a 'ribbon of steel'. The tariff was used to tax materials and manufactured goods entering the country. Its purpose was to protect 'infant' Canadian industries by keeping cheap competitive goods outside the country. At the same time, it also encouraged foreign investment, as non-Canadian companies wishing to tap into the expanding Canadian market were encouraged to build factories and produce goods here in order to avoid the tariff. The tariff was necessary because Canada had a much smaller population than either Britain or the US and did not have the **economies of scale** (see box) necessary to produce goods at a competitive price. Finally, immigration policy actively sought settlers from Central and Eastern Europe to populate the Prairie provinces, both to develop the land and raise grain for the central Canadian market and to serve as a market for the manufactured goods of Ontario and Quebec.

Despite these measures, because of the large size of the country and the small population, it was often difficult to wring profits from business in Canada and the government often had to step in to encourage private investment. For instance, the Canadian Pacific Railway (CPR) was issued a wide range of government payments and subsidies to encourage the building of the transcontinental railway. Similarly, because of the large investment necessary, Bell Telephone was given a monopoly on long-distance telephone service in central Canada so that it might exploit economies of scale when building that system.

Still, it was all but impossible for the government to attract private investment for some activities. In these

ECONOMIES OF SCALE

Economies of scale reflect the fact that the greater the quantity of a particular product is made, the less each one costs to produce. Much of the cost of an industrial product is in setting up the factory that will produce it. Whether one is producing cars, stoves, or matches, buying the real estate on which the factory is located, building the building in which it will be housed, and then designing and creating the machinery that will make the product represent a much greater investment than the raw materials that go into the product. For instance, if putting together a factory for making stoves costs $1 million and the labour and raw materials that go into each stove cost $100, then the cost of manufacturing one stove will be $1,000,100. If 10,000 stoves are produced, then the cost of each stove would be $200 ($1,000,000 divided by 10,000 equals $100 + $100 in raw materials). However, if 1,000,000 stoves are produced, the cost falls to $101 each ($1,000,000 divided by 1,000,000 equals $1 + $100 in raw materials). Consequently, because the United States over the years has had a population roughly 10 times the size of that of Canada, manufactured goods coming out of the US have been cheaper than those made in Canada.

instances, both federal and provincial governments frequently undertook these activities themselves, often in the form of Crown—or government-owned—corporations. For instance, Canada's second national railroad, which served to bolster service to certain areas and bring service to others not served by the CPR, was government-owned. Canada's first transcontinental airline—now Air Canada—was a Crown corporation, as was the first national broadcaster—the CBC. Later, Canada's first satellite company—Telesat Canada—was also a government initiative.

In short, historically, because of the unique features of the Canadian state the government has often taken a strong hand in shaping the economy. At the federal level, these efforts have been motivated by a strong nationalist sentiment. This tradition of nation-building is reflected in the structure of Canada's media industries. For instance, just as the railway was seen as binding Canada physically, so in the 1930s broadcasting was envisioned as building a common Canadian consciousness (see box). Consequently, the government set up the Canadian Radio Broadcasting Commission and later the Canadian Broadcasting Corporation to create a national broadcasting network and Canadian programming—two activities that the private sector was unable to undertake profitably at the time. Later, various policy measures in the magazine, newspaper, publishing, music, film, and telecommunications industries were all undertaken with similar objectives in mind—to help build and strengthen a common Canadian culture. In other words, they were enacted

with nationalist purposes in mind. However, as we shall see, the government record in building and strengthening Canadian culture is patchy at best, and while government policy has often been framed by strong language that claims concern for Canadian culture, it has not always been backed with strong action.

Before considering some of the larger political principles and cultural concerns that underpin the Canadian media, we need to understand the distinctive characteristics of the Canadian state that have shaped the development of its communication system. We have already looked at two of these characteristics: the *vastness of the country* and the *small size of Canada's population*. These geographic and demographic facts have meant that Canada has had to invest in expensive national transmission systems so that Canadians can stay in touch with each other.

A third significant characteristic, derived in part from the size of the country, is Canada's *regionalism*. Canada is not just a country of physical geographic variety; it is a country of various regional cultures. From the disparate French and British colonies scattered throughout what is now Canada grew a 'confederation'. This nation required means of internal communication, but not those in which messages would be generated only from a central point and fed to outlying regions. Each region needed to generate its own information such that the region's particularities would be reflected. This would edify the country as a whole, or such is the ideal.

Canada is also a nation of *two official languages*. The

BROADCASTING AND NATION-BUILDING

In the face of an overwhelming spillover of American programming into Canada, the government set up the Canadian Radio Broadcasting Commission (CRBC) and later the Canadian Broadcasting Corporation (CBC) to build a national broadcasting network and create Canadian programming. In introducing the 1932 Broadcasting Act to the House of Commons—the legislation that created the CRBC—Prime Minister R.B. Bennett outlined what the government saw as the purposes of that legislation:

this country must be assured of complete Canadian control of broadcasting from Canadian sources, free from foreign interference or influence. Without such control radio broadcasting can never become a great agency for communication of matters of national concern and for the diffusion of national thought and ideals, and without such control it can never be the agency by which consciousness may be fostered and sustained and national unity still further strengthened. . . . No other scheme than that of public ownership can ensure to the people of this country, without regard to class or place, equal enjoyment of the benefits and pleasures of radio broadcasting.

right to speak either English or French is now enshrined in our Constitution. But Canadians have committed themselves to more than a freedom of language choice for individuals. They have committed themselves to providing various federal government services, including broadcasting, in both official languages even though in certain communities it is impossible for the audience to bear the cost of service in its own official language. Bilingual government services and bilingual broadcasting channels (not just programs) are a symbol of the right of any Canadian to live and work wherever he or she may wish. They are also a continual reminder to all that we are a bilingual country.

In 1971, during Pierre Trudeau's first term as Prime Minister, Canada also officially became a *multicultural country*. Although it was long in coming, we are beginning to see an acceptance of the desirability of tailoring programming to various ethnic communities. Multicultural television services are mostly distributed by cable rather than broadcast (and are therefore not available to everyone). In contrast, multicultural radio services are broadcast.

A final, never-to-be-forgotten characteristic of Canada's communications environment is its proximity to the US. Economies of scale in media production, coupled with both our acceptance of much the same basic political and economic philosophies and this proximity, have led to a massive penetration of US products and ideas into Canada. Because the US has less tolerance for products that are not recognizably American, the counter-flow—Canadian ideas into the US—has been very limited. In Canada, more American television programming is available to the vast majority of Canadians than is Canadian programming. On most Canadian commercial radio stations, more American material is available to listeners than Canadian material. On virtually all magazine racks in Canada more American magazines are available to the reader than Canadian magazines, in spite of the fact that more than 2,300 magazines are published in Canada (Statistics Canada, 2005). More than 95 per cent of the films screened in Canadian theatres are foreign, mainly American. More American authors than Canadian authors are read by the average Canadian schoolchild. Our proximity to the US and the resultant spillover of American cultural products comprise a major factor to be taken into account in considering Canada's communications environment.

In the face of the challenges posed by these characteristics, Canada has a fairly strong record of achievement in forging a national communications system. Table 3.1 provides a chronology of dates of important communications achievements, including many Canadian firsts.

Each of these developments was cause for some rejoicing and some sense of pride. Each in its own way strengthened east–west links from the Atlantic to the Pacific and was a factor in nation-building and cohesion. Equally important as the technological

THE ECONOMICS OF MEDIA REPRESENTATION

Economies of scale also underlie media production. For instance, much of the cost of producing a magazine or book is in paying the writers, editors, photographers, and typesetters to create the 'first copy'. After that, these initial expenses are spread across the number of copies of that product that are produced. So, if the cost of gathering and putting together all of the material that goes into a particular magazine is $50,000, if 50,000 copies of that magazine are printed, the editorial cost of each magazine is $1.00. However, if 500,000 magazines are printed, the cost falls to only 10 cents per copy. Similar economics apply to film and television, where the 'cost per viewer' is spread over the number of audience members.

Because the market for media products in the United States is roughly 10 times the size of the market in Canada, the cost per reader or cost per audience member for those products is often significantly less in the US than it is for Canadian production aimed primarily for a Canadian audience. Consequently, it is often much more profitable for Canadian distributors of media products to sell American books, magazines, TV shows, and films than those made specifically for the Canadian market. As a result, American media products are often more common in Canada than homegrown versions. It is not because Americans make better media products than Canadians that our markets are overrun with them, it's simply because more money can be made selling them in Canada than producing our own.

Figure 3.1 Some Important Achievements in Canadian Communication History

Year	Achievement
1885	A transcontinental railway
1901	A transatlantic radio link
1927	A trans-Canada radio network
1932	A trans-Canada telephone network
	First Broadcasting Act
1948	World's first commercial microwave link
1956	World's first tropospheric scatter transmission system
1958	A transcontinental television service
	A transcontinental microwave network
1959	First Canadian communications satellite experiment including use of the moon as reflector
1968	Canadian Film Development Corporation
1970	Beginning of fibre optic research
1972	A domestic geostationary communications satellite
1973	First nationwide digital data system
	World's first digital transmission network (Dataroute)
1976	Bill C-58: legislation to help Canadian magazine industry
1990	Completion of a 7,000-kilometre coast-to-coast fibre optic network, the longest terrestrial fibre network in the world
1993	Canadian Telecommunications Act
1996	Launch of the first North American commercial digital radio service
1999	Aboriginal Peoples Television Network established

achievements in building the system are legislative achievements, such as the 1932 Broadcasting Act and the 1993 Telecommunications Act. These statutes gave voice to the public interest in the development of these systems and set in law the public goals and ambitions that underlie them. Still, addressing the needs of all the different regions and peoples of the country has been difficult, particularly in the North, where, as Lorna Roth (2005: 221) notes, 'When first introduced in the 1960's and 70's, television temporarily stalled indigenous self-development by introducing yet another Southern medium devoid of First People's images, voices, and cultural activities.'

These realities continue to present challenges to government, business, and other social groups for creating communication systems that serve all of the peoples of Canada in a fair, equitable, and comprehensive manner.

Canada: Liberal Principles in a Conservative State

In theory, freedom of the press is founded on the notion of free speech, but in practice it derives from the desires of competing elites—the business commu-

nity, government, intellectuals, the church—to have access to the general audience. From an audience perspective, freedom of the press translates into exposure to an ideological spectrum within which individual ideas and policies are normally considered. As we have pointed out, freedom of the press developed in Europe from a power struggle between the nobility and the church on the one side and printers and manufacturers on the other side. Canadian press history is distinctive because of the acceptance of liberal principles of press operation and press freedom prior to the evolution of various separate interest groups. Thus, while printers depended on government printing contracts, the colonial government tolerated, to some degree, their printing of anti-government commentary.

Oddly enough, Canada's tolerance was founded both on its colonial status and on the country's proximity to the United States. That is, as leaders in colonies of Great Britain, the Canadian political elites were enfranchised by their class connections to the mother country. Hence, the colonies in what is now Canada strived to remain abreast of changes in the United Kingdom, which, when the Canadian press was developing, were towards modern liberal democracy. When the enactment of liberal principles became too slow in Britain, Canada turned to the United States for models, which were even more radically focused on the rights of individuals and freedom of enterprise without state interference.

In taking their lead from outside the country, Canadian media pioneers created a press and media culture strong on the individualism inherent in liberal principles and weak on the cultural or nationalist ideas inherent in the same theory. In more concrete terms, the Canadian media were and are strong supporters of **freedom of speech**. They are much less strong in their understanding of themselves as supporting institutions of Canadian society. Certainly, many journalists and media managers would claim that in bringing forward political and financial scandal, in exposing criminals, in praising heroes, they fill that role admirably. But when the sense of individualism clashes with the need to support distinctive Canadian institutions, almost without exception the media can be found on the side of individualism. The support of the media for free trade and against regulation of the economy in the interests of Canadians and Canadian institutions is a case in point.

It could be argued that this theme of the media neglecting to support Canadian institutions is present throughout the history of Canadian broadcasting. For instance, support of cultural distinctiveness was written into successive Broadcasting Acts, only to be gradually worn away by the media, which, with the exception of the CBC, were more interested in importing and distributing programs than in producing Canadian programs. Certainly, there is evidence to support such a viewpoint in various broadcasting histories (see, for example, Vipond, 2000; Raboy, 1990; Weir, 1965; Babe, 1990; Rutherford, 1990; Peers, 1979, 1969). Robert Babe (1990), a communications political economist, identifies an additional factor that contributed to this scenario. He argues that, in part, the configuration of our broadcasting and telecommunications systems is a result of deals made in the US to split patents there among companies in such a way that telecommunications became a separate industry from broadcasting. Patents for radio and telephone transmission in Canada were split in the same way, and hence Canadian subsidiaries of US telecommunication companies controlled the same patents as did their parent companies in the US and operated in parallel with them. In broadcasting, ownership restrictions prevented parallel home-office/branch-plant operations. But they did not stop broadcasters from continually pushing for the right to import US programs in bulk and run essentially parallel operations.

The Mass Media and Canadian Culture

We can now turn to examining the relationship between Canadian culture and Canada's mass media—including government's administration and regulation of them. This relationship is both interesting and complex.

Set at the intersection between people and the different social groups, organizations, and institutions that make up our society, the media are a key vehicle in communicating the depth and breadth of the ways of life—or culture—of Canadians. What exactly is culture? As a number of social scientists point out, this is a very complex word and there are many different definitions. As defined by the Canadian government in a report on Canada's cultural industries, *Vital Links*, culture 'includes the knowledge, beliefs, art, morals, customs and all other capabilities acquired by a particular society' (Canada, 1987: 11). To this we might also add the laws, institutions, and organizations that give society form. In other words, from this perspective, culture is a way or ways of life. In Canada, of course, we have a distinctive set of institutions—such as governments, schools, universities, media, the health-care system—that give Canadian culture form, as well as a wide range of ideas, values, and beliefs that exist within that larger social frame. In other words, Canadian 'culture' is itself a product of many distinctive cultures.

Media, of course, are central to how we come to understand and share culture, and, in a large industrial nation such as Canada, the media are complexly woven into the social fabric. They are the means through which the exchange of ideas, experience, images, and interpretations and perspectives on the world takes place. Indeed, it is generally through the media that we come to know our society, its institutions and organizations, and the other people with whom we share our national culture. For this reason, the media industries are often called cultural industries. Tables 3.2 and 3.3 list the top programs in the English and French television markets for the week of 9–15 October 2006. The figures provide a sense of the popular tastes of these audiences and the size of the audiences for each program. Yet, if we were to take Table 3.2 as an indication of how English Canadians know about themselves and others through television, we would have to conclude that anglophone Canada

Table 3.2 Top Programs, Total Canada (English), 9–15 October 2006

Rank	Program	Network	Average Audience (thousands)
1	C.S.I.	CTV National	4,043
2	C.S.I. New York	CTV National	2,577
3	Desperate Housewives	CTV National	2,468
4	C.S.I. Miami	CTV National	2,462
5	Survivor: Cook Islands	Global National	2,387
6	Criminal Minds	CTV National	2,329
7	ER	CTV National	2,269
8	Amazing Race 10	CTV National	2,172
9	Grey's Anatomy	CTV National	2,100
10	Law and Order: Special Victim Unit	CTV National	1,854
11	CTV Evening News	CTV National	1,573
12	Cold Case	CTV National	1,532
13	H.N.I.C. Game #1	CBC National	1,496
14	Ghost Whisperer	CTV National	1,469
15	Law and Order (Friday)	CTV National	1,408
16	Shark	Global National	1,393
17	Lost	CTV National	1,352
18	Corner Gas	CTV National	1,326
19	Deal or No Deal	Global National	1,276
20	C.S.I.	CTV National	1,261
21	Jeopardy/Access HWD	CTV National	1,258
22	Heroes	Global National	1,247
23	Close To Home	CTV National	1,219
24	Deal or No Deal	Global National	1,150
25	Numbers	Global National	1,117
26	1 vs.100	Global National	1,117
27	Studio 60 on Sunset	CTV National	1,104
28	CTV Evening News (Weekend)	CTV National	1,054
29	The Class	CTV National	1,037
30	Global National	Global National	994

Source: BBM Canada, at: www.bbm.ca.

must be suffering from an identity crisis from the infusion of American-made programming.

Historically, Canadian governments have paid lip service to the importance of media and cultural products in the life of the nation, but as Babe (1990) and others have argued, Canadian governments have not been consistent protectors and supporters of Canada's cultural industries. While they have risen to that role from time to time, they have also enacted policies that have stunted the growth of industries, such as film, broadcasting, sound recording (music), and publishing. Canadian government investment in communications has traditionally stressed telecommunications transmission and technology to serve the broadcasting system and interactive media, from the telephone to the internet. In the 1990s, amid budget cuts to public broadcasting, the federal government spent millions on upgrading transmission networks. In 1998 Canada announced that CA*net 3—a national optical network partly funded by the federal government—would be introduced in October of that year and would be able to deliver the entire contents of the US Library of Congress in one second. The press release announcing this noted that a parallel network in the US would

Table 3.3 Top Programs, Québec French, 9-15 October 2006

Rank	Program	Network	Average Audience (thousands)
1	Tout le monde en . . .	SRC	1,717
2	Occupation double	TVA	1,705
3	Annie et ses hommes	TVA	1,265
4	Lance et compte : La Revanche	TVA	1,252
5	Les poupées russes	TVA	1,188
6	Loft Story Talk Show	TQS	1,162
7	Nos étés	TVA	1,133
8	Le Sketch Show	TVA	1,079
9	Auberge chien noir	SRC	1,010
10	La poule aux oeufs d'or	TVA	978
11	Histoires de filles	TVA	976
12	Occupation double	TVA	976
13	Caméra café	TVA	939
14	Juste pour rire	TVA	929
15	La promesse	TVA	927
16	Les Gags	TVA	923
17	Rumeurs	SRC	874
18	Hockey Canadiens Sam	RDS	868
19	L'école des fans	TVA	861
20	Star système	TVA	853
21	Du talent à revendre	TVA	832
22	Match des étoiles	SRC	824
23	Loft Story	TQS	818
24	Le TVA 18 heures	TVA	812
25	On n'a pas toute la soirée	TVA	809
26	Dieu créa . . . Laflaque	SRC	796
27	Le cercle	TVA	794
28	La fièvre du mardi soir	TVA	787
29	Providence	SRC	767
30	Le petit monde de Laura Cadieux	TVA	761

Source: BBM Canada, at: www.bbm.ca.

require one minute. In 2003, Canada moved onto CA*net 4. The point, government spokespeople noted, was to emphasize Canadian technological leadership.

This commitment to current technology and effective, rapid transmission has been a mixed blessing (see Charland, 1986). In spite of the rhetoric used to justify each new major expenditure, because it has provided a conduit for foreign television and radio programs to reach Canadian audiences it has not necessarily served the cultural needs of Canada and Canadians (see Table 3.2). Within Canada, the impressive telecommunications infrastructure has served pri-

vate-sector growth not just in broadcasting but also in the formation of national newspapers such as the *Globe and Mail* and the *National Post*, which have taken advantage of satellite and other communications technologies to print regional editions of their newspapers simultaneously in different parts of the country. In the case of broadcasting, through the insistence of the CRTC, some cultural benefits have emerged from private-sector growth, but the private broadcasters have been reluctant contributors to cultural goals in that in many categories they have shown a preference to import foreign, mainly American programs rather than contribute to the production of Canadian television products.

The usual rationale for government investment in communication infrastructure is that technological development creates jobs—numerous spinoff technologies lead to the creation of new industries, products, and hence jobs in the information sector. (The jargon is that there are significant **multiplier effects**, meaning that such investment leads to both direct and indirect jobs.) Not insignificantly, Canada's advanced communication infrastructure is also a vivid demonstration to the average Canadian that he or she has access to an equal or superior range of programs and services than does the average American.

It is certainly the case that a ready infrastructure has assisted Canadian business to embrace the internet as a business tool. Not only have new internet businesses been founded, but also traditional businesses have been able to take advantage of Canada's robust technological infrastructure.

However, historically, the difficulty with investing in the technological infrastructure of communications has been that because of the country's small population Canadians have never been in a position to produce enough programs to fill the transmission capacity we have developed. And even if Canadian producers could somehow produce the programs, there

would not be enough money in the pockets of advertisers, the public, and governments to pay for the full range of choice we created through the years. In other words, we have created an information environment that at once keeps us abreast industrially of the most advanced nations and also opens us to inundation by foreign cultural products. We neglected to design a system that would guarantee the development of Canadian culture and cultural production. The reason, it would seem, is an underlying belief on the part of elites in the liberal doctrine of free enterprise—an extension of the idea of liberal individualism. This commitment has overshadowed the concern for a distinctive, diverse Canadian culture.

Enter the Americans, who happen to be close by and also happen to be the world's most successful entertainment and information producers. The selection—and, perhaps most importantly, the price—they offer in such areas as television and film is too good for private business to refuse. For one-tenth the cost of producing a season of half-hour television dramas in Canada, US producers can provide a high-quality program with high ratings and ever-so-attractive stars, complete with press attention and magazine commentary that spill over the border in American media products. While Canadian governments at times have played the role of patron in the name of cultural sov-

CANADA'S NATIONWIDE RESEARCH AND EDUCATION NETWORK

In 1998, Canarie (Canada's Research and Innovation Network) deployed CA*net 3, the world's first national optical internet research and education network. CA*net 3 was among the most advanced in the world when it was built, and its design has since been replicated by many network operators in the research and education as well as commercial domains. However, exponential growth in network traffic, expected growth in new high-bandwidth applications, and planned extreme high-bandwidth grid projects required that a new network be built to support leading-edge research in Canada. To this end, the government of Canada committed $110 million to Canarie for the design, deployment, and operation of CA*net 4.

CA*net 4, like its predecessor, interconnects provincial research networks and, through them, universities, research centres, government research laboratories,

schools, and other eligible sites, both with each other and with international peer networks. Through a series of point-to-point optical wavelengths, most of which are provisioned at OC-192 (10 Gbps) speeds, CA*net 4 yields a total initial network capacity of between four and eight times that of CA*net 3.

In December 2006 Canarie announced the development of ROADM (Reconfigurable Optical Add/Drop Multiplexing) technology with the capability to create almost unlimited bandwidth for major science projects, as well as education and training. Still, however, despite these advances in fibre-optic communication technology, communities that are off the main lines of Canada's fibre-optic grid often experience problems of capacity with their internet service.

Source: www.canarie.ca. Courtesy of Canarie Inc.

ereignty or national development and have provided subsidies and enacted legislation to protect Canadian media products and support producers, they have been reluctant to either impose heavy restrictions on private enterprise or restrict the ability of foreigners to do business in Canada.

Consequently, only in Quebec is the regional culture thoroughly reflected in the media (see Table 3.3). In the rest of the country, the result of this focus on technology, liberal market principles, and lack of determination to ensure a dominance of Canadian media products has been, for decades, a cultural low road (see Chapter 7).

Politics and the Canadian Media Today

As we have seen, the media are traditionally portrayed as playing an important role in the governance of society. This section considers the distinctive role of the media in Canadian politics.

The modern nation-state is a sophisticated information apparatus, with government and the traditional mass media acting as two of its major information arms. More recently, web-based media have provided a considerably enhanced opportunity for ordinary citizens to obtain information and to exchange it with others. The government, in order to govern effectively and to perpetuate itself, both collects and produces information. The traditional mass media collect and produce information to inform the public and the state and to maintain successful commercial ventures. The interactive media allow people who possess the skills and equipment to produce, seek out, and exchange information.

The role of the news media in carrying information between people and the government makes for

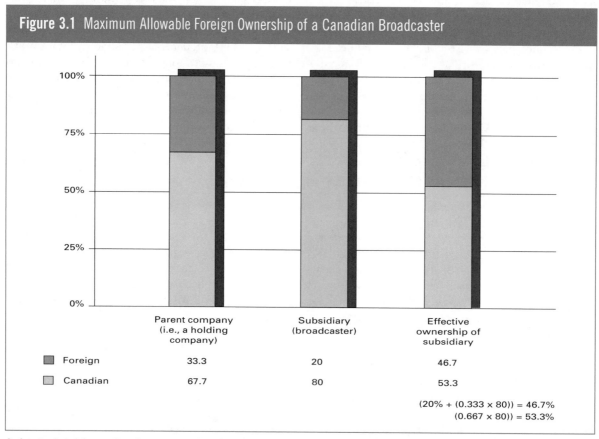

Figure 3.1 Maximum Allowable Foreign Ownership of a Canadian Broadcaster

	Parent company (i.e., a holding company)	Subsidiary (broadcaster)	Effective ownership of subsidiary
Foreign	33.3	20	46.7
Canadian	67.7	80	53.3

(20% + (0.333 × 80)) = 46.7%
(0.667 × 80)) = 53.3%

As free trade between nations increases, so does foreign ownership. As this figure illustrates, according to Canadian law effective ownership of a broadcaster can be as much as 46.7 per cent through indirect ownership (of a holding company) and direct ownership of the broadcaster that is a subsidiary of the holding company. Any increase in allowance of foreign ownership would give majority control to a foreign owner. Within political economic theory, the role of foreign ownership looms large as a factor affecting cultural sovereignty.

extremely close relations with government. The news media depend on the government for both information and advertising. The government depends on the news media to disseminate that information. But the government's desire to keep certain information from them, such as pre-decision information in cabinet documents, gives that relationship a certain ambivalence. At the same time, the desire of the media to maintain their independence and periodically to demonstrate their separate integrity transforms that ambivalence into a love-hate relationship on the part of politicians. The dependence of the media on government for information makes that love-hate relationship mutual. (Several sources provide particularly good analyses of this relationship: Rose and Kiss, 2006; Nesbitt-Larking, 2001; Hayes, 1992; Cocking, 1980; Gratton, 1987; and the proceedings of the Canadian Study of Parliament Group, Canada, 1980.)

In theory, the media act as a counteractive force to potential abuse of power by the state. In pursuit of the public good and in support of democratic theory, the media protect individual privacy from the prying eyes of the state, which, in the name of the community, may venture to collect all kinds of information to ease the job of governance. The media also help, along with the opposition parties in Parliament, to monitor government policy and action (see, e.g., Fletcher, 1981).

The parliamentary press gallery deserves some direct attention in this context. The gallery is the sum total of all journalists who are working on political stories in Ottawa or the provincial capitals and become members of the Ottawa or provincial capital galleries. It is also, as the federal Task Force on Government Information (Canada, 1969, vol. 2: 115–19) noted, 'the most important instrument of political communication in the country'. The press gallery performs two essential roles: to disseminate government information, and to assess the wisdom of government policy and action by reporting and analyzing House debates.

The press gallery and, more generally, the media do not have completely free rein to carry out their roles. They are generally controlled by a set of laws, standards, and professional approaches that dictate their activities. For instance, professional codes of ethics, press councils in some countries, **libel** law, and limited **access to information** are all factors in how and what the media report (see Chapter 9). Restrictions also emerge from the manner in which

journalists operate. Political scientist Fred Fletcher (1981) has noted the effect of the workings of press galleries on news reporting. Until the 1960s, when they came to be seen as compromising if not direct conflicts of interest, press galleries benefited from various incentives, such as retainers paid by governments to journalists, preferred access, and other perks. In recent decades the galleries have emerged as independent from the control of government, and consequently they have become more professional. In turn, however, this independence from government has been compromised by *pack journalism*. The term 'pack journalism' derives from the tendency of journalists to hang around in groups and all chase after the same story at once. As a result, vast areas of government activity are inadequately covered, such as the courts, regulatory agencies, parliamentary committees, and policy-making and adjudication within the civil service. A further shortcoming of the press gallery is that many journalists lack the training to understand certain elements of government. Finally, more recently, in the face of efforts by large media chains to cut down on expenses, the size of the parliamentary press gallery is shrinking. It is now more clearly dominated by a few larger papers and wire services, as well as the major broadcast networks. Most noticeable is the decreased number of regional members whose sole function was to report on matters from the perspective of the region they represented.

In addition to the control exercised upon the media, the media themselves can act in such a way as to impede their role of keeping the public informed. The public's right to know as opposed to the media's tendency to create stories is one such issue. For instance, every decision a government makes that involves the spending of money can be questioned after the fact. Should the government be spending that money? Is it getting good value for its dollar? Who is benefiting? When the media become intent on defeating a government they need only to ask such questions continuously to place the government on the defensive, potentially interfering with its ability to govern, as perhaps was the case with the Liberal sponsorship scandal that led to the fall of Paul Martin's Liberal government in 2005. Meanwhile, the public may be ill-informed about the intent of the government, the context of spending and its relative prudence, and the ways in which government programs actually benefit citizens.

However, in some areas specific regulations govern media behaviour to try and ensure fair report-ing—this is especially true of the media's coverage of elections. Regulations control aspects of political advertising—for example, they exclude dramatization and forbid political ads to be broadcast within 48 hours of an election. There are also restrictions on who can advertise what during a political campaign. For instance, groups are restricted from advertising in favour of one party based on their stance on one issue—for example, abortion. The electronic media must be especially careful to provide equal coverage of all political parties. The print media, however, are free to cover elections as they choose.

There are also less direct measures the govern-ment can use to control the media. For instance, when the government perceives that the structure or operation of the media may be moving against the public interest it can establish a public inquiry to examine media operations, such as it did with the 1970 Special Senate Committee on the Mass Media, the 1980 Royal Commission on Newspapers, and the 2001 House of Commons Standing Committee study of broadcasting. However, while such inquiries are a good vehicle for developing an understanding of the forces shaping the media, they have not proven particularly effective in achieving change (see Skinner et al., 2005).

On another front, since government is the largest advertiser in the country, the withdrawal of advertis-ing can hurt media organizations, especially the print media. The government can also seek to control jour-nalists by giving selective access to people or infor-mation and by exercising favouritism in its monop-oly over government-created information. For exam-ple, inconsistencies in dealing with access to infor-mation can easily be exploited for political motives. Releasing news at 4 p.m. on a Friday afternoon in time for television news allows for the information to get out, but with little comment. The next morning, when the news is old, the newspapers get their shot at interpreting the event or announcement. (The soft form of this sort of manipulation by government is termed 'news management'.) Provincial governments also have some power in this regard. For example, attorneys general can order investigations into what they perceive as media interference with the court system and trials (Canadian Press, 1993c).

Individual politicians can also put their stamp on relations between the government and media. For instance, as the CBC program *The Press and the Prime*

Minister documented, Pierre Trudeau was continually engaged in matching wits with the press. On a day-to-day basis, he was neither an unsophisticated nor a mute observer of the role and failings of the press in Canadian society. At election times he was a master of media manipulation in his presentation of issues and persona. During his time in office, Jean Chrétien was well known for his waffling on issues with the press, leaving reporters and pundits often unsure of where he stood on issues of the day. And during his first months in office in 2006, Stephen Harper was noted for avoiding the media altogether.

Recently, some writers have argued that the line between government and the media is blurring as more and more journalists 'cross over' to take well-paid jobs in government (Rose and Kiss, 2006). Politicians are increasingly hiring former journalists to work as public relations people or 'handlers' to help manage their images and the issues faced by government. This raises questions over whether issues are being fairly and accurately presented by govern-ments, or whether they are subject to 'spin' or inter-pretation that serves the personal or political interests of politicians themselves. As Jonathan Rose and Simon Kiss (2006: 336) ask, 'who is producing the content that we consume in our daily lives? Perhaps public relations officials—whether they are govern-ment, industry, or otherwise—are gaining the upper hand?' In the US, one of the most extreme (or clever, depending on one's point of view) recent examples of 'spinning' a world-changing event was the American government's embedding of journalists with their troops during the invasion of Iraq in 2003. As one critic noted, they did a fine job of reporting both sides of the conflict—both sides, that is, of the soldiers protecting them.

Amid the shifting relations between government and the media, the internet, with its many sources of information and capacity for information-sharing, appears to be challenging the role of the traditional mass media as the 'voice of the people'. For instance, web logs, or 'blogs', have played an increasingly important role in political communication, particu-larly in the US. For instance, Matt Drudge's blog, *The Drudge Report*, broke the story of President Bill Clinton's affair with White House intern Monica Lewinsky, seriously hampering his political effective-ness during his last days in office. Blogsters also uncovered that documents used by CBS news to claim that President Bush 'had shirked his duties as a member of the National Guard during the Vietnam War' were 'of questionable veracity', leading CBS 'to apologize and launch an internal inquiry into how the story had passed internal checks' (ibid., 139). Drawing on the work of blog researchers Drezner and Farrell (2004), Rose and Kiss (2006: 340) point out that 'blogs have significant advantages in the opinion-formation process, often shaping important political events early on. Whereas members of the traditional media must go through some basic processes of vetting and editing before their accounts can be put forward, these constraints are non-existent for bloggers.' At this point, exactly what the impact of new web-based media will be on traditional media in the political sphere is difficult to say.

When placed in the context of the history of the media outlined earlier in this chapter, contemporary tensions, shifts, and changes in the relations among the government, the media, and the public illustrate one thing for sure: the relationship between government and the media is one of ongoing negotiation and change.

Information Needs, Communication Actualities, and the United Nations

Because of our proximity to the US and our frequent contact with American media products, you may tend to believe that the US behaves in its trading relations in a manner consistent with its ideology of free enterprise and free trade. But this assumption is wrong. You may be surprised to learn that other countries are similar to Canada in their concern over the flow of American cultural products inside their borders. You may also be surprised to hear that other countries have stronger restrictions on the importation of cultural goods than does Canada. As well, the US Congress is extremely protectionist. The US engages in judicial harassment by tying up foreign producers with legal challenges when it refuses to accept negative rulings in trade disputes, such as with the long-running argument over US tariffs on softwood lumber.

The United States is the richest and most powerful nation on earth. Moreover, it has an overall ideology that reflects its position of prominence and a tenacious ideological adherence to individual freedom and freedom of enterprise. These and other factors have created a society that is materially richer than Canada and more able to foist its products on the rest of the world. (Nevertheless, it has, at the same time, a very weak social safety net and public healthcare system.)

In Chapter 5 we will explore the impact of cultural products on audiences in more detail, but for now let us advance a few simple concepts on the matter. There is little doubt that continuous exposure to American cultural products presents us with a set of attitudes, perceptions, and ideas, indeed, a world view, inherent in those products. In fact, that is the basic effect in all communication, not just propaganda. It is also the reason why the Motion Picture Association of America attempts to persuade US film producers to use American rather than Japanese automobiles on their sets (Rever, 1995). The problem with continuous exposure to foreign cultural products is that if we lack exposure to other products, other perspectives, other ways to understand the world, other alternatives for acting, then we are open to blindly adopting (or rejecting) the values presented, which may clash with the values and institutions that give form to our own ways of life. Moreover, continuous exposure to foreign media products also affects our sense of media forms, formats, and styles. For instance, we have become so accustomed to the fast-cut, high-action Hollywood style of feature film that those films that don't adopt Hollywood conventions are often considered slow, boring, or too intellectual.

The impact of foreign cultural products has been a long-standing issue for many people and communities. It arises out of a commitment to preserve, develop, and represent one's own culture and nation. The focus on American cultural products derives from the fact that the US is by far the dominant producer of cultural products. While such concern can develop into extreme protectionism, intolerance, and political self-interest, it may also be seen as a commitment to a pluralistic world society being represented in all its heterogeneity. For some time the United Nations Educational, Scientific and Cultural Organization (UNESCO) served as a focus for the articulation of these concerns, for the desirability of nations favouring their own artists, authors, and cultural producers. With the withdrawal of the US and the UK from UNESCO in the early 1980s, and hence the loss of one-third of its budget, this agency tended to steer away from playing such a role. Only recently has the organization managed to regain some of the political momentum it lost during that period (Warnica, 2005).

The position developed by UNESCO on communications problems and prospects, at first with the MacBride Report (1980) and more recently with the Convention on the Protection and Promotion of the Diversity of Cultural Expressions (2005), is that each nation has the right to a national culture or communications policy. A nation must have the capacity to take information produced either by itself or by the world community and analyze it according to its own national needs and priorities. In practice, Canada has not fully committed itself to this need. Yet our investments in high technology, such as the information highway, demonstrate that neither are we entirely without commitment to this end. Canada is in the happy position of being economically able to work towards an information infrastructure oriented to its national needs and the maintenance of its independence. Being already committed to technological development in communications, being economically well-off, and being so near and so like the US, we are in a position to lead in setting boundaries on the US cultural barrage for our own benefit and for the benefit of other nations.

Summary

The evolution of the modern mass media began around 1440 with Gutenberg's development of printing by means of movable type. Printing with movable type facilitated a social movement that saw the eclipse of feudalism and the dawning of the Renaissance, followed by the Reformation, the Enlightenment or Age of Reason, and the Industrial Revolution. The divine right of rulers was replaced with the notion of the *consent of the governed*. The printing press served an important social role from the fifteenth century onward in gathering information and informing citizens.

In making their contribution, the press and, subsequently, other communication media have been influenced by their social and historical location, that is, they have been given form and function by a larger set of social circumstances and events. The rise of industrial society, along with urbanization, increased literacy, and the eight-hour workday, provided the context within which contemporary media took their form and function. In Canada, the development of modern media was further shaped by basic social realities such as our vast, sparsely populated, bilingual, multicultural, and regional country, which lies next to the United States—the world's largest economy and most aggressive exporter of entertainment and information products.

Moreover, while the role of the media in society can be conceived from various ideological perspectives—the fourth estate, liberal, Marxist—in Canadian society the press and then the electronic mass media have developed under a set of liberal principles in a conservative state. Canadians have invested a great amount of public funding in the electronic media to assist in nation-building, and this investment in technological infrastructure has provided Canadians with a high level of communication services. However, it has also paved the way for the importation and distribution of a vast amount of foreign content.

As we shall see in Chapter 7, after years of subsidies and support, magazine and book publishers, filmmakers, and sound-recording artists are, to a degree, increasing their domestic market share and making a mark on the world stage. However, these successes are fragile and require the ongoing support of governments. At the same time, technological change has raised the possibility of giving a greater voice to the people—not only to express themselves but also to own and control information sites that may demand greater responsiveness from both government and the traditional mass media. But whether the potential of this technological capacity will be realized, or whether it will weaken the traditional mass media, remains to be seen.

Canadians must remind themselves that, in taking action to regulate the mass media and to stimulate cultural industries, they are not alone. While efforts to define and protect cultural industries have weakened in the face of growing transnational trade and trade agreements, the struggle to maintain control over their own cultural development remains a key concern for many nations and is still being fought in various venues.

RELATED WEBSITES

Access to Information and Privacy Acts: canada.justice. gc.ca/en/ps/atip/

These two Acts provide a sense of Canada's legislation in these areas.

Canada's cultural industries: www.pch.gc.ca/culture/library/ _statscan/stats_e.htm

This page of the Department of Canadian Heritage site offers statistics on cultural industries such as film and recording.

Canada's Privacy Act: laws.justice.gc.ca/en/index.html

As you will see, the Privacy Act covers much more than internet privacy.

Canarie: www.canarie.ca/canet4/

Canarie is the organization responsible for Canada's high-speed internet backbone. This site provides information on Canarie and on CA*net 3 (and 4).

Department of Canadian Heritage: www.pch.gc.ca

Every Canadian student at all concerned with culture, the media, and heritage should visit the website of the federal government's Department of Canadian Heritage.

John Locke: www.orst.edu/instruct/phl302/philosophers/ _locke.html

Many universities have taken it upon themselves to provide texts free of charge to the world. Many are in the US. This site provides information on and texts written by John Locke.

Milton's *Areopagitica*: www.uoregon.edu/~rbear/areopagiti-ca._html

This important work on censorship by the English poet can be found on a variety of sites that are accessible by doing a Google search on 'areopagitica'.

rabble.ca

Institute for Alternative Journalism: www.alternet.org

There are various alternative news websites, including these two.

FURTHER READINGS

Canada. 1981. *Report of the Royal Commission on Newspapers*. Ottawa: Supply and Services. This dated but most recent Royal Commission on the press brings forward many issues. Its background papers are also extremely informative.

Canada, House of Commons. 2003. *Our Cultural Sovereignty: The Second Century of Canadian Broadcasting. Report of the House of Commons Standing Committee on Canadian Heritage*. Ottawa: Communication Canada. This report provides good background on the history, structure, and problems facing Canadian broadcasting.

Vipond, Mary. 2000. *The Mass Media in Canada*. Toronto:

James Lorimer. This book provides a historical perspective on the Canadian mass media.

Weir, Ernest Austin. 1965. *The Struggle for National Broadcasting in Canada*. Toronto: McClelland & Stewart. As the title suggests, the author presents an account of the development of public broadcasting in Canada and of the political and cultural milieu out of which this regime was established.

Williams, Raymond. 1979. *Television, Technology and Cultural Form*. Glasgow: Fontana Collins. Focusing on the development of television, Williams illustrates how technological development is the product of a broad set of social forces.

STUDY QUESTIONS

1. What was the essence of the Enlightenment?
2. How are the mass media connected to Enlightenment values?
3. How might the modern media be seen as a cultural form inherent to industrial society?
4. What are some of the ways in which the federal government has played a central role in developing both the Canadian economy and the Canadian media?
5. Provide some examples of 'economies of scale' in media organizations.
6. Should governments be able to control the information environment? If so, in what ways?

LEARNING OUTCOMES

- To describe the political/historical roots of the mass media and the connections between communication and education, our conception of human rights, and democracy.
- To reacquaint students with the Enlightenment, what it represents as a world view, and how it relates to democracy and communication.
- To illustrate how the media took form in the context of industrial society.
- To describe the beginnings of newspapers.
- To describe the relationship between the press and the electronic media and the democratic right to freedom of speech.
- To describe the beginnings of the electronic media.
- To introduce the concept of ownership and control of the media and the possible bias inherent in allowing certain sectors of society to participate as media owners.
- To place the Canadian media in their historical context.
- To provide an overview of the structure of the Canadian media and how they relate to Canadian culture and politics.

PART TWO

Content and Audiences

CHAPTER 4

Theoretical Perspectives on Media Content

Introduction

Chapters 4 and 5 provide an introduction to communication theory and illustrate some of the main approaches to the study of media content and audiences. This chapter begins by introducing terms that describe some basic characteristics of the process of communication and media content. It then introduces a number of theoretical and methodological perspectives communication theorists use when studying content. Finally, it considers some of the dimensions of the interaction between media content and social reality.

The phrase 'in the beginning was the word' recognizes the importance of symbolic representation and our ability to develop and use language and other symbolic systems. It also indicates the power of language as a symbolic system and its ability to serve as a medium for the creation, communication, and reception of meaning.

The study of the process and content of communication does not focus on whether a description or set of statements corresponds exactly to what it purports to describe. Communication scholars working in the social sciences are more interested in how something is described, how it is transformed by the medium in which it is communicated, the understanding the receiver develops, and the impact the communication could have. To put this in terms already introduced, social scientific communication scholars are more interested in a social rather than in a technological model of communication. There is no ideal state of complete fidelity between what the receiver understands and what the sender meant to send. Rather, our focus is on the dynamics of the development of a message and the reception of content. This includes the bias of the various media and how the communicators, their immediate reference groups, their culture, their society, and the chosen media transform the message as it is being encoded, transmitted, and decoded. In short, a social theory of communication focuses on the transformation that occurs during the communication process.

Representation and Signification

When we study communication, and particularly communication content, we are generally studying practices or processes of **representation**. What is representation? It's the act of putting ideas into words, paintings, sculpture, film, plays, television programs or any other medium of communication. A picture of a plane crash is not the actual crash itself but a 're-presentation' of that crash. (It's the crash 'presented again'.) A map is not the actual place that it seeks to describe, but a representation of that place. An advertisement for a sports utility vehicle (SUV) is not an SUV but a representation or way of thinking about such a vehicle. Even a 'live' television broadcast of a hockey game or some other sporting event is not the actual game itself but a series of carefully chosen and constructed images, camera angles, and commentary that represent the event.

In putting ideas into words, a painting, a sculpture, a film, a website, a newspaper story, or any other medium of communication, a person selects certain elements to describe the object, event, person, or situation he or she wishes to represent. In other words, representations are, to a large part, simplifications of the objects and events they describe. The person receiving or decoding that communication then uses what he or she knows of what is described and what he or she knows of the system of representation—most often language—to come to an understanding of what was encoded by the sender.

A more rigorous way of thinking about representation is as a process of signification. **Signification** is using signs to make meaning. What's a **sign**? Anything with meaning: a word, an image, a sound, a painting, even things themselves like dark clouds on the horizon. The Swiss linguist Ferdinand de Saussure—sometimes considered the founder of **semiotics** or the science of signs—posited that signs are composed of two elements: the signifier and signified. The **signifier** is the thing that we see, hear, or feel; that is, the image on a screen, sounds, or small bumps on paper. The **signified** is the idea or mental concept we draw from those signifiers; the ideas we take from the content of a blog, music, or words written in Braille. In other words, the process of signification is a process of making meaning. Indeed, from this perspective our whole experience of the world is a process of signification as we translate the signs we encounter into meaning: clouds mean rain; a short chapter in the textbook, not too much homework; an angry parent, trouble.

C.S. Peirce categorized signs into three different types: icon, index, and symbol. An icon looks like the object it describes. For instance, maps and photographs both are icons. An index is related to the object it represents. Smoke is an index of fire and a sneeze is an index of a cold or allergy or irritant. A symbol is a sign that bears no direct resemblance to what it signifies. Words are symbols, as is the image of an apple when it is used to represent something other than fruit, like knowledge or a particular brand of electronic products.

Intertextuality, Polysemy, and the Indeterminacy of Representation

The idea that a sign can represent or signify more than one thing raises the indeterminacy of representation. For instance, to some the image of a sporty SUV might signify or represent luxury, adventure, or sex appeal; to others, environmental disaster. The sound of falling rain might signify or represent a soothing summer's evening or, perhaps, an impending flood. The meaning of any particular sign is not guaranteed but, instead, dependent on the context of its use and interpretation.

In other words, signs do not exist in isolation. Rather, they are either explicitly or implicitly part of larger 'texts' or sets of signs and symbols. Images of SUVs are often found in advertisements that portray them as part of mountain adventures or happy family outings. The melodic splash of rain is often used to establish a mood in music, film, or television programs. In other words, the meaning of these signs is itself given form by its relation to other signs in the context of a larger symbolic system. If we are confronted by images and sounds without this kind of grounding, to make meaning out of them we often supply our own context, drawn from memory and imagination.

The idea that meaning is made in the context of larger symbolic systems draws our attention to two other important elements of the process of signification. The first is the 'intertextuality' of the process of

Adbusters often employs semiotics to create 'subvertisements', ads slightly changed or 'subverted' to expose the negative effects of the products they promote. Here the 'signifier'—the vodka bottle—has been modified to shift its 'signified' from the usual party atmosphere depicted in liquor ads to something less alluring.

making meaning. **Intertextuality** refers to the fact that the meaning we make of one text depends on the meanings we have drawn from other sets of signs we have encountered (see, for example, Kristeva, 1969, or Barthes, 1968). In other words, meaning is grounded in the relationships we find between different texts. For instance, at the expense of stating the obvious, our understanding of the ad for the SUV as a family vehicle is dependent on combining knowledge of the SUV as a mode of transportation and the representation of the people in the image as a family. Folding the two signifiers together—SUV and happy family—creates the signified 'family vehicle'. Similarly, our understanding of the ways vehicle exhaust emissions are related to global warming might also lead us to interpret the SUV as an instrument of environmental degradation. In this way we can see that our past experience—our individual history—provides the backdrop for interpreting the signs and symbols we encounter in everyday life.

The second important point to be made about this process of decoding is that making meaning is an active process. Making the connection between signifier and signified, joining past and present experience, is something that requires active participation on our part. Even though, sometimes, the meaning of things appears obvious, even natural, it is not simply injected into our heads. Rather, it requires active work. We make or create meaning.

Because signs can be open to a variety of interpretations, they are often referred to as being polysemic or having many meanings (see Jensen, 1990). The different types or levels of meaning drawn here are often referred to as denotative and connotative, where **denotative** meaning refers to the first level or most obvious interpretation of the sign and **connotative** meaning refers to the range of other, seemingly less obvious or more subjective meanings that may be drawn.

Advertisements are, of course, a good example of the purposive use of different levels of meaning in the creation of media texts. For instance, as the semiotic analysis of the series of ads for Black Label beer in the Appendix to this chapter illustrates, while at the denotative level these ads are simply about a particular brand of beer, at the connotative level they work to imbue the product with a wide range of meanings drawn from popular culture.

The fact that signs are polysemic in nature highlights the importance of context for the creation and interpretation of meaning. As we shall see, both the social and cultural conditions surrounding the production of media texts, as well as those involved in their consumption, play into the meaning generated from them. Similarly, the fact that any given sign can have many meanings illustrates the **indeterminacy of representation**. On one hand, the meaning of signs and the messages of which they are a part is indeterminate because there is an indeterminable number of ways of representing an object, action, or event—another representation can always be made. On the other hand, they are indeterminate because there is no *necessary* correspondence between the meaning encoded in a particular message by the sender and that decoded by the receiver. Nevertheless, each representation is grounded in a specific context as the person and/or medium doing the representing works to guide the audience or receiver of the message towards a specific or preferred meaning.

There are many factors determining **polysemy**, or the grounded indeterminacy of representation. For instance, different media provide different systems for making meaning. Moreover, one system of representation cannot encompass the full spectrum of the meaning of another. A painting cannot be fully translated into a prose essay, or even poetry. Nor can a sculpture be completely transformed into a photograph or even a hologram. Inevitably, something is lost. In short, a multiplicity of meanings can be generated within one medium, and meaning can be generated within the multiplicity of media.

Polysemy and the indeterminacy of representation tend to lead the study of communication away from the foundations of science and social science and more towards the foundations of interpretation we find in the humanities. In other words, it is concerned more with **rhetoric** (how things are said) and

ONE PERSON'S TERRORIST IS ANOTHER'S FREEDOM FIGHTER

No doubt many in the West assume that the owners of al-Jazeera satellite television were secret allies of Osama bin Laden and al-Qaeda. Much in the same way, one might say that the US television networks were dancing to the tune of the American government when they agreed to block the transmission of al-Qaeda-made videotapes in response to the demand of the US National Security Adviser, Condoleezza Rice. (Similarly, the PMO assumed that Terry Milewski was a fellow traveller with APEC protestors when e-mail was seized in which he expressed attitudes to government apparently sympathetic to their viewpoint.) Al-Jazeera's senior producer puts the matter this way: 'It would be wild to claim that we are friends of al-Qaeda, but at the end of the day we do not answer to such people as Condoleezza Rice. . . . We do not talk about what the king ate for breakfast or how many people kissed his hand like the rest of the Arab media. We are more likely to ask those who didn't kiss his hand why they didn't. That's why all the security chiefs in the West monitor every word of our output.'

INDETERMINACY OF REPRESENTATION

The concept of indeterminacy of representation has roots in theoretical physics and discussions of the concept of time. Both the idea and its relation to theoretical physics can be illustrated by a quotation from an article about time: Paul Davies, 'That mysterious flow', *Scientific American* (Sept. 2002): 47. Following the quotation is a rewording of the passage in communicational terms.

. . . [A]n electron hitting an atom may bounce off in one of many directions, and it is normally impossible to predict in advance what the outcome in any given case will be. Quantum indeterminism implies that for a particular quantum state there are many (possibly infinite) alternative futures or potential realities. Quantum mechanics supplies the relative probabilities for each observable outcome, although it won't say which potential future is destined for reality.

But when a human observer makes a measurement, one and only one result is obtained; for example, the rebounding electron will be found moving in a certain direction. In the act of measurement, a single specific reality gets projected from a vast array of possibilities. Within the observer's mind the possible makes a transition to the actual, the open future to the fixed past—which is precisely what we mean by the flux (or passage) of time.

Source: Excerpted from 'That mysterious flow' by Paul Davies. Copyright © 2002 by Scientific American, Inc. All rights reserved.

Here is the parallel.

A television program (or movie, or song, or book) becomes available and garners an audience of a certain size. Normally, it is impossible to predict in advance how the program will be received. The quantum mechanics of society, that is, knowledge of the content, actors, effects, etc., implies many potential impacts. A close examination of the program and all its variables would suggest that we could assign relative probabilities for each observable outcome, that is, each likely reaction by one or more members of the audience; but that will not tell us exactly how an individual audience member is going to react (i.e., which potential future is destined for reality).

From a social framework, we tend to take note of (i.e., the equivalent of measurement in physics) extreme reactions, such as a copycat crime committed after the release of a movie. In the act of taking notice, a specific (extreme) reality from a vast array of possibilities is projected onto the social consciousness (and for that matter, the individual consciousness). The many and varied reactions of all audience members (i.e., the meaning-making that goes on by all audience members) are not attended to and, in both the individual and the social consciousness, do not make the transition from the possible to the actually noticeable, even though they, too, exist. Moreover, the extreme reaction of one member leads to an imputed causality (between the program and the actions of one, or a few, audience members) and a discourse on the effects of media content. Meanwhile, the rich interaction among meaning-generating systems—society, the media, and individuals—proceeds, yet is little discussed, except as a theoretical communications concept.

hermeneutics (how things are interpreted) than with 'truth' per se.

In the study of communication the importance of a statement is not limited to whether it predicts events, can be refuted by others, or generates other interesting hypotheses—all standards of scientific study and the social sciences. What is interesting is what and how any means of communication selects and re-presents or re-constructs something, and what gives a particular representation its force, its ability to persuade, or its attractiveness. Whatever makes a particular novel, painting, or film more popular or revered than another, or even a novel more 'powerful' than a film, cannot be satisfactorily discussed by reference to the relative 'truth' of each communication. Such media and individual works are discussed by communication scholars in terms of their rhetorical force, in terms of the nature or style of their representation.

For instance, if we compare media, movies quite consistently add a specific sense of reality that another medium, such as print, cannot provide. As well, movies often reach a wider audience. However, what movies gain on those two dimensions they often lose in subtlety, character development, and room for imaginative play when compared to print. In regard to other media, the discussion of abstract ideas changes when one moves from books to the popular press or to television. Television demands a pluralism of sight, sound, and personage that is partially there in radio and absent in print—more than a few minutes of the same person talking, no matter what the visuals, begins to undermine the speaker's credibility or at least viewers' interest. Just the opposite seems to hold for print—a single 'voice' will more readily elicit a reader's trust and understanding.

Communication Theory as Social Theory

In studying the process of communication we often draw on social theory, and particularly communication theory, for helping us to understand how processes of communication are nuanced and operate. What is social theory? Generally, it is a representation of the social world; a set of ideas about how the world is organized and functions. While we all have ideas about how the world works, often our assumptions are fragmentary and contradictory. Take, for instance, common-sense proverbs such as 'many hands make light work' and 'too many cooks spoil the broth'. While they both purport to provide a way of understanding and approaching work, they offer contradictory perspectives on how to do so. In contrast, social theory strives to offer rigorous, logical explanations of elements of the social world. It is a representation of the world that attempts to provide a systematic and comprehensive explanation of the relationships between individuals, social groups, and the world around them.

What is the purpose of social theory? At one level, it is to provide understandings of how things work and why things are the way they are. At another level, it is to use such explanations to guide action; to alleviate social problems and improve the quality of life or to construct social policy. To paraphrase Karl Marx, 'The purpose of social theory is not to simply understand the world but to change it', and change it in a progressive manner that makes things more egalitarian and provides more equal access to the fruits of our society for all citizens.

As a kind of social theory, communication theory

is a way of representing the complex process of communication. It is a way of trying to understand the different forces that contextualize and give form to human communication and, particularly for our purposes, mass communication.

There are, however, a wide variety of communication theories. Some are elements of larger theories of society (liberal and Marxist theories, for instance) and offer broad claims of the role and purpose of various forms of communication in society as a whole, such as theories of the press. Others offer only partial explanations of the process of communication, such as the semiotic explanation of the process of signification discussed above. Some provide simple, highly abstract perpsectives, such as Shannon and Weaver's model of communication that was outlined in Chapter 1 (Figure 1.1), which posits that communication both begins and ends with individuals. Others, such as the social model of communication also outlined in Chapter 1 (Figure 1.2), illustrate the process of communication as given form by a great many factors and variables.

To provide a better understanding of the variety of ways different theories both approach and envision the process of communication we will now turn our attention to another model of communication.

The Encoding/Decoding Model

As we have seen, mass communication is a process that involves both **encoding** or creating media messages and **decoding** or interpreting them. While these are both active processes, in each of these moments a range of social institutions and forces serve to frame or contextualize the ways in which messages are constituted and the ways in which people make meaning out of them. Drawing from Stuart Hall's (1993) discussion of this process, Figure 4.1 illustrates some of the key elements involved in it. Please note, however, that although the diagram displays these pieces of the process as individual parts, in reality all of these parts are interrelated. For instance, as we saw in Chapter 3, communication media are integral to the societies of which they are a part, not separate or distinct technical systems. Similarly, as we will see, the professional values of media workers are woven between organizational and technical imperatives, not ideas separated or distinct from social context. However, for purposes of illustration, we have abstracted the process of communication from this

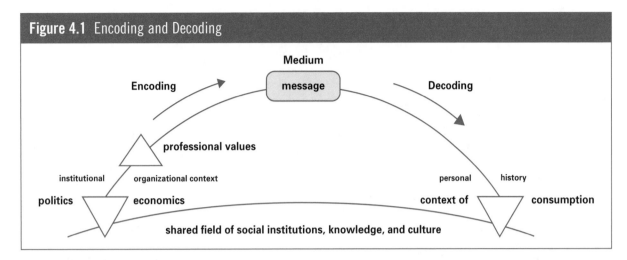

Figure 4.1 Encoding and Decoding

larger social context and exploded its pieces to high-light the different roles that each plays. Each of these pieces is described below.

First is the shared field of social institutions and knowledge, or culture, within which the media system operates. This is the general social milieu in which we live. It is comprised of things like language and social customs: ideas we hold about gender, family, and work as well as the laws, regulations, and other social processes and structures that frame and animate both society and the ways we think and act in the world. To a large part these are the elements of what we referred to as 'industrial society' in Chapter 3. At another level, they might be thought of as 'culture', or the 'ways of life' that make up our society. Certainly the ways that media producers and consumers each experience and draw upon this larger social milieu are not the same; often they are quite different. However, this milieu does provide a common field of referents for people to draw on and to make meaning from.

Second are the broad political and economic processes that contextualize how the process of media production is undertaken. On the political side, we would include specific laws and regulations that frame the way media organizations operate and what media professionals do: things like libel laws, copyright, and media ownership regulations. In the case of broadcasting, we would include the Broadcasting Act and the regulations promulgated by the CRTC; with film, distribution regulations; and with newspapers, ownership regulations. As we saw in Chapter 3, each medium operates in a specific legal and regulatory context that informs the way its products are created. On the economic side, we are concerned with the ways in which the drive for profits, or commercial forces, impinge on production. As we have seen, the economies of scale enjoyed by American producers help flood Canadian markets with American media products. All of these political and economic circumstances influence the ways media products in Canada represent the world.

Third is the institutional or organizational context within which media messages are created. Here we might consider the ways in which organizational mandates or imperatives frame what media organizations do and the products they create. For instance, the National Film Board is guided by its mandate to 'represent Canada to Canadians'. This purpose underlies all of the products it produces. Similarly, as laid out in the Broadcasting Act, the CBC's mandate guides that organization's actions. Private broadcasters and other media have profits as their motive. Hence, both the ways their resources are organized at the organizational level and the media products they produce reflect that imperative.

A fourth dimension of influence on the way media represent the world is the professional values that guide media producers. Media professionals are guided in their practices by specific ideas about the characteristics of the products they create. Journalists go to journalism school to learn how to identify newsworthy events and produce news reports. Similarly, writers working on situation comedies, soap operas, and other program genres are governed by assumptions and guidlelines as to how those programs are structured.

Fifth, as we have discussed, the medium through which representations are communicated can have great influence on the form and structure of ideas and information. Telling a story in a novel is quite different from telling it in a film. Radio addresses audiences quite differently compared with television or newspapers. News is often presented quite differently on the web than in traditional media.

Finally, at the level of decoding, the context of consumption—where and by whom media products are consumed—has impact on the meaning that is made from them. Age, education, family background, religion, gender, race, ethnicity: all of these elements of one's background or 'history' can play on how media messages are decoded. Moreover, much of this personal experience is social experience, that is, experience drawn from the larger field of social institutions, knowledge, and culture.

Again, while the encoder's and decoder's experiences of this field may be vastly different, it does provide a common set of 'referents'—that is, ideas, situations, and circumstances that can be referred to or represented in media products. Consider the television program *The Simpsons*, which is broadcast in a large number of countries and a number of different languages around the world. The culture and institutions found in these countries are often quite different, yet people in these different places are able to decode the meaning from this program and share in its humour. How so? To a large extent this is because the show's writers draw on a set of characters and circumstances familiar to all those people. The program focuses on a typical nuclear family—father, mother, and three children—who live in a typical American town and lead a typical life: homemaking, working, going to school, getting into trouble. In other words, both the characters and the situations they encounter are stereotypes—representations of life in an industrial society that many recognize and to a degree understand, even though they may not live like that or approve of the stereotyping. In other words, in creating the program, its writers draw on a range of ideas familiar to a very diverse group of people. And, in large part, the wide appeal of that program depends on their ability to find common points of knowledge and understanding in the midst of that diversity.

As a social model of communication, the encoding/decoding model draws our attention to the fact that the process of communication is given form by a range of social factors. Individuals, who work in a particular institutional and organizational context, employ professional values to construct media messages that draw on social knowledge supposedly shared by their intended audience; the messages then

MEDIA/CULTURE BINDING

The media interact with everyday life in various ways. Catchy tunes played countless times or repeatable phrases that float through one's head at the oddest times are frequent—and intended to be. The media teach us about politics, life in other cultures and places, how to kiss, how to smoke, how to rob banks, how to play with toys, how to dance. The list is endless (see Meyrowitz, 1985, and his 'effects loops'). But the interaction is not a one-way process. The media draw their content out of the real lives of real individuals and groups. In an example that captures this relation well, the famous writer and semiologist, Umberto Eco, looked at it this way:

1. A firm produces polo shirts with an alligator on them and it advertises them.
2. A generation begins to wear polo shirts.
3. Each consumer of the polo shirt advertises, via the alligator on his or her chest, this brand of polo shirt.
4. A TV broadcast (program), to be faithful to reality, shows some young people wearing the alligator polo shirt.
5. The young (and the old) see the TV broadcast and buy more alligator polo shirts because they have 'the young look'.

- *Which is the mass medium*? The ad? The broadcast? The shirt?
- *Who is sending the message*? The manufacturer? The wearer? The TV director? The analyst of this phenomenon?
- *Who is the producer of ideology*? Again, the manufacturer? The wearer (including the celebrity who may wear it in public for a fee)? The TV director who portrays the generation?
- *Where does the (marketing) plan come from*? This is not to imply that there is no plan but rather that it does not emanate from one central source.

Source: Eco (1986: 148–50).

are delivered through particular technical systems to audience members with particular social backgrounds. In turn, these individuals draw upon social knowledge accrued through their various histories to decode the messages and deploy that information in their lives.

This model is useful in understanding the ways that certain theories envision the process of communication. Few theories claim to explain the influence of all of these different dimensions on that process. Rather, they focus on how a number of those elements work to determine how the media operate and the influence they have.

In this context, a central consideration of media and communication theory is the relationship between agency and structure. To put this another way: can people generally encode whatever ideas and meanings they want into media messages and programs? Or, do the structures and processes in which people live and work determine the range and character of the messages and ideas they produce? This is a key question for trying to explain how media systems operate. However, as a number of researchers have pointed out, social structure is both 'enabling' and 'constraining' (see Giddens, 1984). For instance, language provides a structure for communication, a set of words and rules for communicating. While that structure is constraining in that we can only communicate in that language if we correctly enact its vocabulary, it is also highly enabling because it allows the communication of a vast range—an almost infinite number—of ideas. Similarly, while working as a reporter at a large newspaper is constraining in that one has to adhere to editorial policies and professional values regarding what kinds of events constitute news, how to write a news story, etc., as well as organizational rules and deadlines, it also is enabling because it allows one to write about a wide range of changing events and circumstances on a daily basis and because the material one writes will be read regularly by thousands of people.

Theories of the Media, Theories of Society

As noted, different theories take different approaches to the study of the media. In this section we consider four perspectives on the media and society. The first two—the libertarian theory of the press and social responsibility theory—draw on liberal theories of society to consider what they believe to be the social conditions necessary to create a responsible press. The second two perspectives—**political economic theory** and the **mass society thesis**—are to a large part themselves theories of society and thereby illustrate what they see as the dominant social influences on the structure of the media and media content. The point to consider here is not which of these theories is the right or 'true' perspective on the media and society, but rather the insight that each brings to the analysis.

LIBERTARIAN THEORY

The **libertarian theory** of the press is based on the Enlightenment concepts of agency and the free will of individuals, which are derived from such liberal philosophers as John Locke (1632–1704), John Stuart Mill (1806–73), and David Hume (1711–76). Its fundamental assumption is that individual freedom is the first and foremost goal to be sought. Despite the fact the government can play social roles that are enabling and constraining (e.g., 'enabling' in that it supplies education, etc.; 'constraining' in terms of taxation and laws and regulations governing behaviour), libertarians are highly suspicious of the state. Limiting the powers of the state and other impediments to individual action, so libertarian philosophers maintain, will create the most advantageous situation for all. Of course, what they overlook is that under this arrangement some people—those with more wealth and power—are 'more equal'—that is, have more opportunities—than others.

Libertarian theory sees the mass media as an extension of the individual's right to freedom of expression and, hence, as an independent voice that makes government responsible to the people. The media do so by feeding information to people so that, come election time, performance can be rewarded or punished. In a non-political context, libertarians see the mass media as assiduous pursuers of free speech. Freedom of speech is seen as one of the most important of all freedoms; and while it may result in problems and difficulties in the short term, libertarians see it as the best way to preserve freedom and the rights of all citizens.

In striving to ensure distance between the government and the mass media, the libertarian concept of the media places it in the hands of private citizens. The rights to publish and free expression are seen as fundamental rights of citizenship and must not be tampered with, particularly by government. However, in the face of the overarching importance placed on freedom of expression, there is little concern for the fact that in the course of media production and operation, the private sector has its own interests—those of developing markets and accruing profits—to consider, which are above the interests of the people, of society, or of the government of the day. Consequently, rather than allowing journalists to dedicate themselves to 'serving the people', privately controlled media maximize their own interests as private, profit-oriented corporations.

SOCIAL RESPONSIBILITY THEORY

While also drawing on liberal theories of society and the libertarian theory of the press, **social responsibility theory** arises from the perception that the libertarian arrangement fails to produce a press that is generally of benefit to society. The concept was originally put forward by a non-governmental US commission, the (Hutchins) Commission on the Freedom of the Press (1947).

In Canada, the Kent Royal Commission on Newspapers (Canada, 1981) explained the social responsibility theory well, pointing out that as newspaper publishing began to be taken over by big business, the notion of social responsibility was born of a need to fight against the potential of a new authoritarianism by big-business ownership of the press. The Kent Commission defined the concept of social responsibility as follows:

> The conjoined requirements of the press, for freedom and for legitimacy, derive from the same basic right: the right of citizens to information about their affairs. In order that people be informed, the press has a critical responsibility. In order to fulfill that responsibility it is essential that the press be free, in the traditional sense, free to report and free to publish as it thinks; it is equally essential that the press's discharge of its responsibility to inform should be untainted by other interests, that it should not be dominated by the powerful or be subverted by people with concerns other than those proper to a newspaper serving a democracy. 'Comment is free', as C.P. Snow, one of the greatest English-speaking editors, wrote, 'but facts are sacred.' The right of information in a free society requires, in short, not only freedom of comment generally but, for its news media, the freedom of a legitimate press,

doing its utmost to inform, open to all opinions and dominated by none. [C.P. Snow was, for years, editor of the *Manchester Guardian*.] (Canada, 1981: 235)

Ironically, although an American commission into press freedom (led by university president Robert Hutchins) coined the term 'social responsibility', it is much better accepted in Canada and in Europe than in the US. This is because, in the US, the First Amendment to the Constitution states that 'Congress shall make no law ... abridging the freedom of speech, or of the press.' Being the first of the constitutional amendments, it sits at the top of the hierarchy of rights. The Canadian Constitution does not allow for such a hierarchy of rights whereby one right takes precedence over another, for instance, the freedom of the press versus the right to a fair trial. Thus, in Canada and Europe it is possible to limit free speech based on a consideration of its consequences. For instance, in Canada, reporters must be careful not to discuss a crime in such detail as to jeopardize a person's right to a fair trial. (See Chapter 9 for a further discussion of press freedom.) However, despite the fact that the social responsibility theory of the press might be seen as the dominant theory of the media in Canada, as discussed in Chapter 8, exactly what the dimensions of press responsibility are in Canada and how they might be either taken up by or imposed upon the private corporations that make up the large part of Canada's media remain the subject of public debate.

THE MASS SOCIETY THESIS

As we saw in Chapter 3, as a consequence of industrialization in the nineteenth century, people were uprooted from traditional rural ways of life to live in cities. For many writers of the time, however, this new way of life was without cultural foundation. Cut free from the context of a traditional (feudal) agricultural way of life and the social values, customs, and bonds that gave that life form and function, people were seen in the new industrial context as a collection of isolated individuals—an undifferentiated 'mass' society within which no assumptions about social order and people's place and function in it commonly were held. As Broom and Selznick (in DeFleur and Ball-Rokeach, 1989: 160) put it:

> Modern society is made up of masses in the sense that there has emerged a vast mass of segregated,

isolated individuals, interdependent in all sorts of specialized ways yet lacking in any central unifying value or purpose. The weakening of traditional bonds, the growth of rationality, and the division of labor, have created societies made up of individuals who are only loosely bound together. In this sense the word 'mass' suggests something closer to an aggregate than a tightly knit kinship group.

In this state of social atomization and seeming moral disorder, the masses were regarded by the social elite of the day as somewhat threatening, as though through their new-found political and economic power—the extending franchise or right to vote, their increasing importance in the industrial division of labour, and their rising power as consumers to whom manufacturers are increasingly directing the outputs of their production—they posed a severe threat to the existing cultural order and the abilities of intellectuals and other elites to sustain their ways of life. The nature of this perceived threat varies from writer to writer. For some it simply appears to be a general state of anarchy, a breakdown of social order. Others express concern that these people are easily subject to manipulation and easy targets for totalitarian social and political movements. From this perspective the rise of the Nazis in Germany and Stalin in Russia were products of the rise of mass society. In this context, media are seen as a unifying force in society, a means of conjoining minds in common cause and action, although generally not towards positive ends.

Through the early twentieth century this perspective wound its way through a range of academic disciplines and had a strong impact on early communication theory. To a large extent, it framed new media such as radio and film as part of a new 'commercial' or mass culture where media content is simply an unsophisticated commercial product designed to placate the masses with cheap entertainment and, through advertising, incorporate them into a new consumer-oriented way of life. As we shall see in Chapter 5, underlying these conceptions of the purpose of mass media was also a rather unsophisticated vision of audiences.

POLITICAL ECONOMY AND MARX

Before economics became a free-standing social science, it was seen by early proponents, such as Adam Smith (1723–90), as inexorably tied to politics. In the same way that the management of a family's resources and the power dynamics associated with it might be called domestic political economy, so the organization of a nation's resources, involving as it does both overall political decisions and economic management, could be called national political economy. As capitalism became entrenched in the nations of the West, capitalist political economy first came to be called 'capitalist economics' and then, simply 'economics'. The argument for separating politics and economics, to oversimplify matters, was that the market should operate as a system of resource allocation independent of political systems. Hence, we have economics *tout seul*. However, not all writers agreed with this premise. In the early to mid-nineteenth century, as capitalist industry was introducing massive social change in Europe, Karl Marx argued that the capitalist system was premised on a set of social relations in which politics and economics were inextricably linked.

Modern Western societies, Marx argued, were characterized by a new and revolutionary mode of production—industrial capitalism—in which scientific techniques, applied to the mass production of an ever-increasing range of goods (or commodities, in Marx's terms), created wealth for the owners of capital. In Marx's analysis, industrial society is organized around the reproduction of capital, that is, the creation of 'surplus' or profits from productive activities. This tends to create two main classes: capitalists, or the owners of the means of production (factories, commercial property, etc.); and workers, those who, because they don't own productive property, must sell their labour power to capitalists. Marx argued that this system of production generally serves the interests of the capitalists—a tiny fraction of the population—and that, as workers, the vast majority are exploited by the capitalists. They can be fired at any time and for whatever reason, and they have to fight to squeeze a living wage out of industrialists.

As Marx saw it, modern capitalism transformed all aspects of life, particularly at the political level, as both government and the structure of the state increasingly came to represent the interests of capital. New laws were enacted to protect private property, particularly the productive property of capitalists. Labour legislation laid the legal framework for relations between capital and labour. Taxation raised funds for creating infrastructure—roads, railways, canals, harbours, and communication systems—that kept the wheels of commerce moving. Schools were constructed that taught people the skills necessary to become productive workers. And when workers rebelled through strikes or some other form of civil disobedience the police force could be called upon to restore order.

At the heart of a Marxist analysis of modern society is a belief in the possibility of a better life that could be shared by all—a life that is blocked by the private appropriation of wealth. On the one hand, techniques of mass production seemed to offer the possibility of the end of scarcity. Material abundance could be available to all if the techniques of modern manufacturing were somehow regulated with everyone's interests in mind. On the other hand, Western society has not realized this possibility. A bitter paradox is created when huge quantities of grain sit in prairie elevators, powdered milk in storage, and butter in freezers while thousands of people live in hunger in Canada and millions live in extreme hunger or near famine elsewhere in the world.

Marx's ideas have shaped the political life of the twentieth century throughout the world. In most European democracies the development of mass parties tended to be split in two—those that represent the interests of the owners of property and those that represent the interests of workers. Experiments in socialism, more specifically communism (a political application of Marx's ideas), lasted for 70 years in Russia and continue in China, Cuba, and elsewhere in the world. Although the Russian system of authoritarian state socialism clearly has failed, Marx's ideas have not been entirely discredited and Communist and socialist parties still command strong showings in elections in European countries and elsewhere in the world. Marx's emphasis on the fundamental importance of understanding how economic life tends to structure other elements of social life remains a substantial and important contribution.

Writers working from Marx's analytic legacy are critical of the ways in which the structure of society affords benefits—wealth and power—to some groups of people over others; hence the term 'critical' political economy. In particular, critical political economy focuses on the ways in which the allocation, production, distribution, and consumption of social resources enable and constrain social action. That is, it is concerned with the way the ownership and control of society's resources—particularly pro-

ductive resources—give owners a larger say in the form and direction society takes than those without such control.

As described in more detail in Chapter 5, with respect to the media, critical political economy is concerned with the ways in which the media support dominant interests in society, helping them maintain power and control. In contrast to the ways in which libertarian and social responsibility theories of the press argue that the media can and should have a relatively independent place in the political and economic processes that govern society, critical political economy argues that in capitalist societies the media are a key institution in promoting capitalism and in helping maintain social inequality (see Mosco, 1996).

Perspectives on the Study of Content

A number of perspectives have been developed and used to study media content. A few of the more popular perspectives are discussed in this section—literary criticism, structuralism, semiotics, and post-structuralism; discourse analysis; critical political economy; organizational analysis; content analysis; and media form or genre analysis. For the most part, these perspectives are drawn from larger theories of communication and communication media. Here, however, we will generally consider how they address the encoding of media messages and the larger social and linguistic forces that they see as coming to bear on the production process. Again, the existence of this multiplicity of perspectives underscores the importance of the notion that it is not which one of these is the correct perpsective but rather what insight each brings to the analysis of media content.

LITERARY CRITICISM

Simply put, **literary criticism** is the study and interpretation of texts. It explores the different ways that texts can be read and understood. Its roots reach back to when written records first emerged. As soon as something is recorded, it is open to interpretation and discussion. Major movements and changes in world history have focused on examinations and re-examinations of texts. For example, Martin Luther challenged the interpretation of the Bible by the Roman Catholic Church and the right of the Catholic Church to control access and to be the sole interpreter of the scriptures. Similarly, in China from the Sung dynasty (AD 900) forward, there existed official interpretations of classic Confucian texts and unofficial versions were banned.

Debates in literary criticism have been particularly important for communication studies and the study of content because they draw our attention to the various ways meaning might be drawn from texts. For instance, should texts be seen as simply the intention of the author or might the meaning found there be other than the author intended? Might texts be seen as the product of forces seemingly outside of the author, like language and culture? What weight does one put on the role of the reader in decoding the text?

One of the traditional modes of criticism is to view texts as the presumed intention of the author. From this perspective, interpretation focuses on trying to uncover what the author consciously had in mind, as expressed in the text. (Freudian analysis purports to explain what the author had subconsciously in mind.) Here, the text is treated as the specific product or vehicle of an individual author-creator—the novels of Jane Austen, the plays of Shakespeare. This approach spread to film studies (the films of Alfred Hitchcock) and became known as **auteur theory**, which focuses on the creative control of the director and treats the director as the creative originator of the film.

In the early twentieth century a variant literary criticism, aptly named New Criticism, gained prominence. From this perspective analysis is confined to the texts per se; authorial intention is not considered. Instead, close readings of the works are conducted to discover the ways in which they are ambiguous and carry a multiplicity of meanings. More recently, literary criticism has incorporated concepts from fields such as linguistics, sociology, and anthropology and debates the place of a wide range of factors (including language and culture) in the interpretation of content.

STRUCTURALISM, SEMIOTICS, AND POST-STRUCTURALISM

In the 1950s and 1960s a perspective known as structuralism became dominant in the social sciences and humanities, especially in the fields of linguistics, anthropology, sociology, psychology, and literature. In the analysis of media content, the aim of **structuralism** is to discover underlying patterns or structures that shape both texts and genres; to try to see beneath the surface of texts and uncover common linguistic or thematic patterns that give them form. Here, the author is viewed primarily as a vehicle who enacts the extant rules of language and culture in the creation of his/her work (or life). From a structuralist perspective, to a large extent, we don't speak language so much as language speaks us.

An early and seminal work exemplifying structuralist principles was that of the Russian folklorist Vladimir Propp. In the 1920s, Propp collected over 400 traditional tales from Europe and showed how they all had a similar narrative structure. First, he identified a set of basic (lexical) elements (all stories have certain, similar items): a hero or heroine, a villain, a helper. Second, he described the motifs that propel the narrative from beginning to end. Thus, something must happen to set the hero (usually male) in motion: at some point the villain will disrupt the hero's plans; and at some point the hero will receive aid from a helper (who may or may not be female) to overcome the obstacles in his way. Propp was able to reduce the apparent complexity of a great number of different stories to a simple set of underlying narrative elements that could be combined in a strictly limited number of ways (see Propp, 1970). The structural analysis of narrative has subsequently been applied to all manner of stories, including James Bond novels and films (Eco, 1982a; Bennett and Woollacott, 1987), romantic novels (Radway, 1984), and soap operas (Geraghty, 1991). Figure 4.2 illustrates structuralism at work in the romance genre.

Once narrative structures and surface elements were identified, Propp and other structuralists were able to identify common themes that recurred in stories from all over the world. The magical union of strength and beauty, power in two forms, is a good example of a myth to be found in virtually all cultures. Structuralists would attend to its basic structure. The male embodiment of spiritual and bodily strength (usually a prince) grows up in his kingdom. The female embodiment of beauty and perceptiveness (a princess) grows up in her kingdom. One or both may be disguised in a certain way (a frog prince, a pig princess) or confined (Sleeping Beauty, Cinderella), sometimes as a result of immature vulnerability (plotting by unworthy usurpers, innocence). An event, story, or intervention of some sort induces one (usually the male in a patriarchal society or the female in a matriarchal society) to set out on a quest, sometimes purposeful, sometimes not. The

Figure 4.2 The Narrative Logic of the Romance

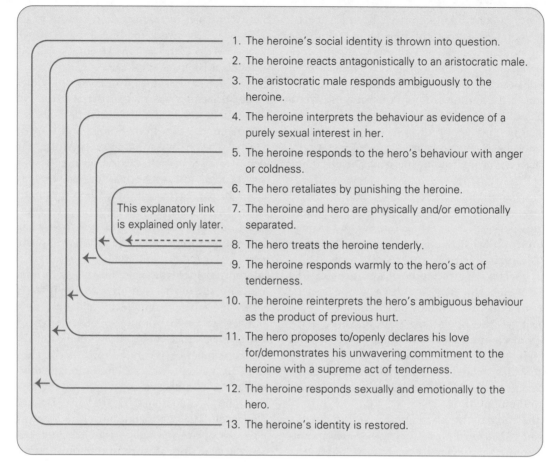

1. The heroine's social identity is thrown into question.

2. The heroine reacts antagonistically to an aristocratic male.

3. The aristocratic male responds ambiguously to the heroine.

4. The heroine interprets the behaviour as evidence of a purely sexual interest in her.

5. The heroine responds to the hero's behaviour with anger or coldness.

6. The hero retaliates by punishing the heroine.

This explanatory link is explained only later.

7. The heroine and hero are physically and/or emotionally separated.

8. The hero treats the heroine tenderly.

9. The heroine responds warmly to the hero's act of tenderness.

10. The heroine reinterprets the hero's ambiguous behaviour as the product of previous hurt.

11. The hero proposes to/openly declares his love for/demonstrates his unwavering commitment to the heroine with a supreme act of tenderness.

12. The heroine responds sexually and emotionally to the hero.

13. The heroine's identity is restored.

From Janice A. Radway. *Reading the Romance: Women, Patriarchy, and Popular Literature.* Copyright © 1984, 1991 by the University of North Carolina Press. Used by permission of the publisher.

less purposeful the quest the more the coming union is written in the stars or blessed by the gods in the form of an unconscious urge in the seeker. The seeker finds the sought (the object of his or her dreams, again evidence of divine blessing) and recognizes her or him by virtue of her or his or both of their inner senses, inherent kindness, or nobility. This something not only confirms the union but confirms the special qualities of both seeker and sought, which befits them to rule others (divine right of kings). The children of the union are, of course, very special, since they inherit the qualities of both.

Such myths live on. The most obvious twentieth-century example of the myth of the prince/princess ascending the throne would be the courtship and marriage of Charles, Prince of Wales, and Diana, a commoner who became Princess of Wales. However, as with so many myths, the story ended in tragedy. So powerful are such myths that US film stars have handlers who build up their mythological identity by counselling them only to accept certain roles. Some pursue a particular type of character, e.g., Arnold Schwarzenegger, others pursue versatility, e.g., Brad Pitt.

Another influential scholar in the field of structuralism was the earlier mentioned Swiss linguist Ferdinand de Saussure. Saussure developed what was later seen as the structural analysis of language (1974). Saussure proposed that language could be scientifically studied in the abstract, as an underlying set of linguistic structures (*langue*, in his terms) that could be combined together by any native speaker to produce an utterance (*parole*). As he argued, 'Language is a system of signs that express ideas, and is therefore comparable to a system of writing, the alphabet of deaf-mutes, symbolic rites, polite formulas, military signals, etc. But it is the most important of all these systems' (Saussure, in Silverman, 1983: 4–5). To better understand this system he proposed a science of signs—**semiotics.** For Saussure, meaning is made in the difference between signs. In other words, given particularly that symbols bear no relation to that which they represent, the only way to tell what something is, is by knowing what it is not (see Silverman, 1983). Anthropologist Claude Lévi-Strauss extended the structuralist formula into social interaction and claimed to show in his work 'not how men think in myths, but how myths operate in men's minds without their being aware of the fact' (Lévi-Strauss, 1969: 12). In other words, the point is that words carry preconceived ideas, or 'signifieds', about things and thereby provide a frame or screen for interpreting the world. From this perspective, one can begin to see why structuralism sometimes claims that people are 'spoken' by the language they use rather than the other way around.

As we have seen, based on the sign (signifier/signified) a semiotic analysis distinguishes between two levels of meaning: the denotative and the connotative. Using this schema, Roland Barthes (1972) has famously decoded ideological meanings in things from wrestling and striptease, to the Louvre, television, popular novels, and advertisements. Through making connections between the images found in everyday media and the ideologies of bourgeois capitalist society, Barthes strove to uncover the ways that popular culture promoted dominant ideas and values.

Take, for instance, the ad that portrays the SUV as a family vehicle that can be used for city transportation and country adventure. From Barthes's perspective, the ad not only represents the SUV as a part of family life, but also draws upon a deeper more subtle set of assumptions and values—another order of connotations. Based on the notion that the meaning of the ad is found in the differences between the images that it contains and possible alternatives, underlying the ad are ideas such as: the nuclear family is the natural and dominant social unit; private vehicles are a preferred mode of transportation; and the domination of nature is both a legitimate and fun leisure activity. Social issues such as what comprises a 'family' in this day and age and the range of environmen-

tal damage caused by private vehicles are smoothed over, buried under these contemporary social myths. In other words, the text positions the reader to the objects in the ad in a particular way and encourages a specific way of reading, or understanding, those objects. From this perspective, by accepting the idea that the SUV is the perfect family vehicle, not only are you accepting the obvious premise of the ad, but you are taking up the baggage of these underlying ideas as well.

Through the 1970s and 1980s semiotic analysis, à la Barthes, became the preferred way of reading cultural texts (see, e.g., Williamson's analysis of advertisements, 1978).

While both structuralism and semiotics provide key insights into the ways in which language structures both the form and content of communication perhaps their biggest shortcoming is how they underplay the importance of the particular in favour of the general—for instance, *langue* in contrast to *parole*. The roles of the individual speaker and listener, or producer and consumer, of communication, as well the context of the message's creation, in the process of communication are ignored.

Beginning in the 1960s, **post-structuralism** emerged as a critique of the idea that there is a consistent structure to texts and that the process of encoding somehow fixes or solidifies meaning for the decoder. A number of the main proponents of post-structuralism were themselves once structuralists, among them Roland Barthes.

For post-structuralists, meaning is made in the act of decoding and, thereby, is the purview of the reader or audience member. What sense is to be made of any particular word, image, or sound is the product of those interpreting those signs and depends on the perspective(s) they bring to the task. For instance, women may interpret content differently from men, gays differently from heterosexuals, children differently from adults. From this perspective, understanding texts involves 'deconstructing' them to uncover the possible play of differences they contain. Meaning is never fixed in content. It is always fluid, as fluid as the next reader makes it. In semiotic terms, post-structuralism argues that signs have come undone and that signifiers can no longer be said to have specific 'signifieds'. Take for instance the SUV ad. Who cares about the happy heterosexual family symbolism seemingly bequeathed on the vehicle by the advertising company? With one look at the ad's description of its spacious interior and stylish appointments, perhaps a gay environmentalist group will decide that this is the perfect mode of transportation for getting its members to their latest waterfowl habitat recuperation project in the mountains.

This is the point made by Barthes in his famous essay, 'Death of the Author' (1977). ('Auteur theory' has not died but has become understood as only one window on the reality of the text.) Since the text only becomes meaningful in the act of being read and understood, the source of meaning, Barthes argued, is the reader. The effect of this startling reversal was the 'empowerment' of the reader or audience. No longer chained to the dull task of trying to find out what Shakespeare 'had in mind' when he wrote Hamlet (an impossible task anyway, argued Barthes), the reader was free to create his or her own meanings, to open up rather than close down the meaning of the text. Gone was any notion of a true or authentic meaning of the text. Texts were polysemic and had a number of different possible meanings. The conception of reading also changed from the passive absorption of the text's imposed meaning to an active exploration of the text's possibilities.

As illustrated in Chapter 5, this shift in interpretation parallels a shift in the ways audiences are viewed in terms of their relation to media content.

DISCOURSE ANALYSIS

Discourse analysis is another perspective with a long history, dating back more than 2,000 years to the discipline of *rhetorica*. *Rhetorica* was oriented to effective persuasiveness and dealt with the planning, organization, specific operations, and performance of speech in political and legal settings (van Dijk, 1985, vol. 1: 1). A passage, speech, or performance can succeed or fail based on the impact it makes on its audience.

Generally, drawing from structuralism, discourse analysis focuses on how language, as a system of representation, provides us with a particular perspective or 'position' in the social world. It posits that language is a kind of structure, and that by being inside that structure, language provides us with a particular view of the world. Today there are many strands of discourse analysis at play in communication studies (see van Dijk, 1997). A major stream focuses on specific instances of language use and their relationship to social power. Another, following the work of Michel Foucault, considers how specific modes of language use bind our ways of thinking and become 'sedi-

mented' into specific institutions and relations of social power.

The first of these modes of analysis points to how particular patterns and conventions of language usage become taken for granted and considers how these patterns serve as larger frames of reference to shape our experience and understanding of the world. For instance, discourse analysis has been used to illustrate the gendered character of language—chair*man*, fire*man*, fisher*man*—and demonstrate through historical referents how this kind of language has supported patriarchal forms of domination in society. Hence, today, out of concern for promoting more egalitarian relationships, we use gender-neutral language—chair, firefighter, fisher. This type of analysis also provides a way of understanding how particular elements of media content work together to create a larger perspective on, or way of seeing, social events and circumstances. For example, a discourse analysis of federal election coverage might look at all of the different kinds of media content focusing on the election—coverage of debates, polls, editorials, news stories—and analyze the ways in which different leaders and parties are treated in that coverage. Were they given equal time/space? Were the views of one party or leader given more favourable or sympathetic treatment than others?

At another level, discourse analysis also provides a framework for understanding how specific kinds of language use fit into larger social practices—for example, how prime ministerial television appearances are discursive elements in a larger political struggle. Here, a discourse analyst might note that beyond the content itself, political debates represent a challenge mounted against the incumbent to dislodge that incumbent from a discourse of power. On the other side, it is the job of the incumbent to constrain the pretender in a discourse of questionable power-seeking. From this perspective, language is a system of power that is utilized to help enact or create a new set of social relations. It is a key stepping stone on the path to changing relations of social power; in this instance, changing the government.

This second type of discourse analysis has a more structuralist character and argues that, in the form of ideas or sets of ideas, discourse (language) becomes a way of knowing the world and, in turn, a way of controlling it. In a series of studies that includes histories of madness, prisons, and sexuality, Michel Foucault (1995, 1988, 1980) illustrates how through making crime, madness, and sex into objects of scientific inquiry and discipline, the 'knowledge' or ideas generated from these inquiries becomes a vehicle to control action and behaviour. As ways of thinking and being in the world, discourses become 'sedimented', or structured, into institutions and organizations. They become rules and regulations that govern our lives and our ways of seeing and being in the world. In this way, words move from being simply ideas to becoming disciplining social practices. Consider how the idea of 'education', for instance, has become sedimented or structured into particular practices, objects, and institutions, such as classes, textbooks, and schools or universities. By this account, we live immersed in discourse, like fish in water, with its invisible currents shaping and determining much if not all of our lives as language, in the form of ideas, takes on a life of its own. At the personal level, larger social discourses frame our ideas, hopes, and desires. Our identities are given form by the discourses of which we are a part. From this perspective, media content can be seen as part of these larger discursive formations, part of the social mechanism through which norms, values, and other ideas about how the world 'should be' are circulated and reproduced.

CRITICAL POLITICAL ECONOMY

Working from the Marxist perspective that the media generally serve to support private capital and the dominant interests in society, writers in the field of critical political economy have approached the media from a number of directions (see Mosco, 1996). For instance, in the 1970s Dallas Smythe pointed out that in contrast to the seeming fact that the purpose of the media is to serve the interests and tastes of audiences, that is, to inform and entertain people, the product from which private broadcasters and newspapers draw the balance of their income from is 'audiences' and that the real business of privately owned media companies is selling audiences to advertisers. From this perspective, media can be seen to serve the interests of owners, not the public at large. As he argues:

> The capitalist system cultivates the illusion that the three streams of information and things are independent: the advertising merely 'supports' or 'makes possible' the news, information, and entertainment, which in turn are *separate* from the consumer goods and services we buy. This is untrue. The commercial mass media *are* advertising in

their entirety . . . . both advertising and the 'program material' reflect, mystify, and are essential to the sale of goods and services. The program material is produced and distributed in order to attract and hold the attention of the audience so that its members may be counted (by audience survey organizations which then certify the size and character of the audience produced) and sold to the advertiser. (Smythe, 1995: 9)

Taking a somewhat broader perspective in their book *Manufacturing Consent: The Political Economy of the Mass Media*, Ed Herman and Noam Chomsky (2002: 2) argue that there are five political, economic, and organizational 'filters' at play in the US news media to ensure that the news works in favour of political and economic elites:

1. the concentration of ownership of the media in the hands of a few large private corporations;
2. the media's dependence on advertising as their principal source of revenue;
3. the media's reliance on government and business elites as sources of news and opinion;
4. 'flak', or negative feedback from powerful established interests when the news plays against their interest;
5. strong belief in the 'miracle of the market' as a means to satisfy social needs and desires (xvii). As they argue, the model 'traces the routes by which money and power are able to filter out the news fit to print, marginalize dissent, and allow the government and dominant private interests to get their messages across to the public'.

On other fronts, the political economy of communication has been employed to illustrate how disparities in information and media hardware underlie disparities in wealth between countries of the global North and South (Hamelink, 1995), why the Canadian media are generally dominated by American product (Pendakur, 1990), and how corporate media generally represent a rather narrow range of perspectives and opinions (Hackett and Gruneau, 2000).

In sum, the main point made by critical political economy is that the larger political and economic relationships that govern society reach down to structure not only the ways in which the media operate but also the very ways they represent the world to us.

Organizational Studies and Professional Values

The study of media organizations or of professional values is not in itself, a theoretical perspective. However, organizational structures and processes, as well as professional values, can have a range of impacts on content production and, as such, are important sites of study when it comes to understanding the forces at play on the creation of content.

Because of the social and political importance associated with news, news organizations are perhaps the most studied of all types of media organization. Taras (1990: 19) illustrates some of the dimensions of organizational influence in this area.

> Events and issues are like light being filtered through a prism, the prism being the news organization; how the light is reflected depends on the particular characteristics of the organization through which it passes . . . . News, in short, is recontextualized to fit the product needs of the institution presenting it . . . . Print reporters work within a hierarchical structure where the final authority about their assignments, whether their articles will run, and where they will appear are in the hands of superiors. Personal values are modified to fit the needs of the organization. The weight of bureaucracy constrains individual initiative and imposes the imperatives of organizational culture.

As Taras goes on to point out, 'organizations themselves are shaped by a number of factors, among them the nature of the medium, markets, and competition, and whether they are public or private corporations' (ibid., 20). In turn, these organizational imperatives all serve to shape media content. (Chapters 8 and 9 provide more insight in this regard.) Studies illustrate that other kinds of media content, too—such as children's programs, nature programming, and feature films—are shaped by such forces (see Cottle, 2003).

Professional assumptions regarding the proper or 'correct' form that media production should take also shape content. Taking again news for an example, as Shoemaker and Reese (1996: 93) point out, 'because there is no formal mechanism for enforcing professional standards or for prescribing formal schooling' journalists are not professionals in the same sense as lawyers or medical doctors. However, a number of generally informal professional criteria govern their work, such as voluntary codes of ethics and shared understandings of what kinds of events and circumstances comprise 'news'. Similar professional codes and practices guide the efforts of other media workers (see Cottle, 2003). Consequently, professional values also have influence over the ways media content is constructed. However, exactly what impacts organizational imperatives and professional values have on media content and whose or what interests they serve are 'empirical' problems, that is, questions that require specific investigation and measurement.

Content Analysis

Like organizational analysis, content analysis is not actually a theory of media content, either. Rather, it is a method of examining media texts. It is often used in conjunction with such approaches as discourse analysis to identify the specific characteristics of media content, such as how particular people, social groups, or places are framed or treated in news stories and what's either included or left out of particular stories or television programs (see Krippendorf, 2004).

Content analysis emphasizes the quantitative aspects of media content, specifically, the number of occurrences of a particular category of phenomenon. For instance, what places (cities, provinces, or countries) are covered in news stories? What kinds of subjects are covered? What sources do reporters quote or draw on in writing a story? (Are some politicians quoted more than others? Are some think-tanks called on more than others?) How often are minorities covered in news stories? How are they covered?

The system of choosing works as follows. First, the analyst determines the variables to be measured. Variables may include things like the general subject or theme of a story; the particular people, places, or events represented; whether these things are framed or treated in a positive or negative light; who are the sources or experts quoted. The researcher then sets up units of analysis—phrases, sentences, paragraphs, column inches, etc.—and counts these variables and perhaps their relation to other aspects of content, such as pictures or long pieces with prominent placement. On the basis of frequencies of occurrence in one or more media products (newspapers, TV news programs, etc.), the analyst can provide a reading of the media treatment of an issue over time. What's left out of a story might be just as important as what is included.

For instance, a 1996 study by NewsWatch Canada illustrated that over a six-month period on CBC and CTV television newscasts 'right-wing think-tanks received 68 per cent of all references while left-wing think-tanks received 19.5 per cent' (Hackett and Gruneau, 2000: 204). While these statistics don't tell us what the news stories were about, they illustrate that right-wing sources were consulted or referred to more often over this period.

In another instance, a content analysis focusing on the coverage of Latin America in the US press over time revealed that the dominant definition of news—what was most often reported about Latin America—was disasters, such as earthquakes and volcanoes. Over the 1970s there was a gradual shift towards a focus on dictators and banana republics. And more recently, there has been a further shift towards a broader and more accurate collection of information. Such an analysis is revealing not only in terms of the triviality of the news definition of an entire continent but also in terms of the significant absences—the failure to offer any serious account of the economic, political, or social developments of that region of the world. Likewise, content studies of social representation in media products have pointed to the fact that the people identified by reporters as 'experts' on subjects are mainly white, professional males. In contrast, black males are often portrayed as criminals, athletes, or musicians. Other studies illustrate both a general lack of representation of people of colour in mainstream Canadian media, and that when they are represented it is often in the form of stereotypes (Jiwani, 2006).

As can be seen from these examples, content analysis is generally used as a method to uncover evidence of some kind of bias in news reports or other media content (see Gans, 1979; Tuchman, 1978; Schlesinger, 1978).

Genre or Media Form Analysis

Another framework of analysis that can be used as a complement to any of the above frameworks is derived from McLuhan's notion of the medium as the message. The presentation of meaning is constrained by the medium itself and how it structures and carries content. Beyond that, it is also constrained by the genre within a particular medium, e.g., action movies or chick flicks as a subset of all movies.

Each medium organizes and encourages particular elements of content and particular relations between

ON ORSON WELLES

Paul Heyer has created an interesting text/audio analysis of Orson Welles's *War of the Worlds* that is a media form analysis in that it deals with the intuitive understanding Welles had of radio as a medium. Heyer's article is in *Canadian Journal of Communication* 28, 2 (2003): 149–65. Or go on-line at: www.cjc-online.ca.

those elements. These elements and relations are both distinct to each medium and forever shifting with the creativity of the practitioners. A good comparative example (which combines both genre and media form) is the television news team of on-air reporter and camera operator versus the single newspaper reporter. The news team intrudes more on the event and operates within the constraints of a television news story, which demands good visuals. On the other hand, a newspaper story depends for its strength on elements such as a logical presentation of the facts and thorough analysis. The following subsections examine a number of major media forms and their biases.

THE ADVERTISEMENT

Advertising is an invention of profound significance to capitalist society. It lies at the very foundation of the commercial mass media, financing the production and distribution of a wide range of information and entertainment. For a surcharge paid on consumer products (the cost of ads is built into the cost of products), an advertising industry of immense size and power was developed first in the United States and then worldwide.

While in the past advertising was a way to increase sales by supplementing or making known consumer satisfaction, it has increasingly become the means whereby producers create needs, launch products, and maintain sales. Because so much is at stake and the constraints of space or time are so great, there is an astonishingly high investment involved in the making of advertisements. It is not uncommon for a 30-second television advertisement to cost more to produce than a 30-minute program. Millions of dollars of production investment in the advertised product hang in the balance. And, of course, there is the cost paid to media outlets to have the advertisement seen or heard again and again.

Advertisements attempt to create a relationship between products and potential consumers, particularly when the products are essentially identical in their basic defining characteristics, such as taste and alcohol content for beer or cleaning capacity for detergent (see Leiss, 2005). In such cases, advertising companies identify what image consumers have of themselves and the product and what is appealing about that image. They then design ad campaigns based on an idealized version of that image. Attributes are identified for the product—for instance, with beer, the purity of the ingredients or the esoteric technology of the brewing process—that appeal to the consumer's self-image. At the same time, advertisers attribute flattering characteristics to the depicted consumers. Often missing in this representation is the obvious distinctive attribute of the product that one might think would be the basis of choice, such as the taste of a beer.

Three other types of advertising are significant. The first includes advertisements for a company rather than its products—usually called institutional advertising. These ads are designed to propagate a favourable corporate image and promote the virtues of a corporation rather than a particular product or product line. In some cases, such as in advertisements for the energy industry, the responsible nature of the individual company or the industry as a whole is put forward explicitly with regard to concerns that have either been expressed by the public or that the corporations have discerned through market research.

The second type of advertisement includes those that masquerade as pieces of reporting. They have been called a variety of names, one of which is **advertorials**. These advertisements present descriptive material on, for example, the contribution of a company to the larger economy. They are usually prepared for print publications, apparently written by a journalist, but in fact written by an employee or agent of the company or agency that is the subject of the article. Television infomercials, half-hour programs pushing particular products, are similar to advertorials. They now account for over $1 billion in sales in the US.

The third type of advertising is called **product placement** or **plugging**. Traditionally, Hollywood film producers have portrayed themselves as putting out 'pure entertainment', meaning that they did not systematically attempt to promote products. But now product placement is part of the financing formula of filmmaking and is defended as an injection of reality into the movie world. As US media commentator Mark Crispin Miller (1990) has noted, plugsters choose projects that offer them maximum control,

THE LANGUAGE OF MOVIES AND TV

Part of the structuring process of each media form is that it develops a language the audience comes to understand. The following are examples of 'languages' the audience has come to learn through TV and film content.

- All police investigations require at least one visit to a strip club.
- All beds have L-shaped sheets to allow the man to bare his chest and the woman to hide hers.
- Ventilation systems are perfect hiding places. They reach to every part of a building, are noiseless to enter and easy to move along both horizontally and vertically, and no one thinks to look there.
- German accents are sufficient should you wish to pass for a German military officer.
- When alone, foreigners speak English to one another.

- All women staying in haunted houses are compelled to investigate strange noises in their most revealing underwear.
- Cars that crash almost always burst into flames.
- Any person waking from a nightmare sits bolt upright.
- All bombs are fitted with large time displays that indicate exactly when they are to go off.
- You can always find a chainsaw if you need one.
- Having a job of any kind ensures that a father will forget his son's eighth birthday.
- Any lock can be picked easily unless it is on a door to a burning building in which a child is imprisoned.
- The more a man and woman hate each other initially the greater the chance they will fall in love in the end.

Adaptation of 'A sampler of one-liners and true facts', by Gary Borders, *The Daily Sentinel* (Nacodoches). (Gary B. Borders)

LOOKING FOR AD SPACE

As if the space over urinals was not enough, *Time* magazine used escalator handrails in the Metro Toronto Convention Centre to remind people of its existence. The ING bank used the floor of a major walkway serving all three of Vancouver's Seabus, Skytrain, and West Coast Express public transit systems. Some enterprising entrepreneurs, operating seemingly on the wrong side of the law, scattered ads for fake photo IDs on the streets and sidewalks in the nightclub district of Vancouver, and boxers and other athletes sometimes temporarily tatoo their bodies with ads while under the camera's gaze.

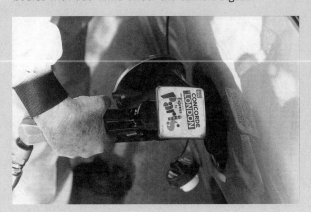

even telling the film producers precisely where they want to see their clients' brands. One of the biggest factors in plugging is how lucrative it can be for filmmakers. For instance, James Bond switched from an Aston Martin to a BMW in *Golden Eye* because BMW offered up a $15 million ad campaign to advertise the movie and the car. In fact, agreements with eight promotional partners netted $100 million in free publicity for this film (*Vancouver Sun*, 6 Dec. 1997, E12). (For a good analysis of product placement, see Wasko et al., 1993.)

The expansion of plugging in movies illustrates how the basic relationship between content and advertisement has been distorted over the years—a change that has been underplayed by communication researchers. Advertisers buy audiences—that everyone acknowledges. What they do not acknowledge is that they purchase audiences in certain frames of mind. No advertiser is going to support a publication, broadcasting program, or website with content that conflicts

with their products or that may cause the audience to adversely react to their products. For instance, airlines have regularly stipulated that newspapers and magazines not run airline ads next to copy describing plane crashes or hijackings. Such advertiser interference upsets journalists, program producers, and editors, but as direct government funding continues to dry up for public broadcasting and as the drive to make greater profits in film and other media increases, the influence of advertisers will continue to grow.

THE NEWS STORY

The news story is a distinctive genre that differs in its structure according to the medium within which it appears. Nevertheless, all news stories share certain fundamental characteristics. Canadian sociologists Richard Ericson, Patricia Baranek, and Janet Chan (1989) developed a set of criteria to describe the characteristics that make events newsworthy. Peter Desbarats (1990: 110), former dean of journalism at

FAVOURABLE COVERAGE AND PUFF EDITORIALS

Another part of plugging is the role newspapers have in promoting their advertisers. In fact, favourable coverage of advertisers is expected of newspapers.

If you look at real estate sections, they are nothing but promotional sections for various parts of the housing industry. So accepting are most Canadians of such favourable coverage that in face of the scandal surrounding leaky condos in British Columbia, no one publicly took the newspapers to task for not having exposed this problem, which had been growing over the years through a lack of responsibility on the part of builders and building inspection codes. One journalist lost his job after writing a critical article on the subject years before it became an admitted issue. Of course, his employer denied the connection.

Not only do commercial media shy away from critical coverage, they often supply quite positive coverage to complement ads. Newspapers regularly run 'special editorial supplements' as separate sections of the paper in which the positive attributes of everything from cars to movies to whole industries are trumpeted in seeming 'news' stories. And on television, video press releases advertising new products such as detergents and movies can be found masquerading as news items on news programs.

the University of Western Ontario, summarizes these criteria:

- Simplification: an event must be recognized as significant and relatively unambiguous in its meaning.
- Dramatization: a dramatized version of the event must be able to be presented.
- Personalization: events must have personal significance to someone.
- Themes and continuity: events that fit into preconceived themes gain in newsworthiness.
- Consonance: events make the news more readily when they fit the reporters' preconceived notions of what should be happening.
- The unexpected: unexpected events that can be expected within frames of reference used by reporters are newsworthy.

A more traditional description of the characteristics of the news story posits that such stories are organized according to an **inverted pyramid**. This means simply that a summary of the seemingly most 'important' information—'who', 'what', 'where', and 'when'—is placed at the beginning, followed by the context—'how' and 'why'—towards the bottom.

As Taras (1990: 20) points out, the content of news stories is also determined by the rhythms of the workday.

Time is an essential consideration in determining the shape a news story will take. The sources that can be reached for interviews and whether facts can be checked, the issues researched, and conclusions drawn are all determined by the time that reporters have available to them. Deadlines impose closure.

In the print medium, a journalist tells the story. This places the journalist, and indeed the paper, squarely between the event and the reader. With television news, the visual presentation actually structures the story and a text is built around the visual impact.

The camera never lies, or so we are led to believe. In fact, the camera always lies because it gives the audience the sense that the picture they see is the whole picture. The camera **frames,** and producers edit the story. The video production of news, or of any other material, puts some things in the picture and keeps other things out. It can emotionalize with the extreme close-up or provide a 'more objective' panorama. It can present the authoritative distance of the medium close-up against a neutral backdrop or include an entire visual environment and attendant mood. The camera tells only its own version of the truth.

SOAP OPERAS

Developed at the beginning of the 1930s in the early days of commercial radio, soap operas were a popular cultural form designed to socialize a home-confined, female audience with disposable income into the art of consuming (Williams, 1992; LaGuardia, 1977). Along with news, soaps are the most analyzed

NEWS TABLOIDS

The inverted pyramid has aided the development of newspaper tabloids. They gain their name from the half-sized format of the pages, which makes them easy to read en route to work by public transit. The tabloids are meant to be quick and impressionistic, often complemented by soft porn and low-level boosterism of actual and potential advertisers. More than broadsheets, they play into the predispositions of their readership, which are determined by market research. Events are often overdramatized and are interpreted as signals that things are often out of control. Headlines regularly emphasize the bizarre, as the examples cited here illustrate.

Teacher swallows live baby mice

People near death hear the same heavenly music

Psychic killed in car wreck brings herself back to life

Wife disguises self as chair to catch cheating husband

Elvis dies, again

73-year-old woman gives birth to triplets!

We've found the fountain of youth! Tomatoes, raisins and aspirin.

---

kind of narrative genre on TV. They have been of particular interest to feminist studies because they are a preferred form of entertainment for female viewers in many countries. Analysis has concentrated on the form and content of soaps and on the pleasures they offer viewers.

A basic difference in plot characterizes the narrative structure of soaps compared with classic narrative: soaps have no sense of an ending. In sharp contrast to the 'closed' stories of classic narratives, soaps are 'open', never-ending narratives, which sometimes go on for years—even decades. In the US, the daytime soap *All My Children* has been running since the late 1930s—first on radio and then, since the 1950s, on TV. In the UK, the BBC radio serial *The Archers* has been going since 1948.

Today, in the US, a distinction is drawn between daytime and prime-time soaps. The former are shown in the afternoon and achieve relatively small but loyal audiences of female viewers and college students. The latter are shown at peak viewing times in the evenings and often have strong family audiences. (See Geraghty, 1991, for an excellent early account of the structure of soaps.)

Over time and after much study, academic perceptions of soaps have changed. At first, they were considered the epitome of that commonly criticized aspect of television that echoes the mass society thesis: trivial, mindless entertainment. Gradually, however, just as the pleasures offered by other forms of popular culture such as films, magazines, sports, and other forms of television were legitimized as valid

pastimes, so too soaps were viewed in a more positive light (Radway, 1984).

MUSIC VIDEOS

In a fashion similar to the soaps, music videos, particularly rock videos, emerged because producers wanted to socialize an audience into purchasing their product. The difference between the soaps and music videos is that with videos the product to be purchased is part of the promotional vehicle used to bring it to the attention of the audience. Music videos are visually enhanced versions of the CDs and tapes that the audience is intended to purchase.

As with each of the media forms discussed in this chapter, rock videos have evolved from other media forms. Movies featuring rock stars, beginning with Bill Haley and His Comets in *Rock Around the Clock* (1956), early Elvis Presley films such as *Jailhouse Rock*

ISOLATING ELEMENTS OF MEDIA CONTENT

A good exercise, and an excellent methodology that provides insight into the workings of some media, is to isolate one element from its context. Turn off the sound of a movie and watch the visuals; record the soundtrack of an investigative TV program and listen just to the words (a transcription is even better); or read the lyrics of a song you have not heard.

(1957) and *King Creole* (1958), and Richard Lester's iconoclastic 1960s movies with the Beatles, as well as filmed recording sessions and concerts, were the precursors of the rock video. Rock videos are successful because they make cheap television, just as playing music produces cheap radio. The cost of production is generally shouldered by record companies or the bands themselves and with videos as content the cost of a half-hour original television show dropped from $2,000–$2,500 a minute to about the same amount for a half-hour. The beauty of music videos is that they assemble quite sizable, high-consuming audiences, whose attention can then be sold to advertisers. Moreover, they promote sales of music products.

Performers such as Madonna, whose record companies can afford lavish extravaganzas to promote their songs in this genre, are at a considerable advantage over less-established artists. Carefully choreographed and staged videos guarantee heavy rotation on video playlists.

As media content, rock videos provide viewers an entry point to popular culture. They provide examples of what clothes and accessories to buy, how to behave, what expressions to use, and so forth. In providing material for imaginative creation, music videos complement fashion photographs and magazine illustrations. Viewers provide individual interpretation and inject a dynamism built on popular music, ridding the pictures of their frozenness in time (see Goffman, 1974; Fornas et al., 1988). As James Curran (1990: 154) has remarked, 'rock music is viewed as a laboratory for the intensive production of identity by adolescents seeking to define an independent self.'

REALITY TV

A genre that is enjoying increasing popularity recently is reality-based television. As a program category, reality TV encompasses a wide range of different types of programming including: game shows, talent searches, cooking and food programs, sports, lives of celebri-

'WHAT WON'T YOU DO?'

In his book, *The Highwaymen: Warriors of the Information Superhighway*, journalist Ken Auletta interviewed a number of highly placed media moguls, that is, media leaders who answer only to themselves. In Chapter 4, 'What won't you do?', Auletta asked these individuals just that—in reference to what type of material they would not allow to be aired. What is notable about these interviews is the number of media heads who apparently accept that the media have an impact on the audience and audience behaviour, but, true to the American spirit of freedom of speech, reject the notion of interfering with content.

Auletta begins the chapter with an anecdote. In 1979 Lawrence Gordon produced a movie, *The Warriors*, about street gangs. He had good reason to believe that, like his later films, *Die Hard*, *Predator*, *Field of Dreams*, and *48 Hours*, it would be a tremendous box-office success. In the first week, three killings were linked to the movie. Gordon said to Auletta, 'People went out and pretended they were warriors.' The film was recalled. Gordon commented, 'I'd be lying if I said that people don't imitate what they see on the screen . . . I would be a moron to say that they don't, because look how dress styles change. We have people who want to look like Julia Roberts and Michelle Pfeiffer and Madonna. Of course we imitate. It would be impossible for me to think they would imitate our dress, our music, our look, but

not imitate any of our violence or our other actions.'

Here is how some interviewees answered the question 'What won't you do?':

Rupert Murdoch, owner of the Fox Network and the British Sun newspaper, which publishes pictures of bare-breasted women on page three every day, replied, 'You wouldn't do anything that you couldn't live with, that would be against your principles. . . . It's a very difficult question if you are a man of conscience. If you thought that you were doing something that was having a malevolent effect, as you saw it, on society, you would not do it. We would never do violence such as you see in a Nintendo game. When I see kids playing Nintendo, and they're able to actually get their character on the screen to bite his opponent in the face, that's pretty sick violence. . . . Is the violence of *Lethal Weapon* OK? I think so. If it involves personal cruelty, sadism—obviously you would never do that. The trouble is, of course, that you run a studio, and how free are you to make these rules? The creative people give you a script and are given last cut on the movie. The next thing, you have a thirty-million-dollar movie in the can which you may disapprove of.'

Oliver Stone, director of such films as *Platoon*, *The Doors*, *Natural Born Killers*, and *JFK*, said, 'Off the top ties, talk shows, hidden cameras, hoaxes, and a 'day or week in the life' of prominent personalities.

Reality TV sometimes assumes a documentary style and focuses on 'real-life', unscripted situations. Other times, plot and narrative structure are achieved through editing and/or having subjects participate in planned circumstances. Other traditional narrative techniques, such as characterization, are achieved through focusing on people with seemingly outlandish personalities and jobs or by careful behind-the-scenes casting of participants.

On American television, and consequently on the Canadian small screen as well, the genre has its roots in early programs such as *Candid Camera* (1948) and *Ted Mack's Original Amateur Hour* (1948). But the genre has always enjoyed at least a marginal presence on the television dial, with shows like *American Family* (1973) and *Cops* (1989), right up to the present and such shows as the enormously successful *Survivor* series and the game show *Who Wants To Be a Millionaire?*. The more recent popularity of the genre is very much an international phenomenon with programs from the British, Japanese, and American television markets cross-fertilizing each other as well as giving impetus to spinoff programs in smaller markets such as those in Canada and Australia.

For producers and television networks, a key attraction of reality TV is cost. With no expensive actors to pay, no high-priced sets to create, and no expensive special effects, reality-based television is a good antidote to the ever-fragmenting TV market and the shrinking viewers and ad dollars accruing to individual broadcast stations in the sea of choices now available to viewers. Much of the cast of these programs work for nothing and the sets or locations require little preparation. Meanwhile, on the decoding side of the equation, reality TV shrinks the distance between program and audience as, increasingly, ordinary people become television stars and videos and other material created by non-professionals are used in television programs.

---

of my head, I'd pretty much do anything . . . I don't view ethics from the outside, only from the inside. What you would find shocking I probably would not. For me it's a question of taste. . . . You can do anything as long as you do it well. I think Hitler would make a great movie.' Does Stone reject the notion that there is too much violence in movies? 'Yes and no', he says, 'Yes, there's too much violence when the violence is badly done. I go back to my aesthetic defense. If it's badly done it becomes obscene. It's not real. If it's well done, it has impact, it has a dramatic point, then it has meaning. It's valid.'

Michael Eisner, chairman of Disney, proffered that while he is not interested in making violent movies, 'I believe there is nothing you should not be allowed to do. . . . I don't believe, strongly, that the government has any right to be involved in anything, or almost anything [related to entertainment].' Later, Eisner added, when asked whether there is a distinction between real and cartoon violence, 'I don't think that anybody thinks that movies like *The Terminator* are real . . . I'm not sure that they don't relieve pressure more than they create it. I don't know the answer to that. I don't want to sit in judgement. I don't think about it that much.'

Michael Ovitz, chairman of Creative Artists Agency, demurred when asked the question, stating that decisions are made on a day-to-day basis. Also, he said that seeing a violent film is a question of choice, and that violence in movies is often 'not real'. However, as to the impact of movie violence he noted, 'I absolutely think it has an impact on kids. It becomes a framework on which children build. I remember all the things of my childhood. They've been my framework for my own value system . . .'

Ted Harbert is president of the entertainment division of ABC, which broadcast a movie, *Between Love and Hate*, that ended with a youth firing six bullets into his former lover. Harbert said in justification, that a network, like a newspaper, offers choices: '. . . adults can handle that type of television. Children can't. This will sound like a paradox, but I don't believe we have to program the network and absolve parents of responsibility, as if it were our problem and not the parents' problem. Parents have to be responsible for what their kids watch.'

Auletta's interviews demonstrate that media moguls give very little serious thought to the social implications of the content they produce. When they are asked to reflect upon the subject, their responses are often simplistic, contradictory, and inconsistent with their professed personal beliefs.

Source: Ken Auletta, *The Highwaymen*. Copyright © 1997 by Rigatoni, Inc. Reprinted by permission of Random House Inc.

Media Creating Meaning: Possibilities and Limitations

In drawing on the larger field of social knowledge and events the media are constantly influencing us: they select certain events to bring forward; they create an image of those events; and they create a discourse within which events and issues are defined (see Mills, 2004; Mitchell, 1988). But beyond influencing our view of reality, do the media have the ability to create a reality quite at odds with the facts? Such a scenario is explored in the movie *Wag the Dog*, in which a Hollywood producer is commissioned to wage a small, bogus war to divert attention from the domestic difficulties of the American President. Though this movie perhaps exaggerates the lengths to which the media will go to 'create' meaning, they have at times attempted to create meaning that conflicts with common perceptions.

Perhaps a more disturbing scenario played out in the United States in the days following the attack on the World Trade Center and the US invasion of Iraq. A series of polls conducted in the summer of 2003 in the US found that 48 per cent incorrectly believed that links between Iraq and al-Qaeda had been found, '22 per cent that weapons of mass destruction had been found in Iraq, and 25 per cent that world opinion favoured the US going to war with Iraq' (PIPA/Knowledge Network, 2003). However, no evidence has ever been found to support any of these assertions. In other words, the poll illustrated that the American people were badly misinformed as to the circumstances surrounding the invasion of Iraq. The poll also found that people's misperceptions varied significantly depending on their source of news, with 80 per cent of those reporting the Fox network as their major source having one or more of these misperceptions, while only 23 per cent of those depending on public broadcasting networks had one or more. In excess of 50 per cent of respondents were found to believe also that Iraq was at some level involved in the attacks—a perception that US intelligence agencies say is unfounded. Moreover, people holding these misperceptions were more likely to support the war. Can the US media be held directly responsible for promoting these misconceptions? The poll provides no direct evidence that they have done so. However, it does illustrate that the media have done little to educate the public on the facts of the situation.

In any event, as one Canadian example illustrates, it is not necessarily possible for the media to promote particular public perceptions even if they attempt to do so. In the late 1980s, a tentative constitutional agreement, the Meech Lake Accord, which proclaimed Quebec to be a 'distinct society' and gave that province and (de facto) the other provinces greater powers vis-à-vis Ottawa, had to be ratified by all the provincial legislatures in order to become entrenched in the Constitution. Despite the support of most politicians and pundits for the agreement, many Canadians had reservations about its contents (Coyne, 1992). In the end, the agreement failed to be ratified in time. Despite this defeat, then Prime Minister Brian Mulroney, in his determination to change the Constitution to placate nationalist sentiment in Quebec, convened a second round of negotiations. These resulted in the Charlottetown Accord, a similar but wider-reaching agreement reached in August 1992 between the provinces and Ottawa after consultation with public groups and Aboriginal leaders. The agreement was taken to a national referendum with the political and media elites of the country threatening the public with dire consequences if they failed to support it. The *Globe and Mail* ran an alarmist editorial in its 1 September edition, and on 24 and 25 October the *Financial Post* ran a letter signed by its senior executives that implored Canadians to vote in favour of the accord. On 26 October, Canadians, including the majority of Quebecers, chose not to ratify the accord, effectively banishing constitutional reform from the political agenda.

This Canadian example illustrates just the opposite of **media/culture binding**. It represents a dramatic breakdown in the ability of the political and media elites to establish a reality or a discourse that is persuasive enough to command allegiance. It also illustrates the limitations on the media's ability to create meaning for their audience.

Media and Reality: Where Lies the Difference?

Few people in this era would identify so strongly with the characters and interaction in a novel that they would confuse the world of the novel with their day-to-day world. The intermingling of media realities and lived realities is more likely to happen in television, film, or even magazines. Soap opera characters, for example, regularly receive letters from viewers

ART AND LIFE

For years, some Canadians have thumbed their noses at Americans for voting Hollywood celebrities into office, such as Sonny Bono (a mayor and then a member of the US House of Representatives), Clint Eastwood (the mayor of Carmel, California, for a time), Arnold Schwarzenegger (the governor of California), and, best or worst of all, former US President Ronald Reagan. But in Vancouver in the fall of 2002 politics and movies were so intertwined that it was difficult to tell who was real and who was not.

First came the successful TV series, *Da Vinci's Inquest*, based on the former coroner of Vancouver, Larry Campbell. Then Vancouver's mayor, Philip Owen, became convinced that Vancouver should set up safe injection sites for heroin and other drug addicts. This stance—a bit of sand in the face of the US government of George Bush the younger and its war on drugs, which managed to net even the President's niece, Noelle Bush, Florida Governor Jeb Bush's daughter—and perhaps other incidents caused the 'political party' Owen represented, the Non-Partisan Association (which does not canvas widely for members), to oust him. Then Larry Campbell decided to run for mayor and bill himself as the actual Da Vinci. And then came a documentary called *Fix: Story of an Addicted City*, which premiered at the Vancouver Film Festival to sold-out crowds. Finally, Philip Owen, still the mayor, asked his supporters at a fundraiser to pay $100 each to attend a screening of the film with the proceeds going to assist the filmmakers in seeking theatrical release for the documentary.

advising them of the intent of other characters in the program, or gifts for their upcoming television 'marriages'. Some observers have suggested that this means the viewers do not distinguish between real life and the soaps. Or, it may be that the viewers want to enter into the construction of the plot or that they want to test the production system. If they warn the character of the intent of another, will a warning be built into the plot? If they send gifts, will their gifts be included in what the couple receives in a future program?

Comedian Rick Mercer, then of CBC's *This Hour Has 22 Minutes*, made comic use of audience involvement and undermined credibility of the Reform/Alliance Party idea to call for public referenda on certain issues. The party was of a mind that if 3 per cent of Canadians (approximately 900,000) signed a petition asking for a referendum, then the government should be obliged to hold a referendum. Mercer asked his audience to visit a website and express their opinion on whether the party leader at that time, Stockwell Day, should change his first name to Doris. Over a million people visited the website and agreed that he should change his name. The Canadian Alliance, not surprisingly, did not ask for a referendum from the federal government on the subject.

In another example of the blending of media and reality, in 1939 Orson Welles produced a radio play called *The War of the Worlds* in which he presented, in documentary style, a pseudo invasion of Earth by Martians. Many listeners phoned in, some as the program was being aired, to report sightings of the landings of other Martians. Some listeners seemed genuinely to fear for their lives (Cantril, 1940). After all, the program aired at the beginning of World War II, when the Nazis were mobilizing using both radio and film. And great uncertainty existed about Stalin and Communist power. Radio broadcasting was still in its infancy, and although intellectuals had been railing against it or enthusiastically endorsing it, they certainly were not minimizing their assessments of its impact on society. In short, while the reaction of some audience members was quite real—there was considerable panic—the treatment of the reactions fed a vision of the media that is as real now as it was then: the media have the power to cause people to do things they otherwise would not do.

More recently, social theorists have argued that the distinction between media representation and reality has blurred, even collapsed altogether. Working in the 1960s Guy Debord argued that we had begun living in a 'society of the spectacle'—that is, a media and consumer society 'organized around the consumption of images, commodities, and spectacles' (Best and Kellner, 1997: 84). As he points out, much of how we understand life, much of what we know and enjoy, is created by others and presented to us in commodity form. The watching of sports events substitutes for the actual playing of games. Our knowledge of world events is mediated through newspaper stories and what we see on TV. Our experience of nature is gleaned through theme parks, zoos, aquariums, and travel programs on television. Our experience of other cultures is generally confined to travelogues and 'ethnic' restaurants and festivals. Computers and the web have accelerated this process. Cards and other games are played on-line as simulations of real events. Even sex slips into the realm of the virtual. Indeed, as Debord points out, 'in the modern conditions of production, life presents itself as an immense accumulation of spectacles' (in Best and Kellner, 1997: 84), almost all of which are sold to us—'mediated' through the market. At the heart of this system, of course, are the media: the source of myriad representations of the real.

Writing some years later, Jean Baudrillard pushed Debord's thesis even further. He thinks that the line between the real and its representation has become so blurred that it is now impossible to tell the difference between them (Baudrillard, 1995). As he argues, modern life has been taken over by simulation, and the 'real' world folded in among so many representations, that it is not possible to tell where one begins and the other ends. From this perspective we are living in a 'simulacra', a hyperreal world where reality has been substituted by symbols and signs that refer only to other symbols and signs rather than to a grounded, objective reality. How true is Baudrillard's thesis? How will you decide?

Media Representation and Reductionism

As we discussed in the opening pages of this chapter, the act of representation necessarily involves a process of simplification as media technologies and production techniques are deployed to compress the world into words, sounds, and images easily packaged by the media industry.

To make events and issues both understandable and seemingly important to the general public, they are simplified and dramatized. This dual requirement can be handled by the creation of dichotomies. Thus we have war and peace, individual freedom and totalitarian control, free speech and censorship, pro-life and pro-choice, separatism and federalism, **liberalism** or **conservatism**, good or evil, right-wing or left-wing, progressive or traditional, sexually exploitative or reflecting of family values, and so on, ad infinitum. Such dichotomies simplify by dividing the world in half instead of more realistically presenting the world as a complex multi-dimensional affair.

Take, for instance, an issue such as unemployment. There are many mitigating factors that inform unemployment, such as government policy, age, gender, education, ethnicity, and geographic location. To try to reduce the complexities of the issue to a simple dichotomy—say, the need for community support structures against the desirability of individual freedom (or lower taxes)—becomes a formidable challenge. So, too, considering the best way to treat adolescents who have engaged in criminal activity requires thought that goes far beyond getting tough or going soft on crime, as the media often portray it. The complexity of the solution to troubled youth even goes far beyond understanding the youth's family history and personality. It extends into styles of child-rearing, the education system, the nature and extent of employment, the society that perpetuates poverty, the role of religion, the presence of degrading portrayals of people in the various media, and so forth. In fact, it extends to our very understanding of what an adolescent is.

Dichotomies not only simplify and stereotype, they dramatize by introducing tension, by the creation of sides battling each other for control. In media presentations, spokespersons for the environment line up against the forest companies, feminists against patriarchal society, First Nations against European immigrants, workers against employers, the poor against the rich, the taxpayers against the government, the middle class against those receiving welfare assistance, the government against Her Majesty's Loyal Opposition. In fact, matters are much more complex than these dichotomies suggest and not easily packaged as media spectacle.

The media's treatment of issues creates the impression that the audience can understand all the issues through short news stories and sound bites. Yet, when people participate in the institutions of society—helping out in a school, a soccer club, a Brownie group, or a political party—they come to understand just how difficult running social institutions can be, how full of compromise an institution must be, how challenging it is to keep people focused on the central task, and how difficult it is to maintain morale. When people do not participate in social institutions or become actively involved in issues of public concern, relying instead on the media to inform them about their community, their nation, and the world, the simplification needed to tell the story quickly and the dramatization needed to capture their attention not only provide an inadequate rendering of the complexity involved, but also, in dichotomizing, polarize public opinion into inflexible camps.

Media simplification and dramatization are reductionist, although these characteristics are not solely due to media practice, as Lawrence Habermehl (1995) points out in *The Counterfeit Wisdom of Shallow Minds*. They reduce people and events into something they are not. They encourage negative and hostile reactions in those who otherwise lack knowledge of the situation and especially in those who do not otherwise participate in society. Dramatic tensions encourage us to form firm opinions on debates of which we know only what the media tell us, of which we possess only a shallow simulation. Journalists and others who seek peaceful solutions to social and international conflict point out that such treatment of wars and other complex political tensions makes it appear that there is no middle ground in social conflict and that efforts to resolve problems peacefully are hopeless and futile. The media create this scenario and take no responsibility for it.

11 SEPTEMBER 2001

If there are significant differences between the real world and the media world, it is nonetheless true that much of our experience of historical events is tied up with media accounts of those events: news reports, books, movies, popular music, and radio and television documentaries. How many people recollect or know of the assassination of US President John F. Kennedy from the amateur film shot by Abraham Zapruder, resurrected by TV news clips or embedded in Oliver Stone's film *JFK*? Or the arrest of O.J. Simpson from the live CNN broadcast of the police chase along that Los Angeles freeway? Or the Persian Gulf War from the highly orchestrated Pentagon press conferences with their computerized images of 'precision bombing'?

Part of the shock of 11 September 2001 is surely tied to our ability to 'witness' the events of that day thanks to saturation media coverage, and especially the continual television coverage that provided such clear images from so many angles that many people said 'it was like watching a Hollywood movie.' Yes, it was like watching a Hollywood movie because it was so fantastic, so unbelievable, so unexpected, but also because we could watch it all unfold on our television screens. If we didn't see the first airliner hit the north tower, that crash nevertheless succeeded in drawing media attention to the World Trade Center so that many of us were watching when the second plane hit 20 minutes later, streaking across the blue sky of a spectacular late summer day, exploding into the south tower as if its hijackers were performing for the cameras.

We can relive that day through its media imagery—the twin towers burning; office workers clinging desperately to remote window ledges; the jumpers; the towers collapsing, almost perfectly, one by one, in a cloud of smoke and debris; monochromatic images of dust-drenched survivors; firefighters working the breached wall of the Pentagon; the smouldering crash site in a field near Shanksville, Pennsylvania. And the stunned faces of the survivors and direct witnesses to this tragedy.

That day—11 September 2001—is no longer a simple date on the calendar. The shorthand expression 9/11 refers to a brutal act of defiance against the world's sole remaining superpower, a challenge to its omnipotence and, just as importantly, a challenge to a way of life built on professed values of democracy, justice, and liberty. If the hijackers won unprecedented media coverage for their attacks on the most potent symbols of American economic, military, and political power (the plane that crashed in Pennsylvania was heading towards Washington), 9/11 remains on the media stage as we struggle to understand why it happened, what the attacks mean, and how the United States and other Western countries can or should respond, or have responded, to them. The media will continue to be heavily implicated in how we come to understand 9/11.

For students of mass communication, 9/11 is a media event in another sense. It is an opportunity to see how the media perform in a crisis situation, how the news media, particularly, live up to their professed responsibility to inform us as citizens as our democratically elected governments combat terrorism. What we have seen to date is not encouraging.

We have seen frequent examples of media reductionism, whereby any consideration of root political causes for 9/11 are dismissed and the whole affair is framed as a simple case of good versus evil, with George W. Bush personifying the forces of good and Osama bin Laden the forces of evil. 'Either you are with us, or you're with the terrorists', as the President so succinctly put it. When

Canadian Prime Minister Jean Chrétien suggested, on the first anniversary of 9/11, that such terrorist attacks were the product of a world divided between prosperous and arrogant Western nations and a humiliated 'poor world' (Canadian Press, 2002), *Globe and Mail* international affairs columnist Marcus Gee (2002) scoffed, insisting that 'evil' was the only explanation for the 9/11 attacks: 'No act of US foreign policy, no economic grievance, can explain the hate-filled ideology that led to the murders of Sept. 11. This was an act of evil perpetrated by evil men.'

We have seen the power of language to define events. When the United States captured hundreds of men during the fighting in Afghanistan and held them in a rudimentary, offshore military prison at Guantanamo Bay, Cuba, it maintained the men were 'illegal combatants' as opposed to 'prisoners of war'. POWs have rights guaranteed by the Geneva Convention. Illegal combatants have no such rights and can be tried and punished by secretive military tribunals, which maintain a lower standard of proof than US court proceedings, and which shield evidence and witnesses from all forms of public scrutiny (Thompson, 2002).

We have seen normal channels of justice derailed. More than 1,200 people of Middle Eastern descent were initially detained without trial in the US, without their identities being revealed, and many without even access to legal counsel ('When violating rights', 2002). Among those was Canadian Maher Arar, who was apprehended by the US on the basis of faulty information provided by the RCMP and secretly deported to Syria to be tortured— a procedure labelled 'extraordinary rendition'. After almost a year of incarceration and torture in Syria, Arar was returned to Canada, where a 34-month federal inquiry cleared him of any wrongdoing and pointed the finger directly at the RCMP and its too-cozy relationship with American surveillance agencies. Still, the US insisted that Arar was on its security watch list as a threat (McCharles, 2006), even after the Canadian government in early 2007 formally apologized to Arar and awarded him compensation of over $10 million. In addition, the hastily crafted Patriot Act of 2001 permitted then US Attorney General John Ashcroft to expand surveillance of telephone and internet communications, increase wiretap activity, and examine financial and medical records in the interests of combatting terrorism (Lapham, 2002). The parameters of debate in mainstream news coverage and commentary have narrowed significantly since 9/11. Describing journalists as 'security guards deciding what could and could not be seen on camera', *Harper's* editor Lewis H. Lapham (2002: 7) searched in vain for news coverage that would provide '[i]nformed argument about why and how America had come to be perceived as a dissolute empire; instructive doubts cast on the supposed omniscience of the global capital markets; sustained questioning of the way in which we divide the country's wealth; a distinction drawn between the ambitions of the American national security state and the collective well-being of the American citizenry.'

Speaking to journalism students at Concordia University in Montreal, former *New York Times* reporter Chuck Sudetic put it more simply. The news media failed to ask three basic, yet crucial, questions: Why? Why here? Why now? We are still wondering. Just as we must wonder what the real outcomes, in the ensuing years, will be of the American–British war on Iraq.

Challenging Standards: Pornography, Erotica, and Freedom of Speech

In discussions of pornography a distinction is often drawn between pornography and erotica. The former is put forward as unacceptable, the latter as permissible. The argument usually goes something like this: there is nothing wrong with having material (literature, films, videos, music, art, websites) designed to be sexually stimulating; there is, however, something wrong with portraying the sexual exploitation of women, children, and men. While such a stance is considered by many to have obvious merit, one difficulty with the pro–erotica stance is that, in real life, erotic feelings are often a component of a private moment. The hawking of wares in which that link between the sexual and the private is broken challenges ideas about sexual relations fundamental to many cultures.

Equally deserving of consideration is the role of erotica or soft porn in advertising. The continuous representation of ideal male and female body types in advertisements appears not only to support parts of the vast clothing, beauty, and drug industries, but also to encourage problems of individual self-worth and disease (excessive body-building, non-medical use of steroids, anorexia, and bulimia). We are familiar with the use of the female body to sell products as diverse as alcoholic beverages, perfume, food, designer fashion, and tobacco products. The emergence of 'himbos' merely extends the target market from females to males: 'His erect nipples are exploited in the furtherance of fragrance and his washboard belly used to flog everything from kitchen cleanser to wrist watches' (Cobb, 1993).

In the same manner in which exploitative sexual portrayals and violence may challenge community standards, so do other portrayals that may not reflect others' perception of the world. Some will be offended by family portrayals of same-sex parents; others by a portrayal of racially based organizations; still others by an unpatriotic portrayal of their nation or a satirical representation of their religion. Such portrayals provide the viewer with another perspective on life besides the one he or she experiences and may encourage a striving for excellence and tolerance as well as a change in common perception. On the other hand, they may discourage an allegiance to community values in favour of the values of a world of signification.

Given the possible effects of such portrayals, the question becomes whether and how much they should be controlled and by whom. Different countries address this question differently, with the most distinctive being the United States. With the First Amendment of the US Constitution stating that Congress shall make no law respecting an establishment of religion, or prohibiting or abridging the freedom of speech, control over pornography is limited indeed.

In Canada media portrayals of particular events and people have also been the subject of public debate. For instance, in 1992 and for some time after, there was great discussion about a documentary film, *The Valour and the Horror*, a CBC miniseries that presented an unromantic view of Canada's involvement in World War II. Many veterans, some of whom were senators, wanted to have the film banned because it insulted their memories of the war. A great war of words ensued in the media about the film (available through the NFB). Most frightening were the hearings on the film conducted by the Senate Veterans' Affairs Committee. Clearly, certain senators were not in the least interested in freedom of speech and used every power they had to threaten the filmmakers, including taking them to court for **defamation** of character.

More recently the CBC found itself mired in a similar debate over its 2006 production of *Prairie Giant*, a biography of Tommy Douglas, the father of medicare and a number of other Canadian social programs. In this instance, one of the descendants of one of the historical characters in the film took issue with the way that character was portrayed, claiming that it was inaccurate and defamatory. In response to these accusations the Corporation cancelled a rerun of the series and suspended sale of the DVD. At the same time, both the Directors' Guild of Canada and the Writers' Guild attacked the CBC's actions, claiming that they amounted to censorship and attacked artistic and creative

WHY TV GETS IT WRONG

In 1994, in the *Globe and Mail*, Graham Fraser wrote an article with the above title. He began the article with the following: 'Vision Statement: TV pretends to expand horizons and clarify a difficult world. Instead, it simplifies to the point of banality and ignores what it can't grasp.' He then quoted the late E.B. White, a New York writer who said (in 1938), 'We shall stand or fall by TV, of that I am quite sure.'

Fraser's points were many. He noted that TV 'frames and focuses the way Americans think about the world. Its grammar and rhetoric shape public debate' and appear to define and limit government action. Television simplifies by conveying emotion, not reason: it has difficulty with abstractions such as religious beliefs and even foreign languages. At times it barely pays attention to critical issues and areas and when it does it treats them in an either/or framework. He quoted respected news commentator Robert MacNeil: 'bite-sized is best; complexity must be avoided; nuances are dispensable; qualifications impede the simple message; visual stimulation substitutes for thought.' Wars must be brought to a speedy conclusion before the audience gets bored. TV can anaesthetize viewers as horrific scenes from war are shown over and over again until what is ultimately horrible becomes a visual cliché.

In times when the lives of thousands are at stake, as they are in Afghanistan, Iraq, and parts of the Middle East, it is truly frightening to think that we live by the dynamics of television and the type of understanding it is capable of delivering.

freedom (Ross, 2006). At the time of writing, it is not clear how this controversy may be resolved.

Summary

Social models of communication attempt to understand the variables or the context affecting the formation or encoding of messages and their understanding or decoding. This chapter has examined a number of different perspectives on the social elements of communication, in other words, the dynamics of meaning-creation and of interpretation.

The study of the creation and interpretation of media content is the study of representation, or, as the semioticians would have it, signification. Such study examines how symbols, such as the words and ideas contained in language, are constructed and used to interpret the world of objects, events, persons, and even representations. This realm of making meaning is not subordinate to that of physical objects because physical objects gain their meaning through systems of symbol.

The study of representation involves understanding the nature of polysemy, intertextuality, and grounded indeterminate systems. In less technical words, it involves understanding how messages are open to a variety of interpretations, how interpretations depend on other representations, and how there are bound to be a finite but unpredictable number of interpretations of the object, event, or phenomenon being represented.

Several approaches are used to analyze media content. Some of the main categories are literary criticism; structuralism, semiotics, and post-structuralism; discourse analysis; critical political economy; organizational analysis; content analysis; and genre/media form analysis. Each has particular strengths and draws out various forces playing on content.

The media are bound to society through a process of interpenetration of media content and lived reality. Often they massage and present material from the margins of society to make it acceptable and available to the mainstream. The media are not free to create non-existent social values even though they may affect the manner in which social values are played out. The interpenetration of reality and media representation is problematic, especially with regard to violence and pornography. The simplification, reductionism, and dramatization of issues also create unacknowledged problems.

Appendix: A Semiotic Analysis of a Black Label Ad Series

The following award-winning ad series was part of a multimedia blitz on television and radio and in print in Ontario and Quebec in the late 1980s. The television and print ads had a tremendous impact. Not only did the sales of Black Label beer double, but also the world of advertising was effusive in its praise for the campaign and the semiotic principles deployed in this ad are now mainstays of the advertising industry.

Tattoos, jeans, and plain T-shirts, grainy black-and-white photographs with a single red highlight, billiards, bars, a short black leather skirt, reflective sunglasses with colourful frames, black vinyl LPs, western string bolo ties, single figures, at times no figures, a partial view of the product label, legend, black: these are some of the elements or signifiers drawn from a selection of the print ads that the agency Palmer Bonner created for Carling's Black Label. What do they mean?

Think in dyads, that is to say, opposites. Once you know the images are from a beer ad, think of how beer ads usually look. Most often they depict groups of attractive 25–35-year-olds on the scene, on the make, and often in humorous situations. These more traditional ads spare no expense and present both human props and product in the lushest production that money can buy and video and computer technology can produce. The setting is well-lit and everything is crisp, clean, life-embracing. Front and centre in the picture in full living colour is 'the product'. And if the viewer is besotted with the beauty of the actors and the set, then the music blasts the message in his/her ears.

All of this works for the mainstream. But other groups in society reject or at least do not respond to these ads and/or drink other beers. Carling Breweries and its advertising agency, Palmer Bonner, began this campaign with the knowledge that on Queen Street West in Toronto and St-Denis in Montreal there appeared to be one such non-responding group. How did they know? Because Black Label already had a high market share in those locations.

Corporations don't obtain such information out of idle curiosity only to dismiss it with a shrug. Most often, when sales figures show unusual patterns, they seek to find out why and to define, if possible, the characteristics of the consumers behaving this way (in an effort to capitalize on the trend). This is exactly what Carling and Palmer Bonner did. With this distinctive pattern of sales they set out to find who was drinking Black Label and why.

Black Label drinkers, it turned out, came from two groups. The first group contained individuals who were some or all of the following: creative, non-conformist, individualist, intellectual. As well, they tended to be anti-commercial, not inclined against homosexuals, oriented to the inner city. Their lives allowed them to play out these traits either through their employment or their unemployment. The second group of Black Label drinkers consisted of hangers-on to the first group, those who, for the most part, lived other lives but longed for and sometimes visited their ideological brethren on Queen Street West and St-Denis. Moreover, it appeared that while the membership of the first group was small, the second group was potentially large. Indeed, the agency came to believe, partly as a result of their focus group work, that a little of the focal values of the first group could be found in all of us.

The identification of the characteristics of Black Label drinkers was interesting and illuminating, but it presented a conundrum. If, as the research showed, one of the major reasons people drank Black Label was because it wasn't advertised, how could one ever hope to advertise the brand and increase sales? The agency and its client elected a strategy that seems obvious in retrospect. They would advertise the lifestyle of the drinkers; flatter those who lived it; understate the product identity; avoid too frequent exposure of any single ad; involve confirmed consumers and others in the ad by mental participation (filling in missing elements); and ensure that the creative elements of the ad reflected aspects of the lifestyle and were consistent with the values of the brand loyalists.

Why go to all this trouble if an identifiable population was already loyal to the brand and take the chance of alienating them? Because, the agency and the brewer reasoned, many more of the second group and perhaps some of the first group could be sensitized to the brand without alienating the brand loyalists. And, perhaps, the ads might strengthen the loyal-

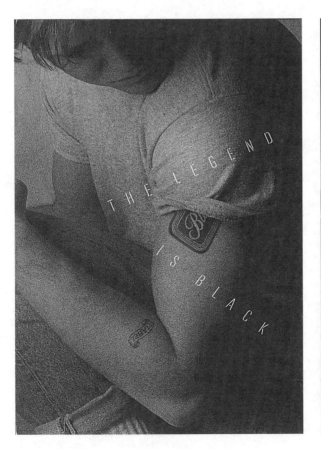

ty of the first group to Black Label.

The message of the ads was simple: 'If you look closely at this ad and you really know what is going on you'll know who we are depicting, that they are a real group in society, that they stand for something, and that they drink a certain brand of beer. You, too, can show your alliance with the values of this group by adopting elements of their lifestyle you don't already share, starting with drinking the same beer they do.'

The ads themselves are black and white, albeit with a red highlight. They are also grainy. Why? The lack of full colour immediately distinguishes the ads from all other beer ads. The graininess assists. Brand identification is obscured, not obscured enough for anyone who has been in a beer store not to know what it is, but visually obscured. Yet, by colour and placement the brand label is the focal point of the picture. In ad number 1 the beer label is in the form of a tattoo—now there's loyalty and commitment. In all the ads no beer bottle is in sight, but what does appear, if you even notice it, in thin, white, broken let-

ters that don't impinge on the eye, is the phrase 'The Legend Is Black'. The male and female models are in-style, 'of a type', but certainly not mainstream.

Each of these elements, led by the black-and-white grainy and red-highlighted photo, complements the others to add up to a whole-picture depiction of the brand loyalists and their preferred brand of beer. Of course, there is no one to challenge the company on whether the group it has identified actually drinks more Black Label than any other beer. No other company has identified the group and its associates as a target market.

Ad number 2 presents a grainy, black-and-white photograph of a black billiard ball in the foreground, slightly out of focus, with part of the Black Label painted on it complete with red, presented upside down with only the first four letters of the word 'Black' visible and with the last letter disappearing around the curve of the ball. The photograph was taken at slow speed with two balls apparently moving in the background. Around the curve of the ball, again visually understated in white, broken, sans-serif type,

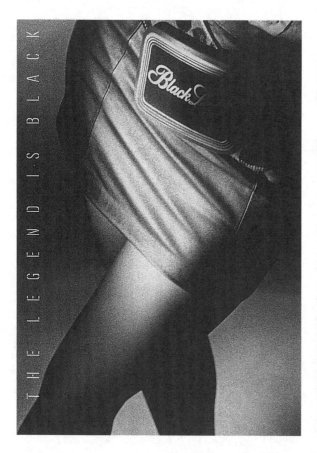

'The Legend Is Black'. 'Legend'? Why 'legend'? And why not a straight-out, simple and direct, non-ambiguous, 'The Beer Is Black Label'?

Ad number 3 shows a grainy, black-and-white photograph of a woman, the photo cropped across her hip and waist. She is wearing a Black Label (sort of) belt buckle/clasp, deliberately partially obscured by a black shadow to show only 'Black L'. Her legs are crossed in a way that leads the viewer to the beer label buckle/clasp, and the miniskirt is, of course, tantalizing. Note that we have yet to see and will not ever see the full unobscured face of a model. Up the right-hand side of the picture, in horizontal, white, broken, sans-serif type is again, 'The Legend Is Black'. Legend? With miniskirts that hearken back over two decades, black-and-white graininess reminiscent of black-and-white TV, even the red, white, and black of the label in contrast to the pastels of postmodernism that were picked up by some of the alcoholic 'coolers'—there is a suggestion of history—the overall style seems to echo a form of industrial art.

In ad number 4, the grainy, black-and-white extreme close-up is of a male model wearing reflective sunglasses in which 'Black' is mirrored in the tell-tale script of the label. The letters of 'The Legend Is Black'—which, by the way, play on 'the legend is back' (and reviving itself in the marketplace)—are at about a 45-degree angle down from left to right to the less radical off-angle of the sunglasses, which run up from left to right. The model's face is unexpressive.

Ad number 5 is the same type of photograph, this time of an LP disc with 'Black' in the place of the record label. Its minimalism and the predominance of the black of the LP lead the eye more readily to the white, broken letters that follow the curve of the LP about one-third of the way through the playing surface.

Finally, in ad number 6, we see an extreme close-up of the chest of a male model. His shirt cuff and part of his hand are coming across where the bottom of his face would be, which adds a visually interesting top border. The shirt is well worn and 'of a style', and the model is wearing three western string or bolo ties, all slightly askew. The top tie has a Black Label slide

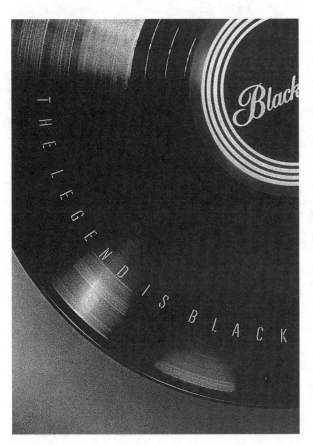

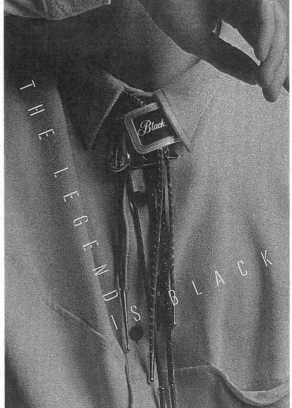

presented in a by-now-typical fashion, with only the word 'Black' visible. 'The Legend Is Black' is in the usual form, but radicalized somewhat by its angle of presentation and by being laid out in the form of an upper case 'L'.

The campaign—whether consciously or not—played on black as a sign (in the semiotic sense of the word), just as the brand loyalists were doing in their choice. Obviously, the whole campaign would have been different if the brand was Green Label. Black is oppositional, of the night, associated with evil, danger, rejection, rejection of colour. Our everyday language is full of allegory carried by black, as a black mood, a blackened reputation, a black mark, a black sky, a black sheep.

With black at the centre of the campaign, adding understated signifiers of the lifestyle of the brand loyalists as oppositional (in dyadic relation to) both to mainstream culture and to mainstream beer ads, Carling (later Molson) and Palmer Bonner (later Bozell Palmer Bonner) had a winning campaign. It was not based on demographics—that is, it did not try to reach as great a percentage of 25–35-year-olds as possible—and it was not intended to knock Labatt's Blue out of its top place. Rather, it was based on psychographics, designed to pick up market share by appealing to a segment of the market that possessed a certain set of attitudes. It also helped Bozell Palmer Bonner get established and, for a while, become the talk of the industry. What it 'signified' was that people who shared the values of the brand loyalists would share their beer.

While this ad campaign was put together some two decades ago, the semiotic strategies it deployed are still used by advertisers today. (Black Label Ad. Photos provided courtesy of Molson Canada.)

RELATED WEBSITES

Advertising Standards Canada: www.canada.com
A listing of Canadian advertising codes and guidelines, as well as information and reports on public complaints, can be found at this site.

Freedom Forum: www.freedomforum.org
This organization is committed to pursuing free speech and freedom of the press.

House of Commons Standing Committee Report on Communication and Culture: www.media-awareness.ca/eng/ISSUES/VIOLENCE/RESOURCE/reports/fraydoc.htm
Parts of the Committee's report, *Television Violence: Fraying Our Social Fabric*, are available at this site.

Media Awareness Network: www.medi-awareness.ca
The Media Awareness Network provides information and insightful analysis of various media issues, including violence in the media.

The Semiotics of Media:
www.uvm.edu/~tstreete/semiotics_and_ads/contents.html
A website on semiotics created by Prof. Tom Streeter of the University of Vermont.

FURTHER READINGS

Auletta, Ken. 1997. *The Highwaymen: Warriors of the Information Superhighway*. New York: Random House. Based on a series of interviews of media managers, Auletta's book is a biting commentary on the social responsibility of the media.

Eco, Umberto. 1986. 'The multiplication of the media', in Eco, *Travels in Hyperreality*. New York: Harcourt Brace Jovanovich, 148–69. This and the other essays provide delightful insights into the unrealities of representation.

Leiss, William, S. Kline, and Sut Jhally (rev. Jacqueline Botterill). 2005. *Social Communication in Advertising*, 3rd edn. New York: Routledge. This is an excellent history of advertising and the different ways advertising constructs relationships between people and products.

Mosco, Vincent. 1996. *The Political Economy of Communication*. Thousand Oaks, Calif.: Sage. A good overview of the history and application of the political economy of communication.

Media, Culture and Society. This journal is the pre-eminent British media studies journal founded in the 1970s by five young media scholars.

STUDY QUESTIONS

1. Use the encoding/decoding model to analyze a popular TV program such as *The Simpsons*. What kinds of shared ideas and social values do the programs writers draw on to tell the story? Why do you think the writers picked these to include in the program? How do the scheduling and structure of the program reflect the fact that it is a commercial television program?

2. Perform a semiotic analysis on a magazine advertisement for an automobile, cologne, or company. What are the signifiers used in constructing the ad? What are the signifieds? How do these work together to construct meaning? How many different meanings can be made from the ad?

3. Compare the libertarian, social responsibility, and political economic theories of the media. Which one seems to provide the most accurate perspective on how the media operate in our society?

4. Perform a content analysis on a major news story (the story may be covered over a number of days, in a number of articles, in a number of publications). Who are the major sources quoted in the story? What perspectives appear to be left out?

5. Select an up-market newspaper or magazine (for example, the *Globe and Mail*) and a down-market publication (for example, one of the *Sun* chain newspapers, but not the *Vancouver Sun*). Identify the major differences in treatment. Then turn to the various theoretical perspectives in this chapter and apply the most appropriate model. If your work is done as part of a group, compare and discuss your selections of theoretical models and findings.

6. 'Calvin Klein is a pernicious influence on society. The ads of this company demean and exploit human beings.' Discuss this statement. Be sure to include a consideration of polysemy.

7. Following Baudrillard, to what extent do you think that reality has been replaced by symbols and signs that refer only to other symbols and signs rather than to a grounded objective reality?

LEARNING OUTCOMES

- To inform students that the aim of the study of content is not to seek one true meaning of statements but rather to illustrate how rich statements are in their possibilities for interpretation.
- To introduce students to the concept of social theory as a means of uncovering the complexity of social communication.
- To introduce a number of terms often used in the analysis of content, including signification, indeterminacy of representation, intertextuality, polysemy, rhetoric, sign, signifier, and signified.
- To introduce different theories of the press.
- To introduce, for class discussion, various theoretical perspectives including literary criticism; structuralism, semiotics, and post-structuralism; discourse analysis; content analysis; critical political economy; and media form/genre analysis.
- To expand media form analysis into genre analysis, that is, a discussion of advertisements, news stories, television in comparison to print as a news medium, investigative television in comparison to print, soap operas, and music videos.
- To explain how the media select from the social world and represent those elements, thereby binding themselves to the culture of which they are a part.
- To provide a discussion of the constraints within which the media operate or, said oppositely, the degree to which the media can manipulate.
- To draw attention to the inherent reductionism in media treatment of any issue.
- To illustrate a semiotic analysis (through the appendix to the chapter).

CHAPTER 5

Theoretical Perspectives on Audiences

Introduction

As we have seen, media weave through our lives at many levels. At the political level, they help frame and animate our understanding of the events and circumstances that define citizenship, how society is organized politically, and our role and purpose in that organization. At the level of culture, media play on our knowledge of social groups, gender, and racial and ethnic distinctions. They also collude in our understanding of social roles (mother, child, teacher), organizations, and institutions. They address us as fans and devotees of particular media personalities and types of programs. And economically, they position us as consumers. In all these ways media frame and animate our sense of identity and provide an understanding of ourselves in relation to others and the world. By and large, however, the media address us as audiences, that is, as sets or groups of individuals for whom their content is designed. Media seek audiences: sometimes to inform, sometimes to enlighten, other times to entertain, and usually to sell to advertisers or pay a fee for the receipt of content. More recently, with the explosion of new, sometimes interactive media choices, people are increasingly able to set the terms of their participation as audience members and even contribute to media production. Still, to a large part, the overarching relation is one where content is designed for consumption by specific groups or types of individuals. However, as we shall see, how people interact with or interpret that content is another matter.

Media audiences are of interest to both academic

Ever since the television became a common household item, researchers have been interested in studying how audiences interact with this medium. (Library and Archives Canada/Richard Harrington/National Film Board of Canada. Photothèque collection/Accession 1971-271/PA-111390)

and industry researchers. Scholars and social scientists seek to understand the nature of the interaction between the media and their audiences; what audiences do with media content; how they engage with television, books, magazines, and music; how media influence perceptions and understandings of the world; and how they guide or influence social action. Members of the industry have a different agenda. They want to know the size and the demographic characteristics (age, gender, ethnicity) as well as other attributes of particular audiences, such as education, income level, and purchasing patterns, so they can define the product they are selling (the audience to the advertiser). Industry members also want to know how audiences respond to audience-building techniques so they can understand how to attract larger audiences or audiences with specific characteristics.

This chapter explores approaches to the audience. It begins with the academic perspectives and then turns to a discussion of industry measures of audiences. It ends with an appendix that provides a case study of audience measurement practices in the Canadian consumer magazine industry.

A Theoretical Synthesis of Meaning-Generating Systems

Audience members do not accept all of what they see or hear—whether the facts of a news story or the general portrayal of society and its values that a film, television show, or novel may contain. Not everyone who sits down in front of the TV brings all his or her critical faculties to bear on every program watched, nor to every piece of pulp fiction. And neither is it the case that audiences are generally composed of fragile beings desperately seeking simulated social contact and meaning through the media. Watching television, reading books or magazines, listening to music, and so on are largely casual leisure activities. And no research has ever shown that the media have the power to induce audience members to act against or outside their will.

Media–audience interaction is probably best thought of as a sometimes energetic, sometimes passive engagement between audience members and the media. Insofar as the media draw relations between audiences and a larger set of social values and institutions, this interaction also takes place at a social or cultural level. From this perspective, audience members, the media, and cultures can be usefully conceived of as closely woven **meaning-generating entities**.

Let us take an example. A young woman, home early from classes, tunes into WWE on TV to find Johnny Nitro and Ray Mysterio throwing each other around the wrestling ring. No one is home, least of all her brother, who left the television on this channel the day before. Though normally not a fan of wrestling, she can't find the remote so she watches for several minutes. Within those few minutes she finds that the bout is nothing special. 'Boring', she thinks, and looks harder for the remote.

While it may not seem like it, this instance exemplifies many of the elements of meaning generation. That is, our protagonist collects, analyzes, and synthesizes information in seconds. She immediately recognizes the scene and the characters and can sense if anything special is happening in this action soap opera directed at young men. She transforms the material on the screen by reconstructing the events in her terms and then re-expressing them, first by her implied lack of interest, and then by her renewed efforts to find the remote.

Is this interaction complex and multi-dimensional? Somewhat. Implicitly and from experience, our protagonist knows wrestling is not targeted at her. The fact that there are no ads relevant to her proves it. Were different, more interesting wrestlers in the ring, or were either of the wrestlers bellowing at the crowd, she might stay tuned for a little longer. Or were she at her boyfriend's house and he wanted to watch, she might stay with the program a while longer. The interaction is also mediated by choice. What do the other channels have to offer? What is in the fridge? How soon is her next assignment due? And so on. Also, her whole frame of mind in assessing whether to watch is characterized by her degree of engagement (very small) and subject to context that is situational (as explained above) and historical (she knows what wrestling is generally about and what tends to happen). Her action in looking for the remote, her sighs of boredom, her flop down on the couch in the first place are all part of her meaning generation.

Given these media–audience dynamics, where does culture as an active, meaning-generating entity figure in this scenario? Cultural dynamics play themselves out in the woman's vision of herself and the relevance of the program to her. Also, the fact that the program is aired in the first place and commands vast audiences is part of a cultural dynamic. Finally, the very scene of these modern gymnasts/gladiators heaving each other around in an action theatre of the absurd constitutes a cultural dimension.

Because the relation between media, audiences, and cultures is based on interaction and is not predetermined, any consideration of the interaction of audience behaviour, media content, and cultural form must take place within a very broad framework—one that has the potential to encompass any and all elements of the interaction. Audience interpretations of media content derive from at least the following factors: (a) the social background or 'history' of the audience member; (b) her/his current state of mind; (c) the social situation, or context, within which the media consumption is taking place; and (d) the text or content (see Lindlof, 1991). Given these criteria, we are able to understand the possible roots of our female viewer's behaviour. Nevertheless, a par-

ticular part of her personality or attitude in that moment might have caused her to behave differently. Also, days later she might make some comment derived from her brief exposure. The point of the analytical framework is not to predict audience reaction but rather to understand it.

Culture is a key element in this meaning-generating system. The individual's cultural milieu works to create identity through acting as the reference point to a host of factors, including social and familial customs, laws, various institutions that mediate interaction, governing structures, and opportunities afforded by cultural and physical geography. It is an ever-shifting totality derived from the wealth, history, and present-day attitudes and actions of groups and individuals. Through interactions based in this context, people then generate meaning in a particular style and in relation to the events of the day.

A TREATISE ON FAME

Is fame a media phenomenon? Is it a produced phenomenon or an interactional phenomenon between a celebrity and an audience?

Globe and Mail columnist Doug Saunders traces it back to Goethe, who with the publication of his novel *The Sorrows of Young Werther* caused Germans to imitate the dress and mannerisms of the protagonist and become obsessed with the author's private life. Fame is probably as old as humanity. What about Jesus Christ? His wrestling with fame was featured in the musical *Jesus Christ Superstar*. What about Mohammed? What about Ulysses and, for that matter, the Greek pantheon of gods?

Saunders suggests some other historical figures who had the quality of fame. Franz Liszt, in 1841, hired Gaetano Belloni to handle his tours, perhaps the first example of agents and managers. In turn Liszt was hired by Phineas T. Barnum, a man of fame himself, for millions of dollars to tour with 'The Greatest Show on Earth'. Charles Dickens had fame in 1858 in his author tour of Britain, the US, and Canada. Florence Lawrence also had it in 1910 when she became the first actor to receive a movie credit in her own name. In 1911 the first fan magazines were launched, which helped intensify fame for such actors as Toronto-born Mary Pickford. In 1942, singer Frank Sinatra started near-riots with his appearances and arguably became the first pop star. Orson Welles gained fame as a radio star with the broadcast of

War of the Worlds. In 1948 Milton Berle became a TV star. In 1960 John F. Kennedy became as much a political celebrity as a US President. In 1968 Pierre Trudeau followed suit in Canada. In 1990, following in the footsteps of other sports celebrities such as Babe Ruth, Michael Jordan signed a $100 million contract for endorsements of other products. And in 1997 US TV networks split their coverage between two celebrities, Bill Clinton giving his State of the Union address and the verdict on the trial of O.J. Simpson.

What may be a new twist on the peregrinations of fame is its explicit exploitation.

In the second part of his three-part series in the *Globe and Mail* (18 Dec. 2000, A11) Saunders talked about the renting of fame. Bo Derek (once ranked a '10' for her beauty by her marketing manager, who was also her husband) was hired to help George H.W. Bush reach a certain segment of the voting population of the US in his run for the presidency. President Bush's son, George W. Bush, used celebrities such as Arnold Schwarzenegger and Chuck Norris, just as Bill Clinton used Barbra Streisand and Richard Dreyfuss. The stars themselves sometimes have political advisers.

Understanding the dynamics of fame is interesting in itself. Understanding the appeal of celebrity is a separate and perhaps even more intriguing question.

Stated succinctly, lived reality at the level of the individual, the group, and the culture interacts with media realities through a constant process of mutual selection, restylization (or appropriation), transformation, and redisplay. This interaction is a continuous process of meaning-making and, as such, is a central element of human existence in modern society.

The study of audiences in all their manifestations and interactions can be approached in many different ways. We will examine six academic approaches to the audience: Marxist analysis and the Frankfurt School; effects research; uses and gratification research; (British) cultural studies; feminist research; and reception analysis (see also McQuail, 2000; Alasuutari, 1999; Lindlof, 1991; Jensen and Rosengren, 1990). As with the perspectives on content we examined in the last chapter, the point here is to provide an overview of some of the main ways audiences have been approached by researchers, as well as illustrate some of the key issues audience research has raised, not to present a comprehensive review of these perspectives.

Effects, Agenda-setting, and Cultivation Analysis

Early studies of the media following World War I (1914–18) presupposed media to have direct **effects** on human behaviour and attitudes. Fuelled by the success of propaganda campaigns during the war, which seemed to indicate that the masses would believe almost anything they were told, researchers posited the 'magic bullet' or 'hypodermic needle' theory of communication, built on the idea that media could basically inject ideas into people's heads. This perspective was supported by the social science of the day, which, on one hand, subscribed to the mass society thesis and, on the other, was animated by early behaviourist conceptions of psychology that saw human behaviour as a simple response to external stimuli. The success of newspaper and early radio advertising in stimulating demand for the growing range of products generated by industry during the interwar period added credence to this idea.

But while the success of war propagandists and early advertisers seemed to demonstrate that people were easily swayed by media suggestion, studies conducted after World War II (1939–45) found that the impact of media messages on individuals was weak

and, if anything, acted to reinforce existing ideas and beliefs rather than alter opinions. In a review of effects research published in 1960, Joseph Klapper, a respected media researcher of the day, concluded that 'mass communication does not ordinarily serve as a necessary or sufficient cause of audience effects, but rather functions through a nexus of mediating factors' (cited in McQuail, 2000: 415).

Having found weaker effects than anticipated, researchers undertook the task of reconceiving the relations between media and audiences and began to look for more diffuse, indirect effects. Working in this vein in the early 1960s, Bernard Cohen argued that news 'may not be successful in telling people what to think, but it is stunningly successful in telling its readers what to think about' (cited in Croteau and Hoynes, 2003: 242). For example, the front page of the *Globe and Mail* (and presumably, to a lesser extent, the *National Post* and the *Ottawa Citizen*) plays a significant role in what questions are asked that day in the House of Commons, as does the CBC news. This idea that the media serve an **agenda-setting function**, that they work, selectively, to draw the public's attention to particular events and circumstances, has gained a measure of credibility among media researchers.

On another front, beginning with George Gerbner (1969, 1977) researchers have also examined the effects of viewing behaviour on people's conception of social reality, a perspective that has evolved into what is called **cultivation analysis**, wherein content is studied for its ability to encourage or cultivate particular attitudes in viewers towards particular persons or perspectives (see Morgan and Signorelli, 1990). For instance, Gerbner's work illustrated that people who watch a great deal of television overestimate the amount of violence in society and tend to have a 'bunker mentality' to protect themselves from what they perceive to be a violent world. However, in spite of the broad acceptance of Gerbner's work, certain British studies (e.g., Wober and Gunter, 1986) have not been able to replicate his findings.

Effects analysis has been greatly criticized, essentially because researchers have not identified clear, strong effects of media exposure. In short, the problem rests on the fact that the effects approach abstracts the process of communication from its social context and tries to draw a straight line between sender and receiver. Just as the Shannon and Weaver model of communication discussed in Chapter 1 was shown to be too simplistic to account for the myriad influences on the ways media messages are constructed, so the effects model does not illustrate the many influences on decoding. From this perspective, human agency is reduced to a simple reaction to content; there is no consideration of how a larger set of social characteristics and forces—age, gender, education, etc.—come to bear on media reception. For example, in regard to media seeming to have a negative effect on someone's actions, what in the person's background could make her or him vulnerable to internalizing a message in a specific way or perhaps to act in an aberrant fashion? Obviously, from this perspective, discussion of the effects of media on individuals can be problematic.

Research on agenda-setting suffers from similar problems. It offers no explanation for how or why the media select what they will cover or what forces might be at play to help sensitize audiences to be receptive to messages. As the encoding/decoding model outlined in Chapter 4 illustrates, the media draw their material from a larger set of social circumstances. Perhaps the news agenda is set in this context, by local, national, and world events. On the other hand, perhaps the agenda is set by public or audience demand, or possibly it is an interaction between media institutions, audiences, and this larger set of social circumstances. In short, the effects tradition of media research raises more questions than it answers.

Moreover, when concerns over media effects are raised it is interesting who gets condemned and who does not for putting forward certain media constructions. German film director Leni Riefenstahl, who died at the age of 101 in September 2003, was never forgiven for her movies *Triumph of the Will* (1934–5) and *Olympia* (1936–8), which portrayed Hitler's Nazis in a heroic light. In contrast, D.W. Griffith, whose *Birth of a Nation* (1916) portrays African Americans as ignorant and crude, is considered a pioneer of American film. Oliver Stone has also escaped condemnation for his movie *Natural Born Killers* (1994) even though copycat crimes were committed in its wake. Stanley Kubrick, on the other hand, withdrew *A Clockwork Orange* (1971) from circulation in Britain after some of its violence was re-enacted in real life (*Globe and Mail*, 22 Aug. 2002). The debate around such movies can often deteriorate into a crude effects theory discussion. Little attention is paid to the social circumstances—such as poverty, inequality, racial dis-

crimination, child and sexual abuse—that animate real-life violence.

Uses and Gratification Research

Uses and gratification research (U&G) began both as a response to findings of limited effects and as a reaction to the growing concern, rooted in the mass society debates, that 'popular culture'—the wide variety of new television, radio, and musical content that started to gain popularity in the 1950s—was undermining or debasing audience tastes (Blumler and Katz, 1974). Based in social psychology, instead of foregrounding what media do to audiences, its central question is, 'What do audiences do with the media?' The underlying premise was to focus on the agency of audience members and explore their motivations in the active selection of media content. Take, for example, two university students who decide to see an action movie after their last exam of the semester. They are not even at the movie yet but uses and gratification theory is already relevant. Going to a movie provides a good chance to relax, get together with friends, enjoy whatever is of interest in the movie, and go out for a coffee afterwards to socialize. Movies give people a chance to talk about other, related interests.

In contrast to effects research, the U&G approach is more attentive to audience variables, that is, the orientations and approaches audience members bring to their selection and interpretation of media content. Given its roots in social psychology, U&G has concentrated on the micro (personal) and meso (group or institutional) levels of social existence, with little attention paid to the macro level—the social, ideological, cultural, or political orientations of the audience. Work during the eighties spoke of never-ending spirals of uses and effects in which audience members look to the media for certain information (Rosengren and Windahl, 1989). Having gained this information, they behave in a particular way and then return to the media for further information, and so on. In fact, the two areas—effects research and uses and gratification research—have been growing increasingly closer together and are, to a degree, complementary.

But while U&G put more emphasis on agency than effects theory, it still focused on abstracting media consumption from the larger social context. Media consumption is reduced to an individual process or relationship. The influence of larger social factors on either why only particular forms of content are presented or why particular audience members choose particular kinds of content are ignored or not fully explored. Moreover, U&G is open to the charge of being functionalist. That is, it is built on the assumption that media function to serve some kind of need on the part of audience members and then sets out to discover what that need is. There is no account of either the larger social origins of this seeming need or the ways the process of media consumption itself plays into a larger set of social forces and institutions. In other words, not considered are the larger social purposes or role of media and how audience uses and understandings of media are given form by a larger set of social conditions.

Marxist Analysis and the Frankfurt School

As discussed in Chapter 4, Marxism sees society as animated by a set of social forces based on capitalist forms of production. Working from this larger frame, Marxist perspectives on the media, such as those seen in Chapter 4, generally focus on how the media work to support dominant interests in society, helping them maintain power and control over time. Consequently, Marxist perspectives don't generally focus on media–audience relations per se and/or on the ways media interact with or impinge on the agency of individual audience members. Rather, Marxist critics consider the ways in which media work to integrate audiences into the larger capitalist system.

One of the most far-reaching and influential Marxist-based critiques of twentieth-century media and culture comes from a group known as the **Frankfurt School**. The leading members of this group of intellectuals were Max Horkheimer, Theodor Adorno, and Herbert Marcuse, and their ideas were formed in the interwar period (1920–40) (see Jay, 1974, for a critical history of the work of the Frankfurt School up to the 1950s). At first they worked at the Institute for Social Research attached to the University of Frankfurt (hence the Frankfurt School), but when Hitler came to power, because they were Jews and their ideas were fundamentally out of step with fascism, they had to leave Germany, eventually settling in the US. Adorno and Horkheimer found faculty positions at Columbia University, where they remained until after World War II. (In the late 1940s Adorno and Horkheimer returned, with great honour, to Frankfurt, where they continued to work in the university until the 1970s.) Marcuse (1954, 1964) settled in San Francisco, where he made his major contributions, remained in the US, and became an intellectual hero of the counterculture in the 1960s.

These intellectuals argued that capitalist methods of mass production had a profound impact on modern cultural life. Capitalist methods had been applied, in the last century, to the manufacture of the necessities of life, that is, material goods like machinery and clothing. Beginning in the 1920s, though interrupted by the Great Depression and World War II, capitalism was applied to the production of what we now call consumer goods, a new range of goods, products, or commodities. With the help of advertising, families were persuaded that the essence of modern life was the acquisition of such goods—the family car, gas and electric ovens, fridges, washing machines, the latest fashions in clothes, and other personal items. New forms of mass communication such as cinema, radio, and photography (in newspapers and magazines), complete with formulaic and commercial content, became woven into this way of life. These new forms, on one hand, were subject in their development, manufacture, and distribution to capitalist methods of mass production; on the other hand, they displaced older high cultural forms of leisure and entertainment such as symphonies, the ballet, plays, poetry, and great literature. At the same time, the media also served as a key vehicle for celebrating and helping integrate people into this new commercial way of life. Adorno and Horkheimer pooled these developments together under an umbrella term: the culture industry (Adorno and Horkheimer, 1977 [1947]).

The Frankfurt School argued that through such developments industrial capitalism penetrated ever deeper into cultural life and began creating a whole, ready-made way of life. In this context, people's wants and desires were both created and satisfied through the marketplace. Building on the concerns of the mass society theorists that industrial society heralded a loss of social and cultural values, Adorno and Horkheimer saw marketers rushing to fill this void with a never-ending parade of commodities. The problem, however, was that this new way of life itself was devoid of any deeper meaning or understanding of the world. The pleasures derived from consumption were fleeting, lasting only as long as it took for new commodities to come on the market. The distinctions between different makes, models, and brands are largely illusory and based on quickly shifting styles rather than substantive qualities or characteristics. Popular films and music are all formulaic, their plots and rhythms easily recognized and understood. And in the ongoing churn of the market, no lasting relationships or deeper understandings of the world might be made.

From this perspective culture and the media serve only one master: capital. All culture is a product of industrial capitalism and the guiding logic is one of profit for the capitalist. There is no active audience, nor is there the possibility of the media acting as a venue for democratic discussion of issues of public concern. Media effects, uses, and gratifications are all buried under the larger domination of culture and the media by the rhythms and needs of capital. Audience members are seen as little more than cultural dupes, or as Smythe (1995: 9) puts it, unpaid 'workers' for the capitalist 'consciousness industry' who are inexorably drawn, via the media, into a prepackaged world where choice is simply an illusion that supports this domination. (For a critique of this reading of Adorno and Horkheimer, see Gunster, 2004.)

The Frankfurt School members have been accused of cultural elitism and pessimism. Perhaps most importantly, from this perspective there is little or no human agency. The audience is simply a tool of the capitalist economy, and very few people today would suggest that the culture industry (a useful term) has the entirely negative effects that the Frankfurt School claimed it did.

Nevertheless, the members of the Frankfurt School were right to point out the importance of analyzing this industry as integral to capitalism and to question critically its impact and effect on contemporary cultural life. The issues they addressed have a continuing relevance. Since they first developed their analysis, we have seen the continuing expansion of the cultural industries to the extent that they now circulate throughout the world. The *Lord of the Rings* movie trilogy, for instance, was not just a movie of special effects and important ideas; it was a marketing extravaganza. Equally, Disneyland, Walt Disney World, Disneyland Paris, and Tokyo Disneyland are part of a global process whereby tourism and entertainment converge in a marriage of the leisure and culture industries to reduce the world to a series of theme parks. Thanks to TV we've all been there and done that, and it all looks the same, partly because you can stay in the same hotels and buy the same things in the same shops in the same shopping malls around the

ON THE BIRMINGHAM SCHOOL

An article by Norma Schulman on the beginnings and impact of the Centre for Contemporary Cultural Studies at the University of Birmingham can be found on the website of the *Canadian Journal of Communication*: www.cjc-online.ca. For Schulman's article, follow the links through back issues to vol. 18, no. 1 and to the full text of the article: www.cjc-online.ca/viewarticle.php?id=140&layout=html.

world. The trends the Frankfurt School identified years ago today dominate the globe.

British Cultural Studies

British cultural studies began as a reaction against the ways Marxist and other media theories both downplayed the role of human agency and discounted the seeming pleasures of popular culture. The impact of the growing mass culture in post-war Britain, particularly on the working class, was of interest to a number of intellectuals in the 1950s, such as Richard Hoggart (1992 [1957]) and Raymond Williams (1958). To advance his concerns, Hoggart established a small post-graduate Centre for Contemporary Cultural Studies at the University of Birmingham, which his colleague Stuart Hall took over in the late 1960s. Hall's work in the 1970s with graduate students in what came to be called the **Birmingham School** of cultural studies was increasingly influential and largely defines what is today known as cultural studies.

There are many accounts of the short history of British cultural studies from the 1950s to the present (see Turner, 1990; McGuigan, 1992; Storey, 1993; Schulman, 1993). Two main lines of development can be identified: the analysis of working-class culture, particularly the culture of young working-class males, and then, in response to feminist critiques at the Centre, the analysis of young working-class females (Women's Studies Group, 1978). A central concern was the use of mass culture, by both sexes, to create and define gendered identities. What clothing you chose to wear, the kind of music you listened to, whether you had, for instance, a motorcycle or a scooter—these things helped create your image and define your personality. Instead of individuals being manipulated by the products of mass culture—as the Frankfurt School had argued—it was the other way around. Individuals could take these products and manipulate them, subvert them, to create new self-definitions. The classic study of this process is Dick Hebdige's *Subculture: The Meaning of Style* (1979), which looked at how young, white, working-class males created identities for themselves through music: from mods and rockers in the 1950s and 1960s through to punk and beyond in the 1970s. Cultural studies paid particular attention to the ambiguous relationship between musical styles and social identities and to the embrace of black music and the culture of young, black males by young, white, working-class males. This is captured beautifully in the 1991 film *The Commitments*, based on the Roddy Doyle novel, when the protagonist, Jimmy Rabbitte, has assembled a group of working-class Dublin youth to become an R&B band and asks them to repeat after him, 'I'm black and I'm proud.' But while cultural studies illustrated that the appropriation of meaning was much more complex than previously thought, it also demonstrated that social forces and institutions worked in complex ways to help reproduce the dominant order. For instance, in his classic study of an English high school Paul Willis (1977) shows how rebellion against established authority leads working-class youth to working-class jobs.

On the media front, another important strand in the study of contemporary culture was analysis of film and television. In the 1970s the British Film Institute's journal, *Screen*, put forward a structuralist-inspired analysis of film arguing that how a story was told (through techniques of editing, visual images, and so forth) controlled and defined the viewer. The narrative techniques of cinema subtly but powerfully imposed their meanings on the spectator, who could not avoid being 'positioned' to see the film in a particular way. (The notion of 'position' refers particularly to the point of view constructed for the viewer through filmic techniques—how the viewer is 'put in the picture'.) In a classic analysis of Hollywood movies, Laura Mulvey (1975) argued that the pleasures of this kind of cinema were organized for a male viewer and that women (both in the storyline and as objects to be looked at) were merely instruments of male pleasure—objects of a male gaze.

Stuart Hall and his students, undertaking an analysis of how television and other media worked, wanted to develop a more open kind of analysis. They argued that media content was structured to relay particular meanings—preferred readings—to audiences, but that it was quite possible for audiences to refuse that meaning and develop their own interpretation of what they heard and saw (Glasgow Media Group, 1976).

The key concept in such analysis is **ideology**. (The meaning of ideology has been much discussed—see Johnston, 1996; Larrain, 1979, 1983; Thompson, 1980 [1963].) There are several different definitions of ideology at play. In one sense, it refers to a coherent set of social values, beliefs, and meanings that people use to decode the world (for example, neo-liberalism and socialism). In Marxist terms, it refers to a particular set of ideas, values, and beliefs—those that support the dominant or ruling class. For instance, under capitalism such ideas as 'the poor are lazy', 'capitalism is the only viable economic system', and 'unions and strikes are bad for society' are promulgated. Through this ideological misrepresentation of social reality, the working class is prevented from understanding how they are exploited or oppressed and come to accept the values of the ruling class. In other words, they have been lured into a 'false consciousness', a false understanding of how capitalist society works. Thus, from this perspective, ideology is a way of representing the world to oneself, a set of ideas that one uses to impose order on society and to decide what place different people and groups should occupy in the social order. By presenting versions of social reality that represent the existing order as natural, obvious, right, and just—in short, as the way things are and ought to be—the effect of ideology is to maintain the status quo, that is, the domination of the powerful over the powerless.

In the face of the social unrest of the 1960s and 1970s—the civil rights movement in the US, the rise of feminism throughout the Western world, and the student movement in Canada, the US, and several European countries—some social scientists began to argue that there was more than one form of ideological oppression at play. Not only did ideology keep the workers in a subordinate position, but it also did the same for women, people of colour, and a range of other social groups. Indeed, through their acts of protest, these groups illustrated that they had their own ideas about how the social world should be structured and what their positions in that world should be. In short, they had their own ideologies. Hence, the question became, 'Amid all of these possible competing ideologies why is it that the one that generally helps keep wealthy white males in positions of power seems to prevail?'

Exploring this question in the British context, cultural studies researchers argued that British television reproduced the dominant value system—loosely understood as a paternalistic class-based consensus that believed in the monarchy, the Anglican Church, Parliament, and the rule of law, among other things (Hall, 1978, 1980). For instance, television news and current affairs programs are a major vehicle for reproducing dominant values: powerful **primary definers** (interviewed politicians, experts, the military) are routinely allowed to define the issues, express their opinions, and offer interpretations of events and circumstances (Hall et al., 1978). Alternative or oppositional interpretations of events are seldom, if ever, allowed expression. An extreme example of this in Britain was the banning of members of Sinn Fein (the political wing of the Irish Republican Army [IRA]) from British TV (see Curtis, 1984; Schlesinger, 1983). On the home front, another example is how, in Chapter 4, we saw that NewsWatch Canada found that over a certain period right-wing think-tanks were quoted three times more often than left-wing think-tanks in Canadian television news programs (Hackett and Gruneau, 2004). Similarly, television dramas, films, song lyrics, popular novels, etc. can all be seen as a set of morality tales from which we are to take lessons in what constitutes desirable and undesirable behaviour. Moreover, when media products fail to conform to dominant values they are often seen to cause negative effects, which illustrates the point that a **dominant ideology** helps to define these other perspectives as 'dangerous'.

Hall argued that, despite the fact that they reflected the dominant ideology, these media presentations can be decoded by viewers in very different ways (Hall, 1978). Indeed, as the protests of the 1960s—as well as those of today—demonstrate, all people do not decode either the media or social life in general in the same way. Depending on their social background—gender, class, race, ethnicity, culture—people often hold different and/or competing ideologies and articulate meaning differently. In other words, although a dominant ideology may be reflected in media products, there is no necessity that they be read or understood that way.

While this idea that audiences decode information in a range of different ways is now taken as a given, a study by David Morley (1980)—a graduate of the Birmingham School—was an important step in establishing this perspective. Morley looked at how viewers of a 1970s BBC program called *Nationwide* interpreted, made sense of, or decoded the program. He found, as Hall had suggested, three different responses: dominant, negotiated, and oppositional. Some viewers accepted the values of the program, which stressed national unity and strong family values, suggesting that Britain was essentially a nation of white, middle-class families living in suburbia. These viewers accepted the program's preferred meaning, this consensual, harmonious representation of British society that systematically filtered out the conflicting interests of marginalized social groups (that is, marginalized by this definition). Other viewers took a rather more critical or negotiated view of the program, while a few groups of viewers (notably young blacks) rejected it altogether.

Spurred by the work of the Birmingham School, through the 1980s and 1990s the cultural studies approach increasingly concentrated on how audiences made sense of the media (White and Schwoch, 2006; Lee, 2003). Audience theorist Ien Ang's (1985) study of how Dutch viewers responded to *Dallas*—an American prime-time TV soap opera of the day—is a well-known example. The approach rejected the strongly deterministic view of the Frankfurt School and the journal *Screen*, stressing that media consumption was an active process. It also illustrated how, far from being the lowly, simple cousin of high culture, popular culture was a rich and dynamic field, filled with a complex range of social meanings.

Feminist Research

Feminist media studies have much in common with cultural studies (see Franklin et al., 1992). The feminist approach developed from French writer Simone de Beauvoir's *The Second Sex* (1957 [1949]) and the writings of Betty Friedan (1963) in the US. Like Marxism, feminism is deeply critical of the character of modern societies, which, it argues, are based on fundamental inequalities. But where Marxism locates the roots of inequality in capital ownership and class division, feminism points to the male domination (patriarchy) of society as the root of profound human inequalities and injustices. These inequalities are pervasive aspects of modern life: men have economic, political, and cultural power; women do not. Men generally control public life, while women occupy the resigned marginal spaces of private life and domesticity.

How is it that these values (of patriarchy) continue to have such power? To answer this, critics studied how cultural products can contribute to normalizing the oppression of women. Advertisements were one obvious place to look (Williamson, 1978), and film, television, and popular fiction provided other avenues (Media Education Foundation, 2002). Feminist researchers developed the idea of gendered narratives (Laura Mulvey's work on film was influential here): types of stories (narrative genres) appeal or speak to male readers or viewers (adventure stories like the Western or James Bond novels are classic examples), while other types appeal to female readers and viewers (Radway, 1984, is the key text). Likewise, they looked at gendered television: feminist audience studies discovered the kind of radio and TV programs that women preferred (see, e.g., Hobson, 1980, 1982). David Morley (1986) studied TV viewers in family settings and discovered a consistent profile of male and female preferences. One principal program category was TV soap operas with their largely female viewing audiences, and many studies have since examined what women enjoy in such programs (Seiter et al., 1989, review previous work).

But while providing key insights into the structure of media texts, some of this early work has been criticized for its lack of theorization of the ways in which women 'read' media texts and incorporate them into their lives. For instance, Ien Ang and Joke Hermes (1991) argue that certain feminists seem to have accepted a crude inoculation model of media effects on women derived from effects theory (i.e., the media inject audiences with meanings) and underline the necessity of investigating how women negotiate with the 'texts' they encounter in the media.

Since its early days, **feminist media research** has expanded to include a wide range of inquiry. For instance, Andrea Press (2000: 28–9) illustrates that feminist scholarship has at least three sometimes overlapping dimensions. The first looks at '[f]eminism, difference and identity' and 'highlights the experiences of those who have remained unheard and gives voice to that which has remained unspoken.' Here, analysis focuses on how media representation and social discourse override or frame out particular perspectives and voices. A second strand of research, 'feminism and the public sphere', emphasizes the 'role of the media

in facilitating—or hindering—public debate', particularly in terms of 'giving voice to those previously unheard, such as women, under-represented groups, and others whose ideas have not previously entered public debate.' For instance, in the context of new media, Shade (in Grossberg et al., 2006: 291) points out, 'There are tensions in gender differences, whereby women are using the Internet to reinforce their private lives and men are using the Internet for engaging in the public sphere.' The third dimension, 'new technologies and the body', considers 'broader questions about media, technology, and the relationship of both to the body' (Press, 2000: 29).

At a more general level, recent feminist scholarship examines how media consumption is woven into patterns of everyday life and how women and other social groups deploy media, along with other facets of their experience, to make meaning of their lives (Hermes, 2006).

Reception Analysis

In the 1980s cultural and feminist studies of the mass media increasingly looked at how audiences made sense of cultural products, how they interpreted what they read, saw, and heard. But it became apparent that to do this, it was necessary to attend not simply to the product itself (the novel, the film, the TV drama), but also, more generally, to the context in which the consumption of the cultural product took place. **Reception analysis** thus takes into account the social setting in which audiences respond to the products of contemporary popular culture and in this way is somewhat similar to uses and gratifications theory. However, rather than emphasizing what use or gratification an audience member gains from media exposure, reception analysis focuses on how he or she actively interprets what the media text has to offer and how media consumption is re-integrated into the personal dimensions of her or his life. As Gray (1999: 31) puts it, this work 'place[s] media readings and use within complex webs of determinations, not only of the texts, but also those deeper structural determinants, such as class, gender, and . . . race and ethnicity. These studies have also shed light on the ways in which public and private discourses intersect and are lived out within the intimate and routine practices of everyday life.'

Reception analysis has been of particular interest to feminist scholars in a number of ways. For one thing, the household is a prime site for cultural consumption by women. When US researcher Janice Radway studied American women readers of romantic fiction she found that they emphasized how the activity of reading became a special, personal time when they left behind domestic chores, responsibilities to husbands and children, and created a time and space for themselves and their own pleasure. They saw it as a moment of self-affirmation (Radway, 1984). This discovery points to the importance of attending to what lies outside the cultural products themselves. The meaning of romance fiction for Radway's readers was something more than the form and content of the stories themselves. It resonated with integral elements of their lives.

In the same way that Radway examined romance reading, work was undertaken on how family members use radio, TV, newspapers, magazines, VCRs, and satellite dishes. It showed that these media can be used for a range of purposes that have little to do with their content. A parent may watch a TV program with a child to nourish their relationship rather than to tune in to what the program is actually about. The dynamics of power relations between males and females, parents and children, and older and younger siblings have been studied in relation to, for instance, who has access to the remote control for the TV or who can work the VCR (Morley, 1986).

Here, the attention is directed towards what the audience brings to a viewing or decoding, the social context, and the act of viewing. Media researchers J. Bryce (1987), Peter Collett and R. Lamb (1986), D. Hobson (1980), and Tania Modleski (1984) have all described how various groups—women, men, families—watch television. Women, for instance, often juggle television-watching with domestic chores. Children often play while watching TV and look up when their ears tell them that the plot is thickening. Men often watch programs not of their own choosing. In some families and at some times, a switched-on television functions as a conversation stopper or mediator rather than a source of watched programming.

British media scholar Paddy Scannell (1988) has analyzed the manner in which broadcasting works at the level of individual audience members to sustain the lives and routines of whole populations, while researchers Roger Silverstone (1981) and John Hartley (1987) have discussed how television provides the basis for symbolic participation in a national community, or sometimes, as in the cases of Belgium, Switzerland, and Canada, an international linguistic community.

More recently, researchers have begun to explore how new media are changing people's perception of themselves, offering new avenues for identity formation. For instance, through a series of case studies, Sherry Turkle (1995) illustrates how computers with their access to chat rooms, on-line games, and other web offerings are providing what Andrea Press and Sonia Livingstone (2006: 189) describe as 'a more malleable notion of "self"'.

Thus, from the perspective of reception analysis, an 'audience' is not so much a group as a set of ever-shifting individuals whose lives (as well as the meaning of media consumption) are structured between media texts and the shifting dimensions and determinants of their own lives. In other words, media are seen as one element in a larger set of institutions, technologies, and discourses that provide the means through which people live their lives.

Industry Audience Research

While academics have had their own reasons for studying mass media audiences, media institutions themselves have long been keenly interested in finding out what people read, listen to, and watch. Such information has practical value. It enables TV or radio stations, for instance, to identify their audiences and discover their listening or viewing habits and preferences. Industry-led research on audiences attends to basic issues, such as when people are available or not to listen or watch, and when exactly they are watching or listening (audience habits). Given this, they can also find out what audiences like or dislike (audience tastes). This information has obvious economic value: the more precise the information they have about their own and their competitors' audiences, the greater are the possibilities to sell these audiences to advertisers or to improve their product (to attract even more advertisers).

Traditionally, such research concentrated on audience size: the bigger the audience for a TV program, the more attractive it would be to advertisers. But since the 1970s, industry researchers have tried to provide more accurate information about what kinds of viewers are attracted to which programs. A program could have a very large audience, but a large portion of this audience may not have much disposable income. A program with a smaller audience with

THEORETICAL PERSPECTIVES ON AUDIENCES

LEND ME YOUR EARS AND I'LL GIVE YOU WHITE BREAD

Why are radio stations as bland as sliced white bread? The answer, according to Bill Reynolds, former editor-in-chief of *eye Weekly* in Toronto, is corporate concentration and vertical integration. Reynolds (2002: R1, R5) notes, 'In 1995, for example, Clear Channel Communications [the dominant radio owner in the US] owned 43 radio stations; now it owns more than 1,200. . . . a subsidiary, Clear Channel Entertainment, . . . has become a prominent promoter, producer and marketer of live events operating out of more than 400 venues in the US and Canada.' This interpretation is really a political-economic analysis of content (see Chapter 4).

'In Canada,' Reynolds continues, 'Corus radio is the largest owner with 52 stations reaching 8.4 million Canadians per week. Corus controls both the classic rock and new rock formats in two major markets—Q107 and Edge 102 in Toronto, and Rock 101 and CFOX in Vancouver. . . . The corporate motivation is to keep those lists [playlists] as tight and familiar as possible, right across the country. . . . Research shows that tight formatting works. Stations carry only 35 'currents', or new songs, and change between three and five songs per week. . . . [For radio] losing one percentage point of market share can mean as much as $1.5 million in lost annual revenue.'

The 'research' of which Reynolds speaks is industry research on the size and nature of the audience, how long they listen, etc. Reynolds goes on to explain that it falls to the radio-promotion representatives of the record companies and, in the US, independent promoters to get untried and untested songs played. The independent promoters actually pay radio stations between $100,000 and $400,000 for the right to represent them and in turn the record companies pay these promoters $800 to $5,000 for each song added to the station (depending on market size). As if that were not enough to insult the listener's right to choose, Clear Channel can charge the independent promoters up to $500,000 per year for the privilege of pitching songs to the conglomerate. Reynolds notes that most claim that pay-for-play does not exist in Canada, but he also notes that if one does not consider the 35 per cent Canadian content requirement, the playlists of Canadian and US radio stations look remarkably similar.

This side of communications businesses does not receive as much attention as it should. The vast majority of the material that audiences see in newspapers or on television, in movie theatres or in magazines, as well as what they listen to on radio, is the result of major marketing efforts of producers.

Of course, in any business things never stand still. University-based radio stations, co-op stations such as CFRO in Vancouver and Radio CINQ in Montreal, and others, such as the Beat at 94.5 FM in Vancouver, are breaking the mould. And deejays at clubs also are a separate force in the music world. But like the big beer makers in contrast to the microbreweries, the availability of mainstream product will continue to dominate.

greater spending power may be more valuable to advertisers than a large general audience. For instance, a program may not reach a mass prime-time audience, yet it may have a strong viewership among young, affluent professionals, and hence can command premium prices on advertisements. The specific makeup of an audience can also attract advertisers. For instance, for the makers of Barbie, an audience of prepubescent girls and their mothers is of great value. This targeting of audiences with very specific demographics is called narrowcasting.

Narrowcasting has been given impetus by the explosion of new broadcast channels. Over the last 25 years, the number of television channels available to Canadian audiences has mushroomed from less than 20 to several hundred. This has led to severe audience fragmentation, as the available television audience has been scattered across this expanding television landscape, not to mention the increasing draw of the internet. For instance, in 1969, 35 per cent of the English-speaking television audience watched the CBC while 25 per cent watched CTV. In 2001–2, however, only 7.6 per cent watched CBC at any given time and CTV was down to 11 per cent (Standing Committee on Canadian Heritage, 2003). As discussed in Chapter 8, fragmenting audiences have put pressure on broadcast companies to find innovative ways to reach large numbers of people. This has led to concentration of media ownership as companies work to reach or re-aggregate audiences through owning a number of different television channels or media outlets. Audience fragmentation has also led media companies that have traditionally owned broadcast and newspaper outlets to buy web-based media, such as News Corporation's 2006 purchase of MySpace.com.

In this context, three important concepts basic to institutional audience research are:

1. reach: the number of potential audience members during a particular program period, i.e., the number of people who are actually watching television during a specific time period;
2. share: the percentage of the audience 'reach' who are watching a particular program during a specific time period;
3. viewing time: the time spent viewing expressed over the period of a day, week, or longer period of time.

Share is generally the most important statistic as it describes what percentage of the available audience is tuned in to a particular program.

Formative research and summative research (see Withers and Brown, 1995) are other approaches to measuring the appeal of TV programming. **Formative research** is undertaken during production, usually by means of focus groups, to obtain reactions to programs in the making. **Summative research** measures the effectiveness of a program after its completion.

Both commercial media outlets and public media institutions conduct audience research. By 1936, for instance, the BBC had set up its own listener research department to answer questions about listener habits and preferences, such as when people get up, go to work, return from work, and go to bed. The same department took over responsibility for television once it was established. Do people watch more TV in the winter than in summer? Do people in certain locations watch more or less than viewers elsewhere? As they answered such questions, media managers could schedule programs to conform to the daily habits and routines of the British people (Scannell, 1988). The BBC also undertook research into audience preferences: what kinds of music did people prefer to listen to—dance band music or orchestral music, opera, chamber music, or other? BBC audience research provided answers to such questions and helped broad-

casters determine how much of each kind of music they ought to play over the air (on early BBC audience research, see Pegg, 1983; Scannell and Cardiff, 1991).

In Canada the CBC took on many of the same research tasks as the BBC but they grew out of a slightly different context (Eaman, 1994). As early as the 1920s in North America, individuals were attempting to set up procedures to measure radio audiences. There was even an early electronic device, the audimeter, designed to record the stations that were being heard in the home.

In October 1936, one month before the CBC began operations, Montrealer Walter Elliott set up an independent market research operation with a partner, Paul Haynes, to serve both the CBC and commercial broadcasters (ibid.). Various other individuals and companies followed over the years, but while they were successful in a commercial context they did not serve the interests of the CBC very well. The most obvious example of their failings came in the form of the ratings of a CBC radio station operating out of Watrous, Saskatchewan. Even though it was well known that this station was listened to throughout the Prairies and even into British Columbia, surveys carried out by Elliott-Haynes showed the audience share to be almost nothing. The main reason for this inaccuracy seemed to be that the company only surveyed urban areas, and it did so within a limited time period and by telephone. Later work showed that CBC in Watrous was in fact the most listened-to station in Saskatchewan.

For years the CBC attempted to use commercial audience research services, though it realized their shortcomings. By 1954 the need for high-quality audience research for public broadcasting had become more than obvious. Moreover, the conceptualization of what information was needed had advanced beyond audience share to qualitative information. So, following the lead of the BBC, the CBC set up its own research department.

Eaman has summarized the types of research undertaken by the CBC over the years:

- the impact of cable on television viewing;
- methodological analysis;
- critiques of other studies;
- indirect indicators of audience demand;
- program balance analysis;
- analysis of Canadian content and gender roles;
- effects analysis;

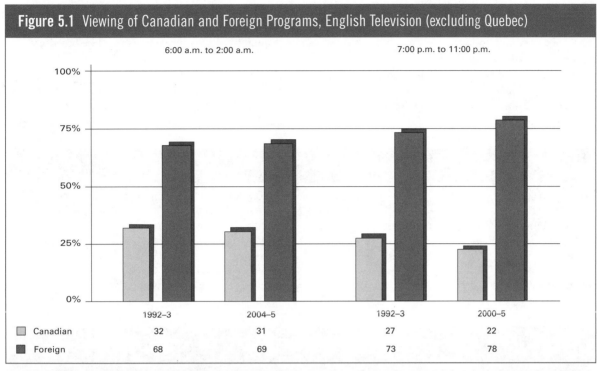

Figure 5.1 Viewing of Canadian and Foreign Programs, English Television (excluding Quebec)

	6:00 a.m. to 2:00 a.m.		7:00 p.m. to 11:00 p.m.	
	1992–3	2004–5	1992–3	2000–5
Canadian	32	31	27	22
Foreign	68	69	73	78

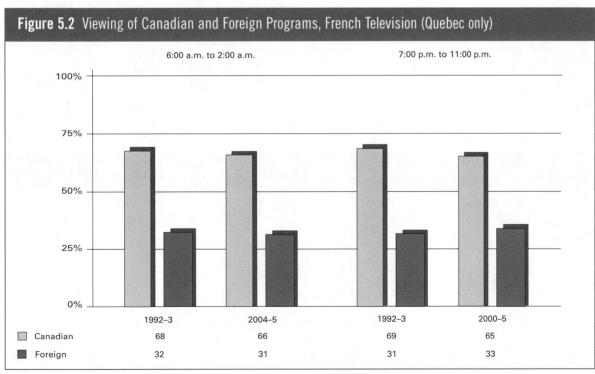

Figure 5.2 Viewing of Canadian and Foreign Programs, French Television (Quebec only)

	6:00 a.m. to 2:00 a.m.		7:00 p.m. to 11:00 p.m.	
	1992–3	2004–5	1992–3	2000–5
Canadian	68	66	69	65
Foreign	32	31	31	33

Traditionally, English Canadians have watched more foreign than Canadian content while Quebecers, partly as a result of language differences, have watched more Canadian than foreign content. Figures 5.1 and 5.2 compare viewership over two periods for overall and prime-time viewing and for English-language and French-language television. Source: Nielsen Media Research in CBC, 'Broadcasting Public Notice CRTC 2006–72 Comments of the CBC/Radio-Canada', at: www.cbc.radio-canada.ca/submissions/2006.shtml

- awareness analysis;
- research on audience maximization;
- audience composition;
- special broadcasts audiences;
- audience behaviour, that is, how often people listen to and/or watch what and when;
- habits and interests of certain age groups;
- comparisons of certain audiences to the general population;
- opinions of programs by audiences;
- opinions of what programs should be broadcast.

Understanding television consumption is important if policy-makers are to ensure there is an ongoing presence of Canadian television products available to Canadians in the current shifting technological envi-

Table 5.1 Viewing of Canadian/Foreign English TV Programming by Environment, 2004–5

6 a.m.–2 a.m.	Satellite	Digital Cable	Analog Cable	Off Air
All programs	100%	100%	100%	100%
Canadian programs	31%	29%	31%	40%
Foreign programs	69%	71%	69%	60%

Source: Nielsen Media Research in CBC, 'Broadcasting Public Notice CRTC 2006–72 Comments of the CBC/Radio-Canada', 1 Sept. 2006, 11.

Table 5.2 Viewing of Canadian/Foreign French TV Programming by Environment, 2004–5

6 a.m.–2 a.m.	DTH/Digital Cable	Analog Cable	Off Air
All programs	100%	100%	100%
Canadian programs	65%	67%	67%
Foreign programs	35%	33%	33%

Note: DTH = direct-to-home satellite
Source: Nielsen Media Research in CBC, 'Broadcasting Public Notice CRTC 2006–72 Comments of the CBC/Radio-Canada', 1 Sept. 2006, 12.

Table 5.3 Audience for Canadian Comedy/Drama Series, 2002–3 Broadcast Year

Rank	Network	Program	Audience (thousands
1	CBC	Royal Canadian Air Farce (Friday)	799
2	CTV	Just for Laughs Gags	680
3	CBC	Da Vinci's Inquest	649
4	CBC	Red Green Show	610
5	CTV	The Holmes Show	556
6	CBC	Just for Laughs	551
7	CBC	American in Canada	536
8	CTV	Cold Squad	523
9	CBC	This Hour Has 22 Minutes	512
10	CTV	Mysteroius Ways (r)	497

Source: Nielsen Media Research from CBC Radio-Canada, Response to Broadcasting Notice 2003–54, 1 Dec. 2003, 5. Available at: <www.cbc.radio-canada.ca/submission/crtc/2003/BPN_CRTC_2003-54_CBCSRC281103_e.pdf>.

Table 5.4 Audience for Canadian Comedy/Drama Series, 2002–3 Broadcast Year

Rank	Network	Program	Audience (thousands
1	CBC	Royal Canadian Air Farce New Year's Special	1,859
2	CBC	Dave Foley's True Meaning of Xmas	1,522
3	CTV	100 Days in the Jungle	1,057
4	CBC	Betrayed	925
5	CTV	Tagged: The Johnathon Wamback Story	900
6	CBC	The Joke's on Us: 50 Years of CBC Satire	817
7	CBC	Talking to Americans	806
8	CBC	CBC All-Star Comedy Homecoming	798
9	CTV	Stolen Miracle	786
10	CBC	Just for Laughs (New Year)	764
11	CBC	Many Trials of Jane Doe	735
12	CBC	Royal Canadian Air Farce Countdown	734
13	CBC	The New Beachcombers	723
14	CBC	Royal Canadian Air Farce New Year's Special (r)	697
15	CTV	A Colder Kind of Death	621

Source: Nielsen Media Research from CBC Radio-Canada, Response to Broadcasting Notice 2003–54, 1 Dec. 2003, 5. Available at: <www.cbc.radio-canada.ca/submission/crtc/2003/BPN_CRTC_2003-54_CBCSRC281103_e.pdf>.

ronment. Research illustrates that despite the growing presence of computers and the web, on average per person television viewing actually increased from about 22 hours per week in 1994–5 to 24.4 hours per week in 2004–5 (CBC, 2006: 4). However, as Table 5.1 shows, foreign programming dominates viewing time on English-language television, particularly in the evening. But as Table 5.2 illustrates, on French television Canadian programming is by far the viewers' favourite. These tables also show that these trends are similar across different program delivery systems. As the CBC (2003: 2) notes, this disparity is at least in part the product of the economics of the Canadian market:

Simulcast rights to popular US sitcoms and dramas can be purchased for between $100–125,000 per hour, which is roughly a third of the cost of licensing a Canadian program. Purchases of these rights also benefit—at no cost—from aggressive publicity that the US networks use to promote these American shows. The popular US series attract large audiences and command premium advertising rates in Canada; the most successful ones generate revenues of between $350–450K per hour, which amounts to three to four times their cost, and five times the revenue that top Canadian programming can generate.

Tables 5.3 and 5.4 illustrate that in the face of this problem the CBC is the dominant provider of English-Canadian drama and comedy programming. As Table 5.3 points out, six of the top 10 Canadian drama/comedy programs were aired by the CBC in 2002–3. Similarly, as shown in Table 5.4, 11 of the most popular English drama/comedy specials over the same time period were shown on the CBC. Consequently, in English Canada the CBC plays a particularly important role in delivering Canadian drama and comedy to audiences.

Today, normal industry or institutional research (the terms are synonymous) adds information on media consumption to survey data obtained through various sampling procedures. Traditionally, media consumption has been measured by means of diaries kept by audience members, in which people log in and out as they watch or cease to watch. In 1993 the BBM Canada (it gets its initials from its former name, the Bureau of Broadcast Measurement) introduced the **people meter**, a sophisticated electronic device to measure listening/viewing every 12 seconds (Enchin, 1993). These new devices have had a significant impact on audience data and have caused some turmoil in the industry. For instance, we now know that far fewer audience members have their eyes and minds glued to the tube than was claimed by those selling audiences.

The data from the people meters therefore caused ad rates to be readjusted. More recently, BBM has introduced portable people meters that track audience members through recording inaudible codes embedded in broadcast programming.

Industry research also introduces categories within which programs are measured. Such categories allow for greater precision in assessing success, but they also demand that programs conform to the categories that are measured. For instance, commercial radio can be divided into the following categories. (Those listed here are categories revised in 2000. They are contained and elaborated on in Public Notice CRTC 1999–76.)

- Category 2 (Popular Music)
  - Subcategory 21: Pop, rock, and dance—includes all types of rock music.
  - Subcategory 22: Country and country-oriented—includes country & western, traditional country, new country, and other country-oriented styles.
  - Subcategory 23: Acoustic—music composed and performed in an acoustic style by the chansonniers and singer/songwriters of our time.
  - Subcategory 24: Easy listening—'cocktail' jazz, soft contemporary jazz, middle-of-the-road, and 'beautiful music'.
- Category 3 (Special Interest Music)
  - Subcategory 31: Concert—includes the whole spectrum of classical music traditions.
  - Subcategory 32: Folk and folk-oriented—authentic, traditional folk music as well as contemporary folk-oriented music that draws substantially on traditional folk music in style and performance.
  - Subcategory 33: World beat and international—music that draws heavily from the traditional music styles of countries throughout the world. It also includes music from the popular, folk, and classical music traditions of countries throughout the world that are played in instrumental form or sung in languages other than English and French.
  - Subcategory 34: Jazz and blues—historic and contemporary music in the jazz and blues traditions.
  - Subcategory 35: Non-classical religious—music of the church or religious faiths; gospel, hymns, contemporary Christian.

Audience Research and the Public Interest

Industry research has its limitations, particularly when it comes to understanding the needs and desires of audiences. Ien Ang discusses such limitations in her book, *Desperately Seeking the Audience* (1991), and captures the problem with the chapter title, 'Audience-as-market and audience-as-public'. Ang notes how industry research tells producers how successful they have been in reaching their audience but leaves them profoundly ignorant about the precise ingredients of their success or failure. Indeed, industry audience research offers little understanding of the motivations, understandings, or relationships audience members bring to bear on programs.

In an article in the *Canadian Journal of Communication*, Toronto media researcher Liss Jeffrey (1994) explores this issue in greater detail. What, she asks, are audience members? Are they individuals with particular psychological traits? Members of specific social, ethnic, age, or religious groups? Members of a society that allows for a fair amount of leisure time? Income earners? People with jobs that are repetitive and not very fulfilling? Persons who can benefit from positive role models? Commodity units to be sold to advertisers? Citizens? Obviously they are all of these. Yet, as Jeffrey points out, when audiences are conceived by programmers as something to be sold to advertisers only some of these audience characteristics are served by the media. True, their demographic characteristics may be known and their degree of attentiveness estimated, but because they are not conceived as citizens who could benefit from certain information and entertainment, they, the public and commercial sectors of programming, and the country all suffer. For instance, in this context, do the media in general impart values that reflect the ideals of society and contribute to its improvement and survival? Do they adequately inform citizens about domestic and international affairs? Do they allow us to see our own achievements or to know about ourselves so that we understand how we can make a contribution to society?

Such questions are important because the greater use society and individuals make of the media, the greater are the media's responsibilities. If audiences are seen only within limited frameworks—for instance, to be entertained but not enlightened—then the media's contribution to society is very limited. Moreover, increasingly, access to the media—particularly broad-

THE AUDIENCE AS MEDIA PRODUCER

As people increasingly turn to the web for entertainment, information, and socializing, large media corporations are turning to audiences themselves to create media content. In October 2006 Google announced that it had agreed to buy YouTube—a website where users upload videos for public consumption—for $1.65 billion. At the time YouTube was delivering over 100 million video views per day and had 65,000 new videos being uploaded daily. Finding ways to 'create value'—or make money—from those people and the videos they contribute to the site was the main impetus to the acquisition.

Earlier in 2006, News Corporation—one of the world's largest media corporations with holdings in film, newspapers, television, magazines, cable, and book publishing—purchased the social networking site MySpace.com for approximately $580 million in cash. With more than 25 million visitors per month, MySpace users put their lives on line through blogs, photo galleries, music, and a wide range of information about their likes and dislikes. It is also a favourite of advertisers. News Corporation plans to integrate MySpace with its news, sports, and entertainment offerings to create a comprehensive interactive commercial media site.

See www.youtube.com and www.myspace.com.

casting—is costly, leaving many people with reduced access and some altogether without. As illustrated in the next chapter with our discussion of the Broadcasting Act, such questions are particularly relevant in Canada where broadcasting has been traditionally viewed as a public service and charged, by Parliament, with specific public duties. Reducing broadcasting service to a simple calculus of the marketplace serves to undermine our knowledge and understanding of the many dimensions of public life, as well as our abilities to participate in it.

The Transforming and Vanishing Audience

As mentioned in Chapter 2, audiences and audience members are being transformed by the internet into users and user groups. Increasing levels of choice and different degrees of interactivity are changing the ways both media and audiences are being thought of. True, website owners such as newspapers, bookstores, e-mail services, and all kinds of other commercial enterprises treat users like audiences. They bombard users with all kinds of advertising, banner ads, pop-up ads, pop-under ads, animated characters, and TV-like ads with sound and motion. But with e-mail, searching for non-commercial information, and participating in discussion groups or other types of messaging, the user is a creator or co-creator of content rather than an audience member.

Similarly, with new communication technologies the distinctions between media producer and audience member are being eroded as audience members are increasingly becoming participants in the production of 'mass' media. For instance, on *Canadian Idol* and other programs, the audience participates in deciding contest winners; on some sports programs, audiences can choose the camera angles they want to watch from; and on other programs people contribute video and other material they have made to the program content.

On the web the distinction between producer and audience is becoming even blurrier as people create blogs, podcasts, games, web cam sites, and other material for public consumption. As P. David Marshall (2004: 22–3) points out, 'Through interactivity, the old division between media form and viewer is broken down more completely as the former viewer is included into the "guidance" of the program, game or internet browser and its outcomes.' Indeed, it is not an exaggeration to say that with these interactive forms of media content the audience 'vanishes', drawn up into the program itself. What do these developments have in store for definitions of audience and audience research? Stay tuned to find out.

Summary

Media–audience interaction might usefully be conceived of as interaction between active, meaning-seeking entities and meaning-generating systems—persons, groups, the media, and cultures. Such a perspective provides a framework for explaining how media, audiences, and culture interact in an orderly but non-deterministic fashion.

MACHINIMA

Machinima (pronounced muh-sheen-eh-mah) is film-making in a real-time 3-D computer-generated environment, often using video game technology. Working within a shared video game, people work either on their own or together to create a film. Action within the game is scripted and then recorded by the various 'actors' from their points of view on the resulting scene. These different shots are then brought together and edited to create the film.

Machinima is an example of 'emergent game play', or the creative use of video game technology in ways that differ from the designers' intent. Machinima films have won awards in numerous film festivals, but because of the ways they subvert the intended purposes of the game they are not always welcomed by game companies.

See www.machinima.org.

The various theoretical approaches reviewed in this chapter bring out different elements of that interaction. Effects research highlights the direct impact of the media on the behaviour of audience members. Marxist research and the Frankfurt School draw attention to the ways production of media and cultural products have the potential to advance the interests of the producers and the elites in society over those of ordinary people. Uses and gratification research tells us what audience members tend to do with media content. Cultural studies describe how audience members select features from the media and use them as meaningful elements in their lives. Feminist research brings forward the gendered nature of narratives and, like cultural studies, explores how the audience member is positioned by the narrative. Reception analysis emphasizes the interpretive structures of audience members, which may derive from personality, content, situation, or other variables.

All approaches to the audience offer information and insight for explaining and understanding, but not predicting, audience behaviour, which depends not only on what the audience brings to the text or content but also on the culturally specific references contained in the material. In academic research, the earliest analyses emphasized what the media did to the audience. More recent studies have asked what audiences do with media content. While cultural studies

oriented to textual content have been dominant for some time, greater attention is now being paid to audience dynamics. Consideration of the social context of viewing, listening, and reading adds yet further elaboration to the articulation of audience variables.

Industry research generates information in precise quantitative measures on the nature of audiences, their size, age, location, education, family income, use of certain products, use of leisure time, and so on. However, the limitations of industry audience research are demonstrated by their inability to understand and meet audience needs with respect to enlightening and socially fulfilling programming.

Understanding internet users and usage is a growing area of inquiry. Already, advertisers have found that certain modes of advertising are largely ineffective and others engender annoyance. How advertisers will meet with internet users on terms acceptable to both has yet to be determined. Meanwhile, while it is clear that new communications technologies and the growing convergence between broadcasting and the web are having dramatic impacts on notions of audience and the role of media in identity formation, as well as the role of media in forms of communication and citizenship, the role and purposes of new media are ongoing sites of struggle among industry, audiences, public interest groups, and policy-makers (see, e.g., Ruggles, 2005; Moll and Shade, 2004). How this struggle will play out remains to be seen.

Appendix: The World's Best Readership Database—PMB, A Case Study

Though our discussion on audience research has focused on the broadcast media, such research is also pursued for print media. In fact, Canada is home to a rich print audience database. It is controlled by the Print Measurement Bureau (PMB), an industry organization run as a non-profit entity by Canadian magazine publishers, advertising agencies, advertisers, and other companies and organizations in the media industry. Industry members sit on the board of directors and various committees and offer guidance in many aspects of the research. PMB's annual study has grown since its first year (1983)—it now evaluates the readership of 118 print publications. Each annual PMB study reports data from a two-year rolling sample of 24,000 individuals aged 12 and over. This means that the results of 12,000 individuals interviewed in 2005 and 12,000 interviewed in 2006 would form the basis of the data reported in the year 2007.

The study's results are based on a nationally representative, stratified, random sample of Canadians. Of the 47,000 census enumeration areas in Canada, 2,000 are chosen that are representative. Variables taken into account include location, ethnicity, age, socio-economic status, and language. Within each enumeration area, 10 households are selected at random and interviewers customarily succeed in getting an average 6.5 to agree to a one- to two-hour face-to-face interview and subsequently to the completion of a printed questionnaire. One respondent is selected from each household in such a way that each member of a household has an equal chance of being chosen.

Readership data are collected for various Canadian English-language and French-language publications such as *Maclean's*, *Reader's Digest*, *Flare*, *TV Guide*, *L'Actualité*, *Elle Québec*, and *Chatelaine*. The at-home personal interview gathers information on reading habits: what publications respondents have scanned/read; the number of times they have read it; the time spent reading an issue; the degree of interest in the publication. Also compiled in the interview are the demographic characteristics of respondents (age, gender, level of education, household income and size, and personal income and occupation) and their habits with respect to other media (TV, radio, public transit, Yellow Pages, newspapers). In a questionnaire completed after the interview, respondents provide information about the products and services they use, their lifestyle and leisure activities, and their shopping habits. Examples of the areas covered are drugs, groceries, home entertainment products, alcohol, other beverages, cars, financial services, home furnishings, and so on. A PMB member can sponsor the questionnaire: in such cases, questions about the purchase and use of certain brands of products would be included (PMB, n.d.). Figure 5.3 summarizes how this information can be interrelated.

Figure 5.3 Interrelationship of Data from PMB Surveys

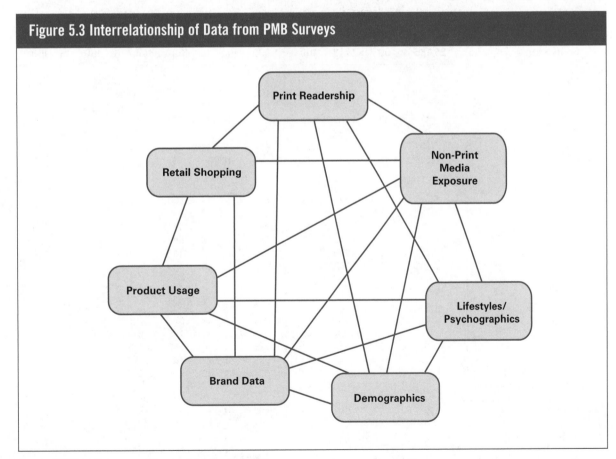

Source: PMB Print Measurement Bureau, Total Canada Age 12+

In addition to access to a comprehensive database with useful information on readers' habits, values, and attitudes on a variety of subjects/products, members of PMB can also request that previously interviewed respondents be contacted again to answer a set of specific questions tailored to the member's interests. These additional data, combined with the annual database, can provide a fuller account of people's tastes and preferences and help members of PMB—whether advertisers, publishers, or other industry organizations—know their market, improve their product/service, design an advertising campaign, and so on. PMB, however, does not collect all the information pertaining to readership. Additional research conducted elsewhere in the industry can tell you what time of day people read magazines, what locations have the most number of readers (hair salons are the top), and so forth.

Magazines use PMB's annual data to understand more fully the nature of their readership. By monitoring their readership, they can, for example, mount subscription campaigns aimed at market segments attractive to advertisers. They may even complement such campaigns with a reorientation of their editorial content and approach. Magazines also use PMB data as a primary tool in selling advertising space to advertisers and ad agencies. The data also allow magazines to gain a sense of the characteristics of the readership of their competitors.

Magazines and ad agencies can carry their use of the data even further. If, for example, an ad agency is buying space on behalf of a computer company, such

Table 5.5 Characteristics of Readership of Six Magazines Sold in Canada

	Unweighted	V%	Weighted	V%	Canadian Geographic				Chatelaine			
					000	V%	H%	I	000	V%	H%	I
Sample	25,165	100	25,165	100	3,507	100	14	100	4,067	100	16	100
Population	25,165	100	27,713	100	4,099	100	15	100	4,476	100	16	100
Age												
12–17	2,171	9	2,542	9	**589**	14	23	**157**	281	6	11	68
18–24	2,090	8	3,106	11	460	11	15	100	473	11	15	94
25–34	3,477	**14**	4,380	16	571	14	**13**	88	740	17	17	**105**
35–49	6,995	28	7,678	28	**1,142**	28	15	101	1,270	**28**	17	**102**
50–64	5,904	23	5,805	21	854	21	15	100	1,082	24	19	**115**
65+	4,528	18	4,202	15	482	12	11	78	631	14	15	93
Education												
No Cert. or Diploma	5,516	22	6,977	25	**976**	24	14	95	781	17	11	69
Sec./High School Grad.	5,706	23	7,119	26	932	23	13	89	1,194	27	17	104
Trade Cert./Diploma	2,539	10	3,212	12	501	12	16	105	492	11	15	95
University/Other Cert.	5,342	21	5,445	20	855	21	16	**106**	1,087	24	20	124
Bachelor's Degree.	3,711	15	3,209	12	549	13	17	**116**	662	15	21	128
Post Grad. +	2,353	9	1,752	6	285	7	16	110	280	6	15	92
Region												
Atlantic	1,460	6	2,055	7	391	10	19	129	400	9	19	120
Quebec	7,474	30	6,621	24	385	9	6	37	298	7	5	28
Ontario	8,711	35	10,738	39	**1,768**	43	16	111	2,169	48	20	125
Manitoba/Saskatchewan	1,445	6	1,843	7	286	7	16	105	307	7	17	103
Alberta	2,352	9	2,755	10	595	15	22	**146**	603	13	22	**135**
British Columbia	3,723	15	3,701	13	694	17	19	127	700	16	19	1117
Gender												
Male	11,482	46	13,643	49	**2,108**	**51**	15	104	**838**	**19**	6	38
Female	13,683	54	14,071	**51**	**1,991**	**49**	14	96	3,638	81	26	160

Note: Highlighted data is discussed in the text.
Source: PMB Print Measurement Bureau, PMB 2006 Readership Volume (Toronto: PMB, 2006).

as Apple, it can statistically establish not only the number of people in a particular city, such as Windsor, who read a particular magazine, but also highly reliable probabilities of how many own a Macintosh, and indeed how many own a Mac, a MacBook, an iMac, Power Mac, or any other Apple product. For that matter, the agency can establish how many readers own other types of computers and how many do not own one at all. Given this information the agency can determine how best to access a particular audience and then buy, for example, a series of ads in one magazine, ads in several magazines, or some other combination.

Just to give a sense of the reality of the business we analyzed some of the data published in 2006. The following discussion is based on Table 5.5.

We have selected six magazines for analysis: *Canadian Geographic, Chatelaine, Flare, Maclean's, Time,* and *Reader's Digest.* We will look at readership (and make mention of circulation). From these figures, taken from *PMB 2006 Readership Volume* (Print Measurement Bureau, 2006), we have selected four variables to examine: age, education, region, and gender. The unweighted figures (column 2) represent the actual number of respondents interviewed. The weighted figures (column 4) represent an adjustment of the numbers so that they more accurately reflect the population as a whole. The sample (row 1) represents the projection of the unweighted figures onto the population as a whole, while the population (row 2) represents the projection of the weighted figures onto the population as a whole. So, for example, the

Flare				*Maclean's*				*Time* (Canada)				*Reader's Digest*			
000	V%	H%	I	000	V%	H%	I	000	V%	H%	I	000	V%	H%	I
1,546	100	6	100	2,516	100	10	100	2,570	100	10	100	6,160	100	24	100
1,811	100	7	100	2,910	100	10	100	2,758	100	10	100	7,206	100	26	100
247	14	10	149	141	5	6	53	186	7	7	73	600	8	24	91
356	20	11	176	337	12	11	103	326	12	11	106	685	10	22	85
410	23	9	143	451	15	10	98	438	16	10	101	1,002	14	23	88
471	26	6	94	776	27	10	96	752	27	10	98	2,009	28	26	101
240	13	4	63	700	24	12	115	651	24	11	113	1,600	22	28	106
87	5	2	32	506	17	12	115	405	15	10	97	1,310	18	31	120
385	21	6	84	467	16	7	64	488	18	7	70	1,579	22	23	87
562	31	8	121	733	25	10	98	713	26	10	101	1,882	26	26	102
159	9	5	76	397	14	12	118	283	10	9	88	961	13	30	115
398	22	7	112	635	22	12	111	585	21	11	108	1,629	23	30	115
228	13	7	109	403	14	13	120	429	16	13	134	757	11	24	91
79	4	5	69	275	9	16	149	260	9	15	149	398	6	23	87
98	5	5	73	269	9	13	125	262	10	13	128	924	13	45	173
68	4	1	16	86	3	1	12	217	8	3	33	374	5	6	22
991	55	9	141	1,399	48	13	124	1,232	45	11	115	3,025	42	28	108
124	7	7	103	274	9	15	142	181	7	10	99	659	9	36	138
271	15	10	150	442	15	16	153	427	16	16	156	1,065	15	39	149
259	14	7	107	439	15	12	113	438	16	12	119	1,159	16	31	120
222	12	2	25	1,446	50	11	101	1,523	55	11	112	3,176	44	23	90
1,589	88	11	173	1,464	50	10	99	1,235	45	9	88	4,030	56	29	110

unweighted number of readers of *Canadian Geographic* projected from the actual interviews is 3,507,000. The projection of readership based on the weighted sample is 4,099,000. All the figures given below the top two rows of figures (sample and population) are based on weighted figures.

V% represents a percentage of the population (calculated vertically in the table) within the individual variable being examined. To take the simplest example, 2,108,000 males read *Canadian Geographic*, which amounts to 51 per cent of all readers and hence a V% of 51; while 1,991,000 females or 49 per cent read the magazine for a V% of 49. A comparison of the V% of an individual magazine to the V% of the weighted population figures indicates how much difference exists between the general population and the readership of the magazine. For instance, while women account for 51 per cent (V%) of the population, only 49 per cent of *Canadian Geographic's* readers are women. The value I represents much the same thing as V%, only more accurately: PMB defines I as 'a measure of the relative degree of association between the two variables [for example, between readership of the publication and a demographic characteristic] relative to a base of 100' (PMB, 1998: n.p.). For example, persons aged 12–17 show an I of 157 for *Canadian Geographic*, which means any sample of persons aged 12–17 would be 1.57 times more likely to be readers of *Canadian Geographic* than if the sample were selected from the population as a whole. And finally, H% is the percentage of the population calculated horizontally in the table within the individual variable being examined. Thus, for example, readers of *Canadian Geographic* aged 25–34 represent 13 per cent of the overall population of readers aged 25–34 of all magazines surveyed.

A sense of the variability in readership of these six magazines can be obtained from the population figures (row 2). *Reader's Digest* leads readership with 7,206,000, which is the highest of any magazine in Canada, followed by *Chatelaine* with 4,476,000, *Canadian Geographic* with 4,099,000, *Maclean's* with 2,910,000, *Time* with 2,758,000, and *Flare* with 1,811,000.

Readership alone, however, does not always tell the full story. Circulation and readers-per-copy (RPC) figures (not included in Table 5.5) can be quite different from readership. For instance, though *Time's* circulation (239,000) is much lower than *Maclean's* (411,000), it has a higher RPC (*Time* gets about 11.5 readers per copy, *Maclean's* only 7.1) (PMB, 2006: 1).

Let us take a closer look at some basic characteristics of the readership of these magazines and some interesting variations from the norm. Later we will turn to readers themselves. One last thing to bear in mind: readership is obviously affected by language, as is apparent in the figures of readership of English-language magazines in Quebec. But do not forget that there are populations of French-language speakers elsewhere in the country.

For *Canadian Geographic* the following points are interesting to note. Examining readership by age shows that in absolute terms the largest group of readers (1,142,000) consists of those aged 35–49. In fact, the magazine has a substantial readership with those aged 25 and above. But it also is very successful with those aged 12–17—589,000 of that age group read the magazine and, as noted above, it has an I of 157. The lower I values for age groups 18–24, 25–34, and especially 65+ indicate that the magazine is less popular among those age groups. In terms of education, again, while the magazine has a lot of readers with no certificate or diploma (976,000), the I values demonstrate that it is relatively more successful in attracting a healthy share of people having some university or other post-secondary certificate (106) and a bachelor's degree (116). In terms of region, while the main market is in Ontario (1,768,000 readers), it is relatively more successful in Alberta with its I of 146 (but only 595,000 readers). The magazine's stronger appeal among males compared to females can be seen in the absolute numbers, the V%, the I, and even the H%.

Chatelaine and *Flare* are most interesting if examined together. The success of *Flare* with young women is apparent in the I figures for those aged 12–34 (149, 176, and 143). But the substantial numbers of readers aged 35–49 (471,000, or 26 per cent of its overall readership) cannot be ignored. As the I values indicate, *Flare* is relatively more successful in attracting young readers than those 35 and older (where the I values drop below 100). However, *Chatelaine* actually has more readers in the 12–34 age range than *Flare* and its I values stay above 100 for the three age groupings from age 25 to 64. In terms of numbers of readers, *Chatelaine* attracts the most readers (4,476,000). The largest percentage of readers (28 per cent) is in the 35–49 age group. The figures also show that *Chatelaine* has relatively greater appeal to those with more education. Looking at the numbers by region, while in 2002 those in Atlantic Canada had the greatest tendency to be readers of *Chatelaine* (I =

134) and those in Manitoba and Saskatchewan had the greatest tendency to be readers of *Flare* (I = 141), now Albertans lead in the percentage readership of both magazines (I values are 135 and 150). In the case of both magazines, Ontarians follow with the second highest number of readers per capita. In interpreting these figures, it is always important to bear in mind absolute numbers of readers in comparison with the relative I values: Ontarians account for about 50 per cent of English-language readers whereas Manitoba and Saskatchewan account for less than 10 per cent. And, surprisingly enough, 838,000 men read *Chatelaine* and 222,000 read *Flare*, 19 and 12 per cent of all readers respectively.

Maclean's and *Time* also make for an interesting comparison, which is made easier by the fact that both their readership figures are somewhat less than 3 million overall. Both magazines' readership data show a substantial number of readers across all age groups, with *Time* appealing to a slightly higher percentage in the 12–34 age range and *Maclean's* appealing slightly more to those aged 65 and above. (An examination of the format changes suggest that this appeal to people over 65 will not be long maintained given the attempt to appeal to younger readers.) While these figures can be read in a number of ways, it might be claimed that younger Canadians seem slightly more inclined to stronger dollops of US content, while older Canadians have a slight preference for Canadian content. A quick look at the I figures show that both magazines appeal to those with more education, with the most educated being the strongest readers of both magazines (I = 149) for both. The fact that the highest I values for both *Maclean's* and *Time* occur among Albertans (in 2002 they were Manitoba and Saskatchewan [138] for *Maclean's*, and Alberta was strongest for *Time*) is interesting. Combined with the *Flare* and *Chatelaine* I values, the high reading levels of Albertans may mean a variety of things. Albertans may have more leisure time for reading magazines, they may have more disposable income, or, in being the province with the most quickly expanding population, magazine reading may be a way of keeping in touch with the rest of Canada. There are probably other factors as well, such as educational levels, and they may be working in combination with each other. Both *Time* and *Maclean's*, by the way, appeal more to males than females (who generally read more than males). The reverse is true for *Reader's Digest*—females prevail.

Both absolute numbers and relative success with certain parts of the population (based on variables like age, education, region, and gender) are important for advertisers (as well as for the magazines themselves). Reaching readers is one thing, but reaching them in a particular environment is also important. The appeal and impact of an ad will be affected by the publication in which it appears. To make the point strongly, it would be surprising to find an ad directed exclusively at the 838,000 male readers of Chatelaine. Yet if it were to appear, it would probably gain attention by virtue of its novelty. *Reader's Digest* deals with this issue all the time—in spite of its ability to deliver more readers, and across many groups, some advertisers are reluctant to advertise in the magazine because they see it as an inappropriate editorial environment. This view stems from various reasons, such as the magazine's condensation of the work of respected writers, its conservative politics, and the dentist office/barber shop/beauty parlour associations some have with the magazine.

Which brings us to a quick analysis of *Reader's Digest* figures. First, while the actual numbers are formidable for those aged 12–17 and over 50, *Reader's Digest* has greater appeal to those 18–49. The magazine is also relatively more successful than other magazines in reaching those with less rather than more education. Note, however, that with I values of 91 and 87, it is also relatively successful with the most educated. By region, even though Ontario accounts for 42 per cent of its readership, the magazine appears to do slightly better, according to I values, in other regions (except Quebec, where the French-language edition is strong). As noted, more women than men read the magazine.

Table 5.5 only touches upon some of the variables that are of interest and that PMB monitors. For instance, the reach of publications over the past year is also calculated. For example, the net reach of *Canadian Geographic* for the past year is 7,814,000. In fact, the magazines surveyed by PMB reach 80.4 per cent of the Canadian population—79.9 per cent of English-speaking Canadians and 81.2 per cent of French-speaking Canadians (PMB, 2006: 1, 71).

The time spent reading a publication is also important, as is the frequency of a publication. Thus, while *Reader's Digest* publishes 12 issues per year, *Maclean's* and *Time* each publish 52. Readers spend 71.12 minutes digesting each issue of *Reader's Digest* (for a monthly total of the same value), while readers

Figure 5.4 How to Read a Cost Ranking (Crank) Report

Target:
A specific user-defined segment of the base population against which all magazines on this run are evaluated. It can be defined by demographics, product usage, or even psychographics.

Percent of Base:
The target market as a percentage of the total base population (e.g., 29.47% of all English adults 18+ are women 25–54).

Rank:
The position of each magazine in the specified category (e.g., with 1,078,000 average issue readers, *Canadian Living* ranks 3rd in composition). Rankings are also shown for CPM and can be interpreted in a similar way.

CPM (Cost Per Thousand):
The cost for each magazine to reach 1,000 women 25–54 (e.g., *Canadian Living*'s CPM is $25.25—calculated by dividing the per insertion cost of $27,220 by the net reach per average issue in thousands: 1,078).

Composition (%):
The percentage of readers of a magazine's average issue who are in the target group (e.g., of all English adults 18+ who read *Canadian Living*, 51.95% are women 25–54).

Coverage (%):
The average issue audience of a magazine as a percentage of the target population (e.g., *Canadian Living* reaches 20.42% of women 25–54—1,078,000 *Canadian Living* readers, divided by the target population of 5,279,000).

Average Audience (000):
The total number of respondents in the target market who are reached by one insertion in a magazine (e.g., 1,078,000 women 25–54 read an average issue of *Canadian Living*).

Cost ($):
The cost of a single insertion in a magazine. This cost can be changed to reflect ad size, colour or b/w, regional rates, or specially negotiated rates. Shown here are national, full-page, four-colour rates.

Projected Population (000):
The projected actual population of the target (e.g., there are 5,279,000 women 25–54 living in Canada).

English Adults 18+

Target: *Women Age 25–54*
Population (000): 5279

Percent Base: *29.47%*

Media	Cost ($) 4C	Avg Aud (000)	Coverage (%)	Composition (%)	Composition Rank	CPM 4C	Rank 4C
Canadian Living	27220	1078	20.42	51.95	3	25.25	1
Chatelaine (Eng)	35695	992	18.79	51.53	4	35.98	6
Reader's Digest	28610	953	18.05	30.57	7	30.02	4
Homemakers	20640	766	14.51	53.19	2	26.95	2
TV Times	61540	632	11.97	29.27	8	97.37	10
TV Guide	19775	597	11.31	33.79	5	33.12	5
Leisureways/Westworld	37900	510	9.66	30.72	6	74.31	9
Maclean's	29995	488	9.24	27.20	9	61.47	8
Time	20530	443	8.39	27.11	10	46.34	7
Cdn. House & Home	12435	430	8.15	57.87	1	28.92	3

Source: 1998 PMB Two-Year Readership Study; Weighted by Population

Reprinted from *PMB Media School* (Toronto: PMB Print Measurement Bureau) by permission of PMB Print Measurement Bureau, Total Canada Age 12+.

Figure 5.5 Sample Products Profile Table

Personally Eat Chocolate/Candy Bars   Base: Total Canada — Age 12+

	Total		Non-User Past 6 Months				User Past 6 Months				Light (1-2)				Heavy (6+)			
	000	V%	000	V%	H%	I	000	V%	H%	I	000	V%	H%	I	000	V%	H%	I
Sample	20415	100	4889	100	24	100	4320	100	70	100	7121	100	35	100	1261	100	6	100
Population	24998	100	5876	100	24	100	17601	100	70	100	8750	100	35	100	1641	100	7	100
Male	12301	49	3198	54	26	110	8194	47	67	95	4033	46	33	94	804	49	7	94
Female	12696	51	2687	46	21	90	9406	53	73	105	4717	54	37	106	837	51	7	100
Age 12–17	2400	10	307	5	13	54	2019	11	84	120	890	10	37	106	355	22	15	225
Age 18–24	2857	11	459	8	16	68	2281	13	80	113	1205	14	42	120	226	14	8	120
Age 25–34	4953	20	1026	17	21	88	3681	21	74	106	1922	22	39	111	268	16	5	82
Age 35–49	7058	28	1591	27	23	96	5064	29	72	102	2609	30	37	106	447	27	6	97
Age 50–64	4139	17	1224	21	30	126	2646	15	64	91	1303	15	31	90	186	11	4	68
Age 65+	3591	14	1268	22	35	150	1911	11	53	76	822	9	23	65	159	10	4	68
EDU - No Cert or Dipl	7957	32	1883	32	24	101	5557	32	70	99	9609	55	25	98				
- Sec/High Sch Grad	6208	25	1404	24	23	96	4458	25	72	102	7980	45	22	102				
- Trade Cert/Dipl	2680	11	707	12	26	112	1816	10	68	96								
- University/Other Cert	4691	19	1036	18	22	94	3418	19	73	103								
- Bachelors Degree	2338	9	571	10	24	104	1635	9	70	99								
- Post Grad +	1124	4	275	5	25	104	716	4	64	91								
Married/Living Together	13888	56	3483	59	25	107	9609	55	69	98								
Single/Wid/Div/Separated	11096	44	2393	41	22	92	7980	45	72	102								
Principal Wage Earner	14757	59	3908	67	26	113	9763	55	66	94								
Principal Grocery Shopper	15558	62	3876	66	25	106	10699	61	69	98								
Professionals	1109	4	287	5	26	110	719	4	65	92								
Sr. Management/Owners	743	3	212	4	28	121	464	3	62	89								
Other Managers	2302	9	502	9	22	93	1630	9	71	101								
Tech/Sales/Teachers/Others	2014	8	440	7	22	93	1448	8	72	102								
Clerk/Secretarial	2786	11	507	9	18	77	2170	12	78	111								
Skilled/Unskilled/Prim	5879	23	1268	22	22	95	4106	23	72	103								
All Other	10364	41	2661	45	26	109	7064	40	68	97								
Employed Full Time	11682	47	2674	46	23	97	8237	47	71	100								
Employed Part Time	3011	12	545	9	18	77	2353	13	78	111								
Atlantic Region	10305	8	400	7	20	83	1553	9	76	108								
Quebec	6265	25	1483	25	24	101	4414	25	70	100								
Ontario	9388	38	2371	40	25	107	6520	37	69	99								
Manitoba/Saskatchewan	1772	7	385	7	22	92	1280	7	72	103								
Alberta	2278	9	432	7	19	81	1654	9	73	103								
British Columbia	3244	13	805	14	25	106	2180	12	67	95								
Montreal	2876	12	700	12	24	103	2028	12	71	100								
Toronto	3682	15	979	17	27	113	2550	14	69	98								
Calgary	706	3	140	2	20	85	528	3	75	106								
Edmonton	725	3	142	2	20	83	537	3	74	105								
Vancouver	1598	6	401	7	25	107	1108	6	69	98								
Comm Size Under 100M	8960	36	1984	34	22	94	6284	36	70	100								
Comm Size 100M–1MM	7881	32	1813	31	23	98	5633	32	71	102								
Comm Size 1MM +	8158	33	2080	35	25	108	5684	32	70	99								

There are 17,601,000 people 12 years of age or over in Canada who have eaten a chocolate/candy bar in the past 6 months.

70% of the 24,998,000 people 12 years of age or over in Canada have eaten a chocolate/candy bar in the past 6 months.

The greatest number of chocolate/candy bar eaters is in the 35–49 age group (29%). 5,064,000 people aged 35–49 have eaten a chocolate/candy bar in the past 6 months.

On a per capita basis, people aged 12–17 are the most likely to eat chocolate/candy bars. They have an index of 225 meaning that they are 125% more likely to eat chocolate/candy bars than their incidence in the general population.

The absolute, unweighted, number of respondents.

000 = Thousands
V% = Vertical Percentage
H% = Horizontal Percentage
I = Index

Source: PMB Print Measurement Bureau, Total Canada Age 12+.

spend 47.40 minutes of their time with each issue of *Time* (for a monthly total of 205.42 minutes). This time per issue, the monthly calculation, and publication frequency are important for both the advertiser and the magazine in calculating how much to charge for ad space. By calculating the levels of media exposure to radio and television and to daily, community, Saturday, and Sunday newspapers, as well as a number of other variables, cross tabulations can be made and the relative salience of the magazine environment approximated.

In some of its instructional materials, PMB provides examples of how its database can be used to determine a plan for, and the cost of, reaching a certain population (PMB, 1998). Figure 5.4, one example, demonstrates how to determine the cost of reaching a certain percentage of the known population of a particular target group. The various important elements of the table are explained in the boxes surrounding the central table.

Based on the data in Figure 5.4, an advertiser might choose to place ads in *Canadian Living*, *Homemakers*, and *Reader's Digest*, reasoning that these three magazines would provide good coverage of the target population with some (but not a great deal of) overlap. On the other hand, if the product were strongly home oriented, *Homemakers* and *Canadian Living* might be chosen instead. All the variables have to be assessed to match an advertiser's product and goals with suitable advertising venues.

Another example, Figure 5.5, illustrates the power of the database to identify the amount and nature of product usage, the exact characteristics of those who are users, and, subsequently, how an advertiser might best reach the market he or she wishes.

As you can sense by the nature of the data and in the terms it is presented, the magazine enterprise, like most commercial media enterprises, focuses on serving advertisers and audiences. The numbers tell the important stories to advertisers and to the financial and advertising sales managers. These numbers, however, are of less or little importance to readers, contributors, and editors, who are more interested in the content of a magazine and its image.

RELATED WEBSITES

Audience Dialogue: www.audiencedialogue.org/
As the website says, it 'exists to provide useful information for communicators of all kinds—broadcasters, publishers, aid agencies, arts organizations, webmasters, and anybody else who's interested in using research-based techniques to make their communications more effective.'

BBM, the Bureau of Measurement: www.bbm.ca/
This site contains all kinds of interesting information on who watches TV and who listens to radio, at what time of the day they listen, how much time they spend listening, in what location, and so forth.

Canadian Journal of Communication: www.cjc-online.ca
CJC provides links to back issues of the journal, including the Norma Schulman article cited in this chapter (vol. 18, no. 1).

Print Measurement Bureau (PMB): www.pmb.ca/
The print equivalent to the BBM, this site is a bit more difficult to navigate but it does provide basic magazine circulation statistics and readership by men and women. You can also download a presentation.

FURTHER READINGS

Ang, Ien. 1991. *Desperately Seeking the Audience*. London: Routledge. This book offers a good summary of audience research.

Jensen, Klaus Bruhn, and Karl Erik Rosengren. 1990. 'Five traditions in search of an audience', *European Journal of Communication* 5: 207–38. This article provides an orientation to the various schools of thought that guide audience research.

Radway, Janice. 1984. *Reading the Romance*. Chapel Hill: University of North Carolina Press. Radway's book is a classic analysis of how women readers use romantic fiction and demonstrates the contribution scholars can make to understanding the interaction between the media and people's lives.

STUDY QUESTIONS

1. In less than 50 words, define each of the following:
   • Effects research
   • Reception analysis
   • Uses and gratification research
   • Cultural studies
   • The Frankfurt School
2. Some reception studies (for example, Radway) appear to describe the interaction between audiences and content as secondary to the tangential actions surrounding the interpretation of content. It is more the act of reading that counts over what the person is deriving from the content itself. Comment on this in relation to other methods of analysis.
3. Which of the perspectives on audiences would you use for writing an essay dealing with the impact of media violence on society? Why?
4. Which of the perspectives on audiences corresponds most closely to your own views?
5. Is there anything to be concerned about in regard to the information that industry organizations collect on audiences, which advertisers consult? Have you ever responded to a market survey? If so, have you always 'told the whole truth and nothing but the truth'? Discuss.

LEARNING OUTCOMES

- To illustrate how the interaction between media content and audience members is a dynamic interaction in which audience members selectively attend to certain elements and actively interpret content elements based on frameworks of understanding they bring to content.
- To point out that media–audience interaction is not predictable but can be explainable after the fact.
- To introduce six ways of studying how the media influence audience members: Marxist analysis and the Frankfurt School, effects research, uses and gratifications research, British cultural studies, feminist research, and reception analysis.
- To describe the types of research carried on by members of the media industries, for example, the CBC.
- To explain how industry members measure audiences and what they measure, for example, reach, share, and viewing time.
- To explain one of the ways in which the Canadian magazine industry measures its audiences and, armed with that information, sells those audiences to advertisers.
- To illustrate what industry data tell us about magazine readers and how many people read what large consumer magazines that are sold in Canada.
- To introduce the idea that industry research tends to treat audience members as consumers.

PART THREE

Major Influences on Media Functioning

CHAPTER 6

Communications Law and Policy

Introduction

Mass communication is a highly structured activity. It takes place in a built environment that includes communication technology, certainly, but also laws, policies, economic principles and pressures, and guiding ideals. Laws and policies establish the rules of the game as laid down by governments, which recognize that mediated communication is a powerful force in society and there must be rules in place to ensure that the media serve not only their owners and content creators but society as a whole. The policy realm, then, establishes both rights and responsibilities. If media workers have the right to freedom of expression, they also have the responsibility to respect people's privacy and laws pertaining to libel, copyright, hate speech, etc. If media owners have the right to a reasonable return on their investment, they also have an obligation not to abuse their power in the market and not to inhibit others from communicating.

Mass communication is not a frivolous activity. As earlier chapters in this book have made clear, communication plays a crucial role in defining the goals, aspirations, and values of society, and fulfills the basic informational needs of a modern democratic society and the individuals who constitute that society. It is the site upon which cultures are formed. In this chapter and the next, we talk about law and policy, which, taken together, can be understood as society's answer to the question: What is communication for? Law and policy are the state's response, developed over many years and by many different governments, to the question of what Canadian society wants from its telecommunication and broadcasting systems, and from its cultural industries. Each society answers these questions in its own way, which explains why the same medium will be structured differently from country to country. All countries use the same radio technology, to take one simple example, but organize their radio systems in particular ways—who can own radio stations, how many stations they can own, over what geographical expanse they can broadcast, what

kinds of programming are permitted, etc.

This chapter provides an overview of how telecommunications and broadcasting operate in Canadian society. We concentrate on the policies and principles that govern their operation, beginning with an examination of the defining laws, or, more formally speaking, statutes: the Telecommunications Act (1993) and the Broadcasting Act (1991). We then examine other statutes that affect telecommunications and broadcasting, as well as policies developed in accordance with the Telecommunications and Broadcasting Acts to ensure that these industries operate according to the goals set out in these defining statutes.

Two further points of introduction. First, the phrase 'communications law and policy' could be used to encompass all of telecommunications, broadcasting, and the cultural industries. However, we use it here to address only telecommunications and broadcasting. Chapter 7 will focus on the cultural industries, by which we mean the remainder of the communication industries: book and magazine publishing, cinema, sound recording, newspaper publishing, and new media. Second, the terms 'regulatory' and 'regulation' generally refer to both policies and laws. However, these terms may also be used in a more restrictive sense to include only policy, creating a distinction between the regulatory framework and the legal framework (i.e., the statutes).

Governing Communications

The legal and regulatory frameworks that govern communications are founded on political, cultural, and economic considerations, which reflect the impact communication has on society. Because politics, culture, and economics may pull in different directions, tensions exist within communication policy. These tensions are derived from attempting, for example, to engage in both nation-building (a political consideration) and the construction of a viable cultural industry (an economic consideration). Or, alternatively, from trying to ensure that Canadian creative artists obtain exposure to Canadian audiences (a cultural consideration) while providing a wide range of programming to all tastes and audience sectors (a more general social consideration).

Besides the Telecommunications and Broadcasting Acts, a variety of laws and policies apply to these communications fields. They include:

- the Canadian Charter of Rights and Freedoms, which guarantees the freedom to communicate, including the right to own media enterprises and to collect and impart information;
- access-to-information legislation, designed to make government-gathered information available for public scrutiny—at both the federal and provincial levels;
- legislation protecting privacy, intended to protect individuals about whom information is collected and stored by governments and businesses;
- limits on free speech, including libel law, which is intended to protect the good name of individuals, and laws restraining the communication of hate against specific groups;
- controls over the production, dissemination, and importation of obscene material, particularly rules intended to protect children from exposure to such materials;
- copyright and patent protection, designed to protect intellectual property and increasingly used to protect electronic communications content, such as television news programs and computer software;
- requirements for public disclosure of company information, intended to protect the interests of investors or potential investors in company shares traded on a stock exchange;
- federal and provincial employment laws, which govern work conditions, training, hiring, employment equity, etc.;
- consumer protection, including rules designed to limit the market powers of large companies and monopolies; and
- contract law and company law.

Such laws in Canada may be federal, provincial, or both, depending on the division of powers described in the Canadian Constitution. They are based on legal conventions established internationally, or on common law inherited from the British system of justice.

The Legal and Regulatory Frameworks of Communication

Telecommunications policy applies to telephone, telegraph and telex, data networks, satellite communications, and the internet. Broadcasting policy applies to radio, TV, cable TV, pay TV, and specialty TV. Both telecommunications and broadcasting policies are very much in flux. The nature of these areas of activity and the increasing overlap among them—a phenomenon known as **technological convergence**—are evolving, especially from a policy perspective. Technological convergence is leading to the revision of policies developed in response to distinctive technologies, industries, and needs to bring them in line with current realities.

Also contributing to a need to revise policies is the general expansion of communication industries. Most notably, public ownership of communication enterprises, which has been a feature of Canadian telecommunications (e.g., Teleglobe, Telesat, Canarie) and broadcasting (the CBC), is being reconsidered. More and more, these enterprises are subjected to funding cuts as Canada and other nations open up their communications markets to private enterprise. Beyond the trend away from public ownership is an expanded opportunity for many different firms to compete for increasingly segmented audiences—old and young, French, English, Italian, and Chinese, sports fans, arts enthusiasts, etc.

A third major reason for policy deregulation and re-regulation stems from the recent enthusiasm of developed nations, including Canada, for liberalized international trade. Canada has signed the Free Trade Agreement (FTA) with the United States, the North American Free Trade Agreement (NAFTA) with the US and Mexico, and various other general trading agreements promoted and administered by such institutions as the World Trade Organization (WTO) and the Organization for Economic Co-operation and Development (OECD). As a result, Canada and other signatory countries must abide by a common set of rules for the creation of communication products and services. These rules are most often set by those with the strongest economies (the United States, Japan, Germany, the United Kingdom), which generally reject as valuable—even as legitimate—the direct intervention by governments in the marketplace. At the beginning of the twenty-first century, we are seeing this dynamic play itself out in magazine legislation

FINDING LEGISLATION ON THE WEB

To access legislation currently before Parliament, go to the Canadian parliamentary website <www.parl.gc.ca> and click on 'Bills'. Then select 'LEGISinfo' from the box on the left-hand side. From there, you can access current House of Commons and Senate bills and search by title or bill number. To access an Act or statute, go to the Canadian Department of Justice website <www.canada.justice.gc.ca> and click on 'Laws' in the top right-hand corner. From there, you can access an alphabetical directory by title and search by subject or keyword.

and media ownership restrictions. However, it is only a matter of time before the US attempts to curtail subsidies for Hollywood film companies shooting in Canada or to have some element of cable-TV policy declared unfair.

Complementing the economic and technological pressures for policy revision are cultural pressures to ensure that the Canadian creative community has a fair chance to be seen and heard and thereby to contribute to the cultural fabric of the country. Expressed another way, Canada and most other nations—the US is the exception—see communications as a field over which they wish to exert control to assert **cultural sovereignty**. Were governments to step aside completely, history teaches us that the communications sphere would be dominated by foreign corporations distributing the most commercially viable content and foreign content emanating primarily from the United States.

Policy Development

The aim of communication policy is not to resolve completely the tensions described above, but to balance economic opportunity with social, cultural, and political goals. For example, the Broadcasting Act states that the Canadian broadcasting system will 'serve to safeguard, enrich and strengthen the cultural, political, social and economic fabric of Canada'; that 'each element of the Canadian broadcasting system shall contribute in an appropriate manner to the creation and presentation of Canadian programming'; and that 'each broadcasting undertaking shall make maximum use, and in no case less than predominant use of Canadian creative and other resources in the creation and presentation of programming.' These goals are an attempt to strengthen Canada's cultural resources, to provide employment opportunities for Canadians, and to promote the val-

ues that Canada, as a nation, stands for.

The Canadian Radio-television and Telecommunications Commission (CRTC), which administers the Telecommunications and Broadcasting Acts, arbitrates among the social, cultural, political, and economic goals of those Acts and the economic and political interests of the organizations that provide telecommunications and broadcasting services. The CRTC sets standards, notably Canadian-content rules for broadcasters, which are designed to ensure that the goals of the Telecommunications and Broadcasting Acts can be met.

In Canada, the process of policy-making for telecommunications and broadcasting is very much open to public participation, in part because Canada professes a strong egalitarianism and recognizes the different interests at play, in part because the CRTC is an arm's-length government agency rather than a department within a government ministry and thus operates with some measure of independence.

The influence of public input, however, seems to be on the decline because the CRTC has become mired in adjudicating between licensees, responding to organized interest groups, coping with international trade agreements and technological change, all while trying to abide by the goals laid out in the statutes. For instance, the CRTC has had to deal with expansion of cross-media ownership: TV companies buying newspaper chains (e.g., CanWest Global) and newspaper companies buying into TV and cable (e.g., Quebecor). These moves have little to do with serving the public and everything to do with personal and corporate ambition.

In addition to CRTC hearings, over the years public input has also been a feature of the various Canadian inquiries, commissions, and committees investigating telecommunications, broadcasting, and the cultural industries. Among those that engaged in public consultation are: the Royal Commission on

National Development in the Arts, Letters and Sciences (chaired by Vincent Massey and Henri Lévesque, 1951); the Special Senate Committee on Mass Media (chaired by Keith Davey, 1970); the Royal Commission on Newspapers (chaired by Tom Kent, 1981); the federal Cultural Policy Review Committee (chaired by Louis Applebaum and Jacques Hébert, 1982); and the Task Force on Broadcasting Policy (chaired by Gerald Caplan and Florian Sauvageau, 1986). More recently, the Information Highway Advisory Council (IHAC) held public meetings and produced a report on economic and social opportunities that the internet offers Canadians (Industry Canada, 1997), the Standing Committee on Canadian Heritage heard public testimony in its study of Canadian broadcasting (Canada, 2003), and the Standing Committee on Transport and Communication conducted two years of public hearings across the country before producing its report on issues concerning the news media in Canada (Canada, 2006a). With the same goal of consultation in mind, the government has begun to establish websites to aid public discussion on policy. The CRTC's own website (www.crtc.gc.ca) provides a wealth of information to citizens and researchers interested in policy decisions.

In the autumn of 1998, the CRTC conducted hearings that illustrated the changing nature of public input. In those hearings, the system of regulations that govern Canadian content was reviewed. In the past, the hearings would have seen the broadcasters on one side and the regulators on the other, with members of the public given the status of interveners. As Doug Saunders of the *Globe and Mail* put it, the situation looked more like this: first were the lobby groups, such as the Friends of Canadian Broadcasting, the Canadian Association of Broadcasters (CAB), and the right-wing Fraser Institute; second came the private broadcast community within which there were substantially different positions; third were the program producers, led by Alliance Atlantis. The lobbyists argued about the overall form broadcasting should take. The private broadcasters and the right wing argued for licences free from obligation. The left wing argued for a public benefit to be derived from the granting of the opportunity (a broadcasting licence) to make money. The broadcasters also argued among themselves over the extent of Canadian-content obligations. And the program producers argued with the broadcasters over who should own the rights to pro-

gramming created in part with public subsidies. With all these various interests in the foreground, the voice of the public was difficult to discern.

Of course, part of the reason for change in the consultation process is opinion polling, especially when polling is used in tandem with fairly sophisticated and informal use of the media by government. Governments hire pollsters to poll continuously. They learn public preferences regarding all of their policies and intentions by asking representative samples of Canadians about them. They also know the political orientations of major media commentators and columnists. Thus, with major policy issues, the government puts out information with a pretty good sense of how the public will receive that information. The government also knows that commentators of various political stripes will contribute to the debate. Through the continuous process of monitoring public opinion, the government can determine where the public stands on any given question and also how best to pitch a policy initiative to engender a favourable response. Without declaring a formal public consultation process, a certain kind of informal public debate can nonetheless take place.

Telecommunications Policy

Telecommunications policy governs telephony, data communication (including the internet), wireless telecommunications (including cellphones), and satellite communications (including links for broadcasters and for data and telephone services). More formally speaking, telecommunications is defined as 'the emission, transmission or reception of intelligence by any wire, cable, radio, optical or other electromagnetic system, or by any similar technical system' (Telecommunications Act, 1993, s. 2[1]). In strictly technical terms, broadcasting is a type of telecommunications, but in policy terms, because broadcasters control the content of their transmissions, broadcasting is treated separately and is governed by a policy section in the Broadcasting Act. Telecommunications is governed by federal statute as a result of a 1989 ruling by the Supreme Court of Canada that all major telephone and telecommunications companies fall within federal jurisdiction because their networks interconnect with out-of-province carriers.

In overview, the Telecommunications Act addresses technological and economic issues, such as providing reliable and affordable services in an efficient and

TELECOMMUNICATIONS ACT, SECTION 7*

The foundation for Canadian telecommunications policy is contained in Section 7 of the 1993 Telecommunications Act. It states:

7. It is hereby affirmed that telecommunications performs an essential role in the maintenance of Canada's identity and sovereignty and that the Canadian telecommunications policy has as its objectives:

   (a) to facilitate the orderly development throughout Canada of a telecommunications system that serves to safeguard, enrich and strengthen the social and economic fabric of Canada and its regions;

   (b) to render reliable and affordable telecommunications services of high quality accessible to Canadians in both urban and rural areas in all regions of Canada;

   (c) to enhance the efficiency and competitiveness, at the national and international levels, of Canadian telecommunications;

   (d) to promote the ownership and control of Canadian carriers by Canadians;

   (e) to promote the use of Canadian transmission facilities for telecommunications within Canada and between Canada and points outside Canada;

   (f) to foster increased reliance on market forces for the provision of telecommunications services and to ensure regulation, where required, is efficient and effective;

   (g) to stimulate research and development in Canada in the field of telecommunications and to encourage innovation in the provision of telecommunications services;

   (h) to respond to the economic and social requirements of users of telecommunications services; and

   (i) to contribute to the protection of the privacy of persons.

* Notes omitted

effective manner, nationally and internationally, and protecting the privacy of users, and the Act underlines the role of telecommunications in maintaining Canada's identity and sovereignty (see section 7 of the Act on this page). It does so by stressing Canada's social and economic particularities, by stimulating research and development in the field in Canada, by affirming Canadian ownership and control of telecommunications infrastructure, and by affirming the use of Canadian transmission facilities.

The historical core of telecommunications is the telephone industry. In Europe this business evolved from nineteenth-century state monopolies in post and telegraph (P&T) services. In Canada, privately owned monopolies used to be the norm—for example, BC Tel in British Columbia, Bell Canada in Ontario and Quebec. These private monopolies existed alongside provincially owned monopolies in Manitoba, Alberta, and Saskatchewan. This core of telephone companies and an ever-decreasing number of smaller companies operated as a national system and, until September 1998, presented itself to the world as the Stentor Alliance.

In addition to the provincial telephone companies were the companies that arose after the long-distance telephone markets and then the local telephone markets were opened up for competition, some as subsidiaries of the major phone companies. These providers included major companies like Cantel and Call-net (now part of Rogers Communications), AT&T Canada, Sprint, Bell Mobility, and Fido. There are also well over 200 radio common carriers providing wireless mobile radio and radio paging services as well as the personal-communications service providers. Then there is the internet, with access either through cable or telephone (hard-wired or wireless) and local access providers as well as a growing number of satellite services.

To provide seamless service to the public, a complex set of rules and specifications has developed to allow both technological compatibility among all these providers and revenue-sharing. The CRTC is the adjudicator of these rules. This includes arrangements made among Telesat Canada (the Canadian satellite communications company), the telephone companies, the cable-TV companies, Teleglobe (formerly the monopoly agency controlling transoceanic telecommunications), and those who purchase their services (e.g., the specialty and pay-TV companies).

COMMON AND CONTRACT CARRIERS

Telecommunication companies are service providers. They offer transmission services for a fee. In many cases they are **common carriers** in that they are obliged to carry any message (content) that any member of the public (company or individual) wishes to send at equitable cost. A **contract carrier** provides transmission services to specific companies or individuals, but is not obliged to provide those same services to other individuals or companies. The banks, for example, contract for telephone and data communication services and obtain bulk rates unavailable to the average citizen. Your internet service provider is also a contract carrier. The company has a contract with its customers but is under no obligation to extend its services to others.

A carrier may not tamper with the message, nor can it be involved in creating any of the messages carried for customers (a requirement that may have to be modified as on-line services evolve). The creation of the 'content' is what distinguishes broadcasters from common carriers; broadcasters are involved in content creation and the selection of content, which they then transmit to audiences. Broadcasters, unlike carriers, are legally responsible for all the content they transmit even though much of their programming may have been purchased from third parties.

The major telecommunication issue for the past two decades has been the transition from monopoly services to competing services. The issues confronting telecommunications in the years to come may very well be twofold: technological convergence, which increasingly blurs the lines between broadcasting and telecommunications; and further commercialization, including either a relaxation or complete abandonment of foreign-ownership restrictions.

TELECOMMUNICATIONS REGULATION OVER THE YEARS

Regulation of telecommunication dates back to the nineteenth century when it was believed that only one company could provide efficient service in any given area. The rationale at that time—one that continued through to the 1980s—was that it made little sense for more than one telephone wire to be strung down every street. Telephone services were declared to be a 'natural monopoly'. To guard against undue exploitation, the monopolies were regulated by what eventually became the CRTC. Governments during the twentieth century felt that both broadcasting and telecommunications (first telegraph and later telephone) were valuable social services. They reasoned that such services ought to be provided to all Canadians at equitable prices—not necessarily the same price everywhere, but neither at prices affordable in urban areas and unaffordable in rural areas. In fact, the failure of commercial companies to commit to providing widespread telephone services persuaded the governments of Alberta, Manitoba, and Saskatchewan to create publicly owned telephone monopolies within their jurisdictions.

By the 1980s it had become apparent that technology had more to offer than telephone companies were providing. It had also become apparent that connections between competitors were possible and that it was feasible for purchasers of bulk services to resell telephone access for cheaper rates than the telephone companies were offering for individual service. Given these realities, in September 1994, in what has come to be known as Telecom Decision 94–19, the CRTC ruled that competition must be the basis for the provision of all telecommunication services, including local voice telephony service. This decision required companies to separate the costs of providing any single service (e.g., local phone service) from those for any other service (e.g., long-distance phone service), meaning that companies would no longer be allowed to cross-subsidize services. Historically, the revenue from long-distance phone services subsidized local phone service, helping to keep local phone service affordable for individuals and small businesses.

Not all aspects of Telecom Decision 94–19 were immediately implemented; the federal cabinet referred some of the rulings back to the CRTC after receiving appeals against the decision. Nevertheless, it marked a major turning point in telecommunications regulation. When Decision 94–19 was put in place, the common expectation was that the cable-TV companies and the telephone companies would compete vigorously in the marketplace. Instead, the focus of competition has been on the vast and continuing expansion of internet services and the burgeoning mobile services sector.

Competition has also led to an unanticipated outcome—the breakup of the Stentor Alliance. When telephone companies had geographic monopolies, their focus was providing service while making a reasonable rate of profit. With competition, they transformed themselves, becoming more technologically innovative and focusing on marketing their services. As competitors established themselves across the country, it became apparent that the territorial boundaries of each of the Stentor companies had become liabilities, just as it would be a liability, for example, if the *Globe and Mail* could only publish in Ontario. Stentor itself had been a cartel of companies committed not to compete with one another. Given that this cartel might be illegal and, more importantly, that its competitors were not similarly constrained, it was no longer logical for a 'no trespassing' pact to exist among Stentor members.

In overview, telecommunications have been transformed dramatically over the last 25 years. The overall function has remained constant, to allow Canadians to communicate with one another and, thereby, to build a nation. However, while in the beginning this goal seemed achievable only through territorial monopolies operating within a tight regulatory framework, with increased wealth, technological sophistication, and an existing infrastructure, the need for monopolies has passed. The dismantling of these monopolies has resulted in enhanced services, more competition, and a demand for less government regulation and greater adherence to the rules of the commercial marketplace.

Ownership is one area where there is pressure to either relax or abolish existing regulations. Enhancing and expanding services costs money, of course, and in early 2003 the House of Commons Industry Committee initiated hearings to review rules restricting foreign investors to minority stakes in Canadian telecommunications companies (Chase, 2003). The law currently prevents non-Canadians from holding more than one-fifth of telecommunications operating companies and one-third of affiliated holding companies. In early 2006, Canada co-sponsored a request to the World Trade Organization to abolish foreign-ownership restrictions on telecommunication services, which would include, of course, Canada's own restrictions (see Sinclair, 2006). The impetus behind such a request is to increase the pool of investment capital flowing into this Canadian industry sector (rendering Canadian companies both more competitive and more valuable) and also to create investment opportunities for Canadian telecom

companies beyond Canada's borders. At the same time, however, it would move regulation of the industry further out of the hands of Canadian governments, assigning this responsibility primarily to market forces. This would make it much more difficult for governments to insist that telecommunication companies serve national political, social, cultural, and/or economic goals.

The Final Report of the Telecommunications Policy Review Panel recommended the Telecommunications Act be amended so that 'market forces shall be relied upon to the maximum extent feasible as the means of achieving the telecommunications policy objectives' (Canada, 2006b: 12–13). One significant consequence of the Panel's neo-liberal free-market thrust was the announcement by Industry Minister Maxime Bernier, in mid-December 2006, that the government would accelerate the deregulation of local phone service by allowing the major players (and former monopolies such as Bell Canada) to establish local rates as they see fit, without any regulatory approval from the CRTC. This rush to deregulation was expected to be in place early in 2007, despite the objections of opposition critics and the smaller service providers (Wong, 2006).

With respect to foreign ownership, the Panel saw 'significant merit' in gradually removing investment restrictions. In a first phase, this would mean giving the federal government the authority to waive restrictions on foreign investment when it is deemed to be in the public interest. A second phase of liberalization was recommended to be taken in concert with similar amendments to the Broadcasting Act (Canada, 2006b: 11-24–11-26).

SATELLITE COMMUNICATION

Canada has been a pioneer of non-military satellite application since the early 1960s. In 1964 Canada joined INTELSAT, the international **consortium** that operated the first satellite communication service with the mandate to provide international communication linkages. The possibility of improving trans-Canada communication links using satellites has appealed to federal policy-makers since at least 1965. A White Paper on satellite policy, issued in 1968, stated: 'A domestic satellite system should be a national undertaking stretching across Canada from coast to coast, north to Ellesmere Island and operating under the jurisdiction of the Government of Canada' (Canada, 1968).

In 1969, the Telesat Canada Act established the joint public-sector/private-sector corporation that was given the responsibility to own and operate the Canadian satellite communication system and to provide communication services to Canadian locations on a commercial basis. Telesat's first satellite was launched in 1972 and shortly thereafter the company initiated the first domestic satellite communication service in the world. By 1995, Telesat had launched five series of satellites.

Telesat is the 'carriers' carrier', a reference to the fact that most of the signals carried on satellite are transmitted on behalf of another carrier, such as a telephone or cable-TV company. Historically, the primary use for satellites was telecommunications traffic (mostly voice telephony and data communication). However, by 1987 it was apparent that broadcasting services were becoming at least as important to Telesat. The vast majority of broadcasting services consisted of the delivery of video signals across the country.

While commercial over-the-air television and radio networks in southern Canada make use of satellite transmission as part of their distribution technology, it is rare for them to abandon their terrestrial links to use only satellites, especially since the development of **optical fibre**. As well, with Telecom Decision 94–19, the door is opening for competition in providing satellite services, so that Telesat will no longer enjoy a monopoly.

Satellite technology was the key to integrating Canada's North into the larger telecommunication and television networks of the south, beginning with the Anik satellite program of the 1970s. If, initially, this meant the delivery of more sophisticated telephone service to some northern communities, it also meant the one-way delivery of CBC programming in French and English to the North, with no native-language or culturally relevant programming on offer (Roth, 2005: 74–88). The first step towards the true 'televisual joining of Canada's North and South' occurred with the establishment of the Inuit Broadcasting Corporation in January 1982 (ibid., 134–5). Aboriginal broadcasting was not enshrined in Canada's Broadcasting Act until 1991, and it achieved two-way flow with the licence approval of the Aboriginal Peoples Television Network (APTN) in February 1999; APTN received mandatory carriage on basic cable throughout Canada and satellite delivery to 96 northern communities (ibid., 204).

Broadcasting Policy

Public policy places a heavy emphasis on being able to exert national control over the broadcasting sector, which includes radio and television in all its burgeoning forms: cable, pay, specialty, satellite. Since the late 1920s, broadcasting policy has been informed by the mandate of nation-building, and it is important to recognize from the outset that the Broadcasting Act (Canada, 1991) defines broadcasting in Canada not as an industry but as 'a public service essential to the maintenance and enhancement of national identity and cultural sovereignty' (section 3[i][b]). This distinction means broadcasting in Canada is perceived as a system of communication, not merely a medium of entertainment. This essential public service comprises three distinct sectors: public broadcasting (e.g., the CBC), private broadcasting (i.e., commercial radio and TV), and community broadcasting (i.e., non-profit, community-service radio and TV). The legal definitions relevant to broadcasting are provided in section 2 of the 1991 Broadcasting Act:

'Broadcasting' means any transmission of programs, whether or not encrypted, by radio waves or other means of telecommunication for reception by the public by means of broadcasting receiving apparatus, but does not include any such transmission of programs that is made solely for performance or display in a public place;

'program' means sounds or visual images, or a combination of sounds and visual images, that are intended to inform, enlighten or entertain, but does not include visual images, whether or not combined with sounds, that consist predominantly of alphanumeric text.

Broadcasting has been recognized since 1932 as federal jurisdiction under the Canadian Constitution, but in the 1970s it was determined that the provinces could establish educational broadcasters provided that these organizations operated at arm's length from their respective provincial governments. This led to the establishment of Radio-Québec (now Télé-Québec), TV Ontario, the Saskatchewan Communications Network, ACCESS Alberta (now privately owned), and the Knowledge Network in British Columbia.

Policy instruments pertain to three specific aspects

BROADCASTING ACT, SECTION 3*

Broadcasting Policy for Canada

[Declaration]

3. (1) It is hereby declared as the broadcasting policy for Canada that

(a) the Canadian broadcasting system shall be effectively owned and controlled by Canadians;

(b) the Canadian broadcasting system, operating primarily in the English and French languages and comprising public, private and community elements, makes use of radio frequencies that are public property and provides, through its programming, a public service essential to the maintenance and enhancement of national identity and cultural sovereignty;

(c) English and French language broadcasting, while sharing common aspects, operate under different conditions and may have different requirements;

(d) the Canadian broadcasting system should

  (i) serve to safeguard, enrich and strengthen the cultural, political, social and economic fabric of Canada,

  (ii) encourage the development of Canadian expression by providing a wide range of programming that reflects Canadian attitudes, opinions, ideas, values and artistic creativity, by displaying Canadian talent in entertainment programming and by offering information and analysis concerning Canada and other countries from a Canadian point of view,

  (iii) through its programming and the employment opportunities arising out of its operations, serve the needs and interests, and reflect the circumstances and aspirations, of Canadian men, women and children, including equal rights, the linguistic duality and multicultural and multiracial nature of Canadian society and the special place of aboriginal peoples within that society, and

  (iv) be readily adaptable to scientific and technological change;

(e) each element of the Canadian broadcasting system shall contribute in an appropriate manner to the creation and presentation of Canadian programming;

(f) each broadcasting undertaking shall make maximum use, and in no case less than predominant use, of Canadian creative and other resources in the creation and presentation of programming, unless the nature of the service provided by the undertaking, such as specialized content or format or the use of languages other than French and English, renders that use impracticable, in which case the undertaking shall make the greatest practicable use of those resources;

(g) the programming originated by broadcasting undertakings should be of high standard;

(h) all persons who are licensed to carry on broadcasting undertakings have a responsibility for the programs they broadcast;

(i) the programming provided by the Canadian broadcasting system should

  (i) be varied and comprehensive, providing a balance of information, enlightenment and entertainment for men, women and children of all ages, interests and tastes,

  (ii) be drawn from local, regional, national and international sources,

  (iii) include educational and community programs,

  (iv) provide a reasonable opportunity for the public to be exposed to the expression of differing views on matters of public concern, and

  (v) include a significant contribution from the Canadian independent production sector;

(j) educational programming, particularly where provided through the facilities of an independent educational authority, is an integral part of the Canadian broadcasting system;

(k) a range of broadcasting services in English and in French shall be extended to all Canadians as resources become available;

(l) the Canadian Broadcasting Corporation, as the national public broadcaster, should provide radio and television services incorporating a wide range of programming that informs, enlightens and entertains;

(m) the programming provided by the Corporation should

  (i) be predominantly and distinctively Canadian,

  (ii) reflect Canada and its regions to national and regional audiences, while serving the special needs of those regions,

  (iii) actively contribute to the flow and exchange of cultural expression,

* Notes omitted

(iv) be in English and in French, reflecting the different needs and circumstances of each official language community, including the particular needs and circumstances of English and French linguistic minorities,

(v) strive to be of equivalent quality in English and in French,

(vi) contribute to shared national consciousness and identity,

(vii) be made available throughout Canada by the most appropriate and efficient means and as resources become available for the purpose, and

(viii) reflect the multicultural and multiracial nature of Canada;

(n) where any conflict arises between the objectives of the Corporation set out in paragraphs (l) and (m) and the interests of any other broadcasting undertaking of the Canadian broadcasting system, it shall be resolved in the public interest, and where the public interest would be equally served by resolving the conflict in favour of either, it shall be resolved in favour of the objectives set out in paragraphs (l) and (m);

(o) programming that reflects the aboriginal cultures of Canada should be provided within the Canadian broadcasting system as resources become available for the purpose;

(p) programming accessible by disabled persons should be provided within the Canadian broadcasting system as resources become available for the purpose;

(q) without limiting any obligation of a broadcasting undertaking to provide the programming contemplated by paragraph (i), alternative television programming services in English and in French should be provided where necessary to ensure that the full range of programming contemplated by that paragraph is made available through the Canadian broadcasting system;

(r) the programming provided by alternative television programming services should

(i) be innovative and be complementary to the programming provided for mass audiences,

(ii) cater to tastes and interests not adequately provided for by the programming provided for mass audiences, and include programming devoted to culture and the arts,

(iii) reflect Canada's regions and multicultural nature,

(iv) as far as possible, be acquired rather than produced by those services, and

(v) be made available throughout Canada by the most cost-efficient means;

(s) private networks and programming undertakings should, to an extent consistent with the financial and other resources available to them,

(i) contribute significantly to the creation and presentation of Canadian programming, and

(ii) be responsive to the evolving demands of the public; and

(t) distribution undertakings

(i) should give priority to the carriage of Canadian programming services and, in particular, to the carriage of local Canadian stations,

(ii) should provide efficient delivery of programming at affordable rates, using the most effective technologies available at reasonable cost,

(iii) should, where programming services are supplied to them by broadcasting undertakings pursuant to contractual arrangements, provide reasonable terms for the carriage, packaging and retailing of those programming services, and

(iv) may, where the Commission considers it appropriate, originate programming, including local programming, on such terms as are conducive to the achievement of the objectives of the broadcasting policy set out in this subsection, and in particular provide access for underserved linguistic and cultural minority communities.

[Further declaration]

(2) It is further declared that the Canadian broadcasting system constitutes a single system and that the objectives of the broadcasting policy set out in subsection (1) can best be achieved by providing for the regulation and supervision of the Canadian broadcasting system by a single independent public authority.

of radio and television broadcasting: technological issues, content, and access. These three areas have engendered and led to the modification of broadcasting as the needs of each have evolved.

TECHNOLOGY

The technological particularities of sending broadcast signals over the airwaves have in every country demanded some form of governing authority to assign broadcast frequencies; this was the point of entry for the state regulation of radio broadcasting in its infancy. Without getting too technical about it, radio is transmitted by waves of electromagnetic radiation at various frequencies. Radio broadcasters, therefore, need to transmit their signals at allotted frequencies in the finite broadcast spectrum in order to avoid interference with one another. Frequency allocation is assigned by national state agencies—e.g., the CRTC in Canada, the Federal Communications Commission in the United States—in co-operation with neighbouring countries.

The first regulatory authority in Canada was the Ministry of Marine and Fisheries, administering the 1913 Radio-telegraph Act. The ministry licensed both transmitters and receivers. The first Canadian radio station to obtain a licence was XWA in Montreal in 1919, an experimental broadcaster established by the Canadian Marconi Co. By 1928, there were more than 60 radio stations operating across Canada under minimal regulation, many of them affiliated with newspapers and electrical appliance dealers (see Vipond, 1992).

As the airwaves became more crowded through the 1920s, prompting disputes over both signal interference (from powerful American stations) and the content of broadcasts (especially religious broadcasts), the Canadian government recognized the need for a more comprehensive approach to broadcast policy. In December 1928 the Minister of Marine and Fisheries, P.J. Arthur Cardin, established the Royal Commission on Radio Broadcasting (known as the Aird Commission after its chairman, Sir John Aird), which was asked to 'examine into the broadcasting situation in the Dominion of Canada and to make recommendations to the Government as to the future administration, management, control and financing thereof.' The Aird Commission held public hearings in 25 Canadian cities between April and July 1929 (Canada, 1929).

Aird studied five central issues—the educational component of broadcasting, international wavelength allotment, advertising, Canadian content, and ownership—and recommended that radio broadcasting in Canada be restructured as a national public system owned, operated, and subsidized by federal government authorities, with provincial control over programming. The Aird Commission hearings prompted considerable debate between those who preferred that radio be run on the principles of a **free market** and those who saw the need for state intervention to ensure that Canadian radio was not Americanized (see Gasher, 1998). Upon release of the Aird Report, these arguments, still with us today, were taken up by the Canadian Association of Broadcasters and the Canadian Radio League, respectively. The Canadian Radio League, under the leadership of Graham Spry and Alan Plaunt, proved to be better organized and more persuasive, and the nationalist view of Canadian broadcasting won the day.

Ottawa created the Canadian Radio Broadcasting Commission (CRBC) in May 1932. The Commission was assigned the ambitious task of regulating, controlling, and conducting broadcasting throughout Canada, but in the throes of the Great Depression it was never given funding adequate to its mandate. The CRBC set up broadcast stations in only six cities—Montreal, Ottawa, Toronto, Vancouver, Moncton, and Chicoutimi—and had to rely on 14 private stations in other cities to distribute its network programs. This mixed system of public and private broadcasting was inherited by the Canadian Broadcasting Corporation (CBC) when it was established in 1936 and remains with us to the present day.

The CBC was the product of a revised Broadcasting Act, which gave the public broadcaster more money (through increased licence fees) and greater autonomy, and accepted the role of private, commercial stations as the local broadcasting complement to the CBC's national network services. By 1944, the CBC was operating three networks—two in English, one in French—and its satisfactory performance prompted subsequent Royal Commissions to adopt CBC Radio as the model for the new medium of television in the 1950s. The Massey Commission (officially, the Royal Commission on National Development in the Arts, Letters and Sciences, 1949–51) described CBC Radio as 'the greatest single agency for national unity, understanding and enlightenment' (Canada, 1951: 279), and, with the CBC assuming responsibility for television as of 1952, the

Fowler Commission (the Royal Commission on Broadcasting, 1956–7) defended Canadian broadcasting's national, public service structure. The Fowler Commission equated the privatization of broadcasting with the Americanization of Canadian radio and television (Canada, 1957: 230–3).

Both the Massey and Fowler commissions heard complaints from the private broadcasting community about the CBC's double mandate as state broadcaster and state regulator. The new Broadcasting Act of 1958 relieved the CBC of much of its regulatory authority, establishing a 15-member Board of Broadcast Governors (BBG) to regulate both public and private broadcasting. The BBG oversaw the rapid expansion of CBC's television service and approved in 1961 a second national television broadcaster, the private, commercial CTV network, and TéléMétropole, a private, French-language station in Montreal. However, continuing regulatory disputes between the CBC and the BBG prompted the creation in 1968 of the Canadian Radio-Television Commission (renamed the Canadian Radio-televi-sion and Telecommunications Commission in 1976), with a clearer and broader mandate to regulate all of Canadian broadcasting.

Today, the CRTC's duties in the broadcasting field include:

- defining categories of broadcasting licences;
- issuing and renewing licences, up to a maximum of seven years;
- modifying existing licence conditions;
- suspending or revoking licences (the CBC licence excepted);
- licensing cable distributors and satellite delivery systems;
- hearing complaints about the broadcasting system;
- reviewing mergers of media companies.

In 1999, for example, the CRTC reduced the length of the licence of Montreal AM radio station CKVL from seven years to three. The broadcast regulator punished the station for the insulting and vulgar remarks of

A BRIEF HISTORY OF TV

1883: Paul Nipkow, a German scientist, invents a perforated spinning disk that can break down an image into a sequence of pictorial elements.

1923: Russian-born Vladimir Zworykin patents an iconoscope, an early electronic camera tube, in the US.

1926: Scotsman John Logie Baird makes a public demonstration of television by broadcasting shadow pictures; two years later he is able to broadcast colour pictures and outdoor scenes.

1928: General Electric presents the first TV drama. Sound is carried on a radio station, and the picture is seen on a three-by-four-inch screen.

1932: An RCA subsidiary begins experimental telecasts atop the Empire State Building; four years later a converted radio station feeds programs to it twice weekly.

1939: The first television sets become available to the American public. NBC begins regular service.

1940: The first official network broadcast takes place.

1941: CBS presents its first newscast, on the bombing of Pearl Harbor; war delays the construction of systems in the United States.

1950: The first community antenna TV service—the precursor to cable TV—begins in Pennsylvania.

1951: CBC initiates regular TV programs in Montreal and Toronto; CBS begins limited colour broadcasts. A videotape recorder is publicly demonstrated for the first time.

1962: Toronto is the site of a trial for closed-circuit pay-TV.

1968: The Canadian Radio-television and Telecommunications Commission is established.

1970s: Japan develops a high-definition television system.

1975: Sony launches its Betamax VCR. The VHS follows a year later.

1982: The CRTC licenses Canada's first pay-TV services.

1999: Web-TV service begins.

Source: *Globe and Mail*, 4 Feb. 1999, D5, which cited *The 1998 Canadian and World Encyclopedia*; *Encyclopedia Americana*; *Les Brown's Encyclopedia of Television*.

'shock jock' André Arthur and the failure of the station's owner, Metromedia CMR Montreal Inc., to take seriously numerous public complaints about Arthur (Canadian Press, 1999). In 2004, the CRTC denied the licence renewal application of Quebec radio station CHOI-FM arguing that the station, and radio host Jeff Fillion in particular, repeatedly aired derogatory comments about women, people of colour, and psychiatric patients, a decision that was subsequently affirmed by the Federal Court of Appeal (Thorne, 2005).

Much of the CRTC's work involves staging public hearings on licence applications and renewals. The hearings are held throughout the year, either at the Commission's head office in Gatineau, Quebec, or in major cities around the country. Each year the CRTC has to rule on thousands of licence applications, renewals, and amendments.

To say that the CRTC merely regulates the broadcasting system to achieve policy objectives set by Parliament understates the extent to which the CRTC has been obliged to interpret policy. It also understates the extent to which the CRTC has established policies of its own in areas such as cable and specialty TV.

Since the 1970s there has been considerable discussion in the policy field about the degree to which the CRTC can and should initiate and resist policy action. There has also been discussion about the extent to which the federal government should maintain policy control over the CRTC. One of the controversial aspects of the 1991 Broadcasting Act is the increased scope it grants for federal cabinet direction to the CRTC. As well as making section 3 of the Act much more explicit, the statute requires the CRTC to implement stated regulatory policy (section 5) and also provides cabinet with the power to issue directions on how the CRTC is to interpret both policy sections. Since 1991, the federal cabinet has taken a much more active role in policy-making in the broadcasting field through its power of direction.

A good example of the cabinet's current powers was evident in the debate over the development of direct-to-home (DTH) satellite services. In 1994, the CRTC decided to exempt from licensing requirements any company that met specified criteria: Canadian ownership; the use of Canadian satellites for the delivery of all services; adherence to priority carriage rules already established for cable TV operators. This decision meant that only one company—ExpressVu—would be exempted, eliminating ExpressVu's principal competitor, Power DirecTV, which was partly American-owned and which intended to use US satellites for the American share of its program delivery.

ExpressVu was owned by a consortium that included BCE (Bell's parent company), Cancom, Western International Communications (WIC), and Tee-Comm Electronics (the makers of the satellite dishes required). Power DirecTV was 80 per cent owned by Power Corp. of Montreal, with the remaining 20 per cent held by Hughes Aircraft, a unit of General Motors in the US. The CRTC's decision to preclude Power DirecTV from entering the DTH satellite business prompted the federal government to establish a three-member panel to review the decision. In April 1995 the panel recommended that DTH competition should be allowed, that the CRTC should license all qualified applicants, and, in effect, that the CRTC could not use its power of exemption to avoid setting up a licensing procedure in an area of major policy significance. In July 1995 the cabinet ordered the CRTC to implement the government's policy on licensing competitive DTH pay-per-view television program undertakings. The CRTC was also required to call for licence applications to carry on DTH distribution and to issue decisions quickly on those applications. Three applications were received—from ExpressVu, Power DirecTV, and Shaw Communications—and, after a public hearing, the CRTC licensed the first two operators in December 1995.

ACCESS AND CONTENT

In recent years, a major shift in broadcasting policy has occurred pertaining to the issue of access, from an original emphasis on signal coverage to an emphasis on participation. From as early as 1936, one of the fundamental principles of Canadian broadcasting policy has been the extension of service to all Canadians, and private broadcasters' place in the national broadcasting system has been to help in providing Canadians in all areas of the country access to the reception of radio, and later television, broadcast signals (see Canada, 1986: 5–14). This has been a technologically and financially challenging task given the size of the country and Canada's sparse and scattered population. Between 1936 and 1950, radio's reach in Canada expanded from 50 to 90 per cent of the population. This policy of full coverage was reaffirmed with the arrival of Canadian television in the 1950s. The federal government adopted a 'single-station pol-

POLICY AND REALITY

Here is a simple example of a mismatch between policy and actuality in the world of the media. Canadian broadcasters are permitted by the CRTC to run 12 minutes of commercials per hour. Guess how many *Blind Date* runs? A study commissioned by the Vancouver Media Directors' Council (not a left-wing organization) and entitled *Blind Date: The 2002 Canadian Television Commercial Monitoring Report* noted that the show carried up to 28.4 minutes of non-program material. The objection of the advertisers who commissioned the study is that such 'clutter' makes advertising less effective and undermines television as a medium. One wonders if the movie-makers who specialize in product placement have such concerns about the medium of film.

icy', whereby no competing television station would be allowed in any market until a national television broadcasting system was established, thus prioritizing the extension of service rather than the encouragement of competition (Raboy, 1992: 111–14).

The notion of 'access to broadcasting' began to assume another dimension in the 1960s, once extensive territorial coverage of radio and television had been achieved and a private television network (CTV) had been established. Access came to mean the inclusion of all Canadians in the content and production of programming. While the issue of Canadian content has been significant since the first decade of radio, the idea of requiring a minimum percentage of broadcast time to be used for transmitting Canadian television productions was instituted by the Board of Broadcast Governors in 1959. Today, Canadian-content regulations stem from the CRTC's obligation under the Broadcasting Act to ensure that each licence-holder makes 'maximum use . . . of Canadian creative and other resources in the creation and presentation of programming'. The CBC's programming, according to the Act, should also be 'predominantly and distinctively Canadian'.

The Canadian-content quota has never been well received by the private broadcasters, who have protested each requirement vigorously and sought to minimize their carriage of Canadian material (see Babe, 1979). The CRTC requires television licensees to have at least 60 per cent of all programming hours given to Canadian productions; private broadcasters are allowed to reduce that to 50 per cent in prime time. Radio regulations will be discussed in more detail in Chapter 7, but, generally speaking, commercial AM and FM radio stations are required to play at least 35 per cent (raised from 30 per cent in 1998) Canadian musical selections, both as a weekly average and between 6 a.m. and 6 p.m., Monday to Friday.

The principal battleground for disputes over Canadian-content quotas has been English-language television, where Hollywood productions are readily available, cheap to buy, and popular with audiences and advertisers. During the 1970s a considerable amount of evidence demonstrated that, while the majority of programs aired by Canadian TV broadcasters were 'Canadian' in the regulatory definition, the English-Canadian audience showed a strong preference for US entertainment series and movies (the audiences for French-language television showed a much stronger preference for Quebec-produced programming, for both linguistic and cultural reasons). A particularly weak programming genre was English-language drama.

Since the early 1980s, several events have improved the situation significantly. The first of these was the establishment of Telefilm Canada's Broadcast Program Development Fund, which encouraged independent producers to create high-quality TV dramas and series. These productions, in a number of instances, have shown a strong potential for export sales as well. The second event was the licensing of a number of specialty and pay-TV services, to be distributed via satellite and cable. All the new services were required to spend a portion of their revenues on programming production. While these services have not always been successful in building audiences, the trend towards specialty programming, or 'narrowcasting', is clear; the CRTC licensed 22 new specialty services in 1996. The third development was the establishment by the private sector of a number of production funds in the 1980s and 1990s, increasing the pool of capital available to production companies and making it easier for them to get airtime.

When significant numbers of Canadians began subscribing to cable television service during the 1960s, the CRTC sought to ensure that Canadian

CANADIANS LIKE THE CBC

According to a May 2004 poll conducted for the Friends of Canadian Broadcasting:

- The CBC received the highest ratings among 13 organizations for public confidence in protecting Canadian culture and identity on television.
- Canadians gave the CBC positive marks in meeting its mandate of providing 'radio and television services incorporating a wide range of programming that informs, enlightens and entertains'. Eighty-one per cent of Canadians rate the CBC as good or better than its Canadian competitors in this area.
- Even though both CBC radio and television were seen as contributing to Canadian identity and culture, CBC television made the biggest contribution according to 58 per cent of respondents.
- Canadians in every region of the country attribute a high level of importance to the CBC's regional mandate, from a low of 67 per cent in Alberta to a high of 88 per cent in the Atlantic provinces.
- Ninety-four per cent of respondents agreed that they would like to see the CBC survive and prosper, and 77 per cent said the CBC provided value for taxpayers' money.
- More than half of respondents (51 per cent) said the CBC funding should be maintained at current levels, while 38 per cent said the corporation's funding should be increased.

These findings reflect strong support among Canadians for the CBC.

Source: Ipsos-Reid, 'Broadcasting Issues and Canadian Public Opinion: An Ipsos-Reid Survey for the Friends of Canadian Broadcasting', May 2004. At: friends.ca/files/PDF/IRMay04.pdf.

broadcasters would have priority for cable carriage. Regulations require cable-TV licensees to provide clear channels for signals in a specified order of priority, with CBC, local, and regional signals favoured over foreign (i.e., US) signals.

The federal Department of Canadian Heritage initiated a review of Canadian content in March 2002, inviting submissions from the public and interested parties in the film and television industries. In a discussion paper entitled *Canadian Content in the 21st Century* (Canada, 2002: 1), the department said 'the time has come to reassess the definition of Canadian content and ensure that the approach that is chosen is up to date and well suited to the challenges ahead.'

The notion of Canadian content has already undergone considerable refinement. In the 1970s and 1980s, there was an increasing recognition of Canada's multicultural makeup and demands were made that the broadcasting system should reflect this reality. As Lorna Roth (1998: 493–502) notes, by the early 1980s one in three Canadians was of non-British, non-French, and non–Aboriginal descent, and the federal government began to enshrine guarantees of cultural and racial pluralism in the Constitution, for example, in sections 15 and 27 of the Canadian Charter of Rights and Freedoms (1982), and in legislation, for example, the Multiculturalism Act (1998).

Inclusion was one of the central themes informing discussions leading up to the adoption of a revised Broadcasting Act in 1991. Marc Raboy (1995: 457) argues that the 'transparency of public debate' between 1986 and 1991 was responsible for enshrining the rights of women, ethnic groups, Native peoples, and disabled persons in broadcast legislation. In section 3 (1) (d)(iii), the Act states that the Canadian broadcasting system should:

> through its programming and the employment opportunities arising out of its operations, serve the needs and interests, and reflect the circumstances and aspirations, of Canadian men, women and children, including equal rights, the linguistic duality and multicultural and multiracial nature of Canadian society and the special place of aboriginal peoples within that society.

Subsequent clauses call for the provision of programming that 'reflects the aboriginal cultures of Canada' and programming 'accessible by disabled persons'. When the CRTC renewed the licences of the CTV and Global television networks in August 2001, the Commission demanded from the networks a plan, to be accompanied by annual reports, to 'address a number of initiatives including corporate accountability, programming practices and community involvement as they relate to the goal of ensuring that the diversity of Canadian society is reflected fairly and consistently in CTV's and Global's programming.' The CRTC also called for the creation of a task force, to be co-ordinated by the Canadian Association of Broadcasters, to address the depiction of Canada's cultural diversity on TV screens (CRTC, 2001). As Lorna Roth (1998: 501) has stated: 'Though it still faces multiple challenges, we might say that the Canadian attempt to deal with "cultural and racial diversity" in broadcasting represents its political willingness to symbolically weave cultural and racial pluralism into the fabric of Canadian broadcasting policy and human rights legislation.'

A Future for Broadcast Regulation?

If spectrum allocation was the original premise for state intervention in the broadcasting sphere, do we still need the CRTC in the era of the 500-channel universe and the internet? The answer would appear to be a qualified yes. In a speech to the Broadcasting and Program Distribution Summit in Toronto in February 1999, Wayne Charman, director general of the CRTC's broadcast distribution and technology division, identified three factors driving changes in the communications industry: globalization, technological change, and business consolidation (CRTC, 1999: 2). The CRTC is adapting to this new environment, Charman said, by assuming a more flexible approach to regulation. 'We have broadened our scope to include both protection [and] promotion using constraint wherever appropriate and competition wherever possible.'

Recent regulatory decisions suggest that the CRTC will not likely run out of things to do anytime soon. The Commission, for example, has been active in adopting measures pertaining to: television violence (e.g., anti-violence rules for video games, a V-chip-based classification system for programming); alcohol advertising; third-language and ethnic TV programming; Canadian content on radio; the conversion of television broadcasters from analogue to digital services; and, as discussed above, abusive commentary on the radio airwaves. The CRTC has expanded Canada's national television system by approving for inclusion in nationally distributed basic cable and DTH satellite packages the private, French-language TVA network (1998) and the Aboriginal Peoples Television Network (1999). In November 2000 the CRTC approved 200 new digital TV services, including 21 category-one licences, which distributors are required

to carry. These included the Women's Sports Network (WSN) and PrideVision, aimed at Canada's gay and lesbian community. Two pay-per-view and four video-on-demand services were also approved, increasing both the diversity of the TV dial and the choices available to viewers (CRTC, 2000). The CRTC has also had to rule on recent corporate mergers of media companies that have resulted in considerable cross-ownership of media properties in a number of major Canadian markets (for more discussion, see Chapter 8). A study of the Canadian broadcasting system by the Standing Committee on Canadian Heritage (known as the Lincoln Committee after its chairman, MP Clifford Lincoln) recommended that the CRTC be directed to strengthen its policies on the separation of newsroom activities within cross-owned media to ensure editorial independence, called for the CRTC to establish a mechanism to ensure the editorial independence of broadcasters, and asked the federal government for 'a clear and unequivocal policy statement' on the subject of cross-media ownership (Canada, 2003: 409–12).

While spectrum allocation may have been the original premise for broadcast regulation, Robert McChesney (1999: 26) reminds us that technology was not the only reason for state intervention. 'Many of those who struggled for public broadcasting in its formative years did so not on technical grounds of spectrum scarcity as much as a profound critique of the limitations of the market for regulating a democratic media system.' If anything, concerns about a free-market approach to governing the media spectrum have intensified in recent years as a consequence of trends towards corporate concentration and media convergence, issues that will be taken up further in Chapters 7, 8, and 9.

Summary

This chapter began by explaining that communications law and policy form part of the structure within which mediated communication takes place, and emphasized the importance of laws and policy instruments in defining the goals, aspirations, and values of society, and in fulfilling the basic informational needs of a modern democratic society and the individuals who constitute that society. Although this chapter concentrates on the Telecommunications and Broadcast Acts, and the role of the CRTC in regulating both sectors, we noted that a number of laws and policies apply to these particular fields of communication, including the Canadian Charter of Rights and Freedoms, access-to-information legislation, privacy laws, copyright, and various limits on free speech. Telecommunication policy applies in numerous areas—telephone, telegraph, telex, data networks, satellite communication, the internet—and broadcast policy applies to all forms of radio and television. Discussion of the policy-making process highlighted the inputs from the public and industry players. The section on telecommunication policy described several elements of the Telecommunications Act, explained the distinctions between common and

contract carriers, highlighted the relatively recent policy shift that has taken place from monopoly to competition in local and long-distance telephone governance, and discussed the implications of the advent of satellite communications. The section on broadcasting policy described the history of the initial regulation of radio and then of television in all of its forms, focusing on three overarching themes: technological issues, content, and access. The chapter concluded with a brief discussion about the future of broadcast regulation, given the contextual influences of globalization, technological change, and business consolidation.

RELATED WEBSITES

Broadcasting Act: www.crtc.gc.ca/eng/LEGAL/BROAD.htm
The full text of the current Act can be found here.
Canadian Department of Justice: www.canada.justice.gc.ca
The Justice Department website includes enacted statutes.
CRTC: www.crtc.gc.ca
The CRTC provides an excellent site with information on all aspects of regulation, as well as on upcoming hearings.

Parliament of Canada: www.parl.gc.ca
Information on current legislation can be found at this site.
Telecommunications Act: www.crtc.gc.ca/eng/LEGAL/TELECOM.HTM
This is where the full text of the Act can be found.

FURTHER READINGS

Babe, Robert. 1990. *Telecommunications in Canada*. Toronto: University of Toronto Press. This is a comprehensive account of the history of the technology, institutions, and government policies related to telecommunications in Canada.

Canada. 1986. *Report of the Task Force on Broadcasting Policy* (Caplan-Sauvageau Task Force). Ottawa: Minister of Supply and Services. This thorough and accessible report led to revision of the Broadcasting Act.

———. 2003. *Our Cultural Sovereignty: The Second Century of Canadian Broadcasting*. Report of the Standing Committee on Canadian Heritage, June. Ottawa: Communication Canada Publishing, June. At: www.parl.gc.ca/InfoComDoc/37/2/HERI/Studies/Reports/herirp02-e.htm. This document provides a thorough overview of the history of broadcast regulation in Canada and the state of the broadcast industry currently, as well as recommendations for future policy directions.

———. 2006. *Final Report of the Telecommunications Policy Review Panel*. Ottawa: Industry Canada. This report provides a good overview of telecommunications policy and regulation, addresses current issues facing the industry, and provides recommendations for future policy directions.

Gasher, Mike. 1998. 'Invoking public support for public broadcasting: The Aird Commission revisited', *Canadian Journal of Communication* 23: 189–216. This article tests the Aird Commission's claims to speak on behalf of Canadians by examining the actual testimony before the Royal Commission.

Raboy, Marc. 1990. *Missed Opportunities: The Story of Canada's Broadcasting Policy*. Montreal and Kingston: McGill-Queen's University Press. Raboy presents a thorough and readable history of Canadian broadcasting policy.

Roth, Lorna. 2005. *Something New in the Air: The Story of First Peoples Television Broadcasting in Canada*. Montreal and Kingston: McGill-Queen's University Press. This book charts the emergence of television service to Canada's Aboriginal peoples and describes the policy process leading to the establishment of the Aboriginal Peoples Television Network.

Vipond, Mary. 1992. *Listening In: The First Decade of Canadian Broadcasting, 1922–1932*. Montreal and Kingston: McGill-Queen's University Press. The brief but fascinating history of Canadian radio prior to the establishment of a national broadcaster is detailed in this work.

STUDY QUESTIONS

1. What are communication law and policy and what purpose do they serve?
2. What is the fundamental policy distinction between telecommunications and broadcasting?
3. What is meant by 'rationalizing' policy, and why has it been necessary in recent years?
4. What role does the Canadian public play in policy development?
5. What has been the effect of telephone deregulation since the 1980s?
6. What is the significance of broadcasting in Canada being defined by the Broadcasting Act as a 'public service'?
7. What was the significance of the Aird Commission of 1928–9?
8. How has the definition of 'access' to broadcasting shifted over the past 70 years?
9. What purpose does broadcast regulation serve in the age of the internet and dozens of specialty services delivered via cable and satellite?

LEARNING OUTCOMES

- To introduce law and policy as a principal structuring force in the Canadian communications environment.
- To situate law and policy with respect to other structuring forces, such as economics and technology.
- To define, and distinguish between, the telecommunications and broadcasting regimes.
- To explain the role of the CRTC and to outline its principal functions.
- To explain the policy concepts of common and contract carriage.
- To underline how the notion of public access to broadcasting has evolved historically.
- To explain the rationale behind Canadian-content regulations in radio and television.
- To consider the future of broadcast regulations in a digital environment.

CHAPTER 7

Cultural Industries Law and Policy

Introduction

Like telecommunications and broadcasting, the cultural industries—that is, cinema, music recording, publishing (book, magazine, and newspaper), and new media—are vehicles for the circulation of ideas. The term 'cultural industries' derives from the involvement of each of these industries in large-scale commercial manufacturing, distributing, and retailing cultural materials.

This chapter introduces Canada's cultural industries and describes the particular rationales governments use to justify their respective policy and regulatory instruments. It examines cinema in both historical and contemporary contexts, looking at emerging trends in the industry and in film and video policy. Music recording is considered in regard to the organization of the industry, the influence of broadcasting on music recording, the position of Canadian musicians in the context of the big recording giants, and what changes in the ways Canadians consume music mean for law and policy. Under book publishing we look at some history and current government support programs that have helped Canadian book publishers and Canadian authors, many of whom have become recognized around the world. The discussion of magazine publishing focuses on the legislation that has been necessary to ensure that Canadian magazines have room in the marketplace. It reviews the challenges mounted by the US and Canada's policy responses, and ends with an assessment of the future. We also describe several key elements of newspaper publishing as a cultural industry. The chapter closes by considering the burgeoning new media sector and the kinds of policies needed for active Canadian participation in these media.

Traditionally, artistic expression relied for its survival on patrons prepared to support it and artists able to create original works. For centuries, members of the social elite—in business, politics, the church—have acted as art patrons. But in the modern era, with the establishment of democratic governments that wished to express the will of the people and encour-

age creativity, the state has come to share this role more and more with the elite. Given the importance of ideas in our society, the economics of the mass market, the demands of Canadian audiences, the power of companies involved in providing cultural products, the high value placed on human creativity, and the goal of nation-building, governments have developed certain regulations and policies to support specific cultural industries.

The cultural industries have in common with broadcasting and telecommunications some of the general policies and laws that regulate communications, such as copyright law, privacy laws, and the Charter's clause on freedom of speech. In addition, regulatory and funding bodies have been established to support specific cultural sectors.

The Policy Process

In the cultural industries, the policy-making process is much less open than in telecommunications and broadcasting (with the exception of open websites). Basically, the industry lobbies government for supportive policies and the government responds, usually by granting something—but not everything—the industry has requested. Occasionally, mechanisms are put in place to test public opinion—such as the Ontario Royal Commission on Book Publishing (1972), the Applebaum-Hébert committee on cultural policy (1982), the Magazine Task Force (1994), and even the debate surrounding Bill C-55 on magazines (1998–9). But much more often, policy is developed by consultants undertaking investigations into the functioning of an industry and making recommendations for appropriate policy. There are many such reports at both the federal and provincial levels.

In Canada, while there were earlier attempts, such as the Aird Report that led to the establishment of a public radio broadcaster and John Grierson's report on film that led to the establishment of the National Film Board, cultural policy effectively dates back to the comprehensive Royal Commission on National

Development in the Arts, Letters and Sciences (1951). This Commission, chaired by Vincent Massey, led to the founding of a body, the Canada Council, with the responsibility to provide funding for artists (as well as for research in the humanities and social sciences). In the late 1960s, as the baby boomers came of age and with impetus from centennial celebrations and Expo 67, pressure increased drastically on governments to provide opportunities for Canadians to participate in both artistic expression and in the various cultural industries. The federal government and some provincial governments began to examine the cultural industries as well as their support of them—for example, funding for the National Film Board and preferential postal rates for Canadian books, magazines, and newspapers (that date back to the 1840s). Throughout the 1970s, various cultural policies were put in place and, while vibrant industries have been a long time in establishing firm financial foundations, Canada can now boast an impressive performance in film and television production and sound recording, and in writing and publishing books, magazines, and newspapers. These achievements have not been attained without considerable effort and investment from politicians, government officials, cultural industries personnel, creative artists, and support from the Canadian public.

Nevertheless, there were and still remain barriers to the sustenance of a vibrant cultural industry in Canada, particularly with respect to policy. In 1983, Paul Audley suggested in his book, *Canada's Cultural Industries*, that two major challenges faced Canadian cultural policy: financing and distribution. A proper level of financing was required to create high-quality cultural products because established, foreign-owned producers in film, music, books, and magazines could sell their products more cheaply, which made it difficult for Canadian talent and products to compete. And even if such materials were developed by Canadians, access to distribution channels, that is, cinemas, radio airplay, bookstores, and magazine racks, was severely restricted both by business practices and by the sheer volume of imported products. In the case of books, for example, foreign companies had moved into Canada and established branch plants (wholly-owned subsidiary companies) to serve the Canadian market with what appeared to be Canadian products.

Given the barriers to the Canadian cultural industries and the nature of cultural products themselves, a substantial body of research dedicated to the analysis of Canadian cultural policy has emerged (see, e.g., McFadyen et al., 1994). That literature has identified a number of rationales behind the development of Canadian cultural policies. These rationales, discussed below, include democratic participation, cultural development, public service, and market failure (for a detailed review of the latter three, see Lorimer and Duxbury, 1994).

Quebec-based media scholars Marc Raboy, Ivan Bernier, Florian Sauvageau, and Dave Atkinson (1994) argue that it is the government's responsibility to enhance **democratic participation** by providing citizens with access to the ideas and creativity of their own community. To fail to do so is to prevent citizens from fully and knowledgeably participating in their community. A more local form of this model is called the community development or animation model: it emphasizes the value of self-knowledge in forming a dynamic community. Support for cultural industries is also often justified by making reference to the notion of **cultural development**. Here, it is argued, the state has a responsibility to provide citizens with access to

POSITIONS ON CULTURAL INDUSTRIES POLICY

There is an abundant literature on the ins and outs of cultural industries policy. For example, Canadian political economist Abraham Rotstein (1988) and west-coast-based economist Steven Globerman (1983) have opposing views on market failure. Rotstein argues against using economic concepts because, he reasons, they are inappropriate for cultural and artistic activities. Applying economic concepts to culture is rather like applying religious concepts to the marketplace. Globerman, on the other hand, argues that cultural activities should, like all other activities, be made subject to marketplace realities. If audiences are too small or they are unwilling to pay enough for the service, then it should cease to exist.

ART FOR ART'S SAKE

An often-used rationale for some cultural support policies is 'art for art's sake'. This means that art should be supported by governments, or anyone else with funds, not for any motive other than for the sake of art itself. It is argued further that to do so is to celebrate human creativity and human freedom to create.

Art in the form of music or writing can be the foundation of publishing or sound recording. Filmmaking can also be the product of artistic rather than commercial motivations. In fact, in many instances, artistic aims are melded with communicational aims to create wonderful artistic works. We have not included 'art for art's sake' as a rationale for the support of cultural industries because we feel that, while it is a viewpoint related to the overall endeavour of producing cultural objects, it is one step away from being a rationale for cultural industries policy. Some would disagree.

their cultural heritage and to favour the creation of works that reflect and enrich that heritage. A public service approach stresses the role of government to assist the nation in preserving its heritage and its efforts towards human betterment—goals often left unaddressed by the constraints of business practice, such as profits. The notion of market failure is a more clearly economic justification for government intervention and encompasses two ideas. First, there may be structural barriers to the participation of domestic businesses in domestic—and international—cultural markets. Thus the government has the responsibility to step in and assist new or 'infant industries' to establish themselves in the marketplace. Second, the market rarely reflects the true value of a work of art, which has lasting value as a public good, so it is seen as legitimate for governments to intervene to encourage production of such works.

Whichever rationale is used, cultural industries policy, like broadcasting and telecommunications policy, attempts to balance three sets of factors—the economic, the political, and the cultural (including the artistic). This balancing act, however, is difficult. First, all three sets of factors are nearly always simultaneously at work. Second, in Canada, economic interests in the cultural industries usually involve foreign businesses while cultural interests usually involve the national creative community—two parties seldom in agreement. Third, Canada is a trading nation and in recent years Canadian governments have enthusiastically pursued international trade agreements, which can often conflict with cultural goals. In the negotiations leading up to the signing of the Canada–US Free Trade Agreement (FTA) and the North American Free Trade Agreement (NAFTA), Canada managed to persuade its trading partners that the cultural industries should be exempt from full compliance with the requirements of free trade. The Canadian government insisted that Canada must retain the right to take policy and program action to support its cultural industries. The value of this exemption has been debated, particularly inside the cultural industries sector (see analysis by Carr, 1991), because of the extensive opportunities in the trade agreement for retaliatory actions by the US. In 1998 the value of that cultural 'exemption' was tested within the WTO by a US attack on Canadian magazine policy. As we will see, it was found to be lacking. More and more, however, Canadian governments at both the federal and provincial levels are accepting the tenets of free trade and an overall market approach to the production and distribution of cultural goods and services.

The Canadian cultural industries, and the laws and policies established to regulate and support them, can be divided into six sectors: cinema, music recording, book publishing, magazine publishing, newspaper publishing, and new media.

Cinema

Federal and provincial governments in Canada have been sponsoring motion-picture production in one form or another since early in the twentieth century, and Ottawa has operated a national film production organization continuously since 1918. Canada, however, has been much more successful in the spheres of industrial and documentary film production—e.g., films produced by the National Film Board, founded in 1939, have won 12 Academy Awards (Table 7.1)—than in the higher-profile domain of dramatic, feature-length film production, the kinds of movies we see in our theatres. There, Hollywood is the dominant player in the Canadian market, occupying better than 90 per cent of screen time in Canada's commercial movie theatres. Even though directors like Atom Egoyan, François Girard, Patricia Rozema, Deepa Mehta, Mina Shum, Léa Pool, and Denys Arcand have given renewed vigour to Canadian feature filmmaking since the early 1980s, domestic films have averaged only between 3 and 6 per cent of box-office revenues in Canadian cinemas. In a sense, our own domestic cinema is foreign to Canadian audiences.

Although at the federal level the primary policy concern in the post-war period has been increasing the production and distribution of Canadian feature films for theatrical, home video/DVD, and television release, provincial governments—most notably in Quebec, Ontario, and British Columbia—have instituted programs to encourage Hollywood producers to locate their film and television productions in such cities as Montreal, Toronto, and Vancouver (see Gasher, 2002a; Elmer and Gasher, 2005).

It is important to understand that Ottawa has perceived cinema for most of its history as a medium of nation-building. The first state-sponsored films in Canada were tools to promote immigration from Britain to settle the Prairies. Motion pictures are believed to have played a key role in Canada attracting three million immigrants between 1900 and 1914. Early films were also used to lure industry and investment capital (Morris, 1978: 133–5).

The use of film as a medium of propaganda during World War I led governments to play an increasing role in film production, and Canada became the first country in the world with government film production units, although Ottawa consistently rejected calls to curtail American monopolization of the commercial film sector. A distinction was made by state officials between the purposeful films of government production and entertainment films (Magder, 1985: 86).

Having previously contracted out film projects, Ontario established the Ontario Government Motion Picture Bureau in 1917. The Bureau purchased the abandoned Trenton Studios in 1923 and ran them until 1934 (Morris, 1978: 70–1). British Columbia established its own Educational and Patriotic Film Service in 1919, becoming one of the first provinces to use film to promote immigration (ibid., 149).

In 1918, the federal government established the Exhibits and Publicity Bureau within the Department of Trade and Commerce for 'the production, acquisition and distribution of motion pictures'. This agency's *Seeing Canada* series, launched in 1919 and aimed primarily at foreign audiences, was designed to attract industry and capital to Canada (ibid., 131–5). The Exhibits and Publicity Bureau became the Canadian Government Motion Picture Bureau in 1923 and was absorbed by the National Film Board of Canada in 1941 (ibid., 161). The establishment of the NFB under the direction of John Grierson in 1939 entrenched the state as a producer of films for nation-building purposes.

Table 7.1 The National Film Board's Academy Awards

Films

Year	Title (Director)
1941	*Churchill's Island* (Stuart Legg)
1953	*Neighbours* (Norman McLaren)
1978	*Le Château de sable* (Co Hoedeman)
1979	*Special Delivery* (John Weldon, Eunice Macaulay)
1980	*Every Child/Chaque enfant* (Eugene Fedorenko)
1983	*If You Love This Planet* (Terre Nash)
1984	*Flamenco at 5:15* (Cynthia Scott)
1995	*Bob's Birthday* (Alison Snowden, David Fine)
2004	*Ryan* (Chris Landreth)
2007	*The Danish Poet* (Torril Kove)

Other Categories

Year	Award
1989	Honorary Oscar in recognition of NFB's 50th anniversary
1999	Technical achievement to NFB scientists Ed H. Zwaneveld and Frederick Gasoi and two industry colleagues for the design and development of the Film Keykode Reader

Source: www.nfb.ca

John Grierson (r), founder of the National Film Board, examines posters produced by the NFB in 1944. During World War II, the NFB was an important agency of propaganda in support of the Allied war effort—its films were distributed theatrically in Canada and the US. (Courtesy Library and Archives Canada, PA-179108)

Increasingly in the post-war period, the federal government has been called upon to address the commercial film sector. The aftermath of World War II demanded that the government redefine the mandate of the NFB—which during the war years was a propaganda agency—and address the American domination of feature film, particularly in the face of a balance-of-payments crisis with the United States. The Emergency Foreign Exchange Conservation Act of 1947, which imposed import restrictions on a number of US goods, excluded motion pictures, even though $17 million of the $20 million taken out of Canada that year by the motion picture industry went to the US. A lobby group from the Motion Picture Export Association of America (MPEAA) and Famous Players Canada Corporation convinced Minister of Trade and Commerce C.D. Howe that Hollywood could help resolve the problem it had helped to create. Rather than impose screen quotas or withholding taxes, Ottawa negotiated the Canadian Co-operation Project with Washington and the resourceful MPEAA.

The deal required Hollywood to: produce a film on Canada's trade-dollar problem; provide more complete newsreel coverage of Canada; produce short films about Canada; release NFB films in the United States; include Canadian sequences in its feature films; make radio recordings by Hollywood stars extolling Canada; and work with a Canadian government officer in Hollywood to co-ordinate the project (Cox, 1980: 34). Anthony D. Smith (1980: 52–3) writes:

> It is hard today to believe that Canada allowed itself to be thus fobbed off, but it is a matter of historical fact that a representative of Canada was specially appointed to reside in Hollywood and supervise small changes of dialogue and location in American films: escaping convicts would trudge their way to Canada rather than Oregon, lovers would elope to Ottawa rather than Chicago, stars would spend glamorous weekends in the Canadian Rockies.

The Canadian Co-operation Project expired in 1951 when Canada's currency reserves crisis eased (Pendakur, 1990: 141).

The first serious attempt by the Canadian government to stimulate indigenous feature-film production was the establishment of the Canadian Film Development Corporation (CFDC, now Telefilm Canada) in 1967. The CFDC was mandated to: invest in Canadian feature-film projects; loan money to producers; present awards for outstanding production; support the development of film craft through grants to filmmakers and technicians; and 'advise and assist' producers in distributing their films (ibid., 148). In sum, the CFDC was designed to ease the burden of funding feature-film production in Canada.

Private investment in film production had been encouraged by Ottawa since 1954 through a 60 per cent capital-cost allowance, a tax deduction available to investors in any film, no matter the source. The law was revised in 1974 to increase the write-off to 100 per cent, but only for investments in Canadian feature films. The impact of the capital-cost allowance is debatable in terms of the program's cultural and economic objectives. Citing figures based on tax-shelter productions from 1974 to 1986, Manjunath Pendakur (ibid., 170–3) acknowledges that the capital-cost allowance boosted film production ($660 million in eligible investment for 432 feature films) and the size of average film budgets (from $527,000 prior to 1974 to $3.5 million by 1986). But the tax shelter was less successful in increasing either the production of identifiably Canadian feature films or their distribution and exhibition. The 1985 *Report of the Film Industry Task Force* (Canada, 1985: 28–9) concluded that the capital-cost allowance, in fact, 'widened the gap between production and market'. Because the introduction of the 100 per cent capital-cost allowance coincided with the CFDC's decision to drop its demand for a distribution agreement as a funding prerequisite, the capital-cost allowance in effect reduced the importance of distributor participation in Canadian film projects. As a result, 'while the supply of Canadian theatrical properties increased considerably, many were totally unmarketable.' Investors proved to be more interested in tax savings than in cinema; when returns on investment were not forthcoming and the economic recession of the early 1980s hit, private investment in film production dried up.

Canadian governments have been reluctant to impose protectionist measures on the film industry, even though Ottawa heard repeated calls for screen quotas in Canadian movie theatres throughout the twentieth century. Part of the problem, certainly, is that the operation of movie theatres falls under provincial jurisdiction, and a nationwide screen quota would demand co-ordination among the 10 provinces. But there really is no public appetite for reducing in any way Hollywood's stranglehold on the Canadian market. Most Canadians—including francophones in Quebec—believe that going to the movies means going to Hollywood movies, and until at least the late 1980s there was probably not a large enough stock of quality Canadian features to warrant a quota.

Neither the 1984 *National Film and Video Policy*, tabled by Liberal Communications Minister Francis Fox (Canada, 1984), nor the 1985 *Report of the Film Industry Task Force* (Canada, 1985), delivered to the Conservative government of Brian Mulroney, favoured quotas, preferring instead to target the structural issues of distribution and **vertical integration**. That is, the problems Canadian filmmakers had in gaining access to Canadian theatre screens was explained by the fact that the same companies that owned major Hollywood studios also owned Canada's principal theatre chains—Famous Players and Cineplex Odeon—and the distribution companies that supplied those theatre chains with films.

By the early years of this decade, these same two theatre chains controlled three-quarters of the Canadian box office. In June 2005, Cineplex purchased Famous Players in a $500 million consolidation deal (Shecter, 2005), making Cineplex by far the dominant theatre chain in the country, with 132 cinemas and 1,301 screens. A condition of the deal, imposed by government, was that Cineplex sell 35 theatres in 17 cities to ensure competition, and the company was expected to control about 60 per cent of the Canadian box office alone. The deal also made Cineplex the leading company in Canada in digital cinema advertising. Cineplex Entertainment is a subsidiary of Onex Corp. (www.onex.com).

In the 1980s, television became by far the largest source of revenue for private Canadian film and video companies, thanks to Canadian ownership and Canadian content regulations, the CBC's inherent interest in Canadian materials, and the licensing in the 1980s of pay-television and specialty channels devoted to broadcasting feature-length films. The CRTC expanded the market to Canadian film producers by licensing its first national pay-TV networks—First

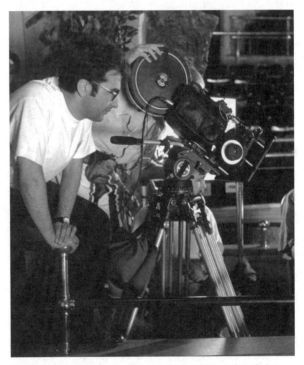

The Canadian film industry has grown over the last decade in particular. Independent filmmaker Atom Egoyan has gained critical acclaim and international recognition for his films such as *The Sweet Hereafter*, *Ararat*, *Exotica*, and *Felicia's Journey*. (Photo: Johnnie Eisen)

Choice and C-Channel—in March 1982 (Magder, 1993: 202). A year later, the CRTC licensed three cable services specializing in movies: SuperChannel (in western Canada), The Movie Network (in eastern Canada), and the French-language Super Écran (Canadian Cable Television Association, 1995).

Producers committed to film production on a full-time basis began to explore a variety of funding sources, specifically, co-production between the private and public sectors and hybrid film-television production. The 1981 film *Les Plouffe*, for example, received one-fifth of its budget from the CBC and was released in three versions: as a six-hour TV mini-series; as a French-language feature film; and as an English-language feature. The principal backers of the 1982 feature film *The Terry Fox Story* were broadcasters Home Box Office and CTV. Ted Magder (1993: 200–1) writes: 'Feature film producers were now more eager than ever to obtain major funding from broadcasters, who had become an important source of film capital.'

In recognition of the promise television held, the federal government in 1983 altered the mandate of the Canadian Film Development Corporation. The federal Department of Communications introduced the $35 million Canadian Broadcast Development Fund, to be administered by the CFDC, which later that year changed its name to Telefilm Canada to reflect its new emphasis on television. While the sum of money in the Broadcast Fund may not appear significant, it increased considerably the ability of production companies to access other sources of investment and it encouraged Canadian film producers to look more and more to television production. Magder (ibid., 211) argues: 'In a very real sense the Canadian government had solved the problem of distribution and exhibition by gearing production activities to the regulated market of Canadian television.'

The Chrétien government's Mandate Review Committee, chaired by Pierre Juneau, stated in its January 1996 report that Canadian movies reached their largest audiences through CBC television channels (Canada, 1996: 31). Elizabeth McDonald, president of the Canadian Film and Television Production Association, reported in July 1996 that Canadian feature films earned 40 per cent of their revenues from pay television (Rice-Barker, 1996: 27).

Building audiences was the central theme of a new feature-film policy introduced by the federal Heritage Ministry in October 2000 (Canada, 2000). The ambitious goal of this policy, entitled *From Script to Screen*,

was to capture 5 per cent of the domestic box office within five years—compared to a paltry 2.1 per cent in 1999—and to increase audiences for Canadian features abroad. 'Now that the Canadian industry has come of age and the building blocks of a vibrant industry are in place, it is time to focus on securing a larger share of our own market.'

The policy amounted to a doubling of the Canadian government's investment in the industry, from $50 million to $100 million annually. The new Canadian Feature Film Fund, administered by Telefilm Canada, supports screenwriting, production, marketing, and promotion. The biggest investment—$40 million annually—goes to the Project Development, Production and Marketing Assistance Program. A 'performance-based component' to this program allocates money to producers and distributors based primarily on their track records of success at the box office, but also recognizes the degree of Canadian content and critical acclaim achieved. A 'selective component' funds the production and distribution of innovative and culturally relevant projects by new filmmakers. The policy also supports screenwriting, professional development, promotion, and film preservation.

The goal of meeting 5 per cent of domestic box office was achieved in 2005. Telefilm Canada reported a domestic share of 5.2 per cent of theatrical revenues, but also reported a significant discrepancy between French-language and English-language films. French-language films produced in Quebec claimed a 25.6 per cent share of the market, while English-language films accounted for just 1.1 per cent. In 2005, nine Quebec films earned more than $1 million at the box office (Dillon, 2006). The two solitudes were in evidence again in 2006, when the Montreal-produced, bilingual action film *Bon Cop, Bad Cop* set an all-time Canadian box-office record of $11.36 million, 90 per cent of which was earned in Quebec movie theatres (Kelly, 2006b). Meanwhile, the producers of the *Trailer Park Boys* movie anticipated a big hit in English Canada in 2006, but decided there wasn't enough interest in Quebec to warrant releasing a dubbed version (Kelly, 2006a).

In spite of the popularity and increasing sophistication of home theatre technology and movies on DVD, theatrical revenues increased in Canada in 2004–5. Revenue from distribution to movie theatres amounted to $446.3 million, a 16.6 per cent increase from two years earlier. Revenue from the wholesaling of DVDs and videocassettes was unchanged at $1.8 billion (Canadian Press, 2006).

TRENDS IN CINEMA POLICY

Since the early 1980s, Ottawa has been gradually ceding its leadership role in the film policy field to the private sector and the provinces. Even though Telefilm remains the single most important source of film funding, no film can be made with Telefilm money alone. Filmmakers find themselves tapping half a dozen sources of funding to get their films made.

Canada's major banks and broadcasters have become important sources of financing for both project development and film and television production. These funding sources include Astral Media Harold Greenberg Fund, Bell Broadcast and New Media Fund, Bravo!Fact, Cogeco Program Development Fund, Independent Production Fund, and Rogers Documentary Fund and Telefund.

Canada's provincial governments have adopted a two-track film strategy. Every province in the country has a film office to promote it as a location for film and television production, primarily to Hollywood producers. In addition, the provinces provide development, production, and/or post-production support to indigenous producers through such funding vehicles as grants, loans, direct investment, and tax credits on labour costs (see *Playback*, 2006).

Music Recording

The music recording industry shares many of the characteristics of other cultural industries in Canada;

it is comprised, on the one hand, of small domestic companies that occupy a minimal and fragile share of the domestic consumer market and, on the other hand, of a few large, multinational companies that dominate the production and distribution of recordings, mainly of foreign origin. A significant distinction, however, is the considerable exposure Canadian recording artists receive—on radio, on music television, on the internet, in mainstream record stores—and the number of recognizable Canadian stars the industry can boast.

Canada is the sixth-largest market for recorded music in the world, accounting for $946.4 million in sales (2003 figures). Canadian-produced recordings accounted for about 22 per cent of those sales, with foreign recordings making up 72 per cent and classical music the remaining 6 per cent. Four multinational companies—Universal Music, Sony BMG, EMI Group, and Warner Music—dominate the Canadian recorded music industry, controlling between 80 and 90 per cent of sales. Canadian companies, however, are responsible for 90 per cent of Canadian-content recordings (Canadian Independent Record Production Association, 2006).

With a weak market base from which to operate, Canadian recording companies find themselves in a vicious circle. Lack of profit on past productions means an inability to raise capital for future investment, which means relatively low budgets for current projects and consequently leads to an inability to attract or keep Canadian stars loyal to their labels. This results in insufficient marketing budgets to promote their products, low consumer awareness of

Table 7.2 Who Gets How Much of Your Dollar When You Buy a CD?

Amount	Recipient
4%	Retailer's profit
7%	Label's profit
9%	Manufacturing costs
12%	Recording artist and songwriting payments
12%	Record company distribution, sales, and overhead costs
13%	Promotion and marketing costs
19%	Recording, video, and production costs
24%	Retail store costs

Source: CRIA data, 2003, from Cathy Allison, *The Challenges and Opportunities of Online Music: Technology Measures, Business Models, Stakeholder Impact and Emerging Trends* (Ottawa: Canadian Heritage, Copyright Policy Branch, 2004), at: www.canadianheritage.gc.ca/progs/ac-ca/progs/pda-cpb/pubs/index_e.cfm.

The Be Good Tanyas—Trish Klein, Frazey Ford, and Samantha Parton—are a Vancouver-based alternative country/folk/bluegrass/blues group, and are among numerous Canadian musicians who have found niche markets and gained international acclaim for their recordings and concert tours. Courtesy of Nettwerk Records. (Photo: Maria Coletsis)

their recordings, and low profitability on subsequent recordings. The size of the domestic market means, however, there is scope for larger sales if Canadian companies could increase their share.

One technique that the independent label Battle Axe Records has used to promote the music group Swollen Members is to build momentum in the small Canadian market through releasing on vinyl, running a side business of providing deejays to clubs and special events who play Battle Axe recordings, promoting clothing on stage, riding the coattails of other stars, touring, and building markets through managed appearances. In this way, in the summer of 2002, Swollen Members achieved platinum-level (100,000 records) sales. The achievement of platinum gave the band an entree into the US market, which in turn multiplied sales back in Canada.

Communications scholar Will Straw (1996) has argued that the structure of the recording industry in Canada is undergoing major changes. The international success of Canadian stars, such as Céline Dion, Shania Twain, Diana Krall, Sarah McLachlan, Bryan Adams, and Alanis Morissette, coincided with an expansion of the domestic market for Canadian-content recordings in the 1990s, the opening up of the global market to diverse music styles (e.g., industrial

noise, rap, country), and the emergence of warehouse-sized super-stores that carry a range of recordings to appeal to every taste. While some predicted that with the consolidation of vertically integrated multinational recording companies the global soundscape would become more homogeneous, Straw (1996: 114) concludes instead that the large multinationals are exploiting relatively autonomous music markets and directly signing artists to serve those markets. For some time, bands like the Tragically Hip, Nickelback, and the Barenaked Ladies continued to be more popular in Canada than in the US, yet they remained attractive properties to major record labels. In the case of Nickelback, their US fame eventually surpassed their renown in Canada.

A result of this 1990s restructuring of the music industry has been the displacement of smaller, independent recording companies, which used to rely on unknown and marginal acts to develop niche markets. Straw portrays a two-tiered industry structure, divided between majors and small independents, both operating internationally:

> As major firms construct global audiences from national niches, small independent firms that had hitherto dominated these niches in their own countries find their room to manoeuvre shrinking. To survive they, too, must move into international markets, licensing their own products in other territories, selling publishing and other rights on a country-by-country basis, and picking up the inventory of other small national labels for distribution. (Ibid., 104)

Historically, the most important policy development for Canadian recorded music was the CRTC's establishment in 1971 of Canadian-content quotas for radio, which required popular music stations to play a minimum of 30 per cent Canadian music. The quotas were a response to the under-representation of Canadian recording artists on Canadian radio stations; as of 1968, Canadian music accounted for between 4

MUSIC DOWNLOADING

If the internet is celebrated for the ways in which it has liberated mass communication, it has also been derided for how it has set free some forms of content, such as recorded music. Downloading popular music—and thus bypassing the cash register at the local music store—has become a favoured computer application, particularly among young people whose disposable income is no match for their insatiable appetite for the latest music and video clips.

MP3 technology, which allows people to share and exchange sound-recording files over computer networks, was developed by the International Organization for Standardization in Geneva in 1992. In March 1998, MP3.com began making the music of small, unknown bands available on the World Wide Web, but this led also to the posting and downloading of the old and new music of established artists. Not surprisingly, the music industry, and some musicians, cried foul, citing copyright infringement and fearing a significant drop in retail sales.

Yet, at the same time as the major recording companies began fighting copyright infringement, they also began searching for ways to profit from file-sharing. For example, the Recording Industry Association of America initially sent cease-and-desist letters to people posting music on-line and asked artists to support their fight against file-sharing. But in December 1998 the five major recording companies at that time—BMG, Sony, Universal, Warner Music Group, and Warner Bros—announced the Secure Digital Music Initiative to seek ways to work with file-sharing technology.

By 1999, two kinds of websites were providing music for downloading—corporate, user-pay sites such as Getmusic, Bugjuice, and Twangthis, and free, rogue sites such as Napster. In June 1999, the American Society of Composers, Authors and Publishers (ASCAP) established a licensing agreement with MP3.com, selling performance rights to internet sites. And in December 1999 the Recording Industry Association of America sued Napster for copyright infringement, following up a month later with a similar suit against MP3.com.

Faced with both court action and revenue shortfalls, Napster announced a partnership with the German media company Bertelsmann AG and began to transform itself into a membership service with royalties paid to songwriters and music publishers. In May 2002 Bertelsmann purchased all of Napster's assets and completed its conversion to a commercial subsidiary.

The legality of file-sharing in Canada remains subject to dispute. Under the Canadian Copyright Act, it is illegal 'to reproduce, authorize the reproduction of, or communicate to the public by telecommunication' a musical work protected by copyright without the permission of the person who holds that copyright. However, the Act exempts 'private copying' for private use. The Federal Court ruled in March 2004 that downloading music for personal use and making that file available to others from your computer does not violate the Copyright Act. This ruling has been appealed and the music industry is lobbying for legislative change to the Copyright Act to restrict file-sharing (see CIPPIC, 2006).

---

and 7 per cent of all music played on Canadian radio at a time when the popular music scene was exploding (Filion, 1996: 132). A points system known as MAPL was devised to determine whether or not recordings qualify as Canadian. That is, a 'Canadian selection' must meet at least two of the following conditions:

- the music is, or lyrics are, performed by a Canadian;
- the music is composed entirely by a Canadian;
- the lyrics are written entirely by a Canadian;
- the musical selection consists of a live performance that is either recorded wholly in Canada or is performed wholly and broadcast live in Canada;

- the musical selection was performed live or recorded after 1 September 1991, and a Canadian who has collaborated with a non-Canadian receives at least 50 per cent of the credit as composer and lyricist according to the records of a recognized performing rights society.

Of course, the regulations are not universal. The quota level is lower for radio formats in which Canadian recordings are not as readily available (e.g., jazz, classical music) and higher for French-language broadcasters. The quota for English-language popular music stations was raised to 35 per cent in 1998, and the CRTC ruled that this level had to be maintained from

Table 7.3 The Canadian Audio Visual Certification Office (CAVCO) Points System

For a creative series to be recognized as a Canadian production, a total of at least six points must be allotted according to the following scale. Points are allotted for each Canadian who rendered the services.	Points awarded
Non-animated productions (live action)	
Director	2
Screenwriter	2
Lead performer for whose services the highest remuneration was payable	1
Lead performer for whose services the second highest remuneration was payable	1
Director of photography	1
Production designer	1
Music composer	1
Picture editor	1
Animated productions	
Director	1
Screenwriter and storyboard supervisor	1
Lead voice for which the highest or second highest remuneration was payable	1
Design supervisor (art director)	1
Camera operator where the camera operation is done in Canada	1
Music composer	1
Picture editor	1
Layout and background where the work is performed in Canada	1
Key animation where the work is performed in Canada	1
Assistant animation and in-betweening where work is performed in Canada	1

Whereas MAPL is the points system for music, CAVCO is the points system for film and video production. If a production receives six points it becomes eligible for a tax credit. Source: Department of Canadian Heritage. Reproduced with the permission of the Minister of Public Works and Government Services Canada, 2006.

6 a.m. to 6 p.m. on weekdays and that selections had to be played in their entirety to qualify. At the same time, the quota for French-language music stations was raised from 50 to 55 per cent.

Although the quota system recognizes the importance of radio airplay to record sales, radio's primacy as a promotional vehicle has been challenged since the 1980s by music video stations (MuchMusic and MusiquePlus in Canada) with their attendant marketing value and, more recently, by a combination of MP3 players and internet sites—iPods and other MP3 players allow people to carry with them, and listen to, their own customized library of music. Websites permitting bands to upload their music provide a much more diverse spectrum than conventional radio, with its limited, mainstream genres, can muster.

The Canadian recording companies, represented by the Canadian Independent Record Production Association (CIRPA, www.cirpa.ca), have always insisted that the Canadian-content rules on broadcasting (radio

and television) are essential to their survival and those of the artists they record. With respect to recording artists, the major recording careers of some Canadian performers and composers were launched through significant airplay on Canadian radio and, more recently, on music video television. If it can be argued that Céline Dion and Bryan Adams no longer need to rely on quotas for airplay, it must also be acknowledged that less mainstream acts and up-and-coming performers do. Providing exposure to bands through radio and TV (as well as, increasingly, through newspaper reviews) in their home markets gives them wider exposure, legitimacy, and a fan and financial foundation to pursue international recognition. The problem for the Canadian recording industry (as opposed to the artists) is that the international success of Canadian performers has not always meant success for Canadian recording companies. Most often emerging international stars leave their original label behind. If necessary, a major recording company will buy out an artist or band's contract and offer them far more investment than a small Canadian company could ever afford. Hence, Canadian labels depend for their survival on the new Canadian artists they discover and for whom they can get exposure through Canadian-content rules.

A second significant policy measure was the establishment in 1982 of the Fund to Assist Canadian Talent on Record, which became known as FAC-TOR/MusicAction when a French-language component was added (www.factor.ca). With the encouragement of the CRTC, the fund was created by several radio broadcasters (CHUM Ltd, Moffatt Communications, Rogers Broadcasting Ltd) in partnership with two major industry associations (CIRPA and the Canadian Music Publishers Association, www.cmrra.ca) to channel money into the Canadian music industry. The funds provided are used, for example, to produce demo tapes and promotional video clips and to organize promotional tours by musicians. In 1986, the federal government established the Sound Recording Development Program (SRDP), which provides about $5 million each year to FACTOR/MusicAction (see www.pch.gc.ca).

The 1996 Task Force on the Future of the Canadian

Music Industry acknowledged that gaps in the federal government's policy apparatus compromised the effectiveness of Canadian-content regulations and the Sound Recording Development Program. Specifically, the Task Force identified three areas of future policy concern: 'grossly inadequate' copyright legislation; the absence of incentives to strengthen independent recording companies (which are responsible for 70 per cent of Canadian-content recordings); and the absence of Investment Canada guidelines for the industry.

In May 2001 the Department of Canadian Heritage announced a new Canadian Sound Recording Policy, entitled From Creators to Audience (www.pch.gc.ca/progs/ac-ca/progs/pades-srdp/pubs/policy_e.cfm). More than the title echoes the federal government's new feature-film policy, described above. Here, too, the goal is to provide support at every level of the sound-recording process—from the development of creators to the building of audiences, as its title suggests. A three-year, $23 million program administered, coincidentally, by Telefilm Canada, it established an eight-part Canada Music Fund, which absorbs the pre-existing Sound Recording Development Program and promised to:

'A MAJOR LABEL DEAL IS LIKE HAVING A CREDIT CARD AT 66 PER CENT INTEREST'

After enduring years of unfair contracts that caused performers such as Prince to change his name and tattoo 'Slave' on his face, in March 2002 top musicians played five venues in Los Angeles to raise money to legally transform musicians from what Don Henley of the Eagles called 'indentured slaves' to a position of greater power (*Globe and Mail*, 2 Mar 2002, R1). Journalist Doug Saunders explains the matter approximately in this way. A typical major-label contract calls for seven albums over seven years with a six-figure advance that is repaid out of royalties of 10 per cent of sales revenues. While this works smoothly for some artists—each year a record comes out—for others, a label may withhold release by months or years for 'marketing reasons', thereby extending the time span of the contract. Meanwhile, the artist cannot release a record with another label, and tours and other appearances often are determined by the release of a record. Record companies charge their entire direct operational costs, including the costs of touring, marketing, distribution, and video production against the 10 per

cent royalty of the artist. As a result, the repayment of advances can take decades and top musicians can take home less than $100,000 per year. As Saunders says: 'An estimated 90 per cent of musicians fail to earn back their advances, meaning that all they have gained from their big-label contract is expensive debt. In the words of one veteran record producer, "A major label deal is like having a credit card at 66 per cent interest."'

The label can cancel the performer's contract and keep the work unreleased or sell the contract to another company. Nor are the labels scrupulously honest. Artists ranging from Peggy Lee to Meat Loaf have hired private auditors and obtained up to $10 million settlements for undisclosed sales. Perhaps the tide will turn. Mariah Carey was paid $28 million by Virgin Records to walk away from her contract. David Bowie bought himself out of his contract and finances himself with bond issues. And Billy Joel says, 'I got signed to a deal with a company that was sucking my blood for 25 years. I just don't want that to happen to nobody else, okay?'

- build community support and skills development of creators;
- support the production and distribution of 'specialized music recordings reflective of the diversity of Canadian voices';
- provide project-based support to new emerging artists;
- develop the business skills of Canadian music entrepreneurs;
- ensure the preservation of Canadian musical works;
- support recording industry associations, conferences, and awards programs;
- and monitor industry performance.

As in the film industry, federal government policy stops short of addressing structural factors that allow the major recording companies to dominate the Canadian market in the first place.

Currently, the most important issue for the recording industry, in Canada and around the world, is the downloading of music. While usually cast as a problem of fans pirating music, the phenomenon is a far richer one and is a measure of the high level of demand for music, as well as established consumption patterns—for example, the expectation created by radio that a person should be able to listen to a piece of music before purchasing it. Increasingly, knowing the technology is already there, consumers are also demanding the right to purchase single songs and even the components that make up songs (see Chapter 10).

The development of sites such as Napster (not New Napster) flouted copyright regulations but clearly demonstrated that the recording industry was not providing sufficient flexibility to customers. In the end, iTunes demonstrated that many were quite willing to pay for single tunes. Between April 2003 and the end of 2006 Apple sold approximately one billion songs through ITMS. More recently, the legitimacy of people not just downloading but recombining the musical elements of others in a mash-up has become an important issue.

The essential issue with music, it would seem, is that industry interests and copyright law have established a regime that does not adequately fit with technological flexibility and human behaviour. Music is created not just for listening but for others to play, that is, to pick up instruments and give voice to lyrics. There was a time when music was played, not sold. Subsequently, music was sold as notes on a page to encourage others to buy the sheet music and play it. Most recently, beginning in the twentieth century, it was sold as recordings. Once heard, tunes run around in our heads, we sing, we dance, we whistle, we bond with others by making music together. Before digital technology, high-fidelity reproduction required sophisticated recording equipment; now, many more can record and exchange music. Obviously, for one person to make money from the investment of creativity, time, and energy of others is unfair. But it is plainly unworkable for artists and recording compa-

COPYRIGHT

Copyright is a form of protection for intellectual property that accrues to an author on making a 'literary work' public. It is a right that is granted for a specified time to an author (or another appointed person or body) to print, record, or perform an original creation (artistic, literary, musical). No registration is required in Canada, not even a copyright mark (©).

Copyright provides weak protection. That is to say, it protects the expression of the idea, not the idea itself, and hence allows for someone else to paraphrase and not breach copyright. But were that same person to copy what was written, word for word, then the person would be guilty of both plagiarizing and of breaching copyright.

Copyright is intended to adjudicate between the author's right to benefit from his or her intellectual work and society's right or need to know. It lasts a long time, currently 50 years after the death of the author.

Copyright has two associated rights, a moral right and a property right. Moral rights, which have nothing to do with morality, ensure that the author of a work will be recognized as the author in perpetuity—even if someone else holds the other set of rights contained in copyright, the property or economic rights. Moral rights also allow the author to retain control over the products or services with which his or her work will be associated. Moral rights also forbid mutilation or transformation of a work over the objection of the author.

Property rights for copyright are those rights that allow for the reproduction of original work, often for financial gain. They may be sold, assigned, and divided in any way the rights-holder may wish. These rights can allow someone besides the author to make money. For example, Michael Jackson, who now owns some early Beatles material, can profit from allowing this music to be used for commercial purposes.

nies to attempt to make illegal the natural desire to share and to try to thwart the opportunity to recreate music a person has heard.

Given the talent of recording artists and the technological, financial, and marketing investment and creativity that music companies can bring to a recording—including its presentation—it would be surprising if musicians could not find a way to make a living from their work. With increased access to production and distribution systems, a wider variety of performers has access to the music market.

Book Publishing

While copyright law in Canada dates back to the Imperial Copyright Act of 1841, public policy directly oriented to book publishing did not expand from that beginning until much later. In 1951 the Massey Commission (the Royal Commission on National Development in the Arts, Letters and Sciences) allocated a scant 10 pages to publishing. The matter was not examined again by the Canadian government until 1966: at that time it was categorized as an adjunct to the pulp and paper industry. The industry was valued at $222 million (Ernst and Ernst, 1966). Within the next four years, and in the context of the positive social and cultural environment created by the Massey Commission, book publishing was recognized as a cultural endeavour.

The process of national cultural self-realization that began with the Massey Commission reached fairly quickly into the arts, including writing, with the founding of the Canada Council in 1957. In 1966 a cultural consciousness of publishing began to dawn, and by the 1970s governments and the industry began to review existing laws and policies and to develop support measures. In 1972 the Canada Council included publishing within its mandate and provided funding to publishers to help them meet the deficits they incurred by publishing titles of cultural significance to Canadians. That same year, the report of the Ontario Royal Commission on Book Publishing echoed a belief that had already been forming—that book publishing was important culturally. In its final chapter the Commission noted:

> the Canadian book publishing industry simply makes too small a contribution to the gross national product for economic considerations to earn it any priority over many other fields of

enterprise. But from the cultural standpoint, the fact that book publishing is the indispensable interface between Canadian authors and those who read their books places it squarely in the centre of our stage. . . . Government assistance [to book publishing], in whatever form, can be justified only to the extent that furnishing it will enrich and protect the cultural life of the people of Ontario and Canada. (Ontario, 1972: 219–20)

In 1977 the federal office of the Secretary of State produced a report on the book publishing industry (Canada, 1977a), to be followed in 1978 by reports on English- and French-language educational publishing (Canada, 1978a, 1978b). By 1980 the Association of Canadian Publishers (ACP) had been formed (its membership was restricted to Canadian-owned firms), and it produced a strategy document in 1980 that echoed many of the findings of the Ontario Royal Commission and called for many of the same funding interventions (Aldana, 1980). By the late 1980s most provinces had joined Ontario in examining the size and nature of book publishing activities within their boundaries.

From the early 1970s onward three elements of book publishing were at least tacitly recognized and they became the foundation for the development of law and policy. They were (and are):

- Book publishing is a strategic industry in that it has a substantial influence on the articulation and development of culture.
- The structure of the Canadian market, especially the English-Canadian market, makes it difficult for domestic publishers of Canadian authors writing on Canadian subjects for a Canadian reading public to survive. Survival is difficult essentially because Canadian authors and publishers must compete with run-on copies of imported books on non-Canadian or universal subjects from other English-speaking markets, particularly the US and UK markets, where set-up costs are amortized on print runs much larger than could ever be contemplated in Canada. Moreover, set-up costs are recovered in the exporter's domestic market.
- Within the well-established Canadian framework of a mixed public- and private-sector economy, a role for government intervention has been created so that Canadians do not have to pay a premium for books on Canadian subjects and can have

access to books on Canadian topics and to Canadian authors of comparable stature to published foreign authors.

On the foundation of these understandings, three types of interventions were considered and then implemented, and are still in effect today.

First is economic or industrial support. This financial support targets the bottom line. It is designed to assist publishing firms over the long or short term to improve their financial performance by such means as increasing market analysis and effort, choosing better-selling titles, establishing exports, co-publishing, training, selling rights, and so forth. The critical variables are: increase revenues while holding down or decreasing costs, and increase market share or establish other means for long-term survival. A review of industrial policies indicates that the focus on financial variables has not been exclusive—nor should it have been. In other words, in the same way that the strategic interests of the country are considered when government assistance is designed for the aerospace or pharmaceutical industry, or, for that matter, roads, so the cultural nature of book publishing has been taken into account in industrial programs.

By far the majority of funding for book publishing at the federal level has flowed to industrial support programs, which are directed at Canadian-owned book publishing firms, and these programs have been run directly out of government departments at both the federal and provincial levels. A commitment to stimulate a heterogeneous industry in terms of size, location, and genre orientation has evolved as an accepted feature of industrial book publishing support programs. To be specific, policy-makers have supported a variety of firms: from the very small to the large, those operating across all provinces or locally, in major cities and outside them, and controlled by a variety of individuals with a range of cultural and financial orientations.

The content of the books published is not considered in industrial support programs. This can best be seen in the objectives and current criteria on which industrial support is based. For instance, with the Book Publishing Industry Development Program (BPIDP), established in 1986 by the Department of Canadian Heritage, the objectives are to increase efficiency and long-term economic viability, to increase the competitiveness and facilitate the expansion of Canadian-owned firms, and to pre-serve a diversity of genres. The eligibility criteria for funding include:

- a minimum of 15 published Canadian-authored trade books with a minimum of 12 new releases published over the preceding three years; or, 10 Canadian-authored scholarly books with a minimum of six new releases over the preceding three years;
- a minimum level of eligible sales—$200,000, or $130,000 for official-language minority publishers and Aboriginal publishers;
- a sales-to-inventory ratio, for its own titles, equal to or greater than the minimum ratio established for the appropriate commercial category;
- financial viability.

This support is provided in tandem with export marketing assistance and, formerly, a postal subsidy program. Export assistance is provided by paying approximately 50 per cent of publishers' expenditures on export efforts.

The second type of support for book publishing is cultural. Cultural support differs from industrial support in both design and impact. Cultural support has a direct concern with specific types of publishing. As the Canada Council mandate terms it, it is support of 'artistic production in the literary arts and the study of literature and the arts'. For the Council, this includes poetry, fiction, drama, titles for children and young adults, literary criticism and literary biography, creative or literary non-fiction, CD-ROMs or cassettes with particular characteristics, and art books of certain types. Special note should be taken of the inclusion of creative and literary non-fiction. The Council has concluded that the development of a national literature of non-fiction deserves support.

Unlike industrial assistance and structural intervention, cultural support does not favour firms of a certain status, nature, size, or financial performance. Rather, once a firm is eligible and published works are deemed of sufficient professional quality, publishing firms receive support based on the number of books published and their professional quality. In fact, the program penalizes those firms that receive industrial support from BPIDP. The Canada Council reasons that this encourages small firms (which usually develop new authors) and does not overly discourage large firms to participate in bringing forward cultural titles.

Provincial support for book publishing contains

both industrial and cultural elements. For example, Manitoba and a number of provinces in the Atlantic region signed regional economic development agreements with the federal government. Under the terms of these agreements, both levels of government contributed funds and services to help book publishers develop their businesses. On the other hand, in British Columbia and Saskatchewan, the main focus of support is cultural and the programs of support are modelled after the Canada Council support programs.

Structural support is the third type of support that Canadian governments have put in place for Canadian publishers. The Copyright Act itself and the so-called distribution right for book publishers constitutes a structural support and was incorporated in the 1997 revisions of the Copyright Act. It was designed to prevent Canadians, especially libraries and booksellers, from importing multiple copies of books for which a Canadian firm has distribution rights. **Reprographic rights**, which compensate authors and publishers for photocopying, are another structural support measure that has assisted the industry.

In 2002 the federal government expanded its structural support by creating Booknet Canada, which describes itself as a not-for-profit agency dedicated to innovation in the book industry supply chain (www.booknetcanada.com). Booknet was created to assist the industry to computerize its business-to-business operations, also known as the supply chain. One goal was to create a standardized way of communicating product descriptions (known as bibliographic metadata) so that a book publisher can go to its database of production information, including title, author, price, book size, binding, content category classification, draw out the information as well as a recognizable tag telling another computer what it is, and send the required information in a predetermined manner so that it would be properly recognized by the receiving computer. This investment of several million dollars over a period of years was to help in the transition to using computerized information systems in the industry. As of 2006 it has been a modest success. While various businesses in the supply chain are now computerized (e.g., publishers, bookstores, and wholesalers), many have idiosyncratic requirements that undermine the efficiency of the system. Booknet is a structural support measure in that it is a government investment designed to reduce the overall transactional costs for the industry.

Each of these support measures—structural, cultural, industrial—has its own dynamic. Structural support policies usually become invisible once implemented. They become part of the environment within which publishers, book retailers, or other businesses operate: they are taken for granted just like any other principle of doing business. Industrial support encourages publishers to focus on their identities as businesses, that is, the financial elements of their enterprise—the size of markets, costs of production, distribution efficiencies, and overall performance. Cultural support programs encourage publishers to focus on the reasons for which they are in this unique business. That is, whether in New York, London, Tokyo, or Paris, book publishing companies rarely turn profits anywhere near as large as those of any other industry, cultural or otherwise. For publishers, publishing most often represents an extension of the creation of meaning. Publishers attempt to create resonance (as judged by both the critics and the market) for the meaning created by the author. Publishing is not usually conceived as a means to get rich—which is not to say that large multinational conglomerates, such as HarperCollins, Bertelsmann, Macmillan, and Pearson, are not doing exactly that.

What has been the result of these book publishing support policies? The pessimists point to the continuing low profitability of the industry and a lack of substantial increase in market share for the Canadian-owned sector. But there are definite positive signs, especially if one takes a cultural perspective. The most obvious sign is the rising profile of Canadian writers within and outside Canada. Up to the 1960s it was difficult to find a recently published novel set in Canada or written by a Canadian in many bookstores. And international notice of Canadian authors outside of literary circles was also extremely limited. Canada could boast no writing community, and no authors of world stature who were recognized as Canadian writers in the same way that, say, the Group of Seven Canadian painters were recognized. Today, the field has been transformed. There are about 20 to 30 well-known and respected Canadian writers who are known in and outside Canada—and not just in English-speaking countries. They include Margaret Atwood, Alice Munro, Robertson Davies, Ann-Marie MacDonald, Anne Michaels, Michael Ondaatje, Guy Vanderhaeghe, W.P. Kinsella, Mordecai Richler, Yann Martel, Margaret Sweatman, Jane Urquhart, Douglas Coupland, Margaret Laurence, Rohinton Mistry, Antonine Maillet, and Mavis Gallant. Besides these

STRUCTURAL SUPPORT INTRODUCED THROUGH THE BACK DOOR

In the early 1990s the Competition Bureau allowed a man named Larry Stevenson to purchase and amalgamate what were then Canada's two main bookstore chains, Smithbooks and Coles. Upon being given this **effective monopoly** of the chain store segment of the market, Stevenson set out to build a series of big-box bookstores called Chapters. From a public perspective his venture was a great success. More books became available in more locations throughout the country. From an industry perspective, Stevenson's operation was something between a limited success and an unmitigated disaster. While providing retail space for publishers, as the retailer of as much as 60 to 70 per cent of a publisher's books Chapters was able to dictate its own terms of payment. Thus, while publishers billed Chapters to pay within 90 days—60 days longer than in normal businesses—Chapters began to extend the payment time to 120 days or longer. To avoid paying altogether, it could ship the books back to the supplying publisher and reorder them the next day, further extending the payment time by another 90 days. Publishers were powerless to act since to do so would have meant losing the majority of their sales. This business behaviour on the part of Chapters put the ability of publishers to publish in jeopardy and in one instance, according to the monitor put in charge of restructuring General Distribution Services, led to the company's demise.

In 2001, Heather Reisman and her husband, owners of Indigo Books and Music, bought Chapters in a hostile takeover. Reisman's husband is the very rich and successful Gerald Schwartz, who owns Onex, a diversified company with holdings in such industries as electronics manufacturing, theatrical exhibition, sugar refining, and automotive products. In 2002 Onex had revenues of $23 billion and 98,000 employees worldwide. The two are also well-known supporters of the Liberal Party—for example, they contributed $75,000 to Paul Martin's leadership bid. While many publishers were relieved at the change of ownership, they were also concerned with the even greater concentration of ownership in book retailing. So was the Competition Bureau, which asked Reisman to sell off some of her stores. She agreed, but there were no serious buyers. Thus the Bureau let her keep the stores at the same time as it worked out a performance agreement in which she agreed to pay her bills within a certain period and to behave in a certain way towards her suppliers, the publishers. According to one perceptive analyst, the result was the beginning of a regulatory regime in book retailing, at least one governing the behaviour of Indigo/Chapters. A different way of putting it would be that the government had allowed such concentration of ownership in book retailing that it was forced to create structural support in the name of a set of rules for this national book chain monopoly.

---

are famous non-fiction writers such as Farley Mowat, Michael Ignatieff, and John Ralston Saul, to mention only a few. These authors, all prize winners, many at the international level, are published in other languages and read around the world.

Another way to measure the effects of book publishing policies is to view the growing success of Canadian book publishers, whose exports now total over 30 per cent of their domestic sales. Canadian-owned firms are increasing their share of the domestic market. Canadian-owned, English-language firms seem to be publishing fewer titles but achieving greater sales per title. Increasing numbers of movie producers are purchasing the right to make Canadian novels into movies, and the movie version of Michael Ondaatje's *The English Patient* captured nine Academy Awards in 1997. Nevertheless, while the publishing industry is culturally vibrant, it remains financially

vulnerable. Without continued contributions from governments, this $4 billion industry (at the retail level) would face financial ruin.

Magazine Publishing

The magazine industry is interesting for a number of reasons. At a first level, magazines are powerful builders of community. Their regular, periodic publication, their specializations, their ability to provide readers with exposure to a variety of writers, and their advertiser-funded ability to provide high-quality editorial content complemented by attractive graphics for a low price all give them a significant power to build a community through loyal subscribers and purchasers. Regular readers often gradually identify with the point of view of the magazine, thereby consolidating their membership in that community.

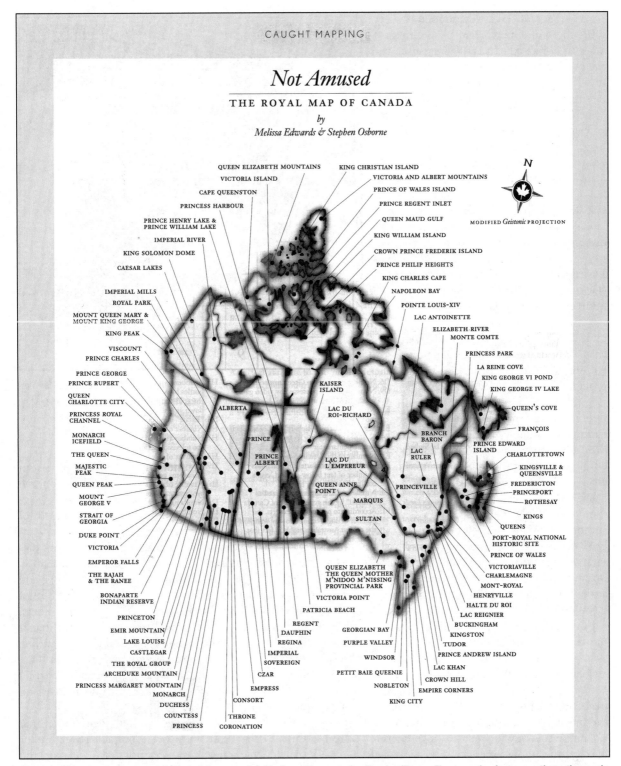

CAUGHT MAPPING

Not Amused

THE ROYAL MAP OF CANADA

by
Melissa Edwards & Stephen Osborne

Geist magazine has been successful in building a readership for a literary and cultural audience. The magazine features a thematic map in every issue, as well as a variety of other creative and engaging elements. A recent map featured locations named after royalty. Reprinted from *Geist* magazine, issue 63. Visit www.geist.com.

At a second level, this community of subscribers and purchasers allows magazines to attract advertisers to buy space in their magazines. Having created a community, the magazine sells to its advertisers the passing attention of its readers, which is, hopefully, focused on the advertisement and shaped by the editorial content of the magazine. Thus, advertisers can reach their desired market—whether those interested in reading a weekly selection of Canadian news (*Maclean's*), a monthly collection of Canada's photogenic regions, flora, and fauna (*Canadian Geographic*), a monthly discussion of social issues from a left-leaning political perspective (*Canadian Dimension*), a taste of literary non-fiction (*Geist*), or a monthly look at Canadian business (*Report on Business*).

These two attributes of magazines—their creation of demographically identifiable communities and their selling of those communities to advertisers—combine to provide a third level of interest in magazines that could be termed 'the national interest'. National magazines create a national community—one that is aware of the latest changes to affect them, that engages in debate about the implications of those changes and about what other opportunities and challenges exist that might affect them. National magazines not only build a national community of authors, historians, and news junkies, but also doctors, engineers, youth, and practitioners in various fields, such as welding, small-appliance repairs, house-building, nursing, and so on. Also found on newsstands across Canada are magazines serving computer enthusiasts, cyclists, golfers, water and snow skiers, science fiction enthusiasts, body builders, do-it-yourselfers, snowboarders, and countless other special interests.

The characteristics of the known readers and subscribers—that is, the target market—determine the content created and circulated in magazines. Given that Canada's population is one-tenth that of the US, the inevitable subordination of Canadian interests to US interests is easy to predict. While that is not so bad in magazines about water skiing, in those dedicated to social and political matters few Canadians would be happy seeing only one-tenth of the space available devoted to a discussion of Canadian issues. The

This cartoon, illustrating the debate surrounding Bill C-55, demonstrates how vociferously the US government pursued the market interests of its magazine companies and how much US magazines wanted access to the Canadian advertising market. (Aislin, *The Gazette*, Montreal)

inevitable shaping of Canadian opinion by American magazines has led to a national social policy concern surrounding the Canadian magazine industry.

Early magazine publishing policy consisted of copyright and postal subsidies to free up the log-jam of costly distribution for magazines. These subsidies provided a foundation to build the Canadian nation and keep Canadians in touch with one another and with the outside world. On the basis of a great deal of invested energy by authors, editors, and publishers, and assisted by lower postal rates, a Canadian magazine (and newspaper) industry was able to grow. The market never excluded foreign magazines. In fact, both readers and authors looked to foreign magazines as much as Canadian magazines for informative and entertaining material.

While postal subsidies worked well for a long time, by the 1950s and early 1960s advertising rather than circulation and subscriptions had become the driving force in the magazine industry. At that time Canada's magazine industry was dominated by foreign magazines to such an extent that no national weekly newsmagazine—only *Maclean's*, a monthly—existed. The nearest approximation was the Canadian edition of *Time*, in which a few pages of Canadian material were added to the front of the magazine.

By 1961 the relative underdevelopment of a domestic publishing industry, including magazines, had been recognized, and the Royal Commission on Publications, chaired by Gratton O'Leary, was set up to examine the situation in detail and bring forward recommendations. The O'Leary Commission identified the main difficulty of establishing a domestic magazine industry to be the unfair advantage of foreign magazines in the marketplace. Foreign magazines, such as *Time*, develop editorial content for their own market, paid for by selling ad space to advertisers in the US. They may then take this content, spruce it up a bit by adding a Canadian section, and sell a Canadian edition to readers in Canada after having collected another set of ads (from Canadian businesses) for the Canadian edition (some pan-North American advertisers always stay on to access both markets). The only added costs, because the initial costs have already been absorbed by the US edition, are the printing, the selling of ads, and the small amount of new editorial content. In contrast, Canadian magazines have to pay the whole cost of producing and editing an original magazine, the full cost of selling the ads, and the full cost of printing a short run.

In 1965, the government of Canada decided to address this unfair advantage of foreign magazines and to provide a stronger advertising base for the Canadian magazine industry (American-produced Canadian editions were 'poaching' advertising dollars away from fully Canadian magazines). It brought forward Bill C-58, which allowed Canadian advertisers to claim advertising as a tax-deductible expense only if that advertising was placed in Canadian periodicals. Two criteria determined what qualified as a Canadian periodical. The first was that ownership had to be at least 75 per cent Canadian. The second was that no more than 20 per cent of the content of a magazine could come from one or more issues of one or more periodicals that were printed, edited, or published outside Canada. This bill passed and became section 19 of the Income Tax Act.

The government enacted further legislation in 1965—Customs Tariff Code 9958 (Customs Tariff, 1965, Schedule VII). This tariff forbade the importation of any split-run magazine, that is, any magazine that had been prepared for a foreign (usually the US)

market and had had some or all of the advertising stripped out and replaced by advertising targeted at the Canadian market. Further, it forbade the importation of magazines that contained more than 5 per cent of advertising directed solely at the Canadian market. This legislation was silent on advertising placed by multinational companies and targeted at both Canadians and US citizens. Thus, many multinational companies created ads with both markets in mind. The net result was that multinationals spent far less per capita on magazine advertising in Canada than they spent in the US. A study by Carleton University professors I.A. Litvak and C.J. Maule (1978), which examined the big four North American car makers, placed the per-capita value of magazine advertising in Canada at about one-fifth that spent in the US.

These two policies worked well until 1993, when Time Warner had the clever idea of beaming its editorial content by satellite, not across but above the border, to a printing plant in Canada and selling ads for the resulting magazine, a 'Canadian edition' of *Sports Illustrated*. In so doing, it was getting around the letter, though not the spirit, of the law. Time Warner was still subject to the provisions of section 19 of the Income Tax Act, that is, Canadian advertisers would not be able to declare their advertising expenses as business expenses. However, *Sports Illustrated* was able to address this problem by slashing the advertising rates that a Canadian magazine would normally charge for reaching an audience like that of *Sports Illustrated*. Canada Customs ruled that the resulting magazine was technically not a split-run.

While *Sports Illustrated* went ahead and built up its Canadian sales to 125,000 copies, the Task Force on the Magazine Industry, set up in 1993 and chaired by Patrick O'Callahan, was given the mandate 'to review federal measures to support the Canadian magazine industry [and] ... to propose measures that will enable the government to effectively carry through on its policy objective of ensuring that Canadians have access to Canadian information and ideas through genuinely Canadian magazines' (Canada, 1994: 4). More specifically, the mandate of the Task Force was to recommend ways to bring section 19 of the Income Tax Act and Tariff Code 9958 up to date and thereby to ensure a flow of adequate advertising dollars to Canadian magazines.

After reviewing the industry, the Task Force recommended ill-advisedly that an 80 per cent excise tax

A 2002 ad campaign of Magazines Canada included this full-page ad with the incongruous element of poodles, rather than huskies, pulling a dogsled to make the point that 'it's not the same if it's not Canadian'. (Genuine Canadian Magazine—www.magazinescanada.ca)

This 2007 ad campaign from Magazines Canada is less amusing than the 2002 poodle ad but it is designed to encourage subscriptions rather than emphasize the unique value of Canadian magazines. (Genuine Canadian Magazine—www.magazinescanada.ca)

(payable by the printer or distributor) be placed on advertising space sold by foreign magazines to advertisers who were directing their advertising to Canadian audiences. The government looked favourably on this and brought forward Bill C-103, to apply the 80 per cent excise tax on all foreign publications.

In 1996 the US challenged this legislation, magazine postal subsidies, and the provision of Tariff Code 9958 against the importation of split-runs within the World Trade Organization. The WTO, after appeal, ruled in favour of the US. Determined to protect Canadian magazines, the Canadian government responded with alternative measures. In place of postal subsidies, the Department of Canadian Heritage now provides postal grants to qualifying Canadian-owned and -controlled magazines. These grants are deposited directly into the magazines' accounts with Canada Post. Second, in 1998 the government brought forward Bill C-55, which became the Foreign Publishers Advertising Services Act (passed into law in 1999) and would allow only Canadian magazines to provide advertising space to those seeking to reach Canadian consumers. Because advertising is defined by the WTO as a service, not a good, the same provisions do not apply. Moreover, the Act proposed fines of up to $250,000 for publication of split-run magazines.

The reaction of the US to Bill C-55 was immediate. Knowing that it was unlikely to win if it protested Bill C-55 within WTO, the US lobbied hard and, when that failed, threatened massive retaliation, far beyond the financial restriction that US magazine firms would have to live with, in short, a trade war. In statements to the press the US challenged the legitimacy of Canada's new measures, noting that Canada should not have brought forward legitimate legislation to protect its magazine industry given that its first attempt was judged to be illegitimate by the WTO. (It is common practice for the US to interpret international agreements according to the letter, not the spirit, of the law.) The Minister of Canadian Heritage, Sheila Copps, responded in kind, saying that if the US continued to undermine legitimate cultural concerns and the development of Canadian policy, the world would see the US as a bully, which would threaten the legitimacy of international trading agreements.

Though Bill C-55 cleared the House of Commons in March 1999 and went on to the Senate for consideration, negotiations between Canada and the US continued and commentary flourished. On 26 May 1999, Trade Minister Sergio Marchi and Copps announced that a bargain had been struck, one requiring substantial amendments to Bill C-55 and, indeed, to the Income Tax Act. US magazines were given the right to create and sell split-runs in Canada. These split-runs, in which certain ads are pulled and replaced by Canadian ads, are allowed to have 18 per cent of their ad space devoted to advertising directed solely at Canadians (phased in over three years). Should US magazine owners want to increase their access to Canadian advertisers, then they would be required to get permission from the Department of Canadian Heritage, set up an office in Canada, and increase their Canadian editorial content (supposedly to at least 50 per cent). In contrast with the past, Canadian advertisers will now be able to deduct their advertising costs in split-runs of any magazine as business expenses.

Besides giving away an undetermined percentage of the advertising market to the US (with no discussion of other foreign countries), the deal also almost guts section 19 of the Income Tax Act. This legislation, which required 75 per cent Canadian ownership of Canadian publications, was also changed. Foreign owners are now able to acquire up to 49 per cent of 'Canadian' publications (magazine companies are controlled with much less than 49 per cent ownership).

What did the Canadian magazine industry get in this deal? Ministers Marchi and Copps claimed that it represented a victory for Canada: they had achieved recognition from the US of Canada's 'right in trade to protect our culture'. The fact that this is exactly what the cultural exemption in NAFTA was supposed to do was not mentioned. The ministers also prom-

ised a fund to assist the Canadian magazine industry with its anticipated loss of $98 million per year in ad revenue (Canadian Magazine Publishing Industry, various press releases). In December 1999, Copps announced a $50 million assistance fund (*Vancouver Sun*, 17 Dec. 1999, C12). By 2000 the fund had been named the Canada Magazine Fund and it had been reduced to $35 million.

The beginning of this fund was inauspicious—it really represented the government buying off the industry rather than creating justifiable policy (and potentially facing a trade war from the ever aggressive US government). However, some unexpected value appears to be emerging. The Fund, which is being made available to associations as well as individual magazines, is encouraging national projects that otherwise would never get off the ground. For example, in 2002 the Canadian Magazine Publishers Association mounted an ad campaign to draw attention to the value of Canadian-published magazines. In 2007, it mounted another campaign, 'Buy 2, Get 1 Free', in which Canadians were invited to buy two subscriptions and get a third free. Such national projects are bolstering Canadian periodicals and increasing the interest of Canadians in reading them.

Concern over the gutting of policy by international trading rules extends beyond magazines into all sectors of cultural policy. For nearly two years (early 1997 to early 1999), a select group of cultural and new media industry representatives met at the behest of the Department of Canadian Heritage and the Department of Foreign Affairs and International Trade to discuss and develop an overall strategy document. The group was called the Cultural Industries Sectoral Advisory Group on International Trade

AN INTERNATIONAL INSTRUMENT ON CULTURAL DIVERSITY: WHAT IT CAN DO

An international instrument on cultural diversity can:

- recognize the importance of cultural diversity;
- acknowledge that cultural goods and services are significantly different from other products;
- acknowledge that domestic measures and policies intended to ensure access to a variety of indigenous

cultural productions are significantly different from other policies;

- set out rules on the kind of domestic regulatory and other measures that countries can and cannot use to enhance cultural and linguistic diversity; and
- establish how trade disciplines would apply or not apply to cultural measures that meet the agreed upon rules.

(SAGIT). The result was a report entitled *Canadian Culture in a Global World: New Strategies for Culture and Trade* (see www.dfait-maeci.gc.ca/tna-nac/canculture-en.asp). The report brings forward two main recommendations. The first is for the government to continue to use the strategy of exempting culture in international trade negotiations. This is really the fallback position in case the second, new, and more radical recommendation fails. That second recommendation is to negotiate 'a new international instrument that would specifically address cultural diversity, and acknowledge the legitimate role of domestic cultural policies in ensuring cultural diversity'. Such an instrument, the report noted, would distinguish between cultural products and policy and other trade products and policy. Thus, it would aim to outline and regulate the policy measures that countries can take to ensure access to natural cultural products (see www.unesco.org/culture/en/diversity/convention for the text of the resulting convention).

The international community received this policy initiative with some interest. As noted in Chapter 1, in October of 2005 UNESCO, the United Nations Educational, Scientific and Cultural Organization, adopted a Convention on the Protection and Promotion of the Diversity of Cultural Expressions and sent the document to its member nations for approval by their national governments. At the time of writing it is difficult to find any report of substantial progress in gaining signatures from UNESCO's 191 member countries.

Newspaper Publishing

It is not quite accurate to say that the newspaper industry in Canada is unregulated, but it is the closest thing we have to an industry that operates exclusively on market principles. Historically, the vast majority of newspapers in Canada have been organized commercially, even if their owners were political movements, trade unions, churches, or wealthy families. Beginning in the late nineteenth century, newspapers became mass media seeking to maximize readership and revenues, and as the twentieth century

The arrival of the *National Post* on the market in the autumn of 1998 increased readers' choice for a national daily newspaper and brought greater competition among Canada's newspaper chains. (Source: *Globe and Mail*, 30 Oct. 1998. Reprinted with permission from *The Globe and Mail*.)

progressed, corporate newspaper chains were forged from previously independent family-owned newspapers. In 1967, for example, Paul Desmarais's Power Corp. bought *La Presse* from the Berthiaume family and the Montreal daily became the flagship of a newspaper group that included *Le Nouvelliste* (Trois-Rivières), *La Voix de l'Est* (Granby), and *La Tribune* (Sherbrooke). Similarly, the Southam chain expanded to eight dailies when it bought the *Montreal Gazette* in 1968 from the White family, which had owned the *Gazette* for 98 years. Increased concentration and decreased competition in the newspaper industry prompted two federal government inquiries: the 1969–70 Senate Special Committee on Mass Media (the Davey Committee) and the 1980–1 Royal Commission on Newspapers (the Kent Commission). These inquiries will be discussed in further detail in Chapters 8 and 9.

Today, the newspaper industry is dominated by media conglomerates. For the most part, newspapers have become merely one sphere in a broad domain of commercial interests extending far beyond journalism as corporate owners perceive their media properties as avenues for profit and the promotion of their other goods and services. The increasingly concentrated and corporate ownership of the press in Canada, especially since the late 1990s, has prompted governments to reconsider policy measures to ensure the editorial independence of the press and a healthy range of news, information, and opinion. The ownership of Canada's community weekly newspapers, too, has become increasingly concentrated. According to statistics compiled by the Canadian Community Newspaper Association in January 2005 (CCNA, 2005), three companies—Sun Media Corp. (76 titles), Torstar Corp. (70 titles), and Black Press Group Ltd (66 titles)—owned almost 30 per cent of the community weekly newspapers in the country (212 out of 713). The community newspaper holdings of two groups—Torstar Corp. and CanWest Global Com-munications, companies which also own daily newspapers—accounted for more than 45 per cent of total community weekly newspaper circulation.

The Quebec government conducted hearings on press concentration in February and March of 2001 and produced a report in November of that year, *Mandat d'Initiative portant sur la Concentration de la Presse* (Quebec, 2001). In the fall of 2002 the Quebec government's Ministry of Communications and Culture established an advisory committee to recom-mend legislative measures that could be introduced as early as the spring of 2003. The June 2006 report of the Standing Senate Committee on Transport and Communications (Canada, 2006a) made a number of recommendations to limit corporate concentration and cross-ownership across the media spectrum. Noting that Canada was 'atypical among large democracies', the Committee encouraged the federal government to develop the same kind of regulatory mechanisms that impose ownership restrictions in the democracies of Britain, France, Australia, Germany, and the United States (ibid., 24). The report concluded: 'Excessive levels of concentration and the domination of particular markets by one media group engender distrust in the very institutions that Canadians rely upon for their news and information' (ibid., 63).

During the 1990s, three companies—Hollinger, CanWest Global Communications, and Quebecor—moved to the forefront of the daily newspaper industry. Hollinger, an international company that counted among its properties the *London Daily Telegraph*, the *Jerusalem Post*, and the *Chicago Sun-Times*, launched an aggressive buying spree in 1992, quickly acquiring majority ownership of Southam Inc., which was at the time Canada's largest daily newspaper chain. By 1999 Hollinger owned 97 per cent of Southam and controlled 59 of Canada's 105 daily newspapers, including a new national newspaper, the *National Post*, which it launched in October 1998. This rapid expansion, however, overextended Hollinger, and by April 2000, Conrad Black, the company's bombastic chairman, announced his decision to sell off the bulk of Hollinger's community weekly newspapers and a number of its smaller dailies in order to reduce the company's debt. Hollinger's major dailies were initially excluded, but in July 2000 CanWest Global struck a $3.5 billion deal to acquire 13 metropolitan dailies and Hollinger's internet properties, magazines, and community publishing operations, as well as 50 per cent of the flagship *National Post*. A year later, CanWest purchased the remaining half of the *National Post*.

CanWest, founded in the early 1970s by I.H. (Izzy) Asper as an independent television company, has become the principal media conglomerate in the country with Canada's largest chain of daily newspapers (CanWest MediaWorks), a national television network (Global Television), and an internet portal (www.canada.com) that brings together on the World

Wide Web the content of its television and newspaper divisions. CanWest, which also operates radio and television stations in Australia, New Zealand, Great Britain, and Turkey, has subsidiaries involved in new media and digital television (see www.canwestglobal.com).

Quebecor, similarly, has risen from modest beginnings to become a central player in the Canadian media landscape. Company founder Pierre Péladeau started his empire by buying the Montreal community newspaper *Le Journal de Rosemont* in 1950—with, as legend has it, money borrowed from his mother—and rapidly expanded his holdings in daily newspapers, television, and printing. When the company outbid Torstar in 1998 to take control of the Sun Media Group, Quebecor became the second-largest newspaper company in Canada with 25.4 per cent of the readership market and a major internet portal (www.canoe.ca). In September 2000, Quebecor outbid Rogers Communications for Groupe Vidéotron, a $4.9 billion transaction that included Quebec's largest cable television distribution company and the French-language TVA television network (see www.quebecor.com).

Finally, another giant entered the newspaper market in 2000. Telecommunications conglomerate BCE Inc. (Bell Canada Enterprises) bought the country's second-largest and most prestigious daily newspaper,

ONE PUBLISHER-EDITOR RELATIONSHIP

Journalists and newspaper readers have long laboured under the mistaken assumption that, on the whole, owners of newspapers do not interfere with the editorial stance taken in their newspapers. The actions of the Aspers, owners of CanWest Global Communications Corp., in creating national editorials flew in the face of this myth. It outraged editors working for them and journalists across the nation (and elsewhere), and moved a group of 40 former executives of Southam Inc. (the foundation of the Aspers' newspaper holdings) to take out full-page ads questioning whether the Aspers were threatening freedom of the press. Subscriptions plummeted. It also caused investors to question the wisdom of holding CanWest Global stock and their stock price fell precipitously.

David Estok has noted the Aspers' apparent backing away from the frequency of these national editorials and also noted:

> That the Aspers wanted to use their newspapers to express their opinions about current events on the editorial pages is normal and perfectly natural. That the Aspers used such a blunt instrument, bullying tactics and firing people to get their way is less so.

In other words, it is not the principle of editorial freedom that needs protection, just the finesse with which it is carried out. This is tantamount to accepting what many have argued is unacceptable: direct influence of editorial stance by an owner.

A view of a more genteel wielding of influence has been brought forward by Max Hastings in *Editor: An Inside Story of Newspapers*. Hastings is a former editor of the *Daily Telegraph*, a UK newspaper owned by Conrad Black, the man who sold the Aspers their newspapers. Hastings recounts how Black would phone him at any hour and quiz him on the *Telegraph*'s coverage of certain people, especially the rich and/or powerful, and sometimes thugs and scoundrels. He also tells of the difficulties he experienced in shaping coverage of members of the Board of Directors of the *Telegraph*. Perhaps most telling is his account of Black's real concern over the publication of a piece in another of Black's holdings, the *Spectator*, describing Hollywood as 'Jewish town'. Various Hollywood luminaries demanded space in both the *Spectator* and the *Telegraph* to denounce the author. In response to Hastings's opinion that they should be allowed space to reply, Black was reported to have said, 'You don't understand, Max. My entire interests in the United States and internationally could be seriously damaged by this.'

This one sentence captures both Black's sense of legitimacy of his role in determining editorial policy and his acceptance that his financial interests could or should be determinants of the content of his newspaper holdings. Even if Hastings is willing to soften his vision of Black—Black once wrote a note to Hastings addressed to 'Sir Max Hastings OM, CH, KBE, DSO and Cluster MA (Oxon)' from 'His Most Eminent Beatitude the Grand Mufti of the Telegraph'—the portrait of owner influence is clear. Ultimately, freedom of the press belongs to those who own one.

the *Globe and Mail*, from the Thomson Corporation. Having also acquired the CTV national television network, BCE formed a new subsidiary, Bell GlobeMedia (see www.bce.ca). The economic implications of this consolidation will be discussed in Chapter 8 and what it means for journalism specifically will be addressed in Chapter 9.

Beyond the scale of these new companies, though, what has really grabbed the attention of policy-makers is the extent to which a new generation of newspaper owners has taken to meddling with the editorial content of its newspapers. If, in the past, the owners of the Southam and Thomson chains left their editors alone to run their own newspapers—provided they were making money—Conrad Black and the Asper family have been far more interventionist, even politically engaged. Black, for example, took great interest in the editorial content of his newspapers, to the point of writing his own letters to the editor and the occasional book review. He chose the editors of his newspapers as much for their political views as their journalistic competence, and he was constantly on the phone to them, questioning decisions, criticizing, and advising.

Black was also a newsmaker in his own right. An imposing figure with strong opinions to match his considerable intelligence, he used the platform newspaper ownership afforded to assert his right-wing views, criticizing labour unions, 'lazy' journalists, Canadian and Quebec nationalists, and especially the governing Liberal Party under Jean Chrétien (see Barlow and Winter, 1997). Black took a hard line against striking *Calgary Herald* workers during an eight-month dispute in 1999–2000, insulting their union representative and denigrating their motives (see Ferguson, 2000; Canadian Press, 2000). When Black was offered a British peerage, after having become a British citizen for this purpose, Prime Minister Jean Chrétien cited precedent dating to 1919 that meant a Canadian could not accept a British lordship. Black then sued Chrétien and lost, renounced his Canadian citizenship, and moved to England, where he became Lord Black of Crossharbour (Arab, 2002).

Black, of course, has been making news of a different sort since 2003, when he stepped down as chief executive officer of Hollinger International after an internal company inquiry determined that he and several other senior executives had received more than $32 million (US) in unauthorized payments.

Since that time, Black has been sued by Hollinger, a number of Canadian investors, and the US Securities and Exchange Commission for a range of alleged fraud, racketeering, and false accounting practices. Black is also facing criminal charges from the US Attorney's Office in Chicago. In 1999, Black was the third largest newspaper publisher in the world. The only significant newspaper holding of Hollinger International is the *Chicago Sun-Times* and Hollinger Canadian Newspapers has been reduced to holdings of 10 small daily newspapers accounting for less than 1 per cent of daily newspaper circulation in Canada (Challands, 2005).

Editorial interference has taken a more radical turn under Black's successors—CanWest founder Izzy Asper (who died in 2003) and his son and successor, company president and chief executive officer Leonard Asper. If Black at least tolerated diversity of opinion, even criticism, in his newspapers, the Aspers have been far less respectful of contrary views. In August 2001, CanWest terminated Southam News national affairs columnist Lawrence Martin, claiming it was an effort to avoid redundancy and reduce costs and not for anything he had written. But *Maclean's* said Martin was fired for his persistent criticism of then Prime Minister Jean Chrétien over 'Shawinigate', an issue involving the receipt of federal funds by a resort hotel in Chrétien's Shawinigan riding (see Lindgren, 2001). Later the same month, *Montreal Gazette* publisher Michael Goldbloom announced his resignation. Though he was vague about the reasons, Goldbloom told his staff that 'CanWest has a more centralized approach to its management, and there are some aspects of the operations where we have had different perspectives' (Sweet, 2001).

The Aspers breathed new life into government inquiries into corporation concentration in December 2001 when they decided to run 'national editorials' up to three times per week in 14 of their major daily newspapers. The editorials were to be commissioned by CanWest's head office in Winnipeg. Member newspapers were not only ordered to run them, but the editorial boards of their newspapers were also prohibited from publishing any subsequent editorials dissenting from the views expressed in the national editorials.

CanWest's national editorial policy was a radical departure from Southam's long-standing commitment to the editorial independence of each of its member newspapers and an attempt by head office to assume control of the editorial voice of its newspapers. The policy was met with condemnation from journalists, academics, politicians, and newspaper readers. Journalists at the *Montreal Gazette* signed and published a petition criticizing the national editorials, staged a by-line strike, and established an independent website to draw attention to the issue (see Gasher, 2002b). A group of 40 former Southam executives, including the company's former chief executive officer, took out a full-page newspaper advertisement in June 2002 to protest the policy (Damsell, 2002). The Féderation professionelle des journalistes du Québec called for a federal parliamentary inquiry.

With the spotlight on CanWest, the company made its own situation worse by refusing to cover the controversy it aroused—forcing people to inform themselves about what was happening at CanWest by reading competing newspapers—and by providing critics with considerable evidence of its intolerance for editorial dissent. For example, four of its columnists—Stephen Kimber at the *Halifax Daily News*, Doug Cuthand at the *Regina Leader-Post*, Michael Johansen at the *St John's Telegram*, and Lyle Stewart at the *Montreal Gazette*—subsequently quit the chain, citing continual editorial interference from CanWest managers. The issue came to a head in June 2002 when CanWest fired *Ottawa Citizen* publisher Russell Mills (Zimonjic, 2002; Regan Shade, 2005). Mills maintained he was fired because of a four-page *Citizen* article that was critical of the Prime Minister and an editorial that called for Chrétien's resignation. CanWest's national editorials quietly disappeared after the Mills firing. No public explanation was offered for what appeared to be a change in policy in the face of significant public pressure. (Consult the archives of the website www.yourmedia.ca for an extensive collection of material written about the CanWest national editorial policy.)

While the constitutional guarantee of freedom of the press appears to leave governments little legislative latitude, the Quebec government, for one, has shown a determination to act. Quebec is particularly sensitive to the issue because two companies—Quebecor and Power Corp.—own all but one of the French-language dailies in the province (the exception is the limited-circulation *Le Devoir*), accounting for 97 per cent of circulation. Unfortunately, Quebec's November 2001 report on press concentration (Quebec, 2001) was a timid effort, calling primarily for newspaper companies to publish a statement of principles and steps they are taking to ensure editorial diversity.

Besides legal interpretations of freedom of the press, which bind governments in their regulation of the press, there is also an ideological inhibition at play. As Enn Raudsepp of the Department of Journalism at Concordia University points out, for most of the 500 years of press history, the state has been seen as the institution that the press has required freedom from and protection against. Today, however, when media conglomerates are larger and more powerful than many national governments, it is time to consider state regulation of the business practices—rather than the editorial practices—of newspaper owners in a monopolistic industry. Raudsepp (2002: 28) argues that Canadians have two choices: 'We can continue to allow the inevitable drift to a business big brother—or we can try to develop a national consensus about the quality of the news and information we expect from our media and then take steps to ensure that we get it.'

New Media

As noted in Chapter 2, the term 'new media' encompasses both decentralized production of media products and interactive media spawned by digitization. This sector has greatly expanded over the past five years from games and learning materials delivered on CD-ROMs and DVDs to blogs, wikis and social networking of all kinds, video and audio streaming, podcasting, **mash-ups**, and dynamic informational databases.

New media have also spawned new calls for state regulation, particularly in the domains of hate speech, pornography, and terrorism, all of which are prevalent on the internet. In its *Report on New Media* of May 1999 (see www.crtc.gc.ca/ENG/NEWS/SPEECH-ES/1999/S990517.htm), the CRTC declared that it would not regulate new media. Operating from the simple definition of new media as 'services delivered over the Internet', the Commission conducted 10 months of hearings in 1998–9 to determine the answers to three questions:

1. Do any of the new media constitute services already defined by the Broadcasting Act or the Telecommunications Act, and if so, how should they be regulated?

2. How do the new media affect the regulation of the traditional broadcasting undertakings of radio, television, and cable?
3. Do the new media raise any other broad policy issues of national interest?

The CRTC determined that, for the most part, the internet is not subject to either the Broadcasting Act or the Telecommunications Act. For those materials that do fall under the legal definition of 'broadcasting'—e.g., digital audio services and audiovisual signals—'the Commission has concluded that regulation is not necessary to achieve the objectives of the Broadcasting Act.' There is, for instance, a wealth of Canadian content on the internet—an estimated 5 per cent of the world's websites are Canadian—and the CRTC ruled that new media have had no detrimental impact on either radio and television audi-

ences or advertising. The Commission further determined that websites specializing in 'offensive and illegal content', such as pornography and hate messages, are already covered by Criminal Code provisions.

If the CRTC report kept a door open to future intervention, it was in the domain of public access to the internet. While the issue of internet access is complex—it includes questions of literacy, computer skill, hardware affordability, and the services of public libraries, which are beyond the CRTC's purview—the Commission noted that it is already studying telecommunications issues relating to access and affordability in remote, high-cost service areas such as the North. 'The Commission intends to address issues relating to whether access to the Internet should be considered as "basic" service for subsidy purposes in its decision in that proceeding.'

In the context of the definitions we surveyed in

THE DIGITAL DIVIDE

Canada is one of the most 'wired' countries in the world. And while it may sometimes seem that *everyone* is connected to the internet—especially to those of us with easy internet access who regularly use computer networks while working or studying—this is clearly not the case. Even in an affluent country like Canada, internet access is far from universal, and tends to be most common among urban residents, those with money, those who are more educated, and those with children. If we take into account factors such as high-speed versus low-speed access and computer skill levels, the picture is even more uneven. When we look at the *global* internet map, the so-called digital divide is greater again.

Based on the 2005 'Canadian Internet Use Survey' conducted by Statistics Canada, 68 per cent of adult Canadians used the internet for personal, non-business reasons in the 12 months prior to the survey (Statistics Canada, 2006). This means that close to one-third of adult Canadians did not.

Canadians living in Canada's largest cities were more likely to use the internet than those in small towns and rural areas. For example, internet use was 77 per cent in Calgary and Ottawa–Gatineau, 75 per cent in Halifax and Toronto. Rural and small town areas averaged 58 per cent internet use in 2005.

Statistics Canada cited income, education, age, and the presence of children as key determinants of internet use. For example, 88 per cent of adults with household

incomes of $86,000 or more used the internet in 2005, compared to 61 per cent of adults occupying households with less than $86,000 in income. Eighty per cent of adults with some post-secondary education used the internet, compared to 49 per cent with less education. Eighty-five per cent of adults under 45 years old used the internet, compared to only half of those 45 and older. And 81 per cent of persons living in households with children used the internet, compared to 61 per cent of households without children.

Of those Canadians who accessed the internet from home in 2005, e-mail (91 per cent) and general browsing (84 per cent) were the most popular uses, followed by those seeking information about: weather or road conditions (67 per cent), travel (63 per cent), news or sports (62 per cent). Fewer Canadian internet users played online games (39 per cent) or used chat or messenger applications (38 per cent).

As more and more social, political, educational, and economic activity moves into cyberspace, those without ready internet access become further and further excluded from these activities, not only within Canada but around the world. The term 'digital divide' refers specifically to the gap between the information rich and the information poor. While we might assume that this gap is becoming narrower with time, evidence suggests that, in fact, the gap is widening (see van Dijk, 2005).

Chapter 2, the inclination of the CRTC not to regulate makes sense. The decentralization of media production and the rise of interactive media provide opportunities for broader participation. To venture into regulation would run counter to those currents. At the same time, as podcasting becomes commercialized, as it is almost bound to do, and social networking entities such as MySpace and YouTube or even music downloading sites such as Rhapsody and iTunes stabilize their dominance, the CRTC may find the need for regulation reasserting itself. But again, what will work against regulation is the wider range of products such sites make available—the long tail phenomenon we introduced in Chapter 2 and discuss at greater length in Chapter 12.

Summary

The cultural industries include cinematic production, sound recording (sometimes referred to as music recording), book and magazine publishing, and sometimes newspaper publishing. Arguably, cultural industries also include new media, by which we mean everything from websites to blogging to audiovisual production and exchange.

The beginnings of cultural industries policies can be traced back to the early 1950s and the report of the Massey Commission, but policy development began in earnest in the 1970s. At least four rationales can be identified for cultural policies: democratic participation, cultural development, public service, and market failure. In parallel with the multiplicity of reasons governments use to support cultural industries, the support policies and programs for each industry are many and varied. In cinema, investment in production and incentives for distributing Canadian productions are significant. In sound recording, Canadian-content regulations have been an effective policy instrument. For book publishing, structural, industrial, and cultural support measures have created a vibrant sector. In magazine publishing, ownership control through the Income Tax Act and provisions to exclude split-runs have been effective until recently. With the passage of Bill C-55, split-runs are possible but foreign publishers are limited in the amount of space they can sell to Canadian advertisers. In time, the net effect of this policy will become clearer.

Ownership and control of the distribution system are key concerns for cultural industries. In cinema, the tendency of theatres to show US movies is well documented. In bookstores, on magazine racks, and in record stores, US products dominate. Only with regard to newspapers is there clear Canadian dominance and that dominance exists because of the local nature of news and as a result of section 19 of the Income Tax Act, which was weakened in the aftermath of Bill C-55 in 1999. Financing has also been a problem for the cultural industries: in nearly every field, government-sponsored subsidy programs have been required.

Canada's cultural industries are gaining acceptance within and outside Canada. The great debate on whether cultural industries should be assisted by government funds, and on what basis, seems to have abated. It may be revived should the Harper Conservatives gain a second term in office, but the obvious cultural and spinoff economic advantages the country gains from supporting cultural industries keep those who believe in government inaction at bay. New understandings of the marketplace, outlined in Chapter 12, are finally allowing market economists to see what the rest of the world has known for some time—that nations must invest in cultural articulation to work against the dramatic advantages held by the cultural industries in large, rich countries (such as the US and UK but also France, other European countries, and Brazil) and that India and China are gaining because of their vast size.

Canada's participation in international trading agreements has made building the cultural industries more, rather than less, problematic. The US—and to some extent other nations, such as the UK, but notably less so other European countries—has demanded greater access beyond its already dominant position in Canada's cultural markets (which the Americans term 'entertainment markets'). As a result, the future of Canada's cultural industries and broadcasting (with spectrum scarcity becoming less relevant) is potentially threatened. In 1999 the federal government brought forward a strategy paper published in the name of an advisory group of members of the cultural industries. This paper calls for the development of a new policy instrument designed to protect domestic cultural industries from the full rigours of international trading rules. The pace of acceptance of the New International Instrument on Cultural Diversity is slow but it has not fallen off the world's agenda.

RELATED WEBSITES

Canada Council: www.canadacouncil.ca

The Canada Council provides information on grants made to artists and the cultural industries.

Canadian Independent Record Production Association (CIRPA): www.cirpa.ca

CIRPA is the trade organization representing the independent sector of the Canadian music and sound recording industry. For over 25 years it has been the collective voice of independent music in English-speaking Canada.

Canadian Musical Reproduction Rights Agency Ltd (CMRRA): www.cmrra.ca

The CMRAA is a non-profit music licensing agency that represents the vast majority of music copyright owners (usually called music publishers) doing business in Canada.

Department of Canadian Heritage: www.canadianheritage.gc.ca/index_e.cfm

To access information about Canadian cultural industries go to the federal government's Canadian Heritage site and follow the links to Arts and Culture and then to the cultural industry of your choice.

Foundation to Assist Canadian Talent on Record (FACTOR): www.factor.ca

FACTOR is an industry-sponsored strategy to assist the development of an independent Canadian recording industry through funding to allow Canadian songwriters and recording artists to have their work produced.

National Film Board of Canada (NFB): www.nfb.ca

As the site says: 'Created in 1939, the National Film Board of Canada (NFB) is a public agency that produces and distributes films and other audiovisual works which reflect Canada to Canadians and the rest of the world. It is an exceptional fountain of creativity, which since its very beginnings has played a crucial role in Canadian and international filmmaking. Its founder and the first Government Film Commissioner, John Grierson, wanted to make the NFB the "eyes of Canada" and to ensure that it would, "through a national use of cinema, see Canada and see it whole: its people and its purpose."'

Telefilm Canada: www.telefilm.gc.ca

Telefilm Canada is a cultural investor in film, television, new media, and music. Its annual budget is $230 million.

FURTHER READINGS

Audley, Paul. 1983. *Canada's Cultural Industries: Broadcasting, Publishing, Records and Film*. Toronto: James Lorimer. Audley's book was the first to examine the cultural industries in Canada and provides an important historical perspective on the issues at that time, with particular emphasis on the production and distri-bution of Canadian cultural materials.

Dorland, Michael, ed. 1996. *Cultural Industries in Canada: Problems, Policies and Prospects*. Toronto: James Lorimer. Modelled on Audley's book, this edited collection reviews Canada's cultural industries with a focus on public policy and political economy.

STUDY QUESTIONS

1. Explain the four rationales for supporting cultural industries. How do they differ from one another? How might each lead to different policies?
2. Identify the main support policies for each of the cultural industries.
3. What effect has Canadian cultural industries policy had in your life?
4. What is the net impact on Canadian culture and Canada's cultural industries of international trade agreements designed to promote free trade?
5. Market economists and cultural theorists both claim that democracy is a foundation for their position on government support for cultural industries. How can this be? Outline the nature of democracy as both see it and identify which you think is the more robust use of the term.
6. You are responsible for developing a new strategy document for Canada's cultural industries, including the new media. Write a position paper.
7. How does the CRTC's decision not to regulate new media conform to its regulatory policies in other media, such as telecommunications and broadcasting?
8. To what extent does the 'digital divide' shape the growth of the internet?

┌─────────────────────────────────┐
│   LEARNING OUTCOMES   │
└─────────────────────────────────┘

- To introduce the cultural industries—cinema, music recording, and book, magazine, and newspaper publishing—and their characteristics.
- To describe the various rationales that governments use for investing in cultural industries—democratic participation including community animation, cultural development, public service, and market failure.
- To indicate that investments by government in cultural industries attempt to balance economic, political, and cultural factors.
- To review the support the federal and provincial governments provide for cinema—Ottawa's early support for documentaries through the National Film Board; Ottawa's more recent support for Canadian feature films created by Canadians; the support of the provinces for bringing US productions to Canada; and likely future directions.
- To explain how it is not quality of content that prevents Canadian movies from being seen but rather industry structures, particularly vertical integration.
- To review the nature of Canada's music recording industry.
- To describe the role of radio in Canada's music recording industry.
- To review the characteristics of Canada's book publishing industry and the nature of the support that the federal government has provided for that industry over the years.
- To introduce the concepts of copyright, intellectual property, and reprographic rights.
- To review the characteristics of Canada's magazine publishing industry, the key policies that have supported it over the years, the diminution of those regulatory policies as a result of technological development, and the resulting actions of the federal government to support the industry.
- To describe, briefly, the characteristics of Canada's newspaper publishing industry.
- To introduce new media to the policy framework, particularly with respect to the issue of public access.

CHAPTER 8

The Structure and Role of Ownership

Introduction

Though we use the term 'mass media' quite often, we can easily forget how diverse a sector this is. We could be talking about a small, family-owned community newspaper or a national television network. There is no natural or inevitable way to organize the mass media; their structures evolve through time, and different societies organize their media in particular ways. The United Kingdom, France, the United States, and Canada—all Western, liberal democracies—structure their mass media in distinct ways in response to particular social needs, desires, and pressures. Even within the same country, we see different rules applied to different media, as discussed in Chapters 6 and 7. This chapter suggests that mass media institutions are not simply products of technology, but are organized according to the characteristics of the given medium, the resources it draws upon, and the socio-political context in which it operates.

Nevertheless, all media organizations have something in common. No matter how they are organized, they participate in the economy, that sphere of society in which, in the words of media economist Robert G. Picard (1989: 8–9), 'limited or scarce resources are allocated to satisfy competing and unlimited needs or wants.' Picard goes on to identify four groups that the media serve:

> 1) media owners, the individuals or stockholders who own media outlets; 2) audiences, those who view, listen to, or read media content; 3) advertisers, those who purchase time or space to convey messages to audiences; and 4) media employees, those who work for the firms. (Ibid., 9)

We could add to this list a fifth group: governments. Through their cultural policy apparatus, governments adopt guidelines and laws that compel media organizations to serve the needs and wants of national or regional constituencies. In the Canadian case, this has meant ensuring Canadians have access to both the cultural and economic opportunities that participation in the media affords.

It is amid these currents and countercurrents that we consider the various forms of media ownership in this chapter, and especially public ownership and private-sector commercial ownership: their goals, methods of operation, and strengths and shortcomings within the context of the interests of the society as a whole.

Allocating Resources

When we think of resources, we usually think of water, minerals, fish, or trees—things used to produce goods and services subsequently offered to consumers for a price. How such resources are managed and how they are organized economically bear closer scrutiny because similar principles apply to the resources that the mass media harness.

Water, for instance, is a resource essential to life—not only for human consumption, but also for the maintenance of plant and animal life—and is therefore considered an especially precious resource. Careless or excessive use can lead to life-threatening shortages of clean water. For this reason, governments have generally assumed control of its exploitation—how and for what purpose clean water is used. Management of this resource can take any number of forms, such as municipal governments assuming responsibility for drinking water, provincial governments taking charge of hydroelectric power, and provincial governments regulating the industrial use of water by private companies. Water's inherent value also explains why governments in water-rich countries like Canada have been nervous about opening up the export of water to commercial enterprise, even though there's a market for it, and even though the United Nations estimates that one-quarter of the world's population has no access to clean drinking water (Reuters, 1998).

Resource industries like fishing and forestry tend to be in the hands of private enterprise, but the natural resources these industries draw upon are considered to be commonly owned—i.e., public property as opposed to private property. As such, these industries are regulated by governments to ensure that resource supplies are not exhausted and that the environmental impact of their extraction is minimized. Of course, such regulation often fails, either because it is based on imprecise or bad science (the depletion of fisheries) or because it was not designed or administered stringently (the clear-cutting of large tracts of forest). Governments grant such resource companies the right to use a specified quantity of a resource, in a specified fashion, for a limited period of time.

The private ownership of resources is usually allowed when a resource is not particularly scarce. Thus private ownership by one person will not prevent private ownership by others, as is the case with land in Canada. Even agricultural land, as important as it is for the food supply, is privately owned, and agricultural producers decide what to grow based on their own best estimates of what the market will demand at harvest time.

The media use resources, too. Sometimes these resources are commonly owned, and sometimes they are privately held. For example, radio stations rely on the radio spectrum—that portion of the electromagnetic spectrum used to carry radio signals—to transmit their programs to audiences. As we discussed in Chapter 6, the radio spectrum is a finite resource and therefore requires some form of management—radio licensing—to avoid signal interference between stations. While an individual radio station may be a private enterprise operating on a commercial basis, it requires a licence to use the airwaves, which remain public property.

Television broadcasting has, historically, largely followed radio's model. Television broadcasters, whether public or private, require a licence—again, the airwaves are public property. When television signals were received exclusively via over-the-air transmission, there was a need to manage the broadcast spectrum to avoid signal interference. There was also a political-cultural imperative from the start. The regulation of the broadcast spectrum permits the federal government to ensure that Canadians have access to Canadian programming and enjoy a broader selection of programming than a free-market regime could be expected to provide. Now that most Canadians receive their television signals through cable transmission or satellite, signal delivery is less a policy issue than is the maintenance of a diverse offering of programming.

Newspapers, on the other hand, are organized on a completely different basis, in large part because the resources they employ are privately held: they buy newsprint from pulp and paper companies, print their newspapers on privately owned printing presses, and deliver them with their own trucks. Within Western democratic societies like Canada, newspapers operate entirely within a commercial marketplace and require no permission from any government to publish.

Like the newspaper industry, magazine and book publishing is organized as commercial enterprise, employing private resources. The difference is that magazine and book publishers tend to function in larger regional, national, and international markets and thus face much higher distribution costs and much more foreign competition. Government subsidies—federal and provincial—have been put in place to maintain a diverse offering of Canadian magazines and books.

Much of the excitement about the internet derives from its infinite and varied capacity for content; there is room in cyberspace for every kind of content, whether or not it has mass or narrow appeal. No one owns cyberspace, and while universal public access remains a concern, particularly in the developing world, the costs of participation are relatively low in the affluent world. In Canada, for instance, it is far cheaper to launch an on-line publication than a printed version. In this case, the material resources employed are privately owned computers and telephone or cable lines.

Individual Freedom, Public Interest, and the Free Market

Western democracy is founded on the freedom of the individual, both as a political actor and as a participant in the economy. Western democracies, for the most part, have free-market economies, in which individuals are at liberty to produce and consume according to their own interests, although governments reserve the right to temper market forces when they feel it is in the public interest, however that interest may be defined. For instance, it was the opinion of the R.B. Bennett Conservative government in 1932 that broadcasting was an area in which public ownership should prevail. The Bennett government, in spite of its private-enterprise orientation, was not convinced that private control of radio would best serve the interests of all Canadians, particularly if it meant the American domination of Canada's airwaves.

Between the 1930s and the present, a great deal has changed. For one thing, governments are eager to assign more and more areas of the economy to market forces, particularly in the cultural realm, but also in the fields of health care and education. Second, the belief in free-market economics is on the rise worldwide and even former Communist-bloc countries are keen to become part of international organizations devoted to freer trade. Third, with increased wealth and advancements in technology, the task of providing communication services across vast distances has become easier. And fourth, the globalization process, which is producing what David Morley and Kevin Robins (1995: 1) describe as 'a new communications geography', calls into question conventional notions of community; people's sense of belonging to the national community has changed. All in all, it is becoming more and more difficult for national governments to assume control of cultural production on behalf of their constituents.

The basis for private ownership derives from both classical and contemporary economic theory. In *The Wealth of Nations* (1937 [1776]), Adam Smith sought to explain how society managed to secure and produce all that was necessary for survival without any form of central planning. Smith formulated a set of basic 'laws' of the marketplace, and is perhaps best known for identifying the market's **'invisible hand'**, whereby 'the private interests and passions of men' are directed to serving the interests of society as a whole. As Robert Heilbroner (1980: 47–67) explains, Smith's laws of the marketplace 'show us how the drive of individual self-interest in an environment of similarly motivated individuals will result in competition; and they further demonstrate how competition will result in the provision of those goods and services that society wants, in the quantities that society desires, and at the prices society is prepared to pay' (ibid., 53). Smith argued, in other words, that self-interest drives people to whatever work society is willing to pay for, and that this self-interest is regulated by competition. No one participant in the market can become greedy, because prices for goods and wages for workers are kept in line by competition. Similarly, competition regulates the supply of goods, preventing both overproduction and underproduction. Smith 'found in the mechanism of the market a self-regulating system for society's orderly provisioning' (ibid., 55).

While even in Smith's day there were price-fixing combines and large-scale producers who disrupted the competitive balance among producers, for the most part, eighteenth-century England conformed to Smith's model. As Heilbroner writes: 'Business was competitive, the average factory was small, prices did rise and fall as demand ebbed and rose, and prices did invoke changes in output and occupation' (ibid., 56). Contemporary society, however, does not conform to Smith's model. For one thing, market competition has given way to market dominance—hence the term **monopoly capitalism**—as huge corporations seek to minimize, even eliminate, competition among producers and large labour unions seek to minimize competition among workers. For another, governments have entered the marketplace with their own notion of self-interest, disrupting the neat functioning of Smith's 'invisible hand'. Government intervention, that is, has been quite visible in seeking to direct the economy to serve particular interests, whether those interests are job creation for its citizens or maximizing export opportunities for domestic producers.

While neo-classical economists appeal to societies to revive the laissez-faire credo—leave the market alone to regulate itself—Smith's model has become increasingly divorced from economic reality as his 'laws' of the marketplace have been consistently violated by all parties over the past two centuries. The idea that the mass media simply serve the needs and wants of audiences, who base their consumption decisions on universally accepted notions of merit, is an attractive one. But the evidence suggests that in the cultural sector of the economy, too, Smith's 'laws' of the marketplace have little application.

MARKET ECONOMICS AND CULTURAL PRODUCTION

Perhaps the most fundamental problem is the tendency of many people, and particularly economists, to apply the free-market perspective to sectors of the economy in which it may not be appropriate. Economists often argue that if films, books, TV programs, magazines, and sound recordings cannot survive in the marketplace, then they do not deserve to survive. To intervene to support what large audiences are not interested in, the argument goes, is to use the state to subsidize the tastes of the elite. While the merits of **economism**—the perception of cultural production as commercial enterprise—can certainly be debated, further consideration takes us back to the notion that private ownership is most often applied when management of a resource is not deemed critical to either the resource's or the community's survival. This is a key point because it goes to the heart of how we perceive cultural production and what role we assign the mass media in society.

In its comprehensive survey of state involvement in cultural activity in Canada, the Applebaum-Hébert Committee (Canada, 1982: 64–71) noted that governments often intervene in the cultural sphere in cases of market failure, when the market does not or cannot adequately serve the cultural needs of society. Markets, for example, do not recognize the longevity of cultural products, which may be produced by one generation and maintain their value through subsequent generations. Think of the number of artists— Van Gogh, Mozart, Gauguin, Rembrandt—who are today recognized for their genius, yet who were not adequately compensated for their creations in their own lifetimes. Markets may also fail to accommodate 'infant industries'—new, domestic industries that cannot compete right away with well-established and large-scale transnational industries. The Canadian feature-film industry is a good example of an industry that continues to struggle to find a market in the context of Hollywood dominance of this country's commercial theatre screens. Cultural production, Applebaum-Hébert argued, also confounds market economics because it entails a large element of risk and requires a substantial investment of a society's resources, and because the public has a 'limitless variability of tastes'. The most common instance of market failure in the cultural sphere, however, involves the market failing 'to register the full benefits conferred' by cultural activity:

> . . . the fact can be demonstrated that, historically, those cultural activities that have conferred the most lasting benefits, and which have been seen, in retrospect, to have done most to illuminate their times, have more often than not served only minority interests in their own day. On grounds either of market failure or of diffuse social values, the case for [state] intervention applies with special force to the satisfaction of minority preferences. (Canada, 1982: 69)

Free-market or laissez-faire economics tends to reduce all goods and services to the status of commodities, objects that attain value through marketplace exchange. While we often believe a market

economy to be especially responsive to consumer demand for choice, the cultural theorist Raymond Williams (1989: 88) reminds us that the capitalist organization of communication imposes 'commercial constraints', so that 'you can say that at times freedom in our kind of society amounts to the freedom to say anything you wish, provided you can say it profitably.' Commodities, by definition, are validated through sale. As Yves de la Haye (1980: 34–5) argues, when cultural activities are organized commercially, their purpose becomes the generation of profit. If we perceive books as, first and foremost, commodities of exchange, then their value is measured in retail sales and revenues generated. By this reckoning, the best-selling biography of a Hollywood movie star is more valuable than a critically acclaimed history of Kosovo. Yet few would deny that the book on Kosovo is more valuable in terms of its contribution to human understanding than the trivial celebrity biography; the NATO countries went to war over Kosovo, after all.

Economism confines the notion of value to exchange value, and dismisses as 'externalities' any other kinds of benefit (or liability) that may accrue from cultural production. While he was US President, Bill Clinton summoned film and television producers to the White House in the wake of the Columbine school shooting in the spring of 1999 to ask that Hollywood assume some responsibility for the harm that film and TV violence may induce. Such costs—to society, to individuals—are simply excluded from market transactions. At the same time, the benefits of educational programming can be underestimated in the marketplace.

Economism also casts individuals as consumers playing a narrow role in the economy, rather than as citizens with a larger role to play in democratic society. We may read books or watch movies for any number of reasons—entertainment or pleasure, certainly, but also for personal growth, education, insight, and critical understanding. Books, television programs, theatrical performances, and museum exhibits are not simply goods or services that we buy and sell, but crucial opportunities for the kind of communication that is fundamental to the notion of culture. In other words, cultural products are more than commodities. They are expressions of a culture as a way of life and as a system of beliefs and values. They are expressions of ideas and images that help a culture to imagine itself and to articulate its priorities. If excluded by the so-called 'realities' of the marketplace, certain forms of cultural expression can be marginalized, even silenced.

Historical Background: Function and Ownership

The roots of media institutions are found in two places. The first is the need of the state to circulate information about the rights, duties, responsibilities, obligations, and freedoms of the state, the community, and the individual. The second is in the social, cultural, economic, and political opportunities communication affords.

Gutenberg's printing press was an invention that responded to a social structure that created room for individual initiative, to a thirst for learning, to a growing literacy, and to an opportunity to make the Bible and other manuscripts available to a wide, literate audience. Some researchers argue that printers were among the earliest capitalist entrepreneurs in that they took risks by printing materials and tried to recoup their investments through sales (Eisenstein, 1979).

The establishment of the commercial press in Canada was a response to the opportunity to print, under contract, official government information and to make such information widely available. Taking Britain and the United States as its models, the press in Canada soon evolved into an institution capable of responding to other social and political pressures for the distribution of information and ideas. The press was by no means an isolated example; cinema in Canada, too, was originally a medium exploited by governments for political and commercial propaganda, and only later became a more independent form of art, information, and dramatic entertainment.

Given these roots, the intensive involvement of government in the press and printing is not difficult to understand. In seventeenth-century Britain, while ownership of printing facilities was not exclusive to the public domain, the government used laws and taxes to control press output so that it would reflect the interests of the ruling elites. Taxes on paper and the disallowance of type founding were two indirect mechanisms that controlled the dissemination of information. However, as printers as a group became less and less dependent on government largesse, and with the general economic and political rise of the bourgeoisie, intense, insistent pressure grew for the freedom of printers to pursue their economic interest.

FREE PRESS, FREE MARKET

From the beginning of printing to the present day there has been a struggle between 'the media' and 'the state' for control of communications. Each has compelling reasons to want control of the generation and distribution of content. The state needs to disseminate information to govern, to command allegiance from its citizens, and to generate a sense of community among its inhabitants. Reading a newspaper, for example, keeps us informed about our government's activities and offers us a depiction of our society: who our fellow citizens are, what they look like, what they think, what they value, etc. (see Anderson, 1989). The media want to speak either for their owners in pursuit of markets or for the ordinary citizen, to raise a voice against some form of mistreatment. The battle for press freedom was fought on the foundation of individual freedom and the relation between freedom of speech and democracy, with the press putting itself forward as a separate estate representative of a distinct set of interests, not those of church, business, or landowners, but those of 'the people' (see our discussion of the 'fourth estate' in Chapter 9).

Yet simultaneously, the press was fighting for the economic interests of private press owners. It would seem that the press won recognition, at least in part, on the basis of the conjoined interests of individual free speech and the generally accepted liberal theory and commercial practice of the day; intellectuals like John Milton, John Locke, and John Stuart Mill were the early proponents of the libertarian theory of the press (see Osler, 1993). Specifically, individuals—in this case, press owners—wanted to have the right to pursue their own interests, and in doing so they would create benefit to society through the workings of Adam Smith's 'invisible hand'. They would be free to pursue economic markets by participating in a free market of ideas.

Within the context of liberal-capitalist economic theory, the press asked for nothing more than any other business. But in dealing with information, which even during the Industrial Revolution was recognized as somehow different from other commodities, the press found it prudent to fight and win the battle on non-economic grounds, on the basis of the rights of individuals to free speech.

The state never did give up its right to produce and disseminate information, and, indeed, well into the twentieth century the so-called 'free press' was closely aligned with political parties (see Sotiron,

1997). In various European countries the interconnections between government and the press are still close. For example, when Silvio Berlusconi was Prime Minister of Italy (1992–4, 2001–6), his Mediaset company owned three of the country's four national private television networks, as well as newspapers and radio stations. Berlusconi was critical of the one major channel he didn't own, Italy's state television network RAI. When he was re-elected in May 2001, Berlusconi lobbied to pack RAI's board with loyal directors, and during the summer of 2002 he caused an uproar when two RAI journalists he had publicly criticized were subsequently fired (Bagnall, 2002; Wallace, 2002).

Organizing Structures

No media industry in Canada is governed exclusively by free-market economics. Governments, both provincial and federal, are implicated in one form or another in the structure of every media industry: as proprietor (CBC, NFB); custodian (museums, galleries, theatres); patron (commissions, grants, sponsorships);

catalyst (tax incentives, subsidies); or regulator (CRTC) (Canada, 1982: 72). The result is that our mass media are organized as a complex mixture of public and private enterprise.

Newspaper publishing comes closest to an exclusively private enterprise, but even here section 19 of the Income Tax Act ensures that Canadian newspapers remain Canadian-owned; the newspaper industry is protected from foreign takeover and foreign competition. Newspapers are considered by the state to be relatively untouchable because they are so closely associated with the historical struggle for freedom of mediated forms of expression. In the post-war period, governments in Great Britain, the United States, and Canada have all ignored reasoned calls to intervene in the newspaper industry to ensure a better balance between the press's freedom to publish and the citizen's right to be informed. Both the Davey Commission (Canada, 1971: 255–6) and the Kent Commission (Canada, 1981: 237) raised concerns about ownership concentration in Canada's newspaper industry and proposed legislative mechanisms to address the problem. The Standing Senate Committee

Table 8.1 Daily Newspaper Ownership Groups, January 2006

Publisher	Number of Newspapers	Share of Canadian Dailies	Total Weekly Circulation	Share of Total Weekly Circulation[c]
Hollinger Canadian Newspapers LP	10	9.90	308,898	0.98
Osprey Media LP	21	20.79	1,862,741	5.93
Brunswick News Inc.	3	2.97	609,213	1.94
FP Canadian Newspapers LP	2	1.98	982,561	3.13
Transcontinental Inc.	11	10.89	985,775	3.14
CanWest MediaWorks	13	12.87	8,898,120	28.35
Halifax Herald Ltd	1	0.99	731,031	2.33
Power Corp. of Canada	7	6.93	3,077,551	9.80
Bell Globemedia	1	0.99	1,970,216	6.28
Black Press	1	0.99	111,900	0.36
Horizon Operations (BC) Ltd	5	4.95	591,573	1.88
Torstar Corp.	4	3.96	4,372,010	13.93
Sun Media (Quebecor)	17	16.83	6,588,079	20.99
Sing Tao Newspapers	1	0.99	n.a.	n.a.
Independents	4	3.96	302,069	0.96
Totals	**101**	**100**	**31,391,737**	**100**

Notes: Shares are rounded to nearest two decimal places; n.a. = not available.
Source: Canadian Newspaper Association, 2006, at: www.cna-acj.ca. Reprinted by permission of the publisher.

Table 8.2 Canadian Daily Newspaper Holdings, January 2006

Owner	Region	Title	Total Weekly Circulation
Hollinger Canadian Newspapers LP	Quebec	*Record*, Sherbrooke	24, 375
	BC	*Cranbrook Daily Townsman*	16,860
		Alaska Highway News, Fort St John	18,950
		Daily Bulletin, Kimberley	7,965
		Nelson Daily News	15,880
		Peace River Block Daily News, Dawson Creek	11,334
		Daily News, Prince Rupert	15,350
		Trail Times	21,620
		Kamloops Daily News	79,722
		Citizen, Prince George	96,842
	Group Circulation		**308,898**
Osprey Media LP	Ontario	*Expositor*, Brantford	131,430
		St Catharines Standard	187,739
		Niagara Falls Review	106,027
		Tribune, Welland	85,560
		Barrie Examiner	61,044
		Chatham Daily News	80,130
		Cobourg Daily Star	26,160
		Standard-Freeholder, Cornwall	86,358
		Kingston Whig-Standard	165,432
		North Bay Nugget	91,153
		Intelligencer, Belleville	90,511
		Observer, Sarnia	118,951
		Sault Star, Sault Ste Marie	113,742
		Sudbury Star	107,903
		Daily Press, Timmins	57,132
		Sun Times, Owen Sound	101,925
		Port Hope Evening Guide	14,316
		Packet & Times, Orillia	48,234
		Daily Observer, Pembroke	34,662
		Peterborough Examiner	130,177
		Lindsay Daily Post	24,155
	Group Circulation		**1,862,741**
Brunswick News Inc.	NB	*Times & Transcript*, Moncton	226,781
		Daily Gleaner, Fredericton	148,883
		New Brunswick Telegraph Journal, Saint John	233,549
	Group Circulation		**609,213**
FP Canadian Newspapers LP	Manitoba	*Brandon Sun*	103,059
		Winnipeg Free Press	879,502
	Group Circulation		**982,561**
Transcontinental Inc.	NS	*Amherst Daily News*	18,821
		Daily News, Halifax	156,491
		Cape Breton Post, Sydney	157,254
		Evening News, New Glasgow	47,820
		Daily News, Truro	41,185

Owner	Region	Title	Total Weekly Circulation
	N&L	*Telegram*, St John's	242,922
		Western Star, Corner Brook	44,670
	PEI	*Guardian*, Charlottetown	124,476
		Journal Pioneer, Summerside	54,540
	Sask.	*Times-Herald*, Moose Jaw	53,400
		Prince Albert Daily Herald	44,196
	Group Circulation		**985,775**
CanWest MediaWorks	Quebec	*Gazette*, Montreal	1,004,983
	Ontario	*National Post*	1,447,475
		Ottawa Citizen	973,347
		Windsor Star	438,976
	Sask.	*Leader Post*, Regina	307,065
		Star Phoenix, Saskatoon	330,455
	Alberta	*Calgary Herald*	873,574
		Edmonton Journal	913,026
	BC	*Vancouver Sun*	1,095,975
		Province, Vancouver	923,135
		Nanaimo Daily News	51,192
		Times Colonist, Victoria	509,887
		Alberni Valley Times, Port Alberni	29,030
	Group Circulation		**8,898,120**
Halifax Herald Ltd	NS	*Chronicle-Herald*, Halifax	731,031
	Group Circulation		**731,031**
Power Corp. of Canada	Quebec	*La Presse*, Montreal	1,504,772
		Le Nouvelliste, Trois-Rivières	253,616
		La Tribune, Sherbrooke	195,409
		La Voix de l'Est, Granby	97,145
		Le Soleil, Québec	599,095
		Le Quotidien, Chicoutimi	207,855
	Ontario	*Le Droit*, Ottawa	219,659
	Group Circulation		**3,077,551**
Bell Globemedia		*Globe and Mail*	1,970,216
	Group Circulation		**1,970,216**
Black Press	Alberta	*Red Deer Advocate*	111,900
	Group Circulation		**111,900**

Owner	Region	Title	Total Weekly Circulation
Horizon Operations B.C. Ltd.	BC	*Penticton Herald*	54,843
		Daily Courier, Kelowna	113,125
	Alberta	*Lethbridge Herald*	138,259
		Medicine Hat News	83,496
	Ontario	*Chronicle-Journal*, Thunder Bay	201,850
	Group Circulation		**591,573**
Torstar Corp	Ontario	*Guelph Mercury*	85,404
		Hamilton Spectator	643,275
		Record, Kitchener-Waterloo	406,676
		Toronto Star	3,236,655
	Group Circulation		**4,372,010**
Sun Media (Quebecor Inc.)	Quebec	*Le Journal de Montréal*	1,909,510
		Le Journal de Québec	716,676
	Ontario	*Brockville Recorder and Times*	71,484
		Daily Miner and News, Kenora	16,000
		London Free Press	617,508
		Ottawa Sun	348,334
		Beacon-Herald, Stratford	62,448
		St Thomas Times-Journal	46,572
		Toronto Sun	1,355,969
		Simcoe Reformer	42,165
		Woodstock Sentinel-Review	42,582
	Alberta	*Calgary Sun*	470,355
		Edmonton Sun	511,404
		Fort McMurray Today	21,534
		Daily Herald-Tribune, Grande Prairie	38,030
	Manitoba	*Daily Graphic*, Portage La Prairie	17,214
		Winnipeg Sun	300,294
	Group Circulation		**6,588,079**
Sing Tao Newspapers (Canada 1988 Limited)	Quebec	Sing Tao Newspapers	n.a.
	Group Circulation		**n.a.**
Independents	NB	*L'Acadie Nouvelle*, Caraquet	101,495
	Quebec	*Le Devoir*, Montréal	176,495
	Manitoba	*Flin Flon Reminder*	12,500
	Yukon	*Whitehorse Star*	11,579
	Group Circulation		**302,069**

Note: n.a. = not available.

Source: Canadian Newspaper Association, at: www.cna-acj.ca. Reprinted by permission of the publisher.

on Transport and Communications (Canada, 2006a) revisited this question in 2003 and, besides echoing previous commissions on the topic of corporate concentration, added corporate consolidation and cross-media ownership to the list of concerns about conglomerate ownership (see Chapter 7). The Kent Commission, specifically, proposed a Canada Newspapers Act to balance the rights and responsibilities of a free press and recommended legislation both to correct the worst cases of corporate concentration and to prohibit the further concentration of ownership. Magazine publishing in Canada is distinguished from the newspaper business in this regard by its dependence on both government subsidies (e.g., preferred postal rates, direct grants) and protectionist legislation (the Income Tax Act) for its survival in a marketplace dominated by American publications (see Dubinsky, 1996).

Table 8.1 summarizes the Canadian daily newspaper ownership groups while Table 8.2 provides a comprehensive summary of the holdings of these Canadian companies, testifying to the high level of corporate concentration in this segment of the economy. CanWest MediaWorks, the country's largest publisher with 13 daily newspapers including the *National Post*, controls close to 30 per cent of all weekly newspaper circulation, while the top five companies together control almost 80 per cent of weekly circulation. The country's five independent newspapers together account for less than 1 per cent.

The state presence is much more apparent in the broadcasting sector. Radio, for example, has private, commercial stations operating alongside publicly owned broadcasters (i.e., CBC and Radio-Canada) and community stations. CBC and Radio-Canada compete with the commercial broadcasters for audiences, but they do not compete for advertising. Public radio in Canada has been commercial-free since 1974, leaving the public broadcaster wholly dependent on federal government funding for its operations. Community radio stations are run by non-profit societies with a democratic management structure, and raise money from a combination of advertising, government subsidies, and fundraising activities such as radio bingo. As discussed in Chapter 6, all radio stations—private, public, and community—are regulated by the CRTC; they are required to meet the specific conditions of their broadcast licence as well as Canadian-content quotas. The domestic sound recording industry, though owned by private interests, has of course been the principal beneficiary of Canadian-content regulations on radio.

Television, too, is a mix of private, public, and community broadcasting stations. A significant difference here is that the stations of CBC and Radio-Canada, including Newsworld and Le réseau de l'information (RDI), compete with the commercial broadcasters for both audiences and advertising. This competition for advertising has long been a sore point with the private broadcasters, who feel the CBC

MARKETING

Whether or not media organizations are organized as commercial enterprises, great efforts are expended in identifying audiences, maximizing their numbers, determining their content requirements, and, in the case of media that carry advertising, matching audiences to appropriate advertisers. There is no point in offering an information service no one seems to want or need, just as there is no point in advertising luxury automobiles to people with limited incomes. While audience tastes remain difficult to predict, media organizations leave as little to chance as possible, employing focus groups, customer surveys, and opinion polls to target their products more precisely.

In Quebec, for example, the trade magazine *Infopresse* publishes an annual media guide that includes data on: advertising dollars spent on each medium; the largest advertisers for each medium; audience ratings for radio and television stations; circulation figures for newspapers and magazines; internet site visits, including pages viewed and the amount of time spent per visit (Infopresse, 2006). For example, the guide lists Sympatico-MSN (news.sympatico.msn.ca/Home/) as the most popular website among Canadians, visited by 85 per cent of Canadian internet surfers, with an average of 379 page views per visitor per month, and with each visitor spending an average 601.3 minutes per month on the site.

This kind of information helps media managers understand how to sell audiences to advertisers and helps advertisers determine which media platforms are most effective in reaching the consumers they want to target for their products and services.

encroaches on their business, specifically when the public broadcaster goes after programming particularly attractive to advertisers—e.g., professional sports, blockbuster Hollywood films—but seemingly unrelated to the CBC/Radio-Canada mandate. This topic was raised during the CBC's licence renewal hearings before the CRTC in 1999, and again by the Lincoln Commission's comprehensive study of Canadian broadcasting (Canada, 2003). Even supporters of public broadcasting argue that advertising competition distorts the public broadcaster's mission. Both private and public television in Canada is regulated (e.g., licensing, Canadian-content quotas, advertising limits) and both private and public broadcasters benefit from federal and provincial subsidies for the creation of Canadian film and television programming. Specialty channels form the sector of the ownership picture that will bear closest scrutiny in the years ahead.

The film industry in Canada is a special case because it has both public and private production houses, but the distribution and exhibition sectors of the industry are organized along principles of private enterprise. As noted in Chapter 7, governments in Canada have been involved in film production—as patrons, catalysts, and regulators—since early in the twentieth century. Hollywood began to dominate the burgeoning commercial film industry in the 1920s and this did not sit well with Canadians in a period of strong Canadian nationalism. The federal government established the National Film Board of Canada in 1939 as a means of asserting a greater Canadian presence on cinema screens. The NFB has largely been confined to producing the kinds of films that tend not to be shown in commercial theatres—documentary, experimental, animation, and sponsored films—leaving the production of dramatic feature-length films to the private sector. If there has been competitive tension between the NFB and private-sector producers, it has been over contracts for sponsored films, which are films commissioned by government departments and corporations for educational and marketing purposes. But even the private producers of feature films in Canada rely heavily on government loans and subsidies for production, distribution, and marketing, and public television has been one of Canadian cinema's most dependable exhibition venues.

Until recently, telephone service was defined by Ottawa as a 'natural monopoly' and Canada had both private (e.g., BC Telephone, Bell Canada) and provincial state monopolies (e.g., Sasktel, Manitoba Telecom

Services) operating side by side. The CRTC, however, began to deregulate the industry in the late 1980s, first opening up long-distance telephony to competition and in 1994 opening all telephone services to competition.

Even art galleries, theatres, concert halls, and museums, insofar as they can been seen as mass media, are characterized by a mix of public and private ownership, with content generated by both public-sector and private-sector sources. The international web of computer networks we call the internet has no single owner, but it, too, counts on both public- and private-sector initiatives for its operation and its content. Cyberspace is a medium of exchange for all kinds of communication and defies any simple structural category.

Ted Magder (1993: 10–11) argues that state intervention in the cultural sphere has been motivated by two objectives: national identity and economic growth. The Canadian Pacific Railway remains a powerful symbol in Canada because it was one of the first national institutions asked to serve both goals simultaneously; the building of the railway was a private enterprise heavily subsidized by Ottawa and designed to bind a sparsely populated and vast country together. If the CPR permitted the transportation of people and goods back and forth across Canada, the federal government imagined that a national radio broadcasting network would allow for the transcontinental dissemination of ideas, values, and images. In fact, the metaphor describing the CBC as a 'railway of the airwaves' has been evoked many times.

The goals of creating a Canadian national identity and stimulating economic growth remain in perpetual tension in the communication sphere, and the various ownership structures of the media in Canada speak to Ottawa's ongoing struggle to keep both objectives in view. Where the Canadian people fit into this picture is an important question. Canadians are, at the same time, citizens, audience members, and taxpayers, and their support for both private enterprise *and* public service exacerbates the tension around ownership structures.

Public Ownership

The central difference between public and private forms of ownership pertains to their bottom lines. Public ownership is devoted to providing communication as a public service. Private ownership is devot-

PUBLIC OWNERSHIP

Public ownership is a slippery term. It can be used to mean either ownership by a government on behalf of its citizens—'the public'—or ownership by a group of self-interested shareholders. The term 'public ownership' is used in business to denote companies that make a public offering of shares in search of investment capital. It is in this sense that they are publicly owned and must make available to the public financial information about their business operations, through press releases and audited annual reports.

Of course, these two forms of ownership are fundamentally different. The government-owned institution is devoted primarily to public service, while the shareholder-owned entity is devoted primarily to generating returns for its shareholders, who are free to trade their shares at any time. The government-owned institution is answerable to all citizens, whether or not they use the service provided. The shareholder-owned company is responsible primarily to its shareholders and secondarily to the customers it serves. References to public ownership in this chapter pertain to government-owned or controlled media, and we use private ownership to refer to commercial institutions, whether they are owned by a group of shareholders or by individuals.

ed to providing communication for profit. Regardless of the mix of private and public enterprise described above, this distinction is fundamental and needs always to be kept in view if we are to make the link between the ownership structure of a medium and the purpose of the communication it provides.

The idea of public service is to employ the mass media for social goals. This can mean the provision of universal and equitable service to all Canadians, as in the telecommunication, radio, and television industries. It can mean foregrounding the educational component of communication, which informs all cultural policy to some extent. Or it can mean ensuring a Canadian voice in film, radio, TV, publishing, and popular music, where there is a clear risk of being drowned out by American voices. Communication as public service is inherently inclusive, addressing audiences as citizens rather than consumers, and asserting citizens' rights to communicate and be informed.

The public service ideal, of course, is not without shortcomings when it comes to putting principles into practice. In Canada, public service has often meant national service—i.e., communication in the service of nation-building. As Marc Raboy (1992: xii–xiii) notes, in the broadcasting sector this has meant the subordination of other social and cultural goals to national economic and political interests, specifically, 'the political project of maintaining "Canada" as an entity distinct from the United States of America and united against the periodic threat of disintegration posed by Quebec'. It has also meant the concentration of film, radio, and television services in central Canada, creating a hierarchical distinction between the 'national' preoccupations of Ontario and Quebec and the 'regional' concerns of the other provinces and territories.

The central ethic of the public corporation is connected to the democratic ideal. More specifically, it is to provide a public service to both the users of the service and to the population as a whole. Under such an ethic, charges are sometimes levied for services rendered, and at other times costs are covered through general government revenues. In still other instances, revenue raised by general taxes is combined with user fees. On the consumer's side, user fees are often determined in part by what others must pay and in part by how much the service actually costs. For example, while rural users often pay more for telephone services, they do not pay the full amount of what it costs to bring the service into sparsely populated areas. In this way an attempt is made to provide universal and equitable access encompassed by the notion of common carriage. It is surely a national achievement to bring radio and television services to every Canadian community of at least 500 people—even if all of them cannot ever consume enough to form a market sufficiently attractive to advertisers to pay for the service. Not to provide such services would threaten the maintenance of national sovereignty; if we find ourselves unable to provide such services, another nation, most likely the United States, might. Or, some Canadians would simply be deprived.

A public service ethic also means that the object of public corporations is not to demonstrate the existence of a market or pursue profit as a primary goal. In most countries profit-making by publicly owned corporations is forbidden, and in others certain or all public media corporations are prevented from accepting advertising. These restrictions exist to ensure that the public corporation is not compromised in its ability to serve the public by its need to seek advertising revenue. It also guards against competition between the public and private sectors for advertising income.

Public service means that economics is only one factor to be considered in a larger equation. The other major element of the equation is the determination of the public interest, not in a unitary or authoritarian fashion, but in a way that reflects the many and varied interests and viewpoints that are part of any society (see McQuail, 1991, for an attempt at outlining the public interest in the context of media performance).

This public interest ethic means that the publicly owned outlet must weigh its public service mandate—such as appealing to all ages and people in all locations, training top-level journalists, or meeting the needs of audience members to be responsible and contributing citizens in society—against economic pressures. The public corporation can consider, on the merit of the case itself, whether it will carry children's programs without advertising support, develop socially oriented programs for the poor, or underwrite programming for the aged. After making this decision, it must find the means to carry it through.

PUBLIC ENTERPRISE

Public enterprise has a long and distinguished tradition in every Western country. Its most common use has been in instances when a national social need was clearly identified, yet a market was not organized or seemed incapable of adequately serving the needs of the country. In communications the establishment of a national broadcasting service such as the CBC is the classic example. Educational institutions, the postal service, and health services are others.

As Herschel Hardin (1974) points out, Canada has made extensive use of public enterprise throughout its history, with the most common form being the Crown corporation. At times, as in the case of the Canadian Pacific Railway, Canada has combined public enterprise or public support with private enterprise to produce the same end: public service. As Robin Mathews (1988) notes, we practise a brand of capitalism tempered by socialism.

Public ownership of the media has followed in this

tradition. Its general purpose has been to bring information and entertainment, images, and symbols, reflective of the variety of the country and the variety of the world, to the greatest number of citizens possible, especially through broadcasting. The social value was that the audience might generally benefit from such exposure and that compatriots might see themselves as members of a single nation.

While the prime example of public ownership in the Canadian media is the CBC, there are other examples in the National Film Board of Canada, community radio stations, and the provincial educational broadcast networks. Originally a radio operation, the CBC was set up essentially because of a fear of inundation by programming from the United States. As for television, it was not apparent how Canadian production and display could be a money-making venture. The CBC extended its activities into television to bring information reflective of the variety that makes

Robert Rabinovitch was appointed president and CEO of CBC/Radio-Canada in 1999. Although CBC/Radio-Canada is funded primarily through parliamentary appropriation, the Corporation's autonomy is assured through the authority conferred by Parliament upon its Board of Directors and the appointment of a President and CEO who cannot be fired except by Parliament. This principle of 'arm's length' is critical to CBC/Radio-Canada's role as a news-gathering organization. (Courtesy CBC/Radio-Canada, Ottawa)

up Canada to the greatest number of Canadians, so that we might all see ourselves as members of a single and independent nation.

FORMS OF PUBLIC OWNERSHIP

The characteristic model of broadcast ownership is a national public **monopoly** or, in cases such as Canada, a national public broadcaster existing side by side with private-sector broadcasters. In either case, the organization and finances of the national public broadcaster may be controlled by the state. However, the broadcaster is independent from government in its program policies. The CBC, for example, has a board of directors appointed by the government of the day but the board acts independently of that government. The original BBC model was adopted by France, Italy, the Scandinavian countries, and Japan, and by Commonwealth nations such as Australia, New Zealand, Zimbabwe, and India. In Belgium and Switzerland, as in Canada, each linguistic group has its own service. In Germany, where the states or Länder are responsible for broadcasting, a number of regional monopolies come together to form the national networks (Rolland and Østbye, 1986).

The dynamics of cultural identity have played a major role in the formation and design of broadcasting systems, especially of their public components. Often, when regional cultural identity is important—as it is in Norway, Germany, and France—room is created for regional productions. National cultural identity is predominant as a concern in Italy, the Netherlands, France, Finland, and Denmark. The French have seen themselves as bastions against Anglo-Saxon or English-language imperialism and are therefore strongly protectionist. They also support domestic production subsidies both in France and in the European Union. Italy has expressed its concerns in terms of 'cultural colonization'. Many European countries have established quotas governing national and imported content. Denmark and Finland have favoured variety in importation over quotas to keep foreign content from overwhelming national culture (Bakke, 1986).

The creation of public-sector institutions and their predominance over the years have ensured a firm commitment to the public service ethic. But more recently these state monopolies have been challenged by issues of fiscal constraint and economism. That is, should governments spend public money to promote and protect indigenous cultural activity in this man-ner? And, is cultural production an appropriate sphere of state activity? We have seen a shift since the early 1980s from what Colin Sparks (1995) terms a 'culturalist discourse'—which perceives cultural production as first and foremost a cultural activity—to an 'economistic discourse'—which defines cultural production as commercial enterprise. Among those promoting the wholesale appropriation of cultural production by the private sector are the same media proprietors who stand the most to gain from such a shift.

Private Ownership

Private-sector ownership takes two basic forms. The ownership of a company can be closely held, either by an individual or by a very small group (often family members). Or the ownership of a company can be widely held by a large group of shareholders, who buy and sell their interest in the company through the stock market. In the latter case, a company will form a board of directors answerable to its shareholders.

The general ethic of the private or commercial media outlet is survival and growth in a marketplace driven by profit. This ethic does not derive merely from the personality traits of private-sector owners. Commercial corporations are organized for the purpose of earning returns for their owners, whether those owners are individuals or groups of shareholders. Because the bottom line in the private sector is profit, private media companies have greater latitude than public media institutions in changing course to pursue more lucrative markets, whether those markets are in the sphere of communications or not. Thomson Corp., for example, was once one of Canada's two principal newspaper chains, and the company was a significant newspaper owner in the United States and Great Britain. But Thomson redefined itself in the 1990s as an information company, gradually withdrew from the newspaper industry, and moved its assets to more promising business opportunities elsewhere, specifically in the markets of financial, legal, and scientific information (Thomson Corp., 1998, 1999).

FORMS OF PRIVATE OWNERSHIP

Even within the private sector there is a considerable variety of ownership structures. The single enterprise is, as its name suggests, a business form in which owners confine themselves to one business with no connections to other companies. It is a single, independent firm that usually operates on a small scale.

IF KIDS CAN, THEN NELVANA AND CORUS CAN SURVIVE CONVERGENCE IN TORONTO

Once upon a time, there was a small publisher of children's book in Toronto called Kids Can Press. It was run by two wise women and they were successful in finding and publishing quality Canadian titles. Along the way, they published a series of stories about Franklin the Turtle™. In a neighbouring land, another Canadian company called Nelvana developed some very clever animation and visual effects technology that came to the notice of the big Hollywood moguls. Both companies were successful. Nelvana made lots of money because it was in the movie business where successful companies make lots of money. In the book business, especially in Canada, making gobs of money is extremely rare, so Kids Can made less. 'It's a living', said the wise women, 'and it's fun.'

One day, Nelvana met Kids Can. More importantly, Nelvana met Franklin the Turtle. Nelvana said: 'We can take Franklin to places he would never go in the book world. Why don't we buy your company for more money than you ever dreamed of? You can continue running the company, and we will take Franklin into the new lands of television and licensed merchandising. And we will all live happily ever after.'

So Nelvana did buy Kids Can. It paid $7 million, a sum virtually unheard of in the land of Canadian book publishing, and it took Franklin into television and licensed merchandising.

Now modern stories never begin and end that simply, because, for one thing, time passes, and, for another, the world changes. It seems that, indeed, in the land of television broadcasting and TV program distribution in Canada, changes were afoot. As a result of a decision of a queen's council of advisers (a.k.a. the CRTC), one company was able to obtain control of one of Canada's two private television networks, CTV. The triumphant company renamed itself Corus. Once the singing of joy was over, Corus thought that it would be a good idea to invest in program production to broadcast to its stations and to sell to other networks around the world from whom it purchased programs. Corus looked for a good production company to buy and it spied Nelvana. So Corus said to Nelvana, 'Why don't we buy your company for more money than you ever dreamed of? You can continue running the company.' So Corus bought Nelvana. It paid Nelvana $540 million.

All was happy in the land for about two years because Kids Can was one of Canada's leading children's book publishing companies, Nelvana was Canada's leading cartoon production company, and Corus was one of Canada's leading television-based entertainment companies. However, one morning Corus woke up to a world market filled with cartoon-based television programs. Thus it came to pass that Corus, which had declared a $100 million profit in its third quarter of 2001, declared a $190 million loss in its fourth quarter of 2002 and felt it necessary to take a further write-down of $200 million on its assets. Also, it saw its shares drop from a high in 2001 of nearly $40 to a low in October of 2002 of $20.

So, one blustery day in October 2002, the admirals from Corus said to the captain of Nelvana, 'We want Franklin to work harder. We would like to see Franklin generate about 25 per cent of revenue, not the 7 per cent he is now generating. He could do so by sailing more aggressively into the world of licensed merchandising. If Bob the Builder™, Barney the Dinosaur™, and Thomas the Tank Engine™ can generate 39 per cent profit for London-based HIT Entertainment PLC, we think Franklin can do more. Besides, as you know, we do own the rights to Babar the Elephant™ and Little Bear from the Berenstein Bears™ and they are willing to help.' The captain of the Nelvana ship pondered. Finally he said, 'Why don't I sail into port and someone else can captain the Nelvana ship. I will act as a retired admiral.' So the captains of Corus said, 'We are sorry to lose you, but maybe it would be best for all of us.'

So Corus drew up some new maps for sailing more aggressively into the land of merchandising. And they set out to find a new captain for Nelvana. As for Kids Can Press and Franklin, well, they sailed on, because, in the world of children's book publishing, there are always new authors, always new titles, and always new readers who love to fall in love with creations such as Franklin the Turtle.

Source: Keith Damsell, *Globe and Mail*, 26 Oct. 2002, B1. Reprinted with permission of *The Globe and Mail*.

Examples of this form of ownership of newspapers, radio stations, and even some television stations were quite common until media barons like Roy Thomson began acquiring them to form chain operations. Some examples still exist, particularly among magazines, community weekly newspapers, and small-town radio stations. But single enterprises are fewer and fewer as chains both large and small gobble them up or force them out of business.

Chain ownership is the linking or **horizontal integration** of a number of companies in the same business—typically, newspapers, radio stations, or television stations—occupying different markets. Chains are usually geographically dispersed, but sometimes members of the chain will occupy the same location and aim for distinct audiences. Vancouver's two daily newspapers, the *Sun* and *Province*, for example, are both part of the larger CanWest chain, but they seek different readers and advertisers within the Lower Mainland of British Columbia. Member companies in a chain may have agreements to buy and sell services from each other. CanWest newspapers, for instance, share editorial content (stories and pictures) among member papers and have their own wire service, CanWest News Service. In addition, chains often consolidate administrative resources, so that accounting and marketing services or departments responsible for technological innovation will be able to serve all members in the chain. Such sharing of resources offers chain operations tremendous cost advantages over single enterprises. Typically, chain ownership provides the advantages of reducing competition and creates economies of scale (see Rutherford, 1992).

Chain ownership is a common form of media organization in Canada. CanWest MediaWorks, owned by CanWest Global Communications Corp., runs a chain of 13 daily newspapers across Canada, including the *National Post* and major dailies in Victoria, Vancouver, Edmonton, Calgary, Regina, Saskatoon, Ottawa, and Montreal (www.cna-acj.ca). CanWest also owns the Global Television Network, which is comprised of a chain of 11 stations in eight provinces (www.canwestglobal.com).

Vertical integration is the concentration of firms within a specific business that extends a company's control over the entire process of production. A vertically integrated company, for instance, will have subsidiary companies involved in every aspect of an industry. The most common example of vertical integration is the commercial film industry, in which the major Hollywood companies not only own production studios and distribution companies, but have subsidiaries involved in theatrical exhibition, television, and video/DVD rental to ensure their films reach audiences. The advantages inherent to vertical integration are substantial. A vertically integrated company ensures itself of both resource supplies and sales markets, and it minimizes other uncertainties related

Ownership trends in the media industries as well as the contrast between well-capitalized private commercial organizations and starving public media organizations are aptly illustrated in this cartoon. (Bob Krieger, The Province)

Table 8.3 Converged Media Companies

Quebecor Inc.

PUBLISHING
- Newspapers: Sun Media Corporation newspaper chain with 8 metro dailies, over 50 community newspapers in Quebec, and nearly 200 across Canada
- Magazines: *7 jours, Clin d'oeil, Dernière Heure, Échos Vedettes*, among others
- Books: Combined, Québecor Media's publishing houses publish the largest number of titles in Quebec. These houses include Les Éditions Internationales Alain Stanké, CEC Publishing, Éditions du Trécarré, among others.

TELEVISION
- Videotron: cable TV provider with 1.4 million subscribers in Quebec; its cable network covers 80 per cent of the province and is the largest in Quebec.
- TVA: owns 6 of 10 stations in the TVA network, as well as the specialty channel Le Canal Nouvelles, among others. It is the largest French-language TV network in North America.
- SUN-TV: Quebecor acquired the Toronto-based English-language station CKXT-TV in 2004 and rebranded the station as SUN-TV, to identify with the *Toronto Sun* newspaper.

NEW MEDIA
- Canoe.inc: operates CANOE network of internet properties, including canoe.ca portal, and reaches 6.4 million users monthly.
- Nurun: web business applications
- Vidéotron: internet service provider

RETAIL
- Archambault: retail chain of 14 book, music stores; owns Camelot-Info computer bookstores chain, Paragraphe bookstore in Montreal, and two music and video distributors.
- SuperClub Vidéotron: retail chain of video sales and rentals with over 180 locations

CanWest Global Communications Corp.

PUBLISHING
- Newspapers: *National Post* national daily newspaper;11 metro dailies, 2 small-market dailies, 2 free dailies in Ottawa and Vancouver, and 21 community newspapers
- Magazines: *Financial Post Business* (*National Post*); *TV Times* (newspaper insert); *Shout!* (distributed in Aboriginal schools); *Swerve* (*Calgary Herald*); *Saturday ed* (Edmonton)
- Books: CanWest Books publishing company, launched in 2004

TELEVISION
- Global TV Network: 11 stations in 8 provinces
- 3 independent stations (CH Hamilton, Vancouver Island, Montreal)
- 2 CBC affiliates (Kelowna, Red Deer)
- Network Ten (Australia)
- TV3 and C4 (New Zealand)
- Specialty channels Prime TV, Men TV, Mystery, DejaView, Lonestar, Fox Sportsworld Canada, Xtreme Sports, COOL TV, and TVTropolis

RADIO
- 91.5—The BEAT (Kitchener)
- 99.1 COOL FM (Winnipeg)
- Original 106 (UK)
- Super FM, Metro FM, Joy FM, and Joy Turk FM (Turkey)
- MORE FM network of 21 stations (New Zealand)
- Complete ownership of Radioworks group with four networks comprising 27 stations (New Zealand)

NEW MEDIA
- canada.com: internet portal for news and information
- On-line shopping: on canada.com and local shopping through newspaper websites
- Internet Broadcasting Systems

FP DataGroup	Medbroadcast	celebrating.com
FP InfoMart	working.com	connecting.com
LifeServ: website	driving.ca	dose.ca
	remembering.ca	

BCE Inc.

TELEPHONY
- Bell Canada: conventional telephone service
- Bell Mobility: wireless telephone service
- Bell Digital Voice: VOIP service

NEW MEDIA
- Bell Globemedia Interactive: family of websites, including sympatico.ca and globeandmail.com
- Sympatico: internet service provider

TELEVISION
- CTV: national television network of 21 owned and three independent affiliates
- TQS, and 17 specialty channels: Report on Business TV, The Comedy Network, MTV, The Sports Network (TSN), Réseau de sports (RDS), Discovery Channel, and others
- Bell ExpressVu: satellite TV service

Rogers Communications Inc.

TELEVISION
- Rogers Cable: Canada's largest cable TV provider, with 2.3 million customers in Ontario, New Brunswick, and Newfoundland and Labrador
- Ethnic TV stations OMNI 1 and OMNI 2 (Ontario) and OMNI 10 (Vancouver)
- Shopping Channel
- Rogers Sportsnet
- Infomercial producer Mix Productions (Quebec)
- Minority interests in specialty channels Viewers Choice Canada, Outdoor Life Network, Biography Channel Canada, and others

RADIO
- Rogers Broadcasting: 46 radio stations across Canada, including 3 new FM stations in Halifax, Saint John, and Moncton

BCE Inc. (cont'd)	**Rogers Communications Inc.** (cont'd)
PUBLISHING – *Globe and Mail*, national daily newspaper – *Report on Business Magazine* – *Globe Television*	**TELEPHONY** – Rogers Wireless: 6.2 million wireless telephone subscribers as of 31 Dec. 2005 **PUBLISHING** – Rogers Publishing: over 70 periodicals, including *Maclean's, Chatelaine, Flare, l'Actualité*, and Canadian business and trade publications **NEW MEDIA** – Rogers Yahoo! Hi-Speed Internet: cable-based internet service provider **RETAIL** – Rogers Video: chain of video sales and rentals in over 300 locations **OTHER** – Sports Entertainment group: combined operations of the Rogers Centre entertainment venue (formerly known as the SkyDome) and the Toronto Blue Jays
Sources: www.quebecor.com; www.canwestglobal.com; www.bce.ca; www.rogers.com.	

CONVERGENCE

Convergence is an economic strategy in which media conglomerates take advantage of the digitization of content and government deregulation to reduce operating costs and expand market share. Media content is now produced digitally, so that newspaper stories, radio programs, photographs, recorded music, and television programming can be cobbled together as a content package on media companies' websites. At the same time, the CRTC has increasingly permitted media conglomerates to own newspapers and radio and TV stations in the same markets.

The advantages of convergence for the media conglomerate are potentially enormous. A single company can offer advertising buyers a number of media platforms from which to develop an ad campaign, as well as package deals for those who advertise in more than one medium. It offers audiences one-stop shopping for news and entertainment, creating a recognizable media brand and encouraging brand loyalty among consumers. Similarly, convergence allows media to cross-promote one another. 'In Canada, with two or three companies you can cover the country', Phillip Crawley, publisher and chief executive officer of the *Globe and Mail*, told the Canadian Newspaper Association's annual meeting in Calgary in 2002 (Brethour, 2002).

A converged company can save costs by reducing its workforce because content created for one medium can be repurposed for use in a sister medium. Increasingly, for example, newspaper reporters are being asked to prepare news stories that can appear on the company's website and be twinned with a TV report on the company's local newscast. CanWest Global, which owns a national television network, a chain of daily newspapers, and an internet portal, has used its convergence strategy to reduce administrative costs and to encourage content-sharing among its newspaper, TV, and web newsrooms (ibid).

Of course, what appears to the eyes of media executives as an advantage may be detrimental to workers and audiences. Journalists working in shrinking newsrooms are being pressured to produce more stories each day, and stories that can be used in more than one news medium. CanWest Global president Leonard Asper has been widely cited for envisioning a future in which journalists 'wake up, write a story for the Web, write a column, take their cameras, cover an event and do a report for TV and file a video clip for the Web' ('The complications of convergence', *Globe and Mail*, 4 Aug. 2001, A12). In other words, convergence strategies compel fewer workers to produce more and varied content without very much consideration for how much time and effort is required to produce high-quality news content, not to mention any consideration for essential differences between media.

But besides the qualitative implications this entails, there are quantitative concerns as well. In spite of claims to the contrary, audiences are faced with fewer distinct choices among mainstream information and entertainment sources. By pooling their production, distribution, and marketing resources, media conglomerates raise the barriers to entry for would-be competitors. Telecommunications researcher Kevin G. Wilson (2002) argues that convergence 'has produced horizontal concentration as there are fewer players in the respective telephone, cable, TV, radio, Internet and publishing industries, and vertical concentration because most of the remaining companies are now owned by one of the five convergence "champions"'—BCE Inc., Rogers Communications, Shaw Communications, CanWest Global Communications, and Quebecor Inc.

Because Canada's major media companies have accrued considerable debt burdens in expanding the quantity of their media properties, the quality of their content has suffered as resource cutbacks and layoffs have inevitably followed takeovers. Since spending over $3 billion to buy the Southam newspaper chain in 2000, for example, CanWest Global has been trying to divest assets to ease a $3.8-billion debt load (Canadian Press, 2003). Its attention to reducing debt resulted in an increased share price in early 2004 (Edwards, 2004). Similarly, Quebecor, 'engulfed in debt problems' in the aftermath of its October 2000 purchase of cable company Videotron, was forced to sell more than $1 billion in assets. Quebecor Media recently recovered from three years of cost-cutting in every division, but still carries $1 billion in high-yield debt (Silcoff, 2003). BCE, too, remains saddled with a debt of $17.6 billion, which represents an onerous two-thirds of the company's market value (Lewandowski, 2003). Nonetheless, Bell Globemedia bid $1.7 billion in July 2006 to add to its broadcast holdings through the purchase of CHUM Ltd (Schecter, 2006).

CanWest Global Communications has made a concerted effort to emerge as a national player by cross-promoting its national television network (Global), its daily newspaper chain (CanWest MediaWorks), and its internet portal (canada.com). The portal consists mainly of content from its newspaper and television newsrooms, and in several of its urban markets—e.g., Vancouver and Montreal—its newspaper and TV newsrooms co-operate on

featured news series. For example, during the summer of 2001, the Montreal *Gazette* and the 5:30 p.m. Global newscast teamed up on a series called 'Hot Neighbourhoods'. *Gazette* business reporter Mary Lamey appeared on Global's newscast to talk about one of Montreal's booming real estate markets, then the next morning she and *Gazette* columnist Mike Boone would write about that neighbourhood in the newspaper.

Quebecor has probably been the most successful Canadian company in exploiting the financial possibilities of media convergence. In 2003, it introduced the Quebec television ratings hit *Star Académie* on its TVA network. With the popular Julie Snyder as host and producer (as well as girlfriend of Quebecor CEO Pierre-Karl Péladeau), the 'reality' series brought together 14 aspiring singers being trained for stardom. The series consisted of four 30-minute weeknight 'documentaries' and a 90-minute prime-time special on Sunday night. The 13 April 2003 finale attracted an audience of three million viewers, almost half of the Quebec population. Quebecor promoted the show through its publications—e.g., through both advertising and news coverage in Montreal's best-selling daily newspaper *Le Journal de Montréal* and in the supermarket magazine *7 Jours*—and profited from audience members using either its Netgraphe web portal or the telephone to vote for their favourite contestants. The Quebecor music company Select later produced a CD, which sold 500,000 copies and, of course, was available in Quebecor's music and bookstore chain Archambault (Baril, 2003). *Star Académie* was the ratings leader in Quebec during the 2005–6 television season; its 2005 gala was the top show, attracting 2.4 million viewers, and the 2005 daily 'documentary' was third, with an average audience of 1.6 million. TVA had eight of the top 10 televisions shows in 2005–6 (Infopresse, 2006: 40).

What does convergence mean? Kevin G. Wilson (2002) writes: 'The stewardship of Canada's economic and cultural nervous system is literally in the hands of a handful of heavily indebted companies that have yet to demonstrate that the patchwork of companies they have assembled are capable of generating any beneficial synergies.'

to the circuit of production (Mosco, 1996: 175–82). Following the lead of the vertically integrated Hollywood film companies, Canada's largest audiovisual company, Alliance Atlantis Communications (www.allianceatlantis.com), produces, distributes, and broadcasts filmed entertainment.

Conglomerate ownership is characterized by large companies with a number of subsidiary firms in related and unrelated businesses. Besides the advantages of scale conglomerates afford their owners, shareholder risk is reduced because the conglomerate is not dependent for its profits on any one industry.

Convergence is the name given to the economic strategy media conglomerates employ in an attempt to create synergies among their media properties (see Table 8.3). Quebecor Inc. (www.quebecor.com) is an example of a conglomerate because it has interests in businesses not directly related to newspaper publishing: e.g., television broadcasting (TVA, SUN-TV), new media (Canoe), cable television service (Videotron), and music retailing (Trans-Canada Archambault).

Tempering the Profit Motive

Because private-sector media companies operate on the basis of profit maximization, governments have seen fit to introduce policy measures—both regulations and inducements—to ensure the private sector makes a contribution to the production and dissemination of Canadian cultural products. Even the establishment of a Royal Commission can apply moral suasion to address an identified shortcoming in a particular industry.

In television broadcasting, for instance, American television programming is far more economically attractive to Canadian broadcasters than indigenous programming. First of all, it is generally 10 times cheaper for a Canadian broadcaster to buy an American show than to produce its own program. This is because American TV producers can recoup their costs of production in the huge, US domestic market, then offer their programming at bargain rates to foreign television networks. Second, there is much less risk for Canadian broadcasters in buying American programs that already have a track record of attracting audiences and advertisers than in developing their own shows from scratch. Finally, Canadian broadcasters can benefit directly from the publicity and media coverage that successful American TV shows generate. If Canadian broadcasters had to produce their own shows, they would have to market them, too.

As we discussed in Chapter 7, the vertical integration of the commercial film industry makes it difficult for Canadian feature films to penetrate exhibition markets. Because the same companies that own Hollywood movie studios have ownership ties to Canada's principal theatre chains, these companies have a vested interest in granting preference to their own films. The commercial theatres are also more inclined to book Hollywood films to benefit from both audience familiarity with what Hollywood produces and the publicity these films generate through

fan magazines and televised entertainment programs like *Entertainment Tonight* and *E-Talk Daily*. English Canada has never succeeded in developing a comparable celebrity culture that would turn Canadian actors and directors into household names. In Quebec, however, French-language magazines like *7 Jours* and *Dernière Heure* and television programs like *Flash*, *Star Systeme*, *La Fureur*, and *Tout le monde en parle* generate sizable audiences and have turned Québécois performers into stars.

In other cultural industries, the private sector's reluctance to invest in Canadian cultural production is less easy to quantify, but as illustrated in Chapter 3, economies of scale give book and magazine publishers marketing their wares in both Canada and the US tremendous cost advantages over those selling only in the Canadian market, rendering distinctly Canadian products much less profitable for book and magazine retailers. The success Canada has had in developing, with considerable state intervention, a popular music industry and a vibrant literary tradition since the 1960s seems to suggest that a certain amount of prejudice is at play in the private sector as well. That is, in spite of all evidence to the contrary, some media owners simply do not believe Canadians can produce popular and profitable forms of entertainment, and thus prefer to take the safer route of importing cultural products for which someone else has already done the work of building a market.

There is no denying the tensions between the public good and the private commercial interest. The Broadcasting Act recognizes these tensions by assigning social responsibilities to all licence-holders, including minimum Canadian-content regulations and special additional responsibilities for the public sector. Section 19 of the Income Tax Act provides recognition in the form of effectively restricting majority ownership of Canadian newspapers, magazines, and broadcasting stations—i.e., any medium that accepts advertising—to Canadians (although this requirement has been diluted considerably and there is pressure on the federal government to ease this restriction further to increase the pool of potential buyers and thereby decrease the number of Canadian properties owned by concentrated media companies—see Chapter 7). The public goals of communication are also recognized in the form of postal grants to qualifying Canadian publications and in the support policies of the Department of Canadian Heritage (formerly the Department of Communications) for cultural industries, even if these programs are under review by a federal government committed to balancing its books and under pressure from the United States through World Trade Organization challenges. In the area of film, support policies, targeted programs, and public agencies such as the National Film Board and Telefilm Canada are recognition of public goals. Complementary provincial support policies demonstrate how deeply felt these public goals are. In telecommunications, the notion of common carriage also reflects public goals.

Policies directed at the production and broadcasting of high-quality indigenous programming have had varying success from country to country. Only in specific instances have governments and industry been able to identify mechanisms that simultaneously encourage high-quality indigenous content and either increase or maintain profits. Until the late 1980s in Canada, the private sector could not be persuaded by any form of policy to develop and sell high-quality indigenous television programming. In contrast, the United Kingdom was more successful,

Figure 8.1 Cross-Ownership in Nine Canadian Cities by Market Share of Local Television Newscasts and Local Newspapers

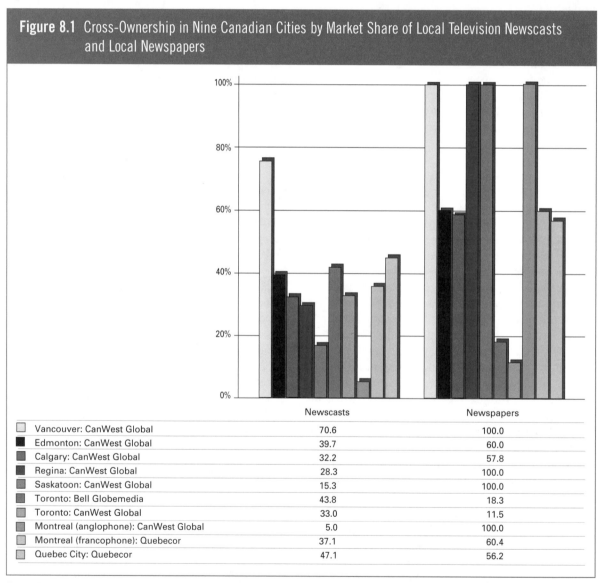

	Newscasts	Newspapers
Vancouver: CanWest Global	70.6	100.0
Edmonton: CanWest Global	39.7	60.0
Calgary: CanWest Global	32.2	57.8
Regina: CanWest Global	28.3	100.0
Saskatoon: CanWest Global	15.3	100.0
Toronto: Bell Globemedia	43.8	18.3
Toronto: CanWest Global	33.0	11.5
Montreal (anglophone): CanWest Global	5.0	100.0
Montreal (francophone): Quebecor	37.1	60.4
Quebec City: Quebecor	47.1	56.2

Figure 8.1 is a clear illustration of concentration of ownership in the provision of news via television and newspapers in major Canadian cities. The possibility of a plurality of messages being delivered by a variety of media owners is very restricted in many Canadian cities.

with Australia somewhere in between. The status of the United Kingdom as a centre of English-speaking peoples, the articulation of the notion of the public interest, and the concomitant role of export markets have contributed greatly to the ability of its private sector to produce attractive programming.

In spite of its limited abilities to pursue cultural goals, the private commercial sector is making continuous gains in its participation in media industries. One factor in this is a general reorientation underway in industrialized economies. In the post-war years, the industrialized world followed one element of Keynesian economics, that is, state spending to encourage economic growth. However, once their economies were humming, Western states never stopped spending more than their net revenues. The result was that nations saddled themselves with potentially crippling debts. A general trend in Western countries since the early 1980s has been to look for areas of state involvement that can be cut at a savings to the public purse. Publicly owned media have been one area in which public spending has been cut, while services have been expanded through increased private participation.

Another factor is that, over time, public (and existing private) corporations have identified which audiences can be served by what means to make what level of profit. Program types, employee levels, and working relationships have all been established. The knowledge infrastructure now exists and can be transferred to new firms through the hiring of qualified personnel.

As well, new technologies (specifically, communication satellites, computer applications, and fibre optics) have been developed that challenge the ability of states to control electronic communication and their legitimacy in doing so because, through innovation, limits on carrying capacity (radio spectrum scarcity) are quickly disappearing. In the case of satellites, when a signal from space can deliver programs to all homes in a country, in the context of international covenants affirming the freedom to receive information, what should be the position of the state?

In the face of insistent requests from the private sector to be allowed to engage in profit-making activity that can serve a market, if not the public good, it is difficult for states to argue that cultural goals directly contradict such activities. This is especially the case in the presence of technology able to facilitate the activities. Whenever audiences watch or listen to a program, however limited in enlightenment that program may be, cultural content is being transmitted. In addition, basic human rights to have broad access to information come into play, specifically the right of an individual to receive information.

Implications of Private Media Ownership

For those who believe that communication in all its forms involves much more than satisfying markets, the appropriation by private enterprise of a greater and greater share of the mass communication sphere is of great concern. While economists argue that the free-market organization of cultural production is the most efficient means of giving consumers what they want, political economists maintain that the commercial organization of cultural production limits choice and discriminates between those members of the public who have disposable income to spend on advertised products and those who don't. This is particularly the case when corporate concentration limits the number of, and distinctions between, producers and distributors (see Mosco, 1996: 182–205).

In the realm of the mass media, private enterprise is seen as having two particular social benefits. First, in keeping with Adam Smith's invisible hand, it is said to stimulate the provision of affordable goods and services for which consumers have expressed a need or desire through their purchasing decisions. Second, because advertising subsidizes the media, consumers are able to receive content either for free (e.g., radio) or at a minimal cost (e.g., daily newspapers).

These benefits, of course, are not as straightforward as they may seem. First of all, anticipating consumer demand is an inexact science, notwithstanding polls and focus groups. Consumers can only make choices among those already offered—supply to a large extent governs demand—and media managers have been frustrated time and again in trying to determine which new services will attract consumers. Media economists have demonstrated, for example, that most major Hollywood movies lose money, and the studios depend on their blockbuster hits to make up for their far more numerous flops (Leblanc, 1990: 287). The same applies to television series; each new fall season introduces more losers than winners, shows that are cancelled after only a few weeks. Advertising and other forms of publicity, of course, play a role in generating excitement and consumer demand around new films, TV shows, music recordings, and book releases, but consumer tastes remain very hard to anticipate.

Second, it is simply not accurate to say consumers receive some media programming for free, thanks to advertising. Instead, consumers pay for it in a round-about way. Even if we do not directly hand over any money to a radio station to listen to its programming, we pay for that programming nonetheless every time we buy an advertised product. Advertising costs, in other words, are built into the sale price of potato chips and breakfast cereal, so that a share of the money we spend on groceries, snacks, clothing, beer, gasoline, and cosmetics is in turn used to pay for media programming.

Media economists also argue that we pay with our time—we literally pay attention—whenever we watch television or listen to the radio, and that time, that attention, is what advertisers seek access to

(Picard, 1989). This is a key point to understanding how commercial media work within the economic system. In order to generate profits, managers of commercial media seek to attract audiences to their programming to sell those audiences to advertisers. Putting it another way, communications theorist Dallas Smythe (1994: 270–1) argues that what advertisers buy is not simply air time or newspaper space, but 'the services of audiences with predictable specifications who will pay attention in predictable numbers and at particular times to particular means of communications'. Through increasingly sophisticated audience measurement techniques, media managers collect data on their audiences—not only the size of the audience is determined, but demographic factors such as income, education, age, and sex—and sell advertisers access to the kinds of audiences that will be interested in buying their product or service. Mass media content, then, is merely 'an inducement (gift,

As this cartoon illustrates, the increase in media offerings—in this case, as provided by specialty-TV channels—is largely an illusion. (CAM/Regina Leader Post. Reprinted by permission.)

bribe or "free lunch") to recruit potential members of the audience and to maintain their loyal attention'. Smythe writes that 'the free lunch consists of materials which whet the audience members' appetite and thus (1) attract and keep them attending to the programme, newspaper or magazine, and (2) cultivate a mood conducive to favourable reaction to the explicit and implicit advertisers' messages.'

Private ownership of the communications media raises four particular concerns. The first is that private enterprise casts cultural production as commercial enterprise, whereby the goal of communication becomes the generation of profit. This form of organization imposes commercial constraints on communication. Communication as commercial enterprise creates pressures to maximize entertainment value and to minimize difficulty and complexity, and to provide communication in an advertising-friendly or consumption-friendly environment. In the medium of television, for example, competing programs are only a click of the remote away. Programming that is difficult, challenging, or slow-paced may have trouble holding audiences, and could be hard for broadcasters to support. This includes newscasts, which, according to the expectations of commercial enterprise, need to maximize ratings in a competitive environment even if that means sacrificing the quality and integrity of their journalism.

A second concern is that the increasing convergence of media properties reinforces the profit motive and moves owners further and further from their core areas of business. That is, conglomerates are in business to make money rather than to make movies or newspapers or books or radio programs. The goal of the conglomerate is to serve shareholders and paying customers, rather than society at large. By privileging the profit motive above all else, the creation of conglomerates weakens the owners' commitment to core areas of business; media properties may become a lesser priority within the conglomerate than, for example, its real estate holdings. Managers can therefore revise the conglomerate's mandate, as Thomson has done by moving away from newspapers into more specialized media, or abandon media industries altogether for more lucrative industries.

Related to this is a third concern. The broader a conglomerate's reach, the more businesses it is involved in, the greater the chance for a conflict of interest between its media business and its other holdings. Critical themes—e.g., environmentalism, labour practices, poverty—in newspaper and magazine stories, TV documentaries, or radio programs could threaten the earnings or community standing of the conglomerate's other holdings. In such cases, the conglomerate's media properties will feel pressure to avoid certain subject areas, depriving the public of a full airing of important social issues or confining their discussion within safe parameters.

Finally, the trend towards corporate concentration has reduced substantially our sources of information at precisely the same point in history when our dependence on communications media for our knowledge of the world has increased. The plethora of TV and radio channels, books, magazines, newspapers, music recordings, and DVDs available to us is largely illusory; it disguises the fact that many of these media are the products of a mere handful of large corporations. If we are to take seriously our role as citizens in democratic society, we should be encouraging the greatest variety of information sources possible, as well as an increase in distinct media channels for us to express ourselves.

Taken together, these trends of private ownership have reduced our sources of information and narrowed the range of what can be said and how it can be expressed.

Media Democratization

The idea of democratizing the media has a history dating back at least to the 1960s and 1970s, when co-operative radio stations, film and video collectives, and alternative or 'underground' newspapers were established. Recently, however, the relative accessibility of the internet, the inadequacies of both public and private forms of ownership described above, and the hyper-commercialism that has accompanied globalization have combined to reinvigorate movements for media reform and the establishment of alternative media organizations.

Proposals for reforming the existing media—especially in the field of news and information—include: imposing limits on ownership, and especially cross-media ownership; amending the Competition Act to account for diversity in the expression of news and ideas; legislating a code of professional practice or a code of ethics for media organizations; restructuring provincial press councils and/or establishing a National Media Commission;

and enacting right-of-reply legislation, which would permit editorial redress for persons misrepresented in the media (Skinner, 2004: 16–17). David Skinner argues that 'these reforms would help ensure some diversity in corporate news voices, provide journalists some independence from their corporate employers and provide some checks on the relationship between the media and the public' (ibid., 18). Reform initiatives, however, leave standing the fundamental structures of public and private media institutions.

The other means by which groups seek to democratize the media is through the establishment of alternative media outlets, defined as 'independent and/or community-minded media with a self-espoused mandate to serve a particular range of social groups and/or interests' (ibid., 23). Examples include Co-op Radio in Vancouver and the myriad independent media centres sprouting on the World Wide Web. If these are to be viable alternatives, Skinner argues, they need to create an infrastructure based on sound economic models and strategies, for example, by forming associations and strategic partnerships to combine production and distribution resources (ibid., 24–5).

Summary

There is no natural or inevitable way to organize mass communication. The media are social institutions structured in various ways according to their technological characteristics, the resources they draw upon, and the socio-political context in which they operate. If all media organizations have something in common, however, it is that they participate in the economy by generating profits for media owners, by providing communication services to their audiences, by advertising goods and services, and by providing employment.

The mass media in Canada are owned both privately and publicly, but all operate in a mixed economy. No media industry in Canada is governed exclusively by free-market economics. Even newspaper publishing, which comes closest to an exclusively private enterprise, is subject to federal government regulations regarding ownership intended to protect newspapers from foreign takeover and foreign competition. Nor is any media organization in Canada immune to the demands of the marketplace; even the publicly owned CBC must pay attention to ratings and advertising revenues.

The critical difference between public and private forms of media ownership pertains to their bottom lines. Public ownership is devoted to providing communication as a public service, to employ the mass media for social and/or national goals. Private ownership is devoted to providing communication for the profit of media owners. These distinctions are fundamental because they speak to the role communication is assigned in Canadian society. The economistic view perceives communication, first and foremost, as commercial enterprise, subjecting all forms of cultural production to commercial criteria of supply and demand. The culturalist view regards cultural products as much more than commodities to be exchanged in the marketplace. They are expressions of a culture as a way of life and as a system of beliefs and values. They are expressions of ideas and images that help a culture to imagine itself and to articulate its priorities. As private enterprise has encroached on more and more areas of mass communication in Canadian society, concerns have been raised over the increasing commercialization of cultural production, conglomerate ownership of media organizations, conflicts of interest between media companies and other businesses owned by the same parent, and corporate concentration.

Moves to democratize the media have assumed two forms: media reform, which seeks to find ways to diversify and render existing media organizations more accountable; and alternative media, that is, the establishment of new independent media outlets dedicated to serving defined communities.

RELATED WEBSITES

Alliance Atlantis Communications Inc.:
www.allianceatlantis.com
> This site provides corporate information and news about programming from Alliance Atlantis.

Broadcast Dialogue: www.broadcastdialogue.com
> This site offers directory and contact information for all Canadian radio and television stations.

Canadian Community Newspaper Association: www.ccna.ca
> Industry news and ownership information can be found at this official site.

Canadian Newspaper Association: www.cna-acj.ca
> Like the CCNA site, this official site of the CNA provides industry news and ownership information.

CanWest Global Communications Inc.:
www.canwestglobal.com
> This site describes the history of the company and lists its vast media holdings.

FURTHER READINGS

Gasher, Mike. 1997. 'From sacred cows to white elephants: Cultural policy under siege', in Joy Cohnstaedt and Yves Frechette, eds, *Canadian Themes* (Montreal: Association for Canadian Studies) 19: 13–29. This article traces the thematic shifts in Canadian cultural policy from the Aird Commission to the Applebaum-Hébert Report.

Heilbroner, Robert L. 1980. *The Worldly Philosophers: The Lives, Times, and Ideas of the Great Economic Thinkers*. New York: Simon & Schuster. This is a very readable reference guide to history's leading economic theorists.

Mosco, Vincent. 1996. *The Political Economy of Communication: Rethinking and Renewal*. London: Sage. Mosco's theoretical work applies contemporary political-economic thought to communication and cultural industries.

Skinner, David, James Compton, and Mike Gasher, eds. 2005. *Converging Media, Diverging Politics: A Political Economy of News Media in the United States and Canada*. Lanham, Md: Lexington Books. This collection of essays provides a current comparison, overview, and critique of the political economy of the news industries of the United States and Canada.

STUDY QUESTIONS

1. Why are the same media organized differently in otherwise similar countries like Canada, the US, Great Britain, and France?
2. What did Adam Smith mean by the 'invisible hand' of the market? To what extent does his economic thinking apply today?
3. What is the rationale for state intervention in the cultural economy?
4. What are 'externalities' and how are they pertinent to the discussion of media economics?
5. What are five ways in which Canadian governments are implicated in the structure of the media industries?
6. To what extent does advertising on CBC television distort the public broadcaster's central mission?
7. What are the principal distinctions between public and private forms of ownership?
8. What are three forms that private ownership of the media can assume?
9. What is media convergence and what does it imply for media content?
10. Why is it often more beneficial for Canadian television networks to buy US programs than to produce their own?
11. What does it mean to say that media sell audiences to advertisers?

LEARNING OUTCOMES

- To explain that there is no natural and inevitable way to organize media.
- To demonstrate the extent to which all media participate in the economy.
- To show that media are not simply products of technology, but are also shaped by the resources they draw upon and the socio-political context in which they operate.
- To point out that no media industry in Canada is governed exclusively by free-market economics.
- To underline the fundamental distinctions between public and private forms of ownership.
- To discuss the implications for media content of public and private forms of ownership.
- To provide a critical evaluation of the increasing privatization and deregulation of the Canadian media.
- To identify media reform initiatives and the emergence of alternative media movements that seek to alter the Canadian media landscape.

CHAPTER 9

Journalists as Content Producers

Introduction

Content producers are central to the whole media enterprise. Journalists, radio hosts, magazine photographers, television producers, film editors—all have vastly different job descriptions and work environments, but they all participate in the manufacture of the content we see in our newspapers, books, and magazines; hear on our radios; and see on our television, computer, and cinema screens. The stories and images we see, whether based on fact or fiction, are never presented simply or 'naturally', but are instead highly constructed. This process of construction involves a series of choices about what stories to tell and how to tell them. It comes into play both when content producers are trying to portray reality as accurately as possible and when they are trying to emphasize a particular point of view or style of presentation. After all, no story tells the whole story and no picture gives the full picture. This chapter posits journalism as a particular practice of content production and, as such, considers who Canadian journalists are and the cultural, legal, and institutional contexts of their work.

News as Content Production

Like other forms of content, news is produced, and much like other mass media—cinema, TV—news production is a form of storytelling. News items are usually referred to as 'stories', and, like other kinds of stories, they consist of characters, conflicts between characters, and temporal and geographical settings. This has implications for how we think about news and for the role journalism plays in society. News stories, while based on actual events and real people, never simply 'mirror' reality, as some journalists would contend. A mirror, after all, shows us only what is placed before it, nothing more and nothing less; the person holding the mirror may have control over where to point it, but the depiction the mirror offers is always a simple and direct, if unorganized, reflection. The mirror metaphor and the associated notion of 'reflec-

tion' do not adequately describe the role of journalists as content producers. If news media were mirrors, all news reports about the same event would be identical to one another. Clearly, they are not.

Nor is news simply gathered. Such a conception of journalism underestimates the degree of selection that goes into producing a news report and the extent to which events must meet a news organization's particular standards of 'newsworthiness'. Each day news reporters and their editors or producers face an infinite number of events from which to fashion their news stories. They receive far more invitations to press conferences than they could possibly cover and they receive far more press releases than they could ever use. Journalists make choices about what to cover based on what they perceive to have 'news value', what fits within their news organization's particular areas of coverage (politics, business, sports, crime, the arts), and what they believe will interest their audience. The values journalists apply to assess newsworthiness were described in our discussion of media form in Chapter 4. To reiterate, deciding what is news is a subjective operation, involving reporters and their editors or producers in a complex process of selection. While news judgement is most often exercised intuitively by journalists under time pressure in the field, media scholars have identified a number of criteria that render some events news and others not news. Melvin Mencher (2000: 68–76), for example, identifies seven determinants of newsworthiness: timeliness (events that are immediate or recent); impact (events that affect many people); prominence (events involving well-known people or institutions); proximity (events that are geographically, culturally, or 'emotionally close' to the audience); conflict (events pitting two sides against one another); peculiarity (events that deviate from the everyday); and currency (long-simmering events that suddenly emerge as objects of attention).

Figure 9.1 illustrates the process by which an event becomes news. It demonstrates that within a veritable universe of daily events going on around the world, only some are selected by journalists as worth reporting. As Jaap van Ginneken (1998: 31) makes clear, journalists' perceptions inform these decisions. 'News is something which is (perceived as) "new" within a specific society, and not something which is (perceived as) "nothing new". It is something which is (perceived as) unexpected, extraordinary, abnormal, not something which is (perceived as) expected, ordinary, normal.' To cite a simple example, normal rush-hour traffic volume on an urban freeway is not news, while the unusual case of a seven-car pileup that kills three people and closes the freeway for an hour is.

This process of selection has compelled some theorists to perceive journalists—especially middle managers, such as editors and news directors—as **gatekeepers**, people who sift through a huge number of events and decide which events will be covered and which stories will be broadcast or published. While gatekeeping is an evocative metaphor, it is only a partial explanation of the news production process, applicable only to some stages of selection. A newspaper assignment editor, for example, chooses among an assortment of scheduled daily press conferences, meetings, and speeches and decides which will be 'staffed' by a reporter and which will not. This is a form of gatekeeping. Similarly, wire editors will sort through hundreds of wire-service stories from around

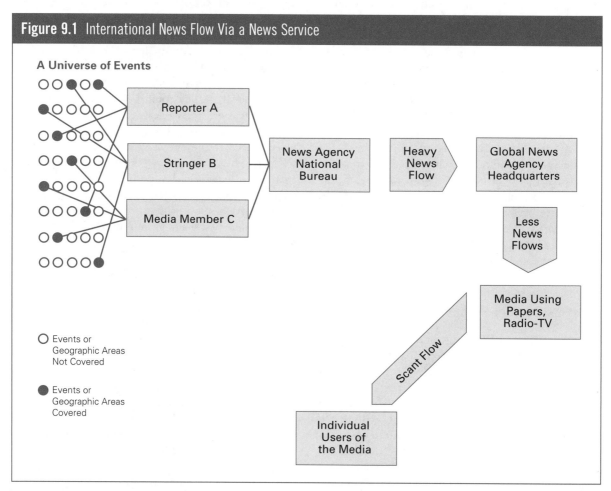

Figure 9.1 International News Flow Via a News Service

Of the many news events, only some are covered by reporters, 'stringers', or members relaying stories to the bureau of the global news agency. Editors there forward important news items to the world headquarters of the agency. Editors at world headquarters select what they think newsworthy. Finally, individual readers, listeners, or viewers decide what international news they will be attentive to. What began as hundreds of events and items has gradually dwindled to only a handful.

Source: Al Hester, 'International News Agencies', in Alan Wells, ed., *Mass Communications: A World View* (Palo Alto, Calif.: Mayfield Publishing, 1974). Reproduced with permission of the author.

the world each day to select those to be considered for publication. This, too, is gatekeeping.

However, there are limitations to the metaphor of gatekeeping for describing the process by which news is produced. While it accounts for the question of *what* the news organization will cover, it leaves aside the equally important issue of *how* an event will be covered. It ignores, for example, the extent to which wire-service stories are revised by copy editors and the different 'play'—length and prominence—they receive from one news organization to the next. The same news item may occupy the first two and half minutes of the six o'clock news on one channel, complete with interviews and illustrative footage, and warrant only 15 seconds of the anchor's narration on another channel. Same event, but different news stories. Newspapers, too, assign relative importance to news stories by how they play them—whether as a front-page story with a bold headline above the fold or as a back-page brief. Again, the same event may receive completely different treatment from one newspaper to the next.

The gatekeeping metaphor also ignores the creative nature of content production. Every news organization establishes an identity for its audience and its advertisers through the style of journalism it practises—serious and thorough, entertaining and concise, etc. Developing and maintaining that identity is achieved by establishing a certain kind of editorial presence through the assignment of resources and the shaping of content. Tabloid newspapers like the *Ottawa Sun* and *Le Journal de Montréal*, for example, pay a considerable amount of attention to crime stories, covering the police beat and the courthouse quite heavily. Their news stories are relatively short and written in a lively and provocative style, and their pages are filled with bold headlines and lots of photographs. More sober broadsheets like the *Globe and Mail* and *Le Devoir*, on the other hand, pay much more attention to political, foreign affairs, and cultural reporting. They tend to feature much longer, in-depth stories and fewer photographs. These two kinds of newspapers are interested in very different kinds of stories and news presentations. Examining how this editorial style is created opens the selection process up to many more factors than the notion of gatekeeping can accommodate. Nonetheless, the gatekeeping metaphor draws our attention to the refusal, or negative-selecting function, of editors and producers. In other words, we need to think about what is left out of the selection process.

A more precise way to think of journalists as content producers is through the metaphor of the frame. That is, through the use of words, images, and sounds, journalists 'frame' reality. If we think of the empty newspaper page or the blank television screen as a picture frame, it is journalists who decide how to fill that frame each day, by inserting into the frame particular stories, visuals, and graphics and by leaving out much more material. They decide not only which events to include in the news frame, but also how to depict those events: how much coverage to provide, what prominence to assign the story in the newspaper or broadcast, what aspects or angle of the story to emphasize.

The metaphor of the frame implies there are borders or limits to what a news organization can properly present as news. These limits are defined by such practical considerations as the size of the 'news hole' (the amount of editorial space available in print journalism) or 'news block' (the amount of air time available in a news broadcast), the costs involved in producing the coverage (does it involve travel and hotel accommodation?), and the availability of reporting staff. These limits are also governed by the more subjective criteria of an event's news value and how well it suits the news organization's particular areas of coverage. We would expect a news organization specializing in arts coverage to send its own reporter to the Toronto International Film Festival or the Juno Awards presentations, rather than rely on the Canadian Press wire service, just as we would expect a news organization specializing in sports to send its own reporter to the Stanley Cup final, regardless of which teams are playing. News coverage is also governed by a given news organization's various political stances, whether or not they are explicitly stated. Think about how news organizations may react differently, even if the distinctions are subtle, in their coverage of labour–management disputes, same-sex marriages, cuts in social spending, or international trade disputes. In her groundbreaking study of news practices, media scholar Gaye Tuchman (1978: 1) used the frame metaphor to emphasize the necessarily restricted view of the world journalism provides:

Like any frame that delineates a world, the news frame may be considered problematic. The view through a window depends upon whether the window is large or small, has many panes or few, whether the glass is opaque or clear, whether the window faces a street or a backyard. The unfolding scene also depends upon where one stands, far or near, craning one's neck to the side, or gazing straight ahead, eyes parallel to the wall in which the window is encased.

No news organization can cover every event from every possible angle. Therefore, what stories it includes and excludes can reveal a great deal about the news judgement it applies when producing its daily news package.

Ideals of Journalism

If news, then, is constructed, much like other kinds of media content, it is also subject to particular ideals that distinguish journalism from other forms of storytelling. Journalism has a fundamental guiding ideal: the quest for truth. That ideal is centred on the search for information and based on a commitment, in the words of the Kent Commission, not only to treat 'events and persons with fairness and impartiality, but also [to consider] the welfare of the community and of humanity in general in a spirit devoid of cynicism' (Canada, 1981: 23–4).

The performance of this truth-seeking function is the foundation for freedom of the press, facilitating the circulation of information and ideas for the benefit of all and extending the basic democratic right of freedom of expression granted to all individuals into the realm of the mass media. As scholars Robert Martin and Stuart Adam (1991: 27) note, freedom of expression can be seen as 'an essential pre-condition to the creation and maintenance of democracy itself. . . . A democratic society must not only permit, but encourage, the widest possible participation of all its members in its economic, social, and cultural affairs.' Freedom of the press is a notion that is both informed by and supportive of democracy. The flip side of the *right* to freedom of the press is the news media's *responsibility* to inform Canadians as engaged citizens—rather than consumers or spectators—in a democratic society.

The struggle for freedom of the press is ongoing and journalists are at the forefront of efforts to extend public access to information in both formal and informal ways. Journalists are often highly dependent on official sources and their own contacts for information, and the news media's role as 'fourth estate' grants journalists their moral authority to gain access to the people and institutions that populate their reportage: politicians, bureaucrats, police officers,

FREEDOM OF THE PRESS

Constitutional guarantees and universal declarations are important, but they define freedom of the press in largely abstract terms. The real, concrete meaning of freedom of the press is derived from its daily exercise by those journalists who push at the boundaries of what can be broadcast and what can be published.

Journalists—reporters, photographers, editors, producers, publishers—exercise freedom of the press when they report what is truly new and important to the public interest, when they broaden the range of debate, when they expand the horizons of what can be reported, imagined, revealed, criticized. Journalists also exercise freedom of the press when they hold their own news organizations to the ideals of their journalistic calling, especially when that news organization may have to pay a political or economic price for its reportage.

Freedom of the press would be meaningless as a human right if journalists never exposed scandal, if they never revealed information government officials preferred not to divulge, if they never quoted critics of powerful people and powerful institutions, if they never drew attention to hypocrisy, greed, or arrogance—if, in other words, they never gave anyone cause to restrict press freedoms. As journalism educator John Miller (1998: 115) puts it: 'Freedom is like muscle: use it or lose it.'

The right to freedom of the press is exerted not only in exceptional, headline-grabbing cases—e.g., the Somalia affair, Shawinigate, the Pentagon Papers, the Watergate scandal—but on a daily basis, in countless small ways. Journalists are giving meaning to freedom of the press every time they reveal more than their sources are willing to share with the public, every time they undermine the propaganda disseminated by corporate and political communications officers, every time they introduce factual evidence to accompany decision-makers' opinions.

To exercise freedom of the press, then, is to give it concrete meaning, even when—especially when—it means discomforting news sources, antagonizing public officials, prompting court challenges, even irritating fellow journalists.

community leaders, celebrities, Parliament, the court system, the stock exchange, and so on.

The term 'fourth estate', which refers to the role the news media play in the governing of a democratic society, originates with the press struggle to gain access to the proceedings of the British Parliament in the late eighteenth and early nineteenth centuries. Even after the right of freedom of the press had been won in Britain—formally recognized in the Bill of Rights of 1689—journalists were prohibited from Parliament, which prevented public scrutiny of the government's affairs. Throughout the eighteenth century, however, this prohibition was repeatedly defied, until the right to report on parliamentary proceedings was recognized on a de facto basis after 1771 and legally confirmed in 1803. The role of the press in Parliament was institutionalized with the construction of a press gallery in 1831 (Osler, 1993: 61). Thomas Babington, Lord MacCauley, is believed to have coined the term 'fourth estate' in 1828, when he wrote:

> The gallery in which the reporters sit has become a fourth estate of the realm. The publication of the debates, a practice which seemed to the most liberal statesman of the old school full of danger to the great safeguards of public liberty, is now regarded by many persons as a safeguard tantamount, and more than tantamount, to the rest altogether. (Quoted in Brucker, 1981: 30)

This was a recognition of the place of journalism in representing citizens as a kind of watchdog over their governors.

The news media today fulfill the role of a fourth estate by reporting on legislative debates and other government business, and by pressuring governments to increase access to information. All legislatures in Canada have press galleries populated by print, radio, television, and on-line reporters, and journalists also regularly attend the public meetings of municipal governments. Of all the coverage the news media provide, political reportage is considered to be the most closely related to journalism's role in democratic society: providing citizens with the information they need to be independent and self-governing.

The guiding ideals of journalism are socially produced and thus evolve over time. Today's highly regarded ideals of independence and objectivity have their historical roots in the period between about 1880 and 1920, when newspapers were transformed from a partisan press supported by political patronage and subscriptions from like-minded readers into a mass, commercial press that gradually became more and more dependent on advertising revenue (see Sotiron, 1997). In this period, urbanization and increased literacy rates created sizable markets of potential newspaper readers in Canada's growing cities; technological advances in printing (for instance, faster rotary presses) made it possible to increase the size and speed of press runs; and the extension of railway lines facilitated regional delivery of both newspapers and newsprint. The result was that newspapers increased their circulations, which made them increasingly accessible to readers, more attractive to advertisers, and less beholden to political parties.

As newspapers became *mass* media, they could no longer afford to be seen as propaganda sheets for political parties because that would risk antagonizing both potential readers and advertisers. Historian Minko Sotiron (1997: 4) writes: 'This period in Canadian history marked the transition from the politically oriented newspaper of the nineteenth century to the corporate entity of the twentieth.' Newspapers gradually began to assert their independence from political patronage—even if they maintained a clear political leaning—by cutting their formal political ties and by making a clearer distinction in their pages between 'objective' reporting and commentary (see also Schudson, 1978).

Today, the ideal of objectivity remains central to journalism's code of conduct, even though it is undermined somewhat by the fact that news reportage is the product of the subjective processes of selection and interpretation discussed earlier in this chapter. How can any news report be objective when it has been produced by journalists who subscribe to both personal and institutional values? It may be tempting to dispense with the notion of objectivity altogether. But communications scholar Robert A. Hackett (1996: 40–3) argues that in spite of declarations that objectivity is passé and has been replaced by 'advocacy' or 'critical' journalism, 'the ethos of objectivity, broadly conceived, continues to dominate North American journalism. Audiences and sources continue to expect their news to be free from the taint of personal bias.' Although notions of 'fairness' and 'balance' are often substituted for objectivity, Hackett remarks that 'very few journalists would want to be accused of lacking objectivity.'

There are more sophisticated ways to think about journalistic objectivity. Hackett and Yuezhi Zhao reject the traditional 'positivist' model of objectivity, which perceives truth as the relatively simple product of direct observation and accurate recording. The positivist model asserts that all that stands between reality and journalistic accounts of that reality is good reporting practice, an assertion that fails to account adequately for the mediating presence of the journalist, the language he or she employs, and the socialization he or she has undergone (Hackett and Zhao, 1998: 109–66). Hackett and Zhao, however, also reject the 'conventionalist' or postmodern position, which dismisses objectivity as unattainable because the real world cannot be perceived directly, that is, without the mediation of conventional concepts, theories, ideologies, and values, without the mediation of language (in all its forms), and, often, without the mediation of people describing the world on our behalf. 'Whereas positivism claims that it is possible to have direct knowledge of the world through sense experience, conventionalism says that the subject is always separated from direct perception of the world by the mesh of categories, concepts, or conventions that grid and filter our perceptions of it' (ibid., 116). Instead, they propose a critical realist approach to objectivity, a position that acknowledges the limitations of both positivism and conventionalism, but nonetheless insists that the real world is accessible and knowable. Coming to know the truth about the world, they maintain, is a never-ending process, with knowledge constantly produced and revised, subject to the mediation of our categories, concepts, values, and conventions, and emerging only as a result of 'the interactive or dialectical to and fro between subject and object, concepts and reality' (ibid., 129). In other words, if knowledge about the real world cannot be taken at face value through direct observation, and if knowledge production is always subject to various layers of mediation, knowledge and truth can nonetheless emerge through careful and reflexive investigation. 'The world is knowable—but not at first sight' (ibid., 130).

Plenty of disagreement remains among journalists and scholars about the translation of journalistic ideals into practice. How well do the news media live up to their responsibility of informing the public? To what degree are the news media independent and objective? Abstract ideals are also subject to material constraints, and the extent to which we rely on the media for information about our world—the extent to which we live in 'second-hand worlds', as the American sociologist C. Wright Mills once put it—underlines the importance of scrutinizing our sources of information. Who are journalists and under what legal and institutional constraints do they practise?

Newsmakers

Journalism is often described as a profession, even though, unlike the teaching, medical, and legal professions, it has no regulatory body and requires no mandatory formal training. Anyone who practises journalism, whether as a freelancer or as a staff member of a news organization, is a journalist. This does not mean, however, that the occupation is wide open. While there are any number of independent websites and special-interest publications at which hobbyists can work, there are a limited number of mainstream news organizations in Canada where journalists can earn a decent living, and their hiring practices reveal that journalism remains an exclusive occupation. Increasingly, news organizations expect their new recruits to have a degree from one of the growing number of post-secondary journalism programs in Canada.

The most recent data available portray those who populate the newsrooms of Canada's news organizations as predominantly young, white, middle-class males with a higher level of education than the Canadian average. Canada has approximately 12,000 journalists working full-time, 30 per cent of whom work for daily newspapers, 27 per cent for radio, 22 per cent for television, 18 per cent for weekly newspapers, and about 3 per cent for news magazines and wire services. The national public broadcaster is the single most important employer of news workers; CBC/Radio-Canada alone accounts for 19 per cent of all journalists in Canada (Pritchard and Sauvageau, 1999: 15–21).

In a survey of more than 500 journalists conducted in May 1996, researchers David Pritchard and Florian Sauvageau determined that the average age of journalists in Canada is 39.7 years. Seventy-two per cent of Canadian journalists are men, with a high of 77 per cent in daily newspapers. Men outnumber women in all media, with the most equitable split in television news, where 64 per cent of journalists are men, 36 per cent women. While 56 per cent of Canadian journalists hold a university degree, this percentage ranges from 65 per cent at daily newspapers to 41 per cent at community weekly papers. One of the most remarkable observations made by Pritchard and Sauvageau in sketching their demographic profile is the fact that 97.7 per cent of Canadian journalists are white (ibid., 15–19).

A more recent, but far less comprehensive survey of daily newspapers conducted in 2004 by Diversity Watch (Miller and Caron, 2004) found that non-whites constituted 3.4 per cent of news-gathering staffs at the 37 papers responding to the survey questionnaire. Of the 61 minority journalists the survey found, 57 of them—over 93 per cent—worked for large dailies (circulation over 100,000). The same survey determined that 34 per cent of news workers at Canadian daily newspapers were women. In both cases, the percentage of women and visible minority journalists fell well short of their share of the Canadian population.

In the state-regulated broadcasting sphere, inclusivity is a prominent theme of the Broadcasting Act (1991). Section 3(d)(iii) of the Act declares that the Canadian broadcasting system should:

> through its programming and the employment opportunities arising out of its operations, serve the needs and interests, and reflect the circumstances and aspirations, of Canadian men, women and children, including equal rights, the linguistic duality and multicultural and multiracial nature of Canadian society and the special place of aboriginal peoples within that society . . . . (Canada, 1991)

As discussed in Chapter 6, federal broadcast legislation has shifted its priority from the extension of radio and television services to all parts of the Canadian territory to one that enshrines the 'broadcasting rights' of three specific groups: women, Native peoples, and multicultural/multiracial communities. Lorna Roth (1996: 73) writes: 'Each has the right to be fairly portrayed on the airwaves and equitably represented on staffs throughout all broadcasting services—public, private, and community.' Research, however, indicates that the Canadian news media remain far from attaining this goal.

However, a 2004 study by the Task Force for Cultural Diversity on Television found that visible minorities comprised just 12.3 per cent of anchors and 8.7 per cent of reporters and interviewers in English-language news. Another study determined that more than 90 per cent of television news direc-

tors were white (Khakoo, 2006).

Inclusivity is an important issue in a period of globalization and in a country as culturally and racially diverse as Canada, and newsmaking should bear some resemblance to the makeup of Canadian society, both in the content generated and in the people employed. Clearly, *who* reports the news has implications for both *what* gets covered and *how*.

As the preceding section of this chapter outlined, there is considerable room for interpretation in judging the news value and the appropriate presentation of a particular event or issue. Therefore, journalists' life experiences—their assumptions, their biases, their prejudices, their values—affect their reportage. In a report to the Canadian Race Relations Foundation, researchers Frances Henry and Carol Tator (2000: 169) concluded that journalists were not objective, detached, or neutral in their reporting. 'They are highly selective in their writing. Often their own sense of social location, experiences, values and world views, as well as the interests and positionality of publishers and newspaper owners, act as an invisible filter to screen out alternative viewpoints and perspectives.' A relatively young reporting staff, for example, may be less aware of, and less sensitive to, issues that pertain to an aging Canadian population, such as the future of the Canada Pension Plan or the costs of prescription drugs. A predominantly male newsroom may be less receptive to issues of particular relevance to women—e.g., child care, reproductive rights, sexism—and may be prone to patriarchal views of the issues that especially involve women, such as sexual assault, spousal abuse, pay equity, etc. (see Meyers, 1997).

Henry et al. (2000: 296–310) argue that the media are particularly important sources for information about Canada's visible minority communities. But because few Canadian journalists are non-white and because Canadians of colour are rarely interviewed by journalists unless the news item directly concerns race, minority men and women are largely invisible in Canadian newsrooms and Canadian news coverage. This invisibility 'communicates the message that they are not full participants in Canadian society.' Communications research has repeatedly determined that when people of colour are visible in news reportage, they are often depicted in negative and stereotypical ways. Henry et al. write: 'A pervasive theme of both news and [dramatic] programming is the portrayal of people of colour as "the outsiders within," reinforcing the "we-they" mindset.' People of colour lack access to the media to make their voices heard. Journalism educator John Miller (1998: 137) argues that this results in 'blind spots' in news coverage: 'If few women or visible minorities are in positions where they can determine what newspapers cover and how, issues affecting them are probably not going to receive proper attention or get on the agenda for public debate.'

The point is not to turn the news media into organs of advocacy for the disenfranchised. Instead, Kovach and Rosenstiel (2001: 108) explain: 'The ultimate goal of newsroom diversity is to create an intellectually mixed environment where everyone holds firm to the idea of journalistic independence. Together their various experiences blend to create a reporting richer than what they would create alone. And in the end that leads to a richer, fuller view of the world for the public.'

The Legal and Policy Contexts of News Production

Freedom of the press is one of the most fundamental rights of a democratic society, and journalism in

Canada is practised in a free press environment. Section 2 of the 1982 Canadian Charter of Rights and Freedoms protects both freedom of expression and freedom of the press under the heading 'Fundamental Freedoms':

2. Everyone has the following fundamental freedoms:
    (a) freedom of conscience and religion;
    (b) freedom of thought, belief, opinion and expression, including freedom of the press and other media of communication;
    (c) freedom of peaceful assembly; and
    (d) freedom of association.

This does not mean, however, that journalists are free to report whatever they want, or that news organizations can publish or broadcast with impunity. Press freedom in Canada is constrained by laws that ensure journalists' freedoms do not compromise the security of the state or the freedoms of other Canadian citizens. As journalist and legal scholar Michael G. Crawford (1990: 3) notes: 'The danger in the term "freedom of the press" is that it implies a special right has been imparted upon the news

MEDIA BUSTERS MUFFLED

In Canada, one of the world's most concentrated print media markets, direct-action media critics are becoming the story that dares not go to press.

In January [1999], reporter Mike Roberts of British Columbia's *Province* newspaper went to work on a story about Guerrilla Media, a covert band of Canadian culture jammers who publicize their media criticisms by wrapping mainstream newspapers in mock covers as they await sale in distribution boxes.

With research complete, Roberts sat down with his editors to discuss the approach he should take to writing the piece. 'We'd rather you didn't,' is the response he recalls.

Roberts says his editors at the paper—owned [at the time] by Conrad Black, the media titan who [controlled] 60 per cent of Canada's dailies—told him they didn't want to give publicity to an organization that breaks the law. Given that *Province* reporters regularly cover such protests as sit-ins and blockades, the reason Guerrilla Media was made an exception is 'an interesting question,' says Roberts.

Reporters tread carefully around their employers' vested interests, Robert notes. 'I was cognizant that this story

would be a tricky one to get through,' he says. 'That's the first time that situation has arisen with me at the paper. That's the first time I've been asked to not do a story.'

Adele Weder, a Vancouver-based freelancer, experienced a similar Blackout after accepting an assignment from Conrad Black's new Canada-wide daily, the *National Post*. This time, the topic was *Adbusters* magazine, including its campaign against Black, the *Post*, and corporate concentration of media ownership.

In May, Weder told *Adbusters* editor Kalle Lasn that her article had been accepted by her editors and would be published once she gathered quotes from *Post* editor-in-chief Ken Whyte and from Black himself. Shortly thereafter, Weder was told the story would not be going to press.

'They told me they killed it,' said Weder. 'I'm disappointed with the cancellation of the piece, but it's not my place to comment on what might have happened.'

In the *Post* offices, 'killed' is considered too harsh a word. Harriet O'Brien, the section editor in charge of Weder's assignment, says the piece was 'held over'—so far for three months and counting.

media which is above the rights of the general public. That is not the case.' The news media have no greater privileges than the average citizen. Journalists, instead, are recognized by the Canadian courts as 'members and representatives of the public'. Journalists are also subject to constraints based on the specific conditions of their employment and the predominantly commercial organization of the news industry. In law, freedom of the press is a right of media proprietors. While journalists in the field produce the stories, it is their employers who exercise the constitutional power of freedom of the press, deciding whether or not to run a particular story, deciding how any given story might be handled. Every reporter has a story to tell about a proprietor's interference in news coverage.

Freedom of the press is a core right of all modern democratic states. But this core tenet of liberal democracy is not interpreted exactly the same way by all democracies, compelling journalists to work within both national and international legal and policy frameworks. At the international level, Article 19 of the Universal Declaration of Human Rights (1949) provides the ethical foundation. It states:

para. 1: Everyone shall have the right to hold opinions without interference.

para. 2: Everyone shall have the right to freedom of expression; this right shall include freedom to seek, receive and impart information and ideas of all kinds, regardless of frontiers, either orally, in writing or in print, in the form of art, or through any other media of his/her choice.

para. 3: The exercise of the right provided for in para. 2 of this article carries with it special duties and responsibilities. It may therefore be subject to certain restrictions, but these shall only be such as are provided by law and are necessary for the respect of the rights or reputation of others or for the protection of national security or of public order or of public health or morals.

Article 12 of the declaration also deals with press functioning by addressing infringement of privacy and attacks on honour and reputation. It states: 'Everyone has the right of protection of the law against such interference and attack.' These two rights, free speech and the right to privacy, always exist in tension with one another. Journalists may have rights,

---

O'Brien did acknowledge that the story warranted internal discussion that went at least as high as Whyte (neither Whyte nor Black could be contacted by presstime). 'We established that *Adbusters* was launching a campaign against the *Post* and especially Conrad Black,' says O'Brien. 'There was a sensitivity there.'

Asked whether that sensitivity played a role in the piece being held, O'Brien chose to duck and cover: 'Possibly,' she said.

Noam de Plume, a pseudonymous spokesperson for Guerrilla Media, says reporters and editors seem to be taking a see-no-evil, speak-no-evil approach to Conrad Black's most confrontational critics to prevent run-ins with corporate management.

'The gatekeeping, when it has to be, is very controlling,' says de Plume. 'They're saying the criticism that we're leveling at them is something they don't want to discuss in a public way.'

Scott Uzelman of News Watch Canada, an academic research group that monitors media 'blind spots,' says the Blackout of culture-jamming critics is a blunt example of monopoly media's inability to report fairly on its own powers and responsibilities. Last year, News Watch published a study of how coverage of Conrad Black's empire in a major daily newspaper changed after that paper was bought by Black. Not surprisingly, they found the paper's coverage became far less critical; what's more, that paper took a year to acknowledge the group's study, finally printing an op-ed on the subject in the weekend magazine section.

Uzelman argues that it all points to the need to revisit the tired idea that government interference poses the greatest threat to journalists' freedom to report dissenting opinions. 'The same ideal isn't applied to the media themselves, which are increasingly large corporations,' Uzelman notes.

So Canadians shouldn't hold their breath for a Conrad Black newspaper to assign an investigative series on the effects of media concentration?

'If that happened, I would probably drop dead with surprise,' Uzelman says.

—*James MacKinnon*

Source: *Adbusters*, No. 27 Autumn, 1999: 27, www.adbusters.org. Reprinted by permission of Adbusters Media Foundation.

but they also have legal obligations and ethical responsibilities.

Canada's media laws are the product of two historical contexts, the European and the American.

THE EUROPEAN CONTEXT

The member states of what is now called the European Union have followed very closely the model provided by the Universal Declaration of Human Rights in drafting their own statements on rights and freedoms. The European Convention for the Protection of Human Rights and Fundamental Freedoms (conventions.coe.int/treaty/en/Treaties/Html/005.htm), adopted by the Council of Europe in Rome in 1950, included articles asserting the rights to freedom of thought, conscience, and religion (Article 9) and to freedom of expression (Article 10). The European Union's Charter of Fundamental Rights (ue.eu.int/df/default.asp?lang=en), adopted in December 2000, ensures the rights to freedom of thought, conscience, and religion (Article 10), freedom of expression (Article 11), as well as the related rights of academic freedom (Article 13) and the right to education (Article 14). Article 11, specifically, states:

1. Everyone has the right to freedom of expression. This right shall include freedom to hold opinions and to receive and impart information and ideas without interference by public authority and regardless of frontiers.
2. The freedom and pluralism of the media shall be respected.

Neither of these documents, however, defines these freedoms in absolute terms. Each contains qualifiers pertaining to such areas as privacy and national security, and they preserve the right of states to license radio and television broadcasters. Article 10 of the European Convention, for example, stipulates duties and responsibilities pertaining to national security, territorial integrity, public safety, the prevention of crime, the protection of health and morals, and the maintenance of the authority and impartiality of the judiciary.

Perhaps the clearest and most explicit statement pertaining to the rights of the news media in the European context comes in the Declaration of Rights and Obligations of Journalists, adopted by the European Union in Munich in 1971. The so-called Munich Charter asserts: 'All rights and duties of a journalist originate from the right of the public to be informed on events and opinions. The journalist's responsibility towards the public takes precedence over any other responsibility, particularly towards employers and public authorities.' The document lists a set of duties and rights that provide considerable insight into the meeting of journalistic ideals and day-to-day practices. In summary they are:

Declaration of duties:
1. To respect truth because of the right of the public to know the truth;
2. To defend freedom of information, comment and criticism;
3. To report only known facts and not to suppress essential information;
4. Not to use unfair methods to obtain news, photographs or documents;
5. To respect the privacy of others;
6. To rectify any published inaccurate information;
7. To protect persons who provide information in confidence;
8. Not to engage in **plagiarism**, calumny, slander, libel and unfounded accusations, nor accept bribes in any form;
9. To distinguish between journalism and advertising or propaganda;
10. To resist editorial pressure from unqualified persons.

Declaration of rights:
1. Journalists claim free access to all information sources, and the right to inquire freely into all events affecting public life;
2. Journalists have the right to refuse subordination to anything contrary to the general policies of the information organs of which they are contributing members;
3. Journalists cannot be compelled to perform professional acts or express opinions contrary to their convictions or conscience;
4. Editorial staffs must be informed or consulted about major editorial changes;
5. Journalists are entitled not only to the advantages resulting from collective agreements but also to an individual contract of employment, ensuring sufficient material and moral security to guarantee their economic independence (Clement Jones, 1980).

This 1971 document not only stipulates the basic principles upon which European journalists could reach consensus, but also identifies five areas of constraint within which journalists work: international and national law and information policy; the orientation, actions, and preferences of the government of the day; the policies, practices, and attitudes of owners; the philosophies, practices, and attitudes of colleagues, including editorial managers; and pressures from societies and subgroups within society. If, then, these rights and obligations are interpreted differently from country to country, from news organization to news organization, and from journalist to journalist, they nonetheless provide a model for the vigorous and responsible practice of news production, as well as a reference point for critics and scholars of the news media.

THE AMERICAN CONTEXT

A parallel initiative to the 1971 European statement of rights and responsibilities of journalists was long in coming to the Americas. But on 11 March 1994 the Inter American Press Association (IAPA) sponsored the Hemispheric Conference on Free Speech in Chapultepec, near Mexico City. Out of that conference came the Declaration of Chapultepec, 'a commitment to freedom of speech and of the press, an inalienable human right and fundamental principle, to ensure the very survival of democracy in the Americas'. Several points from the Declaration's preamble are worth noting:

> Without democracy and freedom . . . justice is demeaned and human advancement becomes mere fiction.
>
> Freedom must not be restricted in the quest for any other goal. It stands alone, yet has multiple expressions; it belongs to citizens, not to governments. . . .
>
> We, the signatories of this declaration, represent different backgrounds and dreams. We take pride in the plurality and diversity of our cultures, considering ourselves fortunate that they merge into the one element that nurtures their growth and creativity: freedom of expression, the driving force and base of mankind's fundamental rights. . . .
>
> Without an independent media, assured of guarantees to operate freely, to make decisions and to act on them fully, freedom of expression cannot be exercised. . . .

> Even the constitutions of some democratic countries contain elements of press restriction.
>
> While defending a free press and rejecting outside interference, we also champion a press that is responsible and involved, a press aware of the obligations that the practice of freedom entails. (IAPA, at: http://216.147.196.167/projects/chapul-declaration.cfm)

The principles enunciated within the Declaration follow along the same lines. Here are three of the 10 points:

- No people or society can be free without freedom of expression and of the press. The exercise of this freedom is not something authorities grant, it is an inalienable right of the people.
- Every person has the right to seek and receive information, express opinions and disseminate them freely. No one may restrict or deny these rights. . . .
- The credibility of the press is linked to its commitment to truth, to the pursuit of accuracy, fairness and objectivity and to the clear distinction between news and advertising. The attainment of these goals and the respect for ethical and professional values may not be imposed. These are the exclusive responsibility of journalists and the media. In a free society, it is public opinion that rewards or punishes. (Ibid.)

The Declaration of Chapultepec excludes any state role except that of ensuring freedom. Certain statements signal the heavy hand of the US contingent, such as, 'Even the constitutions of some democratic countries contain elements of press restriction' and 'The exercise of this freedom [freedom of expression and of the press] is not something authorities grant, it is an inalienable right of the people.' The European declarations demonstrate a much better balance between responsibilities and freedoms (www.sipiapa.org).

As Martin and Adam (1991: 27) explain, the Canadian tradition of freedom of expression is a balancing act of the American individualistic view and the European collectivist conception. A Canadian notion of freedom of expression encompasses individuals' rights of expression to promote and encourage 'the widest possible participation of all its members in its economic, social and cultural affairs'. But it also perceives freedom of expression 'not merely as a commodity possessed by individuals, but as an essential pre-condition to the creation and maintenance of democracy itself'. That is, the right of freedom of expression is granted to individuals insofar as they are actors in a free and democratic society. This freedom is not absolute. Section 1 of Canada's Charter of Rights and Freedoms notes that the Charter's guarantees are 'subject only to such reasonable limits prescribed by law as can be demonstrably justified in a free and democratic society'.

Canadian Law and Journalism

While enjoying freedom of the press, Canadian journalists are also subject to national and international law, and they are compelled to subscribe to a variety of ethical codes that deal with the business of news production. These codes serve as guidelines rather than regulations, and while they may indeed encourage responsible journalism, their primary goal is to ward off legislative intervention.

In the electronic media, the Canadian Association of Broadcasters has a Code of Ethics, a Sex-Role Portrayal Code for Television and Radio Programming, a Broadcast Code for Advertising to Children, and a Voluntary Code Regarding Violence in Television Programming, all of which are administered by the Canadian Broadcast Standards Council (CBSC). The Code of Ethics contains 18 clauses dealing with such issues as: the diversity of the audience; abusive and discriminatory material; the vulnerability and impressionability of children; participation in worthwhile community activities; the nature of educational efforts; the accuracy of news; the presentation of public issues; the content of advertising; subliminal devices; conformity with advertising codes; the distinction between advertising and news and public affairs programming; portrayal of each gender; and the public responsibilities of broadcasting. In addition, Advertising Standards Canada administers voluntary codes on advertising and jointly administers with the CBSC the Broadcast Code of Advertising to Children (www.mediaawareness.ca/eng/indus/advert/bcac.htm).

The Radio and Television News Directors Association of Canada (RTNDA) also has a 14-point Code of Ethics. Its preamble states: 'Free speech and an informed public are vital to a democratic society. The members of the RTNDA Canada recognize the responsibility of broadcast journalists to promote and

to protect the freedom to report independently about matters of public interest and to present a wide range of expressions, opinions, and ideas.' To that end, RTNDA members follow a code pertaining to: accuracy, comprehensiveness, fairness, and authenticity; equal treatment of minority populations; independent reporting; conflicts of interest; privacy; the integrity of the judicial system; correction of errors; intellectual property rights; and confidentiality of sources. For example, Article 8 states:

> Broadcast journalists will treat people who are subjects and sources with decency. They will use special sensitivity when dealing with children. They will strive to conduct themselves in a courteous and considerate manner, keeping broadcast equipment as unobtrusive as possible. They will strive to prevent their presence from distorting the character or importance of events. (www.cbsc.ca/english/codes/rtndarevised.htm)

The written press is guided by a different set of institutions. Canada has six regional press councils—representing British Columbia, Alberta, Manitoba, Ontario, Quebec, and the Atlantic provinces—to address public complaints (Saskatchewan and the territories have no press councils). However, press councils have no regulatory authority, relying instead on publicity and moral suasion to encourage ethical behaviour by member newspapers and their journalists.

Newspaper companies in the past have adopted their own codes of ethics, but this practice has largely been abandoned for fear that it increases publishers' legal liability. As journalism educator John Miller (1998: 115–22) has recounted, the Canadian Daily Newspaper Association attempted to abolish its Statement of Principles in the mid-1990s. Initially drafted in 1977 as a code of ethical standards for its members, this Statement was intended to be updated when the CDNA met in 1993. Instead, the CDNA's legal and editorial committees voted to abolish it altogether. Public pressure, however, compelled the CDNA's board of directors to adopt a diluted version in September 1995 (Cobb, 1995: A12). This Statement of Principles (see Stott, 1995: A7) reads as follows:

> *Preamble*: The statement of principles expresses the commitment of Canada's daily newspapers to operate in the public interest. A newspaper is a vital source of information and a private business

enterprise with responsibility to the community it serves.

Freedom of the Press is an exercise of every Canadian's right to freedom of expression guaranteed in the Charter of Rights and Freedoms. It is the right to gather and disseminate information, to discuss, to advocate, to dissent. A free press is essential to our democratic society. It enables readers to use their Charter right to receive information and make informed judgements on the issues and ideas of the time.

Independence. The newspaper's primary obligation is fidelity to the public good. It should pay the costs of gathering the news. Conflicts of interest, real or apparent, should be declared. The newspaper should guard its independence from government, commercial and other interests seeking to subvert content for their own purposes.

Accuracy and Fairness. The newspaper keeps faith with readers by presenting information that is accurate, fair, comprehensive, interesting and timely. It should acknowledge its mistakes promptly and conspicuously. Sound practice clearly distinguishes among news reports, expressions of opinion, and materials produced for and by advertisers. When images have been altered or simulated, readers should be told.

Community Responsibility. The newspaper has responsibilities to its readers, its shareholders, its employees and its advertisers. But the operation of a newspaper is a public trust and its overriding responsibility is to the society it serves. The newspaper plays many roles: a watchdog against evil and wrong-doing, an advocate for good works and noble deeds, and an opinion leader for its community. The newspaper should strive to paint a representative picture of its diverse communities, to encourage the expression of disparate views and to be accessible and accountable to the readers it serves, whether rich or poor, weak or powerful, minority or majority. When published material attacks an individual or group, those affected should be given an opportunity to reply.

Respect. The newspaper should strive to treat the people it covers with courtesy and fairness. It should respect the rights of others, particularly every person's right to a fair trial. The inevitable conflict between privacy and the public good should be judged in the light of common sense and decency.

The Canadian Newspaper Association adopted the same Statement of Principles when it replaced the CDNA and the Newspaper Marketing Bureau in July 1996 (www.cna-acj.ca/about/sp.asp).

In a study of Canadian journalism ethics conducted in 2001–2, researcher Bob Bergen (2002: 10–11) could identify only one daily newspaper, the *Toronto Star*, that operated according to a set of well-publicized principles. More typical, Bergen said, was the *Ottawa Citizen*, which had a 19-page Ethics and Policies manual that its journalists were expected to follow. Bergen also examined 65 collective-bargaining agreements and found that 59 contained clauses allowing journalists to take specified actions when ethical issues arose (ibid., 33).

In the present climate of increased concentration of ownership and increased commercialization of the news media, governments are pressuring converged media companies to make public statements of their journalistic principles. For example, when the CRTC renewed the television licences of CTV and CanWest Global in August 2001, it imposed a number of conditions, including the requirement that the two networks adhere to a Statement of Principles and Practices governing the cross-ownership of TV stations and newspapers. While the CRTC conceded that better journalism could result from pooling the resources of the companies' TV and newspaper newsrooms, it was also concerned about the possibility of a reduction in editorial diversity. The CRTC demanded that CTV and Global maintain separate management of their broadcast and newspaper newsrooms and create 'independent neutral monitoring committees', which would address complaints and report to the CRTC annually. The two companies were required to spend $1 million each on promoting the committee and the Statement of Principles and Practices (CRTC, 2001).

The Quebec government, which is particularly sensitive to the high levels of corporate concentration among French-language news media, is also pressing news organizations in the province to publish ethics codes as part of a larger attempt to ensure 'the quality and diversity of information'. Minister of Culture and Communications Diane Lemieux established an advisory board in September 2002, charged with providing recommendations that could be drafted into legislation as early as the spring of 2003 (Dutrisac, 2002). No such legislation, however, has emerged and the topic has largely vanished from the Quebec political agenda.

As discussed in Chapter 6, a study in 2003 of the Canadian broadcasting system by the Standing Committee on Canadian Heritage (the Lincoln Committee) expressed concern about both corporate concentration and cross-media ownership, particularly as it threatened news organizations' editorial independence. Most recently, the June 2006 report of the Standing Senate Committee on Transport and Communications (Canada, 2006a) made a number of recommendations to limit corporate concentration and cross-ownership across the media spectrum. Noting that Canada was 'atypical among large democracies', the Committee encouraged the federal government to develop the same kind of regulatory mechanisms that impose ownership restrictions in the democracies of Britain, France, Australia, Germany, and the United States (ibid., 24). The report concluded: 'Excessive levels of concentration and the domination of particular markets by one media group engender distrust in the very institutions that Canadians rely upon for their news and information' (ibid., 63).

In addition to the codes of ethics and regulatory bodies that guide Canadian newsmakers to provide fair and accurate reporting, particular Canadian laws aid or constrain the newsmaking process. These statutes are designed to protect the public interest and cover areas such as access to information, libel, privacy, and contempt of court.

ACCESS TO INFORMATION

Access to information laws have recently been enacted in North America as a way of extending the right to freedom of information. The basic principle is that, in the name of democracy, most government information should be available to the people. Exceptions should be rare and are justified only when public access to information might pose a risk to national security, the privacy of individuals, or the confidentiality of certain political discussions (e.g., the advice of public servants to cabinet ministers). The reason for the existence of two terms—**freedom of information** and **access to information**—reflects two different governing traditions. 'Access to information' is appropriate to countries such as Great Britain and its former colonies, like Canada, in which information is collected and created by the government (the Crown) and is seen to be the property of the Crown unless the Crown is prepared to release it. In the United States, the same kind of information is seen to be the property of the people because 'the people' are paramount in the US Constitution. Thus, 'freedom of information' is a more appropriate label.

ACCESS TO INFORMATION

Excerpt from the Access to Information Act*, R.S.C. 1985, c.A-1, ss. 2, 4, 10, 13–27:

Purpose of Act

2 (1) the purpose of this Act is to extend the present laws of Canada to provide a right of access to information in records under the control of a government institution in accordance with the principles that government information should be available to the public, that necessary exceptions to the right of access should be limited and specific and that decisions on the disclosure of information of government information should be reviewed independently of government.

(2) This Act is intended to complement and not replace existing procedures for access to government information and is not intended to limit in any way access to the type of government information that is normally available to the general public.

* Notes omitted

The Act discusses right of access to government records. Right of access is granted to Canadian citizens and landed immigrants, but that right can be extended to other persons. The Act defines the circumstances under which access can be refused, requiring the government to state the reason. Exemptions are defined under 'Responsibilities of Government'. They include the non-release of documents obtained in confidence from other governments, those that could be injurious to the conduct of intergovernmental affairs, documents related to the detection or committing of crime, sensitive business information such as trade secrets, and certain financial information. Under 'Personal Information', exemptions are granted in accordance with the provisions of the Privacy Act. Under 'Third Party Information', 'Operations of Government', 'Statutory Prohibitions', and 'General', a limited set of other exemptions is included, such as the results of product testing and the possibility that the government may wish to publish the information itself (Martin and Adam, 1991).

The federal government and all the provincial governments have access to information legislation, which outlines what kinds of government information are subject to scrutiny and how journalists and ordinary citizens can obtain access. Typically, this involves submitting an access to information request to the pertinent government department or agency and awaiting a response. Sometimes, repeated requests must be made to focus the inquiry of the specific information sought.

In 2002, the Canadian government concluded an 18-month review of its access to information legislation. While the Access to Information Review Task Force determined that the legislation was 'basically sound in concept, structure and balance', it also discovered 'an overwhelming need for more rigorous process, clearer and more widely understood rules, and greater consistency in outcomes, both for requesters and for government institutions' (www.atirf-geai.gc.ca/report/report2-e.html). In July 2006 the Canadian Association of Journalists asked the Stephen Harper government to strengthen the federal Access to Information Act to increase government openness and accountability (micro.newswire.ca/release.cgi?rkey=1407047759&view=42015-0&Start=0).

Access to information laws are important to journalists and the general public for two reasons. First, governments are ravenous collectors of information and have considerable data at their disposal, ranging from budget and expenditure documents to tax returns and detailed census statistics. This information is required by journalists to ensure a full understanding of the social, political, and economic issues they cover. Second, much of a government's daily work and decision-making occur outside of public meetings. In order for journalists to monitor government activities and report them to Canadians, they need to know what happens beyond the confines of public meeting halls. Again, this access to information is required to report on and evaluate government performance.

LIBEL

While freedom of expression laws define the positive foundation of journalism, libel and other restraint laws define the negative constraints within which journalists must operate. **Libel** is defined as the publication or broadcasting of 'a false and damaging statement'. Such a statement must be seen to discredit or lower the public perception of an individual, corporation, labour union, or any other 'legal entity' (Crawford, 1990: 15; Buckley, 1993: 112). The common issues surrounding libel include the determination of the nature of the libel, the damage done, those who bear responsibility, appropriate compensatory action, as well as considerations of personal privacy and the public interest.

In most countries, responsibility for libel extends beyond the author to editors and producers in their role as people who review submissions and decide what to include and not to include in putting reports together for publication or broadcast. Responsibility also commonly extends to the proprietor and can even include distributing companies such as wholesalers and newsstand or bookstore owners.

Libel law serves to protect against falsehood the reputations of those who are the subjects of published or broadcast reports. At the same time, it seeks to ensure that journalists live up to the ideals of fairness and accuracy in their pursuit of truth.

Libel Chill

The term **libel chill** refers to the effect that the threat of libel action can have on the news media, particularly in the coverage of powerful individuals and organizations. This threat can be effective in discouraging journalists because, as analyst Nancy Duxbury (1991) points out, under British and Canadian libel law the **burden of proof** rests with the accused ('reverse onus', in legal parlance). Once a libel action is mounted, in other words, the onus is on the journalist to defend him or herself. Free comment about powerful people can exact a hefty price if those powerful people choose to contest journalists' reports about them in the court of law. Whether or not the court decides in favour of the plaintiff, the journalist must endure the anxiety associated with such an action.

The plaintiff, on the other hand, risks little from a libel suit, beyond increased publicity and general speculation about guilt or innocence. According to David Potts, a libel lawyer who served as junior counsel for the plaintiff in a case involving the Reichmann family, review commissions looking into libel law have been satisfied that the only way to protect the average citizen is to retain libel laws in their current form. The Reichmanns, extremely wealthy real estate developers, were profiled in a lengthy article in the November 1987 issue of *Toronto Life* magazine. They mounted a $102-million lawsuit, naming the author of the article, the publisher of the magazine, and the magazine's managing editor (*Globe and Mail*, 11 Dec. 1989, B1). In February 1991, the case was resolved before going to court—but only after the publisher had spent $1 million in legal costs. *Toronto Life* printed a retraction on page 1 of its March 1991 edition that stated, in part: 'Let us unequivocally and categorically say that any and all negative insinuations and allegations in the article about the Reichmann family and Olympia & York are totally false.'

A more recent concern about 'on-line chill' involves the legal liability of websites that publish reader comments and host discussion forums. The BC-based website P2Pnet.net was hit with a defamation suit for comments posted to the site by its readers. The legal question raised is whether websites can be compelled to remove allegedly libelous content under the threat of legal liability. Legal scholar Michael Geist writes: 'Under current Canadian law, intermediaries can face potential liability for failing to remove allegedly defamatory content once they have received notification of such a claim, even without court oversight' (Geist, 2006).

The easiest way to avoid libel suits is to avoid publishing or broadcasting contentious material. While some news organizations prefer to stick to 'soft news' in order not to antagonize anyone, others continue to encourage investigative journalism as a way of both attracting audiences and fulfilling their truth-seeking mission. While libel law can be seen to work as a censoring device (hence the term, 'libel chill'), others argue that libel law contributes positively to the reporting of what would be agreed upon, by a community of fair-minded people, as the truth.

PRIVACY

Libel and personal privacy are closely connected, and often the trade-off between personal privacy and public interest is the central issue behind libel cases. Section 7 of the Charter of Rights and Freedoms states: 'Everyone has the right to life, liberty and security of the person and the right not to be deprived thereof except in accordance with principles of fundamental justice.' Section 8 protects against 'unreasonable search or seizure'. In addition, the federal government, all 10 provinces, and all three territories have acts to protect privacy, pertaining to such issues as eavesdropping, surveillance, wiretapping, and use of personal documents.

Contempt of court is also connected closely to **invasion of privacy**. For instance, in Britain the media must be quite circumspect in their discussion of cases before the courts for fear of being charged with contempt. On the other hand, the royal family suffers from Britain's lack of a privacy law (witness news photographers' obsession with the late Princess Diana) and the public's seemingly insatiable appetite for 'news' about the royals. In Canada, controls on the media in commenting on cases before the courts are generally less stringent than in Britain, but much more stringent than in the United States, where the O.J. Simpson murder trial and the impeachment proceedings against President Bill Clinton resembled media feeding frenzies. In the 1990s, cameras moved into US courtrooms and made mass media spectacles of such high-profile cases as the O.J. Simpson murder trial and the William Kennedy Smith rape trial. Now, with Court TV, the lurid details of some court cases in the US are standard fare on the menus of satellite and cable television.

In Canada the courts can move in to prevent ongoing news coverage in order to protect citizens. In May 1999, for example, a Calgary court ordered *Alberta Report* magazine to stop publishing stories about genetic, late-term abortions, i.e., those prompted by prenatal diagnoses of abnormality, at Foothills Hospital. The Calgary Regional Health Authority had complained to Alberta's Court of Queen's Bench that the stories were endangering the lives of hospital staff (Foot, 1999: A4).

A Canadian Supreme Court ruling expanded considerably the bounds of privacy legislation. The Court ruled in April 1998 that 'it is against Quebec law to publish an identifiable picture of a person no matter how harmless, taken without his or her consent, unless there is an overriding "public interest".' The Supreme Court was upholding a 1991 Quebec court decision to award $2,000 to a Montreal woman whose picture was taken without her consent while she sat in the doorway of a building. The photograph was published in the Montreal literary magazine *Vice Versa* as part of a story on urban life (Cherry, 1998: A4). The ruling means that individuals' privacy is protected even when they are in a public place. Journalists must walk a fine line between notions of personal privacy and public interest. People's lives are not fair game for journalists, unless a clear case for the public's right to know can be argued. Journalists, of course, flirt with this fine line all the time, especially in their coverage of major entertainment and sports figures, where reportage often delves into celebrities' personal relationships.

CONTEMPT OF COURT

Contempt of court refers to instances when the judicial process is interfered with and/or the courts are disobeyed (Buckley, 1993: 110). Here again, two fundamental democratic rights come into conflict: the right to freedom of the press and the right to a fair trial. Section 11(d) of the Charter of Rights and Freedoms states that any person charged with an offence has the right 'to be presumed innocent until proven guilty according to law in a fair and public hearing by an independent and impartial tribunal'. To ensure these conditions are met, the justice system has at its disposal a number of measures, some of which affect the ability of journalists to report the news in its entirety. For example, judges in Canadian courts can impose publication bans on court proceedings and the press is not permitted to identify juveniles involved in court cases or to identify the alleged victim in a rape trial (see ibid., 96–111). So while journalists help to render the judicial system open and transparent, their rights in this regard are not absolute.

Making News (and Profits?)

Besides being affected by the legal and ethical imperatives described above, most journalists in Canada work for commercial news organizations and, as such, are also implicated in generating profits for their owners. Decisions about what a comprehensive news package entails will always be made in concert with the need to maximize audiences and attract advertising. Advertising, after all, pays most of the bills of mainstream news organizations and pays all of the bills in the cases of community newspapers, which are distributed free of charge, and commercial radio and TV stations. Even the CBC, a public broadcaster that receives the bulk of its funds for operation from government—59.1 per cent in 2004–5—must pay attention to audience ratings to maintain public confidence and to attract advertisers, even though advertising and program sales accounted for less than one-quarter of CBC's radio and television services' revenues in 2004–5 (www.cbc.radio-canada.ca/annualreports/2004-2005/pdf/financial_e.pdf).

Like producers of romantic fiction, news organiza-

tions target particular market segments in order to assemble an audience that will be attractive to advertisers. For example, tabloid newspapers like the *Ottawa Sun*, the *Vancouver Province*, and *Le Journal de Montréal* target younger, blue-collar readers and give extensive coverage to crime stories, popular entertainment, and sports. Their judgement of news and their writing style will be tuned accordingly. On the other hand, broadsheet newspapers like the *Globe and Mail*, the *Calgary Herald*, and *La Presse* aim for a more sophisticated readership and give much more coverage to politics, business, high culture, and world affairs.

No news organization has an unlimited budget. This means that the news value of an event must always be weighed against the costs required for coverage, particularly if the story necessitates travel. The maintenance of permanent news bureaus, whether in Beijing or Ottawa, is expensive and the coverage those bureaus produce has to warrant the costs involved, in terms of the quality of the reportage and/or the prestige that accrues to the news organization for having far-flung correspondents. At the same time, no news organization has unlimited time or space to tell its stories, and news judgement must also account for this. A television newscast is always the same length, whether it is a slow news day or a busy one. Newspapers vary in size from day to day, but this is primarily a product of how much advertising they sell. This is why newspapers are so thick during the Christmas shopping season—it is a busy time for retailers even though it is a typically slow time for news—and relatively thin in the slow shopping months of January and February.

Besides these structural factors affecting news decisions, ideological factors also come into play. Owners, managers, and journalists all subscribe to certain beliefs about how the world works and, regardless of how objective and fair a journalist tries to be, these beliefs influence what gets covered and how. During the 1988 federal election, for example, when free trade with the United States was the central issue, most daily newspapers favoured the Canada–US Free Trade Agreement and their support was evident, both in the editorial pages and in their 'objective' news reportage. The *Vancouver Sun*, to cite a specific instance, went so far as to refuse to cover an anti-free trade rally in Vancouver that attracted more than 1,000 people, denying these dissenting voices space in its pages. In a similar vein, the pro-Canada rally that preceded the 1995 Quebec referendum received very different news coverage from the feder-alist press (*Montreal Gazette*, *La Presse*) and nationalist press (*Le Devoir*) in Montreal.

More often, though, such bias in the judgement of news assumes subtler forms and may not be readily detectable to readers and viewers, many of whom may share the bias. Jaap van Ginneken (1998: 60–3) iden-tifies five categories of 'values' that are promoted con-tinuously and, hence, tend to predominate in the news coverage of the Western democracies:

1. The economic values of free enterprise and a free market;
2. The social values of individualism and social mobility;
3. The political values of pragmatism and modera-tion;
4. The lifestyle values of materialism and autonomy;
5. The ideological values that the West's point of view is based on scientific reason, while the views expressed in developing and non-Western coun-tries are based on dogma.

These values, van Ginneken asserts, are widely shared among Western journalists, with the result that they are taken for granted and through news media dis-course become 'naturalized'. As these perceptions are subscribed to, particularly by those in power, they form a society's 'dominant ideology'. Alternative views, such as the belief in the necessity of market regulation or the balancing of individual with collec-tive rights, become, by definition, deviant or 'unnatu-ral'. North American news stories dealing with the 'pink revolution' that has swept Latin American poli-tics and policy in recent years tend to support van Ginneken's contention in this regard.

As we have been suggesting throughout this chap-ter, news stories are selective representations of the universe of daily events going on around us. Both the stories that are told and how they are told owe some-thing to the prevailing values that define newswor-thiness, the particular style and budget of the news organization, and the beliefs and ideas that tend to predominate in society (see Figure 9.2). In any con-sideration of the question, 'What is news?', a number of factors are at play. Not all events occurring in the world are considered newsworthy by journalists, and therefore only events that meet certain criteria of news value will be considered as potential stories. At the same time, not all potential news stories are of interest to all news organizations. Some newspapers carry very little coverage of sports and crime news, while others specialize in these areas. The structure of the news organization will also have an impact on the newsroom budget, which will determine what stories it can afford to cover with its own staff, especially if travel and lodging are required. Finally, all societies subscribe to certain collective beliefs and values, which form a dominant ideology, and as members of society, journalists, too, have certain beliefs about the way the world works and should work. Events that confirm such beliefs are more likely to be seen as news stories—and presented as a kind of 'proof'—than events that contradict the dominant ideology. These latter events, when covered, are often present-ed as sorry deviations from the norm. This distinction was clearly evident, especially in the US media but also in Canadian news reports, in the aftermath of the American-led war on Iraq in 2003. Stories highlight-ing the American troops as liberators received sub-stantially greater and more favourable coverage than did those that focused on looting and anti-American protests. Of course, in some instances of news cover-age, what goes around comes around, so that three or four short years later one would have been hard-pressed to find news reports in the Western press

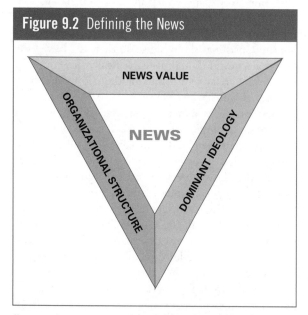

Figure 9.2 Defining the News

NEWS VALUE

ORGANIZATIONAL STRUCTURE

NEWS

DOMINANT IDEOLOGY

News can be seen as a product of the complex tension among: the factors that inform news value; the economic, time, and space constraints of organizational structure; and the beliefs that com-prise the dominant ideology in society.

touting the American and British invasion as liberating or successful.

Ownership and Control

A specific economic constraint in commercial news production is corporate concentration. As discussed in Chapter 8, our news comes from a handful of corporations that have media outlets in a number of Canada's major cities (or 'markets', from their perspective) and that are increasingly committed to **convergence**, or the delivery of news and information across a range of media platforms—newspapers, magazines, radio, television, internet.

Media ownership confers control over the content of news at two levels. **Allocative control** is exercised by publishers, shareholders, and directors, who allocate resources—labour and capital—to a news organization. They determine such things as the overall mandate or philosophy of the news organization, its annual operating budget, its anticipated profit margin, and its capital expenditures for technological upgrades. They also hire senior managers who share their views on the mandate of the news organ-

NEWS ON-LINE

Today, it seems, everyone has a website: organizations, companies, governments, elementary school classes, our next-door neighbour, even the royal family (www.royal.gov.uk). For the news media, in Canada as elsewhere around the world, the internet is a particularly attractive medium of diffusion; it provides instantaneous, global distribution, the ability to update stories constantly, and the capacity to combine text with sound and still and moving images. Websites offer audiences hypertext links to other relevant information sites and archives of past stories, and invite more immediate audience response to coverage. The web is populated by bloggers, podcasters, alternative media, and media reform groups.

Though it seems obvious that the internet is playing an increasingly significant role in the distribution of news and information, no one knows for sure how this medium will evolve, what precise journalistic role it will play, or who will do most to develop the internet as a news medium: established, mainstream news organizations or new, independent and innovative players. What is certain is that the development of this medium will require human and capital resources. The commercial media, which have considerable resources at their disposal, will demand that their on-line sites generate revenues, and their development will be governed by what is commercially viable rather than by what is technologically possible. Many sites, such as that for the *Globe and Mail*, now charge a subscription fee, at least for access to the full editorial product. The real innovations in on-line journalism are most likely to emerge among organizations driven by motives other than profit, such as those committed to particular political goals, including those dedicated to media democratization.

There are thousands of news organizations on-line, in some form or another, throughout the world. Today you can

read abridged, on-line versions of most major Canadian dailies and community newspapers, and through their sites you can link to other, related information sources, submit a letter to the editor, participate in on-line discussion groups, sign up for a subscription, or place a classified advertisement. Some newspapers have stand-alone sites—e.g., the *Globe and Mail* (www.theglobeandmail.com), *Le Devoir* (www.ledevoir.com)—while most are part of internet portals—e.g., the CanWest dailies (www.canada.com) and the Sun Media papers (www.canoe.ca)—and grouped together on aggregated sites.

The internet may seem to be a promised land for newspapers especially, because it eliminates the printing and delivery costs of publishing a hard-copy edition and it opens up a potential global audience. But audiences have been reluctant to pay for the kind of on-line content they are accustomed to accessing for free, many people still prefer reading a hard-copy edition, and on-line publishing means local papers compete for audiences with internationally known newspapers like the *New York Times*, *The Times* of London, and *Le Monde*, as well as broadcasters like the CBC and the BBC. Most news organizations on-line have not fully exploited the potential of the internet, providing few hypertext links, few audiovisual offerings, and minimal opportunities for interactivity, preferring to post an on-line version of their 'old media' form with little if any original content.

A number of alternative news sites have capitalized on the accessibility of the World Wide Web to expand the sphere of journalism. They include indymedia organizations in Canada (e.g., hamilton.indymedia.org, quebec.indymedia.org) and abroad, as well as international news providers like The Real News (www.itwnews.com), Paper Tiger Television (www.papertiger.org), and the Guerrilla News Network (www.guerrillanews.com).

ization and will ensure that it is enacted. **Operational control** is exercised by editors and producers who decide on a day-to-day and story-to-story basis how to employ the resources allocated. Such decisions include who to hire (at entry levels), who to assign to which news production tasks, and which stories to cover (Murdock, 1990: 122–3). Of course, these two levels are not mutually exclusive and some owners are more involved than others in daily news production.

It must be acknowledged, though, that newsrooms are complex work environments and the time pressures associated with daily journalism limit the amount of *direct* influence owners and managers can exercise over the journalists in their employ. Reporters, who spend much of their time in the field gathering information and conducting interviews, enjoy considerable latitude in generating ideas and developing their stories. Control over reporting staff is best seen as *indirect*. That is, it consists of a socialization process in which individual journalists—once hired and assigned to a particular department—learn what kinds of stories their supervisors want, and, more importantly, what kind they do not want (see Schulman, 1990). Every reporter has a tale to tell of producing a tantalizing story that was never published.

Corporate concentration is a growing concern around the media world and has attracted renewed attention in Canada in recent years. Thanks to mergers, takeovers, buyouts, and closures, fewer and fewer companies control the production of news. This has a number of implications for the process of newsmaking and the quality of information we receive (see Skinner et al., 2005). First, critics argue that as the sources of news and comment diminish, so does the diversity of such information. Alternative and oppositional voices risk being ridiculed, marginalized, or ignored altogether. Second, corporations are responsible to shareholders who are primarily interested in profit maximization. This can affect the quality of news coverage if managers are stingy with their newsroom budgets and/or their news organization avoids controversial

PAPER CHAINS

The problem of corporate concentration in the media is particularly acute in the newspaper industry. The four largest newspaper companies in Canada control 73 per cent of the total weekly circulation of the country's daily newspapers (Table 9.1). CanWest MediaWorks, which owns 13 dailies across the country (among them the *National Post*, the *Vancouver Sun*, and the *Ottawa Citizen*), accounts for close to one-third of total weekly circulation.

Quebecor became Canada's second-largest publisher of daily newspapers in January 1999, with papers in eight of the top 10 Canadian markets and more than one-fifth of total weekly circulation. Quebecor, which achieved this standing by buying Sun Media, publishes such newspapers as the *London Free Press*, *Le Journal de Montréal*, and the Sun newspapers in Ottawa, Toronto, Winnipeg, Calgary, and Edmonton (Lamey, 1999: F1–2). Together, Torstar Corp., which publishes four newspapers including the national circulation leader the *Toronto Star*, and Power Corp., which publishes seven French-language newspapers including *La Presse* in Montreal, account for another fifth of total daily newspaper circulation in the country.

Table 9.1 Holdings of Canada's Largest Newspaper Chains, 2006

Name of Company	Number of Dailies	Percentage of Total Weekly Circulation
CanWest/Southam	13	28.35
Quebecor/Sun Media	17	20.99
Torstar	4	13.93
Power Corp.	7	9.80

Source: Canadian Newspaper Association, 2006, at: www.cna-acj.ca/. Reprinted by permission of the publisher.

stories for fear of antagonizing audiences and/or advertisers. A third concern is the potential for conflict of interest between a corporation's news business and the other businesses it owns.

Quebecor, for example, which owns *Le Journal de Montréal*, the city's most popular daily newspaper, the TVA television network, and the canoe.ca internet portal, became a participant in its own news stories during the summer and fall of 2002 when 1,500 of its employees engaged in a bitter strike against Quebecor's cable television subsidiary, Vidéotron, the largest cable supplier in Quebec. Similarly, CanWest Global media outlets found themselves compromised when pro-Palestinian activists prevented former Israeli Prime Minister Benjamin Netanyahu from speaking at Concordia University in September 2002. CanWest media properties like the *Montreal Gazette* and Global Television vigorously covered, and commented on, the low point in Netanyahu's speaking tour, a tour sponsored by the Asper Foundation. The Foundation's president, the late Izzy Asper, was the founder and, at the time, executive chairman of CanWest Global, as well as the father of the company's president and chief executive officer, Leonard Asper.

Other conflicts of interest can arise relating to ownership. For instance, the Montreal newspaper *La Presse* has long been suspected of compromise in its coverage of the federal Liberal Party because the president of the company that owns the newspaper, André Desmarais, is married to former Prime Minister Jean Chrétien's daughter. In a specific instance, Chrétien's Chief of Staff, Jean Pelletier, complained directly to Desmarais about criticism of the Prime Minister by *La Presse* columnist Chantal Hébert (see Richer, 1999).

Journalist and scholar Ben Bagdikian (1990: xxii) has characterized corporate concentration as a conflict of interest between the public's need for information and corporations' desire for 'positive information'. Put another way, Peter Desbarats (1996: 61) writes: 'This concentration of ownership has created concern that the goals of media-owning corporations may at times run counter to freedom of expression and the long-term interests of society.'

Conflict between the rights and the responsibilities of the news media characterized much of the twentieth century, and governments in the UK, the US, and Canada have all conducted investigations into patterns of media ownership in the post-World War II period. As discussed in Chapter 4, the report of the Hutchins Commission on Freedom of the Press in the United States is recognized as a foundational document for what is known as the social responsibility theory of the press (Commission on Freedom of the Press, 1947). This theory extends the core democratic right of freedom of the press to include the right of citizens to be adequately informed by the news media.

Canada's Special Senate Committee on Mass Media, known as the Davey Commission (Canada, 1971: 3), concluded that media diversity defied the logic of market economics: 'More voices may be healthier, but fewer voices are cheaper.' Among the Davey Commission's principal recommendations was a press ownership review board, 'with powers to approve or disapprove mergers between, or acquisitions of, newspapers and periodicals' (ibid., 71). But, given the federal government's refusal to regulate either Canada's free press or the free enterprise in which news organizations engage, no such panel was ever established.

In 1980 the Royal Commission on Newspapers, known as the Kent Commission, was created in direct response to a 'rationalization agreement' between Canada's two premier newspaper chains of the period, Southam and Thomson, which left Southam alone in the Ottawa market and Thomson alone in the Winnipeg market. In line with the social responsibility theory of the press, the Kent Commission concluded that freedom of the press is not the owner's or editor's right to free speech, but is part of the people's right to freedom of expression and is 'inseparable from their right to inform themselves'. In the aftermath of the Royal Commission hearings, federal Consumer Affairs Minister Jim Fleming proposed a Canada Newspapers Act (1983), which would establish a national press council, offer grants to encourage newspapers to open bureaus across Canada, and impose ownership restrictions. But the legislation was opposed by the vocal publishing lobby and was never adopted by the Liberal government of the day (see Miller, 1998: 37–40). The Kent Commission's critique of the newspaper industry was sound, but to regulate the press is to redefine the legal meaning of freedom of the press, which democratic governments have so far refused to do.

As mentioned above, the 2003 Lincoln Committee report on broadcasting in Canada contained a number of recommendations to shore up editorial independence, particularly in instances of cross-media ownership (Canada, 2003). Similarly, the final report of the Standing Senate Committee on

Transport and Communications (Canada, 2006a) encouraged the federal government to enforce more diligently existing regulations concerning corporate concentration and cross-media ownership, and to expand the mandates of the CRTC and the Competition Act to include mechanisms for both the open review of media company mergers and for greater restrictions on media ownership.

In their defence, news media owners assert that a wealth of information sources—print, radio, television, magazines, and especially today the internet—makes corporate concentration less of a concern than it was when the Davey and Kent Commissions conducted their hearings. There is some merit to this argument. More newspapers, magazines, radio stations, and TV channels are available to us than ever before, and the internet gives users access to websites from around the world. Alternative sources of information are available.

But in assessing this argument we need to consider two points. First, there is considerable information-sharing among news media. That is, print and broadcast organizations depend heavily on the same wire services—Canadian Press, Associated Press, Agence France Presse—for regional, national, and international news, so that frequently the same story is used by various newspapers, radio stations, television outlets, and websites. Chris Paterson argues, in fact, that convergence has resulted in the increased concentration of information delivery on the internet.

> Comparative analysis of international news stories from major news Web sites with wire stories reveals a dearth of original journalism (or even copy-editing) and near total dependence by major Web news providers (like MSNBC, CNN, Yahoo and others) on wire service reporting and writing. The multitude of on-line information providers evidence burgeoning 'cybermediation' of a limited diet of news, rather than the outright disintermediation evidenced in other cyberspace sectors. (Paterson, 2005: 146; see also Paterson, 2001)

In other words, an increase in the quantity of news sources does nothing to ensure an increase in the diversity of news sources.

Distinctions between print, broadcast, and on-line coverage of local stories are similarly minimized because competing news organizations often set the news agenda for each other: they monitor each other's coverage, they cover the same local events, and they cite the same information sources. It is not uncommon, in other words, to read the same news story in two different newspapers and then also to hear a condensed version of the same story delivered by radio and television news readers. We may think we are benefiting from a broad range of news coverage, but all too often these media are getting their stories from the same source.

In addition, a considerable amount of internet information comes from the same government and corporate sources used by the conventional media, and this information is often packaged by websites established by print and broadcast outlets. The news portal Canadian Online Explorer (www.canoe.ca) was established in 1996 by Sun Media, the chain that owns the Sun newspapers, and it is now owned and operated by Quebecor. As such, its content reflects it

The role that journalists play in society has changed with twenty-first century war and instant communication. Journalists all around the Middle East could instantly report on the progress of the US-led war against Iraq. *Kansas City Star* photographer Jim Barcus was at Tactical Assembly Area Champion Main in Kuwait when this photo was taken in March 2003. He's wearing his desert goggles and thigh-mounted gas mask pouch. The latter is required by the 82nd Airborne, the unit in which Barcus was embedded. (The Kansas City Star)

ownership connections. Similarly, CanWest Global decided in September 2001 to fold the stand-alone websites of its daily newspapers into a single portal (www.canada.com), bringing together the sites of CanWest's daily newspapers and the Global television network. The existence of an abundance of information sources, again, does not equate with information diversity.

While a promising development in this regard is the emergence of a number of alternative and independent news sources, particularly on line, these newcomers cannot match the news-production resources (i.e., human and capital resources) that the mainstream commercial news organizations can muster, nor, yet, can they boast the authority that the mainstream news sector has won through many decades of service.

Corporate concentration is considered to be less of a problem in radio and television news because two important features of Canada's broadcasting industry mitigate against its domination by one or two companies. The first is the existence of the CBC/Radio-Canada as Canada's public broadcaster, for which there is no parallel in the newspaper or magazine industries. With radio and television outlets in French and English, the CBC serves Canada well with news and information programming, even if some would argue that the CBC could do a much better job in these areas. The greatest threat to the quality of its broadcasting in recent years has been the reduction in its funding from the federal government—a decrease of almost 10 per cent over the past 10 years, from $963.2 million in fiscal 1995–6 to $877 million in 2004–5. The uncertainty of and the net reduction in its government funding have forced the CBC to reduce staff and to make its television programming more appealing to advertisers. The second difference is that the broadcast industry is regulated by the CRTC, which, in enforcing the Broadcasting Act, can impose ownership restrictions and broadcasting standards on licence-holders. Some questions remain, however, about how much power the CRTC has to interfere with corporate mergers.

Corporate concentration has some sup-

porters outside the industry. David Demers (1999) argues that corporate ownership and good journalism are not necessarily mutually exclusive. Newspaper chains, Demers maintains, benefit from 'economies of scale and superior human and capital resources',

As demonstrated by this *Toronto Star* advertisement, individual media organizations, as well as individual journalists, can tell vastly different stories about the very same event. (Reprinted with permission—Torstar Syndication Services)

which can result in both quality reporting and industrial stability. One clearly positive result of corporate concentration is its pooling of considerable capital resources. This permits newspapers like the *Globe and Mail* and *La Presse* to establish the kind of editorial budgets that an independent news organization simply could not afford. These two dailies, for example, have permanent news bureaus across the country and around the world and they have the resources to send their reporters and columnists wherever the action is. This is important as readers expect quality newspapers to contribute independent voices to major news stories such as the 11 September 2001 terrorist attacks, the conflicts in Afghanistan and Iraq, and global trade agreements. Very few metropolitan dailies have foreign correspondents, relying instead on wire-service copy to supply them with both national and international news and analysis from a relatively small stable of syndicated columnists. But size does not always mean better coverage. For instance, if we compare Canada's national television networks, the CBC does a much better job than either CTV or Global of bringing a distinct, Canadian perspective to regional, national, and international news coverage.

News as Storytelling

One way of looking at journalism is as a practice of meaning production. There is always a distinction between events and stories about events, between reality and stories about reality. Journalists represent reality; they cannot reproduce it. They are thus storytellers, using words, images, and sounds to depict reality (people, places, ideas, institutions, events). As Kovach and Rosenstiel (2001: 149) put it: 'Journalism is storytelling with a purpose. That purpose is to provide people with information they need to understand the world. The first challenge is finding the information that people need to live their lives. The second is to make it meaningful, relevant, and engaging.'

But what this implies is that the choices journalists make among the words, images, and sounds at their disposal will attribute particular meanings to the events they cover. A reporter covering a demonstration, for example, will define that event in different ways, depending on whether the participants in the demonstration are described as 'a small group', 'a crowd', or 'a mob'. Similarly, the specific observations and quotations cited in the story and the visuals chosen to illustrate it will define the event in a certain

way. And this applies regardless of how 'objective' the reporter tries to remain. No story, after all, can tell the whole story.

In this vein, researchers Elizabeth Bird and Robert Dardenne encourage us to think of news stories as myths, stories that we tell ourselves in an effort to make sense of often complex phenomena, to assert and maintain cultural values, and to determine notions of right and wrong. Journalists, for example, often refer explicitly to mythical tales—Cinderella stories and battles between David and Goliath are frequently called upon—to assign meaning to events and offer the news audience a kind of shorthand to understanding. Allusions to Cinderella and the Biblical David, for example, help to perpetuate and reinforce the value of social mobility, which, as we noted earlier in this chapter, has been identified by van Ginneken as one of the predominant values in the Western media's news coverage. Every time we read a real-life Cinderella story, it adds credence to the myth of social mobility. Every time we hear that another David has defeated another Goliath, it reinforces the idea that ordinary people can bring down giants, that power relations are fragile, possibly even illusory. Bird and Dardenne (1997: 346–7) write: 'While news is not fiction, it is a story about reality, not reality itself. Yet because of its privileged status as reality and truth, the seductive powers of its narratives are particularly significant.'

This is not to suggest that journalists simply make up or invent stories out of thin air. Rather, the point is to emphasize that there is always a difference between an event and a story about an event. Events are usually messy, complicated, hard to understand, with no clear beginning, middle, or end. In reporting on such events, journalists seek to impose an order on events, to render them comprehensible and meaningful, to frame them in particular ways, to contain the events within the 60 seconds of a television news report or the few hundred words of a newspaper article. In answering to the demands of storytelling, journalists impose a narrative structure on events—the 'who' of the story becomes character, the 'what' becomes plot, the 'where' and 'when' become setting, the 'why' becomes motivation, and the 'how' becomes narrative (see Kovach and Rosenstiel, 2001: 156)—and this imposition runs the risk of oversimplifying complex phenomena. Any news story is merely one depiction of an event among an infinite number of other possible depictions, making it all the more important that alternative news sources remain available to us.

Summary

Journalists are content producers and storytellers (not unlike the storytellers who work in other mass media forms). News is not simply gathered; it is constructed or produced.

Journalism, as a form of storytelling, is based on real people and real events. But rather than mirroring reality, as is often suggested, the news media instead frame reality, selecting particular events, particular people, and particular aspects of a story as newsworthy while excluding many others, attributing meaning to events in particular ways.

Journalism shares some of the characteristics of other forms of storytelling but it is also distinguished by the following features: its guiding ideals of truth-seeking, independence, and objectivity; the ethical and legal rights and obligations of the practice in a free press environment; and the institutional context of news production. Freedom of the press, one of the linchpins of news reporting, does not mean that journalists are free to report whatever they choose or that news organizations can publish and broadcast with impunity. Such constraints as privacy and libel keep news producers in line with accepted notions of integrity.

Given the selective nature of the news production process, it is important to understand where news reports come from. Journalists in Canada are not representative of the population at large. Instead, they tend to be young, male, white, and well-educated, and they work predominantly for commercial news organizations with large corporate owners. These factors have implications for both what and how news is reported, as well as for what may not be reported.

Finally, there is an argument to be made for perceiving news reports as myths—stories that are told over and over again and that contain reality within a culturally acceptable framework of understanding. This view originates in a tradition of study that perceives texts—all kinds of texts—as cultural constructions, as a way of creating bridges between fictional and non-fictional forms of storytelling.

RELATED WEBSITES

Canadian Association of Broadcasters: www.cab-acr.ca
The CAB represents Canada's private broadcasters. The site profiles industry sectors and highlights industry and social policy issues.

Canadian Broadcast Standards Council: www.cbsc.ca
The Canadian Broadcast Standards Council was established by the CAB and aids in the application of broadcast standards. The site contains CBSC codes, policy decisions, and annual reports.

Canadian Newspaper Association: www.cna-acj.ca
The Canadian Newspaper Association is a non-profit trade and lobby organization representing Canadian daily newspapers.

Canadian Online Explorer: www.canoe.ca
Canadian Online Explorer, the property of the media conglomerate Quebecor, is an on-line news service and internet portal established in March 1996. A French-language version was added in September 1999 (www2.canoe.com/index.html). Both sites offer visitors a daily news package (updated throughout the day) featuring all the departments of a regular daily newspaper.

Canada.com: www.canada.com
Canada.com is a news portal that brings together news highlights from CanWest Global's daily newspapers and the Global television network.

CanWest Global Communications: www.canwestglobal.com
CanWest Global is a diversified media company with television, radio, film, and newspaper holdings in Canada, New Zealand, Australia, Ireland, and the United Kingdom.

Cyberpresse: www.cyberpresse.ca
This French-language news portal brings together news highlights from the seven Gesca-owned daily newspapers.

Globe and Mail: www.globeandmail.com
The *Globe and Mail* is Canada's leading national newspaper. Its website includes stories from its daily print edition as well as breaking news dispatches.

National Post: www.nationalpost.com
Canada's other 'national' newspaper, owned by CanWest Global, posts stories from its print edition on its website.

Quebecor Inc.: www.quebecor.com
Quebecor is a diversified media company with holdings in television, the internet, newspaper, magazine, and book publishing, as well as book and music retailing.

Radio and Television News Directors Association of Canada: www.rtndacanada.com
The RTNDA represents Canada's broadcast journalists and news managers. It establishes broadcast standards and ethics guidelines, and lobbies on behalf of broadcast journalists.

Toronto Star: www.thestar.com
The Toronto Star is Canada's largest-circulation daily newspaper. The site contains a selection of stories from the print edition as well as breaking news.

Universal Declaration of Human Rights: www.un.org/50/decla.htm or www.un.org/Overview/rights.html
The full text of this important document can be found at these sites.

FURTHER READINGS

Canada. 2006. *Final Report on the Canadian News Media*, vol. 1. Standing Senate Committee on Transport and Communications. Ottawa: Senate Committees Directorate, June. This report contains a great deal of current information about news media ownership and practice, as well as recommendations to government to ensure that the commercial goals of news organizations do not preclude high-quality, independent journalism.

Hackett, Robert A., and Yuezhi Zhao. 1998. *Sustaining Democracy? Journalism and the Politics of Objectivity*. Toronto: Garamond Press. This book provides a critical examination of the relationship between journalism and democracy, with a particular emphasis on the philosophical underpinnings of objectivity as an ideal.

Kovach, Bill, and Tom Rosenstiel. 2001. *The Elements of Journalism: What Newspeople Should Know and the Public Should Expect*. New York: Crown Publishers. This well-written and concise book diagnoses several fundamental problems with the state of journalism in the United States, but the problems it addresses and the recommendations it makes are quite applicable to the Canadian context.

Schudson, Michael. 1978. *Discovering the News: A Social History of American Newspapers*. New York: Basic Books. This oft-cited study of the transformation of journalism in the late nineteenth and early twentieth centuries, while based on American newspapers, provides an explanation of the emergence of objectivity that applies to Canadian journalism as well.

Skinner, David, James Compton, and Mike Gasher, eds. 2005. *Converging Media, Diverging Politics: A Political Economy of News Media in the United States and Canada*. Lanham, Md: Lexington Books. This collection of essays compares the state of commercial journalism in Canada and the United States, offers critical case studies on instances where commercial goals detract from journalistic quality, and concludes with a consideration of emerging alternative media and media reform movements.

Tuchman, Gaye. 1978. *Making News: A Study in the Construction of Reality*. New York: Free Press. Tuchman's analysis of how journalists gather information and produce news is a groundbreaking study.

van Ginneken, Jaap. 1998. *Understanding Global News: A Critical Introduction*. London: Sage. This critical study details how and why news circulates internationally, and includes discussion of the implications of news flows.

STUDY QUESTIONS

1. What does it mean to say that news content is highly constructed?
2. What are some of the implications of this process of construction?
3. In what sense is news production a form of storytelling?
4. What is wrong with the mirror metaphor or the reflection thesis of journalism?
5. Why is gatekeeping an inadequate metaphor for news judgement? To what extent is the term useful, and what are its limitations?
6. What does freedom of the press mean in the Canadian context? Is it an absolute right?
7. Does objectivity remain a viable ideal for journalists?
8. To what extent are news stories selective representations of the world?
9. In what ways do media owners and managers exercise editorial control?
10. What does it mean to say news stories define events?

LEARNING OUTCOMES

- To explain that journalism, like other forms of media content, involves the deliberate and selective production of news stories.
- To point out that events are selected as news based on specific criteria of newsworthiness.
- To propose the metaphor of the 'frame' as a better explanation for news production than the mirror or gatekeeping.
- To describe, and problematize, some of journalism's core ideals, such as the search for truth and the code of objectivity.
- To survey the demographic characteristics of journalists in Canada to point out that they are not representative of the population as a whole.
- To describe the legal framework of news production in Canada and to explain what freedom of the press means in the Canadian context.
- To explain that most journalists in Canada work for commercial news organizations governed by the profit motive and to explore what this implies for news production.
- To provide a more sophisticated understanding of what kind of editorial control owners and managers exercise.
- To position journalism as a narrative form that draws on a number of storytelling conventions.
- To point out that news organizations produce meaning, defining the events that they cover.

CHAPTER 10

Communication Technology and Society: Theory and Practice[1]

Introduction

We live in interesting times. We are in the midst of one of the most dramatic shifts since the Industrial Revolution. Western society, indeed the whole world, is in the midst of a major change in the nature and organization of society facilitated by information and communication technology. The impact of computing technology and digital media on the structure of society, the economy, and media is vast and only partially understood. Only with time will we come to fully appreciate the new realities, new opportunities, and new challenges presented by the digital age.

This chapter begins by defining technology in general and communication technology in particular and by discussing how communication theorists view technology. It then provides an overview of the development of communication technology and explores some recent technological developments in communication, reviewing the categories of activity these developments are affecting. The chapter concludes with some observations on communication technology and society.

Technology Defined

Somewhat surprisingly, technology is difficult to define. It is more than just apparatuses, gadgets, machines, or devices. The Canadian physicist Ursula M. Franklin, in her 1989 CBC Massey Lectures entitled 'The Real World of Technology', focused on technology as practice. Franklin stated:

> Like democracy, technology is a multifaceted entity. It includes activities as well as a body of knowledge, structures as well as the act of structuring. Our language itself is poorly suited to describe the complexity of technological interactions. The interconnectedness of many of these processes, the fact that they are so complexly interrelated, defies

our normal push-me-pull-you, cause-and-consequence metaphors. How does one speak about something that is both fish and water, means as well as end? (Franklin, 1999: 5–6)

Franklin pointed out that technology is about 'the organization of work and people', and that it involves 'procedures, symbols, new words, equations, and, most of all, a mindset'. This perspective reminds us not to look at technology in isolation, as a kind of thing that has specific effects on people, but rather to see technologies as parts of an ongoing way of life, with deeply tangled causes, effects, interpretations, and motivations.

Thirty years ago, US communication scholar Langdon Winner (1977) noted that technology encompasses at least three elements:

1. pieces of apparatus;
2. techniques of operation to make the apparatus work; and
3. social institutions within which technical activities take place.

Even before Winner proposed this three-part definition of technology, Raymond Williams (1975) had argued that technology reflects the overall organization of society. Television technology, for example, he claimed is an extension of the Industrial Revolution. By offering programs to fill our leisure time, it feeds and maintains the mass society that industrialization created. This kind of explanation is clearly not about television as a particular kind of electronic device, but rather about the complex network of practices that television-in-context has become for us.

Thinking about Technology

In recent years, insights into technology and society have been more systematically organized and their articulation has gained some sophistication. In

---

1. The authors wish to thank John Maxwell for his co-authorship of this chapter. John is assistant professor in the Master of Publishing program at Simon Fraser University and recently completed his Ph.D. dissertation on the history of the origins of personal and educational computing.

Questioning Technology, philosopher Andrew Feenberg (1999) provides an account of the major and current conceptual frameworks and orientations social scientists and philosophers use to think about technology. His analysis provides four main perspectives on technology: instrumentalism, determinism, substantivism, and critical theory. A fifth perspective, constructivism, is closely related to critical theory.

Instrumentalism sees technology as a value-neutral tool that can shorten the path to natural ends or, alternatively, social goals. For example, we need a drink of water: a cup works better than either our hand or putting our face in a pool of water. We need to get from Long Beach on Vancouver Island to The Beaches in Toronto: a plane or two in combination with cars and buses gets us there faster and more easily than walking and swimming.

Conversely, technological **determinism** holds that technology operates according to an inexorable logic inherent in the technology itself. Technology here is seen as part of the natural evolution of a better world. It is easy to see examples of determinist thinking in the trends towards miniaturization and mobility: the mobile phone you carry today will inevitably be replaced by one that is smaller or lighter and allows you to do more with it—or so we commonly think.

From the determinist perspective, human control over the exact direction of technological development seems weak and causes a good deal of anxiety. In a stance related to technological determinism, **substantivism** claims that not only does technology operate according to its own inherent logic, but also that this logic is at the expense of humanity. The harsh social realities of the Industrial Revolution, the development of nuclear weapons, and more recently the threat of environmental disaster have given substantivist critics much to think and write about to bolster their perspective. Take the automobile, for example: the availability of mass-produced cars in the early twentieth century led to the development of large-scale infrastructure (roads, highways, suburbs, shopping malls) designed with cars and car travel in mind. But we now live in a world where the urban sprawl (not to mention air pollution and dependency on foreign oil reserves) brought on by a car-oriented culture is very difficult to escape from; more efficient and more environmentally friendly modes of mass transit are notoriously difficult to design and build, simply because urban density is so low in the suburbs (com-

pared with urban density in Europe or Asia, where rail travel is much more economically feasible). The structure has become self-reinforcing: the only way to live in car-oriented suburbs is to drive a car.

Taking their position to a logical conclusion, Feenberg reports that substantivists view the modern condition as reflective of the essence of modern technology—its rationality, its efficiency, its priority on control and calculability. The more pessimistic or dystopian of the substantivists argue that technological thought and action threaten non-technological values as they extend ever deeper into social life. We become slaves to the machine. Thus, it is not uncommon in universities and other institutions for rules to be built around the capacity of the technology to keep processing information in an orderly way—and not around what is best for professors and students. For instance, graduate students working full time on their theses may find themselves not classified as full-time students and hence may be faced with loan repayment. Even when solutions for working around particular regulations are put in place, with staff changes the rationales for these solutions may be forgotten or deemed not to be worthwhile as the years go by. As Jacques Ellul expressed it, technique has become autonomous. McLuhan expressed the same point by saying that human beings are 'the sex organs of the machine world'.

Consider this summary Dizard has written of Ellul's position (best exemplified in Ellul's book, *The Technological Society* (1964):

1. All technological progress exacts a price—while it adds something, it subtracts something else.
2. All technological progress raises more problems than it solves, tempts us to see the consequent problems as technical in nature, and prods us to seek technical solutions to them.
3. The negative effects of technological innovation are inseparable from the positive. It is naive to say that technology is neutral, that it may be used for good or bad ends; the good and bad effects are, in fact, simultaneous and inseparable.
4. All technological innovations have unforeseen effects. (Dizard, 1985: 11)

While these points have a ring of truth, they also reflect an inevitability and a pessimism. As we will see, there are challenges to both inevitability and pessimism. A complementary viewpoint to Ellul's can be found in the writings of Canadian philosopher George Grant. In *Technology and Empire*, Grant argued that the foundation of all modern, liberal, industrial, and post-industrial societies is to be found in technique and technology. In 1969 he claimed that the dominant doctrine of modern **liberalism** was 'the belief that human excellence is promoted by the homogenizing and universalizing power of technology' (Grant, 1969: 69).

But neither instrumentalism nor substantivism is adequate. Technology is *not* neutral as the instrumentalists claim. Our ways of life *are* changed even when we purchase something as small as an iPod or a cellphone. Edwin Black (2001) has described how IBM made it possible for the Nazis to undertake censuses that provided both ethnic background and addresses—allowing the Nazis to round up Jews and send them to the gas chambers when the time came. **Critical theory** claims we do have choices to develop technology, to shape its development, to use it, and to engage with it to a greater or lesser extent. IBM did not have to facilitate the collection and storage of data to increase the efficiency of rounding up Jews. But in playing the particular role it did, it contributed to a world in which technology can be criticized as dehumanizing and even murderous.

Feenberg (1999) argues that theorists Herbert Marcuse and Michel Foucault—a French scholar who was part of the 'New Left' movement of the 1960s—opened up the opportunity to think about technology and technological development as something other than an outside force that could only be slowed or quickened by society. Rather, they made it possible to conceive of technology as existing inside society. In other words, technology is an integral part of society, just like religion, education, culture, economics, and politics. It emerges as a manifestation of society in the same way as do social habits and institutions, economic and political systems, and is thus subject to the same kind of criticism.

This twofold notion—that technology exists within society and that social forces and political decision-making can control both the nature of the machines that emerge and their usage—means that technology develops in what Feenberg calls a **socially contingent** manner. In other words, technology arises and takes a particular form depending on the dynamics of the society in which it emerged—which may include rejection, as happened with fax machines when they were first invented and with movable type

in China prior to Gutenberg, the European credited with the invention of movable type. Rather than pointing to a good or a bad essence of technology, critical theory sees technology as offering up possibilities in the context of which society must choose a course of action. Such sites of struggle raise issues of power, control, and freedom that society must address.

Constructivism has emerged out of the shortcomings of both instrumentalism and substantivism. Today, a constructivist framework largely prevails in studies of technology. Constructivists argue that technology is socially constructed. That is, it is constructed by members of society and shaped by social forces. They argue that the contest for the site does get addressed and that many paths lead out from the first forms of a new technology. There are always viable alternatives in the form technology will take and the uses to which it will be put. They go on to say that to succeed, technology must have a technical and a social logic; in other words, new tools (or systems) succeed where they find support in the social environment.

The difficulty in understanding the nature of technology is that once a tool or system finds a supportive environment, most often it undergoes a process of **closure**. Closure refers to the fixing of a product or system into a socially recognized object, producing a 'black box', an artifact or way of doing things that is no longer called into question. And once a black box is closed, or 'naturalized', as sociologists Bowker and Star (1999) put it, its social origins and alternatives are quickly forgotten and the artifact or system appears purely technical and inevitable—as if it was bound to emerge in the form it has taken. It becomes part of the taken-for-granted environment. This notion both of purity (independent from social forces) and of inevitability (that it would emerge in the form it did) is, Feenberg claims, a **determinist illusion**. In a different society, or at a different time in history, or in the hands of different developers, a certain piece of technology might have been differently configured. Differently configured, the telephone could readily have served as a broadcast receiver for musical events just as phones are coming to be news cameras; cameras, sound recording devices; and computers, burglary tools.

The constructivist view of technology maintains that technology arises within and under the control of society. Said slightly differently, specific practical and political choices are involved in development of technical systems. For example, the **deskilling** of work is neither inevitable nor an accident of technological advance. Deskilling resulted from developers breaking down tasks into simple components. This allows an employer to replace people doing complex tasks with less skilled people each performing one simple part of a complex task. This simplification allows the employer to pay less. Arguably, done well, it may actually increase the reliability of production. Equally arguably, decent living wages for workers may be undermined and job satisfaction may plummet. But this way of thinking about systems is not inevitable or inescapable. Rather, it has a particular history in the development of mass production and factory management. The constructivist motto is, thus, 'it could have been otherwise.'

The nature of a constructivist view has been captured well by Wiebe Bijker (1993). In fact, as Felczak (2006: 6) notes, Bijker actually extends the constructivist formulation as follows:

> Society is not determined by technology, nor is technology determined by society. Both emerge as two sides of the sociotechnical coin, during the construction process of artifacts, facts, and relevant social groups.

Bijker claims that what we call a machine is, in reality, a shorthand expression for a **socio-technical ensemble** and, he says, 'it should, in principle, be possible to sketch the (socially) constructed character of that machine.' Similarly, the term 'social institution' is shorthand for a different socio-technical ensemble and 'it should be possible to spell out the technical relations that go into making that institution into a stable setup' (Bijker, 1993: 125).

This means that any machine—a chainsaw, a bicycle, a hair dryer, an iPod, a cellphone, or the Hubble space telescope—arose out of a socially defined intention of its developers (e.g., to use the Hubble to see far into space), who were able to create a particular technical device for intended and sometimes unintended uses, hence a socio-technical ensemble.

Felczak makes two further points. One is derived from sociologists John Law and Michel Callon (1988). If machines are socio-technical ensembles, then it follows that engineers are social activists. They design machines that reconfigure social relations and hence change society. On the other side of the equation, in the context of information technology, social scientific investigation can embrace an activist element just as some scientific inquiry does, for example in the health sciences (see Lorimer et al., 2000). Thus, rather than being after-the-fact commentators on socio-technical ensembles, social scientists can engage in the development of socio-technical ensembles and thereby participate in defining their nature and contours for the benefit of society. Imagine if the health sciences confined themselves to describing the symptoms of diseases and did not look for the causal factors and means whereby those causes could be neutralized.

Technology and Western Society

The notion that the distinguishing feature of Western society is its embrace of technology requires some explanation. It might be more accurate to say that Western, i.e., capitalist, society promotes technological invention that can be applied to real or imagined social needs for the purpose of first, profit, and, secondarily, job creation, which in turn allows for the consumption (i.e., purchase) of the invention. From our morning alarm through the manufactured food of our breakfast, our transportation to highly engineered buildings, and our use of computers and personal communication devices, we live amid technology. As well, the society within which we live embraces technology in health care, in upholding the law, in finance, and in culture and entertainment. Some claim that we embrace technology because the rank of nations in the world economy is profoundly affected by an ever-continuing great technological race. But is Western society unique in its relationship to technology? Probably not—all cultures and societies can be seen as being based on tightly integrated technologies. Sociologist of science Bruno Latour suggests that what distinguishes modern society from so-called traditional societies may be the size and scope of our socio-technical ensembles, rather than any qualitative difference in the way people think or cultures act.

As successive layers of technology have taken root in Western society and successive layers of infrastructure have been laid down, we should not be surprised to find that our dependency on these systems has grown. So enthusiastic is the acceptance of technology by Western, especially North American, society that a person might say the Western world, and increasingly the world as a whole, is firmly in the clutches of the **technological imperative**, that is, we have convinced ourselves that we should continuously develop new technologies and apply them broadly, and they will lead to a better life. Furthermore, development of technology in Western society is usually a deliberate attempt to create material objects, interventions, or systems that, in changing or improving situations, allow the developer to reap financial reward. In this sense, technological development is a business—and the economies of Western nations are wrapped up intimately with the innovation, development, and promotion of new technologies. One result is that the technological distance between developed and developing economies in communication (and those that are not developing at all) has been increasing. This gap, which from time to time is brought forward for discussion, is often called the **digital divide**.

Recalling Winner's three-part definition of technology, we can see that technologically oriented societies affirm and embrace machinery, the social organization necessary to adopt that machinery, and the acquisition of the requisite skills and techniques needed for its operation for private financial benefit largely without social or political interference. The enthusiastic acceptance of technology is so complete that both analysts (e.g., Gilder, 1991) and the general public believe as truth the projections about the future of society based on technological capacity. This is a straightforward example of technological determinism: if technological development (usually conceived of as developing and adopting some kind of apparatus) can do something, society will take full advantage of this technological capacity and will be shaped fundamentally by the apparatus.

For instance, technological determinism would argue that landing a man on the moon changed society fundamentally: it was seen as the beginning of the colonization of space by humanity. Similarly, the internet was presumed to democratize the world more completely than ever before. Of course, both socio-technical ensembles have had profound impacts on society, but the extent to which they have met expectations is not borne out. This is the kind of technological determinism we all tend to engage in from day to day. What is important to remember is how this perspective glosses over the fundamental complexity of the real world.

In the first place, determinism fails to consider that the technology does not drop out of the clear blue sky or from the head of some unworldly genius.

Rather, it is derived from specific efforts to solve problems or find opportunities. For instance, the very global-sounding (albeit gendered) 'man went to the moon' could be more accurately framed as 'the US government contributed enormous funding to military-industrial contractors in order to establish American technological superiority in the Cold War with the Soviet Union by putting a human being on the moon.' In the second place, technological determinism ignores the role of state and institutional control over the industrialized application of technology. As is apparent, the internet can as easily be used for dictatorship or terrorism as for democracy. If politicians wish, they can enact policy so that a certain technology (e.g., the internet) can only be used in certain ways (e.g., for Canadian content), and hence, with certain consequences (e.g., contributing to the cohesiveness of Canada or to massive rejection of such a policy by many Canadians). Such control is not just in the hands of governments; corporate interests may exercise their power to shape technological systems in order to preserve market influence; Microsoft found itself in trouble with the US Department of Justice for its monopolistic business practices.

THE DANGERS OF TECHNOLOGY AND TECHNOLOGICAL HUBRIS

Implicit in our everyday perspective on technology is the notion that technology can transform society for the good, in other words, that it contributes to progress. But as Ellul points out, the consequences of the transformative dynamic of technology usually go unrealized in its initial application. Antibiotics are a well-known example. While antibiotics have been a godsend in terms of public health, we now understand that strains of antibiotic-resistant bacteria have emerged precisely because of our use of antibiotics. Each winter, following the SARS scare of 2004–5, health officials worry that a drug-resistant strain of flu may cause a world pandemic. Similarly, the development of monocultures, single varieties of plants that are most productive and produce the most economically harvestable crop, makes food supplies extremely vulnerable to failure. The sinking of the *Titanic* was a famous example of technological hubris. The *Titanic* was viewed as unsinkable because it was an example of the latest and greatest technology.

In communication, similar issues surround the limitations of technology. For instance, while a lot more people are able to access vast amounts of information, as economies of scale come to dominate, information with only a limited audience tends to disappear. Specialty magazines disappear from newsstands, and scholarly monographs, that is, books written by scholars that focus on narrow yet important subjects, such as the influence of ethnicity on modern farming communities, have a very difficult time getting published. The control systems of the large producers tell them that they can make more money elsewhere. National, provincial, and regional news, as well as information about our neighbours down the street, ceases to reach us as we turn more and more to local (the primary broadcast area of the station or channel) and global (CNN or BBC) broadcasting. Finally, elements so mundane as the number of hours one might spend sitting in front of a computer or TV, or the lack of socialization involved in working from home, may have considerable unanticipated consequences when multiplied throughout society. For one thing, the physical health of people deteriorates. Again, this is what Ellul meant by the inseparability of the good and bad effects of technology.

Centralization, Decentralization, and Control

The question of who owns and controls technologies was a critical issue even before Karl Marx in the nineteenth century wrote about the means of production. Before the Industrial Revolution the means of production were somewhat more natural—the land, seeds of known crops harvested and stored over the winter, and tools. Landowners controlled the means of the production of food—the land itself—while peasants worked the land. The owners taxed the peasants a portion of their crops so the owners became rich and the peasants stayed alive—just—to work the land the following year. As Chapter 2 made clear, communication technologies have traditionally been owned and controlled by large corporations and/or governments. There has been a shift away from a centralized model (the mass media), in which a single entity owns and controls the generation of content and technology used to produce that content. Increasingly, individual members of society and organizations are availing themselves of production technology and opportunities to generate their own content, and opportunities for media-based interaction have expanded enormously. Meanwhile, large corporations are ferreting out investment opportunities in the portal sector—the aggregation of content and hence the aggregation of audiences sufficiently large to create a viable attention-selling business.

To put the matter in slightly different terms, it is important to be careful in assessing the nature of change that technology is bringing about because the forces of profit-seeking inherent in large corporations will be working hard to recreate sufficiently large audiences to trigger economies of scale in (centralized) production. This, of course, can then bring vast profits to the corporations. In short, the new media are a contested site and media entrepreneurs will be looking for ways to shape the organization of technology to their financial advantage.

Technical Convergence: Old Myth, New Reality

Traditionally, communication has been divided into several different industries based on the black-box type closure (see Chapter 10) that came to exist around a particular communicative process—person-to-person communication, newspapers, books and magazines, voice communication to wide audiences, sound communication, and audiovisual communication to large, usually home-based audiences. Thus, telephone systems were designed to facilitate point-to-point communication offering limited **fidelity** (telephones need only transmit a recognizable voice) but sophisticated switching. Broadcast technology was designed not only to carry signals from a single point to multiple points but also to have a satisfactory level of fidelity so that listening for a long time to voice and especially music would be an enjoyable experience. No switching between senders and receivers was required, just stream of signals flowing outward from a single source. Recording technology was developed to yield the highest possible fidelity but distribution was determined by consumer purchase. And just as recording technology increased in its fidelity over the years from wax cylinders to 78s to LPs to tapes to CDs and now DVDs, so radio improved as

CANNED MUSIC

It is said that the phrase 'canned music' came from the fact that wax cylinders were stored in cans to protect them.

stations migrated from AM (amplitude modulation) to FM (frequency modulation) and then to digital radio.

While no doubt many assumed there was a technological basis to this division of responsibilities between telephone and broadcast, as Babe (1988, 1990) has pointed out, this was a myth—no such technological determinism existed. Telephone systems could easily have been turned into broadcast instruments as they were in the very first example of voice telephony by Reginald Fessenden (see Fessenden, 1974) and in early radio forms, and as they were used in the former Soviet Union. As we saw in Chapter 2, social and political forces achieved several different technical closures to allow the formation of viable communication industries.

The separation of communication functions into separate industries and the development of technology that best suited the functions of telephony, broadcasting, and sound and video recording have served society well. This separation is now many decades old, and government regulation largely takes the resulting industry structure for granted. Such industrial and technological separation has prevented the overall control of communication by one set of companies by spreading ownership somewhat broadly. Imagine if the CBC or CTV were your telephone and cable company as well as one of five or so major recording labels.

With digitization and the development of digital media infrastructure, the traditional technological separation of telephony, broadcasting, and cable as well as music and movie purchase for home consumption ceases to make sense, leaving an industrial and regulatory structure that is open to criticism and change. Telephone companies now provide TV programming, and cable TV companies are offering telephone service. Meanwhile, your cellphone can be a camera, a text-messenger, an MP3 player, and a GPS unit.

Digital media devices such as cameras, computers, musical instruments, radio, television, cable, GPS units, and telephones are all information machines that essentially do the same job—collect, code, and thus transform information into digital form. They are merely specialized computerized transceivers (transmitters and receivers). For instance, through sampling and/or synthesis, an electronic keyboard can almost reproduce any sound. A digital audio file is essentially the same as a digital image; no technical reason prevents you from manipulating a song in an image-edit-ing program or from adding effects like reverb to a photograph. Each device is a computer specialized to a particular sound and/or image and/or text format. What they share in common is digitization, and hence the ability for one device to send output or receive input from another is what is meant by the term **convergence**, which also refers to the tendency of communication companies to treat different forms of digital media—television, radio, telephones, news—as the same substance.

Where, historically, we have seen communication industries arranged around significantly different technological underpinnings, the advent of digital media means everyone is working with the same foundational technologies, everything mediated by computers and computer networks (and increasingly the internet itself). The resulting reconfiguration of communication industries presents considerable challenges for policy.

TECHNOLOGY AND POLICY

In the beginning years of the twenty-first century, we are once again facing many of the same choices that people confronted at the turn of the last century. Just as social and political variables in the form of policy, not technology, determined that telephone and broadcasting would be separated into two industries (see Babe, 1988, 1990), so policy and market forces will encourage an industrial structure that, hopefully, is of the greatest benefit to Canadians (or, possibly, the greatest benefit to the producers). The challenge for policy is ever-strengthening forces of globalization (see Chapter 11)—communication systems controlled by a very few transnational corporations that would dwarf the largest we see now. The two central issues are: (1) to ensure that the needs of the public and of cultural and national groups are met, and (2) to ensure that certain businesses do not become too powerful and thereby thwart the participation of others and prevent further social and technological development. The attempt of Microsoft to dominate in nearly every software market is a case in point. Some feel that the success of Google is equally threatening.

While allowing for convergence and competition sounds like a good idea, it is difficult for the CRTC to respond with appropriate policy. For example, both telephone and cable companies provide internet access to consumers and are known as 'backbone providers'. They also provide connectivity to small internet service providers (ISPs), who also sell access to

A BRIEF COMPARISON OF SATELLITE RADIO SERVICES

XM Radio Canada
- Number of channels: more than 80, eight of which are Canadian-produced.
- Monthly subscription cost: $12.99.
- Receiver cost: prices start at $79.99 (after rebate).
- Run by Canadian Satellite Radio in partnership with XM Radio in the US.

Sirius Canada
- Number of channels: 100, 10 of which are Canadian-produced.
- Monthly subscription cost: $14.99.
- Receiver cost: prices start at $69.99.
- A partnership between the CBC, Standard Radio, and Sirius Satellite Radio US.

Source: www.cbc.ca/story/arts/national.

the public. Similarly, the cable companies now own some of the specialty channels as well as provide access to these to their competitors—clearly a conflict of interest that the cable companies exploit to the degree that they can get away with it. Government policy sets the rules of the game, determining whether, for instance, cable companies can own specialty channels.

Satellite radio is an interesting recent case in point. In the fall of 2005 the CRTC licensed two services in Canada, Sirius radio and XM Radio Canada. The CRTC initially ruled that the services would be required to carry at least eight original channels produced in Canada, 25 per cent of which were to be in French, and a maximum of nine foreign channels for each Canadian one. After some protest by citizens' groups and a referral back to cabinet the services agreed to increase the Canadian content.

There is a significant international component to policy issues. For instance, while different countries have different laws on free speech, privacy, access to information, and so forth, the internet breaks through those laws by being universally available. Were international bodies truly out to respect the laws and cultures of member nations, great effort would be expended to find a way of building 'metatags' on information so that its flow could be controlled. However, this is on no agenda of any international body with any power.

DATA AND METADATA

The separation of information about a phenomenon and the phenomenon itself reorganizes space and power because control is most likely to reside where the information (and control) reside. This separation can also be termed a separation of data from metadata, or, less usually, content from metacontent where 'meta' means 'of a higher order'. Consider a few examples of the separation of data and metadata. A thermostat exists in the living area of a house and a furnace in an out-of-the-way corner, perhaps the basement. The thermostat gathers the data, the temperature. It then feeds that information to a control system that determines whether the air is above or below the pre-set temperature (the metadata): it then sends a signal to a switch on the furnace to turn it off or on. Another example is a public library. A library physically houses thousands and thousands of books. But a library also manages a large database: the catalogue of its books. With digital technology, it becomes more and more possible to manage the catalogue, making even more information available and adding value at several points. It does not, however, help with the physical collection; many libraries today struggle to keep the actual physical collection in sync with the catalogue. A third example is perhaps the oldest: the census a government takes to keep track of its citizens. It is probably impossible to serve the individual and at times idiosyncratic needs of several million people living out their lives independently, so a central institution like a government must represent them centrally, on paper in a computer file. With at least a basic set of metadata about the population—e.g., age structure, family status and size, income range, workforce structure, mother tongue—government can make decisions based on its assessment of what that population actually wants or needs. The question, of course, is how well the metadata represent the reality of the people out there.

In each case, local phenomena and knowledge are replaced with knowledge further away from the phenomena. This replacement of one kind of knowledge in the hands of one set of people with another kind of knowledge in the hands of another set of people (or machines) can have far-reaching consequences. Particular local knowledge—a whole information system, based on a vast storehouse of information coded in behaviour, feelings, superstitions, and understandings used to retrieve the past, explain the present, and foretell the future—is set aside. Relevant data are identified, metadata (decision-making) models created, monitoring programs set in place, laws passed, and authority anointed. In this process knowledge is formalized, and communication and information-processing systems are put in place to focus power on those with formal knowledge. This process can, and often does, eclipse local culture. It shifts control from a multiplicity of scattered points, each in close proximity to a phenomenon, to a central location that controls activities in a far-flung hinterland. Ideally, the centralization of control improves things for everyone. However, as illustrated, for example, by the federal government's control over both the east coast cod fishery and the west coast salmon fishery, through inadequate systems and technological hubris both fisheries have been negatively impacted. The Newfoundland fishery was effectively destroyed even as fishers were arguing for years that the fish were disappearing. Centralization of control can have its downside.

Once the central processing centre has gained appropriate levels of information, it can begin to replace the on-location decision-maker. The central processing centre can also introduce a further level of sophistication. It can bring in information about other locations—for instance, the state of world production, the state of markets, or even the state of government subsidies or restraints in other countries. It may even be able to predict events more accurately based on its knowledge of distant but related events.

The social and economic impact of the separation of data and metadata is extensive. First, metadata become a separate product that can be bought and sold. Second, as noted, increased power accrues to the location of the metadata. Third, homelands of indigenous peoples distant from the centres of power and control are turned into frontiers of industrial society, whether in the Arctic (now a source of both oil and diamonds) or the Amazon (increasingly a source of minerals and useful plant-based drugs). This kind of top-down, instrumental logic in the service of greater efficiency and control was powerfully critiqued by philosopher Martin Heidegger in the 1940s, who saw

KNOWLEDGE FRAMEWORKS AND UNDERSTANDING

An article in a recent issue of *The New Yorker* tells the story of Ted Ames, who was born into a fishing family on the Maine coast. As a result of his small stature his parents encouraged him to obtain an education. Because of his close connection to his family and community, he pursued biology in the hope of obtaining a job related to the fishery. In the course of his studies he realized that the centralized knowledge that science brought to the east coast fishery neglected the wisdom of generations of fishers. Sampling techniques, for example, took no account of spawning grounds and fish behaviour. It was as if any patch of fish habitat was equal to any other patch. Ames's research led him to some work done at Memorial University of Newfoundland that identified the spawning grounds of cod. The findings were surprising in that, just like salmon, it seems that cod return to their place of birth to reproduce. The problem is that bottom-dragging trawlers have been destroying the spawning grounds, and those that are left, or that have recovered to some degree, are less and less known to modern fishers with their sonar. In short, both scientists and fishers were losing the local (or traditional) ecological knowledge of fish behaviour so neither group had any particular wisdom on how to rebuild the cod fishery.

Ames decided that this knowledge could be and needed to be captured. By interviewing older fishers, he combined their wisdom with his knowledge of biology and, as an ethnobiologist and practising fisherman, received a half-million-dollar 'genius' award from the MacArthur Foundation in the process. The result: a fuller understanding of the factors influencing the reproduction and survival of cod and more informed efforts towards the recovery of the fishery in the Gulf of Maine.

Source: Wilkinson (2006); see also www.fishhistory.org/publicPapers.php.

the natural and traditional world increasingly framed as resource stockpiles. Whatever intrinsic value might have been there, Heidegger opined, had been subsumed into an all-consuming rationality.

The Special Case of the Internet

The internet presents challenges for traditional conceptions of communication technology and industries, in its starting assumptions, its structure, and the ways in which people are using it. The sheer size of the internet today means that how it differs from older communication models represents a major shift in the way we must think about communication media.

The foundations of the internet were laid in the United States in the 1960s, when large amounts of Cold War-era government funding were poured into the new computer science departments at American universities. Researchers at the time were interested in developing interactive computing. The original ARPAnet project (*circa* 1969) connected computer systems at five US universities, enabling information exchange and message-sending between them. This project grew into the 'internet' through the 1970s and early 1980s, by which time most of the underlying technological infrastructure in use today had been worked out.

In terms of the evolution of a particular sociotechnical ensemble, a number of interesting features of the early internet shape how it works today. First, the internet was developed as a *peer-to-peer system*; there is no central control point in the network, unlike even the telephone system, which maintains centrally managed switching. The internet, by contrast, is arranged like a mesh or web, in which points on the network are multiply and redundantly interconnected: the route by which any particular piece of information travels is decided by software rather than by the physical connections, and all points on the internet are equals or peers, at least in theory. The internet trades information units called **packets**, which are something like envelopes with 'To:' and 'From:' labels on them. Network software reads these address labels and makes decisions about how to transfer packets along. Furthermore, these packets are like sealed envelopes; the contents are only important to the computer systems at either end of a transmission. The internet is therefore described as an end-to-end architecture, with the network itself remaining ignorant or at least ambivalent about what is being transferred; this is

called **network neutrality**.

An interesting feature of the internet is that it has existed for much of its life as a publicly funded system, first in the US, and today in most other countries as well. However, since the mid-1990s, more of the internet is made up of corporate, for-profit components, while substantial chunks worldwide are still run by governments and/or academic institutions. This has given the internet a different character than large-scale corporate media like television, and effective corporate control of the internet is still limited, though this is in flux as corporate interests make larger and larger investments in internet infrastructure. The internet is certainly not free from large corporate involvement. The dot-com boom of the late 1990s was a gold rush of stock market speculation in companies that were founded to computerize anything capable of being computerized. Investors flocked to ideas rather than viable business and lost a tremendous amount of money doing so. And after the dot-com movement ended (the bubble of speculation and hopes for instant riches burst) in 2001 because there were no viable businesses behind many companies, the largest corporations maintained their investments and profit-making in the internet. The areas of economic growth so far have to do with network provision—that is, the companies that own the connections and charge for access—and the web search engines. In 2005, Google became the largest media company in the world by market valuation (the total value of all shares held): at $80 billion US, it was larger than Time Warner, Disney, or Viacom. It is interesting to consider that this is for a company that most of us use every day without paying a cent.

A second significant feature of the internet is that its underlying technologies have for the most part been developed and released non-commercially as open systems and more recently as **open source** software. This means that the software, standards, and protocols that make the internet run are not owned or controlled by any one party, but, rather, are publicly available just like published academic research. The major internet engineering process has for decades revolved around a system of requests for comments or RFCs. The RFC is effectively a peer-review system where contributions of software and system design are openly circulated, reviewed, and improved upon by a community of engineers much like Wikipedia is open to participation in its content. The result is that anyone wanting to contribute to the process can do so.

Over the past decade, this process has grown into a general strategy for software development, with a rich variety of components available as open source—that is, free for examination, modification, use, and distribution, without typical commercial trappings such as licence fees, trade secrets, or usage restrictions.

This model of systems development has proved enormously successful for the internet itself, but it also has cultural implications. In a world in which works—text, music, video, and so on—are stored and transferred digitally, and consequently can be copied and distributed globally in an instant and for almost zero cost, traditional conceptions of copyright and intellectual property have become increasingly problematic, especially for century-old industries that have grown up around a more traditional copyright landscape. Into the legal battles that result from the technological change comes the open-source movement, bringing with it a completely different sensibility about how and by what terms works should be circulated and exchanged.

With regard to internet usage by the general public, the World Wide Web (as in WWW or, simply, the web) emerged as an internet application in the early 1990s and quickly grew to be the largest user of internet **bandwidth**—the capacity of a network for carrying information. The web provides a friendly interface to the internet, and grew in its first decade to the point where it allows for an almost infinite number of niche audiences to access content of interest to them. For much of the web's first decade, its basic model was a simple page-delivery system. However, its increasing interactive capability, in terms of both web content being served up by user choices and other applications acting more like desktop computer software, has transformed users into webmasters. The biggest trend in recent years has been the rise of **blogging**—ranging from personal diary entries to serious reflective analyses of current issues. The most interesting aspects of the blogging phenomenon are not the content of blogs themselves so much as the sheer numbers of bloggers (the Pew Internet Project released the results of a 2006 survey claiming that there were as many as 12 million bloggers in the US alone; the blog search service Technorati counted 49 million blogs as of July 2006) and the interlinking among blogs, which means that 'what people are talking about' has become measurable in a way never seen before.

The web's status as a new mass medium comes to the fore when we consider the impact of blogging on journalism. It is easy enough to see bloggers as jour-nalists—or at least reporters or editorialists—and the mainstream media have had to take note of this fact, either by attempting to distance themselves from blogging by appealing to ideals of quality, objectivity, and journalistic ethics or by incorporating bloggers in their offerings. A segment of the blogging community (or 'blogosphere' as it has been called) has responded to this challenge by branding itself as 'citizen journalism' and noting that the combined voices of thousands of observers (some expert) have at least as good a claim to objectivity and accuracy as does the journalism profession. The main difficulty with the blogosphere is, like the internet itself, that there is no guarantee of truthfulness or validity of any single contribution. In the journalism profession there is a commitment to certain procedures directed at objectivity, fairness, reliability of sources, and so on (see Chapter 8; also see the discussion of the Maher Arar case at the end of Chapter 12). Dan Gilmore's 2004 book, *We the Media*, has provided good coverage of this phenomenon.

It is important to remember that the web is not equal to the internet, and dozens of other applications or services are used by millions of people daily, from the 'old'—electronic mail and on-line discussion forums—to new forms such as multi-participant role-playing games, peer-to-peer file-sharing systems, instant messaging, and distributed computing systems. Increasingly, we are seeing traditional media formats like video and telephone services appearing as internet-based applications. There are few technical obstacles to these developments; internet-based television content seems mostly slowed by copyright and licensing ambiguities, and internet telephony, or VOIP (voice-over internet protocol), is becoming better known.

Perhaps the most intriguing characteristic of the internet is that no single trend is at work; rather, innovation and creativity seem to be occurring in hundreds of directions at once. Cable TV proponents once promised a coming 500-channel universe. The internet offers millions of possibilities. And, while the internet introduces a new level of decentralization of services and control, it is important to remember that a unified network is a tool that can facilitate an even greater concentration of databases, brands, and discourses.

Technological Development: Rationales and Realities

In societies that embrace technology through their social organization, the freedom of individuals and business is seen to propel technological development. Free to do so, individuals and businesses respond to economic opportunity and provoke our curiosity with objects and the way things work. But for any technology to be seized upon and heartily embraced by society, especially when they are major public infrastructure projects such as the deployment of worldwide communication satellite systems, requires the allocation of resources in the short term with the promise of long-term gain. The usual rationales to encourage our eager acceptance of technology are based on some idea that a particular technology will improve the lot of humankind. The specific areas in which that improvement is purported to arise for communication are customarily health, culture, and education. In health, the wide dissemination of preventive, diagnostic, curative, and emergency information is stressed. In culture, the inexpensive and more extensive dissemination of quality products is highlighted. In education, the availability of better information designed more effectively for the learner, with the possibility of interactivity and supplemented by motivational devices and workplace relevancy, is just a beginning. Other positive impacts are claimed in the areas of self-direction, social interaction, international and inter-ethnic tolerance, and even cognitive skills.

The realities of major technological development of infrastructure are somewhat different, as theorists might predict. As we all know, television and radio can open the world to people at its furthest reaches, especially now with satellite transmission and particularly to areas with low literacy rates. However, achieving the goal of universally available television—'to educate, inform, empower, amuse, and enlighten'—is another matter. Take, for instance, something as simple as the teaching of reading. In other cultural contexts, reading may be regarded as a selfish or indulgent activity insulting to those around the reader because it shuts them out, just as television is seen to do in our own society. There is nothing universal about the appeal of technologies. And in addition to cultural barriers are economic ones. For example, educational programming most often must be paid for by scarce public funds, which means their availability is limited. In contrast, entertainment programs promote consumerism and are commonly funded through advertisements and are widely available.

This is not to discount developments in communication or to claim that they cannot broadly serve the interests of culture, education, and health. However,

neither satellites nor the internet nor any other technology is likely to bring about a new egalitarian world. These technologies have brought about extensive efforts at distance education both in the developed and developing world—for instance, in China, India, Mongolia, Indonesia, and Thailand. In some instances they have been successful in raising the levels of skills and knowledge of students. But the efforts of people ultimately make the difference. While distance education may use computers and digital communication, because such technology can cope so easily with distance, they are not necessary components of distance education programs. Satellites (and wireless communication in general) also have the major advantage that they can help serve large, sparsely populated developed countries or developing countries that lack a land-based communication infrastructure. But again, no amount of technology of any kind will make a bit of difference without knowledgeable teachers and without a nurturing recipient society.

The introduction of computers into the classroom and access to the internet have become symbols of modernization, just as television was a generation or two earlier. The individualization of the learning process has also been stressed. Most importantly, and obviously, these technologies change the nature of the classroom from a closed-off laboratory of learning to a window on the world of organized and spontaneously produced information, opinion, and analysis. The 'One Laptop Per Child' project from the Massachusetts Institute of Technology, which plans to distribute millions of inexpensive laptop computers to children in developing nations, is premised on just such a rationale. Nevertheless, the correlation between the rationale for technological development and how it is manifested in reality is not always true. Nowhere is this more obvious than in situations where technology is introduced from one part of the world to another, where the knowledge of the technology is either limited or non-existent.

TECHNOLOGY TRANSFER

The export of new technologies from one country to another, especially from developed economies to developing economies, is usually referred to as **technology transfer**. The problem with most of the thinking behind technology transfer is the tendency to reduce technology to 'machines' or 'devices' and to ignore the wider social and cultural contexts in play. Indeed, the 'problems' of 'technology transfer' (both problematic terms) have themselves contributed to the development of the richer definitions of what technology actually is that were introduced at the beginning of this chapter.

Research on technology transfer reveals a number of insights. Generally speaking, direct causal correlations between the introduction of a technology into developing economies and changes in social behaviour (for example, between the availability of birth control devices and actual usage) cannot be easily identified. Combinations of technology with other changes can change behaviour. For example, economically speaking (and only economically), in many rural and agricultural settings it is seen as a net asset for families to have more children whereas in a city they are a net expense. Hence, birth control information with a change of circumstances may have an effect as urbanization gradually changes the orientation to size of family.

Relatedly, technically oriented approaches to the introduction of technology (skills training, explanation of the equipment) are limited in their effectiveness. The socio-cultural element is missing in the ensemble. E.F. Schumacher's classic work, *Small Is Beautiful*, has elaborated much of this dynamic. Nor does the local manufacture of equipment in developing economies, designed to give people insight into how it is assembled and a sense of ownership, necessarily remove barriers to its adoption and maintenance. Equipment can be assembled under direction and without any understanding of its operation or how it might fit into the practices and contexts of daily living. The importation of 'turnkey operations'—where the importing country simply opens the box and turns the machine on—often proves of limited value for lack of prior study of the social context. Finally, such transfers, if they do work, often create substantial long-term dependency relationships as the receivers of the technology continue to rely on those supplying it for instruction on its use and maintenance.

In the end, this discussion leads us right back to the beginning. Technology is not merely machinery—each artifact or system is a socio-technical ensemble, in Bijker's words, or, in Franklin's conception of technology, is a social practice.

Technology, International Law, and Copyright Law

By international covenant, countries currently have the right to participate in communication development and also to protect themselves from it, a protection that has been set aside in free trade agreements such as those that apply within the European Union. For example, should an unwanted satellite signal spill over so that it is transmitting inside its boundaries, a country can object. Japan has adjusted some of its satellite footprints in response to such objections. Shaping the footprint of Rupert Murdoch's Star TV satellites is just one of the restrictive conditions under which the Murdoch conglomerate operates in China.

Countries have the power also to forbid the importation or exportation of any other form of information, either material or immaterial. These rights to protect groups, which are largely dependent on national status, are termed **collective rights**.

Existing in tension with these collective rights are **individual rights**. Building from the foundation of the United Nations' Universal Declaration of Human Rights (paragraph 19), all individuals have the right to 'seek, receive and impart information'. The challenge is this: while the collectivity has the right to act in its own interests, individuals within the collectivity have the right to do so as well, and these interests may be contrary to those of the collectivity as a whole. Thus, while Canadians as a group might want regulation to ensure a predominance of Canadian broadcast signals, many individual Canadians might want the freedom to choose what broadcast signal to tune into. Once individual rights to 'seek, receive and impart', especially to 'impart', are extended to commercial information producers and then extended to corporations on the basis that corporations have the status of persons (in most legal respects), problems arise. Not only is there the force of individuals who do not want the state to interfere with individual freedoms but also corporations avidly pursue their 'individual freedom'. This pits the political, social, and cultural interests of the collectivity against the demands of producers, both individuals and business interests.

Technological developments represent a continual challenge for legal systems and policy-makers. The foremost challenge is to respect both collective and individual rights and to ensure that the greatest number of citizens gain the maximum benefit. At times and in some countries, creating universal benefit means assisting dissemination. At other times in other countries it may mean denying people access to certain technologies and content in order to promote a more universal distribution of other content via alternative technology. For example, in Europe, cable TV was a long time in coming. One reason it was not introduced earlier is that it would have undermined state monopolies (Collins, 1992).

Other rights enter into the picture in technological development. Personal privacy is one. The most obvious example of invasion of privacy is that which takes place when someone with a scanner intercepts a cellphone conversation. Similarly, someone may intercept your credit card number as it is being transmitted along the internet. But other aspects of privacy are equally important. Profiles of individual consumer behaviour gained by tracing a consumer's spending patterns potentially infringe on personal privacy. Indeed, a whole industry is developing because we have the technological capacity to monitor all sorts of information. It is commonly called **data mining**. For now, we should note that determining the level of privacy to be protected and then protecting personal privacy are complex matters.

Protection of 'intellectual property' has also become a salient issue with the digitization of content and the incredible opportunities that now exist for distributing that content. Copyright, a legal and commercial framework that emerged in the era of print, when it was relatively difficult (that is, capital-intensive) to produce and distribute copies of works, now faces major conceptual challenges in a digital world where copies can be made and distributed at almost zero cost.

TECHNOLOGY AND COPYRIGHT LAW

Digital technology, which allows for easy, inexpensive, and almost perfect copying and distribution of digital files over the internet, has brought forward a new dynamic that is a powerful challenge to copyright law. Combined with the manner in which people use the internet—many provide content with no real wish for financial gain—this technological capacity has encouraged an emergent culture of sharing. Everything from the design of web pages to software source code to digitized music and video is shared on-line—sometimes on an enormous scale.

Copyright law begins with a different premise than does the internet, dating back to a time when monarchs and church leaders wanted to control (not to facilitate) the circulation of ideas. Copyright in England, for example, began with the Statute of (Queen) Anne of 1710 (see www.copyrighthistory.com/anne.html). Copyright law vests in the creator not outright ownership but the right to control the copying

of a work. In other words, it is a temporary monopoly property right—the right to benefit financially from the sale of copies of a created literary work—and a more long-lasting, moral right—the right to be associated with the work (e.g., named as the author). In Canada, this includes the right to restrict use of the work in association with other events, products, organizations, and so forth. Copyright law also establishes public or user rights as a way of balancing the rights of society with the rights of the creator. This balance is based on the notion that ideas emanate from the social whole and the individual gives expression to them through the intellectual work of articulating them in written form, photographic reality, or any other copyrightable form. The most important manifestations of user rights are two. First, copyright limits the term of the monopoly property right. Second, it circumscribes creators' rights by protecting only the expression of the idea, not the idea itself; hence, others may paraphrase. It also introduces a user right called fair dealing—in the US the equivalent right (which is not identical to the Canadian right of fair dealing) is fair use. Fair dealing allows users to quote a passage in reviewing or studying a work; it allows a person to make a copy for purposes of study. The fair-dealing principle represents a balancing of freedom of speech (to talk about a copyrighted product) with the property right of the creator—to benefit from the dissemination of his or her work.

In short, there is an inherent conflict between copyright law and the internet and other digital technologies that ease and affirm the sharing of information. Indeed, the operation of computers—which make temporary copies of materials that you see on your screen—is to some degree in conflict with copyright law. So powerful has been the desire for free sharing of information that actual internet practice is in clear conflict with copyright law, so much so that schoolteachers are cautioned against using any internet materials for fear of a lawsuit against their school boards by Access Copyright, the main rights collective of creators and copyrights holders (Murray, 2005: 652).

The reaction to the internet and digital copying technologies by the copyright industries has been assiduous lobbying to strengthen copyright laws and controls on behalf of rights holders because they perceive their interests to be under threat by digital copying practices. In recent years, in various countries waves of new copyright laws have emerged with an aim to vest more and more control with the rights holder and less with users. A common example is the DVD, which is presented as a 'black box' medium that can only be played on a licensed playback device. In the US, attempts to circumvent the technological barriers built into DVDs and playback devices, even for legitimate purposes, are potential grounds for legal action under the **WIPO copyright treaty**. As of 2006, Canadian law allows for circumvention for legitimate purposes, but should Canada sign the WIPO treaty, our law will likely have the same provisions as that of the US.

Copyright holders have also been successful in some countries, notably the EU and the US, in extending the length of time the copyright holder has to benefit from his/her temporary monopoly.

Rights holders and their organizations tend to mount their lobby efforts in the name of fighting personal and commercial **piracy** and distribution of illegal copies by many in the first instance and by fewer larger-scale operations in the second instance. They have been successful in establishing Digital Rights Management (DRM) mechanisms that do not just put a lock on content but involve monitoring and data collection of individual user behaviour without the user's knowledge. This eavesdropping is forbidden in other contexts, for example, telephone conversations, and raises privacy concerns for users (ibid.). It is also worth noting who the negotiators are in setting user rights and what their positions are. As Murray (ibid., 653) points out, they are most often large public institutions and organizations, such as the Council of Ministers of Education of Canada (CMEC), that both counsel against internet use in schools, because some uses may infringe, and also are prepared to bow to strong assertions of creators' rights by Access Copyright (which are very much open to legal interpretation). The CMEC might better stand up for user rights by, for example, 'contributing to legal clarification by defending reasonable interpretations of users' rights, [rather than bowing] to assertions about the law made by . . . Access Copyright' (ibid., 654).

The matter is not simple in that protection that is either too strong or too weak in protecting creators' rights could disrupt communication and cultural industries. Lack of protection of intellectual property allows cheap consumption of products and simultaneously the deprivation of creators of reward for their intellectual effort. Without reward, the creative industries—book and magazine publishers, television and movie producers, sound recording and distribution

companies—will wither and die. Lack of protection also stands in the way of legitimate business in intellectual property in those countries that turn a blind eye to piracy. In India in the early 1990s, so many small theatres were screening pirated videos that the state introduced a licensing system to attempt to garner revenues. Although this was done, the videos shown continued to be illegal copies. However, as Urvashi Butalia (1994) notes, this should not lead to the conclusion that piracy is rampant in all media in India. On the contrary, at least in book publishing, countries such as India have come to realize that their interests are better served by enforcing copyright laws. The film industry of Egypt, for example, is severely crippled by the numerous bootleg copies made as soon as any film is finished. Nevertheless, the motivation for many countries to take decisive action is not strong—the effect of legislation would be primarily to protect the interests of US industries.

So what is being done and what does the future hold?

ALTERNATIVES TO COPYRIGHT

Lawrence Lessig, a Stanford University law professor, has spearheaded a movement to create a legal framework for the sharing, rather than exploitation, of intellectual property. For several years Lessig was on the US university lecture circuit speaking out against the tendency of large corporations to overly restrict the use of copyrighted materials, including cartoon characters. At the same time, he pointed out that those same corporations, and specifically Disney, had drawn inspiration from the folklore of the past for the characters they were trying to forbid others to use. In a lecture entitled 'Free culture: how big media uses technology and the law to lock down culture and control creativity' (see www.free-culture.cc/freeculture.pdf), Lessig articulates four main points:

1. Creativity and innovation always build on the past.
2. The past always tries to control the creativity that builds upon it.
3. Free societies enable the future by limiting the power of the past.
4. Ours (the US and, by extension, the world) is less and less a free society.

Lessig convinced many that there should be an alternative to copyright and his persuasiveness allowed him to form a foundation to which many have donated. That not-for-profit foundation is called the Creative Commons and its main activity has been the creation of a legal alternative to copyright (see creativecommons.org/). The Creative Commons has developed a number of symbols that can be attached to a work to signify what rights are claimed. A double-c inside a circle indicates that it is being made available under a Creative Commons licence. The Canadian version of the full licence can be downloaded from: creativecommons.org/worldwide/ca/. Contained in that agreement is this key section:

3. Licence Grant. Subject to the terms and conditions of this Licence, Licensor hereby grants You a worldwide, royalty-free, non-exclusive, perpetual (for the duration of the applicable copyright) Licence to exercise the rights in the Work as stated below:
    (a) to reproduce the Work, to incorporate the Work into one or more Collective Works, and to reproduce the Work as incorporated in the Collective Works;
    (b) to create and reproduce Derivative Works;
    (c) to distribute copies or soundrecordings of, display publicly, perform publicly, and perform publicly by means of a digital audio transmission the Work including as incorporated in Collective Works;
    (d) to distribute copies or soundrecordings of, display publicly, perform publicly, and perform publicly by means of a digital audio transmission Derivative Works;
    The above rights may be exercised in all media and formats whether now known or hereafter devised. The above rights include the right to make such modifications as are technically necessary to exercise the rights in other media and formats. All rights not expressly granted by Licensor are hereby reserved, including but not limited to the rights set forth in Section 4(e).

The above section is followed by another section on restrictions, and creators are able to restrict use in a variety of ways. As well, Creative Commons has developed a set of symbols that creators can affix to their material (see creativecommons.org/about/licenses/meet-the-licenses).

The Creative Commons is not the only game in town. GNU, which stands for GNUs Not **Unix**, issues a General Public Licence (GPL) and is generally used by software developers.

The actions of large copyright corporations are also being challenged in the music industry in Canada. Terry McBride, the CEO of Nettwerk Music Group in Vancouver, takes issue with the manner in which the music industry is managing itself in the face of a clear desire of fans to be able to choose the music they want and have it readily available to download. McBride has undertaken a variety of projects, including financing the legal defence of a girl in Texas who was charged with illegally downloading and sharing music files. In September 2006 he masterminded the multi-layered release of a Barenaked Ladies album. As well as placing the CD in music stores, McBride sold the individually recorded vocal, guitar, drum, and other tracks so that fans can actually remix the songs according to their own liking (O'Brian, 2006). Nettwerk sells individual songs from its website, but unlike other services there are no Digital Rights Management restrictions, leaving the consumer to do what he or she likes with the music. The website states:

> Litigation is destructive, it must stop . . . . as per Nettwerk copyrights, we have never sued anybody and all our music is open source to encourage fans to share it with others and help us promote our Artists. As per those Artists we manage on other labels (Majors), we take issue with those labels claiming that litigating our fans is in our interest, as it clearly is not.

Achievements in the Information World

Beyond doubt, communication technology is changing the world. Over the past decade many new devices, services, and capacities have emerged to enhance our ability to communicate and handle information. In the process, social dynamics have changed.

INCREASED COMMUNICATION CAPACITY, SPEED, AND FLEXIBILITY

With satellites, optical fibres, sophisticated switching technologies, and data communication engineering, rather than having an ability to somehow get a message from A to B, we now speak bandwidth and nanoseconds. When applied to radio-based communication systems (like broadcast TV), bandwidth used to mean the proportional amount of a particular band of frequencies allotted to any given station or transmitter. The wider the band, the greater the amount of information—and generally the higher the image or audio quality—that can be effectively communicated. With newer packet-switched systems like the internet, bandwidth refers to the number of digital **bits** sent per second and is a function of how fast the switching machinery can operate. More bits result in more information per second (or nanosecond). For example. CD-quality stereo audio is sampled (digitized) at 44,000 times per second, 16 bits per sample, for each of the two (left and right) stereo channels. Without **compression**, this means that a communication system needs to be capable of sending about 1.4 million bits per second to transmit music effectively. Digital compression reduces the number of bits required to represent the information mathematically. The MP3 format, for instance, reduces the requirements for CD-quality audio to about one-tenth (128 or 192 thousand bits per second), which is easily handled by common 'high-speed' or 'broadband' internet services. Hence we now have the ability to transmit music that sounds perfect to our analogue ears, an ability that, as noted in the previous section, changes music consumption patterns and threatens the traditional manner in which the music industry has operated.

Canada is and always has been at the forefront of communication technology, beginning with such events and people as the first phone call made in the world by Alexander Graham Bell from Brantford to Paris, Ontario, on 10 March 1876; the first transatlantic telegraph message from Poldhu, England, to Signal Hill in St Johns Newfoundland at noon on 12 December 1901; and the first radio broadcast, by Canadian Reginald Fessenden on Christmas Eve, 1906. We were the first nation to launch a domestic communication satellite and the government of

Canada has maintained a surprising commitment to both speed and capacity. According to *Computer Industry Almanac* (2005), there are over 6.7 million broadband subscribers in Canada, ranking eighth in the world (behind much more populous countries).

Only a decade ago no one gave any thought to the idea that to reach a person on the phone that person had to be at a particular location, and the person phoning needed to know or find out where the person he or she wished to reach was. With that technology, most people being phoned actually answered. However, with message services and cellphones, users decide whether they will answer a call or turn their phone off. As well, it is possible to initiate a call from anywhere to any other person, no matter that person's location. Indeed, our communication 'grid' has expanded to the extent that we almost forget it is there. From ubiquitous cellular network access for mobile phones to satellite-based Global Positioning Systems (GPS) to the increasingly common and even overlapping wireless 'hot spots' in cities, in the early twenty-first century we are nearly able to take connectivity (and increasingly bandwidth) for granted. The phenomenon of being unconnected to the wider world has become rare. It demands deliberate action and affects social relations accordingly—'she's decided to be incommunicado.'

INCREASED FLEXIBILITY IN PRODUCTION AND DISTRIBUTION

In Chapter 2 we noted that the traditional, centralized, capital-intensive model of communication media has been eroded substantially in the last two decades by digital media. In the late 1980s, desktop publishing brought layout and design of books and magazines to anyone with a computer and a laser printer. In the mid-1990s the web brought a new form of almost zero-cost global distribution on line.

REGINALD FESSENDEN

Christmas Eve 2006 marked the 100th anniversary of the world's first voice broadcast, by Reginald Aubrey Fessenden (1867–1932), a Canadian inventor born in Knowlton, Quebec. Fessenden's technical achievement was the development of the heterodyne principle, a process of mixing modulated radio signals that is still basic to modern AM radio. By his death Fessenden had developed 500 patents that were effectively infringed on

by emerging large corporations such as RCA, the Radio Corporation of America. In 1928, the US Radio Trust finally acknowledged Fessenden's contribution (what would probably be seen as patent infringement today) and granted him the enormous—but at the same time, paltry, given its centrality to radio broadcasting—sum of $2.5 million. He died in Bermuda four years later.

In the late 1990s inexpensive digital tools revolutionized music and video production and independent producers are increasingly able to reach audiences directly via networking sites such as MySpace.com. Generally, we are seeing producers bypassing the traditional middlemen and connecting directly with consumers. The phenomenon is known as **disintermediation**. But as also noted in Chapter 2, a counter-trend is developing. Some call it reintermediation, in which a new breed of filtering agencies is emerging. A good example is Apple Computer's iTunes music store, which presents a new mechanism for filtering, sorting, and, more importantly, promoting music available on-line. YouTube.com is a video-sharing website that emerged in 2005 and allows anyone to upload and tag (by category or keyword) video clips; the direct result is that hundreds of millions of pieces of video are available for free. These thousands and even millions of reintermediators have established their own brand identity and presence. With the burgeoning of content, the traditional challenges of producing, manufacturing, and distributing product are being replaced by the provision of a wide range of content filtered, organized, and capable of being sampled and remixed in such a way that users can find and acquire what they wish, in a form that they wish it, painlessly and for the time period that they feel is appropriate. What makes this possible is not just a wealth of content, but an enormous increase in the amount of readily available information *about* the content, through blogs, reviews, tags, comments, and cataloguing data. As Chris Anderson points out in his 2006 book, *The Long Tail*:

> Consumers . . . act as guides individually when they post user reviews or blog about their likes and dislikes. Because it's now so easy to tap this grassroots information when you're looking for something new, you're more likely to find what you want faster than ever. That has the economic effect of encouraging you to search farther outside the world you already know, which drives demand down into the niches. (Anderson, 2006: 56)

Production services markets are also changing. China and India are emerging as powerhouses of production to Western specifications. It is only a matter of time before they take over an increasing amount of content creation and design and go directly to the market for confirmation. The entire economic system is reorienting itself to take advantage of easy and cheap communication of all kinds of messages around the world.

MODELS AND DATABASES: CONTROLLING THINGS AND PROCESSES

Computers are and always have been about **models**; the earliest computers were used to construct a model to allow projections of reality. Today, the mother of all information technologies is the **database**—most commonly, the relational database that structures information as collections of rows and columns and the web of interrelations between them. By collecting a large amount of real-world data as they occur and placing this material in a database, one can develop a sophisticated model with an immense amount of power to analyze what has gone before, understand what is happening currently, and predict what will happen next. Google's statistically improbable phrases (SIPs) allow discourse communities to be identified and publications of interest to be brought to the attention of consumers. (Perhaps the best explanation of statistically improbable phrases is to cite some examples. Phrases such as 'content analysis' and 'mass communication' are highly probable in documents dealing with analysis of communication and, although used, highly improbable in normal discourse.) No doubt, the spy services of various nations use the same techniques to try to identify and track terrorists or political and ideological enemies. In the aftermath of the 13 September 2006 shooting at Dawson College in Montreal, in which one woman was killed and 19 other people were wounded by a gunman who then killed himself, some wondered whether analysis of websites might allow prior identification of potential murderers. Others, quite rightfully as well, worry about government monitoring of the communications of citizens.

Analyses of databases of information are replete throughout society. Manufacturing relies on computer modelling and feedback. The emerging field of bioinformatics merges computer science with genetics, as researchers populate vast databases with genetic information, seeking to understand genetics through constructing computer-based models of the human (and many other species') genome. The merging of anthropological techniques (ethnography) with biological data into ethnobiology is allowing two different realms of information to be merged.

Such activities are sometimes referred to as 'topsight' and the pursuit of topsight is one of the major thrusts of high technology today. Every electronic transaction is recorded and the sum total of transactions creates a body of data, which, in turn, can be mined for valuable information. This information can then be used by the person who collects it or it can be sold to another party. The direct recording of information also results in a net decrease in the costs of the transactions. No longer is paying for an item one function, assessing the store's stock levels another, counting cash yet another: with electronic transactions all this and more are rolled into one. Yet, effectively, such activities represent a scaling up of processes normal to small business. The small business often knows its customers intimately: 'The usual, Mr Wodehouse?' Computerization of information allows the intimacy of such interaction to be synthesized. Some feel uncomfortable with such machine synthesis, and many would claim it makes a poor (as well as alienating) attempt at knowing the customer or, for that matter, of knowing its product. People who have ever purchased anything on-line from Amazon, for example, have probably recognized the ludicrous suggestions of what else they might be interested in.

Nuisances, Problems, Dangers

With new capabilities and advantages come new challenges and dangers. Though plenty has been achieved in the past few decades thanks to communication technology, a number of interesting problems have also arisen.

SYSTEM VULNERABILITY

Moving to a computer-dominated, digital world introduces certain vulnerabilities, some a result of human intervention, others a result of nature. A major cosmic event involving substantial electromagnetic disturbances could wipe out the increasingly delicate computer systems on which we rely. As well, gophers have been known to chew through the coatings on optical cables! Satellites are vulnerable to the forces of the universe, as Canada learned when two of its communication satellites were hit with cosmic particles.

Just as thieves exist in the real world, they populate the internet. Systems exist to protect sensitive data like credit card numbers (as well as passwords, PINs, and other identity tokens). Usually, such tokens are encrypted before being transmitted over the network. **Encryption** technology uses complicated mathemat-

ics to scramble a message and render it as incomprehensible as possible. Only with the correct key (a number or string of characters) can the message be unscrambled. But, as with locks on doors, whatever can be encrypted can also be cracked, given enough effort. Most day-to-day encryption (such as that which protects your communication with your bank on-line) is crackable. Practical, real-world data security—as with physical locks—is concerned with making things *secure enough* to make it not worth an attacker's while. Nothing is ever 100 per cent secure.

Computer users—especially those using Microsoft Windows—spend a good deal of time and trouble dealing with viruses. While several companies make anti-virus tools, they are only able to barely keep up with new viruses; one can never be 100 per cent safe. Viruses in combination with encryption-cracking schemes can be particularly nasty, with thousands of virus-infected computers being hijacked to participate in a distributed cracking project.

In January 1999 the Air Miles program and its customers were shocked to find thousands of 'confidential' customer files open for viewing to passing web browsers. While the problem was fixed quickly, the vulnerability of information collected by others is well illustrated by this unintentional breach of security—and this example did not even involve outside hackers breaking into the site. Even though the files do not contain credit card numbers, to make them publicly available is an invasion of privacy. Or is it? Why is it not an invasion of privacy when Air Miles compiles that information and puts it to use? Has Air Miles not invaded the privacy of the consumer in the same way in which that privacy obviously seems to have been violated through its public availability? Looking at the matter a little differently, does the number of people who see the information determine if the privacy is invaded? Air Miles and other organizations with which you deal usually collect information with your agreement. It is part of the fine print that you will find in many products and services. Air Miles rewards you with points for giving them this information. Many organizations sell their data lists to others. That, too, can be seen as an invasion of privacy even if the intent of such organizations is not illegal. These are issues that must be dealt with if we are going to address adequately the issue of system vulnerability.

On 21 October 2002 a massive denial-of-service attack was mounted on the domain-name service (DNS) root servers of the internet. It pirated the use of

6,000 ordinary PCs and considerably slowed down eight of the 13 DNS servers. The system was maintained and certain spokespeople were of the opinion that the perpetrators were attempting to demonstrate what was possible rather than bring about the collapse of the internet (News.google.com, 23 Oct. 2002).

SPAM

The term 'spam' derives from a now-classic sketch by the 1970s-era British comedy troupe *Monty Python* (now available on the internet, appropriately) set in a café whose menu includes only items that contain the tinned luncheon meat Spam (and often little else). The term was used as early as the 1980s to describe the flooding of a communication channel with unwanted content, and today usually refers to unsolicited e-mail (often advertising watches, erectile dysfunction medications and other pharmaceuticals, dating and sex services, and get-rich-quick schemes). The key ingredient in spam is simply the extremely low cost of doing it; sending e-mail to thousands of addresses can be done for very little money. The unfortunate reality is that it is difficult to do anything about it; any schemes to make electronic mail systems more spam-proof do so at the risk of crippling an otherwise superbly useful service.

FRAUD

As if attempts to disrupt normal internet activity by technically defeating a system via spam, viruses, and encryption-cracking were not enough, we must also consider the role of human beings in the techno-social internet ensemble and examine the vulnerabilities of millions of on-line users.

One of the most common examples of on-line fraud is called 'phishing'. You receive an e-mail message from your bank or other company with which you have a relationship in which you are told of some new feature or change to their service. All you need to do, it tells you, is to click on the provided link, log in, and update your account. The problem is that the site you are asked to connect to is not the bank at all, and so when you type in your identification number and password, you are unknowingly giving this information to the people behind the scam. For very little investment (it costs little to send an e-mail to hundreds of thousands of people), even a small percentage of people who respond by following the link and 'logging in' can pay off for these crooks.

Extreme fraud involves stealing the identity of another. According to the Ontario Privacy Commissioner, Ann Cavoukian, identity theft is 'an epidemic' in the US. Identity theft involves collecting enough information on someone that the fraud artist can begin to assume that person's identity. Knowing this to be a possibility, people who make extensive use of the internet routinely provide false information in response to the requirement by certain sites and internet services to provide a user identity in order to protect themselves. The relative instability of identity and authentication schemes on the internet leads to opportunities for fraud on both small and large scales. More robust identification systems have not yet been developed, though various parties are working on an 'identity 2.0' system to replace the tangle of accounts, passwords, and partial identities most of us must contend with on-line, and that make easy work for the fraud artists.

INFORMATION WARS

In late 1998 the Pentagon declared cyberspace the fourth battleground, identifying human decision-making as its primary target. The following year, the NATO war on Slobodan Milošević's regime in Yugoslavia (and especially Kosovo) included an 'infowar' component, aimed at disrupting the communication and information infrastructure. One way to do this is by physically destroying or damaging it; another way is by disrupting it from within, both technically and socially.

The American war on and occupation of Iraq has featured a substantial amount of information war activities—both in terms of deliberate sabotage and disruption of Iraqi communication infrastructure and in terms of the careful management of the information flowing into, within, and out of Iraq. One interesting element of the Iraq War was that once the fighting started, there was little discussion of an information war itself but a great deal about the inaccuracies and insipidness of US coverage, a result of journalists being 'embedded' with American and British forces and not having freedom to report on anything beyond that which they were allowed to see and hear. In the lead-up to the war, a certain amount of attention was paid to such traditional propaganda activities as leaflet dropping, and during the war commentators were surprised at how long the Iraqi state television remained functioning. Also, the spirited denials during the war of Iraq's Information Minister, Mohammed Saeed-al-Sahaf (dubbed 'Comical Ali'), that flew in the face of televised reality were elements of an information war.

Of course, the whole pretext for the war was information-generated rather than action-generated. The US claimed that Iraq possessed or was assembling chemical, biological, and nuclear weapons of mass destruction. The US failed to convince the United Nations but went ahead anyway. In light of the lack of evidence of such weapons of mass destruction, well after the invasion per se had been accomplished, on 22 May 2003, US intelligence agencies began an examination of information sources, not as an act of contrition but as an attempt to determine the quality of information-gathering (Lumpkin, 2003). Such a move completely sidesteps whether invasion was justified.

The point to bear in mind with respect to information war is that, true to the notion of socio-technical ensembles, there is no clear boundary between physical sabotage, system cracking, disinformation, and old-fashioned propaganda. All of these tactics are at the core of conflict strategy in the twenty-first century; they merely target different facets of communication.

The 'So What' of Technological Developments

From the beginnings of radio onward the principal debate over communication was a cultural one. The central question was: What are the effects of the media on society? The next question was: How can society ensure that the media speak to the full range of citizens, with their broad range of tastes and desires for entertainment as well as information and enlightenment? The guiding question appears to have changed, however. Now it is: What economic benefit can we derive from developing and applying communication and information technology?

This transformation is no accident. Technology has combined with the search for profit to create a juggernaut of development that, from 1998 to 2001, was seemingly unstoppable. With the burst of the dot-com bubble, development based on information technology has not stopped. It is just more contained and less visible. Added to the pressure of technology and business are the efforts of the large exporting countries—the US, the UK, the leading economic powers in Asia, and certain directorates within the EU bureaucracy. They have been pushing and continue to push economics and trade in every theatre, particularly the WTO (formerly GATT), the International Telecommunications Union (ITU), EU agreements, the

OECD, the G-8, and the Asia-Pacific Economic Co-operation forum (APEC).

Countries such as Canada and France are also enthusiastic players, except that in the name of culture these countries are attempting to secure a lasting place for domestic cultural industries—publishing, broadcasting, film, video, and sound recording. Canada's concerns for distinctive voices and for speaking to all Canadians exist within this economic context of seeking to ensure a vibrant cultural production industry (see www.parl.gc.ca/information/library/PRBpubs/prb0564-e.html).

As art and culture become, more and more, areas of commodity production, artists and cultural producers are being more fairly rewarded for the use made of their work. However, they are also becoming more involved in the exploitation of their works and hence more conscious of markets and exploitation strategies. Today's visual artists, for example, must address several important questions. Should they sell a hundred signed prints of their work or sign a contract for unlimited reproduction with a royalty on sales of, say, 10 per cent? Which will enhance their reputation as an artist? Which will make them richer and allow them to paint more?

At the same time, and on the less pessimistic side of things, with new technologies come new industries and new players. For every business that fell victim to the march of rail and highways, vast new opportunities were created by the new transportation. Similarly, while lots of middlemen and women will find themselves displaced, job opportunities are opening in new industries. No doubt there is and will continue to be turmoil as people are forced to change jobs, and governments certainly should be looking for ways to assist in this transition. But with each new major technological development, there is an increase in wealth, and if governments do their job of ensuring that the benefits of technology are shared, there will be increased consumption and hence increased jobs.

Reflections on Our Technological Society

As McLuhan said: 'We shape our tools. . . .' Through innovation and the enactment of policy, especially in the context of the evolving power of communication technology, we shape technology, as well as its industrialization. And McLuhan added: '. . . thereafter our tools shape us.' Once in place, once closure has occurred, society appears to slip into the determinist illusion—the logic of any particular socio-technical ensemble begins to play itself out within the context of further policy.

Information and communication technology have created a separate sector of society. Separating information and the communication of it—its transmission, its transformation—has made information the action itself. As a result of business firms collecting our shopping patterns, we can be targeted for relevant information rather than deluged with information that is rather irrelevant to our consumer behaviour. By creating databases of ongoing information, firms decrease the work required to make decisions. By the establishment of internet commerce, information in the form of pictures and words facilitates the purchase of goods and financial transactions from the home. At the same time, information-based interaction on a mass scale is reforming our access to entertainment and knowledge—to symbolic production—as well as the range and location of those with whom we interact.

Such technology-based changes take place in Western society under the driving force of capitalism, which encourages individuals to create technology that will accrue profit for them. One result of this capitalist imperative, however, is that countries place themselves in a weak position in the construction of both society and technology. Effectively, they allow the unfettered pursuit of technological and, hence, market advantage and then consider the need to create compensatory measures. In the context of entertainment products, especially the exploitation of attention-grabbing and arousal-enhancing content, capitalist secular society takes offence (in the name of individual freedoms) at attempts by other cultures to protect their social fabric from excessive sexual display. As members of society we become inured to movie and television violence, which, in turn, inures us to the everyday violence in our cities. We hardly blink an eye at city murders that occur daily, yet we obsess over the harvesting of stem cells and over police officers being killed in the name of protecting society against the excesses of some of its members. In the information arena, technology has made possible the out-sourcing of many thousands of jobs to other areas of the globe while immigration laws prevent workers moving across national boundaries to take up employment. At the same time, databases allow all sorts of functionality, including putting a human face on large business by creating consumer profiles and seeming to know the consumer personally, thereby helping to displace small

business and its attendant employment generation and community-building.

As the constructivists make clear, our management of technology could be otherwise directed. Sweden has a system in place that makes it easy for employers to fire workers, but at the same time a far more generous social support system means that these workers' well-being is not unduly threatened just because they don't have a job. Efforts are now being made to encourage environmentally friendly technology, yet similar efforts to promote employers taking responsibility to retrain workers are not discussed at all. If technology, then policy.

Policy is needed. Independent of the need for band-aid policy to ensure privacy and the need of severe disincentives for such non-violent crimes as identity theft, we need to understand in a very broad sense what the reorganizing consequences of a separate information sector are. We must return to Innis's notion of the bias of information. What biases will be introduced into society by the ability to collect information on just about everything or by the ability to copy easily every information package? Acceptable answers to such questions are difficult to imagine because most observers are either enthusiastic about or resistant to new technology.

Independent of what could be done, it is likely that the development of new ways of doing things, new industries, and new opportunities will continue and so will the concomitant disruptions. The internationalization of markets and, hence, globalization, which we discuss in the next chapter, are also issues to observe. Internet-based companies will arise, but whether they will be worldwide or North American in scope, like Amazon.com, national, like Indigo.ca, or local, like your nearby independent bookseller, remains to be seen.

As noted earlier, the intended and unintended effects of technology are wrapped up together. A price is being exacted even as we 'advance'—there is, for instance, more information, but public access to information, especially on a percentage if not an absolute basis, may actually be diminishing. As well, problems are being both solved and created. For example, banking is faster and less vulnerable to human error, but banking systems are less personal and can crash or be hacked into. Many new, increasingly centralized businesses are being created—large, dynamic, national and international companies with sophisticated information systems, as well as internet companies—while old, perfectly fine, friendly neighbourhood businesses are being destroyed. The locus of control is changing, as is the nature of control. And unforeseen consequences are constantly emerging. Who could have imagined computer viruses before they arrived (except, of course, for the hackers and companies that first created them)? Who, 30 years ago, when the futurists debated what we were going to do with all our new-found leisure time, would have thought that the average professional would be working an increased number of hours per day, per week, per month, and per year? As apparatuses of technology evolve so do new professions—the best examples are the database builders and the website designers.

Perhaps changes in the dynamics of work have been the biggest surprise. Those who have work appear to have to work harder, even though technology seems to have facilitated our workplaces and jobs. And many are economically worse off rather than better off. Communication technology has not translated into a net increase of efficiency. Rather, it is just a new way of doing things that seems absolutely unstoppable. Along the same lines, the digital deficit is something to take very seriously as the developed world surges ahead and developing economies do not keep pace.

Summary

This chapter began with some definitions of technology that emphasize the practical, social, situated nature of technology. We reviewed several complementary theoretical perspectives of technology, including instrumentalism, determinism, substantivism, critical theory, and constructivism. We discussed the limitations of the first four and how theorists increasingly see technology as a phenomenon that, like other areas of social practice such as business, education, health, and families, exists within society and can be controlled by society for its own purposes. We noted how machines can be seen as socio-technical ensembles, as phenomena that have technical elements but are social in their application or manifestation. We emphasized how technology changes things rather than solves problems—positive and negative consequences of technology are always intertwined and, to some extent, unpredictable. We also examined closure and how closure on a particular socio-technical ensemble leads to a determinist illusion, that the machine/system/black box could be only the way it finally became.

Communication technology is closely linked to control, and public policy in the past century has had a major impact on the particular socio-technical ensembles and the resulting industries with which we now live. Digitalization and technological convergence have reopened the same policy problems in the twenty-first century. The answer to how to provide for the greatest social benefit, given the technologies and industries currently emerging, may not be a replication of twentieth-century solutions.

We made particular mention of data, metadata, and databases as key concepts for understanding today's information environment. We also described the fundamentally different dynamic the internet brings to the fore and how this dynamic is challenging copyright law.

The social rationales most often used in favour of technological development highlight health and education. On the other hand, the realities of technological communication systems, once they are introduced, involve commercial exploitation. Communication technology, like all technology, does not immediately transfer to developing societies. Some basic concepts in the regulation of communication technology are individual rights, collective rights, privacy, and intellectual property.

The state of communication technology today is nothing short of astonishing. Optical fibres can be impregnated with rare earths, which serve as natural amplifiers, a process called *rare-earth toping*; cable signals can ride free on power lines; kids' toys have more computing power than the desktop computer of a decade ago; and hundreds of thousands of individuals can come together to create vast information resources or to lobby for socio-economic change.

Computers have combined with communication to make location irrelevant to the efficacy of personal communication. Video, audio, data—any kind of information—can be transmitted with ease to any location in the world and into outer space. Production need no longer be highly centralized because high-quality hardware is relatively portable and inexpensive. Indeed, so inexpensive is it and so available are transmission technologies that protection of intellectual property has become increasingly problematic. Ease of communication is creating not a global village but perhaps a global marketplace of producers in which dominant economies can outsource production to inexpensive labour pools.

Previously complex tasks have been simplified and

made less expensive, and new tasks have emerged that were hitherto undreamt of. Objects can be located and maps can be drawn with ease. Vast pools of information are readily available. Behaviour of all different kinds can be monitored and patterns identified that are even a surprise to those whose behavioural patterns are being monitored.

These developments come at a cost, however. Communication systems can be shut down by natural forces and by sabotage. No information is entirely secure because, just as computers can build walls, other computers can knock them down. Active internet users can become unwitting victims of spam and viruses. Their whole systems can be shut down. With copying being so difficult to control, corporations are vulnerable to piracy and sabotage. Individuals can have their identities stolen and any electronic transaction can be accessed by a determined cracker. But at the same time, homing devices can be attached to private property to prevent loss.

Although communication has a cultural component, the development of communication technologies is firmly within the political and economic domain. Canada, France, and certain other nations continue to attempt to preserve cultural communication against the ravages of information and entertainment exporters led by the US. What the final balancing of interests will be remains to be seen. Indeed, the evolving shape of society, as the dynamics of digital communication technologies play themselves out, also remains a matter of speculation.

It is clear that the unintended consequences of new technologies are rarely thought through by the engineers, scientists, and technicians who develop them. Indeed, the consequences can never be entirely predicted. Yet there has been very little consideration of the macro implications of the development of the information sector. This lack of prior consideration is part of the technological imperative, which assumes that any unforeseen problems can be solved in time by ever newer technological solutions. Even today, for example, we hear such arguments in regard to climate change and environmental degradation. The blithe acceptance by society of technology because it means economic gain, at least for some, blinds us to considering the desirability of technological developments, whether those developments involve health, entertainment, war, fashion, or life itself.

RELATED WEBSITES

Backbone Magazine: www.backbonemag.com/
Backbone is a Canadian magazine with insights into technology and the web.

Book distribution: www.amazon.com; www.indigo.ca; www.chapters.ca
Competing with the huge American on-line bookseller, Amazon.com, is Chapters/Indigo.

CA*net: www.canet3.net/
The CA*net website carries a wealth of information on Canada's data network.

Lawrence Lessig's Creative Commons: creativecommons.org
Lessig's creative commons site is a good lead into any discussion of copyright in the context of new technologies.

MP3: www.mp3.com; www.emusic.com; www.2look4.com
These are websites where one can download MP3 files or obtain software to transform CD tracks into MP3 files. A history of MP3 technology can be found at: www.du.edu/~bopulski/paper.htm. Technical background on the technology can be found at: www.iis.fraunhofer.de/amm/index.html.

Music on-line: www.musicmaker.com; www.customdisc.com; www.theiceberg.com
In 1998 the first two sites listed began providing more than 100,000 legally licensed song tracks by a wide range of artists. Visitors to the sites can pick out tunes and have the on-line companies create custom-compiled CDs to order. The iceberg site uses the internet to broadcast specialized music formats to interested users. Apple has now added its own system.

Convention on Protection and Promotion of Diversity of Cultural Expressions: www.parl.gc.ca/information/library/PRBpubs/prb0564-e.html
This site provides background and analyzes Canada's interests with respect to the convention.

Recording Industry Association of America: www.riaa.com
The RIAA argues against the MP3 trend and has mounted a lawsuit against MP3 distributors.

Wikipedia: www.wikipedia.org
Wikipedia is a credible source of information about the media, and a whole lot else.

Wired magazine: www.wired.com/
Wired magazine is a wonderful course of insight into the media. It touts Marshall McLuhan as its patron saint.

Zero Knowledge Systems Inc.: www.zks.net
If you are really worried about people tracking your internet activity, this outfit can make your internet surfing a totally anonymous experience with four levels of encryption.

FURTHER READINGS

Anderson, Chris. 2006. *The Long Tail: Why the Future of Business Is Selling Less of More*. New York: Hyperion. An examination of market transformations in cultural goods such as books and music when display/retailing costs are reduced to negligible amounts.

Feenberg, A. 1999. *Questioning Technology*. New York: Routledge. An analysis of the nature of technology, including a review of various theories that attempt(ed) to explain technology.

Lessig, Lawrence. 2001. *The Future of Ideas: The Fate of the Commons in a Connected World*. New York: Random House. Lessig argues that established corporate interests are moving with considerable speed and force to shut down the creative and innovative space that the internet created through such means as copyright law.

STUDY QUESTIONS

1. Using a concrete example, such as broadcasting, radio, the internet, or computers, outline the three elements of technology and how they interact with each other to influence society.
2. With technological convergence there are likely to be ever-larger corporations attempting to take advantage of economies of scale. Working against corporate concentration on the internet is open-source software. What is the state of open-source software development and is it a viable alternative to proprietary software?
3. If technology is developed with humanistic concerns in mind, such as serving the health and education needs of society, why does technology seem to end up serving industry? Provide examples in your discussion.
4. What communication technology developed in the past two years has affected your work or personal life?
5. Is the legitimate use of technology impinging on our personal privacy? In what ways?
6. In your opinion, which theories of technology have the most to offer?

LEARNING OUTCOMES

- To point out that some societies, particularly Western society, are more friendly towards technology than others.
- To point out that, within Western societies, attitudes and approaches to technology vary considerably.
- To explain that technology encompasses machines, professional and technical practice, and social institutions.
- To describe how, rather than solving problems, technology changes conditions.
- To discuss technological convergence.
- To review how policy, both in the past and at present, has influenced and is influencing the development of technology.
- To review rationales that governments use to support technological development.
- To introduce the notion of technology transfer.
- To introduce some key areas of technology policy, specifically, individual rights and collective rights, piracy, and trading regimes governing trade in intellectual property.
- To illustrate some recent technological changes and their influence on society.

PART FOUR

Our Evolving Communications World

CHAPTER 11

Globalization

Introduction

Consistent with the title and purpose of this book, we have been talking primarily about communicative practices, policies, and structures within Canada. If we have emphasized that these practices, policies, and structures are in many ways particular to the Canadian social, cultural, political, and economic environment, it should be clear that they are in no way confined to Canada apart from the rest of the world. In an era of globalization, it is becoming increasingly evident that national communication systems are but subsystems within a much larger and increasingly integrated global communication system, influenced and shaped by extra-national social, political, and economic currents. In fact, we could say that globalization and the information or network society are two sides of the same coin, in that the development of new information technologies has been very much part of the global reorganization of the capitalist economy since the mid-1970s.

References to the term 'globalization' abound in our culture. Our political leaders mention it frequently in their speeches and globalization has become a cliché in the business community. But what does it mean? We define 'globalization' as the set of processes by which social and economic relations extend further than ever before, with greater frequency, immediacy, and facility. More specifically, 'globalization' refers to the increased mobility of people, capital, commodities, information, and images associated with the post-industrial stage of capitalism; with the development of increasingly rapid and far-ranging communication and transportation technologies; and with people's improved (though far from universal) access to these technologies. Simply, globalization means we are more closely connected to the rest of the world than ever before in history, even if these connections have significant gaps and are not shared equally by all Canadians, let alone by all citizens of the world.

The activities and institutions we have described under the heading of 'mass communication in Canada' are not, and never have been, exclusively Canadian. Canadians' communicative practices—letters, telephone calls, magazines, newspapers, books, music

recordings, television programming, and films—have always been tied into international circulation. Federal and provincial cultural policy always has been informed both by universal covenants—e.g., freedom of expression, the sharing of the radio broadcast spectrum—and by the policies (sometimes compatible, sometimes adversarial) of neighbouring jurisdictions. Canadian media institutions—radio, television, cinema, music recording, newspaper publishing, and magazine and book publishing—were established and have continued to evolve in the context of other national media (particularly those of the United States). What distinguishes the current epoch is that the reach and the speed of the mass media have increased so dramatically that borders, which in the past partially shielded any one nation's mass media from those of other nations, have either crumbled entirely or have become increasingly porous. Distance is less an impediment to communication than it has been before.

Many are tempted to look at technological innovation as the principal, if not sole, determinant of this global integration; but if technology has played an undeniably significant role in enabling global communications, so, too, have communication law and cultural policy, trade liberalization, and changing social and cultural conditions. This chapter examines globalization in broad terms and considers what globalization means for how we live and how we communicate.

Defining Terms

While globalization often refers to the world's increased economic interdependence—formalized by the World Trade Organization (WTO), the North American Free Trade Agreement (NAFTA), the European Union (EU), etc.—the term refers equally to political, social, cultural, and environmental interdependence. In the workplace, for example, globalization means that many of us work for companies with operations in a number of countries around the world. The specific job we do may be part of a production process organized as a transnational assembly line, and the product or service we offer probably is destined for export markets. Thomas Friedman (2005: 414–38) cites the example of Dell Computers, whose just-in-time production process includes designers, parts suppliers, and assembly stations in six countries.

In the political arena, globalization means that governments are increasingly implicated in events that occur well beyond their own borders. Whether the misfortune is famine, disease, war, or natural disaster, political leaders feel increasingly compelled to aid countries many of us cannot easily locate on a map. As this chapter was being written, politicians were re-evaluating Canada's military mission in Afghanistan and UN Special Envoy Stephen Lewis was criticizing the great disparity between Western countries' military spending in the Middle East and central Asia and their feeble commitments to fighting the spread of HIV/AIDS in Africa.

In the social sphere, globalization means that friendships and family ties extend around the world and that our neighbours come from half a dozen different countries, speak different languages, and worship within different religions. When we shop, we buy clothes made in China, wine made in Chile, and furniture made in Sweden. This means that we are increasingly implicated in world affairs, and not merely through our shopping and buying habits. When Israel re-invaded Lebanon in the summer of 2006, the bloodshed that ensued touched the lives of Canadians with direct ties to those countries; eight members of a Montreal Lebanese family were killed in the Israeli bombing, and thousands of Canadians on extended visits eventually escaped the region at government and, therefore, taxpayers' expense on Canadian and Canadian-hired ships. When Italy won the 2006 World Cup, there were celebrations of comparable fervour in Toronto, Montreal, Vancouver, and Rome.

CANADA'S CHANGING FACE

It should be clear by now that covering Canada, with its vast geography and scattered population, is one of the greatest challenges facing media organizations, whether their content field is music, news, or dramatic entertainment. That task has become even more daunting in an era of globalization when the Canadian population is more heterogeneous than at any time in its history. In releasing its 2001 census figures, Statistics Canada (2003a, 2003b) reported that visible minorities now constitute 13.4 per cent of the Canadian population and the proportion of foreign-born Canadians is 18.4 per cent, the highest level in 70 years. There are more than 200 ethnic groups represented in Canada. Demographers predict that, if current immigration and birth-rate trends continue, visible minorities will comprise 20 per cent of the Canadian population by 2016 (Anderssen, 2003).

These figures are even higher in urban centres such as Toronto, Vancouver, and Montreal, which received almost three-quarters of immigrants to Canada in the 1990s. In Toronto, 44 per cent of the population is foreign-born, making it the most ethnically diverse city in North America. Visible minorities comprise 21.6 per cent of the population of British Columbia and 19.1 per cent in Ontario. Some analysts perceive two Canadas: one in cities like Regina, where the majority are descendants of Aboriginal Canadians and early European settlers; the other in cities like Richmond, BC, where visible minorities (mostly Chinese and South Asians) account for nearly 60 per cent of the population (Galloway, 2003).

But if past performance is any guide, it is unlikely that Canada's media organizations are ready to accommodate such diversity, whether in their hiring practices or in their representational strategies. As we noted in Chapter 9, an astonishing 97.7 per cent of Canada's journalists are white, and it is rare to see visible minorities occupying prominent roles in Canadian television drama. We rarely see Canadians of colour in news coverage unless the news item specifically concerns race, and non-whites remain subject to stereotypical portrayals in dramatic film and television programming and advertising.

This is a matter of great concern because, as Henry et al. (2000: 296) note, the media 'are major transmitters of society's cultural standards, myths, values, roles, and images.' Because racial minority communities tend to be marginalized in mainstream society at large, 'many white people rely almost entirely on the media for their information about minorities and the issues that concern their communities.'

It is a particularly important issue for Canadians, because the communications media have been assigned such a central role in creating a sense of national community, a theme that permeates federal cultural policy. As a socializing institution, the media of mass communication either can continue to exclude people of colour and exacerbate racism and xenophobia, or they can become more inclusive, reflecting Canada's changing face and facilitating our ongoing demographic transformation.

In the cultural sphere, globalization means that some Hollywood movies are as popular in Tokyo and Madrid as they are in Los Angeles. It also means that we come into contact with more and more cultures through such activities as vacation travel and foreign-language acquisition. Newsstands and bookstores, at least in urban centres, offer newspapers, magazines, and books from around the world in several languages; shops specialize in international recorded music and in movies from various parts of the world. The internet connects us to on-line radio stations and podcasts from places we've never been. What we consider to be Canadian art and cultural performance are increasingly infused by an array of international influences. Indeed, many of Canada's leading writers and performers have their roots in such far-flung places as the Philippines, the Caribbean, Egypt, India, and Sri Lanka.

In the environmental sphere, we are increasingly aware that how we use natural resources—air, water, land, minerals, trees, fish—in one corner of the world has significant implications for the rest of the planet. Debates over the Kyoto Accord, an international agreement to reduce greenhouse gas emissions, symbolize both the difficulty and importance of collective struggles to come to terms with how we are degrading the global environment. The quick spread of certain diseases—SARS, HIV/AIDS, Avian influenza, tuberculosis—similarly underscores the relatively close proximity of the world's peoples. A deadly disease originating in rural northern China can reach rural southern Canada within a few days (see Norton, 2007: ch. 9).

The term 'globalization' can be misleading, however, because it suggests that all significant social relations now occur on a global scale. Clearly, this is not so. What the term more properly refers to is an intensified relationship between social activity on local and global scales (Massey and Jess, 1995: 226). Once predominantly local, face-to-face, and immediate, social interactions now commonly stretch beyond the borders of our local community so that 'less and less of these relations are contained within the place itself' (Massey, 1992: 6–7). While we still talk to our neighbours when we meet them on the street, we also communicate regularly with friends, relatives, and associates—by phone, by e-mail—at the other end of the country and on the other side of the world.

Many of the features of globalization are not new. International migration is not new, nor is the mobility of investment capital or the global circulation of cultural products. What is new about globalization is its intensity: the expanded reach, facility, and immediacy of contemporary social interactions. The migration of people, whether regional, intranational, or international, whether voluntary or forced, has become a more common experience, and many of those who migrate return frequently to their countries of origin. Russell King (1995: 7) notes: 'Nowadays, in the western world, only a minority of people are born, live their entire lives and die in the same rural community or urban neighbourhood.' There is a greater circulation today of people seeking to improve their lives, whether they are refugees fleeing intolerable living conditions, youths seeking educational and employment opportunities far from home, or what King calls 'executive nomads' conducting business in markets around the globe.

Investment capital, too, has become increasingly mobile as companies seek business opportunities wherever they can be found and flee from regions deemed uncompetitive or hostile to free enterprise. Regions of the world are seen primarily as markets—sales markets, resource markets, and job markets—and corporate executives demonstrate less and less loyalty to their traditional places of business. American automakers, for instance, do not need to confine their operations to the Detroit area if cars and trucks can be made more cheaply with comparable quality standards in Canada or Mexico. Similarly, if Hollywood producers find the labour costs of the California film unions prohibitive, they can seek lower labour costs in Canada or Australia. For example, recent Academy Award nominees *Brokeback Mountain*, *Capote*, and *Chicago* were filmed in Canada. Corporations, in other words, are becoming transnational. They are less rooted to their 'home' bases than ever before, seeking greater productivity and improved access to international markets wherever these advantages can be found. In the economic realm, Morley and Robins (1995: 109) note that globalization 'is about the organisation of production and the exploitation of markets on a world scale.' *New York Times* columnist Thomas L. Friedman celebrates this in his best-seller *The World Is Flat* (2005: 8). He perceives globalization as the levelling of the 'global competitive playing field', arguing that 'what the flattening of the world means is that we are now connecting all the knowledge centers on the planet together into a single global network, which—if politics and terrorism do not get in the way—could usher in an amazing era of prosperity and innovation.'

Nowhere has capital been more successful at penetrating world markets than in the cultural sphere. Morley and Robins (1995: 1–11) argue that two key aspects of the new capital dynamics of globalization are, first, technological and market shifts leading to the emergence of 'global image industries', and second, the development of local audiovisual production and distribution networks. They refer to a 'new media order' in which the overriding logic of the new media corporations is to get their product to the largest possible number of consumers.

Media images also serve as a reminder of how far our social interactions stretch, the extent to which those relations are technologically mediated, and the implications of such mediation. Morley and Robins (ibid., 141) observe:

> The [television] screen is a powerful metaphor for our times: it symbolizes how we exist in the world, our contradictory condition of engagement and disengagement. Increasingly, we confront moral issues through the screen, and the screen confronts us with increasing numbers of moral dilemmas. At the same time, however, it screens us from those dilemmas. It is through the screen that we disavow or deny our human implication in moral realities.

The screen metaphor also applies to globalization, which screens out large segments of the population. Globalization's impact is decidedly uneven, dividing people along class lines, in particular. While wealthy, educated urban dwellers have considerable access to the fruits of globalization, especially when it concerns economic opportunity, those with less mobility, particularly in terms of declining employment opportunities and falling wages, are unable to pay the price—whether of tropical vacations or of expensive imports. This inequality is something the cheerleaders of globalization, such as Friedman, exclude from their analysis. Not all of us are in a position to reap the benefits of global interconnectivity because we don't all enjoy the same degree of mobility. In fact, many of us are hit hard by the new-found mobility of investment capital—when, for instance, sawmills are closed in British Columbia and automotive manufacturers leave Quebec because their owners can simply shut down, pack up, and move in search of more beneficial investment climates. Zygmunt Bauman (1998: 2) states. 'Globalization divides as much as it unites; it divides as it unites—the causes of division being identical with those which promote the uniformity of the globe.' An integral element of globalization, Bauman maintains, is 'progressive spatial segregation, separation and exclusion' (ibid., 3). The people to whom companies belong are their shareholders, who are free from the spatial constraints of most workers, and even of nation-states. Like absentee landlords, their mobility creates a disconnect between their economic power and any sense of community obligation, whether local, regional, or national (ibid., 8–9). Thus, some people are full participants in, and major beneficiaries of, globalization processes, while a great many others are excluded from the benefits. Indeed, if they are implicated at all, it is as victims of the instability that globalization has created.

Mass Media as Agents of Globalization

Sophisticated and accessible transportation and communication technologies have enabled globalization. If you will recall our discussion of Harold Innis's theories of communication in Chapter 1, transportation and communication networks have the ability to 'bind space', to bring people and places closer together. They enable people to maintain close contact in spite of their geographical separation. Airline connections between major cities can fly business leaders and politicians to a meeting in another city and bring them home in time for dinner. Frequent e-mail communications connect friends and colleagues in remote locations, minimizing the implications of their actual separation.

In business, organizations need no longer be based on the Fordist model, in which assembly-line operations take place in a single, all-encompassing factory. The particular activities involved in the assembly of a product can now be dispersed globally to take advantage of cheap labour, ready supplies of resources, and/or lax regulatory environments. Or, the production process can be moved closer to markets to minimize distribution costs. Through telephone contact, e-mail, fax, and video conferencing, managers can maintain two-way communication with remote operations, disseminating instructions to sub-managers and receiving from them regular progress reports. If need be, the manager can hop a plane for a brief, on-site visit.

Since the end of World War II, increasing mobility has created a new layer of international governance to co-ordinate the increasing number of integrated spheres of activity. Initially this meant the creation of the United Nations in 1945, which deals with military, economic, health, education, and cultural affairs between states. Today the list of international governing agencies includes the North Atlantic Treaty Organization (NATO), the World Trade Organization (WTO), the Association of Southeast Asian Nations (ASEAN), the Asia-Pacific Economic Co-operation group (APEC), the African Union, the Group of Eight (G-8), the Latin American Integration Association (LAIA), the European Union (EU), and many others.

The flip side of this international co-operation is international interference in cases where states' interests conflict. As the 1998–9 dispute between Canada and the United States over magazine policy made clear, globalization means that national governments no longer enjoy uncontested sovereignty within their own borders. This has significant policy implications when issues such as Canadian-content regulations, proposed quotas for theatrical film screens, enforcement of the prohibition of on-line hate speech, or enforcement of copyright laws are raised. Countries can choose to ignore international law—of which China has been accused with respect to international copyright agreements—or they can exert their political and economic might to derail legislation—as the United States does with any country's attempt to protect its domestic film industry from Hollywood's dominance of theatre screens.

The mass media play three important roles in the globalization process. First, they are the *media of encounter*, putting us 'in touch' with one another via mail, telephone, e-mail, fax, etc. Second, they are the *media of governance*, enabling the centralized administration of vast spaces and dispersed places. Third, they constitute a *globalized business* in and of themselves, conducting trade in information and entertainment products.

While face-to-face interaction remains integral to social relations in even the most globalized of environments—on the street, in the park, at work, at school, at public meetings, at the corner store—proximity no longer constricts our social interactions. Communications technologies like the cellular telephone, fax machine, and personal computer bind social spaces and enable people to maintain regular and frequent contact across distance. This is particularly so as these technologies have become more accessible in terms of cost, ease of use, and availability, and as these media have entered the private sphere of the home. The high speed of technologically mediated conversations approximates

Computers linked to the internet are commonplace in offices today, which permits business to be conducted on a global scale: employees can send messages that are transmitted in fractions of a second; managers at head offices can keep an eye on inventory levels and employee productivity in subsidiaries; and clients can get service through corporate websites that are always open for business. (PCPaintbrush PhotoLibrary)

face-to-face communication. As the promoters of the digital age delight in telling us (e.g., Negroponte, 1995), such media enable us to conduct social relations over great distances, and their increasing sophistication minimizes—though does not eliminate entirely—the obstacles inherent in physical separation.

Similarly, as Innis points out, communication media enable the centralized governance of a political community on the scale of the modern nation-state and the centralized administration of a transnational corporation of intercontinental scope. Both national forms of governance and global forms of capitalism require efficient means of communication to establish a coherent agenda; to disseminate instructions and information; to monitor the activities of remote departments; and to receive reports from local managers or governors in the field. This relationship is one of power, in which an authoritative body exercises control over social space and social order (see Drache, 1995: xlv–xlvi). If a country as large and diverse as Canada is difficult to govern, its governance would be virtually impossible without modern communication and transportation technologies. In decreasing the importance of distance, the scale on which governments and organizations function today can also, paradoxically, isolate nearby regions and peoples, if they are not deemed integral to the networks of governance or of commerce (see Castells, 1999c, 2001).

Finally, the media have become a central constituent of globalization in what is called the 'information age'. This means, first, that the cultural industries are conducting a greater proportion of global trade by serving as the conduits for the exchange of information and entertainment commodities. The communication and information sector of the world economy accounted for 18 per cent of global trade in 1980 and steadily increased its share through the 1980s and 1990s (Herman and McChesney, 1997: 38). Second, information and ideas are increasingly important to an economy that has become dependent on innovation in all industrial sectors. Ideas that can lead to new product development, greater productivity, and the expansion of markets have become essential to maintaining growth in a capitalist economy. Corporate management guru Peter Drucker (1993: 8) maintains that the 'basic economic resource' is no longer capital, or natural resources, or labour, but knowledge. 'Value is now created by "productivity" and "innovation", both applications of knowledge to work.'

The economic role that the mass media have come to play has considerable implications for how we define communication (as 'commodity' or as 'cultural form', as discussed in Chapter 8), for who gets to speak (on both the individual and the collective levels), and for what kinds of messages become privileged. As Edward Herman and Robert McChesney (1997: 9) state:

> We regard the primary effect of the globalization process . . . to be the implantation of the commercial model of communication, its extension to broadcasting and the 'new media', and its gradual intensification under the force of competition and bottom-line pressures. The commercial model has its own internal logic and, being privately owned and relying on advertiser support, tends to erode the public sphere and to create a 'culture of entertainment' that is incompatible with a democratic order. Media outputs are commodified and designed to serve market ends, not citizenship needs.

By making information an exploitable resource, the democratic ideal of free speech and freely circulating information has been transformed (at least in many sectors) into the media proprietors' freedom to exploit world markets with that speech and with that information. This transformation has created the network that benefits the global entertainment and information industries. However, these industries tend to produce and distribute specific types of entertainment and information while neglecting other, less profitable, but no less important communication products. In the media view, people no longer constitute audiences or polities so much as they comprise markets. If the overwhelming purpose of assembling audiences becomes to sell those audiences to advertisers, or sell those audience members' names and personal information to marketing firms, then some people—those with disposable income—will become much more valuable as consumers of communication products than other people—those without disposable income—and will thus be better served by these media.

This problem is offset somewhat by the emergence of individuals and small public-service organizations seeking to employ the same communication technologies for quite different purposes—perhaps to combat economic globalization or militarism, or to support environmental or human rights measures.

The same technologies that allow the BBC to broadcast internationally also allow Human Rights Watch to communicate with citizens all over the world, even if independent bloggers, podcasters, and independent-media groups cannot bring the same resources to the arena as News Corp. or Sony. Real News, for example, proposes to use the internet (as well as satellite, digital television, and community-access TV channels) to produce a non-profit global news and current affairs network that will be independent of corporate influence (see www.iwtnews.com).

Global Information Trade

Like other aspects of globalization, the cultural sphere is witnessing the expansion and intensification of a trend that already has a substantial history. This history reveals that international cultural exchanges have always been uneven, with a few sources of communication serving many destinations. This asymmetry intensified dramatically in the second half of the twentieth century as large media companies exploited their increased capacity to reach far-flung markets, treating the world as 'a single global market with local subdivisions'. Herman and McChesney (1997: 41) write:

> The rapidity of their global expansion is explained in part by equally rapid reduction or elimination of many of the traditional institutional and legal barriers to cross-border transactions. They have also been facilitated by technological changes such as the growth of satellite broadcasting, videocassette recorders, fiber optic cable and phone systems. Also criticially important has been the rapid growth of cross-border advertising, trade and investment, and thus the demand for media and other communication services.

Terhi Rantanen (1997) points out that a handful of European news agencies—Havas, Reuters, Wolff—began to dominate global news coverage in the mid-1800s. Herman and McChesney (1997: 12) note that the development of the telegraph and submarine telegraph cables in the mid-nineteenth century meant that, for the first time, information could reliably travel faster than people.

> From the beginning, global news services have been oriented to the needs and interests of the

wealthy nations which provide their revenues. These news agencies were, in effect, the global media until well into the twentieth century, and even after the dawn of broadcasting their importance for global journalism was unsurpassed. Indeed, it was their near monopoly control over international news that stimulated much of the resistance to the existing global media regime by Third World nations in the 1970s.

Herman and McChesney (ibid., 13–14) describe the film industry as 'the first media industry to serve a truly global market'. By 1914, barely 20 years after cinema was invented, the US had captured 85 per cent of the world film audience, and by 1925 American films accounted for 90 per cent of film revenues in Great Britain, Canada, Australia, New Zealand, and Argentina, and over 70 per cent of revenues in France, Brazil, and the Scandinavian countries.

Such developments have been criticized as instances of media imperialism—the exploitation of global media markets to build political, economic, and ideological empires of influence and control. If what used to be called media imperialism is now described in the more palatable language of media globalization, concerns nevertheless remain that the mass communication sphere has come to be dominated by 50 of the world's largest media companies, the majority of them based in Western Europe and North America (McChesney, 1998: 13).

The point we wish to underline here is that the interdependence characteristic of globalization is rarely symmetrical. The flow of information and entertainment products is decidedly uneven, creating a situation in which a few countries produce and profit from the vast majority of media content, leaving most of the world, to a great extent, voiceless. The United States, for example, is the world leader in the production and dissemination of cultural products, and has since the 1940s adopted an aggressive posture in promoting the uninhibited flow of information and entertainment products worldwide. As Table 11.1 indicates, Hollywood films dominate box offices around the world. Any issue of *Weekly Variety* indicates that the theatre screens of the world have become a global market for the same Hollywood films we see in North America, although in some countries, such as France and Japan, audiences support indigenous films. The US information and

Table 11.1 Top Three Box-Office Films, Selected Countries (May 2006)

Country	Title	Country of Origin
Germany	Mission: Impossible III	USA
	Ice Age: The Meltdown	USA
	Scary Movie 4	USA
France	Ice Age: The Meltdown	USA
	Oss 117/Nid d'Espions	France
	Asterix et les Vikings	France/Denmark
Spain	Mission: Impossible III	USA
	Eight Below	USA
	Take the Lead	USA
Australia	Mission: Impossible III	USA
	Ice Age: The Meltdown	USA
	Eight Below	USA
UK	Mission: Impossible III	USA
	Confetti	UK
	Ice Age: The Meltdown	USA
Italy	Mission: Impossible III	USA
	Ice Age: The Meltdown	USA
	Take the Lead	USA
Japan	Umizaru 2: Limit of Love	Japan
	Meitantei Conan: Tanteitachi no requiem	Japan
	Check it Out, Yo!	Japan
Taiwan	Mission: Impossible III	USA
	Silent Hill	Japan/USA/France
	Eight Below	USA

Sources: Box Office Mojo International, 11 May 2006, at: www.boxoffice mojo.com/intl/; Music Charts and Box Office Ratings, 11 May 2006, at: allcharts.org/movies/.

industries at present is commercial television, thanks to satellites, cable distribution, and digital technologies, which are creating more and more specialty channels hungry for content.

Politically, the strong trend toward deregulation, privatization, and commercialization of media and communication has opened up global commercial broadcasting in a manner that represents a startling break with past practice. Throughout the world the commercialization of national television systems has been regarded as 'an integral part' of economic liberalization programs.

Public broadcasting systems, in Canada and around the world, are under siege. Even the venerable BBC, which has come to symbolize the best of public broadcasting, has adopted a commercial strategy. The BBC launched its BBC World Service Television as a global commercial venture in 1991, seeking 'to capitalize upon the BBC brand name, considered to be the second most famous in the world after that of Coca-Cola'. In 1996, the BBC established joint ventures with two American corporations to create commercial TV channels for world markets. Herman and McChesney (ibid., 46–7) write: 'It is clear that the BBC has decided that its survival depends more upon locating a niche in the global media market than in generating political support for public service broadcasting.'

What is emerging is a tiered global media market dominated by US-based companies, which can capitalize on the competitive advantage of having 'by far the largest and most lucrative indigenous market to use as a testing ground and to yield economies of scale' (ibid., 52). These companies are moving from a predominantly US-based production system to an international production and distribution network, localizing content to some extent, but also taking

entertainment industry was worth $350 billion US in 1997 and had supplanted jet engines as the country's principal export (Auletta, 1997: x).

The three media industries with the most developed global markets in the 1990s were: book publishing, with global sales of $80 billion US in 1995; recorded music, with sales of $40 billion US in 1995; and film, which was dominated by the Hollywood studios owned by Disney, Time Warner, Viacom, Seagram, Sony, Philips, MGM, and News Corp. In the late 1990s, the Hollywood production studios were going through the greatest period of expansion in their history. According to Herman and McChesney (1997: 43–5), the biggest growth area among media

Table 11.2 Top Three Albums, Selected Countries (May 2006)

Country	Title and Artists	Country of Origin
Germany	Laut gedacht/Silbermond	Germany
	Wish/Reamonn	Germany
	All the Roadrunning/	UK
	Mark Knopfler, Emmylou Harris	
UK	Eyes Open/Snow Patrol	Northern Ireland
	St. Elsewhere/Gnarls Barkley	USA
	Shayne Ward/Shayne Ward	UK
Italy	Grazie/Nannini G.	Italy
	Confessions on a Dance Floor/	USA
	Madonna	
	Gli Altri, Tutti Qu/Baglioni	Italy
Spain	MÔ/Joan Manuel Serrat	Spain
	Joyas prestadas/Niña Pastori	Spain
	Il Divo/Il Divo	Spain/France Switzerland/USA
Australia	10,000 Days/Tool	USA
	Pearl Jam/Pearl Jam	USA
	Back to Bedlam/James Blunt	UK

Source: Music Charts and Box Office Ratings, 12 May 2006, at: allcharts.org/. Reprinted by permission of the publisher.

advantage of lower costs outside the United States. In the 1980s and 1990s, for example, Canada became an important site of Hollywood film and television production, as American film companies took advantage of the lower dollar and comparable technical expertise north of the border (see Elmer and Gasher, 2005; Gasher, 2002; Pendakur, 1998). The Hollywood animation industry has similarly taken advantage of the cheap yet stable labour markets of India, South Korea, Australia, Taiwan, and the Philippines for the time-consuming and labour-intensive execution of animation projects originally conceived in Los Angeles (Breen, 2005; Lent, 1998).

Herman and McChesney (1997: 52–6) have identified the principal players in the global media market as forming two tiers. The first tier consists of about 10 vertically integrated companies with annual revenues of between $10 and $25 billion US. These companies would include News Corp., AOL Time Warner, Disney, Bertelsmann, Viacom, and TCI. The second tier comprises about three dozen companies with annual revenues of between $2 and $10 billion US.

These companies are most interested in the world's most affluent audiences, the audiences that advertisers want to reach, the audiences with the money to spend on advertised products and services. This means, for example, that the poorest half of India's billion people are irrelevant to the global media market, and that all of sub-Saharan Africa has been written off. '[Sub-Saharan Africa] does not even appear in most discussions of global media in the business press.' Specifically, the global media are most interested in markets in North America, Latin America, Europe, and Asia. China, with a population of 1.2 billion, is the 'largest jewel in the Asian media crown' (ibid., 64–8).

The global media market, of course, does see some two-way traffic. The Globo and Televisa television networks in Brazil, for example, have succeeded in capturing a respectable share of Brazil's domestic market, and their telenovela productions are major exports. Globo owns an Italian television station, has an ownership interest in an American network specializing in Latin American programming, and has joint ventures with AT&T, News Corp., and TCI. Canada, too, has begun to tap export markets in both the film and television industries, even if the financial returns are relatively modest. A renaissance in Canadian feature-film production since the mid-1980s means that directors like David Cronenberg (*Crash, ExistenZ, A History of Violence*), Atom Egoyan (*Ararat, The Sweet Hereafter, Where the Truth Lies*), Deepa Mehta (*Fire, Earth, Water*), Denys Arcand (*Love and Human Remains, The Barbarian Invasions*), François Girard (*Thirty-Two Short Films about Glenn Gould, The Red Violin*) and Jean-François Pouliot (*La Grande Séduction*) have made names for themselves in international film markets. And Canada has become one of the world's leading exporters of television programming. Canada enjoyed record sales at the 1998 and 1999 MIP-TV trade show in France, selling television programming to the US, Britain, Ireland, France, Germany, Australia, New Zealand, South Africa, Israel, Poland, China, Malaysia, and Zimbabwe (Vale, 1998; Binning, 1999).

Theories of International Communication Flows

The predominant explanation for international communication flows has been world systems theory, as articulated by Immanuel Wallerstein (1974). Wallerstein argued that a European, capitalist 'world economy' emerged in the late fifteenth and early sixteenth centuries, an extra-national economy involving long-distance trade that forged links between Europe and parts of Africa, Asia, and what came to be known as the West Indies and North and South America (Wallerstein, 1974: 15–20). The world system Wallerstein described demarcated three zones in the world economy: the core states, whose economy was characterized by industrialization and the rise of a merchant class; the periphery, comprised of state economies based on resource extraction; and a semi-periphery, made up of in-between states whose economies shared some characteristics with both the core and periphery (ibid., 100–27). He argued that 'the size of a world-economy is a function of the state of technology, and in particular of the possibilities of transport and communication within its bounds. Since this is a constantly changing phenomenon, not always for the better, the boundaries of a world-economy are ever fluid' (ibid., 349).

The world system's asymmetry, particularly in regard to trade in cultural materials, drew the attention of communication scholars in the post-World War II period and led to the development of two closely related theories: media imperialism and cultural dependency. Oliver Boyd-Barrett (1977: 117–18) used the term **media imperialism** to characterize the unidirectional nature of international media flows from a small number of source countries. More formally, he defined 'media imperialism' as 'the process whereby the ownership, structure, distribution or content of the media in any one country are singly or together subject to substantial external pressures from the media interests of any other country or countries without proportionate reciprocation of influence by the country so affected.' Media imperialism research grew out of a larger struggle for decolonization in the aftermath of World War II (Mosco, 1996: 75–6).

Cultural dependency is a less deterministic means of characterizing cultural trade imbalances than is media imperialism. Whereas the term 'imperialism' implies 'the act of territorial annexation for the purpose of formal political control', Boyd-Barrett (1995: 174–84) maintains that cultural dependency suggests 'de facto control' and refers to 'a complex of processes' to which the mass media contribute 'to an as yet unspecified extent'.

While both approaches contributed a great deal to documenting international communication flows and drew attention to an obvious problem, neither theory offered a sufficiently complex explanation of the power dynamics behind international cultural trade, nor did they provide satisfactory descriptions of the impact of such asymmetrical exchanges. The media imperialism thesis was particularly crude, assuming too neat a relationship between the all-powerful source countries and their helpless colonies. Ted Magder (1993: 8–9) argues that the media imperialism thesis leads to two distinct questions: 'First, what are the particular social, political, and economic dynamics that establish, maintain, challenge, and modify media imperialism? Second, what effect do the practices of media imperialism have on cultural values and attitudes?' Early media imperialism studies, Magder argues, assumed that the transnationalization of cultural production led to the transnationalization of reception—that audiences around the world would get the same meanings from the same TV shows and feature films. This is not the case. Another shortcoming was its presumption that 'all power flowed from the imperial core, as if the "target" nation were an innocent and helpless victim.' Clearly, some members of the target nation stand to benefit from the economic opportunities cultural imports afford.

Magder qualifies the media imperialism thesis by underlining four points: the imperial centre is rarely omnipotent; the target nation is rarely defenseless; certain actors within the target nation may stand to benefit from media imperialism; and the effects of media imperialism are often unintended and unpredictable. He writes: 'It is not enough to document the internationalization of culture in its various forms; rather the limits, conflicts, and contradictions of media imperialism must also be evaluated.'

While slightly more nuanced, the cultural dependency thesis shared a number of the shortcomings of the media imperialism thesis. Like media imperialism, Vincent Mosco (1996: 125–6) argues, cultural dependency created homogeneous portraits of both the source and the target countries. It concentrated almost exclusively on the role of external forces and overlooked 'the contribution made by local forces and relations of production, including the indigenous class structure'. Cultural dependency also portrayed transnational capitalism as rendering the target state powerless. Like media imperialism, cultural dependency did not adequately account for how audiences in the target countries used or interpreted media messages that originate elsewhere.

Nonetheless, the clear asymmetry of globalization remains an important issue for researchers who study cultural policy and the political economy of communication from a range of perspectives. Current research seeks to account for the heterogeneity of national cultures, the specificity of particular industries and corporate practices, and varying reception practices—how cultural products are actually used by audiences.

Manuel Castells has proposed another way of looking at the contemporary world that places communication technologies at the centre of global economic—and by extension, social and political—interactions. Castells describes a 'network society' that, as its name suggests, depicts a networked, or interconnected, world, which is less inter*national* than inter*nodal*, placing major global cities, rather than nations, at the centre of its analysis.

Castells argues that the internet has allowed people to forge a new kind of sociability—'networked individualism' (Castells, 2001: 127–9)—and a new global geography—'a space of flows' (ibid., 207–8). This interconnected world, then, has considerable implications for the inclusion and exclusion of people and places from the network of global information flows. Internet use, he notes, is highly concentrated within a network of 'metropolitan nodes' (ibid., 228), which become the new dominant hubs of economics, politics, and culture. Castells writes: 'The Internet networks provide global, free communication that becomes essential for everything. But the infrastructure of the networks can be owned, access to them can be controlled, and their uses can be biased, if not monopolized, by commercial, ideological, and political interests' (ibid., 277). For this reason, Castells places new onus on democratic governments to ensure political representation, participatory democracy, consensus-building, and effective public policy (ibid., 278–9).

Saskia Sassen (1998: xxv) sees in this network society 'a new economic geography of centrality' in which certain global cities concentrate economic and political power and become 'command centers in a

global economy'. If Sassen agrees with Castells that this new geography is produced by the internet's most prominent and active users (ibid., xxvii), Sassen is concerned with the conflict that necessarily ensues between 'placeboundedness'—those peoples, activities, and institutions bound to a specific place, often in support of the network infrastructure—and 'virtualization'—those peoples, activities, and institutions capable of exploiting Castells's virtual space of information flows (ibid., 201–2).

A New World Information and Communication Order

Cees Hamelink (1994: 23–8) observes that two features of international communication stand out in the post-war period: the expansion of the global communication system and tensions in the system across both east–west and north–south axes. East–west tensions—i.e., Cold War tensions between the Communist bloc led by the Soviet Union and the Western democracies led by the United States—were most prominent in the 1950s and 1960s. North–south tensions—i.e., tensions between affluent, industrialized nations of the northern hemisphere and the Third World countries of the southern hemisphere—arose in the 1970s as the Third World took advantage of its new-found voice in the General Assembly of the United Nations. A number of UN initiatives led to a proposed New World Information and Communications Order (NWICO), which sought compromise between the American advocacy of the **free flow of information** and the Third World desire for a balanced flow.

The US push for the free-flow doctrine began during World War II when the American newspaper industry campaigned for the freedom of news-gathering; in June 1944, the American Society of Newspaper Editors (ASNE) adopted resolutions demanding 'unrestricted communications for news throughout the world'. Early in 1945, an ASNE delegation travelled around the world promoting their 'free-flow' position. In February 1946, a US delegation to the United Nations submitted a proposal to UN Secretary-General Trygve Lie asking that the UN Commission on Human Rights consider the question of freedom of information. The UN held a conference on freedom of information in Geneva in 1948.

At this stage, the free-flow doctrine met its stiffest opposition from the Soviet Union, which insisted on the regulation of information flows and complained that the Americans' freedom of information position endorsed, in fact, the freedom of a few commercial communication monopolies. Nevertheless, the free-flow doctrine was largely endorsed by the UN, and Article 19 of the 1948 Universal Declaration on Human Rights states: 'Everyone has the right to freedom of opinion and expression; this right includes freedom to hold opinions without interference and to seek, receive and impart information and ideas through any media regardless of frontiers' (ibid., 152–5).

The issue of communication flows was revisited at the behest of Third World countries in the 1970s, when it became clear that the free-flow doctrine was a recipe for Western cultural **hegemony**, as the Soviets had anticipated. Herman and McChesney (1997: 22–4) write: 'By the 1970s the trajectory and nature of the emerging global media system were increasingly apparent; it was a largely profit-driven system dominated by [transnational corporations] based in the advanced capitalist nations, primarily in the United States.' The development and launching of **geosynchronous** communication satellites in the 1960s and 1970s 'fanned the flames of concern about global media.'

> Satellites held out the promise of making it possible for Third World nations to leapfrog out of their quagmire into a radically more advanced media system, but at the same time satellites posed the threat of transnational commercial broadcasters eventually controlling global communication, bypassing any domestic authority with broadcasts directly to Third World homes. (Ibid., 23)

The major global institutions dealing with communication issues at the time—the UN, the UN Educational, Scientific and Cultural Organization (UNESCO), and the International Telecommunication Union (ITU)—all included majorities of Third World countries and sympathetic Communist states. The impetus for a renewed debate on international communication came from the 90-member Movement of the Non-Aligned Nations (NAM). 'The nonaligned position included a socialist critique of capitalist media and a nationalist critique of imperialist media' (ibid.).

The international debate at that time focused on three points, as it still does to some extent. First, historically, communication services together with

evolved information technologies have allowed dominant states to exploit their power. Through historical patterns and enabling technology, such as communication satellites, these dominant states have assumed a presence in the cultures and ideologies of less dominant states. That presence, whether it comes from being the principal source of foreign news or from beaming satellite signals into another country, is strongly felt by developing nations.

Second, the economies of scale in information production and distribution threaten to reinforce this dominance. And any attempt to counteract a worsening situation must avoid feeding into the hands of repressive governments that would curtail freedom of expression and information circulation.

Third, a few transnational corporations have mobilized technology as a vehicle for the exploitation of markets rather than as a means of serving the cultural, social, and political needs of nations. In other words, the large corporations have seized the opportunity to develop and use communication technologies, but they have employed those technologies primarily to exploit the value of audiences to advertisers, and not to provide information, education, and entertainment to these audiences for their own benefit or for the benefit of the larger cultural whole.

Pressure from the Third World compelled the UN to broaden the concept of free flow to include 'the free and balanced flow of information'. International debate over the design of a New World Information and Communication Order (NWICO) coalesced around the final report of the 16-member International Commission for the Study of Communication Problems (the MacBride Commission), established by UNESCO in December 1977 (UNESCO, 1980). The underpinnings of this report are found in two principles that were accepted by a pair of intergovernmental conferences, the first held in San José, Costa Rica, in 1976, and the second in Kuala Lumpur, Malaysia, in 1979 (UNESCO, 1980: 40, 41). They are:

1. Communication policies should be conceived in the context of national realities, free expression of thought, and respect for individual and social rights.
2. Communication, considered both as a means of affirming a nation's collective identity and as an instrument of social integration, has a decisive role to play in the democratization of social rela-

tions insofar as it permits a multidirectional flow of . . . messages, both from the media to their public and from this public to the media.

The MacBride Commission (ibid., 253–68) advocated 'free, open and balanced communications' and concluded that 'the utmost importance should be given to eliminating imbalances and disparities in communication and its structures, and particularly in information flows. Developing countries need to reduce their dependence, and claim a new, more just and more equitable order in the field of communication.' The Commission's conclusions were based on 'the firm conviction that communication is a basic individual right, as well as a collective one required by all communities and nations. Freedom of information—and, more specifically the right to seek, receive and impart information—is a fundamental human right; indeed, a prerequisite for many others.'

The MacBride Commission pointed to an essential conflict between the commercialization and the democratization of communication, and clearly favoured a movement for the democratization of communication, which would include respect for national sovereignty in areas of cultural policy and recognition that the 'educational and informational use of communication should be given equal priority with entertainment.' The report stated: 'Every country should develop its communication patterns in accordance with its own conditions, needs and traditions, thus strengthening its integrity, independence and self-reliance.'

The MacBride Report also criticized the striking disparities between the technological capacities of different nations. Recommendation 27, for example, states:

> The concentration of communications technology in a relatively few developed countries and transnational corporations has led to virtual monopoly situations in this field. To counteract these tendencies national and international measures are required, among them reform of existing patent laws and conventions, appropriate legislation and international agreements.

Finally, MacBride described the right to communicate as fundamental to democracy. 'Communication needs in a democratic society should be met by the extension of specific rights, such as the right to be informed, the right to inform, the right to privacy, the right to participate in public communication—all elements of a new concept, the right to communicate.'

From NWICO to the Present

The MacBride Report proved to be a better manifesto on the democratization of communication than a blueprint for a restructuring of international communication exchange. Even though UNESCO adopted its key principles—eliminating global media imbalances and having communication serve national development goals—the NWICO was poorly received in the West 'because it gave governments, and not markets, ultimate authority over the nature of a society's media' (Herman and McChesney, 1997: 24–6). In fact, the Western countries, led by the United States under Ronald Reagan and Great Britain under Margaret Thatcher, chose in the 1980s the more aggressive path of pursuing liberalized global trade. 'In the 1980s a wave of global "liberalization" gathered momentum, in which state enterprises were privatized, private businesses were deregulated, and government welfare initiatives were cut back.' Even Canada, which was one of the affluent industrialized nations identified by the MacBride Commission as being dominated by cultural imports, began to pursue the neo-liberal agenda of free trade and budget cutbacks in the 1980s under the successive Progressive Conservative governments of Brian Mulroney. Very little changed in Canadian government policy after Jean Chrétien's Liberals assumed power in 1993. Issues like deficit reduction and freer trade continued to dominate the political agenda and the ministers of industry, international trade, and finance enjoyed as much influence over cultural policy as the minister with the culture portfolio, if not even more (see Gasher, 1995b).

International bodies like the World Trade Organization (originally, the General Agreement on Tariffs and Trade) became more important to the major cultural producers than the United Nations—the US and Britain withdrew from UNESCO in 1985—and the rules of the game for international communications were written in such treaties as the North American Free Trade Agreement (NAFTA) and the Treaty on European Union. Herman and McChesney (1997: 30–1) write: 'The political design of all these regional and global trade agreements has

INTERNAL COMMUNICATION IMBALANCES

Even within countries, communication imbalances mean that some regions communicate and others are communicated to. When we refer to the *American* television industry, for instance, we are really referring to an industry based in two media centres: New York and Los Angeles. Similarly, the American film industry might be more properly termed the Los Angeles film industry and is often simply called Hollywood.

In Canada, Montreal and Toronto serve as the country's principal media centres, responsible for most of our film and television programming and book and magazine publishing. Both of Canada's 'national' newspapers—the *Globe and Mail* and the *National Post*—are based in Toronto. Even publicly owned institutions like the Canadian Broadcasting Corporation and the National Film Board concentrate their production and administrative activities in central Canada. Statistics Canada (1998: 11) reports that in 1996–7, broadcasting consumed 80 per cent of the federal government's $1.9 billion budget for the cultural industries, the bulk of which was spent in Ontario and Quebec, 'largely as a result of the concentration of production facilities and related infrastructure located there'.

The CBC's commitment to regional production had been called into question as early as 1957 (Canada, 1957: 75–6) and in her study of the first three decades of CBC television drama, Mary Jane Miller (1987: 327) was unable to discern any coherent CBC policy on the role of regional dramatic programming. The NFB's record on regional production has been even worse. Founded in 1939, the NFB did not establish its first regional production centre until 1965, and it did not have a production presence in all regions of Canada until 1976 (Jones, 1981: 177–8; Dick, 1986: 118–21).

This concentration is especially striking in the film industry. A 1977 study commissioned by the federal Secretary of State (Canada, 1977: 154) noted that 75 per cent of Canada's production companies were located in the Montreal–Ottawa–Toronto triangle and accounted for at least 90 per cent of the country's film production. A number of provinces in Canada, excluded from the 'national' film industry, became film production centres in the 1980s and 1990s by attracting foreign film and TV production on location. British Columbia, for example, which didn't have a film industry until the mid-1970s, has become Canada's largest site of film and TV production primarily by attracting Hollywood location shoots (Gasher, 2002).

Technological factors, too, can affect the quality and equitable distribution of communication services. As much as Canada has tried to institute a broadcasting system accessible to all Canadians, the North has presented a unique challenge. Canada began experimenting with communications in the North because of the irregularity in radio signals. It seems that the same electrical disturbances that produce the northern lights also interfere with radio transmissions. When investigators concluded that reliable communications in the North could not depend on airwaves, satellites became the solution.

Early satellites were designed to enable individuals and communities to communicate with each other. Because the satellites were relatively low-powered, powerful ground stations were required to send and receive signals. Satisfactory results induced further development. The power of satellites was increased, as was their capability of transmitting larger numbers of signals, until it was possible to receive television signals with a four-foot receiving dish. Suddenly, northerners could receive at least as many TV channels as southern Canadians.

been to remove decision-making powers from local and national legislatures in favor of impersonal market forces and/or supranational bureaucracies remote from popular control.' NAFTA, for example, 'requires that government agencies operate on a strictly commercial basis, and it explicitly removes the possibility that governments can take on any new functions.'

The New World Information and Communication Order, in other words, was almost immediately supplanted by what Herman and McChesney (ibid., 35) call the 'new global corporate ideology'.

Its core element and centerpiece is the idea that the market allocates resources effectively and provides the means of organizing economic (and perhaps all human) life. There is a strong tendency in corporate ideology to identify 'freedom' with the mere absence of constraints on business (i.e., economic, or market, freedom), thus pushing political freedom into a subordinate category.

And as the communications media have become increasingly implicated in the global economy, media policy is governed more and more by international financial and trade regimes such as the International Monetary Fund and the WTO.

Changing Notions of Place

The widespread commercialization of cultural production, communication, and information exchange raises a number of questions about the relationship between communication and culture. The perpetual flows of people, capital, goods, services, and images that characterize globalization carry significant implications for how we experience and imagine place, how we define community, and how we constitute identity. Doreen Massey (1991: 24) asks: 'How, in the face of all this movement and intermixing, can we retain any sense of a local place and its particularity?' Globalization has intensified struggles over the meaning of place. This is particularly the case in countries like Canada, whose citizens tend to be more familiar with cultural imports than with the ideas and expressions of their own artists and intellectuals.

As noted above, the various flows we associate with globalization are not new. What globalization has done, however, has been both to increase the traffic—human, material, electronic, etc.—across some borders and to reconfigure others. Thus, for example, the Canada–US Free Trade Agreement was an attempt to facilitate trade across the border dividing the two countries. Although the legal boundary remains, the meaning of the border has changed, at least as far as trade relations are concerned. The signing in December 2001 of the Smart Border Declaration between Canada and the US, whereby the latest communications technology will be used to create a more secure shared border, means that the very term 'border' has taken on a rather changed and less Canadian-determined meaning for the foreseeable future. This applies to cultural exchanges as well; it has become more difficult for Canada to preserve some space within its own market for indigenous cultural products. Technologies like satellite television ignore terrestrial boundaries altogether; satellite TV is confined instead by satellite 'footprints', which mark the limits of a satellite's technological reach.

The heightened permeability of borders has been met, among some, by the desire for a more rooted, or more secure, sense of place. Gillian Rose (1995:

88–116) notes that place has been a privileged component of identity formation. 'Identity is how we make sense of ourselves, and geographers, anthropologists and sociologists, among others, have argued that the meanings given to a place may be so strong that they become a central part of the identity of people experiencing them.' Places, and the experiences we associate with places, both as individuals and as members of a group, inform memory and our sense of belonging. This sense of belonging is critical to understanding the relationship between identity and a particular locale. 'One way in which identity is connected to a particular place is by a feeling that you belong to that place.' We might, therefore, detect a very different sense of belonging between native residents of a place and migrants. Migrants such as refugees and exiles, who have not moved of their own free will, may feel little sense of belonging to their new place of residence.

Culture is another means by which identities of place are constructed and sustained. Stuart Hall (1995: 177–86) argues that we tend to imagine cultures as 'placed' in two ways. First, we associate place with a specific location where social relationships have developed over time. Second, place 'establishes symbolic boundaries around a culture, marking off those who belong from those who do not.'

> Physical settlement, continuity of occupation, the long-lasting effects on ways of life arising from the shaping influence of location and physical environment, coupled with the idea that these cultural influences have been exercised amongst a population which is settled and deeply interrelated through marriage and kinship relations, are meanings which we closely associate with the idea of culture and which provide powerful ways of conceptualizing what 'culture' is, how it works, and how it is transmitted and preserved.

At the same time, Hall explains, 'There is a strong tendency to "landscape" cultural identities, to give them an imagined place or "home", whose characteristics echo or mirror the characteristics of the identity in question.'

> Our sense of place is really part of our cultural systems of meaning. We usually think about or imagine cultures as 'placed'—landscaped, even if only in the mind. This helps to give shape and to give a

foundation to our identities. However, the ways in which culture, place, and identity are imagined and conceptualized are increasingly untenable in light of the historical and contemporary evidence.

If one impact of globalization has been to call into question the notion of 'place' as the basis for identity and/or culture, **postmodernism** and improved networks of transportation and communication facilitate the imagination of communities based on gender, race, ethnicity, sexual orientation, social class, etc. Proximity, in other words, is not a necessary element of identity formation. If culture and identity are not confined to a particular place, it follows that any one place is not confined to a single culture or identity. This has precipitated localized struggles over immigration, language, urban development, architecture, and foreign investment. Mike Featherstone (1996: 66) remarks that 'cultural differences once maintained between places now exist within them.' For example: 'The unwillingness of migrants to passively inculcate the dominant cultural mythology of the nation or locality raises issues of multiculturalism and the fragmentation of identity.' Massey (1995: 48) argues: 'The way in which we define "places", and the particular character of individual places, can be important in issues varying from battles over development and construction to questions of which social groups have rights to live where.'

The conventional container of identity and culture that has come under greatest challenge from the re-imagining of community prompted by globalization has been the **nation-state**. Questions of citizenship and questions of identity have been increasingly dissociated (Morley and Robins, 1995: 19). The emergence of trade blocs in Europe, Asia, and North America and the prevalence of both international and subnational cultural networks have undermined the primacy of the nation-state in contemporary imaginings of community, identity, and culture.

We should not overreact to these changes, however. We still have democratically elected national, provincial, and municipal governments, which continue to pass laws and pursue policies that form the basic framework within which media organizations operate in Canada. These laws and policies are responses to pressures from both the global economy and local cultures. As we discussed in Chapters 6 and 7, laws like the Broadcasting, Telecommunications, and Income Tax Acts, the funding programs of Telefilm Canada and the Canada Council, and cultural institutions like the Canadian Broadcasting Corporation remain pre-eminent in structuring cultural production in Canada. No media industry is untouched by them. Globalization alters the context in which mass communication takes place, but local conditions of cultural production remain pertinent.

Summary

This chapter began with an extended definition of globalization and showed how it was not simply an economic phenomenon, but an intensification of social relations across time and space that touches every aspect of our lives, from how we shop to what we watch on television. We then outlined three roles the communication media play in the globalization process—as media of encounter, as media of governance, and as a globalized business in and of themselves. We subsequently reviewed the predominant theories to explain international communication flows and their implications, beginning with world systems theory, touching briefly on media imperialism and cultural dependency, and concluding with Manuel Castells's notion of the 'network society'.

On this conceptual groundwork, we traced the history of international communication exchanges, concentrating particularly on the period from the 1940s to the present. We discussed the doctrine of 'free flow' promoted by the United States and then explained the rise, and subsequent downfall, of the New World Information and Communication Order, whose proponents sought to alleviate communication imbalances between national communities in the 1970s and to promote the 'right to communicate' as a fundamental human right. Instead, the 1980s and 1990s were characterized by further trade liberalization and the reinforcement of the commercial view of communication as commodity exchange.

The chapter concluded with a discussion of the impact of globalization on how we think about 'place', 'community', and 'identity', given the importance of communication and cultural exchange to our sense of belonging, and expanded on Castells's ideas about the new forms of sociability and the new global geography that characterize our time.

RELATED WEBSITES

European Union: www.europa.eu.int

The official site of the European Union includes an institutional overview, regular news dispatches, and official report.

International Telecommunications Satellite Organization (INTELSAT): www.intelsat.int

INTELSAT provides global communications services with a 'fleet' of 20 geosynchronous satellites.

International Telecommunications Union: www.itu.int

The ITU is an international organization through which governments and private corporations co-ordinate telecommunications networks and services.

UNESCO: www.unesco.org/webworld/observatory/_index.shtml

The principal objective of the United Nations Educational, Scientific and Cultural Organization is to contribute to global peace and security by promoting international collaboration through education, science, culture, and communication.

World Trade Organization: www.wto.org

The WTO governs trade between nations and seeks to promote trade liberalization throughout the world.

FURTHER READINGS

Bauman, Zygmunt. 1998. *Globalization: The Human Consequences*. New York: Columbia University Press. This book looks at globalization from a critical and human perspective, considering its political, social, and economic implications on people's daily lives.

Castells, Manuel. 2001. *The Internet Galaxy: Reflections on the Internet, Business, and Society*. Oxford: Oxford University Press. Written by one of the foremost contemporary theorists on international communications networks, this book examines the internet from a number of perspectives, including its history and how it impacts the way people work, consume media, and interact socially.

Hamelink, Cees J. 1994. *The Politics of World Communication*. London: Sage. Hamelink provides a detailed study of international communication policy formation and the central issues that continue to create conflict among national governments. The book is particularly useful for gaining a broader, international perspective on public policy issues.

Herman, Edward S., and Robert W. McChesney. 1997. *The Global Media: The New Missionaries of Global Capitalism*. London: Cassell. The authors present a critical assessment of the rise of concentrated and converged media conglomerates, supported by documentation on which companies owned which media during the mid-1990s.

Morley, David, and Kevin Robins. 1995. *Spaces of Identity: Global Media, Electronic Landscapes and Cultural Boundaries*. London: Routledge. This is a provocative look at how the globalization of communication has undermined and altered conventional notions of national and cultural belonging. The ideas proposed in this book remain current.

UNESCO. 1980. *Many Voices, One World: Report by the International Commission for the Study of Communication Problems* (MacBride Commission). Paris: UNESCO. The controversial MacBride Report was critical of the free-flow doctrine promoted by the US and proposed measures to ensure more equitable and balanced communication flows between nations.

Wallerstein, Immanuel. 1974. *The Modern World-System: Capitalist Agriculture and the Origins of the European World-Economy in the Sixteenth Century*. New York: Academic Press. This classic iteration of world systems theory describes the emergence of an extra-national economy involving long-distance trade links between Europe and parts of Africa, Asia, and what came to be known as the West Indies and North and South America.

STUDY QUESTIONS

1. Globalization is often used to mean economic globalization. Besides economics, what other glob-alizing forces impact the communications sphere?
2. In what ways are the mass media agents of globalization?
3. Is media globalization the same as media imperialism? Why or why not?
4. What is the argument in support of the free flow of communication? What is the basis for criticism of this position?
5. What was the MacBride Commission's position on international communication flows?
6. What is world systems theory?
7. What does Manuel Castells mean by 'a space of flows'?

LEARNING OUTCOMES

- To define globalization in broad terms, so that it can be understood as a phenomenon that affects many aspects of Canadians' lives.
- To discuss the role of the media in enabling globalization forces.
- To point out that communication exchanges—both nationally and internationally—tend to be uneven.
- To discuss critically the theories of media imperialism and media dependency.
- To address the international communications debate, from NWICO to the present.
- To consider what globalization implies for how we think about community, place, and identity.

CHAPTER 12

Communication in a Digital Age

Introduction

Communication pervades our lives and communication media pervade all facets of modern society. Communication media encompass the purely technical—film, books, magazines, television and radio broadcasting, newspapers—and the wondrous variety on the internet; professional practice in these industries and activities; the formal institutions of communication, such as film production companies, book and magazine publishers, newspaper companies, radio stations, and website producers; and the many individuals who participate in production and/or as audience members. The influence exerted by these media, including workers in the communication industries and media institutions, ranges across all dimensions of society: politics, economics, education, culture, the family, and individual lives. The media also have an enormous impact on our world view and the ability to transform it or introduce bias into it. This is not to suggest that, normally, the media cause us to lose our grip on reality, although there are special cases of distortion and misinformation, especially surrounding war and terrorism. Rather, it is to acknowledge that each medium is an incomplete and imperfect tool of understanding. To study the dynamics of these tools, which we have been doing in this book, is to attempt to understand the distance between what we know and what there is to be known.

Oral discourse takes us into the world of transmitting information and mnemonics, into the character of the speaker—what we can tell and remember of him or her through choice of words, intonation, thought structure, expressiveness, and associated body language (if we can see the speaker). Literacy takes us to the printed word—to linear, sequential, and logical thought, to the analytical engine the eye represents when connected to the brain and when the mind is filled with knowledge and has the capacity to reason. Electronic society in analogue form reopens the oral and recaptures images and sound that, when combined, are quite rich in their simulation of reality. Digital electronic society does all this and more.

Specifically, it offers up textual, numeric, oral, and audiovisual representations that, given a level of investment in hardware and software, can be made instantly available anywhere in the world. In a digital society that records everything, as ours increasingly does, text and numbers are instantaneously available almost everywhere, a reality that has a binding effect on our world. As well, this instant availability of text, numbers, sounds, and images—this ubiquity—allows for the analysis of patterns. It allows for the generation of metatext, i.e., text about text, numbers, sounds, or images by looking, counting, correlating, by applying algorithms or detecting patterns in apparently chaotic or unpredictable events such as brain patterns before epileptic seizures or earthquakes.

From Mass Distribution of Symbolic Products to Mass Communication

The worldwide transmission of messages and the transformation that digital communication offers or foists upon us are the foundation for the remaking of society. As each day goes by and each new information service is offered, we smile (or frown) and accept it. Each change seems so insignificant. Yet, compounded, these many different small changes represent a maelstrom of change so blinding that we cannot see as far as 20 years into the future. Big-box retailers, whether bookstores or hardware stores, are creatures of information technology. They could not exist without electronic data interchange (EDI). With EDI in place they are much strengthened and small suppliers and retailers become even less competitive because they are exceptions to the system. In percentage terms, their cost for participation in the information system used by an industry vastly exceeds the cost of participation of the superstores.

Associated with these changes is a significant social struggle that digital communication has set in motion. Some might shy away from words like 'social struggle'. They might prefer 'new, open, more competitive markets' or even, as the idealists like to put it, a 'new chance for democracy'. But a social struggle it is. As with any technological change, we are not merely throwing out a bunch of old machines and bringing in some new, sleek, quieter, more effective ones—we are setting in motion revision and reformation of professional practice. We are encouraging the reorganization and perhaps the re-establishment of associated institutions. We are opening up for reconsideration of the foundations of governing policy. We are recasting the role of the consumer. And in doing so, we are setting in motion how our overall communication system and a vastly enlarged and somewhat separated information sector will interact with and affect society, politics, economics, community, culture, art, religion—in fact, the whole of our lives and the whole of society.

At the foundation of this massive change is the decentralization of the communication systems of the modern world and the potential for interactivity. Modern electronic communication services and opportunities are toppling centralized mass communication—the creation of highly designed messages at one point that are meant to be received by millions from its position of sole supremacy. The media, practices, and institutions of mass communication are being undermined not so much by the fragmentation of markets but by the rise of a sophisticated publicly accessible transmission system potentially available to everyone—the internet. For example, independent recording labels and bands who sell their music via the internet have been able to get around the control of the recording industry giants—the Sonys, the BMIs, the Universals. Unlicensed internet radio and podcasting in general essentially circumvent the state and commercial apparatus controlling mass broadcasting. Consider, as well, open-source software, which is a concerted effort on the part of digital labourers to undermine the centralized production and market domination of software by the world's richest man, Bill Gates, a centralizer of the first order. These are but a few examples in the growing trend of decentralizing and interactive communications.

The hippies of the 1960s used to cry out: 'Power to the people', and today there are significant new possibilities for the people themselves—the public—to achieve a degree of power and control in their lives and in the body politic. For instance, a software programmer may hit upon an idea that provides a product no one even thought he or she needed, but suddenly with its invention the value becomes obvious. The exploits of such programmers in 1999 and 2000 could be found on the business pages of most news-

papers. With the burst of the dot-com bubble, programmers now find themselves working behind the scenes, with bricks-and-mortar businesses and organizations that can benefit from communicating with other businesses and organizations by means of the internet. The world of mergers and acquisitions, leveraged buyouts, and general 'conglomeratization' has subsided as various companies come to terms with what one company can reasonably handle.

The foundations of this change from mass distribution of centrally produced products to mass communication by people and institutions can be understood by recalling the definitions introduced in Chapter 2:

- Mass communication is the centralized production and dissemination of mass information and entertainment.
- Mass communication is also the decentralized production and wide accessibility of information and entertainment by means of public access to the internet.
- Mass communication is the exchange of information on a mass scale. Its defining attribute is the interactivity that takes place in society among individuals and groups by means of sometimes public access to communication channels.

The latter two meanings of the term 'mass communication' are new. It is not that the processes are new. Decentralized, widespread production of content describes small literary magazines. Widespread person-to-person communication by means of the postal system is ancient. And the telephone and telegraph have been with us since 1876 and 1846 respectively. What is new in the case of widespread production of cultural products is vastly increased ease of access. The greater variation of media text, sound, and image, together with the capacity for immediate transmission, storage, and manipulation, makes electronic person-to-person communication an enterprise of far greater social significance than the telephone and data communication. The social challenge these evolved technologies present is how they can be made available in such a way that they evade capture by the global communications behemoths.

Communication and Democracy

The social change arising from developments in communication interacts with the fundamentals of democ-

Communication pervades our lives and communication media pervade modern society. The power of both the worldwide transmission of messages and the transformation that digital communication offers is the foundation for the remaking/reordering of society. (Scott Greene, Channel Babel, oil on canvas, 1998. Courtesy of the artist and Catherine Clark Gallery, San Francisco, Calif., USA)

racy and society in general on at least three fronts. First is the evolving form of communication institutions and their ownership and control within society. Second is the nature of the transformative bias inherent in any medium, specifically the transformative bias inherent in publicly accessible (to message and meaning production) digital communication media. Third, the possibilities for participation in message-making are significantly expanded by digital media.

The first front on which communication engages democracy evolves from the interaction between communications institutions and society. The history of this interaction can be traced back to the printing press, which, at first, was controlled by the state or governing elite. But as the provision of information and entertainment became a burden to their host institutions, the press was turned over to powerful and determined businessmen who, as a class, developed and exploited the formula of providing engaging content, building interested audiences, and collecting advertising revenues. As the power of the press barons became obvious, the role of the press as an institution in society became a central question of concern. Should the press owners be allowed to use all their potential power to advance their biases in favour of business, certain political parties, and certain policies, such as free commercial speech? Should they be vehicles for inveterate seekers after truth, as the libertarian journalistic community might wish? Or should they act in a more constrained fashion, as self-aware institutions with a privileged position in society and, consequently, a responsibility to act for the social good of all? These questions exemplify the ways in which communication interacts with notions of democracy.

We saw in Chapter 3 how, particularly in Canada, the social responsibility thesis prevailed, at least until the late twentieth century, not only in the press but also in the founding of broadcasting and specifically through the founding of a national public broadcasting service in the CBC. Even more than the press, broadcasting was seen as a potential harbinger of greater social coherence and responsibility in the media, offering enlightenment to individuals and encouraging the pursuit of democratic ideals. To be concrete, public broadcasting gave the state the chance to bankroll a medium of communication on behalf of the people that would counterbalance the commercial media, which are often bankrolled 80 per cent or more through advertising by the business sector.

At the international level, the efforts of UNESCO— beginning in the 1970s and carrying through to the 2000s—to extend the ideals of public broadcasting through a new world order were founded on essentially the same idea of social responsibility. Dubbed fair flows of information rather than free flows (where the strongest in the market were free to dominate), this UNESCO initiative was squelched by the US and the UK. The desire of these two countries to maintain their predominance as exporters of information, entertainment, and ideology to the world overrode any sense either had of social justice or of the value of celebrating diversity on a worldwide scale. Canadian policy, on the whole, decried this imperialism, and, with the help of favourable government policy, we built up cultural industries capable of carrying Canadian creative content to Canadians. Yet, no sooner had such industries been established than they became exporters, larding our cultural products on importing nations.

In the digital age the question is perhaps how extensively and quickly large corporations will move to reconsolidate their predominance and hence their control. As noted earlier, this is already happening through Google, MySpace, YouTube, NetFlix, and so on. Once the extent of that reconsolidation can be ascertained, the next question will be to determine the consequences of that movement for democracy. Currently, production for and participation in the internet are dispersed. At least in North America, website producers include virtually anyone with the

desire to produce a website. Internet providers are often started-from-scratch small businesses. Yet as we have pointed out, certain sites and services are quickly becoming dominant and, once these are commercialized, it will prove to be less exciting for individuals to produce content for the Rupert Murdochs of the world to get richer. We are beginning to see a layering of the internet with services such as Google Scholar, a search service of scholarly articles, books, theses, and abstracts across the disciplines. Such a service is laying the foundation for the yet to be created Google Health, which could be a parallel service to Google Scholar, including a procedure for rating the veracity of the content, and could be accessed within an ad-inclusive or ad-free environment.

The internet (and public communication in general) is a communication medium controlled by many rather than by a few. With the right policy in place, this trend could continue. We have the academic and research community to thank for the internet's public-sector identity and freely available protocols and codes, which make this communication technology very accessible to both those who want to use it and those who want to create for it. Open-source programming represents a movement in the direction of public access to the tools of communication, as do markup languages like html, xml, and even pdf files, all of which combine the content or text with information about the text. There is certainly the opportunity, if the political will exists, to create policy to ensure that the internet remains widely accessible and its control widely dispersed.

Even if control of the internet and other means of publicly accessible communication does not remain dispersed and becomes more concentrated, in a digital age the dominant communication institutions may not necessarily be confined to the business sector. For example, scientists and scholars are taking back control over publication of their work. It is equally possible that a good section of the information infrastructure will remain outside the hands of corporations for some time and be controlled by governments, institutions, and individuals. This would certainly better serve democracy by avoiding the concentration of power in the hands of too few, all of whom are based in the commercial sector of society. The major challenge is to prevent business institutions from adding a last bit of value and marketing push that earns them vast revenues for organizing information.

The dynamics of the digital age will also engage

democracy through the inherent biases of each medium and its operations. For instance, the print medium encompasses newsletters, books, magazines, and newspapers; the nature and size of their publishers; the elements of their distribution systems; the developments that print has encouraged, from poetry through to the essay and scientific investigations; education, legal systems, and religions that have been built around print; and even the individualism and imperialism that are intrinsic to Western civilization. As the more varied digital age comes into greater prominence—with its capacity for sound, image, instantaneity, text, numbers, and levels of metatext—there is bound to be fundamental change in world societies. In terms of democracy, whether the electronic media and their biases will provide human beings with enhanced opportunities, and specifically, enhanced tools for governing themselves, remains an open question.

On the third front of engagement between digital communication and democracy—more potential for participation in message-making—the answer seems clearer. To the extent that democracy includes participation in our own affairs, there is little doubt that digital technology is providing enhanced opportunities for participation. Whether we speak of playing video games versus watching television, or mobilizing opinion against the latest attempt by the business community to have the world run at its convenience or against accepting the plans of our political leaders, there is little doubt that the organization of digital communications at this point in history allows for expanded public participation in formerly cloistered decision-making.

Content and Audiences

The core issue in communication is the creation and distribution of content that engages an audience. If the content does not inform, enlighten, or entertain and/or if no one tunes in, then we have, as the saying goes, a failure to communicate. Authors, publishers, filmmakers and producers, recording artists, record companies, and media moguls have nothing if no one watches, listens, or reads. Nor do advertisers have any power to reach their audiences and stimulate purchasing if no one pays attention. Without communication, politicians have no contact with their polity: they govern a figment of their imagination.

Understanding content and understanding the interaction between content and audiences are there-

fore high priorities. Understanding the nature of content—its ability to engage, its passing or lasting effect—is an easy matter to think about and discuss. However, defining the exact nature of content is much more difficult. Why? Because the manner in which an event, an object, or a person is depicted—in words, a drawing, music, a play, film, a radio broadcast, or a magazine article—is always imperfect. Moreover, there are an indeterminate number of ways in which events, objects, and persons can be depicted.

This phenomenon is termed indeterminacy of representation. A second level of indeterminacy is introduced when we develop approaches to understanding content. Communication researchers use a bevy of analytical stances to wrestle content into some meaningful framework so that they might better understand how it is generated and what biases it introduces into our understanding of reality. Each stance or framework contributes a piece to the puzzle of understanding content. And each framework can be deployed as the situation demands it. However, the puzzle itself, like the universe, is ever-changing. Put differently, our task is not to understand variables affecting communication and remove them in an effort to attain perfect communication, as a mathematical model might lead us towards. Rather, our task is to provide a description of the event, object, or person and the manner in which the event, object, or person is depicted. In so doing, we end up describing the social process involved in the creation and transmission of meaning and the inherent transformation involved.

We can focus, for example, on the life and intent of the author, the dynamics involved in the publication of a manuscript, and the tradition in which an author created a work or body of work. Like structuralists and semioticians, we can also identify the organizational elements of a story by focusing on the terms used (signifiers), events, objects, and persons referred to (signifieds), and the foundational ideas and concepts (signs) basic to our way of understanding. Or, following the lead of the post-structuralists, we can delve into the particularities of the meaning system that has been created.

From quite a different perspective, we can examine the production of content in terms of the interests of the producers and those paying for production. For instance, the business sector, and arguably society as a whole, has an interest in consumerism writ large. Consumption of commercially produced products creates employment and wealth and also allows governments to take a share and influence the development of society. (The limitation in this scenario is the pace of consumption we have generated, which may not be environmentally sustainable.)

The political-economic perspective offers insight into the wide range of social forces that give form to media content, such as government regulation, professional codes and values, and, most particularly, the profit motive. Knowing this gives a better understanding of why certain content exists and certain other content does not.

At quite a different level again, organizational analysis provides insight into how the characteristics of specific organizations—such as whether an organization is mandate-driven or profit-oriented—impinge on media content. We can also gain an understanding of the bias or nature of the organization of communication by understanding the manner in which particular forms, such as news stories, ads, soap operas, documentaries, and music videos, are used within the media: how ads are constructed to draw us in, how news presentation privileges the news anchor or one of the protagonists in a story, how investigative television can present a convincing veracity where there may be none at all, and how soap operas captivate audience members in their presentations of fictional characters. Each of these perspectives contributes to the richness of our understanding of both referents (signifieds) and the symbols (signifiers, most often words) used to describe them.

With the overall understanding these various perspectives make possible, we can then extend our understanding of the nature and roles of the media in society. We can understand, for example, how the media are separate from yet intrinsic to society. We can appreciate the role they play in incorporating content from subcultures and making it part of the culture as a whole, or how they can reject as legitimate perfectly normal styles of living that are a part of any culture. We can also gain a sense of how autonomous the media are in their capacity to create their own realities, what their inherent shortcomings are, and, by extension, how we must build mechanisms to ensure they cannot entrap us in a world of their own construction.

In trying to understand the influence of the media on society, we have looked at only half of the equation. Content is one thing. How it is received is another. Thus, we must also strive to understand how audience members engage with the media—what they take from the media and how. In examining what audience members take from the media we can look at systematic differences between what is presented and what is received. In searching out how audience members interpret media content we can explore their stances: are they true believers, skeptics, cynics, distracted observers, and so forth?

The first principle in understanding content–audience interaction is recognizing that it is an engagement of active systems. Audience members, even when distracted, are, as we have noted, meaning-generating or meaning-seeking entities. They seek information or entertainment; they filter it through established opinions and knowledge as well as through situational variables—fatigue, their assessment of the presentation, other pressing concerns of the day, their anticipation of certain events, their position in the workforce, and so on. Similarly, the media are active generators of meaning insofar as they create programs targeted at certain audiences, with certain intensities, designed to engage audience members in a certain fashion. Moreover, both the media and audience members interact against a background of the values and structure of their society, and this society interacts with other societies and value systems of the world.

Perceived as relatively passive, audiences can be examined for how they are affected by certain content and media exposure. In attempting to increase the precision in defining such effects, the outlooks of audiences can be defined prior to media exposure and their subsequent behaviour and outlook measured. The uses to which audience members put media content and the satisfaction and reward audience members feel they derive from media content can also be explored.

Alternatively, we can begin an examination of media–audience interaction by analyzing some fundamental dynamics of society. Such dynamics can be economic, political, or cultural. For instance, Marxist perspectives on media illustrate how media often serve to promote the dominant ideas and values, while the Frankfurt School's examination of the industrialization of the production of information and entertainment illustrates how economics structures cultural form. The British cultural studies theorists successfully provided insight into social movements and youth subcultures, later expanding to feminist analyses. What distinguished cultural studies was its emphasis on the audience members as active agents. The cultural studies researchers examined the wide social context of media consumption and its meaning, as illustrated by audience members in their actions as well as in their words.

Media audiences can also be explored from the outside, as entities to be appreciated or sought after. A political party, for example, might wish to appreciate them in planning election strategy, or media companies might see them as commodities to be sold to advertisers. Such a perspective emphasizes much different variables. At a first level, the number of people in the audience is of central importance. Then come their age, education, gender, income level, location, and so forth, followed by specific elements such as their attitudes, consumption patterns of particular products, and the time they spend listening, reading, and/or watching. Such information is valuable for the business of buying, selling, renting, and accessing audiences. Yet, it is also valuable in understanding general patterns in society. For instance, the knowledge that information technology magazines are on the upswing informs us about social change.

How the media choose to engage audiences and how audiences engage the media are diverse, and the resulting interaction creates many social issues. The various starting points and perspectives we use to gain insight into what audiences make of content reflect that diversity. True, in simple terms, media content, such as violence, may serve as an igniting spark for extreme anti-social behaviour—a good reason for us to be concerned both about content generation and about how society contributes to anti-social behaviour. But media content may also inspire lifelong ambition, grand humanitarian gestures, respect for individual freedom, social plurality, cultural values, and the building of community. This positive spark is even more important to understand.

As interactive public communication systems increase in importance in society, the content–audience equation is transformed fundamentally. In an increasingly interactive system, the media sphere is much less separated from the general social sphere. The production community is expanding both in the mass media (books, magazines, film, TV, and music production) and in public media (the internet and the web). The result is that the proscenium, or boundary, between the media and the audience is less physical and more temporal. Increasingly, at one time or another, we all are involved in media production of one sort or another.

Four Influences on Media Operations

Having acquired an understanding of the nature of media, their interaction with audiences, and their overall interaction with society, we can turn to four major influences on the shape and role of communication in society: (1) policy, or, more comprehensively speaking, law and policy; (2) the marketplace, specifically ownership and control of communication institutions; (3) the role and actions of professionals; and (4) technology.

POLICY

Policy provides the overall framework for how the three other factors play themselves out. Policy creates a market at the level of ownership. Various companies with access to capital compete to gain access to the marketplace, sometimes simply by setting up shop with a certain amount of capital investment, at other times by meeting certain policy criteria and/or bidding for the right to operate. For instance, broadcasters must bid for a licence, newspaper publishers must be Canadian, and while book and magazine publishers can be owned by anyone, like filmmakers and sound recording companies, they gain access to a privileged position vis-à-vis government subsidies if they are Canadian.

Policy also sets in place a market in the buying and selling of content to audiences. Once established, communication companies seek out audiences, clients, subscribers, and/or purchasers. They create content to ensure a constant market for their products for which, in certain cases such as books and movies, the customer pays, and in other cases, for example, broadcasting, audience members do not pay directly.

Policy also sets up a third market, the market in audiences. Certain communication companies—for example, broadcasters, magazine publishers, and, increasingly, filmmakers—either sell their audiences to politicians (in return for grants) or to advertisers in return for revenue. Once in play these three levels of markets operate in interaction with one another. Working at all three levels—ownership, content, and audiences—policy becomes a powerful and overriding force.

OWNERSHIP

The more successful the company is in attracting an audience (with certain characteristics), the more revenue the company can gain either from sales made directly to that audience or through advertisers. The greater the revenue from content and audience sales, the more the company can generate excess income and acquire other companies. With strategic acquisitions, economies of scale or of supply and demand can be achieved with horizontal and vertical integration. As economies are achieved, profits and revenues can increase further and be accumulated to spur on more growth until the firm becomes so large as to be unmanageable or until it loses its direction or energy for growth and is overtaken by another firm or broken up.

On the public-sector side, the impact of success in producing content and in garnering audiences, even when those audiences are large and/or demographically desirable, does not lead to greater strength or growth, expansion of services, or even a reduction in public-sector spending, replaced as it might be with commercial income in cases such as CBC television, where advertising is utilized. Rather, at least in the case of the CBC, audience success appears to result in audience loyalty, which, at times, is trifled with through experimentation with new programs and formats. In public broadcasting, the criteria for success and the appropriate rewards for such success are, as the cultural studies theorists say, sites of contestation. This means your definition of success and its significance is no better than ours, even though the goals set out for broadcasting in the Broadcasting Act provide some guidance.

The point here is that we all understand commercial success. Our concept of public-sector success is much more nebulous and vulnerable to attack from any who care to attack it. True, in considering public broadcasting, we can speak of citizenship, participation, and reflecting the diversity that is Canada. But all that the public-sector broadcaster can trade on, and indeed, all the publishers of certain genres such as poetry can trade on, is expressions of loyalty by audience members—expressions that can always be dismissed by others. No intrinsic strength that might parallel that of successful corporations is gained from being successful in the public sector or in cultural terms.

Ownership patterns continue to evolve, whether they are public or private. There is no natural or inevitable way to structure ownership of the media. Each medium itself influences the nature of ownership, as does the socio-political context, but the laws and policies within which each medium operates comprise by far the major factor. Of course, there is also the economy. All media, public and commercial, participate in the larger economy.

It would be reasonable to expect the continuation of both public ownership, that is, media owned by the state on behalf of its citizens, and private ownership by individuals or companies. No media industry in Canada is governed exclusively by free-market economics: the industries are organized as a complex mixture of public and private enterprise. The central difference between public and private forms of ownership pertains to their bottom lines. Public ownership is devoted to providing communication as a public service. Private ownership is devoted to providing communication for profit. This distinction is fundamental because it speaks to the purpose of communication. It can be argued that the growing commercialization of communication narrows both the sources and the variety of information available to us.

PROFESSIONALISM

Policy also sets the framework for professionalism in the cultural and communication industries, even though policy in this area is quite limited. Outside journalism, only the policy of recognizing the Canadian nationality of writers, filmmakers, music composers, and recording artists has provided a foundation for the development and expansion of the cultural industries in Canada over the past three decades. Works with Canadian contributors get favourable treatment. Within journalism, the number and impact of policies are more obvious. For example, the role of journalists as seekers after truth in the name of the public interest has been recognized in various commissions of inquiry. Libel law also recognizes the role of journalists, specifically their working constraints under the supervision of an editor who, in turn, is responsible to a publisher.

Somewhat surprisingly, journalists in particular and the media in general are not specifically recognized or given any special privileges with regard to the collection and publication of information and analysis. This lack of special status was confirmed in 1961 when the courts rejected the notion that the media had a duty to publish honest communication on matters of public interest. On 5 May of that year, the Supreme Court of Canada ruled that newspapers did not have any claim to what is called **qualified privilege**, that is, on the basis of its duty to publish (rather than its right to free speech), a newspaper could not claim protection from libel suits (*Globe and Mail*, 6 May 1961, A1). The results of this decision have been significant. Essentially, the decision has created a greater distance between the media and such governing institutions as the courts and the government itself. While diminishing the media's privilege, the Supreme Court, by increasing the distance between the media and the governance of society, placed the media closer to the people themselves and indeed to the private sector. Since 1961, the press and the media in general have increasingly cast themselves as spokespeople on behalf of the public or commercial interests and in a more adversarial role to government.

This distance notwithstanding, journalists and other producers of cultural and information products have a recognized role in society and they make, most certainly, a dynamic contribution to the overall role of the media. Journalists are the most significant group as they attempt to serve the interests of society by informing the public in the name of freedom of speech and access to information. They engender a continuing debate over the nature and quality of the information and analysis Canadians receive and do much to limit the power of both their bosses, the media owners, and governments. Other cultural producers have been instrumental in strengthening the rights of creators through revisions to law and policies, such as the Copyright Act and the provision for public lending rights and for collecting royalties for unauthorized photocopying. In both cases, the efforts of journalists and other cultural producers have expanded their influence on the media.

Noticeably lacking in the consideration of the role of some media professionals, specifically entertainment producers, is any discussion of social responsibility. As the portrayal of violent anti-social acts in the media (as well as their manifestation in reality) reaches ever higher levels, we may see increased consideration of the social responsibility of the entertainment media. After all, if we can have physical environmental impact assessments, why can there not be parallel cultural impact assessments?

Such an effort to introduce social responsibility and thereby to expand the terms of professionalism in the cultural and information industries may be further encouraged by the quickly expanding telecommunications sector. As that sector continues to grow, there will be an increasing need to set professional as well as technical standards. Information workers at the professional level will need to have an overall understanding of the nature, dynamics, and role of their industry and its interaction with society. There is every chance that professional associations will be formed—just as they now exist in engineering, education, and the health sciences. It would be surprising if such professional societies did not define a set of ideals and principles of behaviour as well as call for a broad education to assist their members in contributing to the overall development of society.

TECHNOLOGY

Policy also sets the framework for technology. For instance, technology in world agriculture is currently being transformed by one policy—the right to patent life forms. In communication, issues such as who can use what technology for what purpose, who can control that technology, and how that control can be exploited are critical.

Because technology encompasses machines, techniques, and social institutions, technology has a substantial impact on the structure and functioning of society—not as a positive agent but, like communication itself, as a transformative agent, an agent of change that brings both negative and positive consequences. The most dramatic change communication technology brings about is a shift in the locus of control: the greater the ability to communicate, the further the control system can be from the phenomenon being controlled. As the history of communication illustrates, communication developments have generally led to increased centralization, the subordination of the local to the regional, the regional to the national, and the national to the global. Whether the decentralized internet will lead to decentralized and pluralistic control remains to be seen. With facilitating technology in place, the strongest influencing factor will be policy.

At the level of technology, technological convergence works in the opposite direction, leading to greater centralization. Technological convergence (and permissive policy) allows any company with sufficient resources to serve the full range of communication needs of any individual or company. Consequently, the possibilities for large corporations to strengthen their dominance are considerable. Yet as we have begun to see, what technology provides, human nature may take away. The dual phenomena of an appalling lack of ethics—witness the downfall of

Enron and WorldCom—and the inability of professional groups to work with one another—for example, TV reporters and newspaper reporters—appear to work against the apparent advantages of technologically based convergence. In the end, the issue comes back to the definition of technology, which encompasses not merely machines but also the social organization of professions and institutions. There is every reason for a print journalist to be disdainful of the pretty boys and girls who, with their 'beautiful people' looks and enormous egos, populate the world of television. At the same time, there is every reason why these people see print reporters as social misfits incapable of conjuring up a commanding personal presence in presenting their ideas. At the level of the institution, a newspaper newsroom and a television newsroom are wholly different places, as CanWest Global found when it attempted to merge its television empire with its purchase of newspapers, including the *National Post*.

Where current technological developments in communication are taking us is difficult to say. Certainly, on a daily basis we are increasing our ability not only to transmit information but also to collect it and turn it into communication, information, and entertainment products and services. Such products and services developed by companies like Air Miles are changing the nature of our society, primarily by collecting and circulating information about repeated behaviours of which we are currently only vaguely conscious. These same capabilities, of designing products and services based on information analysis, are allowing ordinary citizens to analyze the behaviour of corporations, institutions, and people in power to demonstrate unfairness and inconsistency. And with quantities of information being collected and hooked up to the worldwide communication system the internet represents, certain vulnerabilities have become apparent. For instance, we are more vulnerable to being victimized by virus spreaders, identity thieves, spies, and fraud artists.

POLICY TRENDS

The challenge for policy and for society in general is to balance individual rights, such as the right to privacy, access to information, and free speech, with collective rights, such as the right of a society to allow its citizens to participate in creating and sharing information, to ensure that one foreign perspective does not dominate the means of communication within a country, to encourage communication among different subgroups within society, and to allow citizens to participate in determining the direction of development in their society.

Overall, the policy framework for the communication and information industries has changed over the past decade from a foundation in culture to one in economics. The old framework based on cultural and social goals still officially exists. It can be found in the Broadcasting Act and in the Telecommunications Act. It can be found in justifications trotted out by the federal government in its fights with the US over cultural industries such as sound recording, filmmaking, and book and magazine publishing. It can also be found in Canada Council programs.

In fact, however, the thinking behind the development of cultural, communications, and information policy is mainly economic—at times dressed in cultural language. Indeed, it can only be thus. If, in the final analysis, we are dealing with the market for cultural commodities, whether they are goods or services, policy must be directed at structuring markets so that Canadian producers can survive. The only alternative is to increase the public sector and that appears to be on no one's agenda—no group, no leading individual who has any real voice, no political party. What strictly economic thinking leads to is thinking solely in terms of business enterprises. It leads to assessing cultural contributions on the basis of market success. Thus, Margaret Atwood is taken to be Canada's top author because she sells the most books; the Asper boys, although new to the business, are taken to be Canada's most successful newspaper proprietors because they own the most papers. Critical evaluation of their work plays a role, but there is no arguing with market success, as the saying goes.

As the economic framework becomes ubiquitous, more and more of the cultural world is subject to its criteria for evaluation. At the level of the individual artist, if no one is buying and no gallery is showing, then how can we say that this artist is worth supporting? Or if a publisher consistently performs at a level in the market below that of other firms publishing similar materials, does this firm deserve support? If economic criteria cannot be applied to demonstrate success of institutions such as the NFB and the CBC, then do they deserve our support?

Such thinking leads to the development of what appear to be rogue policies, that is, policies that do not make sense if one examines public attitudes but that are inevitable consequences of the application of policy frameworks. The best example of such a rogue policy, which appeared to lurk in the backrooms of government when the Chrétien Liberals were in their neo-conservative spending-cuts mode, was a dramatic reduction of resources for the CBC that would have led, over a decade, to its demise, at least as we know it today. In 1999, no one would admit to such a policy—no bureaucrat, no politician, no CBC official. Luckily, the concern that this non-policy raised, together with growing evidence of imperfection in the private sector and the self-destruction of the political right as a credible federal government, saved the CBC from an ignominious fate. Still, no one yet will admit that such a policy was being considered.

Whether economics will continue to rule communications policy and culture continue to fade remains to be seen. Perhaps we are living through an economic cycle and cultural values may reassert themselves. Certainly, if one were to look at efforts at global free trade and counteractions to such initiatives, the desire of ordinary citizens to put the fabric of society before the demands of the marketplace is apparent.

Globalization

Current technological possibilities point to an ever more globalized world. Enhanced ease of information accumulation and analysis, communication, and transportation means that our lives are increasingly touched by people in distant places—who we work for, where we shop, what we eat, who makes our clothes, what we watch on television, and where our friends and family are. Bertelsmann, Sony, Disney, News Corporation, Time Warner, and Microsoft are world behemoths that rode a wave of globalization and, until 2001, expanded almost monthly. On a slightly smaller scale, other companies, such as Rogers, BCE (now Bell Canada), and International Thomson, expanded. And at a level of even smaller companies the same trend could be identified. All this came to a halt in 2001 when expansion began to fall apart. The dot-com bubble burst, convergence proved for some to be a house of cards, and accountants and bankers seemed, like Clark Kent, to emerge from their phone booths as steroid-charged, ethically challenged captains of greed and artifice.

One can argue that globalization is the monoculturalization of the world. Increasingly, Peruvians turn to Coca-Cola rather than Inca Cola (actually, Coke

bought it out), Canadians to Nike and other world sports brands rather than CCM and Bauer (again, actually now owned by Nike), Europeans to Disney, Chinese and Russians to McDonald's and KFC. Although in the greater scheme of things monoculture seems less desirable than cultural variety, when brands offer quality control, whether that quality is in a fabric, in the reliability of an electronic device, or in the purity of the water used to make a beverage, it is understandable why brand-name global products edge out locally produced products.

In the end, there are no armies behind globalization. An individual can always choose. In addition, globalization is providing increased opportunity for more producers. Countries like Canada and niche-market artists, such as those from Atlantic Canada, have increased opportunities to participate in the marketplace and to thrive. In concentrating on mass-market goods, global corporations are increasingly creating and dominating mainstream or mass commodity markets. But this, of course, leaves the margins open, and whether marginal beer producers creep into the market because all of the mainstream beers taste the same, or whether Canadian publishers creep into the book and magazine market because their authors speak with different, distinctive voices, globalization has no dictators. While global corporations may not create an ideal world, neither is it a world where plurality is forbidden.

At the personal level, globalization does not mean there is no such thing as local connection. In fact, globalization seems to have prompted a renewed desire for local attachment, rootedness to a proximate and familiar community. For instance, we watch films from around the world but we participate in local drama clubs.

Since the 1940s the global trade in information has been contested ground on the basis of two seemingly incompatible views of communication. On the one hand, communication is perceived as a site of democratization and cultural development. On the other hand, communication is seen strictly in commercial terms, as the opportunity to sell information and entertainment products to ever larger audiences. The move to stress the cultural and democratic elements of communication, led by developing countries in the 1970s, gave way to the assertion of economic interests by the industrialized world. In the 1980s and 1990s, the movement towards a balance in the global flows of information was replaced by a drive for increased commercialization, led by transnational corporations and Western governments (spurred on by a redefinition of democracy as free access for consumers to goods).

Currently, Canada appears to be benefiting from a greater globalization. In addition to our expanded view on the world, information and entertainment markets have opened up to producers other than the US, the UK, and Europe. Some developing countries, for instance, India, Brazil, and Mexico, seem also to be benefiting. But others, especially African countries, are not. Whether a plurality of active producers will be preserved in the global marketplace remains to be seen.

Globalization also carries considerable implications for how we think about 'place' and for how we situate ourselves within communities. Boundaries around places are ever more porous and communities are no longer bound by proximity. In fact, the predominance of place, in the sense of geographic location, as a foundation for community is fading. The implication for cultures, communities, and identities in our global world is beginning to be felt.

Two Horizons of Change

Two significant changes of untold importance are presently occurring in the world of communication. In Chapter 2 we drew attention to the increasing role of interactive communication media. Such media, facilitated as they are by the internet, have the potential to cause a paradigm shift as audience members become content producers and exchangers. This shift in media engagement of the average person may have a profound impact on society, even if portal services such as MySpace come to dominate the market. This shift is worth emphasizing.

The second significant change takes much longer to explain. It is taking place within government and groups of concerned citizens. It is nothing less than a redefinition of the salient attributes and the economics of cultural production.

Economists and economic frameworks play a surprisingly ubiquitous influential role in world affairs. Economics predominates in government, in large businesses, in institutions, and in policy organizations. Economists are the backbone of many consulting companies and their influence is widely felt. To some degree, this makes sense. There is, after all, a financial foundation to the exchange of products and services

in society and economists deal in financial realities. However, the predominance of economists is problematic.

First, most economists feel that the economic dimension of an activity is or should be its defining element. Yet, in instances such as culture or the environment, the cost-benefit analyses of economics fall short of anything resembling a true valuation of worth. A tree, to an economist, may represent so many cubic board feet valued at a certain amount, and this can be determined, yet the same tree limits erosion and flooding, might be home to a rare bird and many other living creatures, and its placement in a landscape may give pleasure—even transcendent value—to a hiker, a photographer, or an artist. The same, of course, is true of a song, a poem, a critical essay. Its value on the open economic market may be negligible, but it might—now or in the future—have tremendous worth to a culture or to a single person.

According to the reasoning of economics, policy directed at cultural industries should be based on an economic analysis because economics can predict human behaviour and policies can be developed based on those predictions that will optimize the allocation of scarce resources. The difficulty here is that when people are motivated by externalities—what economists call non-economic variables such as a love of literature or music—the power of prediction and the efficacy of policy built on economic frameworks fail. Second, economic frameworks are problematic because they are works in progress and are far from perfect. Yet humility and open-mindedness to other frameworks of explanation, even in the face of failure (e.g., saddling the developing world with unpayable debt), are virtually unknown among practising economists.

Thankfully, after years of overly simplistic and plainly wrong thinking about communication and cultural industries, economic thinking is changing. That change in perspective has been captured by two insightful and consequential books. One is *Blockbusters and Trade Wars* (2004) by Canadian lawyer Peter Grant and journalist Chris Wood. The second is *The Long Tail* (2006) by Chris Anderson, editor-in-chief of *Wired* magazine.

Let's look at the Canadians first. The key argument mounted by Grant and Wood is that many, quite fundamental laws basic to economic thinking do not apply in the same way to information and cultural production as they do to other commodities.

They exist as anomalies.

Anomaly 1: Cultural products such as TV programs, movies, and music are not consumed in the sense that they are not destroyed in our use of them. Your listening to music does not deprive the next person from listening to the same music on the same CD. The market for cultural products behaves differently from normal commodities markets.

Anomaly 2: The relationship between first-copy costs and run-on costs is far more dramatically different in cultural production than in the production of other commodities. For it to be the same, each single creation of a CD would require an artist to record anew. Similarly, for normal economic laws to hold, concerts-goers would each suck out a little of the sound so that with a maximum audience there would be no sound left over. For books, the implications of consumption would be that as each page was read (perhaps not by the first, but, let's say by the fiftieth reader) the print would disappear and by the end, the book would collapse into dust. In short, while first-copy costs are enormous for cultural products, subsequent copy costs are often negligible—less than $1 for a CD; about $0.17 for a download—and in many cases, the copy can be used again and again. Compare that dynamic to theatrical performances where the players must gather each night to put on the play. Or consider the creation of clothing where design costs are minimal and material and labour costs are fairly constant.

Anomaly 3: Consumption patterns of cultural products and services are also different. Certain cultural products—blockbusters—command a major share of the market while others don't come close to earning back their costs of creation. And pricing is rarely successful in persuading a person to watch an unpopular movie, read a bad book, or listen to a dull, tedious piece of music.

Anomaly 4: Most often hidden consumer subsidies in the form of advertising or grants (by governments or those with a vested interest) make cultural commodities 'free' (e.g., TV) or available at a much lower price than its cost of production (e.g., magazines, newspapers). Indeed, those with a vested interest can buy their way into cultural products—product placement in movies—so that the cultural consumer inadvertently consumes images that cause him or her to associate a product with a certain social dynamic—e.g., Apple laptops on TV or in movies and powerful people.

Anomaly 5: There is the lack of predictability of appeal of cultural goods that is captured by Grant and

Wood with the phrases 'Nobody knows' (whether a cultural product will succeed in the marketplace) and 'All hits are flukes.' With normal commodities most supplies manage to capture some share of the market at some price.

The above anomalies in cultural product markets are significant. They call into question the appropriateness of applying standard economic theory to cultural products. Yet agencies such as the World Bank proceed apace. Regularly they commission textbooks from Britain and France for African countries that are the former colonies of those nations. (They might, alternatively, help build a publishing industry by restricting the eligibility of bidders to African countries or to firms within a single nation.) Such World Bank policies strengthen powerful entertainment- and information-exporting nations (and multinational companies) while jeopardizing the cultural integrity of less strong nations.

Anomaly 6: But there is one further major problem with the application of standard economic theory to cultural products. Foundational to international economics and trade is the law of comparative advantage. The law of comparative advantage states that the greatest benefit for all is derived through international trade of goods in such a way that countries or regions specialize in those products that they can produce most cheaply in comparison with their trading partners. For example, Canada can produce and sell wheat to countries of the Caribbean and buy bananas from those same countries. Both countries benefit. Or because labour is cheaper in China than in Canada, China can manufacture goods that it can trade for technology from Canada. The foundation of the law of comparative advantage is that each nation has a set of variables that give it an advantage relative to others.

In cultural production, the law of comparative advantage ceases to operate effectively. The advantage consistently goes to powerful, culturally dominant, exporting nations with large domestic markets, where celebrities reside and universal questions are addressed, yet those questions are answered within a particular cultural and socio-political milieu as if that milieu were universal. As well, access to distribution systems is closely guarded, for example, movie distributors book screen time well in advance so that a movie owner has no nights available to screen local movies. Such rigidities work against domestic products and products from non-dominant nations.

Anomaly 7: Economics doesn't encompass everything.

The above anomalies represent inadequacies in economic frameworks themselves. Outside the economics of the matter, in the realm of cultural production, there are highly significant, one might even say *defining*, non-economic factors, again, known and put aside by economists as externalities. For example, people of any country are not born with a set of attitudes and understandings that are typical of their culture or country. They are socialized into a nation and a culture. Social values and perspectives—arrogance, humility, exuberance, respect for others, belief in gender equality, conformity—are introduced to them in schools, in their neighbourhood, in the various socializing institutions of a country and region and through the media. As well as explicit discussion, people come to know about the collectivity to which they belong through the stories they are told and the behaviour they see. If the culture they see in the media or in school textbooks is dominated by a foreign culture, they do not come to know the world through the eyes of their own culture. For example, the US sees itself as the pinnacle of civilization. Inherent in this view is a monoculturalism. Canadians tend to see the world as made up of a variety of cultures, each with its strengths. We are more pluralistic and tolerant. We demand less conformity and we affirm plurality. Thus we are less inclined to go to war, for example, or to attempt to undermine the governments of other countries such as Cuba. These values are introduced gradually as we mature as full Canadian citizens.

In summary, for the reasons that:

1. culture is important for the continuing existence of a nation,
2. market economics do not act normally when the products one is dealing with are cultural, and
3. the law of comparative advantage does not work well in the realm of cultural products and trade,

and because of US efforts to pursue its own interests in spite of having signed trade agreements that disallow actions it takes, the Canadian government, led initially by the then Minister of Canadian Heritage, Sheila Copps, worked diligently to create a regime for international exchange of cultural products. The product of that effort, as we mentioned in Chapter 1, became known as the New International Instrument on Cultural Diversity (NIICD) and was adopted by UNESCO in 2005 as the Convention on the Protection and Promotion of the Diversity of Cultural Expressions (see www.unesco.org/culture/en/diversity/convention).

The essence of the NIICD project was suggested by the policy challenges identified on the 2003 version of the Canadian Heritage website. For the Canadian cultural sector they included:

- ensuring a place for Canadian stories in the domestic and global marketplaces;
- supporting business and investment opportunities while ensuring consumer choice and a diversity of voices and opinions; and
- providing Canadian creators and entrepreneurs with the skills they need to be successful both at home and abroad.

The thrust of the NIICD was described as follows:

by international agreement, [to] recognize the legitimate role of governments to support, promote and safeguard cultural diversity as a key public interest objective. It give[s] countries and communities the flexibility to make their own choices about how they want to evolve—ensuring that nations have all the tools at their disposal to create the right conditions for the creation, production, distribution, promotion and conservation of cultural content while still remaining open to all the world has to offer. The instrument also acknowledge[s] the roles of international organizations, the private sector and civil society in safeguarding cultural diversity.

Effectively, it affirms the distinctive economic and social role of cultural activities. It frees cultural production from a strictly economic model, so that governments can support the production and international marketing of domestic cultural goods and services. And it allows governments to balance the public interest with business interest in investing in cultural production.

The defining nature of cultural production is indeed being re-examined and redefined. In part this attempt at redefinition is succeeding because the economics of cultural production itself is being challenged by new evidence in cultural markets.

Following a groundswell of interest in an article in *Wired* magazine called 'The Long Tail', including mention of the article in *The Economist*, Chris Anderson wrote a book with the same title. The book begins with a bow in the direction of blockbuster hits, which, as Anderson points out, are the foundation of massive media and entertainment industries. Hits rule, he says, and thus the factors that are fundamental to making hits also rule—centralized production, celebrities, massive production budgets, massive marketing campaigns, restricted distribution systems, and formulas that attract the main entertainment-consuming public. Everyone makes money when a hit comes along. An author such as J.K. Rowling makes a tonne of money with each new title in the Harry Potter series; and sharing in the economic windfall are her agent, her publishers around the world, the designers, the editors, the warehouse staff, the booksellers, the movie makers, the lawyers who draw up the movie rights, toy rights, and product rights, the actors, the theatres, in fact, everyone right down to the babysitter who fills in because the usual babysitter must see the latest movie.

So lucrative are hits that the entire industry is hooked on finding the next blockbuster. In search of hits, or at the very least, solid sellers, sales channel and determine retailing opportunity—whether space on a bookshelf, music store shelf, or magazine rack, screen time in a movie theatre, or a time slot or playlist on television or radio. To gain exposure a product must fit an established category that sells. In books such categories are mysteries, biography, romance, politics, self-help; on TV, they are drama, reality TV, news, current events, game shows, sports, and so forth. Once comfortably slotted into a consumer category, the product must perform in comparison with established norms: it must sell at a certain rate from the opening days of its availability, otherwise it vanishes from the mainstream marketplace—unsold.

Cultural industries market works in such a manner because the distribution and display system is both costly and highly competitive. Hits are the high flyers, but for the normal to slow sellers, it is a dog-eat-dog world: sales monitored week by week tell the tale of what products will survive and which will vanish. Moreover, the distribution/display system ends up being highly restrictive in the categories it is willing to display. For example, where the categories of music on display in a music store might be restricted to top 40, alternative, blues, classical, country, easy listening, electronic, folk, hip-hop, jazz, Latin, metal, pop/rock urban, rhythm & blues, clearly this does not exhaust the world of music. Evidence comes from iTunes, where the 'electronic' category is subcategorized into

ambient, breakbeat/breaks, dance, down tempo, drum 'n' bass, electronic cover songs, electronica, experimental, game soundtracks, garage, house, industrial electronic, techno, and trance. And even further, 'techno' is subcategorized into acid, Detroit, electro, gabby, happy hardcore, IDM, intelligent techno, and rave/old skool. Who knew? But some people, apparently, care.

Anderson's point is that the distribution/display costs are much more forgiving in the on-line world. All one does is upload a piece of music with appropriate marketing enthusiasm and it can stay available at a very low cost, selling a few copies each year. This low access cost accounts for the ability of US universities to make standard texts (e.g., Shakespeare's plays) or highly valued but relatively inaccessible archives publicly available at no charge.

Fine and dandy, you might think, but will anyone pay attention to material that does not benefit from vast promotion budgets? As it turns out, the answer is yes, and that is the 'Long Tail'. Figure 12.1 is taken from an on-line essay of Anderson's published under a Creative Commons licence (www.changethis.com/ 10.LongTail). It depicts a typical 'Long Tail' distribution and describes the different sales and different availability at Wal-Mart and Rhapsody: Wal-Mart carries 39,000 titles; Rhapsody well over 200,000. At the left-hand side of the graph are the hits and other best-sellers, with the vertical axis representing the number or frequency of sales. Moving to the right we see the pattern of sales for those titles that are not best-sellers. As the curve suggests, most surprisingly, a very high percentage of the products available are accessed by consumers. Similar data patterns are reported by Ecast, a digital jukebox company. At one point the company noted that 98 per cent of the 10,000 albums that were available sold at least one track every three months. In other words, when a vendor has very low display/distribution costs, and item costs are low but access is easy, consumers choose widely rather than focusing their choices solely on hits. The same pattern is reported by Apple with its iTunes service—nearly every one of the millions tunes it offered in 2004 sold at least a few copies.

Most heartening for a person who values diversity and variety, the pie graphs in Figure 12.1 indicate that the sales of music not carried by Wal-Mart and other major music stores are not trivial. They account for 20 per cent to 25 per cent of the profit for an on-line retailer such as Amazon. True, they may represent as much as 90 per cent of inventory, but when the cost

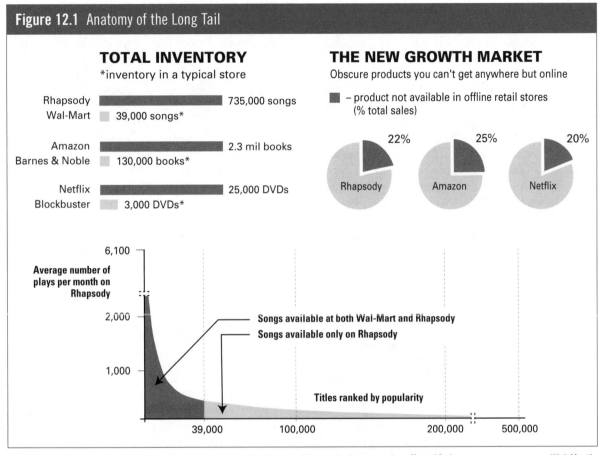

Figure 12.1 Anatomy of the Long Tail

TOTAL INVENTORY
*inventory in a typical store

Rhapsody — 735,000 songs
Wal-Mart — 39,000 songs*

Amazon — 2.3 mil books
Barnes & Noble — 130,000 books*

Netflix — 25,000 DVDs
Blockbuster — 3,000 DVDs*

THE NEW GROWTH MARKET
Obscure products you can't get anywhere but online

■ – product not available in offline retail stores
(% total sales)

22% Rhapsody   25% Amazon   20% Netflix

6,100

Average number of plays per month on Rhapsody

2,000

Songs available at both Wal-Mart and Rhapsody
Songs available only on Rhapsody

1,000

Titles ranked by popularity

39,000   100,000   200,000   500,000

On-line services carry far more inventory than traditional retailers. Rhapsody, for example, offers 19 times as many songs as Wal-Mart's stock of 39,000 tunes. The appetite for Rhapsody's more obscure tunes (charted in dark blue) makes up the so-called Long Tail. Meanwhile, even as consumers flock to mainstream books, music, and films (bottom), there is a real demand for niche fare found only on-line.

of holding and managing the inventory is reduced to close to zero, as it can be with digital products and computerized control, there is a viable business. Anderson (2006: 19) provides some figures for the music industry. He notes that allowing for healthy marketing and on-line delivery costs, as well as profit, music can be sold by the song for $0.79 where the customer gets to choose which individual song to purchase. Purchased on a CD through normal off-line retail channels, a packaged album of 12 (with no choice) would cost $15.21 or $1.27 per song.

In this universe of expanded choice, low cost and easy access combine to produce exploratory behaviour. Such exploration by large numbers of people produces sales of all kinds of products. As Anderson says, these products can be but, on the whole, are not of poor quality. Rather, they are products that appeal to niche markets, whether the customer is looking for

something whimsical or something that is high art. We need, he says, to begin to think about hits and niches, rather than hits and misses. We need to understand that the economics of on-line retailing allow for a fundamentally more inclusive and diverse set of choices than one governed by scarce and expensive retail display space. 'Scarcity (of inexpensive access and distribution) requires hits' (ibid., 8).

This is where the NIICD and the Long Tail overlap. The Long Tail demonstrates that the economics of the matter, that is, market supply and market performance, are not produced by unstructured demand (addressing consumer demand) but rather by the system of production, distribution, and retailing. That system restricts supply and thus focuses demand. When provided with exposure, demand emerges for diverse cultural expression. Thus, as well as providing access to a wide range of cultural products in the name of cultural diversity, the economic rationale for making a wide range of such products available is made clear by the Long Tail of consumer demand: to provide such diversity is merely to meet market demand in a truly unfettered marketplace.

Given that the argument for diversity can be made in economic terms, there is some hope in persuading the many economists who are so influential in world affairs that a different structure is required for the cultural marketplace. Should that argument prevail, a much more heterogeneous market and truly advantageous international trading regime for cultural products may appear on the horizon.

Conclusion: The Media, the State, and Maher Arar—Lessons for Tomorrow?

One final matter of importance to understanding mass communication in twenty-first-century Canada needs to be considered. As many Canadians know, on 26 September 2002, just over a year past the 9/11 plane-bombing of the World Trade Center in New York, a Canadian software engineer, Maher Arar, was taken into custody by US authorities as he passed through—not trying to enter—the United States. He was held incommunicado in the United States for 12 days and then shipped off to Syria where he was tortured for 10 months before finally being released. After his return to Canada, he found himself a further victim. As the Associate Chief Justice of Ontario, Dennis O'Connor, detailed in his Commission of Inquiry report:

> When Mr. Arar returned to Canada, his torment did not end, as some government officials took it upon themselves to leak information to the media, much of which was unfair to Mr. Arar and damaging to his reputation.
>
> Over a period of time, Government of Canada officials intentionally released selected classified information about Mr. Arar or his case to the media. The first leak occurred in July 2003, even before Mr. Arar's return to Canada, and the leaks intensified in the period immediately following his return in October 2003.
>
> There were at least eight media stories containing leaked information about Mr. Arar and/or the investigation that involved him. Typically, the leaked information was attributed to an unnamed government official, an official closely involved in the case, or some similar source. Some of the leaks

sought to portray Mr. Arar as someone who had been involved in terrorist activities, mentioning, for example, that he had trained in Afghanistan. In one, he was described as a 'very bad guy'; in another, the source was reported to have said that the guy was 'not a virgin', adding that there was more there than met the eye.

. . .

> The most notorious of the leaks occurred on November 8, 2003, when information from classified documents was published in the *Ottawa Citizen*, in a lengthy article by Juliet O'Neill that contained a large amount of previously confidential information.
>
> The O'Neill article reported that security officials had leaked allegations against Mr. Arar in the weeks leading to his return to Canada 'in defence of their investigative work—against suggestions that the RCMP and the Canadian Security Intelligence Service had either bungled Mr. Arar's case or, worse, purposefully sent an innocent man to be tortured in Syria.' This rationale implies that officials believe leaking confidential information is justified if it suits the interests of investigators. According to this thinking, leakers get to be selective—picking and choosing what to leak to paint the picture that suits their interests.
>
> There have been several investigations into the sources of the Arar leaks. To date, none of the sources have been identified. All witnesses at the Inquiry who were asked about them denied any knowledge. The sources of the leaks appear to be a complete mystery to everyone and the prospects of identifying those responsible seem uncertain at best. The only remaining investigation is the criminal investigation into the O'Neill leak, which is now two years old.
>
> Leaking confidential information is a serious breach of trust. Obviously, it is important that all available steps be taken to prevent it.
>
> Quite predictably, the leaks had a devastating effect on Mr. Arar's reputation and on him personally. The impact on an individual's reputation of being called a terrorist in the national media is severe. As I have stated elsewhere, labels, even unfair and inaccurate ones, have a tendency to stick. . . .
>
> It seems likely that the smear of his reputation by the leakers has taken its toll. (Canada, 2006c: 46, 47)

The treatment of Arar is bad enough, but what the Commission of Inquiry has revealed is monumental in the history of Canada and the role of the media. The first two issues bear repeating—the official confinement of a Canadian citizen by the US government, his transportation to Syria, his confinement and torture, and the post-Inquiry refusal of the United States to recognize Arar's innocence comprise the first. The second is the behaviour of Canadian officials, not just those who leaked prejudicial information to the media but also those who supplied information to the United States in the first place and refused to fully acknowledge their role in Arar's arrest and confinement.

The tip of the iceberg of a third important issue can be grasped by the resignation of RCMP Commissioner Giuliano Zaccardelli, who admitted to a parliamentary committee that he knew of Arar's innocence within days of Arar's arrest. Not only is it stunning that this head of the RCMP would keep that fact a secret for a year, but also it must surely indicate a complete chain of command within the RCMP from the officers involved in the case right up to the Commissioner himself. No call has been made for a purge of all those involved. Nor has much attention been paid to the role of officials within the Department of Foreign Affairs and International Trade. In other words, even though we know that there was a concerted attempt on the part of a variety of police and government officials to create, and then hide, an injustice, Canadians and their government are content to let one man—Zaccardelli—shoulder the blame. This lack of a robust response in reaction to a gross injustice perpetrated on a completely innocent man is to be condemned. It indicates a willingness to live with the knowledge of institutional corruption in government and our police that has not been quite so apparent heretofore. This is saddening.

A fourth issue has been admirably brought forward by journalism instructor, Andrew Mitrovica, in an article in *The Walrus* magazine. It is the behaviour of the media in the Arar case and, of course, why this issue deserves attention in this book. As of the beginning of 2007, not a single journalist who received erroneous leaks from government officials has revealed his or her sources or apologized to Arar. As Mitrovica (2006–7: 43) says, for those concerned with journalists revealing their sources, 'promises of anonymity are voided when sources are revealed to have lied.' Even those calling for the naming of the sources—Mitrovica credits Jeff Sallot of the *Globe and Mail* with having done so—have not explained their relationships with their sources so that the public can understand how they were given information by persons unknown to them.

The behaviour of members of Canada's media in the Arar affair brings forward several major concepts that we have discussed in this book. Most obviously, they include media responsibility and accountability. As Arar himself has noted, his strength to fight has been maintained by the support of many Canadians who have written to him and supported him in his struggle for justice. The Canadian government in early 2007 issued a formal apology to Arar and his family, along with compensation of more than $10 million, only after lengthy negotiations between the two parties. Yet, where is the call, beyond Mitrovica's article and a few soft supportive journalistic voices, for the media to account and compensate both Arar and the Canadian public for their actions? Where is either some action or a call for accountability from those in the media who were duped, not just by leaks from the RCMP but also by government officials? What are the means by which Canada's media can be made to take responsibility for their actions? Is the symbiotic relationship between the news media and official sources so strong that the media dare not call the government and the RCMP to account? If so, then the media have undermined the basic trust the public places in them to ferret out, as best they can, the real truth rather than allowing themselves to be pawns in the manufacturing of 'truths' convenient to their sources. Will Arar himself have to sue members of the media to hold them accountable for their role? Why was the Commission of Inquiry given terms of reference to stop where it did rather than to interview under oath all those in the RCMP and the federal bureaucracy, compelling them to give a complete account of their actions? And ultimately, what role do the news media have in democratic governance if they are the tools of news providers, this time from government and the police, another time from large corporations or other powerful institutions in society?

Summary

This book has examined the nature of communication in contemporary Canadian society. This final chapter has echoed the major themes, issues, and ideas treated in the preceding chapters. We have also gone beyond the analysis provided in the preceding chapters and discussed the significance of some of the change that digital communication is bringing to Canada and the world, with particular focus on the New International Instrument for Cultural Diversity and the Long Tail of demand for cultural products.

Here we point out that there are good cultural and economic reasons for promoting a diverse marketplace. The chapter concludes by looking at the Maher Arar case, which raises several important and disturbing questions about the relationship between the media and the state in the twenty-first century.

STUDY QUESTIONS

1. If the media themselves introduce a bias, a space or time bias as Innis claimed, and yet other factors exist, such as policy, ownership, and the manner in which content is produced and directed at certain audiences, how do all these factors balance out?
2. Is the world being transformed by the internet, or will the internet soon be largely captured by business so that we will be back to where we started?
3. Are the media a solid foundation for democracy?
4. In any medium—books, movies, TV, music, radio—it is often the case that creators slide into formulaic presentations. Does such content nullify the discussion of content dynamics to be found in Chapter 4?
5. While the media industries look at audiences in one manner, scholars tend to view them in another. Are these two approaches reconcilable?
6. Policy sets a framework within which owners, content producers, and technology act. Which factor is pre-eminent in Canada today and do you expect that the relative power of each variable will shift as we move into the future?
7. Should the Canadian government be supporting Canada's cultural industries?
8. The traditional struggle between owners and content producers is played out most obviously between journalists and management. Are Canada's laws strong enough to best benefit Canadians in this regard?
9. How will your working life be changed by communication technology over the next five years?
10. When all is said and done, is globalization a positive or negative social force?
11. In your opinion, what does the future of mass communication and media look like? Consider some of the following questions when formulating your answer:
    - Who will be the large media owners and what effect will they have on shaping the industry, content, and audiences?
    - How will authors and other content producers be paid?
    - Will the content that is readily available to us be less or more Canadian and will we care about Canadian content?
    - Will people feel they have a greater or lesser opportunity to participate in their community, their nation, their world?
    - Will public broadcasters like the CBC continue to exist, and if so, will they be stronger or weaker?
12. What are the key characteristics of cultural industries and markets that make them different from other types of manufacturing and production?
13. Do you think that the Long Tail phenomenon will last, or is it just a transitory phenomenon associated with a change in technology and organization?
14. The Arar case is not the first time the US government has harassed an innocent Canadian citizen and caused that person major suffering. Nor will it be the last. Try researching E. Herbert Norman, who committed suicide in 1957—what one MP called murder by slander. Consider the degree to which the slanderous myths live on in various accounts of his life and death.

Glossary

Note: In developing added definitions for this edition, especially those relevant to Chapter 10, we wish to acknowledge the contributors to and the creators of Wikipedia. We have found the content provided there highly useful and, after evaluation, have often paraphrased or reproduced it here.

access to information Related to the concept of freedom of information, it refers to the principle that information collected by governments belongs to the Crown and citizens must appeal to governments for access to this information; this is the operating principle in Canada. In the US, 'freedom of information' is the more appropriate term because information collected by governments belongs to the people. See **freedom of information**.

advertorial Promotional material written in editorial form and thinly disguised as normal journalism; newspapers and magazines often provide advertorials as part of an agreement with an advertiser, and they are usually identified as 'advertising features'.

affiliate An independently owned radio or television station associated with either a private or public network of stations; a station not owned by the network.

agenda-setting The process by which priorities are established; it usually refers to elite actors or media owners and managers using their influence to shape governments' priorities.

allocative control The kind of control over media operations exercised by people at the uppermost levels of management—publishers, station managers, chief executives, shareholders, directors—who assign resources of labour and capital to a media organization and determine the organization's overall mandate; it is control over the structural and philosophical context in which media content is produced. See **operational control**.

Areopagitica An essay written by John Milton in 1644 to oppose press licensing in England, expressing faith in the power of truth to prevail through free inquiry and discussion; it remains a foundational document in the libertarian theory of the press and informs discussions of freedom of the press to this day.

audience ratings See separate entries under **share**, **reach**, and **viewing time**.

auteur theory A theory of textual interpretation that assigns primary responsibility for a creative work to a clearly identified author and to the body of work produced by that author; in a complex, collective creative work like a feature film, the author is taken to be the director, as opposed to the producer, the scriptwriter, or the director of photography.

bandwidth The frequency range within which signals are broadcast, typically measured in hertz; with respect to the internet, data transmission rates; the amount of data transferable over a given channel in a given amount of time.

Berne Convention The basis of international copyright law, which requires, among other things, that foreign authors be treated in the same way as domestic authors and that there be a minimum number of years of protection for a copyrighted work.

Birmingham School The media scholars at Birmingham University who developed the Marxist-derived, critical school of thought that became cultural studies.

bits Binary digits, that is, zeros or ones; the basis for the information-carrying capability of most computing systems. A byte is eight bits.

blogs, blogging Usually personal commentaries made public via the World Wide Web on topics of interest to the author or website owner; the word 'blog' is a contraction of 'web' and 'log', as in keeping a log or record of activities. Blogs customarily include text, images, and sound, often including material lifted from other sites, and can be opened for others to make comments as well. Blogging is the activity of creating a blog.

British cultural studies An approach to social analysis that began in the 1950s and was led by scholars Richard Hoggart, Raymond Williams, Edward Thompson, and Stuart Hall; it extended a Marxist class analysis to include race, gender, and other elements of cultural history, and asserted the legitimacy of popular culture forms as objects of study.

broadsheets Full-sized newspapers (as opposed to half-sized tabloids) that tend to be targeted at middle-class or elite readers; this is a conservative newspaper form, with much more text and relatively fewer photos than the tabloid format typically displays.

burden of proof In Western civilization, an accused is presumed innocent until proven guilty and thus the onus for establishing guilt rests with the accusers, usually the state or Crown; in libel law, however, once it has been shown that certain words were written without authorization and they could be damaging, the burden of proof that the words written are not libelous rests with the accused.

Canadian content A legal definition of material that either has been developed by Canadians and/or contains Canadian information; in broadcasting, filmmaking, and publishing, Canadian content is defined by reference to a specific set of criteria designed to encourage the production of Canadian cultural materials by Canadians.

Capital Cost Allowance (CCA) A tax provision whereby investors receive a tax deduction for investing in Canadian film production; it was used to encourage private capital investment in the domestic film industry.

carriage A policy term designed to distinguish between the simple dissemination or transmission of communication (as in telephone service provided by telephone companies) and the production or selection of content; in regulation, this distinction is drawn in order to differentiate between carriage and content activities (e.g., distinguishing between the carriage and content-production or content-selection activities of a television network).

closure With respect to explaining the nature and dynamics of technology, the fixing of a function into a generally accepted form or 'black box', or way of doing things that is no longer called into question. Once closure occurs, a black box becomes 'naturalized', alternatives are quickly forgotten, and the social and technical fit makes the form and functions around which the artifact is organized seem inevitable or predetermined, leading to a 'determinist illusion'.

collective rights Rights accruing to groups of people or communities that are meant to privilege the collectivity over individuals; language laws in Quebec, for example, are designed to protect and promote the language of the French-speaking majority; Canadian-content rules on radio and television are similarly meant to protect and promote the cultural expression of the Canadian community.

commercial media institutions Media outlets organized to produce profits for their owners through the sale of content and/or advertising; regardless of what kind of content the outlet produces, a primary goal of a commercial institution is to produce regular profits.

common carrier A company that provides telecommunications services to all members of the public at equitable rates; such a company is in the business of providing carriage services rather than content.

communication The act of transmitting and exchanging information and meaning through any form of language; while communication typically refers to exchanges through verbal, written, and electronic forms of language, clothing style, gesture, and architecture can also communicate.

compression The process of encoding information using as few **bits** as possible, thereby saving disk space and needed transmission **bandwidth**. The MP3 and ZIP file formats are compressed file formats. In certain cases compression results in a loss of **fidelity** (referred to as 'lossy compression').

concentration of ownership The consolidation of ownership of a number of media organizations by relatively few large corporations; historically, the term has referred to the concentration of the same kind of media properties—newspapers or radio stations—in a few hands, but it increasingly refers to the consolidation of cross-media ownership (e.g., the same company owning both a chain of newspapers and a network of television stations).

conductor A substance capable of transmitting an electric current.

conglomerate A company that contains within it many companies carrying on a variety of businesses not necessarily related to one another: a media conglomerate does the majority of its business in the media; a general or non-media conglomerate has its foundation in non-media firms.

connotative Implicit, suggesting, implying; a connotation is an implied meaning; in communication theory, words and messages are said to have connotative as well as **denotative** (or explicit) meanings.

conservatism A political stance oriented to preserving current conditions and power structures rather than adapting to, embracing, or instigating changed conditions.

consortium A group, usually of institutions, gathered together for a common purpose such as marketing or lobbying policy-makers.

constructivism A point of view that argues that technology is constructed by members of society and shaped by social forces giving it both a technical and a social logic.

consumerism An orientation that emphasizes the role of the individual as a consumer or purchaser of goods and services.

content analysis A quantitative research method that establishes units of analysis—specified phrases, sentences, nouns, verbs, adjectives, paragraphs, column inches, placement, accompanying illustrations, categories of spokespersons quoted or cited—and counts them to indicate the meaning or perspective of a communication.

contract carrier A company that provides **carriage** to a private client, usually a firm, to transmit or communicate signals, but does not offer the same service on equitable terms to others; the opposite of **common carrier**.

convergence In media studies, an economic strategy in which media conglomerates combine the resources and content of two or more different media properties to realize cost savings in content production and cross-promotional opportunities.

conversational analysis Interpretation of social interaction and communication based on a conversation or dialogue model—for example, taking turns in speaking, maintaining and changing topics, and obeying other implicit rules.

copyright The exclusive right to reproduce a work requiring intellectual labour; this right belongs to the author and constitutes: (1) a property right, which may be assigned to others, and (2) a moral right, which may not be assigned but may be waived.

critical theory A point of view that claims that human beings have choices in the development of technology, in its shape, its use, the degree and manner in which to engage with it, and, ultimately, its impact on society.

cross-ownership Ownership of two or more different media in the same market—for instance, newspapers and radio stations.

Crown corporations Businesses owned by federal or provincial governments, but operating at arm's length from government.

cultivation analysis An examination of content for the way in which it may encourage or cultivate a positive attitude in the audience member towards a particular person or perspective.

cultural dependency A relationship in which one country comes to rely on the media products of stronger, exporting countries to satisfy the cultural and entertainment needs of its population.

cultural development Social change that builds on established cultural patterns, reflecting the particular ideals of a culture; an approach based on the state's responsibility to support this process.

cultural imperialism The effort of one culture to impose its ideas and values on another culture, with the effect of undermining the cultural values of the recipient; media and cultural products are a primary vehicle for such imposition.

cultural industries Groups of companies that employ large-scale, industrial methods to produce cultural products.

culturalism The perception of complex phenomena and institutions in terms of their cultural impact and cultural characteristics; such a view foregrounds and privileges the cultural aspect of issues.

cultural sovereignty The capacity of a state or group to govern cultural activity—i.e., form policy, establish laws and conventions—independent of interference from other governments or groups.

cultural studies A field of study derived from a Marxist perspective that extended the analysis of class to race and gender and that, in general, examined the nature of the cultural relations of the society being studied; cultural studies asserted the legitimacy of popular culture forms as objects of study.

DAT (digital audio tape) A consumer technology that allows the recording of sound by digital means in the home.

database A collection of records or information stored in a computer in a systematic, structured way so that a computer program can consult it to answer queries.

data mining The compilation and analysis of data usually collected as part of a financial transaction and aimed at revealing patterns that are useful for a third party to know.

DBS (direct broadcast satellite) A broadcasting system by which a geostationary communications satellite receives signals from earth and sends them back with sufficient strength to be received by residential satellite dishes.

decode The act of separating the code or particular manner in which an idea is expressed from the meaning of the idea—for example, coming to an understanding of what someone has said.

deconstruction The identification of the fullest set of assumptions possible in a communication for the purpose of analysis; taking apart constructed messages in order to better understand them.

defamation Injuring a person's good reputation by means of insults, or interference with the course of justice.

democratic participation A rationale for governments to protect and enhance cultural industries, which is based on the idea that governments have the responsibility to provide citizens with access to the ideas and creativity of their own community because to fail to do so is to prevent citizens from fully and knowledgeably participating in their community.

demographic (1) Used as an adjective, related to the statistical study of populations through the identification of characteristics of a given population (e.g., age, sex, education, income level); (2) used as a noun, it describes a specific group that may be identified through such analysis.

denotative Explicit, literal meaning of a communication; in communication theory, words and messages are said to have both denotative and **connotative** meanings.

deskilling The simplification of complex tasks into components that are readily mastered by workers, who often are working in conjunction with sophisticated machines.

determinism A point of view that sees technology as operating according to an inexorable logic that is inherent in the technology itself.

determinist illusion The notion of inevitability in the form and function of a particular piece of technology, as in, it was bound to develop in the way it did because it is such a perfect device for its current function.

digital A universal code that reduces sounds and images to a series of 0s and 1s; digitization allows the easy transfer of communications from one medium to another, enabling **convergence**.

digital divide The (increasing) difference in the development and use of information and communication technology between rich and poor countries and, in some instances, between the haves and have-nots within a specific society.

direct-to-home (DTH) satellites A broadcasting system using satellites of sufficient power that signals can be received by small, dish-shaped antennae.

discourse analysis A research method that identifies communication patterns and conventions in the production of meaning; that is, what category of person uses what conventions in which context to mean what.

disintermediation The elimination of those involved in between the creator and the final consumer, that is, the elimination of intermediaries such as publishers, libraries, record companies, film distributors.

dominant ideology The set of ideas most commonly used to explain events in a given society; conventional wisdom or conventional explanations of phenomena that are taken by most people as unchallenged assumptions.

economies of scale Efficiencies in costs that can be achieved via repetition of some aspects of the production and distribution processes and the elimination of other processes—for example, the reduction of the per-unit cost of printing 10,000 copies of a book once the presses have been set up, as opposed to printing 1,000 copies.

economism The reduction of complex phenomena and institutions to their economic characteristics; such a view foregrounds and privileges economic values to the exclusion of political, cultural, or other social considerations.

effective monopoly A market in which one firm has become the sole supplier of a particular good or service.

effects research A research method that seeks to identify the direct impacts of the media on human behaviour.

elite The few who are considered superior or more powerful in society or within a particular group in society.

encode To place meaning in a particular code, for instance, language, digital signals, song.

encryption The process of obscuring information to make it unreadable without special (decoding or decryption) knowledge.

fair access The provision to individuals (households or businesses) of telephone and telecommunications services at equitable rates; these rates are averaged into the overall cost of providing service to a country or a region rather than tied to the precise cost of providing individual service.

fair comment Within libel law, fair and bona fide comment on a matter of public interest.

fidelity In sound and electronic engineering, the signal-to-noise ratio, that is, the accuracy of electronic systems in reproducing the input signal—the higher the fidelity the lower is the noise in comparison to the signal.

feminist research A perspective that is critical of the character of modern societies for the male domination of women (patriarchy) that has led to profound human inequalities and injustices.

formative research Research undertaken, usually by means of focus groups, to obtain reactions to television programs and films as they are being made.

fourth estate The media; refers to the role of the media in watching over the other powerful institutions in society.

frame Both a noun and a verb drawing attention to the boundaries a picture, story, or other means of communication places on that to which it refers; these boundaries tend to limit the range of interpretation by audiences or privilege particular readings.

Frankfurt School A school of thought led by the German Jewish intellectuals Max Horkheimer, Theodor Adorno, and Herbert Marcuse, who argued that cultural life in modern times has been profoundly changed by the detrimental impact of capitalist methods of mass production.

freedom of information The principle by which information collected by governments belongs to the people, rather than the state; this is the operating principle in the US. See **access to information**.

freedom of speech The right of any individual to speak freely on matters of concern without fear of retribution; this freedom is not absolute, but subject to certain legal limits.

freedom of the press (1) The freedom of the press and other media to exercise the right to free speech, usually in the name of the public good; (2) the freedom of press and other media owners to pursue market interests unhindered by the state; this freedom is not absolute, but subject to certain legal limits.

free flow of information The doctrine that advocates the rights of producers to sell information to anyone anywhere, and, conversely, the right of any individual to choose to receive any information from any source.

free market (economy/theory) The general approach to commerce that posits that a free market is the most efficient way of serving the best interests of the largest number. See also **invisible hand**.

gatekeeper A person who controls access to media publication or broadcast and determines what gains access according to the identity or character of the media outlet for which he or she works.

geostationary An orbit situated directly over the equator in which objects (i.e., satellites) rotating around the earth remain in a fixed location relative to the earth.

geosynchronous An orbit twice the distance of geostationary orbit, which similarly allows for objects to remain in a fixed position relative to the earth.

global village A metaphor introduced by Marshall McLuhan that captures the sense in which the possi-

bility of instantaneous communication brings societies closer together.

hegemony In simple terms, control by a state or class that is put forward as the natural order.

hermeneutics The science of interpreting meaning.

heterogeneous Composed of difference; opposite of **homogeneous**.

homogeneous Made up of similar parts; opposite of **heterogeneous**.

horizontal integration The combination of a group of companies owned by the same company and operating in the same business but occupying different markets—also known as chain ownership; horizontal integration allows for economies of scale through the streamlining of common needs and business practices.

human agency The notion that human beings control their behaviour through purposive action; humans have subjectivity.

ideology A coherent set of social values, beliefs, meanings; in Marxist terms it is a critical concept that refers particularly to dominant or ruling-class values, beliefs, and meanings, what came to be called the dominant ideology.

indeterminacy (of representation) The inability to account for or describe something fully and completely; the inability to control what a communication can mean.

individual rights Rights that accrue to the individual and that, in the first instance, favour the individual (usually over the community); individual rights include those dealing with free speech and privacy.

information flow A description of patterns of circulation of information commodities or products, for example, movies, magazines, television programs; a summary concept describing the imports and exports of goods, specifically information and entertainment products.

instrumentalism A point of view that sees technology as a value-neutral tool that can shorten the path to natural or self-evident ends or social goals.

intellectual property The set of rights that accrue to an author by virtue of the work expended in the creation of a literary, dramatic, artistic, or musical work; the owned expressions of intellectual work derived from copyright law; intellectual property carries two sets of rights—**moral rights** and **property rights**.

interactivity As a descriptor of media, the inclusion of user-created content as part of what is presented to the audience. While it may be claimed that such devices as letters to the editor are an interactive element of newspapers and magazines, they are placed in separate sections from the content produced by the publication itself. Interactivity is strongest when the boundary between the content producers and the audience is least. To use a theatrical analogy, in strongly interactive media the boundary between the stage and audience vanishes.

intertextuality Pertaining to the referential character of texts; the meaning of phrases, ideas, and points of view derives from the manner in which related ideas, phrases, or points of view have been explored in other intellectual works.

invasion of privacy The seeking after, obtaining, and/or publication of information about an individual that is not public knowledge and that the person has the right to keep private; in some countries this right is protected by law.

inverted pyramid The presentation of a story in a form in which the most important information—who, what, when, where, why, how, and so what—is addressed at the beginning, followed by the development of the story and the context in which it happened; the most common form of news stories.

invisible hand The notion proposed by Adam Smith that the marketplace generally works in the best interests of society by encouraging individuals to pursue their own self-interest and economic opportunity; refers to the self-regulation of a market economy.

langue In semiotics, the shared language system that we use to generate individual utterances.

libel (1) A published written statement that does damage to the good reputation of a person; in France and the US, libel can express true facts, while in the UK and derivative systems, truth is an absolute defence against an accusation of libel; (2) any false or insulting statement.

libel chill The threat, real or imagined, and under which authors and publishers live, that they will be accused of libel and need to expend considerable sums of money to defend themselves, especially when publishing controversial or critical material about powerful people and institutions; this threat often leads to self-censorship as a form of protection.

liberalism A political philosophy in which society is seen as composed of individuals (as opposed to social classes) and that advocates the liberty of individuals as the primary social goal.

libertarian theory A political philosophy that views the sole purpose of the state as enforcing individuals' rights.

literary criticism The analysis of literature—at times dealing with the effectiveness of the author in creating his or her intended response, at other times descriptive of the referential framework of the author when the text was created.

mandate A responsibility granted legally or via another outside authority to pursue a certain purpose—as in a cultural mandate to pursue cultural ends as opposed, for example, to economic ends.

market failure The inability of the free market to reflect the true value of a good or service, for example, a work of art (that may be sold for a small sum during the life of the artist but for increasingly greater sums after the artist's lifetime).

Marxism An approach to studying society that derives from the writings of Karl Marx, who emphasized class as a fundamental dividing element in society, separating and placing in conflict the interests of workers (the class that sells its labour for wages) from capitalists (the class that owns and controls the means of production).

mash-up Any kind of media product—website, song, video—that consists of content brought together from other sources.

mass audience A convenient shorthand term for the great numbers of people who constitute the 'mass entertainment' audience; rather than being conceived as homogeneous, vulnerable, and passive, the mass audience is better conceived as a great number of individuals of heterogeneous backgrounds who use the media for a great variety of purposes.

mass media Newspapers, magazines, cinema, television, radio, advertising, some book publishing, and popular music.

meaning-generating entity Something existing that is complete in itself and seeks information, processes it, and may act on or in relation to it.

media bias The emphasis that a particular medium places on its selection of content elements—for instance, moving pictures by television.

media/culture binding Integration of media with the culture in which they are resident or in which they display products through presentation of elements of that culture.

media imperialism The use of the media to build empires of influence and control. See also **cultural imperialism**.

models As in computer models, a pattern, plan, representation, or description designed to show the structure or workings of an object, system, or concept.

monopoly Exclusive control over the supply of a particular product for a specified market; a market in which consumers have a single source for a product or service.

monopoly capitalism A form of capitalism that encourages greater and greater concentration of ownership, resulting in monopolies and thus negating market competition.

moral rights The set of rights associated with intellectual property that are deemed to be the creator's by virtue of a work being created—they are most often associated with the integrity of the work; moral rights may be held or waived but not assigned to any other person; moral rights are distinct from **property rights** and not considered to be material.

multiplier effects Indirect economic activity that results from a particular industry—for example, movie theatres generate economic activity for popcorn sellers, parking lots, gas stations, and restaurants.

narrowcasting Used in contrast to broadcasting to describe radio and television services targeted at a small or niche audience.

nation-state A sovereign political unit composed of a body of people who share linguistic, historical, and ethnic heritage.

network A group of television or radio stations that work together for mutual benefit—for example, to share programming or to extend distribution to a broader area; network stations are usually, but not necessarily, owned by the same company; increasingly used as shorthand for computer network.

network neutrality A characteristic of communication systems that refers to the network's capacity for transferring data without regard to the form of data being transferred.

new media Technologies, practices, and institutions designed to encourage public participation in information creation, production, and exchange (i.e., communication) on a mass scale by means of either increased access to production facilities (decentralized production) or through **interactivity.** They are usually, but not always, digital media.

open source (software) The production and development of software that allows users and others to see source code and thereby make adjustments to it to suit their needs.

operational control The kind of control over media organizations exercised by editors and producers who are responsible for day-to-day production decisions; these managers determine how best to employ the labour and capital resources assigned to them by upper management, who exercise **allocative control**.

optical fibres Thin filaments of glass made pure enough and shielded on the circumference so that many light patterns can be transmitted simultaneously for long distances (fibre optics).

packets The sending of blocks of data such as symbols, characters, or numbers using variable time intervals separating the transmission of the blocks in discrete recognizable sequences each with addressing and error-checking information attached.

parole In semiotics, the actual words used in a given utterance.

people meter Electronic device that allows audience members to record their media consumption habits.

piracy Theft of intellectual property—often of works by persons in one country by persons based in another country that does not recognize the laws of the first country.

plagiarism Using the words of another without attribution or permission.

plugging or product placement The insertion of identifiable commercial products into the content of entertainment or information media for the purpose of promoting awareness of them.

policy The set of rules, laws, and practices that govern the operation of communication sectors.

political economic theory The study of power within the social relations of production.

polysemy Openness to a variety of interpretations.

postmodernism The view that there is no rational core of meaning at the centre of modern society; a search for the integration of the historical, the contemporary, and the local; a view that no longer affirms the existence of central stories and myths that bring people of contemporary society together.

post-structuralism The theory that uses deconstruction and focuses on the unique and distinctive details of a particular story told by a particular author at a particular time in a particular setting.

primary definers Terms used to define the important elements of a news story; also used to designate those people who are first to assert a meaning to news events; primary definitions tend to be difficult to change.

privacy The right to protect certain aspects of personal life from media discussions; such rights do not exist in Britain in any formal way and are weak in the United States.

private ownership Ownership by individuals or corporations, including of publicly traded companies, as opposed to **public ownership**.

privatization The transfer of publicly owned enterprises into the hands of private individuals or corporations.

probes As used by Marshall McLuhan, probes were new, original, seemingly profound ideas that may or may not have much foundation; by calling his pronouncements probes, McLuhan was indicating that such ideas were works in progress.

property rights The rights pertaining to the ownership of property; intellectual property rights pertain to the ownership and material benefit one may gain from **intellectual property**.

public interest The investment that a national group or other polity has in preserving or developing the best of its values and ideals.

public ownership Ownership by arm's-length government agencies, e.g., the CBC, or by groups of individuals, e.g., co-operatives, which members of the public can join for a token membership fee. Public ownership contrasts to commercial or **private ownership** of commercial companies, some of which are publicly traded and therefore called, in business circles, public companies.

public-sector institutions Government-owned institutions operated by managers ultimately responsible to governments.

public service An orientation, usually of public-sector, volunteer, or co-operative institutions and associations, that places the interests of society above the interests of individuals or specific groups.

qualified privilege Within libel law, the principle that there are occasions when it is in the public interest (in order to promote freedom of expression or public safety) to report on certain persons, even if an individual's reputation may be threatened.

rare-earth doping The use of a group of chemical elements, called rare earths, in optical fibres that share the following characteristic: their electrons rise to a higher than normal energy level when stimulated by a laser and, after stimulation, emit light that can serve as an amplifier to telecommunication signals passing along the fibre.

reach The percentage of audience members who tune into a broadcast program at least once during a specified time period.

reception analysis A research method that investigates how and in what context audiences consume media products.

regime An implicit or explicit set of principles, norms, rules, and decision-making procedures in international trade, often defined in an agreement.

representation The production or construction of ideas or images in a communicative form; the depiction through language of an idea, event, person, institution.

reprographic rights The rights to reproduce, usually by means of photocopying, a copyrightable work.

rhetoric A persuasive form of communication; a research method in which communications are studied as examples of persuasive speech.

Royal Commission A high-level inquiry established by government to investigate problems and recommend solutions.

royalties A percentage of receipts received by copyright owners from those who trade in intellectual property.

satellite footprint The terrestrial area covered by a specific satellite signal.

semiotics The theory of the social production of meaning from **sign** systems; the science of signs; an abstracted form of **structuralism**.

share The percentage of the average audience that tunes into a program or channel over any specified time period.

sign (1) A physical form (a word, gesture, even an object like a rose) used in communication to refer to something else (an object, a feeling) and recognized as such; (2) the totality of associations, thoughts, understandings, or meaning brought about by the use of symbols in reference to an object, person, phenomenon, or idea.

signification The articulation of the connections of, say, an object to its referents.

signified The mental concept of what is referred to—for instance, an object as we think of it when we hear a word (image of table when we hear the word 'table').

signifier The physical form of the **sign**, for instance, symbols such as words.

socially contingent A point of view that emphasizes that technology arises and takes a particular form reflecting the dynamics of the society in which it emerges.

social responsibility theory The notion that the media have a responsibility to make a positive contribution to society and that they occupy a privileged position of which they should be aware.

socio-technical ensemble A term coined by Wiebe Bijker to describe a technical apparatus to reflect the fact that built into all commonly used technology are both social dynamics and technical feasibility (and history).

space bias An idea advanced by Harold Innis, which notes the tendency of certain communication systems and societies to privilege the extension of ideas over space or distance as opposed to time or history.

structuralism A method and theory that emphasizes the formal relations of elements in a meaning system to each other; a particular way of analyzing that attempts to identify the underlying skeletal structure that holds the body of the story together.

substantivism A point of view that sees technology as operating according to its own inexorable logic, and that this logic is at the expense of human concerns and hence humanity.

summative research Research that measures the effectiveness of a program after its completion.

symbolic production The systematic communication of ideas and images through language.

syndication The ability of an organization to sell material for simultaneous publication or transmission in a variety of places—for instance, a newspaper column in various papers or a TV sitcom on different networks.

tabloids Half-size newspapers convenient for reading in limited space that often provide 'bare-bones stories'; tabloids often engage in yellow journalism, that is, the prying into the private and personal lives of the rich and famous in order to uncover scandal. See also **broadsheets**.

technological convergence The capacity of a variety of seemingly different technological devices to perform the same task.

technological determinism The notion that technology is an autonomous and powerful driving force in structuring society or elements of society.

technological imperative The perspective or way of thinking, often said to be typical of Western thought and Western society, that privileges the conceptualization and development of technology and favours the application of technology once it is developed; it perceives technology as a social force.

technology transfer The assimilation of new technologies by societies others than those involved in their development.

time bias An idea advanced by Harold Innis, which notes the tendency of certain communication systems and societies to privilege the extension of ideas over time or history as opposed to space or distance.

Toronto School Marshall McLuhan and Harold Innis lived and worked in Toronto—as such, the Toronto School is said to be composed of scholars who based their research on the ideas of McLuhan and Innis.

transmission Movement from one place to another without disturbance.

turnkey operations Technology that does not require extensive training to operate—you turn the key and it works.

Unix A computer operating system (trademarked UNIX) originally developed in the early 1970s by a group of AT&T employees at Bell Labs and made available to government and academic institutions, thereby becoming—in practice at least—an open system available for widespread and free use. Linux and Mac OS X are operating systems derived from Unix.

uses and gratification research A theory of media focusing on how audience members use the media—for instance, for information, for entertainment, for conversation—and what satisfaction they derive from media.

vertical integration A group of companies linked by common ownership that exist in a supply-demand relation to one another, such as a sound recording company and a radio network.

viewing time The time spent viewing expressed over the course of a day, week, or longer period of time.

Web 2.0 The extension of web applications though the addition of new communication and interaction options that replace static informational sites with electronic communication facilities where people can discuss, collaborate, or otherwise interact.

WIPO copyright treaty One of 23 international treaties administered by the United Nations agency, the World Intellectual Property Organization. WIPO was created in 1967 to encourage creative activity and to promote the protection of intellectual property throughout the world. As of 2007, 183 states were members of WIPO.

Zeitgeist The feeling of the times, the moral character of a period in history.

References

Abercrombie, Nicholas, Stephen Hill, and Bryan S. Turner. 1980. *The Dominant Ideology Thesis*. Boston: Allen and Unwin.

——, ——, and ——, eds. 1990. *Dominant Ideologies*. Boston: Unwin and Hyman.

Adorno, T., and M. Horkheimer. 1972. *Dialectic of Enlightenment*. New York: Herder and Herder.

—— and ——. 1977 [1947]. 'The culture industry', in J. Curran, M. Gurevitch, and J. Woollacott, eds, *Mass Communication and Society*. London: Edward Arnold.

African Internet Connectivity. 2000. 'African country internet status summary', Sept. At: www3.sn.apc.org/_africa/afrmain.htm.

Alasuutari, Pertti, ed. 1999. *Rethinking the Media Audience*. Thousand Oaks, Calif.: Sage.

Aldana, Patricia. 1980. *Canadian Publishing: An Industrial Strategy for Its Presentation and Development in the Eighties*. Toronto: Association of Canadian Publishers.

Allison, Cathy. 2004. *The Challenges and Opportunities of Online Music: Technology Measures, Business Models, Stakeholder Impact and Emerging Trends*. Ottawa: Canadian Heritage, Copyright Policy Branch. At: www.canadian-heritage.gc.ca/progs/ac-ca/progs/pda-cpb/pubs/index_e.cfm.

Anderson, Benedict. 1989. *Imagined Communities: Reflections on the Origin and Spread of Nationalism*. London: Verso.

Anderson, Chris. 2006. *The Long Tail: Why the Future of Business Is Selling Less of More*. New York: Hyperion.

Anderson, Robert, Richard Gruneau, and Paul Heyer, eds. 1996. *TVTV: The Television Revolution, The Debate*. Vancouver: Canadian Journal of Communication.

Anderssen, Erin. 2003. 'Immigration shifts population kaleidoscope', *Globe and Mail*, 22 Jan., A6.

Ang, Ien. 1985. *Watching Dallas*. London: Methuen.

——. 1991. *Desperately Seeking the Audience*. London: Routledge.

——. 1996. 'Dallas between reality and fiction', in Paul Cobley, ed., *The Communication Theory Reader*. London and New York: Routledge.

—— and Joke Hermes. 1991. 'Gender and/in media consumption', in Curran and Gurevitch (1991: 307–28).

Arab, Paula. 2002. 'Black would reclaim citizenship if offered', *St John's Telegram*, 23 May, 1.

Atkinson, J. Maxwell. 1984. *Our Masters' Voices: The Language and Body Language of Politics*. London: Methuen.

Audley, Paul. 1983. *Canada's Cultural Industries: Broadcasting, Publishing, Records and Film*. Toronto: James Lorimer.

Auletta, Ken. 1997. *The Highwaymen: Warriors of the Information Superhighway*. New York: Random House.

Babe, Robert E. 1979. *Canadian Broadcasting Structure, Performance and Regulation*. Ottawa: Economic Council of Canada.

——. 1988. 'Emergence and development of Canadian communication: Dispelling the myths', in R. Lorimer and D.C. Wilson, eds, *Communication Canada*. Toronto: Kagan and Woo.

——. 1990. *Telecommunications in Canada*. Toronto: University of Toronto Press.

Bagdikian, Ben H. 1990. *The Media Monopoly*. Boston: Beacon Press.

Bagnall, Janet. 2002. 'Global concern: Media concentration has become issue in Italy, Britain and U.S.', *Montreal Gazette*, 5 July, B3.

Bakke, Marik. 1986. 'Culture at stake', in Denis McQuail and Karen Siune, eds, *New Media Politics: Comparative Perspectives in Western Europe*. London: Sage.

Bandura, Albert. 1976. *Analysis of Delinquency and Aggression*. Hillside, NJ: L. Erlbaum Associates.

Baril, Hélène. 2003. 'Quebec engranger des profits de Star Académie', *La Presse*, 9 May, D1.

Barthes, Roland. 1968. *Elements of Semiology*, trans. A. Lavers and C. Smith. New York: Hill and Wang.

——. 1972. *Mythologies*. London: Jonathan Cape.

——. 1977a. *Image-Music-Text*. London: Fontana.

——. 1977b. 'The death of the author', in Barthes (1977a: 142–9).

Baudrillard, Jean. 1995. *Simulacra and Simulation*, trans. Sheila Glaser. Ann Arbor: University of Michigan Press.

Bauman, Zygmunt. 1998. *Globalization: The Human Consequences*. New York: Columbia University Press.

Baumgartel, Richard. 1997. 'The Canada rack program', *Canadian Journal of Communication* 22, 2: 289–93. At: www.cjc-online.ca/~cjc/BackIssues/_22.2/baumgart.html.

Barlow, Maude, and James Winter. 1997. *The Big Black Book: The Essential Views of Conrad and Barbara Amiel Black*. Toronto: Stoddart.

BC Film Commission. 1999. 'B.C. film production has record year', press release, 12 Feb.

Beauvoir, Simone de. 1957 [1949]. *The Second Sex*, trans. and ed. H.M. Parshley. New York: Knopf.

Beniger, James. 1986. *The Control Revolution*. Cambridge, Mass.: Harvard University Press.

Bennett, Tony. 1982. 'Media, "reality", and signification', in Gurevitch et al. (1982).

———— and Janet Woollacott. 1987. *Bond and Beyond: The Political Career of a Popular Hero*. New York: Methuen.

Berelson, Bernard. 1972. *Content Analysis in Communication Research*. New York: Hafner.

Bergen, Bob. 2002. *Exposing the Boss: A Study in Canadian Journalism Ethics*. Calgary: Sheldon Chumir Foundation. At: www.chumirethicsfoundation.calgary._ab.ca/downloads/mediafellows/bergenbob/bergenbobindex.html.

Berger, Peter, and Thomas Luckmann. 1966. *Social Construction of Reality: A Treatise on the Sociology of Knowledge*. New York: Doubleday.

Berton, Pierre. 1975. *Hollywood's Canada: The Americanization of Our National Image*. Toronto: McClelland & Stewart.

Best, Steven, and Douglas Kellner. 1997 *The Postmodern Turn*. New York: Guilford Press.

Bijker, W. 1993. 'Do not despair: There is life after constructivism', *Science, Technology & Human Values* 18: 113–38.

Binning, Cheryl. 1999. 'Record sales for Canucks in France', *Playback*, 3 May, 1, 6, 9, 26.

Bird, Roger. 1997. *The End of News*. Toronto: Irwin Publishing.

Bird, S. Elizabeth, and Robert W. Dardenne. 1997. 'Myth, chronicle and story: Exploring the narrative qualities of news', in Dan Berkowitz, ed., *Social Meanings of News: A Text-Reader*. Thousand Oaks, Calif.: Sage.

Black, Edwin. 2001. *IBM and the Holocaust: The Strategic Alliance between Nazi Germany and America's Most Powerful Corporation*. New York: Crown Books.

Blumer, H. 1939. 'The mass, the public, and public opinion', in A.M. Lee, ed., *New Outlines in the Principles of Sociology*. New York: Barnes and Noble.

Blumler, Jay, and Elihu Katz, eds. 1974. *The Uses of Mass Communications: Current Perspectives on Gratifications Research*. Beverly Hills, Calif.: Sage.

Bolan, Kim. 1995. 'Privacy chief wants access to data bases tightened', *Vancouver Sun*, 10 Jan., A1.

Bowker, G., and S.L. Star. 1999. *Sorting Things Out: Classification and Its Consequences*. Cambridge, Mass.: MIT Press.

Boyce, George. 1978. 'The fourth estate: A reappraisal of a concept', in G. Boyce et al., eds, *Newspaper History from the 17th Century to the Present Day*. London: Sage/Constable.

Boyd-Barrett, Oliver. 1977. 'Media imperialism: Towards an international framework for the analysis of media systems', in James Curran, Michael Gurevitch, and Janet Woollacott, eds, *Mass Communication and Society*. London: Edward Arnold.

————. 1995. 'Cultural dependency and the mass media', in Michael Gurevitch, Tony Bennett, James Curran, and Janet Woollacott, eds, *Culture, Society and the Media*. London and New York: Routledge.

Braham, Peter. 1982. 'How the media report race', in Gurevitch et al. (1982).

Breen, Marcus. 2005. 'Off-shore pot o' gold: The political economy of the Australian film industry', in Greg Elmer and Mike Gasher, eds, *Contracting Out Hollywood: Runaway Productions and Foreign Location Shooting*. Lanham, Md: Rowman & Littlefield, 69–91.

Brethour, Patrick. 2002. 'Media convergence strategy praised', *Globe and Mail*, 25 Apr., B2.

British Broadcasting Corporation (BBC). 1987. *Handbook on Audience Research*. London: BBC.

Brown, P., and S.C. Levinson. 1987. *Politeness: Some Universals in Language Usage*. Cambridge: Cambridge University Press.

Brucker, Herbert. 1981. *Freedom of Information*. Westport, Conn.: Greenwood Press.

Bruner, Jerome. 1978. *Human Growth and Development*. Oxford: Clarendon.

Bryce, J. 1987. 'Family time and TV use', in T. Lindlof, ed., *Natural Audiences*. Norwood, NJ: Ablex, 121–38.

Buckingham, D. 1987. *Public Secrets: EastEnders and Its Audience*. London: British Film Institute.

Buckley, Peter, ed. 1993. *Canadian Press Stylebook: A Guide for Writers and Editors*. Toronto: Canadian Press.

Butalia, Urvashi. 1994. 'The issues at stake: An Indian perspective on copyright', in Philip G. Altbach, ed., *Copyright and Development: Inequality in the Information Age*. Chestnut Hill, Md: Bellagio Publishing Network.

Campbell, Joseph. 1968 [1949]. *The Hero with a Thousand Faces*. Bollingen Series. Princeton, NJ: Princeton University Press.

Canada. 1929. *Report of the Royal Commission on Radio Broadcasting* (Aird Commission). Ottawa: F.A. Acland.

————. 1951. *Report of the Royal Commission on National Development in the Arts, Letters and Sciences, 1949–1951* (Massey Commission). Ottawa: Edmond Cloutier.

————. 1957. *Report of the Royal Commission on Broadcasting* (Fowler Commission). Ottawa: Edmond Cloutier.

————. 1968. Department of Industry, Trade and Commerce. *Report on Book Publishing* (Ernst and Ernst).

Ottawa: Department of Industry, Trade and Commerce.

———. 1968. Minister of Industry. *White Paper on a Domestic Satellite Communications System for Canada.* Ottawa: Queen's Printer.

———. 1969. *Report of the Task Force on Government Information.* Ottawa: Supply and Services.

———. 1971. *Mass Media*, vol. 1, *The Uncertain Mirror: Report of the Special Senate Committee on the Mass Media* (Davey Committee). Ottawa: Information Canada.

———. 1977a. Department of the Secretary of State. *The Publishing Industry in Canada.* Ottawa: Ministry of Supply and Services.

———. 1977b. Department of the Secretary of State. *The Film Industry in Canada.* Ottawa: Minister of Supply and Services.

———. 1978a. Department of the Secretary of State. *English Educational Publishing in Canada.* Hull, Que.: Minister of Supply and Services.

———. 1978b. Department of the Secretary of State. *French Educational Publishing in Canada.* Hull, Que.: Minister of Supply and Services.

———. 1980. Canadian Study of Parliament Group. *Seminar on Press and Parliament: Adversaries or Accomplices?* Ottawa: Queen's Printer.

———. 1981. *Report of the Royal Commission on Newspapers* (Kent Commission). Ottawa: Minister of Supply and Services.

———. 1982a. *Report of the Federal Cultural Policy Review Committee.* Ottawa: Minister of Supply and Services Canada.

———. 1982b. *Canadian Charter of Rights and Freedoms.* At: canada.justice.gc.ca/Loireg/charte/_const_en/html.

———. 1984. *The National Film and Video Policy.* Ottawa: Minister of Supply and Services.

———. 1985. Canadian Multiculturalism Act. R.S. 1983 c. 24. At: www.pch.gc.ca/multi/html/act.html.

———. 1985. *Report of the Film Industry Task Force.* Ottawa: Minister of Supply and Services.

———. 1986. Minister of Communications. *Report of the Task Force on Broadcasting Policy* (Caplan-Sauvageau Task Force). Ottawa: Minister of Supply and Services.

———. 1987. Department of Communications. *Vital Links: Canadian Cultural Industries.* Ottawa: Minister of Supply and Services.

———. 1988. *Canadian Voices: Canadian Choices—A New Broadcasting Policy for Canada.* Ottawa: Supply and Services Canada.

———. 1991. Broadcasting Act. At: www.crtc.gc.ca/_ENG/LEGAL/BROAD_E.HTM.

———. 1993. Telecommunications Act. At: www.crtc.gc.ca/ENG/LEGAL/TELECOME.HTM.

———. 1996a. *Information Highway Advisory Council Report.* At: strategis.ic.gc.ca/SSG/ih01015e.html.

———. 1996b. Mandate Review Committee: CBC, NFB, Telefilm. *Making Our Voices Heard.* Ottawa: Minister of Supply and Services.

———. 1999. *Report of the Feature Film Advisory Committee.* Ottawa: Ministry of Canadian Heritage.

———. 2000. *From Script to Screen.* Ottawa: Department of Canadian Heritage.

———. 2002. *Canadian Content in the 21st Century: A Discussion Paper about Canadian Content in Film and Television Productions.* Ottawa: Department of Canadian Heritage, Mar.

———. 2003. *Our Cultural Sovereignty: The Second Century of Canadian Broadcasting.* Report of the Standing Committee on Canadian Heritage, June. Ottawa: Communication Canada Publishing. At: www.parl.gc.ca/InfoComDoc/37/2/HERI/Studies/Reports/herirp02-e.htm.

———. 2006a. *Final Report on the Canadian News Media*, vol. 1. Standing Senate Committee on Transport and Communications. Ottawa: Senate Committees Directorate, June.

———. 2006b. *Final Report of the Telecommunications Policy Review Panel.* Ottawa: Industry Canada.

———. 2006c. *Report of the Events Relating to Maher Arar: Analysis and Recommendations.* Commission of Inquiry into the Actions of Canadian Officials in Relation to Maher Arar. Ottawa: Government of Canada.

Canadian Association of Journalists. 1991. 'Should pilots trust Airbus?', *The Eye Opener* (Ottawa): 2–15.

Canadian Broadcasting Corporation (CBC). 1977. *The Press and the Prime Minister: A Story of Unrequited Love.* TV documentary directed and produced by George Robertson. Toronto: CBC.

———. 1999. *CBC Annual Report, 1998–99.* Ottawa: CBC.

———. 1999. 'It's Time to Talk About the CBC . . . Your Voice Matters', press release, 9 Apr.

———. 2003. 'Response to Broadcasting Notice 2003–54', 1 Dec. At: www.cbc.radio-canada.ca/submissions/crtc/2003/BPN_CRTC_2003-54_CBCSRC281103_e.pdf.

Canadian Cable Television Association. 1995. *1994–95 Annual Report.* Toronto: Canadian Cable Television Association.

Canadian Community Newspaper Association (CCNA). 2005. *Snapshot 2005: One Easy Way To Reach Canadians.* At: www.communitynews.ca/publisher/snapshot2005.pdf.

Canadian Daily Newspaper Association. 1999. *1999 Circulation Data*. Toronto: CDNA. At: www.cna-acj.ca/newspapers/facts/circulation.asp?search=a11.

Canadian Independent Record Production Association (CIRPA). 2006. Sound Recording Market Profile. At: www.cirpa.ca/Page.asp?PageID=376&ContentID=609.

Canadian Internet Policy and Public Interest Clinic (CIPPIC). 2006. File Sharing—FAQ and Resources. At: www.cippic.ca/en/faqs-resources/file-sharing/.

Canadian Journal of Communication. 1995. Special issue on media in Eastern Europe, 20, 1.

Canadian Press (CP). 1993a. 'Front-page story omits who, where, what, when', *Vancouver Sun*, 10 Sept., A8.

———. 1993b. 'Running gags courtesy of nation's courts', *Vancouver Sun*, 3 Dec., A6.

———. 1993c. 'Ontario's A-G orders probe into news coverage in case of serial-rape suspect', *Vancouver Sun*, 1 Mar., A7.

———. 1999. 'CRTC cuts CKVL's license over complaints about host', *Montreal Gazette*, 1 May, C5.

———. 2000. 'Newspaper owner, strike leader go toe-to-toe', *Ottawa Citizen*, 3 Mar., D4.

———. 2002. 'Poverty fueled 9/11 Chrétien warns UN', *Halifax Daily News*, 17 Sept., 10.

———. 2003. 'CanWest Global may sell more assets', *Charlottetown Guardian*, 22 Jan., B11.

———. 2006. 'More Canadians heading to theatres as DVD novelty wears off: StatsCan', *Saskatoon Star-Phoenix*, 29 Aug., C7.

Canadian Radio-television and Telecommunications Commission. 1999. 'The means may be changing but the goals remain constant', speech by Wayne Charman to the 1999 Broadcasting and Program Distribution Summit, 25 Feb. At: www.crtc.gc.ca/_ENG/NEWS/SPEECHES/1999/S990225.htm.

———. 2000. 'CRTC approves new digital pay and specialty television services—more choice for consumers', press release, 24 Nov. At: www.crtc.gc.ca/ENG/NEWS/_RELEASES/2000/R001124-2.htm.

———. 2001. 'CRTC renews CTV and Global's licences—more quality programming and services', press release, 2 Aug. At: www.crtc.gc.ca/ENG/NEWS/_RELEASES/2001/R010802.htm.

Cantril, Hadley. 1940. *The Invasion from Mars*. Princeton, NJ: Princeton University Press.

Carey, James W. 1998. 'The Internet and the end of the national communication system: Uncertain predictions of an uncertain future', *Journalism and Mass Communication Quarterly* 75, 1: 28–34.

Carr, Graham. 1991. 'Trade liberalization and the political economy of culture: An international perspective on FTA', *Canadian-American Public Policy* 6: 1–54.

Castells, Manuel. 1999. *End of Millennium*. Oxford: Blackwell.

———. 2001. *The Internet Galaxy: Reflections on the Internet, Business, and Society*. Oxford: Oxford University Press.

Centre for Contemporary Cultural Studies. 1982. *The Empire Fights Back: Racism in Britain in the 1970s*. London: Hutchinson.

Challands, Sarah. 2005. 'Conrad Black: The rise and fall of a media mogul', CTV.ca News, 17 Nov. At: www.ctv.ca.

Charland, Maurice. 1986. 'Technological nationalism', *Canadian Journal of Political and Social Theory* 10, 1: 196–220.

Chartier, Roger, and Alain Boureau. 1989. *The Culture of Print: Power and the Uses of Print in Early Modern Europe*. Cambridge: Polity Press.

Chase, Steven. 2003. 'Telecom rules get spotlight', *Globe and Mail*, 29 Jan., B1, B10.

Cherry, Paul. 1998. '"A bad day," photographers say', *Montreal Gazette*, 11 Apr., A4.

Chomsky, Noam. 1968. *Language and Mind*. New York: Harcourt Brace.

Clarke, Debra. 2000. 'Active viewers and inactive Canadian scholars: The underdeveloped state of audience research in Canada', *Canadian Journal of Communication* 25, 1.

Clement Jones, J. 1980. *Mass Media Codes of Ethics and Councils: A Comparative International Study on Professional Standards*. Reports and Papers on Mass Communication, Special Issue. Paris: UNESCO.

Cobb, Chris. 1993. 'Himbo: Man as sex object the new vogue: Lean muscular males used to sell products', *Vancouver Sun*, 30 Nov., A1.

———. 1995. 'Newspaper group revises standards; New code reflects Charter of Rights, changing times', *Ottawa Citizen*, 28 Sept., A12.

———. 1999. 'People believe Ottawa hurting CBC, poll shows', *Vancouver Sun*, 20 May, A11.

———. 2000. 'CRTC, CBC in dogfight', *Montreal Gazette*, 7 Jan., A1–A2.

Cocking, Clive. 1980. *Following the Leaders: A Media Watcher's Diary of Campaign '79*. Toronto: Doubleday.

Collett, Peter, and R. Lamb. 1986. *Watching Families Watching TV*. Report to the Independent Broadcasting Authority. London.

Collins, Richard. 1992. *Satellite Television in Western Europe*, rev. edn. London: John Libbey Acamedia Research Monograph 1.

Commission on Freedom of the Press. 1947. *A Free and Responsible Press*. Chicago: University of Chicago Press.

Cottle, Simon, ed. 2003. *Media Organization and Production.* Thousand Oaks, Calif.: Sage.

Cox, Kirwan. 1980. 'Hollywood's empire in Canada', in Pierre Véronneau and Piers Handling, eds, *Self-Portrait: Essays on the Canadian and Quebec Cinemas.* Ottawa: Canadian Film Institute.

Coyne, Deborah. 1992. *Roll of the Dice: Working with Clyde Wells during the Meech Lake Negotiations.* Toronto: James Lorimer.

Crawford, Michael G. 1990. *The Journalist's Legal Guide*, 2nd edn. Toronto: Carswell.

Croteau, David, and William Hoynes. 2003. *Media/Society*, 3rd edn. Thousand Oaks, Calif.: Pine Forge.

Crowley, David, and Paul Heyer. 1991. *Communication in History: Technology, Culture, Society.* London: Longman.

Curran, James. 1982. 'Communications, power, and social order', in Gurevitch et al. (1982).

———. 1990. 'The new revisionism in mass communication research: A reappraisal', *European Journal of Communication* 5, 2–3: 135–64.

———. 1991. 'Mass media and democracy: A reappraisal', in Curran and Gurevitch (1991).

——— and Michael Gurevitch, eds. 1991. *Mass Media and Society.* London: Edward Arnold.

Curtis, Liz. 1984. *Ireland, the Propaganda War: The Media and the 'Battle for Hearts and Minds'.* London: Pluto Press.

Damsell, Keith. 2002. 'CanWest editorial policy blasted in ad', *Globe and Mail*, 6 June, A6.

Darnton, Robert. 1976. *The Widening Circle: Essays on the Circulation of Literature in Eighteenth Century Europe.* Philadelphia: University of Pennsylvania Press.

———. 1979. *The Business of Enlightenment: A Publishing History of the Encyclopédie, 1775–1800.* Cambridge, Mass.: Belknap Press.

———. 1982. *The Literary Underground of the Old Regime.* Cambridge, Mass.: Harvard University Press.

———. 1989. *Revolution in Print: The Press in France, 1775–1800.* Berkeley: University of California Press with New York Public Library.

Dayan, D., and E. Katz. 1992. *Media Events: The Live Broadcasting of History.* Cambridge, Mass.: Harvard University Press.

DeFleur, Melvin L., and Sandra Ball-Rokeach. 1989. *Theories of Mass Communication*, 5th edn. New York: Longman.

de la Haye, Yves. 1980. *Marx and Engels on the Means of Communication (The Movement of Commodities, People, Information and Capital).* New York: International General.

Demers, David. 1999. 'Corporate newspaper bashing: Is it

justified?', *Newspaper Research Journal* 20, 1: 83–97.

Derrida, Jacques. 1981. *Positions.* London: Althone.

Desbarats, Peter. 1996. *Guide to Canadian News Media.* Toronto: Harcourt Brace.

Dick, Ronald. 1986. 'Regionalization of a federal cultural institution: The experience of the National Film Board of Canada 1965–1979', in Gene Walz, ed., *Flashback: People and Institutions in Canadian Film History.* Montreal: Mediatexte Publications.

Dillon, Mark. 2006. 'Canadian films hit 5%', *Playback*, 20 Feb., 2.

Dizard, Wilson P. 1985. *The Coming Information Age: An Overview of Technology, Economics and Politics.* New York: Longman.

Dorland, Michael, ed. 1996. *The Cultural Industries in Canada: Problems, Policies and Prospects.* Toronto: James Lorimer.

Drache, Daniel. 1995. 'Celebrating Innis: The man, the legacy and our future', in Drache, ed., *Staples, Markets and Cultural Change: Selected Essays.* Montreal and Kingston: McGill-Queen's University Press.

Drezner, Daniel, and Henry Farrel. 2004. 'The power and politics of blogs', paper presented at the annual meeting of the American Political Science Association. At: www.utsc.utoronto.ca//farrel/blogpaperfinal.pdf.

Drucker, Peter F. 1993. *Post-Capitalist Society.* New York: HarperCollins.

Dryburgh, Heather. 2001. *Changing Our Ways: Why and How Canadians Use the Internet.* Statistics Canada Catalogue no. 56F0006XIE. Ottawa: Statistics Canada, Mar.

Dubinsky, Lon. 1996. 'Periodical Publishing', in Dorland (1996).

Dutrisac, Robert. 2002. 'Concentration de la presse— Québec demandera à l'industrie de s'autoréglementer', *Le Devoir*, 6 Sept., A3.

Duxbury, Nancy. 1991. 'Why is libel so chilling? An examination of Canadian libel law and the vulnerability of publishers', unpublished paper, Canadian Centre for Studies in Publishing, Simon Fraser University.

Eaman, Ross Allan. 1987. *The Media Society: Basic Issues and Controversies.* Toronto: Butterworths.

———. 1994. *Channels of Influence: CBC Audience Research and the Canadian Public.* Toronto: University of Toronto Press.

Eco, Umberto. 1982a. 'Narrative structure in Fleming', in B. Waites et al., eds, *Popular Culture Past and Present.* Milton Keynes, UK: Open University Press.

———. 1982b. *The Name of the Rose.* New York: Warner Books.

———. 1986. 'The multiplication of the media', in Eco,

Travels in Hyperreality. New York: Harcourt Brace Jovanovich.

Economist, The. 1991. 'The optical enlightenment', 6 July, 87.

Edwards, Stephen. 2004. 'CanWest on mission to woo U.S. investors', *Vancouver Sun*, 10 Feb., D7.

Eisenstein, Elizabeth. 1979. *The Printing Press as an Agent of Change*, 2 vols. New York: Cambridge University Press.

———. 1983. *The Printing Revolution in Early Modern Europe*. Cambridge: Cambridge University Press.

Ellul, Jacques. 1964. *The Technological Society*. New York: Knopf.

Elmer, Greg, and Mike Gasher, eds. 2005. *Contracting Out Hollywood: Runaway Productions and Foreign Location Shooting*. Lanham, Md: Rowman & Littlefield.

Enchin, Harvey. 1993. 'Audience gauge goes high-tech: Electronic measurement of TV viewers, radio listeners seen as revolutionary', *Globe and Mail*, 10 Nov., B4.

———. 1996. 'Cinema chain accelerates growth', *Globe and Mail*, 13 Dec., B4.

Ericson, Richard V., Patricia M. Baranek, and Janet B.L. Chan. 1989. *Negotiating Control: A Study of News Sources*. Toronto: University of Toronto Press.

Eslin, Martin. 1980. 'The exploding stage', CBC-Radio, *Ideas* (Oct.).

Evans, Philip. 2002. 'A bright idea that wasn't: The E-emperor has no clothes', *Globe and Mail*, 25 Apr., A15.

Famous Players. 2002. 'About us'. At: www.famousplayers.com/_fp_aboutus.asp.

Featherstone, Mike. 1996. 'Localism, globalism, and cultural identity', in Rob Wilson and Wimal Dissanayake, eds, *Global/Local: Cultural Production and the Transnational Imaginary*. Durham, NC: Duke University Press.

Feenberg, A. 1999. *Questioning Technology*. New York: Routledge.

Felczak, Michael. 2006. 'Online publishing, technical representation, and the politics of code: The case of CJC-Online', unpublished paper.

Ferguson, Rob. 2000. 'Protests and criticism dog Hollinger annual meeting: Black hears out appeal to end strike in Calgary', *Toronto Star*, 25 May, B1.

Fessenden, Helen. 1974. *Fessenden: Builder of Tomorrows*. New York: Arno Press.

Fetherling, Doug. 1993. *A Little Bit of Thunder: The Strange Inner Life of the Kingston Whig-Standard*. Toronto: Stoddart.

Filion, Michel. 1996. 'Radio', in Dorland (1996).

Fiske, John. 1987. *Television Culture*. London: Routledge.

———. 1989a. *Reading the Popular*. Boston: Unwin Hyman.

———. 1989b. *Understanding Popular Culture*. Boston:

Unwin Hyman.

———. 1989c. 'Moments of television: Neither the text nor the audience', in Ellen Seiter et al., eds, *Remote Control*. London: Routledge.

———. 2003. *Reading Television*, 2nd edn. New York: Routledge.

Fletcher, F. 1981. *The Newspaper and Public Affairs*, vol. 7, Research Publications for the Royal Commission on Newspapers. Ottawa: Supply and Services.

———. 1994. 'The Southam lecture: Media, elections and democracy', *Canadian Journal of Communication* 19, 2: 131–50.

Foot, Richard. 1999. 'Court orders magazine to stop writing about abortion', *National Post*, 3 May, A4.

Fornas, J., U. Lindberg, and O. Sernhede. 1988. *Under Rocken*. Stockholm: Symposium.

Foucault, Michel. 1980. *The History of Sexuality*, trans. Robert Hurley. New York: Vintage Books.

———. 1988. *Madness and Civilization: A History of Insanity in the Age of Reason*, trans. Richard Howard. New York: Vintage Books.

———. 1995. *Discipline and Punish: The Birth of the Prison*, trans. Alan Sheridan. New York: Vintage Books.

Foundation for Media Education. 1992. *Pack of Lies: The Advertising of Tobacco* (35-minute video). Northhampton, Mass.: Foundation for Media Education.

Fowler, Roger. 1991. *Language in the News*. London: Routledge.

Franklin, Sarah, C. Lury, and J. Stacey. 1982. 'Feminism and cultural studies', in Paddy Scannell et al., eds, *Culture and Power*. London: Sage.

Fraser, Graham. 1999. 'CBC hurting private TV, Péladeau argues', *Globe and Mail*, 2 June, A5.

Friedan, Betty. 1963. *The Feminine Mystique*. New York: Norton.

Friedman, Thomas L. 2005. *The World Is Flat: A Brief History of the Twenty-First Century*. New York: Farrar, Straus & Giroux.

Frith, Simon. 1987. 'The industrialization of popular music', in James Lull, ed., *Popular Music and Communication*. Newbury Park, Calif.: Sage, 53–77.

Gallagher, Margaret. 1982. 'Negotiation of control in media organizations and occupations', in Gurevitch et al. (1982).

Galloway, Gloria. 2003. 'Toronto most ethnically diverse in North America', *Globe and Mail*, 22 Jan., A6.

Gans, Herbert. 1979. *Deciding What's News: A Study of CBS Evening News, NBC Nightly News, Newsweek, and Time*. New York: Pantheon Books.

Garfinkel, Harold. 1984. *Studies in Ethnomethodology*.

Cambridge: Polity Press.

Gasher, Mike. 1992. 'The myth of meritocracy: Ignoring the political economy of the Canadian film industry', *Canadian Journal of Communication* 17, 2: 371–8.

———. 1995a. 'The audiovisual locations industry in Canada: Considering British Columbia as Hollywood North', *Canadian Journal of Communication* 20, 2: 231–54.

———. 1995b. 'Culture lag: The liberal record', *Point of View* 26 (Winter): 22–4.

———. 1998. 'Invoking public support for public broadcasting: The Aird Commission revisited', *Canadian Journal of Communication* 23: 189–216.

———. 2002a. *Hollywood North: The Feature Film Industry in British Columbia*. Vancouver: University of British Columbia Press.

———. 2002b. 'Does CanWest know what all the fuss is about?', *Media* (Winter): 8–9.

Gee, Marcus. 2002. 'Don't blame the victim, Mr. Chrétien', *Globe and Mail*, 14 Sept., A17.

Geist, Michael. 2002. 'Cyberlaw', *Globe and Mail*, 17 Oct., B15.

———. 2006. 'Libel case key for Internet free speech', *Toronto Star*, 31 July, D3.

Geraghty, Christine. 1991. *Women and Soap Opera: A Study of Prime-Time Soaps*. Cambridge: Polity Press.

Gerbner, George. 1969. 'Towards "cultural indicators": The analysis of mass-mediated public message systems', *AV Communication Review* 17, 2: 137–48.

———. 1977. *Trends in Network Drama and Viewer Conceptions of Social Reality, 1967–76*. Philadelphia: Annenburg School of Communications, University of Pennsylvania.

Giddens, Anthony. 1984. *The Constitution of Society: An Outline of a Theory of Structuration*. Berkeley: University of California Press.

———. 1987a. *Social Theory and Modern Sociology*. Cambridge: Polity Press.

———. 1987b. 'Structuralism, post-structuralism and the production of culture', in Giddens and R. Turner, eds, *Social Theory Today*. Cambridge: Polity Press, 195–223.

———. 1990. *The Consequences of Modernity*. Cambridge: Polity Press.

Gilder, George F. 1991. 'Into the telecosm', *Harvard Business Review* (Mar.–Apr.): 150–61.

Gilmore, Dan. 2004. *We the Media: Grassroots Journalism by the People, for the People*. Sebastopol, Calif.: O'Reilly.

Glasgow Media Group. 1976. *Bad News*. Boston: Routledge & Kegan Paul.

Global Reach. 2001. 'Global Internet Statistics'. At: www.glreach.com/globstats/index.php3.

Globe and Mail. 1993. 'Court to hear arguments over TV mini-series', 30 Oct., A3.

———. 2001. 'The complications of convergence', 4 Aug., A12.

———. 2002. 'When violating rights becomes the routine', 19 Aug., A12.

Globerman, Steven. 1983. *Cultural Regulation in Canada*. Montreal: Institute for Research on Public Policy.

Goffman, Erving. 1959. *The Presentation of Self in Everyday Life*. Harmondsworth: Penguin.

Goody, J.R. 1977. *The Domestication of the Savage Mind*. Cambridge: Cambridge University Press.

Grady, Wayne. 1983. 'The Budweiser gamble', *Saturday Night* (Feb.): 28–30.

Grant, George. 1969. *Technology and Empire*. Toronto: Anansi.

Grant, Peter S., and Chris Wood. 2004. *Blockbusters and Trade Wars: Popular Culture in a Globalized World*. Vancouver: Douglas & McIntyre.

Gratton, Michel. 1987. *'So, What Are the Boys Saying?' An Inside Look at Brian Mulroney in Power*. Toronto: McGraw-Hill Ryerson.

Gray, Ann. 1999. 'Audience and reception research in retrospect: The trouble with audiences', in Alasuutari (1999: 22–37).

Grossberg, Lawrence, Ellen Wartella, D. Charles Whitney, and J. Macgregor Wise. 2006. *MediaMaking: Mass Media in Popular Culture*, 2nd edn. Thousand Oaks, Calif.: Sage.

Guillermoprieto, Alma. 1993. 'Letter from Brazil: Obsessed in Rio', *New Yorker* (16 Aug.): 44–56.

Gunster, Shane. 2004. *Capitalizing on Culture*. Toronto: University of Toronto Press.

Gurevitch, Michael, Tony Bennett, James Curran, and Jane Woollacott, eds. 1982, 1990. *Culture, Society and the Media*. Toronto: Methuen.

Habermas, Jürgen. 1984. *The Theory of Communicative Action*, trans. Thomas McCarty. Boston: Beacon Press.

Habermehl, Lawrence. 1995. *The Counterfeit Wisdom of Shallow Minds: A Critique of Some Leading Offenders in the 1980s*. New York: Peter Lang.

Hackett, Robert A. 1996. 'An exaggerated death: Prefatory comments on "objectivity" in journalism', in Valerie Alia, Brian Brennan, and Barry Hoffmaster, eds, *Deadlines & Diversity: Journalism Ethics in a Changing World*. Halifax: Fernwood.

——— and Richard Gruneau. 2000. *The Missing News: Filters and Blindspots in Canada's Press*. Ottawa and Aurora, Ont.: Canadian Centre for Policy Alternatives and Garamond Press.

———— and Yuezhi Zhao. 1998. *Sustaining Democracy? Journalism and the Politics of Objectivity.* Toronto: Garamond Press.

Hall, Edward T. 1980. *The Silent Language.* Westport, Conn.: Greenwood Press.

Hall, Stuart. 1980. 'Encoding/decoding', in Hall et al. (1980).

————. 1993. 'Encoding/decoding', in Simon During, ed., *The Cultural Studies Reader.* London: Routledge.

————. 1995. 'New cultures for old', in Massey and Jess (1995).

———— et al. 1978. *Policing the Crisis: Mugging, the State and Law and Order.* London: Macmillan.

————, Dorothy Hobson, Andrew Love, and Paul Willis, eds. 1980. *Culture, Media, Language: Working Papers in Cultural Studies.* London: Hutchinson.

Hamelink, Cees J. 1994. *The Politics of World Communication.* London: Sage.

————. 1995. 'Information imbalance across the globe', in Ali Monhmmedi, ed., *Questioning the Media: A Critical Introduction.* Thousand Oaks, Calif.: Sage, 293–307.

Hardin, Herschel. 1974. *A Nation Unaware.* Vancouver: Douglas & McIntyre.

Hartley, John. 1987. 'Invisible fictions', *Textual Practice* 1, 2: 121–38.

Hastings, Max. 2002. 'Paint it Black', *Globe and Mail*, 19 Oct., F3.

Havelock, Eric. 1976. *Origins of Western Literacy.* Toronto: OISE Press.

Hayes, David. 1992. *Power and Influence: The Globe and Mail and the News Revolution.* Toronto: Key Porter.

Hebdige, Dick. 1979. *Subculture: The Meaning of Style.* London: Methuen.

Heilbroner, Robert L. 1980. *The Worldly Philosophers: The Lives, Times, and Ideas of the Great Economic Thinkers.* New York: Simon & Schuster.

Heinzl, John. 2002. 'Web sites, ISPs lopping pop-up ads', *Globe and Mail*, 23 Aug., B10.

Henry, Frances, and Carol Tator. 2000. *Racist Discourse in Canada's English Print Media.* Toronto: Canadian Race Relations Foundation, Mar.

————, ————, Winston Mattis, and Tim Rees. 2000. *The Colour of Democracy: Racism in Canadian Society.* Toronto: Harcourt Brace.

Heritage, John. 1984. *Garfinkel and Ethnomethodology.* Cambridge: Cambridge University Press.

Herman, Edward S., and Noam Chomsky. 2002. *Manufacturing Consent: The Political Economy of the Mass Media.* New York: Pantheon Books.

———— and Robert W. McChesney. 1997. *The Global Media: The New Missionaries of Global Capitalism.* Washington: Cassell.

Hermes, Joke. 2006. 'Feminism and the politics of method', in Mimi White and James Schwoch, eds, *Questions of Method in Cultural Studies.* Oxford: Blackwell, 154–74.

Hobson, D. 1980. 'Housewives and the mass media', in Hall et al. (1980).

————. 1982. *Crossroads: The Drama of Soap Opera.* London: Methuen.

Hoggart, Richard. 1992 [1957]. *The Uses of Literacy.* New Brunswick, NJ: Transaction.

Horkheimer, Max. 1972. *Critical Theory.* New York: Seabury Press.

Hoskins, Colin, Stuart McFadyen, and Adam Finn. 1997. *Global Television and Film: An Introduction to the Economics of the Business.* Oxford: Oxford University Press.

Houpt, Simon. 2002. 'A lotta promotion genius?', *Globe and Mail*, 27 July, R5.

Howitt, Dennis, and Guy Cumberbatch. 1975. *Mass Media Violence and Society.* London: Elek.

Industry Canada. 1997. *Preparing Canada for a Digital World.* Final report of the Information Highway Advisory Council (IHAC). At: strategis.ic.gc.ca/SSG/_ih01650e.html.

Infopresse. 2006. *Guide Annuel Média 2007.* Montréal: Infopresse.

Innis, Harold. 1950. *Empire and Communications.* Toronto: Oxford University Press.

————. 1951. *The Bias of Communication.* Toronto: University of Toronto Press.

Inter American Press Association/Sociedad Inter-americana de Prensa (IAPA). 1994. 'Declaration of Chapultepec', *Globe and Mail*, 7 June, A13. See also www.sipiapa.org/projects/chapul-_declaration.htm.

Jay, M. 1974. *The Dialectical Imagination.* London: Routledge.

Jensen, Mike. 2000. 'African Internet status', Nov. At: demiurge.wn.apc.org/africa/afstat.htm.

Jeffrey, Liss. 1994. 'Rethinking audiences for cultural industries: Implications for Canadian research', *Canadian Journal of Communication* 19, 3–4: 495–522.

Jensen, Klaus Bruhn. 1990. 'The politics of polysemy: Television news, everyday consciousness and political action', *Media, Culture and Society* 12, 1: 57–77.

———— and Karl Erik Rosengren. 1990. 'Five traditions in search of an audience', *European Journal of Communication* 5: 207–38.

Jiwani, Jasmin. 2006. 'Race(ing) the nation: Media and minorities', in Paul Attallah and Leslie Regan Shade, eds, *Mediascapes: New Patterns in Canadian Communication*, 2nd edn. Toronto: Thomson/Nelson,

302–15.

Jones, D.B. 1981. *Movies and Memoranda: An Interpretive History of the National Film Board of Canada.* Ottawa: Canadian Film Institute.

Jouët, Josiane, and Sylvie Coudray. 1991. *New Communication Technologies: Research Trends.* Reports and Papers on Mass Communication, No. 105. Paris: UNESCO.

Joynt, Leslie. 1995. 'Too white', *Ryerson Review of Journalism* (Spring): 15–25.

Katz, E., and P. Lazarsfeld. 1965. *Personal Influence: The Part Played by People in the Flow of Mass Communications.* New York: Free Press.

Kelly, Brendan. 2006a. 'Trailer Park Boys movie isn't counting on big Quebec crowds', *Montreal Gazette*, 7 Oct., E2.

———. 2006b. 'Bon box office, bad English Canadians', *National Post*, 11 Oct., B3.

Kesterton, W.H. 1984. *A History of Journalism in Canada.* Ottawa: Carleton University Press.

Khakoo, Salza. 2006. 'Colour TV', *Ryerson Review of Journalism* (Spring). At: www.rrj.ca/issue/2006/spring/624/.

King, Russell. 1995. 'Migrations, globalization and place', in Massey and Jess (1995).

Klapper, Joseph. 1960. *The Effects of Mass Communications.* New York: Free Press.

Knelman, Martin. 1977. *This Is Where We Came In.* Toronto: McClelland & Stewart.

Kovach, Bill, and Tom Rosenstiel. 2001. *The Elements of Journalism: What Newspeople Should Know and the Public Should Expect.* New York: Crown.

Krippendorf, Klaus. 2004. *Content Analysis: An Introduction to Its Methodology.* Thousand Oaks, Calif.: Sage.

Kristeva, Julia. 1969. 'Le mot, le dialogue et le roman', in *Sèmiòtikè: Recherches pour une sémanalyse.* Paris: Editions du Seuil.

LaGuardia, Robert. 1977. *From Ma Perkins to Mary Hartman: The Illustrated History of Soap Opera.* New York: Ballantine Books.

Lamey, Mary. 1997. 'Merger of movie-house giants creates King Kong-sized debt', Montreal Gazette, 2 Oct., D2.

———. 1999. 'Sun Media to be spun off', *Montreal Gazette*, 30 Apr., F1–2.

Lapham, Lewis H. 2002. 'American Jihad', *Harper's* (Jan.): 7–9.

Larrain, Jorge. 1979. *The Concept of Ideology.* London: Hutchinson.

———. 1983. *Marxism and Ideology.* London: Macmillan.

Latour, B. 1993. *We Have Never Been Modern*, trans. C.

Porter. Cambridge, Mass.: Harvard University Press.

———. 1999. *Pandora's Hope: Essays on the Reality of Science Studies.* Cambridge, Mass.: Harvard University Press.

Law, J., and M. Callon. 1988. 'Engineering and sociology in a military aircraft project: A network analysis of technological change', *Social Problems* 35, 3: 285.

Leblanc, Jean-André. 1990. 'Pour s'arranger avec les gars des vues, l'industrie du cinéma et de la video au Canada 1982–1984', in Gaëtan Tremblay, ed., *Les Industries de la Culture et de la Communication au Québec et au Canada.* Sillery, Que.: Presses de l'Université du Québec.

Lee, Richard E. 2003. *The Life and Times of Cultural Studies.* Durham, NC: Duke University Press.

Leiss, William. 1990. *Under Technology's Thumb.* Montreal and Kingston: McGill-Queen's University Press.

———, Stephen Kline, Sut Jhally, and Jaqueline Botterill. 2005. *Social Communication in Advertising*, 3rd edn. New York: Routledge.

Lent, John A. 1998. 'The animation industry and its offshore factories', in Gerald Sussman and John A. Lent, eds, *Global Productions: Labor in the Making of the 'Information Society'.* Cresskill, NJ: Hampton Press.

Lessig, Lawrence. 1999. *Code, and Other Laws of Cyberspace.* New York: Basic Books.

———. 2001. *The Future of Ideas: The Fate of the Commons in a Connected World.* New York: Random House.

Levinson, S. 1985. *Pragmatics.* Cambridge: Cambridge University Press.

Lévi-Strauss, Claude. 1969. *The Raw and the Cooked.* London: Jonathan Cape.

Liebes, Tamar, and Elihu Katz. 1986. 'Decoding Dallas: Notes from a cross-cultural study', in G. Gumpert and R. Cathcart, eds, *Inter/Media.* New York: Oxford University Press.

Lievrouw, Leah A. 2000. 'Babel and beyond: Languages on the Internet', *ICA News* (May): 6–7.

Lindgren, April. 2001. 'Move to sell rest of national daily to CanWest "guarantees" its future', *Montreal Gazette*, 25 Aug., C1.

Lindlof, Thomas R. 1991. 'The qualitative study of media audiences', *Journal of Broadcasting and Electronic Media* 35, 1: 23–42.

Litvak, I.A., and C.J. Maule. 1978. *The Publication of Canadian Editions of Non-Canadian Magazines: Public Policy Alternatives.* Ottawa: Secretary of State.

Lord, A.B. 1964. *The Singer of Tales.* Cambridge, Mass.: Harvard University Press.

Lorimer, Rowland. 1994. *Mass Communication: A Comparative Introduction.* Manchester: University of Manchester Press.

——— and Nancy Duxbury. 1994. 'Of culture, the economy, cultural production, and cultural producers: An orientation', *Canadian Journal of Communication* 19, 3–4: 259–90.

Lumpkin, John J. 2003. 'US officials examine the quality of information war planners had before invasion', 22 May. At: www.sfgate.com/cgi-bin/article._cgi?f=/news/archive/2003/05/22/national1251EDT0637.DTL.

McCarthy, Shawn. 1997. 'Cineplex deal may hinge on sale of unit', *Globe and Mail*, 3 Oct., B1, B20.

MacCharles, Tonda. 2006. 'Citing threat, U.S. keeps Arar on watch list', *Toronto Star*, 16 Dec., A1, A10.

McChesney, Robert W. 1997. *Corporate Media and the Threat to Democracy*. New York: Seven Stories Press.

———. 1998. 'The political economy of global communication', in Robert W. McChesney, Ellen Meiksins Wood, and John Bellamy Foster, eds, *Capitalism and the Information Age: The Political Economy of the Global Communication Revolution*. New York: Monthly Review Press.

———. 1999a. *Rich Media, Poor Democracy: Communication Politics in Dubious Times*. Urbana: University of Illinois Press.

———. 1999b. 'Graham Spry and the future of public broadcasting', *Canadian Journal of Communication* 24, 1: 25–47.

McDonnell, Jim. 1983. 'Satellites for development, broadcasting and information', *Communication Research Trends* 4, 2: 1.

McFadyen, Stuart, Adam Finn, Colin Hoskins, and Rowland Lorimer, eds. 1994. Special Issue on 'Cultural Development in an Open Economy', *Canadian Journal of Communication* 19, 3–4.

McFarland, Janet, Jacquie McNish, and Paul Waldie. 2002. 'Look, I just want to resign', *Globe and Mail*, 25 Apr., A1, A10.

McGuigan, J. 1992. *Cultural Populism*. London: Routledge.

McLuhan, Marshall. 1962. *The Gutenberg Galaxy: The Making of Typographic Man*. Toronto: University of Toronto Press.

———. 1964. *Understanding Media: The Extensions of Man*. Toronto: McGraw-Hill.

McQuail, Denis. 1983. *Mass Communication Theory: An Introduction*. Beverly Hills, Calif.: Sage.

———. 1991. 'Mass media in the public interest: Towards a framework of norms for media performance', in Curran and Gurevitch (1991).

———. 2000. *McQuail's Mass Communication Theory*, 4th edn. Thousand Oaks, Calif.: Sage.

———. 2005. *McQuail's Mass Communication Theory*, 5th edn. Thousand Oaks, Calif.: Sage.

Magder, Ted. 1985. 'A featureless film policy: Culture and the Canadian state', *Studies in Political Economy* 16: 81–109.

———. 1993. *Canada's Hollywood: The Canadian State and Feature Films*. Toronto: University of Toronto Press.

Malik, S. 1989. 'Television and rural India', *Media, Culture and Society* 11, 4: 459–84.

Manley, Lorne, Jim Rutenberg, and Seth Schiesel. 2002. 'How Does AOL Fit in the Grand Plan Now?', *New York Times*, 21 Apr., Section 3, 1, 10–11.

Mansell, Robin. 1992. 'Communication and information technologies in the new world order', paper presented at the University of Calgary, Mar.

Marcuse, Herbert. 1963 [1954]. *Reason and Revolution: Hegel and the Rise of Social Theory*. New York: Humanities Press.

———. 1964. *One-Dimensional Man: Studies in the Ideology of Advanced Industrial Society*. Boston: Beacon Press.

Marshall, P. David. 2004. *New Media Cultures*. New York: Arnold.

Martin, Robert, and Stuart Adam. 1991. *A Source-book of Canadian Media Law*. Ottawa: Carleton University Press.

Marx, Karl, and Friedrich Engels. 1974. *The German Ideology*. London: Lawrence & Wishart.

Massey, Doreen. 1991. 'A global sense of place', *Marxism Today* (June): 24–9.

———. 1992. 'A place called home?', *New Formations* 17: 3–15.

———. 1995. 'The conceptualization of place', in Massey and Jess (1995).

——— and Pat Jess, eds. 1995. *A Place in the World? Cultures and Globalization*. New York: Oxford University Press.

——— and ———. 1995. 'Places and cultures in an uneven world', in Massey and Jess (1995).

Mathews, Robin. 1988. *Canadian Identity: Major Forces Shaping the Life of a People*. Ottawa: Steel Rail.

Media Education Foundation. 2002. *Killing Us Softly III* (video). Northhampton., Mass.

Meisel, John. 1986. 'Communications in the space age: Some Canadian and international implications', *International Political Science Review* 7, 3 (July): 299–331.

Mencher, Melvin. 2000. *News Reporting and Writing*, 8th edn. New York: McGraw-Hill.

Meyers, Marian. 1997. 'News of battering', in Dan Berkowitz, ed., *Social Meanings of News: A Text-Reader*. Thousand Oaks, Calif.: Sage.

Meyrowitz, Joshua. 1985. *No Sense of Place*. New York: Oxford University Press.

Miller, John. 1998. *Yesterday's News: Why Canada's Daily*

Newspapers Are Failing Us. Halifax: Fernwood.

———— and Caron Court. 2004. 'Who's telling the news? Race and gender representation in Canada's daily newsrooms'. At: www.diversitywatch.ryerson.ca/home_miller_2004report.htm.

———— and Kimberly Prince. 1994a. *Women's By-line Study*. Toronto: School of Journalism, Ryerson Polytechnic Institute.

———— and ————. 1994b. *The Imperfect Mirror*. Toronto: Ryerson Polytechnic University, Apr.

Miller, Mark Crispin. 1990. 'Hollywood: the ad', *Atlantic Monthly* 265, 4 (Apr.): 41–68.

Miller, Mary Jane. 1987. *Turn Up the Contrast: CBC Television Drama Since 1952*. Vancouver: University of British Columbia Press.

Mills, Sara. 2004. *Discourse*. New York: Routledge.

Milner, Brian. 2000. 'New and old media merge in massive AOL deal', *Globe and Mail*, 11 Jan., A1, A8.

Mitchell, D. 1988. 'Culture as political discourse in Canada', in Rowland Lorimer and D.C. Wilson, eds, *Communication Canada*. Toronto: Kagan and Woo.

Mitchell, Greg. 2003. '15 stories they've already bungled: Mitchell on the war coverage so far', 27 Mar. At: www.editorandpublisher.com/_editorandpublisher/headlines/article_display.jsp?vnu_content_id=1850208.

Mitrovica, Andrew. 2006–7. 'Hear no evil, write no lies', *The Walrus* 3, 10: 37–43.

Modleski, T. 1984. *Leaving with a Vengeance: Mass-Produced Fantasies for Women*. London: Methuen.

Moll, Marita, and Leslie Regan Shade, eds. 2004. *Seeking Convergence in Policy and Practice*. Ottawa: Canadian Centre for Policy Alternatives.

Montreal Gazette. 1997. *The Montreal Gazette: In Touch with English Montreal*. Montreal: Gazette Advertising Department.

Moody's Investors Service. 1997. *Moody's Handbook of Common Stocks*. New York: Moody's Investors Service, Spring.

Morgan, M., and N. Signorelli. 1990. *Cultivation Analysis*. Beverly Hills, Calif.: Sage.

Morley David. 1980. *The 'Nationwide' Audience: Structure and Decoding*. British Film Institute Television Monographs, 11. London: BFI.

————. 1986. *Family Television: Cultural Power and Domestic Leisure*. London: Comedia.

———— and Kevin Robins. 1995. *Spaces of Identity: Global Media, Electronic Landscapes and Cultural Boundaries*. London: Routledge.

Morris, Peter. 1978. *Embattled Shadows: A History of Canadian Cinema, 1895–1939*. Montreal and Kingston: McGill-Queen's University Press.

Mosco, Vincent. 1996. *The Political Economy of Communication: Rethinking and Renewal*. London: Sage.

Mulvey, Laura. 1975. 'Visual pleasure and narrative cinema', *Screen* 16, 3: 6–18.

Murdock, Graham. 1990. 'Large corporations and the control of the communications industries', in Gurevitch et al. (1990).

Murray, Laura. 2005. 'Bill 60 and copyright in Canada: Opportunities lost and found', *Canadian Journal of Communication* 30, 4: 649–54.

Negroponte, Nicholas. 1995. *Being Digital*. New York: Knopf.

Neil Craig Associates. 2004. 'International film and television production in Canada'. At: www.cftpa.ca/newsroom/pdf_studies/2004.10.IntlProductionInCanada.pdf.

Nesbitt-Larking, Paul. 2001. *Politics and the Media: Canadian Perspectives*. Peterborough, Ont.: Broadview Press.

Norton, William. 2007. *Human Geography*, 6th edn. Toronto: Oxford University Press.

O'Brian, Amy. 2006. 'Will this man save the music biz? Vancouver's Terry McBride, who manages a clutch of superstars, found success by learning to ignore his critics', *Vancouver Sun*, 9 Sept., F3.

Olson, David R., ed. 1980. *The Social Foundations of Language and Thought*. New York: Norton.

Onex. 2002. Onex Entertainment Group. At: onex.com/cp/cp_entgp/cp_entgp.asp

Ong, Walter. 1982. *Orality and Literacy: The Technologizing of the Word*. London: Methuen.

Ontario. 1972. *Canadian Publishers and Canadian Publishing*. Report of the Royal Commission on Book Publishing. Toronto: Queen's Printer.

Osler, Andrew M. 1993. *News: The Evolution of Journalism in Canada*. Toronto: Copp Clark Pitman.

O'Sullivan, T., J. Hartley, D. Saunders, and J. Fiske. 1983. *Key Concepts in Communication*. Toronto: Methuen.

Paterson, Chris A. 2001. 'Media imperialism revisited: The global public sphere and the news agency agenda', in Stig Hjarvard, ed., *News in a Globalized Society*. Göteborg: Nordicom.

————. 2005. 'News agency dominance in international news on the Internet', in Skinner et al. (2005: 145–63).

Payzant, G. 1984. *Glenn Gould: Music and Mind*. Toronto: Key Porter.

Peers, Frank. 1969. *The Politics of Canadian Broadcasting, 1920–1951*. Toronto: University of Toronto Press.

————. 1979. *The Public Eye*. Toronto: University of Toronto Press.

Pegg, Mark. 1983. *Broadcasting and Society 1918–1939*. London: Croom Helm.

Pendakur, Manjunath. 1990. *Canadian Dreams and American Control: The Political Economy of the Canadian Film Industry*. Toronto: Garamond Press.

———. 1998. 'Hollywood North: Film and TV production in Canada', in Gerald Sussman and John A. Lent, eds, *Global Productions: Labor in the Making of the 'Information Society'*. Cresskill, NJ: Hampton Press.

Picard, Robert G. 1989. *Media Economics: Concepts and Issues*. Newbury Park, Calif.: Sage.

PIPA/Knowledge Network. 2003. 'Study finds widespread misperceptions on Iraq highly related to support for war'. At: www.pipa.org/OnlineReports/Iraq/IraqMedia_Oct03/IraqMedia_Oct03_pr.pdf.

Plato. 1973. *Phaedrus*, trans. Walter Hamilton. Toronto: Penguin.

Playback. 1998. 'Investment and Finance', 4 May, 36–50.

———. 2006. 'Provincial funding sources in Canada', 3 Apr., 25–30.

Poe, Marshall. 2006. 'The hive: Can thousands of Wikipedians be wrong? How an attempt to build an online encyclopedia touched off history's biggest experiment in collaborative knowledge', *The Atlantic* (Sept.): 86–94.

Popper, Karl R. 1962 [1945]. *The Open Society and Its Enemies*. London: Routledge.

Postman, Neil. 1993. *Technopoly: The Surrender of Culture to Technology*. New York: Knopf.

Pratkanis, Anthony R. 1992. *The Age of Propaganda: The Everyday Use and Abuse of Persuasion*. New York: W.H. Freeman.

Press, Andrea L. 2000. 'Recent developments in feminist communication theory', in James Curran and Michael Gurevitch, eds, *Mass Media and Society*. New York: Oxford University Press, 2–43.

Print Measurement Bureau (PMB). 1998. *PMB 98 Readership Volume*. Toronto: PMB.

———. *PMB 2006 Readership Volume,* Toronto: PMB.

———. n.d. *Introducing PMB*. Toronto: PMB. At: www.pmb.ca.

———. n.d. *PMB Media School*. Toronto: PMB.

Pritchard, David, and Florian Sauvageau. 1999. *Les journalistes canadiens: Un portrait de fin de siècle*. Québec: Les Presses de l'Université Laval.

Propp, Vladimir. 1970. *Morphology of the Folktale*. Austin: University of Texas Press.

Quebec. 2001. *Mandat d'initiative portant sur la concentration de la presse*. Quebec: Secrétariat des commissions, Nov. At: www.assnat.qc.ca/fra/publications/rapports/_rapcc3.html.

Queeney, Kathryn M. 1983. 'DBS: Free flow vs. national sovereignty', *Communication Research Trends* 4, 2: 4–6.

Raboy, Marc. 1990. *Missed Opportunities: The Story of Canada's Broadcasting Policy*. Montreal and Kingston: McGill-Queen's University Press.

———. 1995. 'The role of public consultation in shaping the Canadian broadcasting system', *Canadian Journal of Political Science* 28, 3: 455–77.

———, Ivan Bernier, Florian Sauvageau, and Dave Atkinson. 1994. 'Cultural development and the open economy: A democratic issue and a challenge to public policy', in McFadyen et al. (1994).

Radway, Janice. 1984. *Reading the Romance: Women, Patriarchy and Popular Literature*. Chapel Hill: University of North Carolina Press.

Rantanen, Terhi. 1997. 'The globalization of electronic news in the 19th century', *Media, Culture and Society* 19, 4: 605–20.

Ravensbergen, Jan. 2002. 'BCE set to dismantle multimedia empire: After selling Yellow Pages for $3B, next to go would be CTV, Globe and Mail', *Ottawa Citizen*, 14 Sept., D1.

Regan Shade, Leslie. 2005. 'Aspergate: Concentration, convergence, and censorship in Canadian media', in Skinner et al. (2005: 101–16).

Reuters. 1998. 'U.S. panel on water sees it as commodity', *New York Times*, 22 Mar., 6.

Rever, Judi. 1995. 'France faces off with Rambo', *Globe and Mail*, 4 Feb., C3.

Reynolds, Bill. 2002. 'Why your local radio station sounds like this (white bread)', *Globe and Mail*, 3 Aug., R1, R5.

Rice-Barker, Leo. 1996. 'Victor victorious', *Playback*, 6 May, 1, 5, 14.

Richer, Jules. 1999. 'La presse québécoise en plein marasme: Chantal Hébert sonne l'alarme', *Le 30* 23, 3 (Mar.): 11–13.

Riga, Andy. 2000. 'BCE's Monty a world-beater', *Montreal Gazette*, 16 Feb., D1.

Rolland, Asle, and Helge Østbye. 1986. 'Breaking the broadcasting monopoly', in Denis McQuail and Karen Siune, eds, *New Media Politics: Comparative Perspectives in Western Europe*. London: Sage.

Rose, Gillian. 1995. 'Place and identity: A sense of place', in Massey and Jess (1995).

Rose, Jonathan, and Simon Kiss. 2006. 'Boundaries blurred: The mass media and politics in a hyper media age', in Paul Attallah and Leslie Regan Shade, eds, *Mediascapes: New Patterns in Canadian Communication*, 2nd edn. Toronto: Thomson Nelson, 332–45.

Rosengren, K.E., and S. Windahl. 1989. *Media Matters: TV Use in Childhood and Adolescence*. Norwood, NJ: Ablex.

Ross, Val. 2006. 'No end in sight for CBC's Tommy Troubles', *Globe and Mail*, 4 July. At: www.theglobeandmail.com/servlet/story/RTGAM.20060704.wxdouglas04/BNStory/Entertainment/home.

Roth, Lorna. 1996. 'Cultural and racial diversity in Canadian broadcast journalism', in Valeria Alia, Brian Brennan, and Barry Hoffmaster, eds, *Deadlines & Diversity: Journalism Ethics in a Changing World*. Halifax: Fernwood.

———. 1998. 'The delicate acts of "colour balancing": Multiculturalism and Canadian television broadcasting policies and practices', *Canadian Journal of Communication* 23: 487–505.

———. 2005. *Something New in the Air: The Story of First Peoples Television Broadcasting in Canada*. Montreal and Kingston: McGill-Queen's University Press.

Rotstein, Abraham. 1988. 'The use and misuse of economics in cultural policy', in Rowland Lorimer and D.C. Wilson, eds, *Communication Canada: Issues in Broadcasting and New Technologies*. Toronto: Kagan and Woo.

Ruggles, Myles. 2005. *Automating Interaction: Formal and Informal Knowledge in the Digital Network Economy*. Cresskill, NJ: Hampton Press.

Russell, Nick. 1994. *Morals and the Media: Ethics in Canadian Journalism*. Vancouver: University of British Columbia Press.

Rutherford, Donald. 1992. *Dictionary of Economics*. London: Routledge.

Rutherford, Paul. 1990. *When Television Was Young: Primetime Canada*. Toronto: University of Toronto Press.

Saunders, Doug. 2002. 'Rocking against the suits', *Globe and Mail*, 2 Mar., R1.

Saussure, Ferdinand de. 1974. *Course in General Linguistics*. London: Fontana.

Scannell, Paddy. 1988. 'Radio times: The temporal arrangements of broadcasting in the modern world', in P. Drummond and R. Paterson, eds, *Television and Its Audiences: International Research Perspectives*. London: BFI.

———, ed. 1991. *Broadcast Talk*. London: Sage.

——— and D. Cardiff. 1991. *A Social History of Broadcasting*, vol. 1, *Serving the Nation 1922–1939*. Oxford: Blackwell.

Shecter, Barbara. 2005. 'Cineplex buys Famous Players in $500M "deal of a lifetime"', *Regina Leader Post*, 14 June, A10.

———. 2006. 'CRTC rules for media giant', *Calgary Herald*, 22 July, C3.

Schiller, H.I. 1984. *Information and the Crisis Economy*. Norwood, NJ: Ablex.

Schlesinger, Philip. 1978. *Putting 'Reality' Together: BBC News*. London: Constable.

———. 1983. *Televising 'Terrorism': Political Violence in Popular Culture*. London: Comedia.

Schudson, Michael. 1978. *Discovering the News: A Social History of American Newspapers*. New York: Basic Books.

Schulman, Mark. 1990. 'Control mechanisms inside the media', in John Downing, Ali Mohammadi, and Annebelle Sreberny-Mohammadi, eds, *Questioning the Media: A Critical Introduction*. Newbury Park, Calif.: Sage.

Schulman, Norma. 1993. 'Conditions of their own making: An intellectual history of the Centre for Contemporary Cultural Studies at the University of Birmingham', *Canadian Journal of Communication* 18, 1: 51–74.

Schumacher, E.F. 1973. *Small Is Beautiful: Economics As If People Mattered*. New York: Harper & Row.

Seiter, Ellen, Hans Borchers, Gabrielle Kreutzner, and Eva-Maria Warth. 1989. *Remote Control: Television, Audiences, and Cultural Power*. London: Routledge.

Shannon, Claude E., and Warren Weaver. 1949. *The Mathematical Theory of Communication*. Urbana: University of Illinois Press.

Shoemaker, Pamela J., and Stephen D. Reese. 1996. *Mediating the Message: Theories of Influence on Mass Media Content*. White Plains, NY: Longman.

Siebert, F.S., T. Peterson, and W. Schramm. 1971 [1956]. *Four Theories of the Press*. Urbana: University of Illinois Press.

Silcoff, Sean. 2003. 'Peladeau: A year of redemption', *National Post*, 23 Dec., FP7.

Silj, A., ed. 1988. *East of Dallas: The European Challenge to American Television*. London: British Film Institute.

Silverman, Kaja. 1983. *The Subject of Semiotics*. New York: Oxford University Press.

Silverstone, R. 1981. *The Message of Television: Myth and Narrative in Contemporary Culture*. London: Heinemann Educational Books.

Sinclair, Scott. 2006. 'The GATS Negotiations and Canadian Telecommunications Foreign Ownership Limits', briefing paper. Ottawa: Canadian Centre for Policy Alternatives, 27 Mar. At: www.policyalternatives.ca/Reports/2006/03/ReportsStudies1322/index.cfm?pa=6104ea04.

Skinner, David. 2004. 'Reform or alternatives? Limits and pressures on changing the Canadian mediascape', *Democratic Communiqué* 19 (Spring): 13–36.

———, James Compton, and Mike Gasher, eds. 2005. *Converging Media, Diverging Politics: A Political Economy of News Media in the United States and Canada*. Lanham, Md: Lexington Books.

Skinner, David, and Mike Gasher. 2005. 'So much by so few: Media policy and ownership in Canada', in Skinner et al. (2005: 51–76).

Smith, Adam. 1937 [1776]. *An Inquiry into the Nature and Causes of the Wealth of Nations*. New York: Modern Library.

Smith, Anthony D. 1980. *The Geopolitics of Information: How Western Culture Dominates the World*. London: Faber and Faber.

Smythe, Dallas. 1994. *Counterclockwise: Perspectives on Communication*, ed. Thomas Guback. Boulder, Colo.: Westview Press.

Sontag, Susan. 1999. 'On photography', in David Crowley and Paul Heyer, eds, *Communication in History: Technology, Culture and Society*. Don Mills, Ont.: Longman, 174–7

Sotiron, Minko. 1997. *From Politics to Profit: The Commercialization of Daily Newspapers, 1890–1920*. Montreal and Kingston: McGill-Queen's University Press.

Sparks, Colin. 1995. 'The survival of the state in British broadcasting', *Journal of Communication* 45, 4: 140–59.

Statistics Canada. 1997. *Recent Cultural Statistics (Highlights from Canada's Culture, Heritage and Identity: A Statistical Perspective)*. At: www.pch.gc.ca/culture/library/statscan/stats_e.htm.

———. 1998. 'Focus on culture', *Quarterly Bulletin from the Culture Statistics Program* (Winter). Catalogue no. 87–004–XPB.

———. 1998. 'Hitting a high note: Canadian recording artists in 1998', *Quarterly Bulletin from the Culture Statistics Program* 14, 2. At: www.statcan.ca/english/ads/87-004-XPB/pdf/fcdart.pdf.

———. 2001. *Overview: Access to and Use of Information Communication Technology*. Catalogue no. 56–505–XIE. Ottawa: Minister of Industry, Mar.

———. 2003a. *Immigration and visible minorities*. www12.statcan.ca/english/census01/products/highlight/Ethnicity/Index.cfm?Lang+E.

———. 2005. 'More magazines, higher profit', 14 June. At: www.statcan.ca/english/freepub/11-002-XIE/2005/06/16505/16505_02.htm.

———. 2006. 'Canadian Internet Use Survey', *The Daily*, 15 Aug. At: www.statcan.ca/Daily/English/060815/d060815b.htm.

Sternbergh, Adam. 2002. 'Cutie patootie now kaput', *National Post*, 28 Sept., SP1, SP4.

Storey, J. 1993. *Cultural Theory and Popular Culture*. London: Harvester Wheatsheaf.

Stott, Jim. 1995. 'Today's newspapers a long leap from scan-dal sheets', *Calgary Herald*, 19 Nov., A7.

Straw, Will. 1996. 'Sound recording', in Dorland (1996).

Sutel, Seth. 2000. 'New media marries old', *Montreal Gazette*, 11 Jan., F1, F4.

Sweet, Doug. 2001. 'Publisher stepping down: Goldbloom cites "fundamental differences" with new owners', *Montreal Gazette*, 1 Sept., A1.

Taras, David. 1990. *The Newsmakers: The Media's Influence on Canadian Politics*. Scarborough, Ont.: Nelson Canada.

———. 1999. *Power and Betrayal in the Canadian Media*. Peterborough, Ont.: Broadview Press.

Thompson, Edward P. 1980 [1963]. *The Making of the English Working Class*. Harmondsworth: Penguin.

Thompson, John B. 1999. 'The trade in news', in David Crowley and Paul Heyer, eds, *Communication in History: Technology, Culture and Society*. Don Mills, Ont.: Longman, 118–22

Thompson, John C. 2002. 'No al-Qaeda PoWs while threat looms', *Ottawa Citizen*, 23 Jan., A15.

Thomson Corp. 1998. *Annual Report 1997*.

———. 1999. *Annual Report 1998*.

Thorne, Stephen. 2005. 'Court rejects radio station's case against CRTC', *St John's Telegram*, 4 Sept., A11.

Tiessen, Paul. 1993. 'From literary modernism to the Tantramar Marshes: Anticipating McLuhan in British and Canadian media theory and practice', *Canadian Journal of Communication* 18, 4: 451–68.

Tiffin, Deborah, ed. 2001. *Film Canada Yearbook 2001*. Port Perry, Ont.: Moving Pictures Media.

Tuchman, Gaye. 1978. *Making News: A Study in the Construction of Reality*. New York: Free Press.

Turner, G. 1990. *British Cultural Studies: An Introduction*. London: Routledge.

UNESCO. 1980. *Many Voices, One World: Report by the International Commission for the Study of Communication Problems* (MacBride Commission). Paris: Unipub.

———. *Universal Declaration of Human Rights*. At: www.unhchr.ch/udhr/lang/eng.htm.

Vale, Allison. 1998. 'Cdns. reap sales in France', *Playback*, 19 Oct., 1, 14–15, 19.

Van Dijk, Jan A.G.M. 2005. *The Deepening Divide: Inequality in the Information Society*. Thousand Oaks, Calif.: Sage.

van Dijk, Teun A. 1985. *Handbook of Discourse Analysis*, 4 vols. London: Academic Press.

———. 1997. *Discourse as Structure and Process*. Thousand Oaks, Calif.: Sage.

van Ginneken, Jaap. 1998. *Understanding Global News: A Critical Introduction*. London: Sage.

Vipond, Mary. 1992. *Listening In: The First Decade of Canadian Broadcasting, 1922–1932*. Montreal and

Kingston: McGill-Queen's University Press.

———. 2000. *The Mass Media in Canada*, 3rd edn. Toronto: James Lorimer.

Wallace, Bruce. 2002. 'Mr. Showbiz comes to G8 summit: Few leaders are as colourful, powerful and controversial as Berlusconi', *Montreal Gazette*, 15 June, B1.

———. 2002. 'Recording Industry', in Paul Attallah and Leslie Regan Shade, eds, *Mediascapes: New Patterns in Canadian Communication*. Toronto: Nelson Thomson Learning.

Wallerstein, Immanuel. 1974. *The Modern World-System: Capitalist Agriculture and the Origins of the European World-Economy in the Sixteenth Century*. New York: Academic Press.

Warnica, Richard. 2005. 'Cultural diversity: Canada's UN victory', *The Tyee*, 28 Oct. At: www.thetyee.ca/News/2005/10/28/CanadaUNVictory/.

Wasko, Janet, Mark Phillips, and Chris Purdie. 1983. 'Hollywood meets Madison Avenue: The commercialization of US films', *Media, Culture and Society* 15, 2: 271–94.

Watzlawick, Paul, Janet Beavin, and Don Jackson. 1967. *Pragmatics of Human Communication: A Study of Interactional Patterns, Pathologies, and Paradoxes*. New York: Norton.

Weir, Ernest Austin. 1965. *The Struggle for National Broadcasting in Canada*. Toronto: McClelland & Stewart.

Wilkinson, Alec. 2006. 'The lobsterman: Solving a mystery off the Maine Coast', *New Yorker*, 31 July, 56–65.

Williams, Carol T. 1992. *It's Time for My Story: Soap Opera Sources, Structure and Response*. London: Praeger.

Williams, Raymond. 1958. *Culture and Society: 1780–1950*. New York: Columbia University Press.

———. 1974. *Television: Technology and Cultural Form*. London: Fontana.

———. 1989. *Resources of Hope: Culture, Democracy, Socialism*, ed. Robin Gable. London: Verso.

Williams, Tannis MacBeth. 1986. *The Impact of Television: A Natural Experiment in Three Communities*. Orlando, Fla: Academic Press.

———. 1995. 'The impact of television: A longitudinal Canadian study', in Benjamin D. Singer, ed., *Communications in Canadian Society*. Toronto: Nelson.

Williamson, Judith. 1978. *Decoding Advertisements: Ideology and Meaning in Advertising*. London: Boyars.

Willis, Paul. 1977. *Learning to Labor*. New York: Columbia University Press.

Wilson, Kevin G. 2002. 'The rise and fall of Teleglobe', *Montreal Gazette*, 18 May, B5.

Winner, Langdon. 1977. *Autonomous Technology: Technics-out-of-Control as a Theme in Political Thought*. Cambridge, Mass.: MIT Press.

Winter, James. 1997. *Democracy's Oxygen: How Corporations Control the News*. Montreal: Black Rose Books.

Withers, Edward, and Robert S. Brown. 1995. 'The broadcast audience: A sociological perspective', in Benjamin D. Singer, ed., *Communications in Canadian Society*. Toronto: Nelson, 89–121.

Wober, J. Mallory, and Barrie Gunter. 1986. 'Television audience research at Britain's Independent Broadcasting Authority, 1974–1984', *Journal of Broadcasting and Electronic Media* 30, 1: 15–31.

Women's Studies Group. 1978. *Women Take Issue: Aspects of Women's Subordination*. Birmingham: Centre for Cultural Studies.

Wong, Tony. 2006. 'Canada's phone landscape gets a new regulatory look', *Toronto Star*, 12 Dec., B1, B16.

Woollacott, Janet. 1982. 'Messages and Meanings', in Gurevitch et al. (1982).

York, Geoffrey. 2002. 'Great Firewall of China stifles dissent on the net', *Globe and Mail*, 5 Oct., A14.

Ze, David Wei. 1995. 'Printing as an Agent of Social Stability during the Sung Dynasty', Ph.D. dissertation, School of Communication, Simon Fraser University.

Zerbisias, Antonia. 2003. 'Chaos, or just a little vase they're going through?', *Toronto Star*, 12 Apr., A14.

Zimonjic, Peter. 2002. 'CBC forum debates media ownership: Discussion organized in response to Mills' firing', *Ottawa Citizen*, 23 June, A3.

Index